MW01134377

Poet Be Like God

Jack Spicer. *Photo by Robert Berg (collection of the authors).*

Lewis Ellingham
and
Kevin Killian

POET
BE LIKE GOD

Jack Spicer
and the
San Francisco
Renaissance

WESLEYAN UNIVERSITY PRESS

Published by

University Press of New England

Hanover and London

Wesleyan University Press

Published by University Press of New England,

Hanover, NH 03755

Printed in the United States of America

1 2 3 4 5

CIP data appear at the end of the book

Acknowledgments

Material from Gerald M. Ackerman's unpublished memoir appears here by permission from Dr. Ackerman.

Unpublished letters by Helen Adam appear by permission of Robert J. Bertholf, Curator, The Poetry/Rare Books Collection, State University of New York at Buffalo. Copyright by The Literary Estate of Helen Adam.

Quote from Jack Anderson's memoir/essay, "The Poetry of Jack Spicer" (*Mouth of the Dragon* #9, July 1976), printed with the permission of Mr. Anderson.

Unpublished materials held by the Bancroft Library courtesy of The Bancroft Library, University of California, Berkeley.

All published and unpublished material by Robin Blaser printed with the permission of Robin Blaser.

Unpublished photo (back cover) of Blaser, Spicer, Carolyn and Joe Dunn, Duncan, and Dick Bratset, by Kent Bowker, printed with permission of Kent Bowker.

George Bowering's article "Holes in the San Francisco Fog" is quoted from with the permission of Mr. Bowering.

Unpublished letters of James Broughton printed with his permission.

Continued on page 417

Contents

Illustrations

List of Illustrations

"Poet, Be Like God"

The boys above the swimming pool receive the sun.
Their groins are pressed against the warm cement.
They look as if they dream. As if their bodies dream.
Rescue their bodies from the poisoned sun,
Shelter the dreamers. They're like lobsters now
Hot red and private as they dream,
They dream about themselves.
They dream of dreams about themselves.
They dream they dream of dreams about themselves.
Splash them with twilight like a wet bat.
Unbind the dreamers.
       Poet,
Be like God.

           —JACK SPICER, *Imaginary Elegies*[1]

*T*hree poets met in Berkeley, California, in 1946, as students, rebels, friends: Robert Duncan, Robin Blaser, and Jack Spicer. Together they forged a new kind of poetry—a poetry that would combine an erudite intellectualism with the passionately felt life of homosexual desire. As a joke, they called their common work the "Berkeley Renaissance," but it was not entirely a joke. At bottom they were earnest, and saw themselves as the ultimate heirs not only of modernism but of the entire tide of romanticism. They would be gods, creating new worlds, naming and dispensing them. It was a kind of hubris, one that brought with it its own disillusion and defeat.

But why are the names of Allen Ginsberg, Frank O'Hara, John Ashbery so well known, and Spicer's relatively unacknowledged? Accidents of luck and literary history? Spicer's work is difficult, challenging, and wildly experimental, yet at the same time its lyric directness and imaginative scope speak vividly to many readers. As a student, he wanted poetry to entertain: "The truth is that pure poetry bores everybody. It is even a bore to the poet."[2] And he remains entertaining. His student work, later collected, reveals him as a passionate, blindly lyrical poet with nothing particular to say but a grand way of saying it. After his thirtieth birthday, Spicer began to write seriously, producing in quick order a dozen sequences or "books" of poetry—"serial poems," as he came to call them, with reference both to the serial music of Berio and Boulez and to the radio and movie serials that had entertained him as a teenager in Hollywood. From *After Lorca* (1957), which sets up a dialogue between Lorca and Spicer, to the *Book of Magazine Verse* (1965), a selection of poems quixotically submitted to various reputable magazines of the Establishment, Spicer's conception of the "book" changed from year to year. This body of work collapses notions of self and agency with a greedy, brilliant flair for the absurd. Through his subconcious state, voices from "outside" find human expression, as he allows himself to be overwhelmed by the alterity of a will stronger than his own. The poet's own voice thus has always a quality of abjection, for Spicer disclaims having written the poems. "When someone praises my work I feel like they're talking about my brother," he said once. In absentia he signs the book. When he announced his "dictation" theories, claiming that his poetry was the product of "outside," alien forces, he joined the mystical band of his heroes Yeats, Blake, and Rilke, but became a freak to the hard-edged, career-driven poets of MFA programs and prize committees.

To the crowd at the 1965 Berkeley Poetry Conference a decrepit Jack Spicer improvised a melancholy, shambling speech on "Poetry and Politics." He was fairly drunk, and as he came stumbling down the aisle afterward spectators noticed his fly was open, one dirty shirttail flapping out of unpressed pants. Although he was only forty years old and six feet tall, he looked seventy, hunched over like a man with rickets. His face was swollen and puffy. A cadre of loyal followers drove him home to his one-room apartment on Polk Street, a seedy neighborhood in San Francisco, and put him to bed for his nap. Ten days later, his liver bloated to gargantuan proportions, he collapsed in the elevator of his building. An ambulance took him to San Francisco General Hospital where, admitted without identification, his twitching, sweating body was treated in the poverty ward for the symptoms of a pre-hepatic coma. Days passed without his friends guessing where he was. After ten days, he died.

At that moment he was little known to readers of contemporary American poetry. His work was published in tiny editions, and his personal quirks prevented his publishers from distributing his books beyond a coterie of admirers within the Bay Area. The poetry itself, while often lyrical and "open," had become more difficult and dense since his first volume—*After Lorca*—appeared in 1957. With homophobia raging throughout the land, the frankness of Spicer's homosexual project was as shocking, as repugnant, as Allen Ginsberg's, but he lacked and indeed abhorred Ginsberg's social skills and genius for publicity. Spicer did himself no favors by alienating the important figures in his own world—Charles Olson, Allen Ginsberg, Denise Levertov, Lawrence Ferlinghetti, Frank O'Hara. As a gay male writer, a poet, an alcoholic, an intellectually subtle, widely read man, Spicer struggled from outcast positions for most of his career, rejecting systematically all acceptance that came his way. His untimely death only increased his obscurity. Until the publication of his *Collected Books* in 1975, his poems were almost unavailable, except to those who sought them out with the aid of rare book dealers, or who could find the smudged mimeographed copies of the unpublished work. While the rumors and legends never died, twisting and distorting in the process, they insured his status as that ultimate horror, a cult figure.

In the past twenty years, however, Spicer's influence has grown significantly, affecting poetry throughout the United States, Canada, and Europe. His eccentric theories have enriched the mainstream of modern thought concerning the poem, the function of the poet, the materiality of language, the position of the outsider, the powers of abjection, and the relation between word, image, sentence, and book. His savage isolation and search for purity, which led to his immediate obscurity, were ironically the very qualities that attracted the attention and admiration of succeeding generations of poets. The so-called "second generation" poets of the New York School—Anne Waldman, Ted Berrigan, Bernadette Mayer, Ron Padgett, Bill Berkson, Clark Coolidge—caught on quickly, spurred by the presence among them of several who had known Spicer well—Lewis Warsh, Joanne Kyger, Harris Schiff, Larry Fagin, and others. Poets interested in ethnopoetics and the world voice took a keen interest in Spicer's deep imagery, the surrealism that underlies his thinking. A third group of young writers, some of whom were present at the "Poetry and Politics" lecture of 1965, took to heart Spicer's concept of language as a total system controlling our response to experience, yet divorced from it, the viral model he pioneered with his contemporaries William S. Burroughs and Philip K. Dick; to the young "Language" poets Spicer's work was seen as a forerunner, a proto-genitype. Thanks to these waves of dissemination of his ideas and poetry, today's young poets think of Spicer as a fact of life—like O'Hara or Robert Lowell or Olson or Adrienne Rich.

There were two Jack Spicers, or so it seemed. One opposed the national image of American success, despised bourgeois nationalism; the other embraced a mythic America rooted in crassness and arrogance. One Spicer spoke admiringly of Eugene Debs and John L. Lewis—resourceful men of courage grown from very local U.S. soils, men who attempted to take the best from European traditions to forge a robust labor movement that was American in flavor. But another Spicer enjoyed with colloquial bumptious-ness the national populism represented by such a figure as Huey P. Long of Louisiana, who ruled his state by a formula familiar in the fascist govern-ments of the time. On one hand Spicer claimed Blackfoot Indian ancestry, claimed to be related to Mary Baker Eddy, claimed his father was a Wobbly, called himself an anarchist, was always outspoken, even prideful about his homosexuality in a period when this was dangerous; yet his contempt for "liberalism" was profound.[3]

Can we look to Spicer's Los Angeles origins for the source of his re-gional and (lower) middle-class attitudes about American culture and poli-tics? Movies may have been king in Hollywood, but in Spicer's quieter streets and neighborhoods near Beverly Boulevard and Western Avenue, a Whitmanesque naiveté prevailed among a people, midwestern and south-ern in origin, whose migration had stopped at this final western ocean bar-rier. The class and demographic factors in Spicer's upbringing, derived from family and schools, were issues he regularly raised among his friends, usually by way of unflattering contrasts: his authenticity as "poor" and "American" against another's "rich family" and "fake, silly" culture. Spicer's war was with what he perceived to be the fantasy, the fabricated easiness caught like a disease from (he would have thought "upper") middle-class parents—the families, in his eyes, of most of his friends.

Behind his flamboyant convictions, Spicer lived with a child's awk-wardness emotionally and physically. He couldn't drive a car and, almost spastic in movement, doubtless would have been a hazardous driver.[4] (He told Jim Herndon he had rickets from childhood poverty, which seemed so unlikely—"Vachel Lindsay in disguise"—that Herndon dismissed it as a fabrication designed to convince others of an imaginary lower-class background—a "useful myth," Herndon believed.[5]) He ate convenience food, but was quick to point out its nutritional defects (mainly in economic terms, if he thought it "old" or "junk" or "poor," another capitalist shuck). By contrast, he considered himself rather a gourmet, able to detect uncommon subtleties of flavor in foods, whether in a complicated sauce or in a Tomales Bay oyster fresh and raw.[6] He seemed often to keep the observer in a state of alarm from the threat of at least verbal aggression. But all this was counterposed by his evident intellegence and his candor, openness, wit, and—if he liked one—great charm.

"I want to write a poem as long as California," Spicer announced as a student at Berkeley. In a sense his *Collected Books* are that poem—a long sequence composed out of California history, legend, ambience. This provocative localism ran counter to the international modernism that prevailed in poetry. Spicer used it to portray a distinctive American and western consciousnsess, while he also exposed the many conflicts and tensions this ideology entailed. Oddly, he tried to control disssemination of his poems, demanding less distribution from his publishers. Similar creative tensions characterized the other great poets with whom Spicer worked closely—Robin Blaser and Robert Duncan.

Spicer's writing could not have been born and cannot properly be read outside the context of an earlier generation of modernists. Ezra Pound's long, steady gaze at history, T. S. Eliot's romantic desperation and religious feeling, Langston Hughes's civic directness, Mina Loy's powerful blend of sexuality and war games, Dylan Thomas's tumultuous lyricism, E. E. Cummings's syntactical experiments, Marianne Moore's precision and music, Robinson Jeffers's unearthly Parnassian scream, William Carlos Williams's evangelical Americanism, Laura Riding's austerity, W. H. Auden's wit and brio, all inspired similar themes in Spicer's early and mature work. Yet, in the postmodernist spirit, Spicer kept revising and challenging the tenets of modernism, undercutting the genius of its architects by rewriting their monuments. A new generation of postwar thinkers and poet activists was raising the stakes of the big game. Poetry's new practitioners were serious about the upheavals they wanted to bring about, paralleling in some ways the process that made American painting king in the 1940s, '50s and '60s. Embroiled in the ongoing transformation of poetry, Spicer sought to work a revolution inside the already revolutionary materials of what came to be called "The New American Poetry." He reveled in his status as both an insider and an outsider. His love of low culture manifests itself everywhere, especially as a natural love of California, arising from his feeling that California was, after all, the best and most democratic place on earth.

After his death, the band of poets he had gathered around him dispersed, some to give up poetry altogether. In 1975 Robin Blaser's afterword to Spicer's *Collected Books*, called "The Practice of Outside," located Spicer's theories of dictation and the "Other" within a broader world perspective brought into focus by modern theorists and phenomenologists like Merleau-Ponty, Foucault, and Barthes. At roughly the same time a renewed interest in the pioneering work of male homosexual writers provoked further interest in Spicer's life and poetic practice. In the mid-1980s a large conference was held in San Francisco to celebrate Spicer and his circle. Special issues of the literary magazines *Ironwood* and *ACTS* appeared, packed with useful criticism, original texts, and archival material. In 1993 Spicer's unfinished detective novel was published as *The Tower of Babel*, to wide acclaim. Today Spicer's work, once exceedingly hard to find, is included regularly in anthologies of postmodern poetry and is taught in universities and debated by panels at scholarly conferences. Spanish and French translations have appeared, a sign of popularity overseas.[7] The French techno rock group "Kat Onoma" has made an "opera" out of *Billy The Kid*, his 1958 *chant d'amour*, and Chilean director Raul Ruiz plans to make a film out of the detective novel. Contemporary novelists from Samuel R. Delany to Michael Ondaatje have been influenced by his work, and poets from Charles Bernstein to A. R. Ammons to Susan Howe have acknowledged his influence. Spicer has even been co-opted by trends in gay publishing: a passage from his poem "Jacob" (1959) appears as the epigraph to *Wrestling with the Angel: Faith and Religion in the Lives of Gay Men* (1995), and a line of gay greeting cards uses a line from Spicer's *Language* (1965)—"For you I would build a whole new universe" under a color photo of two buff lovers—it's part of their "Romance Line."

Almost every aspect of Spicer's life deserves extended treatment: his refusal to sign the Loyalty Oath in Berkeley in 1950, which thwarted his academic career, his membership in the clandestine Mattachine Society (one of the first gay liberation groups), his involvement in the "secret" art world of North Beach in the 1950s, his early interest in computers, his immersion in the science fiction of the prewar and postwar eras (including his friendship with the novelist Philip K. Dick), his celebration of an invented bohemia, his opposition to the Vietnam war. He lived a life constricted, in the main, to a few small blocks in San Francisco's North Beach, yet he lived this life in the serene certainty that it would be worthy of full biographical treatment—his letters are studded with directions, only half-ironic, to his future biographers.

The challenge of weeding the half-truths and myths from Spicer's life has been a rich one. Another challenge in telling this life has been to accurately represent the gay subculture Spicer lived and worked in. Currently much work is being done to reclaim "gay history" from the shadows of taboo and deracination. Since Spicer's contemporaries are now in their seventies, some of them are considerably more discreet than others. Among the younger artists who knew and worked with Spicer, we have also had to deal with the fact of AIDS—though it is trivial of course to complain of AIDS as an inconvenience to research when the reality is that it is the extreme crisis of the human spirit. Spicer himself was openly homosexual, but openness meant something different then than it does today. While Robin Blaser has many times warned us away from reducing the meaning of Spicer's poetry to the triviality of who he slept with, Spicer remains in history a telling example of a man at the mercy of a series of homophobic codes and taboos. Over and over, the men and women of Spicer's generation have told us, "You cannot possibly understand what it was like," the coldness and cruelty of life lived at the edge of the sex frontier: the doors shut, the walls without doors, the unthinking callousness with which so many lives were thwarted.

Over the past fifteen years, hundreds of men and women have helped us make this book what it is: a social history, a biography, a literary account. Individuals contributed generously and often. Rare books were given or lent, material assistance of every necessary kind was given. We could not have completed the book without the cooperation of Spicer's brother, Holt V. Spicer, of Springfield, Missouri; Robin Blaser and the late Robert Duncan, whose lives intertwined with Spicer's on every level for twenty years; the late Jim Herndon, Spicer's "Boswell"; Donald Allen, Spicer's friend and editor; Jess, who broke his silence of many years to speak about Spicer to us at last; and Dr. Harry Z. Coren, Spicer's psychiatrist in the last years of his life. From the start, three men inspired and encouraged the writing of this book, giving it context and shape and reality: George Stanley, Stan Persky, and Alvin William Moore (Bill Brodecky). We are especially grateful to the women Spicer loved, including Catherine Mulholland, Ellen Tallman, Mary Rice Moore, and Fran Herndon, and to Spicer's muses, the young— and for the most part, straight—men who inspired his tenderness and his greatest poetry: James Alexander, Gary Bottone, the late Joe Dunn, Landis Everson, Larry Kearney, Graham Mackintosh, Ron Primack, Richard Rummonds, the late John Allen Ryan, and Harris Schiff.

We would also like to thank these others who knew Jack Spicer and provided us with interviews, memoirs, letters, personal accounts, and other memorabilia: Gerald M. Ackerman, the late Helen Adam, Paul Alexander, Jack Anderson, Amiri Baraka, the late Robert Berg, Martin Block, Ebbe Borregaard, George Bowering, Kent Bowker, the late Richard Bratset, David Bromige, James Broughton, Wayne Burns, the late Herb Caen, the late Gail Chugg, the late Andy Cole, the late Robert Connor, Cid Corman, Robert Creeley, Wesley Day, Karen Tallman DeBeck, Pierre DeLattre, James Devlin, N. A. Diaman, Richard Duerden, Harold Dull, Ernie Edwards, the late Larry Eigner, Merle Ellis, Gerald Fabian, Mary Fabilli, Larry Fagin, the late James Felts, Lawrence Ferlinghetti, the late Tom Field, Dora FitzGerald, Nemi Frost, Maxine Gadd, the late Allen Ginsberg, the late Jack Goodwin, Thom Gunn, George Haimsohn, Sam Hardin, Latif Harris, Dave Haselwood, Bobbie Louise Hawkins, Wally Hedrick, Gladys Hindmarch, Ida Hodes, Leni Hoover, Neap Hoover, Andrew Hoyem, Harry Jacobus, Lenore Kandel, Eileen Kaufman, Robert Kelly, Basil King, Arthur Kloth, Joanne Kyger, John Gibbons ("Jack") Langan, Minnette Lehmann, Joe LeSueur, Denise Levertov, Glenn Lewis, the late Dorothy Livesay, Ron Loewinsohn, Stuart Loomis, Michael McClure, Earl McGrath, the late William McNeill, David Meltzer, the late Josephine Miles, Mary Rice Moore, Mary Morehart, the late Ernest Mundt, Armando Navarro, John Norton, Pauline Oliveros, the late Janie O'Neill, Ariel Parkinson, the late Thomas Parkinson, Roy Harvey Pearce, Bern Porter, Harry Redl, the late David Reed, Jerome Rothenberg, Michael Rumaker, the late Jess Sawyer, James Schevill, Hassel Smith, Gary Snyder, Janet Spangler, Josephine [Fredman] Stewart, Knute Stiles, Gaby Onderwyzer Stuart, Richard Tagett, the late Warren Tallman, Jim Townsend, Gael Turnbull, Lewis Warsh, Fred Wah, Diane Wakoski, Philip Whalen, John Wieners, Jonathan Williams, Myrsam Wixman, and Leonard Wolf. We owe great gratitude to Terry Ludwar who, on our behalf, interviewed Gladys Hindmarch, Leni Hoover, Neap Hoover, and (twice) Warren Tallman in Vancouver, B.C.

We thank the following for their hospitality and friendship, for publishing portions of our research, for making that research possible, for sharing their own work with us, for brainstorming sessions, for lending or giving us books and papers, for financial backing, for procuring interviews for us, for answering our questions about everything under the sun, and, in general, for putting up with us over the years: Richard Aaron, the late Steve Abbott, George Albon, A. R. Ammons, John Ashbery, Bill Berkson, Edmund Berrigan, Ernest Besig, Dan Blue, Bruce Boone, Jim Breeden, Manuel Brito, Carolyn Burke, the late William S. Burroughs, Hilde Burton, Lori Chamberlain, Norma Cole, Victor Coleman, Dennis Cooper, Michael Cuddihy, Maria Damon, the late Daniel Davidson, Michael Davidson, Brian De Beck, Raffael De Gruttola, Samuel R. Delany, Darin De Stefano, Steve Dickison, John Dinsmore, Cecilia Dougherty, Rachel Blau DuPlessis, Kenward Elmslie, Clayton Eshleman, Amy Evans, Steve Evans, Thomas Evans, Mark Ewert, David Farwell, Vince Fernandez, Jack Foley, the late Gilbert B. ("Tim") Foote, Betty Forquer, Ed Foster, Raymond Foye, Ben Friedlander, Susan Gevirtz, Alex Gildzen, Peter Gizzi, Robert Glück, Alan Golding, Brad Gooch, John Granger, Barbara Guest, Marilyn Hacker, Lee Harwood, Burton Hatlen, Robert Hershon, the late Leland Hickman, Gerd Hillen, Benjamin Hollander, Earl Jackson, Jr., Lisa Jarnot, Ronald Johnson, Denise Kastan, Jonathan Katz, Martha King, Dawn Kolokithas, the members of the Kootenay School of Writing, Kush, Joel Kuszai, Gerrit Lansing, the late James Laughlin, David Levi Strauss, Herb Levy, Jackson Mac Low, Eric Malone, the late Paul Mariah, John Martin, Ralph Maud, John Arthur Maynard, J.C.C. Mays, the late James Merrill, Roy Miki, Albert Mobilio, Bryan Monte, Laura Moriarty, Andrew Mossin, Jennifer Moxley, James P. Musser, Paul Naylor, Miriam Nichols, Aldon L. Nielsen, Harold Norse, Linda Norton, Peter O'Leary, Michael Ondaatje, Jenny Penberthy, Nancy Peters, Kenneth Pettitt, Kristin Prevallet, Larry Price, Peter Quartermain, the late David Rattray, Vanessa Renwick, Peter Riley, Lisa Robertson, Stephen Rodefer, Renee Rodin, Claude Royet-Journoud, Mark Salerno, Andrew Schelling, the late James Schuyler, Mertis [Golden] Shekeloff, Charles Shively, Aaron Shurin, Ron Silliman, Rod Smith, Rebecca Solnit, Gilbert Sorrentino, Matthew Stadler, Gary Sullivan, Roberto Tejada, Glenn Todd, Joseph and Molly Torra, George Tysh, Carole A. Vernier, Stephen Vincent, Christopher Wagstaff, Anne Waldman, Scott Watson, Steven Watson, Elizabeth Willis, John Yau, Lynette Yetter, Jery Zaslove, and Magdalena Zurawski.

We thank the librarians and cultural workers of the following institutions: Robert J. Bertholf, Michael Basinski, and Wendy Kramer at the Poetry/Rare Books Collection, State University of New York at Buffalo; Charles Watts, Special Collections, W.A.C. Bennett Library, Simon Fraser University, Burnaby, B.C.; William McPheron and Margaret J. Kimball, Special Collections, Green Library, Stanford University; Willard Goodwin, Cathy Henderson, and Barbara Smith-LaBorde of the Harry Ransom Humanities Research

Prologue

Center at the University of Texas at Austin; John D. Stinson, Rare Books and Manuscripts Department, New York Public Library; Gerald Koskovich and Willie Walker, Gay and Lesbian Historical Society of Northern California; Richard C. Fyffe and the late George Butterick, Special Collections Department, Homer Babbidge Library, University of Connecticut; Flora Ito, Public Service Assistant, Department of Special Collections, University of California, Los Angeles; Peter Berg, Head, Special Collections, Michigan State University Library; Richard H. F. Lindemann and Bett Miller, Archive for New Poetry, University of California, San Diego; Anne Caiger and Jeff Rankin, Department of Special Collections, University of California, Los Angeles; J. Kevin O'Brien, Freedom of Information/Privacy Acts Division, Information Management Division, Federal Bureau of Investigation; Laura Moriarty, Poetry Center at San Francisco State University; Bonnie Hardwick and Anthony Bliss, Manuscripts Division, Bancroft Library, University of California, Berkeley; Heather R. Munro, Lilly Library, Indiana University; Betsy Bishop and Dan Meyer, Department of Special Collections, University of Chicago Library; Leslie A. Morris, Curator of Books and Manuscripts, Rosenbach Museum & Library; Kevin Ray, Curator of Manuscripts, John M. Olin Library, Washington University in St. Louis; James Van Buskirk, Director, Gay and Lesbian Center, San Francisco Main Library.

Special thanks go to our editors at Wesleyan University Press, Suzanna Tamminen and Eileen McWilliam, and to Betsey Scheiner, editor *extraordinaire*. Kevin Killian would like to thank Dodie Bellamy for years and years of being what she calls a "Spicer widow" and to tell the world that, for her, he would build a whole new universe.

San Francisco, California
November 1997

Poet Be Like God

CHAPTER ONE

Prodigy Gone Wrong

Dorothy Clause and John Lovely Spicer were two midwesterners who met and married in Los Angeles, where their son Jack was born in January 1925. A younger son, Holt, was born three years later. Although most people thought they made a pleasant, if unremarkable couple, Jack noticed a certain disparity between his parents. They presented him with a puzzle he spent the rest of his life trying to solve: why and how had they come together, and to what end?

John Lovely Spicer worked in hotel and apartment management, assisted by Dorothy, who had been trained as a teacher and taught school for a few years before her marriage. According to Spicer's reworking of the family history, John Spicer had been involved in radical politics until "tamed" by Dorothy's bourgeois drive for middle-class respectability. Certainly John Spicer had had a turbulent youth. Born and raised on a farm in Minnesota in 1882, he had lost his own father early, seen him gored by a bull. His mother's second husband was a tyrant, and John ran away from home after losing his temper and assaulting his stepfather with intent to kill. The next twenty years he spent drifting from job to job, riding the rails, and organizing workers in the Pacific Northwest. The extent of his involvement in the IWW (the International Workers of the World, or, more familiarly, the "Wobblies") will probably never be wholly known. In any case it was over by the time of Jack's birth, although in later life Jack used sometimes to claim that John Spicer had taken him to Wobbly meetings (or reunions) when he was a little boy.[1] Eventually Jack came to view his father as a failure, a man with potential weakened by the American drive to achieve bourgeois status. To his credit, he never attempted to demonize his mother, theorizing that her strength of personality had won out, along with her youth, for she was twelve years younger than John Spicer. Long before Jack was old enough to go to school, his father had traded in his radical dreams for a liberal and polite interest in national and world events.

In general, Jack Spicer's childhood was comfortable and conventional. Throughout the Depression the Spicers lived in one rented single-family home after another in the solidly middle-class neighborhood of Beverly and Western. In later years John and Dorothy lived in the buildings they managed, but while their sons were young they guarded them from the harum-scarum life of "hotel children." The Spicers even had a car, a symbol of some affluence in the thirties—though Jack, whose lack of mechanical dexterity became legendary, never learned to drive.

Ever the teacher, Dorothy Spicer read aloud to her two sons every night—Charles and Mary Lamb's *Tales from Shakespeare*, Hawthorne's *Tanglewood Tales*, and "all of the Oz Books," Holt Spicer recalled. Writers with a true regard for children are rare, and Spicer held them all in great esteem. Lewis Carroll and Edward Lear never left him, and L. Frank Baum's *The Wizard of Oz* and its many sequels remained a touchstone throughout his life. They were California books, which looked back at drab midwestern America with nostalgia and bitterness, triumph and regret, and looked forward to a utopian paradise of technology in the service of progress and human values. Spicer saw his mother as a kind of Dorothy Gale, the unspoiled center of a magical world, the good all-American girl untouched by the vainglory that marks Oz's unsympathetic characters. His own role was more complex: he was ungainly Jack Pumpkinhead, or, in *The Holy Grail*, "like the Tin Woodsman in the Oz books. / Rusted beyond recognition. / I, sir, am a knight."[2]

In later life, teased by Robert Duncan about his putative Calvinism, Spicer triumphantly presented his friend with a souvenir he had kept since childhood—a Sunday school certificate for good attendance.[3] The Spicers felt it important that he and Holt receive a grounding in "religious matters," although they themselves had no affiliation. "The only time we ever went to church as a family," remembered Holt, "was during the brief period of time when my father was working for George Pepperdine and his foundation. In addition to owning Western Auto, George owned a good number of hotels and apartment houses, and my father worked as a supervisor for him. Pepperdine was a pillar in the Church of Christ. He insisted on at least periodic attendance of his own church by his employees, so during a period of time we occasionally attended George Pepperdine's church, which was somewhere in the downtown area, while we were living on the borderline between Los Angeles and Hollywood."

Holt's birth, when Jack was three, created a rupture in an otherwise happy life. Following conventional theories of child development, Jack's grandmother took him back home to the Midwest while Dorothy was pregnant again: it was thought that young children should not be exposed to pregnancy. As an unfortunate result, Jack came to feel that he had been expelled from his own family through no fault of his own. When Spicer reached his thirties, his misery about this expulsion catapulted him into a breakdown and analysis. "There were strong feelings about that, a lot of hatred for the brother who was monopolizing the mother's attention, things one would expect," noted Harry Z. Coren, Spicer's psychiatrist. "Though he thinks the timing somehow wasn't right, it somehow ties in with this trip he took with his grandmother. So it may be a sense of having been apart from his mother, either by a real trip, and/or a sense that his brother was filling his place now; he didn't have as much access to his mom."[4] It did not help that Holt grew bigger, stronger, braver, and more normatively masculine than his older brother. When the boys were young, it was Holt who'd have to rescue Jack from neighborhood bullies. As Holt put it, "I think both of us suffered by early stereotyping. Jack was—I'm not sure how to phrase this—the 'frail genius.' I was the 'normal child.' There is a good deal of truth in that generalization; but, like other generalizations, it is dangerous and can be overworked."[5]

Jack was a bookish boy, and other boys in the neighborhood mocked his learning and pretensions to being a poet. In grade school an insensitive teacher exposed Jack to the further scorn of his classmates by pointing up his naiveté. (He later told a friend, "I never eat raisins. I hate 'em. Do you want to know why? When I was in first, or second grade, we had a rabbit in the classroom, and I came into class after the weekend and went over to the pen and I said to the teacher, 'There are raisins here.' And the kids laughed at me."[6]) He suffered from double vision, reporting that he thought everyone saw *doubly*—"everyone's got two eyes, don't they?" (Later in life, one of the traits that attracted him to Robert Duncan was the positive spin Duncan put on his own eye problems, his glorification of his double vision.) Glasses helped Jack's vision but hurt his image with the other boys, who called him teacher's pet, sissy, four eyes. And his poor coordination made him even more of an outsider, because he could not seem to manage to ride a bicycle like everyone else.

Jack and Holt Spicer at summer camp (mid 1930s? late 1930s?). A sweet, affectionate boy with bad dreams. *Courtesy of Robin Blaser.*

But childhood continued to offer him magical moments. In the evenings, after his homework, he would sit with his family and listen to the radio as night deepened over Los Angeles. In the days before television, radio was king, and from the moment he heard a radio he fell in love with it—this strange outside voice, or bundle of voices, penetrating the airwaves (themselves a mysterious concept), quickening the domestic scene with hints of the outside. He enjoyed the popular singers and comedians of his day—Eddie Cantor, Jack Benny, Sophie Tucker, and a host of others, and tried to model his wit on theirs. He grew addicted to the primitive radio soaps of the thirties and stayed a fan of "Our Gal Sunday" and "Ma Perkins" till they went off the air twenty years later. Radio itself, its intermittent messages, affected him deeply, and formed his sense of art's appeal. Through its serial nature—one "episode" following another at a regular interval—"tune in tomorrow"—radio taught him the contrary pleasures of suspense and timelessness. He bought a phonograph and started listening to classical music, but on radio the music was endless. Radio's mystery shows ("Suspense," "The Shadow") fascinated him and so, of course, did the baseball announcers whose evocative language brought him right behind home plate at Yankee Stadium or Wrigley Field.

He haunted the libraries for the classic and new detective novels and thrillers. Although he never outgrew his love of children's books, as a teenager he broadened his reading to include "adult" writers like Fenimore Cooper, Walter Scott, Galsworthy, Shaw, Sinclair Lewis, Dreiser, Hemingway, Faulkner, as well as Hardy, Thackeray, Balzac, Trollope, and Dickens.[7] He discovered to his amazement that there were real writers, living nearby, right in Los Angeles. At age sixteen he wrote to Aldous Huxley, for example, and sent the writer a birthday present of *The Hidden Teaching Beyond Yoga*, by the contemporary British mystic Paul Brunton. Huxley responded with a comradely letter inviting him to meet his wife, Maria, and join them for dinner at home in Pacific Palisades. An important result of their brief relationship was his sense of communion with another writer at an early age. In addition, studying Huxley's texts on the expansion of consciousness, and learning about Buddhism and Hindu practices through Huxley's popular explications, propelled Jack into a serious study of comparative religion once he went to college.[8]

Games and puzzles fascinated Jack with their rules and laws, and he soon moved from jigsaws to Scrabble to crosswords, which he solved with an alarming ease. Before the age of twelve, he became a regular at the meetings of the Los Angeles Chess Club, challenging the adult members. Because it had its own rules and therefore its own perfections, chess was a way of making sense of a bewildering world. Like most boys, he wanted desperately to be popular among his peers, and his enthusiasm for games won him a certain grudging popularity on the street corners. But he was to be found most often at the library, where he mastered the Dewey Decimal System while still quite young, and in time became an excellent researcher. He had an innate talent for finding things out. "He knew how to use the library in a way that no one I've ever met did," said a later friend.[9] Jack studied railroad and bus timetables and could really work Los Angeles public transit, taking Holt along on day excursions to the farthest parts of the huge city and its sprawling environs.

The Spicers taught their sons the liberal values they had agreed on as a compromise, a patchwork of tolerance for others, racial equality, democracy, "free enterprise," and volunteerism. The Spicers listened to syndicated radio

commentators—Gabriel Heatter, Edward R. Murrow, H. R. Kaltenborn—
and voted for Roosevelt, again and again. "The attitude of our family," recalled Holt,

which we got largely, I think, through our father, [was that] of being very interested
in civil rights and having very affirmative feelings toward all kinds of people, and
tending to be the champion of the underdog, or the person who needed help. My
father and mother tended to share the same interests and biases on important matters. We all used to keep up with national and international news as part of our
way of life. We were very interested in, and very much angered by, the oppression
of the Jews prior to the outbreak of World War II. We tended to be somewhat liberal Democrats and semi-socialists collectively . . . we tended to pull for the underdog; we were very interested in politics and the like.[10]

Jack and Holt were taught to respect their elders, to attend to their teachers, and to be good citizens; and, in the main, Jack agreed with the liberal
mission.

The entry of the United States into World War II brought great changes
to Los Angeles, which converted its huge pool of manpower into further-
ing the war effort. This led to a wave of new arrivals, drawn to the area in
search of lucrative war work, and a consequent housing shortage. After
Pearl Harbor, the Pacific seemed suddenly smaller. Content up to now, and
proud of his achievements within the business community, Jack's father—
now close to sixty—began again to express a certain dissatisfaction and to
exhibit a still-fiery drive toward local anarchist politics. He would take out
a globe and show Jack how Los Angeles was closer to China than to New
York. "Washington doesn't care about us," he would say angrily. "We're too
far away." The war served to underline how independent California was
from the rest of the country; nevertheless, hateful chains of gold bound
California to the rest of the Union. "We were not estranged from everything," Jack later said, quoting his father, "until the railroad took over California between 1870 and 1906."[11] The railroad, celebrated for bringing
Americans closer together, pushed California into a humiliating position of
subservience to the rest of the country, which used it as the "breadbasket of
the nation." There was a touch of the Luddite in both father and son,
which culminated, later in Jack's career, when he sent part of his fingertip
to the Rainier Ale Company, to protest the newfangled invention of the
pop-top beer can.[12]

As Jack continued to imagine a writing career, he became more and
more withdrawn, antisocial, and critical of the world around him. There
was something different about him: the boys in school who mocked him as

a "fairy" or "pansy" had unwittingly pegged him correctly. He wondered about his home, his school, his family—a hundred years ago, what had these spaces been? Empty forest, native peoples. It frightened him to think of it, so he tried not to. But sometimes he forced himself to think about it, and that scared him even more. Jack would watch the young athletes on the playing field, identifying deeply with their mindless quest for perfection, but he was unable to shed his cares as they did. He was bewildered by their taunts, since his sexual nature, slow to develop, veered back and forth between confusion and certainty for the rest of his young manhood, and he did not identify himself as homosexual—not just yet. In his eyes, the way his mother had suppressed his father's IWW activity paralleled the way the U.S. government had cracked down on the Wobbly movement. Of the past, only the music remained, labor songs by Joe Hill—"It's Sister Jenny's Turn to Throw the Bomb, Bomb, Bomb"—and folk songs of his grandparents' era, like "Sweet Betsy from Pike."

For many years of his adolescence, Jack resolutely ignored the claims of his body and staked his identity on poetry. And on magic—the leap between the known and the unknown or unknowable. Hollywood was full of magic, if only you knew where to look, and Spicer's curiosity led him everywhere. He prided himself on his skill with Tarot and read everything he could lay his hands on about the subject—from Eliphas Levi to Aleister Crowley to Charles Williams. He told a Berkeley friend he'd learned Tarot as an adolescent by hanging around a traveling fair, where a "carny" taught him the cards.[13] In later years he planned to write a book on Tarot—a how-to, self-help book that he was sure would make him plenty of money. Jack had an amazing ear and used it to win bets with suckers: after a few minutes conversation with a stranger, he could peg what state and county that man or woman had been born and raised in, computing *heimat* from accent and vocabulary like a Los Angeles Henry Higgins. This skill, like Tarot, was a science that could, and did, pass for magic to the uninitiated.

After high school, Jack attended the University of Redlands for two years. Due to his poor eyesight and a calcium deficiency, he was classified 4-F— physically unfit for service—by the draft board, thus missing out on the central experience of most American boys of his era, military service. His feelings about his exclusion from the service were complicated. He followed every battle of the war, where many of his high school classmates were fighting. His horror grew at the reports of atrocity, slaughter, and heroism that attended each step of the Pacific campaign: the battle of Tarawa in New Guinea in 1944, for example, where four thousand American sailors went in, and only some three hundred came out. The death of a college class-mate became the basis for a novel, *The Wasps*, which he began and aban-doned a few years later.[14] But his feelings about death and war were not solely morbid. The soldiers he met displayed a world-weary eroticism, and the conscientious objectors had a certain eros of integrity as well. Jack fell in love with men of both types: they had each passed a test he had failed.

Redlands, in San Bernardino, was smack in the middle of the citrus belt of central California—the lemons that haunt Spicer's mature poetry grew everywhere, their scent, and the scent of the burning oil from the smoke-pots, permeating his dorm room. He began to drink, just a beer now and then, as do most college boys. The pleasant buzz amused him. He be-friended strangers: on vacations from school he brought home a number of Hawaiian students from Redlands—a generous act, as they had nowhere else to go, and the color of their skin made them unwelcome in many Cal-ifornia towns.[15] Jack's best friend at the University of Redlands was an as-piring musician, Gene Wahl. They made an odd couple—the tall, sham-bling, genially ugly Spicer, and Wahl, the fresh-faced, charismatic All-American boy. Classmates speculated on their friendship, the usual consequence when the attractive attend the plain. On other vacations, Jack and Gene would visit the gay bars and the black after-hours jazz clubs of Los Angeles, where they once saw Billie Holiday sing, and where they heard Charlie Parker for the first time. (It was there, too, that Spicer smoked his first reefer.) After two years Jack and Gene decided to transfer together to the University of California at Berkeley. Berkeley was no one-horse college in the San Bernardino Valley. It was—or so its advertising told them—the "Athens of the West."

Berkeley was undergoing the first wave of expansions in 1945, as a result of the sudden influx of returning GIs, home from the war and soon to be covered by the GI Bill. The university's population almost doubled in one astonishing year (1945–46, Spicer's first there), and the student body was suddenly older on the average, more sophisticated, wilder. At Berkeley, Jack managed to reinvent himself so completely that few of the friends he met in the second half of his life knew anything about his upbringing. He seemed determined to keep his past a secret, to remove even the interest of secrecy from it, so that no one would inquire. Many thought him an or-phan. He made it clear he didn't appreciate questions about "home," only about "California."

Spicer's first friends at Berkeley were Robin Blaser and Blaser's lover James Felts, former students at the University of Chicago who, like Spicer, also arrived in Berkeley in 1945. "From the earliest years," Blaser remembered, "Spicer saw himself as quite ugly. He had certain physical disabilities, an almost spastic characteristic. He saw himself as unattractive and he dramatized that and played it out. He was an astonishing figure. When he first knocked on my door, he was wearing a trench coat, dark glasses, had on sandals, and his feet were stained purple with treatment for athlete's foot."[16] Shocked, Blaser slammed the door, and opened it again only when he heard chuckling on the other side. Spicer was now licensed as a private detective, and made money investigating bartenders for suspicious owners and managers. He was six feet tall, with fine, thinning, gold-red hair, and a doughy face. The calcium deficiency that had kept him out of the army made him hunch over so that he appeared much shorter, his long arms dangling in the characteristic stance of an ape.

Blaser and Felts, intrigued, invited Spicer to share their home, although Robin admits today his immediate interest was in Jack's magnetic pal Gene Wahl. The living situation led to tense difficulties, however, when Robin realized—a comment here, a comment there, "he's no good for you," "he'd be happier somewhere else"—that Jack intended to break him and Jim up. After six months of sniping, Robin asked Jack to find somewhere else to live—it was "either that or lose James Felts," he says. Jack agreed and moved on with a shrug, remaining, indeed, close to Robin for the rest of his life.[17] Spicer seemed to enjoy sowing seeds of discord, unable to stand the sight of a happy couple. And, since most couples have fracture points upon which pressure can be applied, he was remarkably successful in this regard. His progress was littered with the divorces, break-ups, and estrangements of once-happy friends. This tendency was a twisted by-product of Jack's own family romance, the never-to-be-solved mystery of his parents' own happiness together. Jack's relationship to his parents was hidden from his college peers, yet its aftereffects were always in the air.

Spicer's first poetry teacher was Josephine Miles, the only woman in Berkeley's English department and a well-known poet. Miles, only in her early thirties, had long been wheelchair-bound by an aggravated muscular disease. She felt sorry for Jack, as he poured out to her the details of his "terrible life"—he told her, for example, that his parents were professional bridge players in Southern California, making them more raffish and footloose than they were.[18] Miles's strong, careful writing was influenced by older California forebears (George Sterling, Ina Coolbrith, Mary Austin), with an overlay of international modernism by way of Hardy, Eliot, Auden, Wallace Stevens, and Marianne Moore. Privately and poetically, her influence on Spicer was great, and his early poems might be taken for her own. His writing, commented another contemporary, Ariel Parkinson, became a "sinister" version of Miles's incisive line.[19] Miles generously helped him find work off-campus to supplement his slight income from the detective game; and she paid him to help her with word-counting concordances of the great nineteenth century American poets.[20] After studying with Miles for a year, he acknowledged the debt by making her a present of his poetry to date, typed and collated into a bound notebook he grandly called "Collected Poems 1945–6."[21] His poetry was also heavily influenced by a number of other women whom he admired—Edna St. Vincent Millay, Edith Sitwell, Marianne Moore, Mina Loy, Mary Butts, Gertrude Stein, H.D., and Laura Riding. These modernist women writers, too little known even in their own day, were inventors of a new kind of poetry that variously masked or marked sexual difference with a radical approach to logos and gnomos.

On the politically charged Berkeley campus, Spicer found options of every political stripe: a strong socialist party, various factions of Stalinists, Trotskyists, anarchists, and pacifists, angry at the recent use of the atom bomb; and all these groups, he noted ironically, at war with each other. Jack saw radical politics as a chance to keep his father's lost dreams alive and to battle the bourgeois maternal clamp. He was drawn to the Libertarian Circle, a group of "philosophical anarchists" who met every Wednesday night at a flat on Steiner Street in San Francisco, across the bay from Berkeley's campus. The guru and ringleader of this group, Kenneth Rexroth, was forty years old and already a national figure in American poetry. He developed a reading list for the group that included Alexander Berkman, Emma Goldman, William Godwin, Bakunin, McTaggart, and William Reich among the anarchists, as well as Engels, Lenin, Tolstoy, Lao-tzu, Plato, Aristotle, Bacon, Plutarch, and St. Simon.[22] Rexroth occupied a central place in Bay Area letters as an intellectual, a poet, and a man of highly developed political convictions, rather like the father Spicer wished he had. He was the king of San Francisco poetry, and around his throne pretenders bowed and parried and strategized. At these Wednesday night political debates, and in George Leite's Berkeley bookstore, a group of like-minded writers and poets met and began to form connections. On the F train one evening, after a meeting at the Rexroths' home, Robert Duncan nodded to Jack Spicer and the two young men began to talk, at first quietly, then with growing excitement.

Robert Duncan, seven years older than Spicer, had already lived a remarkable life devoted to poetry and sex. He had hitchhiked the United States, meeting other writers, and living out the romantic fantasies of the poet's life he had dreamed of in his native Bakersfield, a dreary town in central California. Duncan had been a student at Berkeley before the war and had already inspired the first of many poetry circles there. On the East Coast in 1940–41, he had edited *The Experimental Review*, and attracted attention from Anaïs Nin, Henry Miller, Thomas Merton, Kenneth Patchen, and Lawrence Durrell. In New York he met surrealist painters who had fled the Nazi invasion of Europe, and worked for a time in an art gallery, so he now knew "everything" about modern art. Duncan had been a gigolo and had even been married. Everything about Duncan was larger-than-life: his erudition, his drama, his talent, and his wit. Duncan was, in Leonard Wolf's words, the "most 'out' man that ever lived."[23] He knocked Spicer off his feet.

Duncan particularly inspired Spicer by his espousal of open homosexuality at a time when it was dangerous to do so. He had declared his homosexuality in the August 1944 issue of *Politics*, earning John Crowe Ransom's rejection from *The Kenyon Review* of a poem that had already been accepted.[24] Both Spicer and Blaser were "fascinated with the piece" by Duncan, finding it "astonishing and marvelous."[25] At times Duncan could pose as a martyr to homosexuality, at other times as a martyr to society's intolerance of it. Yet he gloried equally in the role of satyr, as the boy-chasing, pleasure-loving Dionysus of UC Berkeley.

Duncan, Spicer, and Blaser began to invent their own myth, an insurgence of culture and ease they called—only half-mockingly—"The Berkeley Renaissance."[26] Nothing in Jack's life ever after equaled the combination of high spirits and idealistic hopes of their initial interactions. Duncan's example led the more timid Spicer to explore his own sexuality in ways he'd never dreamed of at Redlands. In fact, he once spoke of 1946, the year he met Duncan, as his year of birth, a comment not only on how much Duncan meant to him, but on how much he wanted to forget his first twenty years on earth. Duncan was equally impressed by Spicer. Spicer's ugliness fascinated Duncan, who considered himself a connoisseur of erotic pleasure, even of decadence. Spicer kept the priapic Duncan at arm's length, however, claiming to draw a kind of Antaean strength from remaining a virgin. Whether or not he planned it this way, this strategy was the one thing that could have held Duncan's restless attention. Duncan never tired of telling the story of his glee when Gene Wahl, who had met

Spicer's family in Los Angeles, confided wonderingly to Duncan: "You know, back home, Jack has a brother who looks like a normal person!"[27] From the beginning Duncan and Spicer quarreled about everything—from Dickens to Tagore to George Orwell—but in a way that satisfied them both, made them hungry for further contact and exploration.

Jack found rooms at the Treehaven Apartments in North Berkeley—a stately, vaguely art deco building with carpeted hallways on the north side of campus, near Robin Blaser and Jim Felts. He spent little time there, however; most of his free hours he spent at 2029 Hearst Street, where Duncan had established a bohemian collective with a young married couple, Hugh and Janie O'Neill. The round table in the O'Neills' house became the spiritual and physical center of the Berkeley Renaissance, as Spicer and Duncan challenged each other into ever more arcane realms of poetry and magic. They were living in a world that seemed charged with beauty and art, and in the magic circle of his new friends, homosexuality was the most glittering fruit of all—not only not forbidden, but positively encouraged. When Jack went home to his parents' hotel on vacations, he played the role of the good elder son, but sought out gay bars—ironically, the Stillwell Hotel, where the Spicers now lived and worked, was located at the very heart of the homosexual bar scene of postwar L.A. In Berkeley, the sexual mores that kept homosexuality a secret were relaxed.

After dinner at the O'Neills', Duncan would read poetry, discuss poetics, or direct them in impromptu performances of Shakespeare or Gertrude Stein. All through the hot summer of 1946, the house was filled with Tarot cards, crystal balls, all the props of magic. Jo Fredman, a graduate student in English, and her husband Fred—a lecturer in Japanese—became part of this magic circle. Fred's copy of the *Kenkyusha*, the classic Japanese-English dictionary, became one of their key sources. Eyes shut, one person thought of a question. Another held out the book so that the leaves opened. A finger dropped at random onto a word, which supplied the answer.

Part of the gatherings' magic was rooted in sexual jealousy and anger. Duncan had developed a crush on Spicer and hoped by sheer brilliance to lure him from his tightly held position on virginity. "I must have been loopy," he said later, "since Spicer was hardly attractive." In turn Spicer became enamored of Hugh O'Neill. Overlapping with his unsettling crush was Duncan's attachment to the now pregnant Janie O'Neill. Years later, Janie O'Neill identified the unpleasant aspect of Spicer that lay hidden underneath the surface of his charm and his beautiful speaking voice. He was like Iago, she said: without realizing it, she began to feel Hugh wanting, and Robert more and more helpful and attractive. "And it was all Spicer's work," she sighed.[28] Like a dog in the manger, Spicer resented Duncan's increasing interest in Janie. Reflecting on Spicer's aversion to Robert Graves's concept of the White Goddess, Duncan wrote:

> Jack Spicer complains
> when the Lady appears
> —The Poet
> allows almost anyone
> in here—She
> is anarchic
> hectic. Who?
> —he sneers—
> is this dish-faced bobby-soxer
> swooning
> when the self-fascinated
> amateur
> Othello
> comforts himself?
> What right,
> or might,
> has this now mother
> now bride
> fat potency
> to interfere
>
> Duncan from imagination's window
>   gazes;
> in this confounding of all things
>   finds grace;
> follows the Moon's irregular
>   phases;
> and sleeps with her wickedness
>   full on his face.[29]

Again Spicer plotted the separation of a couple for his own secret ends. Two "couples," in fact: Hugh and Janie, then Robert and Janie.

The Berkeley Renaissance began in earnest in the autumn of 1946, and included a wide variety of poets; it was far from a solidly homosexual group of writers. Jo Fredman joined Duncan, Spicer, and Hugh O'Neill in writing a "Canto for Ezra Pound," which they mailed to the beleaguered poet at St. Elizabeth's Hospital in Washington, D.C. in December of 1946.[30] There was a group of poets around George Leite, who owned the bookstore Daliel's and produced a magazine of international scope called *Circle*. The Activist poets (including Lawrence Hart, Jeanne McGahey,

Robert Horan, and Rosalie Moore) were tremendously vital, with the two last named each winning the "Yale Younger Poet" awards late in the 1940s. The younger writers drew inspiration from the independence and verve of poet Robinson Jeffers and novelist Henry Miller, both of them at the height of their powers and living respectively in Carmel and Big Sur, just south of the Bay Area. Miller's *Black Spring* was, Spicer believed, the "best work of prose written by an American in the past ten years."[31] Another local figure was the physicist Bern Porter, who had once worked on the Manhattan Project. Turning to the arts, he published the first books of several local poets, including James Schevill, Leonard Wolf, and Duncan himself.[32] Porter, one of many who admired Spicer's work, offered to publish some of it in *Circle*, which he co-edited with George Leite, or in his other magazine, *Berkeley: A Journal of Modern Culture*, but Spicer demurred. "No, no," he responded. "What I do in my head stays there—I don't let it out, ever. The air is bad here in San Francisco. There are so many cultural bums around ready to steal." Porter, who had already published Parker Tyler, Henry Miller, and Anais Nin, invited Spicer to a party in Nin's honor. "No," he said again. "All the cultural bums will be there. I don't want them to know what I'm doing in my head. The San Francisco air is bad, very bad." Shrugging, Porter wished him luck in his career.[33] The poet Leonard Wolf played an early and important part in organizing and promoting the activities of the Renaissance poets. Wolf's poems, collected in the early *Hamadryad Hunted*, were much admired by Duncan and Spicer for the intensity and authenticity of their lyric expression and their use of what Duncan called a "psychic language, a psychic feeling for the dream-like portent and omen of daily experience."[34]

Duncan began and maintained a poetry study group in a rundown boarding house called "Throckmorton Manor." In a long, dark dining room lined with chalkboards he inaugurated the series by reading from and commenting on Pound, T. S. Eliot, Gertrude Stein, Proust, Mann, and Gide. In a later lecture, the Puerto Rican scholar Rosario Jimenez brought Lorca to life by her sensitive reading of him, and Tom Parkinson presented Yeats. Hart Crane was studied, as well as Laura Riding, D. H. Lawrence, Apollinaire, Wallace Stevens, Robert Desnos, William Carlos Williams, and Paul Valery. *Finnegans Wake* was the subject of one memorable group survey.

Spicer lived as a boarder on Tamalpais Road, in the Italianate home of Julia Cooley Altrocchi, a generous and striking woman, the widow of the head of Berkeley's Italian Department. Mrs. Altrocchi was a Vassar graduate and a descendant of the Anglo-Fiorentini, the colony of English and U.S.

expatriates who had gathered around the Brownings at Casa Guidi—though she had never thought it necessary, even when married to Altrocchi, to learn Italian herself. She was a little embarrassed about her one quirk, her firm belief that Edward de Vere, Earl of Oxford, had really written Shakespeare's plays. A warm-hearted and still-young woman, she loved having poets and artists around her. Los Angeles's Stillwell Hotel, where Jack's parents now lived and worked, was a world away from the Florentine/Berkeley elegance of Julia Altrocchi's home. For her a grateful Spicer wrote "A Heron for Mrs. Altrocchi":

> They will not hunt us with snares and with arrows.
> The flesh of the water-bird is tough and is bumb.
> The sound of an arrow, the sight of a hunter
> Only remind us of life without wings.[35]

On campus, under the bust of Lincoln in the Campanile, Leonard Wolf introduced Spicer to Ariel Reynolds. "He was skeletally thin, absolutely white, and he wore an old army jacket that came down to here," she recalled in 1991, indicating a length halfway down her thigh. "This is Ariel," Wolf said. Spicer replied, "And I'm Caliban." An aspiring painter, Reynolds came from a well-to-do Bay Area family and still lived at home, in Piedmont, "in a very beautiful house, and garden, with people who were well-off—my mother and father." Her godfather was Ben Lehman, the refined, aristocratic head of the English Department who had once been married to the actress Dame Judith Anderson. It was a new world for Spicer, the luxury and bourgeois comfort of the Reynoldses, and he visited this Berkeley royalty as often as he could. "We would all go to dinner," remembers Jo Fredman, "and the family didn't know what to think about Duncan! There was always something sexual in his energy, and in the way he read poetry: he turned us *all* on. I was kind of the intermediary . . . I could talk to Mrs. Reynolds, who was complaining about how hard it was to get maids. This was at this little dinner party, where she had this little button, and she was supposed to step on the button and it's supposed to bring the maids from the kitchen."[36] And Spicer's world was a new one for Ariel, who was aghast when she visited his room on Tamalpais Road and saw that he stored his food on top of the toilet tank in the bedroom—his peanut butter, French bread, and milk. He never spoke of his family. Ariel had the impression they were "degenerate," an L.A. version of the southern clans Erskine Caldwell wrote about in *God's Little Acre*. Spicer objected when Ariel became engaged to yet another member of the Berkeley Renaissance, the young

Ariel Reynolds. *Courtesy of Ariel Parkinson.*

professor Thomas Parkinson, himself a poet. "Tom Parkinson!" cried Spicer, "impossible! But a very good poet—unfortunately!" Ariel considered Jack damned by his own naïveté and his extreme discomfort with his body—"it's like the line in Doctor Faustus. Faustus says to Mephistopheles, 'Why aren't you in Hell?' and Mephistopheles replies, 'Why, this is Hell, nor am I out of it.'" Jack gave Ariel a poem, which she kept framed on her dresser at home until her mother destroyed it, sensitive to its allusion to "virgins" and fearing for her daughter's reputation.[37] In 1991 Ariel described the Spicer she knew in 1946:

Jack's mouth was too muscular, too mobile to be "attractive." It was the kind of working instrument his hands were not, and his teeth were gray and yellow. His hair was beautiful—coppery brown, supple and glistening, with a slight wave back from the high white forehead. The whole structure of his face, with high cheekbones and strong jaw, was pleasing. The strength and full development of the head was a marked contrast to the body's aspect of unfinished assemblage. With his height and slenderness, the pale and open face, the rich color of eyes and hair, he had physical distinction, even handsomeness, only, even then, flagrantly and destructively neglected.

   His characteristic expression when I was with him or saw him was of impish

Thomas Parkinson. *Courtesy of Ariel Parkinson.*

glee. He was the great ironist. He was the man outside—Fool, Caliban, Touch-stone, Lucifer. He knew too much to be sorrowful or indignant.

"Football is my only eccentricity."

"Tom Parkinson with glasses—a hippopotamus with a bow tie."

"The food is kept on the toilet tank, because it is functionally convenient."

Every day at lunch, by the Campanile, Jack sat cross-legged, consuming his half-loaf of white French bread and his pint of milk—and laughing.[38]

The Throckmorton Manor series expanded exponentially, and soon po-etry readings were being held all over Berkeley—on Friday nights at the home of Leonard and Patricia Wolf, on other nights in art galleries and bookstores. A spirit of poetry, romance, and magic began to bloom in the very shadow of the university's walls. The excitement of the expansive writ-ing scene of Berkeley in the late forties found its apogee in the Berkeley Writers' Conference, which still seems today a daring use of university re-sources. The English department, responding to the desire of the students for more courses in creative writing, decided to establish a semi-official staff of gifted undergraduate and graduate students to teach their own courses in creative writing. "The reason we had the poetry workshop," explained Tom

Parkinson, "is that so little was being done in terms of teaching writing in the English department."[39] Not much money was involved, for the "teachers" were unpaid; small sums went for rooms in Wheeler Hall, to publish a literary magazine composed of the students' work, and to attract guest speakers—generally, local novelists and poets who gave readings and spoke from their own experience in writing and publishing, such as the British novelist Timothy Pember, who lived in Oakland. These courses were not accredited—the whole enterprise was entirely student-run and directed, although a "faculty advisor" was assigned by the department: Brewster Rogerson at first, and then Wayne Burns. "The scuttlebutt around the department," chuckled Burns, "was that it was the kiss of death to be appointed this, advisor to the Writers Conference—that it was just a preparation for getting rid of you. Which it may have turned out to be."[40] Through a combination of nerve, talent, and luck, a predominantly homosexual clique essentially took over the leadership of the Conference.[41] The young writers involved saw the Conference as a chance to wrest the university framework to their own anarchic ends. They believed that Berkeley was in a middle of a golden age and that they would all emerge world-famous. Spicer, Duncan, and Blaser taught sections, and invited speakers once a month to give readings and lectures. "I was in Spicer's section," Ariel Reynolds recalled. "At the first meeting Spicer gave some rules, discussed writing, and said, 'Now I want you all to bring some poetry to the next meeting.' So, we all did. He said, 'I'm going to read some poems submitted by one of you,' and he read these marvelous poems. I was so impressed: one of the people in this group of students had produced these fabulous poems in the past week! I was just agog. And, of course, Spicer had written them. But he carried it off perfectly, giving the absolutely appropriate stimulation to the class: we all produced quite good work after that."[42]

At a meeting the following year, Spicer played a hoax that had unfortunate repercussions. Mary Morehart, a student of art history, posed as a poet and read poetry Spicer had himself written as an undergrad. The audience, at first skeptical, warmed to her reading and acclaimed her as a fine poet, barraging her with compliments and questions on technique. When the hoax was revealed she found herself *persona non grata* among the poets she and Jack had fooled. "But Jack was jubilant over the joke," she recalled later. "Highly amused, he told me that if the poems were ever published, he would title them 'The Morehart Hoax.'"[43]

Ten years later, when Spicer and Blaser planned a study of the Berkeley Renaissance, they intended to devote a half-serious chapter to "the celebrities who visited Berkeley"—these included young, golden Gore Vidal, paraded

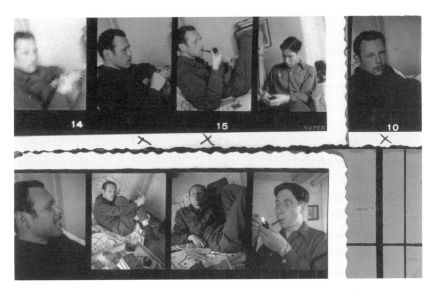

Jack Spicer and Berkeley friends. "Let some curious animal bend and touch that ape / With nuzzling mouth, would not the storm break / And that ape kiss, with dancing in his lips?" *Photos by Mary Morehart.*

around Wheeler Hall by Robert Duncan's friend Anaïs Nin, who introduced him as the "novelist of the future," and wan, shy E. M. Forster, mumbling until Duncan and Jo Fredman broke out the gin at the tea party in his honor at 2029 Hearst Street. In this context, homosexuality was privileged: its glamor and mystery celebrated. When vacations and holidays came, Jack could hardly bear it: he was having so much fun on campus he never wanted it to end. He couldn't bear to be away from his friends for even a weekend. From Los Angeles he wrote to Duncan on Stillwell Hotel stationery, crossing out the "well" in "Stillwell" and substituting "sick."[44]

Ernst Kantorowicz, one of the most brilliant thinkers on campus while Blaser, Spicer, and Duncan were undergraduates, played a significant role in the lives of the three poets. Kantorowicz, professor of medieval history at Berkeley, and author of *Frederick II* and *The King's Two Bodies*, had been a member of the inner circle, the *Kreis*, of the German poet Stefan George in the years before Hitler's rule. George, the last of the great German romantic poets, had built a cult around "Maximin," the beloved youth who had died, still young and beautiful, in George's arms. The circle of largely homosexual artists, teachers, and craftsmen, which included Kantorowicz's teacher, Friederich Gundolf, devoted itself to high standards of scholarship, ability, and performance. In 1933 George died, and soon after Ernst Kantorowicz left Germany (he was Jewish, as well as being a member of the Polish aristocracy).

At Berkeley, Kantorowicz's theories of kingship, accession, and succession to the throne, and the medieval beliefs in the divine right of kings were both provocative and queerly apropos to a young band of poets who saw themselves as inheritors of the kingship of poetry. A masterful teacher, Kantorowicz used various medieval and Renaissance texts to situate the whole range of contemporary attitudes toward the monarchy: for example, this passage from Shakespeare's *Richard II*—

> Was this face the face
> That every day under his household roof
> Did keep ten thousand men? Was this the face
> That like the Sun did make beholders wink?
> Is this the face which faced so many follies,
> That was at last out fac'd by Bolingbroke?
> A brittle glory shineth in this face.[45]

Each question pinpoints another "face" of the king: the first, the feudal lord, the second, the divine body, the third, the human being. "Kantorowicz was of enormous importance to all three of us," said Blaser. "Kantorowicz gave me history. An ability to think historically, to know how large the world is. I had some of that from Catholicism; Duncan from Theosophy; Spicer from Calvinism and the depths of the American. Kantorowicz brought it all to a head and opened into the most extraordinary information. Coming out of that, we have Duncan's *Medieval Scenes* and, of course, *The Venice Poem*. Kantorowicz was fundamental in working against that American thing that works ahistorically and pretends that there isn't really anything but a kind of progression."[46]

Kantorowicz's classes were legendary for their difficulty and their cachet. Thomas Parkinson recalled auditing a class on Anglo-Saxon history. "Someone told me, 'He didn't know any Anglo-Saxon until the summer, don't take that course.' I had had a solid year of very rigorous training in Anglo-Saxon, in *Beowulf* and dramatic philology. But Kantorowicz knew a hell of a lot more than I did! In six weeks he'd learned!"[47] In addition, Kantorowicz was a celebrated gourmet, whose seminar meetings began with hors d'oeuvres and ended with Rhine wine. He was both a dandy and a he-man, leading his students on fishing trips, their knapsacks stuffed with cans of anchovies for *truite bleue*. He discouraged women from attending his classes; his male students thought of him as a god. Spicer learned from Kantorowicz that a measure of casual cynicism often gives wit an edge. He was present one day when the conversation turned to the historian's most faithful disciple, whose wife had recently lost their baby. "He was born dead," someone said, and Kantorowicz quipped, "Takes after his father."[48] Kantorowicz provided a special context for the idealism behind the notion of "the Berkeley Renaissance," as well as some of its more unfortunate aspects—a cold rigor, melodrama, and a certain overdependence on tradition.

In the autumn of 1947, when Hugh O'Neill left Janie and headed for parts unknown, Robert Duncan moved in and helped her prepare for childbirth. Jack was not amused. To escape from the Hearst Street ménage, and to celebrate his B.A. degree, Spicer took a trip to Big Sur and Carmel—Henry Miller country—and began writing an elegiac novel based on his Redlands experience, which he called *The Wasps*. Returning to Berkeley, he moved into another rooming house, this one at 2018 McKinley, where he met Jerry Ackerman, a young student new to the university system. Ackerman, later a well-known art historian, had graduated from Berkeley High School with the budding science fiction writer Philip K. Dick, also a tenant in the McKinley Street house. Ackerman was living with a boyfriend, "Brad." Other students and writers in the ramshackle house included the young surrealist poet Philip Lamantia, the future librettist George Haimsohn, and Robert Curran, a talented student of Wittgensteinian philosophy. Ackerman recalled Spicer holding court, advising all on what books to read, what movies to see, how to study. Spicer made Duncan promise not to come visit him, but this request piqued Duncan's curiosity, and he and Blaser came to pay a call. Duncan's eye fell on the young Ackerman and a new romance was born, much to Spicer's dismay.[49] "Brad" left and Duncan moved in, abandoning Janie O'Neill and her baby. "I remember Spicer pouting and pouting," Ackerman said later, "no longer the center of attention." In addition, Spicer seemed a "little crazy at times—really out of it." For days on end he would stay in bed, the covers pulled over his head, mumbling that the H-bomb was going to fall—a paranoia built up out of the very real fears created by United States politics of the Cold War.[50]

One day Gene Wahl came for a visit, a revenant from Spicer's Redlands past. Once a "famed beauty" whom Spicer, Blaser, and Duncan were always praising, Wahl now seemed seedy, even old, to young Ackerman, who found him "tall, thin, without being skinny, broad-shouldered, with a fine head (even if his hair was thinning)." Disappointingly, he looked "all of 32!"[51] Philip K. Dick, who was clerking at a Berkeley record store, brought in a primitive recording system, and the poets recited poetry and composed impromptu chants for recording. One day, Duncan recalled years later, Dick arrived on his threshold as Robert sat on his bed. With a short, convulsive movement, like Nijinsky's in the *Spectre of the Rose*, Dick arched his back and masturbated in front of an astonished Duncan. "I was the only one he could have shown this side to," he told Thom Gunn.[52] Though Dick's association with Duncan and Spicer lasted no more than a few months, they made a lasting impression on him, and in the 1950s and 1960s the books of Spicer and Dick became mirror images of each other, with the same themes (possession, alienation, the oracular) and, more strikingly, identical images—grasshoppers, Martians, castles and princes, Jewish salesmen, radio waves, ancient wounds, souls, and cities.

As the McKinley Street tenants settled in, Jack began his graduate studies in the English department. Nervously at first, then with more and more confidence, he stepped into a new career as a teacher. "Jack's first teaching assistantship was for Tom Parkinson," Blaser recalled. "His first lecture was on Mary Butts's *Armed with Madness*, that splendid novel about a modern relationship to the grail." Blaser noted shrewdly that Spicer alleviated his anxieties by transferring them to external problems. "When he got his teaching assistantship, for example, he needed a suit. It took I don't know how many fittings and the suit never did fit," Blaser chuckled. "I'll never forget, he would drag me [to the tailor] and we'd go through it all over again."[53] Spicer was a fine teacher, but many of the professors valued him for his library and research abilities, burdening him with backbreaking assignments he came to resent. He complained to a friend that one of the lions of the department had asked him to compile a complete bibliography of D. H. Lawrence and then passed it off as his own work.[54]

More congenial work came from Roy Harvey Pearce, an Assistant Professor in the English department, who was working on the book eventually called *The Savages of America: A Study of the Indian and the Idea of Civilization*.[55] He selected two M.A. candidates—Robin Blaser and Jack Spicer, assigning them to sift through the Bancroft's haphazard collection of Indian documents, circa 1609–1851, with one question in mind: "Will this interest Professor Pearce?" Spicer amused his professor by arriving one evening ready for work, looking "Chaplinesque" in an oversized, baggy, tweed suit, announcing, "Look, Dr. Pearce, I wanted to be Ivy League just like you," unable to detect that Pearce, with his Ph.D. from Johns Hopkins, was only from the so-called "Myrtle League." Spicer, amused by becoming a "data compiler," grew fascinated by the Bancroft's holdings and accounts of Native American lore.[56] The extent of his previous knowledge of the West was not much more than Max Brand novels and John Wayne movies, but his interest in and sympathy for American Indian cultures grew steadily, and soon he sought out and cultivated the eccentric, dying Indian expert Jaime de Angulo, author of *Indian Tales.*

Stuart Loomis, recently released from the army, where he had worked as a psychologist, met Spicer and the other Berkeley poets in the spring of 1947 while attending the clinical psychology department at Berkeley.[57] He fascinated Spicer and Duncan by showing them the recently declassified army psychological profiles, which included the Rorschach inkblot test, that marriage of "science" and the human heart. Loomis discovered that Spicer was already obsessed with pedagogical problems of how to interest students in poetry, and shared with him, over toast and peanut butter in Spicer's messy kitchen, some of John Dewey's educational theory. Loomis suggested that most young people, while indifferent to poetry, are inspired by popular music, sporting events, and movies—in short, by the texts of popular culture. Out of this came Spicer's 1949 essay "The Poet and Poetry—A Symposium," where he announced:

Pure poetry bores everybody. It is even a bore to the poet. . . . Thirty years ago Vachel Lindsay saw that poetry must connect itself to vaudeville if it was to regain its voice. (Shakespeare, Webster and Marlowe had discovered this three centuries before him.) Our problem today is to make this connection, to regain our voices.

We must become singers, become entertainers. We must stop sitting on the pot of culture. There is more of Orpheus in Sophie Tucker than in R. P. Blackmur; we have more to learn from George M. Cohan than from John Crowe Ransom.[58]

This marked the beginning of the populist thread in Spicer's thought, which led in later years to the increasingly multidisciplinary writing workshops he held in later years at the San Francisco Art Institute and in the bar-university of North Beach, and most notably it led to his "Magic Workshop" of 1957.

Spicer was upset by Duncan's breaking of the promise not to visit, and by his cavalier use of the *droit du seigneur.* "Before Duncan came to 2018 McKinley," said Ackerman, "Jack had the rule of the roost in our apartment. When Duncan came in, [Jack] was both dislocated and furious. Literally for months he didn't talk to Duncan. Instead he pouted. At that time I thought he was just mad at Duncan. And I kept saying, 'But, Jack, you should be mad at me!'" Meanwhile, Duncan grew increasingly jealous of

Ackerman's infidelities; he was later to pour his hostility and ire into "The Venice Poem," a masterpiece of obsessional lust and hatred. The two continued living together until the summer of 1949, when the writer Paul Goodman came to teach in Berkeley, sweeping Ackerman off his feet and taking him back to New York with him.

Duncan and Spicer ended their quarrel, and poetry rolled on. "Jack always had these little notebooks he would read poetry from," recalled Ackerman. "You can just imagine—Jack coming in, reading something to Duncan, and then Duncan would give him a lecture. And Duncan would always believe [Jack] was asking for advice, and Jack would always believe he was showing off something good he had done, for Duncan couldn't keep his hands off of anybody's poetry."[59] Spicer's poetry of the period, filled with erotic passions with the lid clamped on, made Duncan impatient. He wanted to open Jack up; to open his poetry and explode it in a thousand directions. Spicer's slow perfectionism, in life and art, frustrated Duncan and, perhaps, made him feel a bit slapdash. To arouse Jack he told stories about his previous homosexual seductions and encounters. An inveterate gossip, Duncan could call on years of rumor and fantasy to fuel the flame. Like many gay men, the McKinley Street boys played the age-old game of deciding which celebrities were homosexually inclined. According to Duncan, they all were—everyone from artists like Salvador Dali (who had been Lorca's boyfriend in the twenties)—to Hollywood stars like Tyrone Power, to modernist masters like Louis Zukofsky (whose secret boyfriend, Duncan claimed, he himself had seduced in New York). Spicer claimed to have had a celebrity encounter of his own—in Fern Dell, at the western end of Los Angeles's Griffith Park, he had been importuned sexually as a teen and offered money for sex by the tragically fallen, still handsome Bill Tilden, once America's greatest tennis player.[60] Spicer played up his virginity to some, like Robert Duncan; and to others he bragged about imaginary sex conquests as most young men will. When Donald Allen met Spicer in 1948, Spicer seemed so intimately knowledgeable about the homosexual scene that Allen was later surprised to learn that Spicer—who spoke of gay bars like a jaded habitué, of sex practices like an old roué—was, at that date, apparently still a virgin.[61]

Leonard Wolf reported back to Duncan and Spicer that the English department was secretly planning to disband the Writers Conference.[62] At issue was the homosexual cast of the Conference, the youth of some of its participants, and more particularly, the proposed publication of a writing magazine called *Literary Behavior*, a takeoff on Alfred Kinsey's recently published landmark study *Sexual Behavior in the Human Male* (1948). Kinsey's findings, now in dispute, seemed to validate the personal experience of gay men across the United States; his book was widely adduced to justify all kinds of pro- and antihomosexual action in Cold War America. The Berkeley controversy centered on one story, now lost, by mathematics student Richard Montague, allegedly so pornographic it made Mark Schorer blush.[63]

Mark Schorer, recalled Duncan, had made a "very personal attack on Spicer" as a "repulsive person."[64] The student-poets demanded a meeting to raise the various issues in a public forum and to plead the case of *Literary Behavior.* "Mark Schorer and Josephine [Miles] both got very angry about it," continued Duncan, "and both said that the university and the department shouldn't pay for the magazine." The meeting, which Blaser, Duncan, and Spicer attended, was long and acerbic. Thomas Parkinson said later: "Mark was by nature rude, and Duncan was by choice rude, so I was more annoyed with Duncan than I was with Mark. Duncan, who could be very nasty as we all know, blew up, baiting Mark and Jo, and to some extent me. I thought everybody was being silly. I said, 'Go ahead, publish it and forget it.' But I got sore because they were all so goddamn rude: it was their rudeness that bothered me."[65] The department withdrew its support and facilities from the Writers Conference. Duncan and Spicer, who never forgot what they regarded as a betrayal of freethinking, each wrote a long poem in the following year about the "war," Duncan's "A Poet's Masque" and Spicer's "The Dunkiad."

While he was still bitter over the squashing of his dreams, Spicer met a dynamic and intriguing woman and began the only serious heterosexual romance of his life. Catherine Mulholland was the daughter of one of California's most famous families. "Kate" Mulholland's family had built the aqueduct from California's Owens Valley to Los Angeles in 1913, a key event in the development of the dry southland of the state, which opened the San Fernando Valley to agriculture and settlement.[66] Kate had grown up on her father's ranch; by the time she came to Berkeley, she'd "had all the solitude I needed."

Kate Mulholland was a doctoral candidate in Berkeley's English department. She was suffering a tragic loss: her boyfriend, Kenny Carruthers, had recently killed himself. As a student at Columbia, Kate had grown used to difficult, sexually confused men: she had been part of the proto-Beat circles of Lucien Carr and Bill Cannastra and had befriended Jack Kerouac and Allen Ginsberg. Now, as she attended the philology classes of Arthur Brodeur in the fall of 1948 and the spring of 1949, she became attracted to the droll, dry wit of her classmate Jack Spicer. "He was so playful about language. I think it was one of the things that appealed to me about him. He had this childlike delight in playing around with language." She found Spicer and Donald Allen congenial companions; the three of them cheered each other up, going to roadhouses and bars, meeting people, attending parties together. Jack had a knack for mimicry, imitating everyone from Dr. Johnson to Liberace to Richard Nixon, then in the throes of the "Pumpkin Papers" crisis. He also responded to Kate's pain; she could open up to him about the loss of her fiancé (indeed she found his interest in Carruthers's suicide a little extreme). Another Berkeley contemporary, Sam Hardin, analyzed Kate's appeal for Spicer:

She was dark-haired, with large eyes. I knew a million people who were in love with her—men *and* women. When you talked with her, you felt like it was just you and her talking, that the rest of the world wasn't there. And this wasn't fake. She really did concentrate when she talked to you. She was a real class act. I didn't know anybody like her who was around. She was a really wealthy, upper-class woman, so she didn't have to have any of that shit about her. She didn't care about money, or class, she was just quite direct about people, and unconventional, but not in a flaunting sort of way. She just did everything her own way, and it had nothing to do with fashion. Kate was just something.[67]

Kate and Jack drank a lot, smoked a lot, visited each other's apartments, took long walks, held hands. One evening at Kate's Berkeley apartment they decided to go to bed together. Undressing, they fell into bed, and then came the disappointment. The spastic quality of his lovemaking—"as if touching was threatening," his extraordinarily small penis, his humiliation and defeat, conveyed his fear to her in a visceral way, reinforcing her own insecurities, and redoubling his self-hatred. Embarrassed, he vanished into the night.

In an attempt to help Spicer to do something about the love affair that tormented them both, Kate persuaded him to consult her psychiatrist, Hal Renaud, who worked on campus at UC's Cowell Hospital.[68] Spicer's poem, "Psychoanalysis: An Elegy," was composed with Kate Mulholland in mind and is Spicer's only specifically "heterosexual" poem. He saw psychoanalysis as a quizzical process, a version of Dada with comic strip roots. "I can't

meet you on Friday," he'd tell a classmate. "I have to see Offissa Pupp"—
the ogre policeman in George Herriman's "Krazy Kat" comic strip. Spicer
made a habit of joking about psychiatrists, and none of them was sacred.
In the late forties, after the *Saturday Review* had published a laudatory
cover story about the American analyst Harry Stack Sullivan, Spicer was
one of the few on the Berkeley campus to resist his allure. Don Allen remembered fleeing a roadhouse one night after Spicer provoked a bunch of
Stack Sullivan admirers to violence with his jeers and taunts.[69] He saw psychiatrists (and dentists) as substitutes for fathers, but didn't know how to
proceed with his own perception.[70]

All through the summer of 1949, Kate was giving serious thought to
marrying Jack. She invited him to her family's huge ranch in southern California, where he got along famously with her father, a man few of her
boyfriends ever could please. But in the autumn Kate surprised everyone,
including herself, by suddenly marrying another man, Gerald Hurley.
When he heard about the marriage, Spicer responded in two revealing
ways. He tried to make Kate jealous by showering attentions on a new pro-
tégée, the beautiful ash-blonde student poet Maureen Strom. At the same
time, he decided, once and for all, to end his own self-hatred by directly
exploring his homosexuality. He vowed to give up the shelter and fortress
of his "virginity" by hell or high water, and his target was the young and
quite attractive poet Landis Everson. "Jack really burned over Landis," recalled Jerry Ackerman. "He went through all the agony of Othello without
probably any—you know, all in fantasy. Landis was very beautiful—don't
you wish we were all nineteen, or twenty?"[71]

At a poetry reading at the home of Gerald Hurley's former roommate,
Jim Townsend, Jack made his first move.[72] "The house lights dimmed," remembered Everson, "and Jack stood up and read a poem attacking me, beginning 'and you, Apollo, have hitched your wagon to the wrong star,' and
ended up, 'the sky is too deep for fucking,' making me out someone who
was coming on to him, leading him on, a prick-teaser—none of which was
true. That was Jack's fantasy. It blew my mind and it embarrassed the fucking shit out of me because every head in the room—and there were probably fifty people in the room—turned and looked at me while Jack pointed
at me and screamed at me this poem. So I left. I didn't know what else to
do. Robin [Blaser] left with me, and walked me home, and put his arm
around me and comforted me. Robin tried to explain Jack to me and I
couldn't understand it."[73] Spicer later described the complexities of their
relationship:

There has been a pattern in my life (one which I must obviously have some part in constructing) of falling in love with a person who has not had homosexual experience, having him use me to find homosexual experience with another person—and then persons. This happened with the first male I fell in love with [i.e., Everson] (some five years ago) in a manner which almost rendered me useless as a person, and has happened twice since then. I am tired of it. Never once was I allowed to go to bed with them. They wanted to be friends.[74]

Like Spicer, Everson was from southern California, but otherwise the two were opposites. Everson was a handsome fraternity boy—a sharp dresser, with his own car, living on GI Bill benefits—everything that Spicer hadn't or wasn't; and Spicer resented it. At the beginning of one break from school Landis drove Jack home to Los Angeles. "Jack was so full of irony and bitterness that just getting into my car caused him to give an ironic smile." Passing through Gilroy, Landis was pulled over, ticketed, and fined. "Well, Jack was absolutely and completely delighted. Because I was shat on, humiliated, by the very society in which I operated, and [in which] he'd like not to operate. It was a vindictiveness against me which showed me where he was coming from. And I always excused him. I saw this was not his problem, but was his way of thinking, as I understood it. A man who writes the line, in his early poetry, that 'Man is so monstrous naked that the whole world recoils' [from the original version of Spicer's "A Night in Four Parts," dedicated to Everson, "for Mr. L. E.—the onlie begetter of these nightmares"], the man who writes that line is certainly talking about only his own subjective view of what nakedness is, how he feels about his own body and other people's bodies—*he* recoils." Jack hated his body, Landis thought. Yet at the same time he didn't *do* anything about it. His body wasn't *that* bad; he could have shaped it up at a gym. But his emotions were those, Landis realized, of a boy of five or six.

Presently Landis thought of a way to get rid of Jack and his embarrassing ardor. He introduced Jack to a friend, George Haimsohn, who shortly afterward took him to bed ("sacrificed himself," as Landis put it). "We all knew it. We all even knew what room it was happening in. The next day Jack walked into Robin's house and we were full of curiosity. His comment on his sexual experience he'd had with George—granted there was no love involved in any of this—was, 'Very interesting.' And that was that."[75] Robert Duncan remarked simply, "George Haimsohn brought [Jack] out."[76] To Haimsohn, Jack was just one of a number of conquests, and hardly the most appetizing one. In the sixties, using a pseudonym, he published a fictional account of the Berkeley Renaissance poets in the 1940s:

[Jack Spicer] was undoubtedly the homeliest man on the whole Berkeley campus. With his scraggly reddish hair, his frightfully thin body and pale colorless face, he looked very much like some odd species of monkey. . . . A whole legion of budding young poets and novelists were placed in this same position [making an embarrassed rejection to a real or implied Spicer advance]. How eager they were for [Jack's] literary advice, his astute criticisms, his helpful suggestions, but not for his body, his love. It was a well-known fact on the Berkeley campus that [Jack], at thirty-three years old, was still a virgin, never having gone to bed with either man or woman. The saddest part of this was that one look at the man and the story seemed quite plausible.[77]

By 1949 Spicer's mood had darkened. The breakup of his affair with Kate Mulholland, the thwarted passion for Landis Everson, the demise of the Writers' Conference, and the growing realization that avowed homosexuality spelled career suicide in academia, all depressed Spicer and gave rise to a small body of early lyric work. Spicer's Berkeley poetry is highly sexualized and passionate, filled with "an overwhelming sense of presence and urgency, the result of incredible intensity of feeling." It speaks of "sexual frustration and humiliation, the great fear of sexual contact, the ridicule of sexuality," and—in a handful of poems—sexual fulfillment.[78] His poetry from 1949 on is unrelentingly morose and astringent.

After the demise of the Writers' Conference, Spicer became increasingly close to a small handful of college men who were left-wing in their politics, largely heterosexual, "jock" types, among them James Herndon, Keith Jones, Dave Fredrickson, and Sam Hardin—big men who loved to drink, cut up, chase women, play football, and organize politically.[79] The artist Minnette Lehmann, then married to Bob Martinson, one of the Marxists, remembered Spicer among these men. "From my point of view, Jack was amorphous. He wasn't sexual. He was not coordinated, but you just wanted to be around him to feel him think. He was not with body. It was like he didn't have a body, is what it felt like. Somehow he was like a *pumpkin*—just this big head, that kind of glowed."[80]

With these football players, many of them studying education on the GI Bill, Jack indulged in several of his most famous Berkeley pranks, including the formation of the Unpopular Front in 1948, an intramural football team he coached.

See, in the thirties [explained Sam Hardin] the Communist Party, attempting to protect itself and to deal with the Fascists, formed what they called Popular Fronts. They would form within a group that was left of center; they would be willing to work with them, see? Of course, any group that tried to work with the Communist Party was always taken over by the Communist Party. So smart leftwing groups wouldn't work with the Communists; you know, they just couldn't trust them, see? So, that was where Jack's name came from: we were the Unpopular Front, and he entered us into the Intramural League as a football team, see? Because he was a football coach, Jack was, see?

We had three quarterbacks: Bruce Dwellie, Jim Herndon, and Tom Winet. The rest of the guys were like me, didn't know anything about football. Or anything else. We just stood around and knocked the ball down if we could. Jack was always trying to get us to play the Statue of Liberty, which was his favorite play, see? But of course, we didn't know shit from Statue of Liberty.

We played against a group who were called the Students for Wallace. They *were* a Communist front group, so they really were the Popular Front. I don't know how we beat anybody, but we did beat them. That was the only game we played. And Jack was very proud that we beat *them*.[81]

In 1949 Spicer got the chance to fulfill a childhood dream when he became the host of his own weekly radio show on KPFA, a newly formed alternative station collectively run in Berkeley. Spicer's show was nominally about folk music, though he sometimes presented poetry readings, and Herndon and Fredrickson were his frequent guests—his backup band, as it were. "He'd talk about a song, tracing a line from a poem that first appears in say, 1500, and then picking it up again in 1900 and comparing the difference. And sometimes Jack would sing—and he was the worst singer in the world. You'd be tuning into the program and you'd hear him, [imitates horrible tuneless voice]—every Saturday night," recalled Sam Hardin. "He'd get Jim and Dave drunk before the program and then once the show began they'd use 'language,' and that's what Jack wanted."[82] After forty weeks KPFA unceremoniously dropped the show, after listener complaints about the uncensored bawdiness of some of the improvised "folk music" Spicer & Co. presented. When the marriage of Jim and Carol Herndon broke up, Spicer and Herndon found an apartment above "The Last Chance," a sorry bar on Oakland's College Avenue—the closest bar to the university. (The university's anti-alcohol policies were so strict that no liquor could be sold within a mile's radius of the main campus.) Though Jim Herndon left the United States for Europe after graduation, and effectively disappeared from Spicer's life for many years, he and his second wife, Fran, subsequently became Spicer's second family.

Jack's studies continued, and he found himself more and more drawn to Anglo-Saxon, Old German, and the cold rigors of philology, perhaps as a respite from the increasing violence and romanticisim of his poetry. With the Singapore-born Dutch national Gaby Onderwyzer, for example, "We never talked about literature," she says. "He was fascinated by philology, and so was I. He was always borrowing my notes. I took these wonderful notes; everything was illegible, in symbols, and yet he understood what I was taking down." She and Spicer talked haughtily about the flimsy major of linguistics. "We were lamenting that the upstart linguistics people, we would say, 'That doesn't tell you anything about language, that you can't pick right up on the bus.' So that's what we had in common. What held us together the rest of the time was my cooking. Feeding him. Not only him, other people too, but he was always included. We had weekly dinner parties, on the weekend: often just mutton, but it was very good. I could make a good curry out of leg of mutton—19 cents a pound, I remember."[83] Spicer also became friends with a fellow English student at Berkeley, Ellen King, who worked with him on the student newspaper, the *Daily Californian*. "The reason I got to know Jack so well right in the beginning was that we were both in love with the same person. Neither of us were doing too well," she laughed. This was another graduate student, named Mel Lyons. Punning on Lyons's name Spicer wrote the beautiful "Orpheus after Eurydice," which uses the Latin tag, "Mella, mella peto / In medio flumine."

After Spicer moved in with Jim Herndon, Ellen was present at a party where Jack wrote a poem, and "I just copied it, because I liked the poem so much."

> The dancing ape is whirling round the beds
> Of all the coupled animals; they, sleeping there
> In warmth of sex, observe his fur and fuss
> And feel the terror in his gait of loneliness.
> Quaint though the dancer is, his furry fists
> Are locked like lightning over all their heads.
> His legs are thrashing out in discontent
> As if they were the lightning's strict embodiment.
> But let the dancing stop, the apish face go shut in sleep,
> The hand unclench, the trembling legs go loose—
> And let some curious animal bend and touch that ape
> With nuzzling mouth, would not the storm break
> And that ape kiss, with dancing in his lips?[84]

"The very peculiar unease of himself," Robin Blaser mused. "The way he saw himself as 'the dancing ape' of the early poems."[85] The image of the ape haunts the iconography of Spicer's student days, and for many of his former classmates this poem, with its wistful beauty and its broad gestural strokes, has remained their favorite of all his work.

Ellen King was one of only a few of Jack's classmates to see anything of his family life, and that only by accident. Through a mutual friend, Ellen's mother had met Jack's mother, and on vacation, Ellen was taken by her mother to visit Dorothy Spicer. Remarking on the name, Ellen said that she had a schoolmate of that name. Proudly, Dorothy drew herself up and announced, "Jack Spicer is my son!" Ellen felt amazed—this pleasant, conventional woman was the mother of Jack Spicer? That was amazing to Jack, too, since his campus life seemed so distant from his Hollywood self. "He was both slightly ashamed of his mother and protective of her," Ellen said. "Liked her, but didn't feel that she would show up well."

Ellen and Jack "used to go to the bars together, and he would say, 'If all of the homosexual men banded together there would be enough of us to vote in a President.' He felt that the numbers were getting larger, that things were getting better. . . ." At the same time, his sense of his own erotic nature was clouded. "I don't know but that he still thought that maybe, maybe something might change, and that he might be with a woman. At that time. And so it didn't seem, at least to me, as if he felt persecuted. He was somehow too apish, or animal-like, to be loved by a man. He thought there was a better chance that women would love him, which they quite did, you know?

"A lot of the people he was close to, like Robin, and Landis Everson, were incredibly beautiful-looking. There was a lot of competition in that sense, with Robert. Robert was quite stunning, too, in those days, and Jack was just totally beautiful in his way but it was not [laughs] the conventional way, certainly. It wasn't anything that men would love."[86]

Spicer began to feel increasingly threatened for his politics as well as his sexual nature. As the Cold War escalated, U.S. universities were becoming involved in self-policing actions designed to prevent communist activity on campus and to avert "outside" political legislation. The University of California Regents in 1950 required professors and staff to sign an oath of loyalty to the constitution with specific anticommunist provisions. Sensitive to oppression from political sources through his experience of the Third Reich, Ernst Kantorowicz balked. Though the *George Kreis* had been anything but communist, he refused to sign the oath, and spearheaded a group of independent-minded professors and graduate students to fight it. When their crusade failed, Kantorowicz left Berkeley for Princeton's Institute for Advanced Study.

For Spicer there was no Princeton waiting with open doors.[87] Refusal to sign the oath was widely considered a noble form of professional suicide— a step that not many had the courage or foolhardiness to take. Reaching back toward his father's early politics and trying, against all common sense, to do the right thing, to make the ethical decision, Spicer followed Kantorowicz's example and publicly refused to sign. Instantly his decision branded him as a leftist, of course, and left those who were in positions to hire at the university level wondering whether they might not be dealing with a risky, unstable personality, at least one too independent to hire safely for a public, or conservative institution.

Although he was not, strictly speaking, fired, it felt like it. Surveying the list of American universities where loyalty oaths were not required, Spicer chose the University of Minnesota, where a sympathetic Berkeley professor, David Reed, helped wangle him a job in linguistics. To a Californian, Minneapolis seemed very far away. Josephine Miles remembered that the "graduate students in the English department here at Berkeley all got together and raised money to buy Jack Spicer an overcoat. He didn't have anything but light summer clothing, and so we bought him this *giant* overcoat."[88] Spicer's decision was brave—everyone said so—but it meant expulsion from his Berkeley paradise. The rest of his career found him grappling with this loss.

CHAPTER TWO

After Berkeley

Spicer's two years at the University of Minnesota passed slowly, far from all friends. In Minneapolis he continued work in Anglo-Saxon, for John Clark, the head of the linguistics department, on a teaching assistant-ship that netted him a total of $120 per month. He taught English, Old English, the History of the English Language, and a seminar course in *Be-owulf*. It was a lonely, isolated life, with an office at Folwell Hall and occa-sional dinners at the Clarks' house.

Only a few months away, and the magic had died. He began the first of several letters to Duncan and Blaser trying to analyze what had occurred among them. What had turned the Bay Area into a kind of enchanted Camelot, and why had it to end? The melancholy underlying this analysis marked Spicer's thought and behavior for the rest of his life. He evoked Kantorowicz's theories of kingship: the three of them—Duncan, Blaser, and Spicer—had been poet-kings, but their reign was over. He touted sev-eral heirs apparent, most of them now lost to poetic history—Arthur Kloth, Harrison Starr, Barton Barber. And anxious for gossip, he asked, Who were the cute boys? The talented new poets? Which "swans" had a chance of replacing them as the kings of poetry on campus?[1]

Together with David Reed of Berkeley's linguistics department, Spicer published an article in the July-September 1951 issue of *Language*, the journal of the Linguistic Society of America. This, recalled Reed, was a close collaboration, each line argued and challenged by the two. It was to be Spicer's only professional publication as a linguist. Spicer and Reed met in New York in December 1950 to present the paper at the LSA Convention there. This was Jack's first taste of New York, where many of his friends now lived. He visited with Glenn Lewis, Landis Everson, George Haimsohn. One Berkeley pal brought him to the ongoing discussion group led by Paul Goodman in Manhattan, where Goodman, the brilliant social theorist, held ad hoc group therapy sessions that seemed designed to browbeat straight boys into acting out on latent homosexual impulses. When Spicer argued with a point made by one acolyte, Goodman jumped in and said, "You're only disputing him because you want to fuck him, own up to it!" Spicer stumbled out into the snowy street, reeling, he said later, as if after an encounter with the Red Queen.[2]

Returning to Minneapolis, he entered a close friendship with Mary Rice, an M.A. student in the Old English class for which he graded papers. Mary was twenty-two years old, from Billings, Montana; she fell deeply in love with him. They moved into a pair of twin studios in a boarding house on East River Road. For the next year and a half the two westerners spent most evenings together, listening to records, following the serials on the radio, talking about books and dreams. Their rent was $60 a month. Mary watched worriedly as Jack ate the same dinner every night—one peanut butter sandwich. At 10:30 they took the streetcar to Herb's, the only gay bar in the city, where they'd have a beer apiece and enjoy the amusing characters. Mary was "naive," she admitted later.[3] There just wasn't much to do in Minneapolis. What Jack saw as Minnesota's claustrophobic provinciality helped him feel closer to his father, for this was the state from whence John Lovely Spicer had fled, back before the turn of the century, running off from the family farm in Albert Lee to wind up in California. To Jim Herndon Jack wrote, "There is no magic in Minnesota."[4]

Slowly but surely it dawned on him that there was no more magic in Berkeley, either. "Perhaps we can figure out what really happened in Berkeley when Berkeley was fully living," he wrote to Robert Duncan. "I'd like to go over some of the days (2029 for example or Venice time) partly because I'm going to be living like a camel on my hump here and partly because I'm going to have to clarify what my poetry was writing about before I can write a new kind of poetry."[5] Isolation accentuated his crankiness and yearning. The gift of poetry had deserted him, once he turned his back on Berkeley. But what other choice had he been given? Gossip reached him that the novelist, poet, and critic Robert Penn Warren had turned down a post at UC Berkeley in protest of the loyalty oath and was due to return to the University in Minnesota at any minute. Warren failed to appear. Spicer felt considerably alone.

Spicer in Minneapolis, lonely and a long way from home. *Photo courtesy of Gary Bottone.*

Every Saturday morning, Mary and Jack haunted a record shop where he spent a dollar on three 78s, by his favorite radio comedians and crooners. Next stop, a liquor store for a half-pint of whiskey, and then "we'd go home and we'd drink it with our coffee, and play those records," Rice recalled. "That was our little Saturday morning party. We used to have some wonderful laughs: he was funny as hell. And he liked, I think, the Montana side of me. He didn't want some pretentious English major—those kinds of people really turned him off. He called me 'Ma Perkins,' and it was my 'Ma Perkins' side that he liked. She was a kind of down-home, folksy— kind of a *simpleton*, you know? And he liked that." Jack would kiss Mary Rice and hold hands with her, and "that was sort of as far as it ever went," Rice said ruefully. "And I just *longed* for him sexually, but it couldn't happen, you know?"

Slowly, Spicer tried writing again, sketches for his long poem in multiple parts, *Imaginary Elegies*, which begins on a punning note with an epigram from Yeats: "All the philosophy a man needs is in Berkeley." The arctic landscapes of the *Elegies* were later revised out of the poem, as if to excise Minnesota's pitiless chill:

> He is bleached by an Apollonian sun
> Until he is white as cold, white as my blindness,
> An Arctic Circle of absolute dreaming,
> Complete with polar bears and Santa Claus and rich with ice.[6]

In the summer of 1951 John Lovely Spicer died in Los Angeles, almost seventy. In later years Jack cried when he thought of his father. Harry Z. Coren, Jack Spicer's psychotherapist fifteen years later, reported a late conversation: "Spicer told me early on that his dad, a year before he died, really had praised him for not signing the loyalty oath. It was a surprise to him. At the time he cried: he was so touched that his father approved of him, unexpectedly so."[7] With his father gone, Jack was free to mythologize him publicly. His friends began to hear that John Spicer had been a card-carrying Wobbly until harnessed to property management by a schoolmarm wife. At the service, Jack's mother told him that she had been offered work managing the Amherst Apartments for the same property management firm that had employed his father at the Stillwell Hotel. When Spicer alighted from the train from Los Angeles, a faithful friend, Arthur Kloth, picked him up from the station in Oakland. Jack didn't mention his father's death. "I'm glad to be back," he said. "In Minneapolis, they think red wine is Manischevitz."[8]

Spicer spent the summer in California, and later that summer, at a Berkeley party, Kloth introduced Spicer to Gary Bottone. Bottone's dark Italianate good looks had the charm of an angel in a Renaissance painting, with the exquisite freshness of a boy in a Baron Corvo photograph. "We sat on a fire hydrant," Bottone recalled, "and—I suppose—were enchanted. I was eighteen or nineteen. Two days later I received a postcard from Jack with the little 'Unicorn' poem on it—and so a correspondence began. I kept the poems and the picture I made him have taken to send to me (I remember his dismay at my request—and his sweet compliance)." Two poems remain, fragile souvenirs of this long-distance love affair. The "unicorn" poem Spicer named "Train Song for Gary."

> The trains move quietly upon
> The tracks outside like animals

I hear them every night.

And sometimes I can almost see
Their glittering unhurried eyes
Move out of sight.

I think that on the day I leave
This town of quiet houses they
Will sound their horns.

I think that then that burning herd
Will turn and follow me towards you
Like unicorns.[9]

Returning to Minneapolis in the fall, Spicer longed for Gary. Every day, Mary Rice watched Jack waiting at his window casually pretending *not* to wait for the mailman. She viewed this spectacle with a mixture of emotions, regret and bewilderment foremost. "I didn't know he was gay for a long time," Mary said ruefully, "not until a friend mentioned it in the school cafeteria. It was the shock of my life. I didn't even know men did such things." When she confronted him, Jack grew upset, flustered. For once he had no funny answer.[10]

Jack stewed. He couldn't write poetry, he claimed, in a state so becalmed by propriety and winter, and he longed to return to California. Most of all he missed his friends, especially Duncan and Blaser. Finally, in 1952, Spicer returned to Berkeley. The loyalty oath had been modified, as Tom Parkinson explained, "to strike out its most objectionable features so that it merely affirmed support of the U. S. and California constitutions, thus becoming a 'constitutional' oath." Referring to a judicial invalidation of the oath made by the California Supreme Court in 1968, Parkinson continued, "the much later [1968] decision was made to satisfy legal and financial claims of faculty non-signers. Many of those non-signers did sign the revised oath (that would be around 1954/5 [actually, 1952] and so did Jack." When California passed the Levering Act, which required only an acceptance of the state and national constitutions with their provisions against forcible overthrow of the government, Jack signed it, allowing him to teach in California. Together he and Mary Rice—who had decided to move to the Bay Area to live with Jack—left Minneapolis and drove through the West. This was Spicer's only extended road trip. (One of the things that separated the Berkeley poets from their Beat contemporaries was their resolute determination never to drive anywhere if they could help it. Duncan, Spicer, and Blaser were all, for different reasons, helpless behind the wheel.) On his lap

Jack carried a large portrait bust of himself, made in Minneapolis by an unknown artist, a terra-cotta head the color and texture of a common flowerpot, now in the possession of Robin Blaser. This "Head of Spicer," in Greek classical or Houdon style, became one of the few possessions Jack carried around from apartment to apartment for the next eight years, until he gave it to Blaser early in 1960. He must have enjoyed watching his head stay so absurdly young while he himself aged so rapidly.

"We were planning to share a house together," Mary Rice recalled. "When we got to Berkeley, I saw the gay thing was going to be overwhelming. I didn't want to be a 'fag hag,' and so I started to date someone else. Even then, the three of us went out to the White Horse bar on Telegraph Avenue almost every night." In the forties, the White Horse, on Telegraph Avenue in Berkeley, had been a center for political talk and student camaraderie.[11] Because of the university's rules about liquor sales, the White Horse, one mile from the campus, vied with the Last Chance as the closest bar. Gay men had started patronizing the White Horse around 1950, and gradually, remembered one patron, "it became de facto gay."[12] Mary Rice gained insight into Jack's reserve when she met Dorothy Spicer on one of Dorothy's very rare visits to Jack in Berkeley. "I had a car then," said Mary, "and we took Dorothy around all week—and she was *ice-cold*, you know. You could see what had happened to him—just an ice cube. Everything went okay, there weren't any fights or anything, we took her sightseeing, but she was just an ice cold woman."[13] Dorothy's middle-class propriety put off the few of Jack's bohemian friends who ever met her; formerly a friendly, outgoing soul, her widowhood seemed to freeze her emotionally in ways neither she nor Jack ever found language to talk about.

On Spicer's return to Berkeley in 1952 Gary Bottone attended his homecoming party, but the thrill was gone. "I was younger, less bohemian, less literary and less 'experienced' than any of Jack's Berkeley friends," he said. "Jack and I tried to make something out of the spell which had been cast on his departure, and I failed. I saw him subsequently with some frequency at the White Horse bar in Berkeley where he wore out a succession of pinball machines. He told me once he wanted to be buried under one."[14] Jack had, in fact, a short attention span. He preferred his boyfriends long distance, or hard-to-get, and preferably straight. Gary was but the first of a long series of young men or boys whom Spicer used primarily as vehicles for poetic expression.

Love failing him, Jack also found that the center of gravity of his poetic universe had shifted slightly west, to San Francisco, where Robert Duncan had moved with his companion, the painter Jess Collins. Asked in 1990 if it was true that he hated Spicer from the moment the two met, Jess chuckled and nodded. "From *before* I met him!"[15] Jess laughed again and launched into the story of the first time he saw both Jack Spicer and Robert Duncan, in 1949. Jess was studying to be a chemist at Berkeley, but dissatisfied with chemistry, he'd decided to try to learn painting. He approached the chairman of the fine arts department with his "meager" portfolio, and the chairman told him, "I'm afraid there really isn't a place for you, Mr. Collins, in our department." Jess was hurt at first, but the chairman swept on by, complimenting his drawing and implying that the department at Berkeley had nothing to teach him, suggesting the California School of Fine Arts in San Francisco instead. Red tape delayed his transfer from Berkeley, but his life changed one day when he wandered into a poetry reading at Wheeler Hall.

At the reading, Robin Blaser read his "Rose" poems, then Landis Everson, and then Duncan stood up and read *The Venice Poem*, which absolutely "floored" Jess. "It took me beyond the planets." At the end of the reading, Duncan asked for comments. An ugly gargoyle who had been sitting hunched over all the way to the right of the front row spoke up in a whiny voice and said that *The Venice Poem* was terrible, a waste of talent. "So I had him placed right then," Jess said. "That was Jack Spicer. And I knew right away I'd never like him."

Jess's transfer to the School of Fine Arts prompted him and Duncan to move to San Francisco—a move that effectively insured that Jess would not have to see Spicer for several years, for Jack refused to cross the Bay to visit Duncan, feeling that Duncan's desertion of Berkeley was a "betrayal" of the whole Berkeley Renaissance ethos. Jess and Robert moved into a huge house at 1350 Franklin Street, near Cathedral Hill, a house its residents named the "Ghost House" for its resemblance to the ornate haunted house drawn by Charles Addams in his New York cartoons. Once the wedding present of California sugar king Adolph Spreckels to his daughter, by the early fifties the "Ghost House" had been carved into inexpensive live/work space for artists. The painters Harry Jacobus and Wally Hedrick lived and worked there too, as did the young filmmaker Stan Brakhage.

Duncan and Jess next moved into James Broughton's former apartment on Baker Street. One evening Jack "marched right in and took over," nonchalantly trying to assume the role he'd once played in Duncan's life—best friend and general pest. When Spicer went home for the night, Jess turned to Robert and laid down an ultimatum—*either he goes or I go.* Robert saw to it that Jack didn't come to the house again. He saw Jack whenever he wanted outside of the domestic life he shared with Jess, but that meant in the bars, not much fun for those, like Robert, who didn't really like drinking much and who grew fastidious and reserved as others got drunk.

Spicer resumed academic work at Berkeley, completing the coursework, but not a thesis, for his Ph.D. in Anglo-Saxon and Old Norse, while working as a teaching assistant for Thomas Parkinson. "I had what I thought was a pretty hefty reading list," recalled Parkinson. "Jack came, and he looked at the reading list, and he started adding books. It was just endless: I mean, that reading list was practically a list of all the important books of the twentieth century by the time he got through with it! And then he spent a lot of time with the kids, lots of office hours. And he gave a couple of weeks of the course (that was the agreement with the T.A.s). And he was simply wonderful. He was really a devoted teacher: very good."[16] Some of Spicer's interaction with Parkinson's students would be today viewed quite equivocally, particularly his involvement with Richard Rummonds, who later published Jack's love letters and poems to him in a small book called *Some Things from Jack.*[17] Rummonds was intrigued by the Berkeley Renaissance, which by 1953 had already acquired the shiny patina of myth, and arranged and edited for publication in *Occident*, the Berkeley literary magazine, a special section called "Four from Before" (Spicer, Duncan, Blaser, and Landis Everson). The appellation made Spicer question his identity as a poet: he felt like a relic in his own time, and he was not yet thirty years old. The Berkeley he had known and loved was dead, and he knew it, but *how* dead?

Spicer found San Francisco unnervingly large, especially since he was not "allowed" to see much of Duncan, and sought refuge in a bohemian bar in North Beach called the Black Cat. As the fifties wore on, the Black Cat became more and more a gay bar, famed for its drag shows featuring Jose Sarria, the "Empress Norton," but in 1952 it was still the playground of artists, writers, and heavy drinkers of all types. Steinbeck, Saroyan, and Truman Capote were reliably reported to stop by as often as they could. "It was a scungy little dive in an alley, at Columbus and Montgomery Street," reported Earl McGrath, one of the young men Spicer met at this time.

It was very romantic, you could hear it, I can always remember my heart quickening when I came near. As you approached you could already sort of pick out the voices of your friends. It was a real drinking establishment. Sailors and hookers and just everything in there. Intellectuals; painters; it was very "modern," in that sense, because you had everything from transvestites to businessmen to girls out on dates with young boys. It was just the sort of a place, you know, to start an adventure. In retrospect it was almost like an existentialist hangout, you know what I mean? It was just before the Beats: existentialism was current thought, everybody was reading Sartre and Camus and all that stuff.[18]

At Berkeley, Jack met the young painter Jay DeFeo, who became an instant soulmate. DeFeo was starting what turned out to be an important career, culminating in her inclusion in the epochal "Sixteen Americans" show at New York's MOMA in 1959–60, and her magnificent painting, years in the making, which she called *The Rose* (two tons of plaster and paint, and the centerpiece to the 1995 Whitney survey of *Beat Culture and the New America*). Her career was blighted by an early arrest for shoplifting paint at a San Francisco hardware store, making it nearly impossible for her to find work. Spicer saw a parallel between her romantic crime and his 1950 refusal to sign the loyalty oath. They were both romantic artists, he postulated, driven, like Rimbaud, to flout society's laws and taboos in the name of a higher ethos. DeFeo's painting, however, was not romantic in the lush style of Jess, Harry Jacobus, Lyn Brockway, or the others in Duncan's salon. Her sparing use of color, her lack of referentiality, and her thick, sensual accent on paint itself, showed a sophisticated awareness of what was happening in New York. Spicer never fully understood DeFeo's painting, but not for lack of trying: early on, he hailed her as one of the frightening harbingers of the new.[19]

Often Jack joined the bridge circle that gathered at George Berthelon's house in South Berkeley on Friday nights. This event became one of the routines that he followed slavishly and superstitiously in order to let his mind roam, so that poems could come when they wanted to. By day Berthelon worked as a mechanic at an East Bay manufacturer of aluminum doors, and by night he ran a big slice of the gay life of Berkeley. Butch by day, and way femme at night. When Jerry Ackerman, returning from New York after his affair with Paul Goodman, had found himself shunned by many of Robert Duncan's friends, it was "landlady" George Berthelon who took him in and sheltered him (and his new boyfriend, avant-garde composer Richard Maxfield). One afternoon, Ackerman and Maxfield were discussing Spicer—he was so ugly, they said, who on earth would have sex with him? Whoever it was would have to be a complete pervert! "How can you talk about your mother that way?" cried George Berthelon, with deadpan glee.[20] Berthelon's home was the setting of many gay parties, where women were distinctly not welcome. Gerald Fabian, a friend of Spicer's from Berkeley, remembered the appalling experience of bringing a woman friend to a party there, or trying to. "Berthelon came out sloshed and made this big scene at us. 'No fish!' I just wanted to knock him right on his ass. Because I was very fond of my friend, and I didn't see anything wrong with taking a woman to a gay party, if she wanted to subject herself to that." Fabian also recalled Berthelon's penchant for boys named "Charles": there was Charles the First, the Second, the Third and so on.[21]

Jess Sawyer, a lecturer with the University of California linguistics department until his death in 1986, recounted the history of what he called "the Old Ladies' Bridge Club." The group consisted of Spicer, Berthelon, Wilben Holther, a professor in the speech department at Berkeley; and John Halvorsen, then associated with the Berkeley English department and later a professor at the university campus in Santa Cruz. Jess Sawyer replaced Edgar Austin, a graduate student in English who lived with Wilben Holther; though Austin continued to visit for awhile, by the late 1950s he had dropped out.[22]

Robert Duncan discussed these times. "Games meant a lot [to Spicer]. This bridge group, by the way, you could never get Robin Blaser or me to be in. It didn't take Jack long to learn we wouldn't be any good as bridge partners. He tried to get some of his bridge partners into the Magic Workshop, but they weren't any good as poetry partners. So bridge was something more than bridge: it's *Alice in Wonderland* for Jack. And poetry was something like a game—a really serious game. Jack was superb with a magic workshop because magic was a game."[23]

"Each of the evenings," recounted Jess Sawyer, "we drank one bottle of gin or bourbon—I don't remember that it greatly mattered which," though he thought bourbon was preferred. "One or the other of us brought this bottle. That duty rotated. We never ate anything. But there was continuous drinking always until we completed that one bottle." The game was fairly set in form:

Jack and Wilben Holther were partners; I was a partner with George Berthelon until he died, later with John Halvorsen. Although I think after George died we switched partners more often in order to even out the differences in our various skills. I would rank the players: first, Jack Spicer; second, Wilben Holther; third, George Berthelon; fourth, me. The bridge was always associated with active and acrimonious post-mortems. The post-mortem of a particularly interesting hand could very easily go on into a second or third hand after the occurrence that was being discussed and analyzed.[24]

Myrsam Wixman, a young friend of Berthelon's from Los Angeles, occasionally watched these evenings of bridge, though he was no bridge player himself. "After each hand they would recriminate, scream and shout; sometimes they would throw the cards. George would scream; Jack would say, 'Well, partner, why on earth did you make that bid!' They were very serious players." Wixman remembered "tiny stakes" in the game, "penny a point or something—exchange two dollars each game."[25]

Literary discussion usually accompanied the bridge. "George was not active in the literary discussions, nor was I," Sawyer recalled, "but Wilben was very keen on following what was going on in the world that Jack was associated with. The first thing that happened each evening before the bridge started was Wilben's catching up on all the local news: who'd written what, what sort of readings and performances were taking place, what things were interesting, gossip about everybody who was busy writing."

Jess Sawyer discussed the players individually. "George Berthelon was the most interesting of us perhaps. He was a thoroughly disreputable character most of us thought—bawdy minded and leering; an excellent bridge player, although erratic and frequently taking chances that involved our losing or being set." Although Berthelon was not involved in the literary talk, he "listened or made snide comments or disappeared into the kitchen organizing glasses and ice cubes for the rest of the evening. He was notorious in a funny sense: for those of the group who were interested in movies, he was a nephew—I believe—of a silent film star, Mae Marsh. Some of her charisma, as far as we were concerned, had rubbed off on George. His bawdiness—his bawdy-mindedness—was always clever and rather beautiful to listen to. In that sense he was a literary person. He apparently was a good cook, but the kitchen was so dirty, the dishes were so dirty, there was so much moss growing, one fled." Sawyer added, "It was quite common for him to have consumed enough alcohol (he was the one who consumed more alcohol than any of the other four of us) until finally his left eye would begin to close. He would not be able to raise it. At this point you knew that a different kind of bridge was going to be played. He tended, then, to make up for my pusillanimity in bidding by simply opening all bids with three no trump. We frequently got beaten because of his outrageous overbidding."

"Wilben Holther, the second best of the bridge players," continued Jess Sawyer, "was a professor in the speech department. He was

very animated and very precise and if I called us "the Old Ladies Bridge Club" it was appropriate for him and me, but not nearly so appropriate for George Berthelon, who was anything but a little old lady in his approach to life, or for Jack Spicer, although even for Jack it was a little more appropriate than for George

Berthelon. Wilben was a rather clean, tidy and neat person. He was big, rather heavy actually; along with Plato's rather big head, severe features—very jolly in a rather nice sort of way. I remember one night we had played at Wilben's—he lived upstairs from George Berthelon. When the bridge playing was all over, everybody had gone, I went to the bathroom and when I came out—Edgar Austin knew I was still there but Wilben apparently thought I had already gone—Wilben had a bottle of alcohol in his hand and a rag, and he was scrubbing the plastic of the chair in which Jack Spicer had sat. I never thought that Jack deserved that much cleaning up [after], but Wilben apparently felt that way about it.[26]

Spicer tended to arrive late. He was

a terribly serious player. His clothes were never very elegant; he always needed cleaning up. Witness Wilben's willingness to clean up after him.[27] But he was also very poor. It was he, I think, who sparked the many post-mortems of the bridge playing. Occasionally Jack was so furious with himself that he would burst into tears. If he played a hand badly—then went through the post-mortem and each time he went through the post-mortem it looked worse—he would eventually feel so angry that he would begin to weep, out of frustration. I suppose the weeping didn't last very long. He was probably embarrassed at such an emotional reaction over a game. But it's evidence of how deadly serious he was about it and how much he enjoyed it and how much it meant to him at that particular time.[28]

Afterward the cardplayers would go to the White Horse. One evening Jack and George Berthelon were having a closing-time drink there when an aging, ex-fraternity boy came in with a few friends "to clean the queers out of the bar." Drunk, he walked up and down challenging queers to come out and fight. The bar closed. "Typhoid Mac," as Spicer dubbed the troublemaker, tried to push Jack to the door. The two got into a fight a block or two up Telegraph toward campus. They fell to the sidewalk; fists flew, clothes were torn, and blood was shed. George Berthelon was standing close by, shouting mad things, finally darting forward to grab, bare, and bite the larger man's calf. "Why'd you do that?" reproached Jack. "I almost had him calmed down." The police came and sent everyone on home.[29]

Spicer's Berkeley circle of gay friends had a San Francisco counterpart, the somewhat *louche* crowd that hung around the apartment of Robert Berg, head of the Ordering Department at the SF State Library. Berg had managed the Campus Textbook Exchange at Cal when Spicer had been a student there, and had staffed it with poets who, he said, needed the money more than anyone else. Now he worked at San Francisco State during the day; cocktail hour began at six, and drunken parties followed. In odd hours he pursued two hobbies, watching old movies on TV, and picking up sailors and Marines to photograph naked against specially designed backdrops. His photographic eye was uncanny for an amateur, and his "physique" nudes are comparable in intensity of feeling and detail to those of a better-known contemporary, George Platt Lynes. Berg was a round man of fearful mien much feared for his diary, which detailed the sexual and amorous escapades of many Berkeley and San Francisco intellectuals, including Duncan, Blaser, and Spicer. In later years he shared the raucous apartment, platonically, with Dick Bratset, who taught English at San Francisco State, and who had known Spicer as an undergraduate at Berkeley.[30]

Politics and the Left still galvanized Spicer. The continuing appeals of Julius and Ethel Rosenberg, convicted in March 1951 of spying for the Soviet Union, dragged on for twenty-six months, during which time the Berkeley intelligentsia mounted a series of fundraising campaigns for their defense. Ultimately all appeals failed, and in July 1953 the Rosenbergs were electrocuted. Outraged and defiant, Spicer and Blaser joined a Trotskyite study group based in Berkeley, until their anarchist leanings saw the joke of it. "The Trotskyite group was run by a guy named Robin Bauer," Blaser recalled. "There were no more than fourteen people if that many, and one said, 'I move that we ban supernaturalist religions.' Oh, God, the absurdity of these things! Jack looked at me and he could see—one, I was displeased; two, I thought this was the most ridiculous thing I had ever heard in my life, and so I whispered, 'I'm papal nuncio,' and Jack said, 'Well, stand up and say so,' and I told them, 'I'm Papal Nuncio of the Bay Area,' and I got thrown out. They never allowed me back as a Trotskyite."[31] When the Mattachine Society began a branch in Berkeley, Spicer saw a possible way of combining his left tendencies with the puzzle of sexual identity that had tormented him all his life.

The Mattachine Society, founded in Los Angeles in the spring of 1951, was one of the very early homosexual rights organizations, and so small was the network of "out" California homosexuals that Spicer knew or knew of several of its founders, particularly Martin Block and the painter John Button. In January 1953 the Mattachine began its own magazine, called *One*, after a quotation from Thomas Carlyle: "A mystic bond of brotherhood makes all men ONE."[32] Several of the first Mattachine members had been communists, and the organization spread on the model of communist "cells," with a branch in Oakland/Berkeley in or shortly after February 1953.[33] Spicer's involvement in the Mattachine soon displaced his alliances to the Berkeley Trotskyites. Both were dangerous enterprises

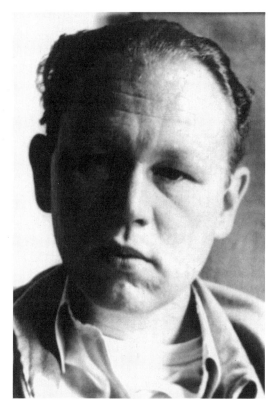

Jack Spicer at the time of his involvement with the
Mattachine Society. *Photo by Edgar Austin (collection of the authors).*

in the Cold War climate of the early 1950s, but the Mattachine offered a
base of identity politics—a human face—that Spicer missed in his other
radical connections, and with great fervor he threw himself into establishing an East Bay beachhead for the Mattachine. Blaser recalled, "I remember
Jack showing me how I should wave a copy of *One*—you know, a gentle
fan—in restaurants and so on, and then that would draw other people to
me, of like mind."[34] The social aspect of the Mattachine meetings appealed
to a number of gay Berkeley men, about ten or twelve of whom met secretly on a monthly basis. "Whoever was host would serve beer or sandwiches, or both, tea, coffee," recalled Myrsam Wixman, "and then there
was a lot of schmoozing about the gay life, its pleasures and perils. There
was some political discussion of the position of gay people in society, and

especially in the East Bay and San Francisco, and about the value of an organization like the one that was being formed in uniting homosexuals to
stand up for their rights, and meet other people similarly inclined, politically and sexually."[35] Blaser was unsympathetic to the "social aspect"—"I
don't know why, since I was going to psychiatrists and having plenty of
troubles of my own"—what a later generation of feminists would call its
"consciousness raising." The meetings, he recalled, were "strikingly like
present-day group therapy."[36]

With Wixman, Spicer attended the notorious Mattachine convention of
April-May 1953, held at the First Universalist Church in Los Angeles.
Called to adopt a constitution for the group, the convention was highly
charged and filled with cloak-and-dagger secrecy that mirrored the paranoia and anticommunist hysteria pervasive in California at that time. "Jack
and I," recalled Wixman, "traveled down with at least two or probably
three other men to L.A., taking the Santa Fe train, which stopped on University Avenue." A group of sorority girls, noisy and animated, boarded the
train at Berkeley too. The gay men, gathering in the lounge area of the car,
took some white paper cones from the restroom sink, filled them with
whiskey, and sat nervous and disgruntled, watching the girls' antics with
disdain. "Fish," Spicer growled, "always travel in schools." At Bakersfield,
the men were transferred to a Santa Fe bus which took them into L.A.'s
Union Station, where they were met by organizers who transported them
to different "safe houses." Spicer and Wixman were driven to Laurel
Canyon, near Beverly Hills, to a secluded cottage offered by a pair of sympathetic young men who worked in the film industry. Everything was
hush-hush, and many used pseudonyms. "They were very amiable hosts,"
Wixman remembered, and at night, with the blinds drawn, a long night of
drinking began. In the morning cars arrived to take them to the First Universalist Church. Though both Wixman and Spicer had family living in Los
Angeles, they had been instructed not to notify their relatives that they
were in L.A. The convention's atmosphere was tense, electric, and conducted in shadow. "This was the kind of secrecy which attended the movements of a lot of gay people who were involved."

The convention had its humorous moments, as when during one debate
about the closet "one young fellow from the Los Angeles area got up and
said that if the names of the members, especially prominent members or
organizers of the organization were put out into the open, he said—he
meant to say, obviously, 'There are many people here who are new who
might be valuable members in the organization who would not touch the

organization with a ten-foot pole were their names made public, and their sexual inclinations broadcast'; but he made an unintentional slip of the tongue and said, 'They won't touch it with a ten-inch pole—I mean, ten-foot pole.' It got a good laugh, of course, from the crowd."[37] But generally the mood was dark, and the convention disintegrated into an acrimonious debate between communist, socialist, and anticommunist factions, and wound up ousting the original radical founders.[38] Spicer adopted an anarchist stance which he later expanded into "Three Marxist Essays" (1962):

Homosexuality is essentially being alone. Which is a fight against the capitalist bosses who do not want us to be alone. Alone we are dangerous.

Our dissatisfaction could ruin America. Our love could ruin the universe if we let it.

If we let our love flower into the true revolution we will be swamped with offers for beds.[39]

"Jack really did a great deal with the Mattachine," Blaser recalled, "attending meetings, organizing them and so on, for well over a year. He took an activist position in it. As far as I know, he never hid that aspect of himself."[40]

In the fall of 1953 Spicer took a new post, one that eventually brought him to San Francisco to live. He was hired as the head of the new humanities department at the California School of Fine Arts, a job secured through recommendations by Tom Parkinson.[41] The animation that had characterized his Berkeley triumphs had deserted him, replaced by a cynical gravity. His circle of friends was changing. Blaser had completed his studies in library science, and was soon to move to Boston to work at the Widener Library at Harvard. Duncan was busy with Jess. He was involved in new writing experiments, and an increased interest in "Eastern" poets like Robert Creeley, Charles Olson, and Denise Levertov. For now, Jack had to think about his career.

When Spicer was hired by the California School of Fine Arts, he arrived in the middle of a battle that had gone on for eight years. The California School of Fine Arts had existed in one form or another since 1874, and such disparate artists as Emily Carr and Diego Rivera had worked there, but by the end of World War II the institution was financially and artistically moribund. The curator Douglas MacAgy, hired as director in 1945, brought the place back to life by mandating an emphasis on contemporary art, and by hiring an extraordinary faculty that included Clyfford Still, Edward Corbett, David Park, Hassel Smith, and Clay Spohn. In addition,

MacAgy lured Ad Reinhardt, Mark Rothko, Salvador Dali, Man Ray, and many others to CSFA for more or less extended periods. (He spent three years trying to lure Marcel Duchamp out of retirement and onto the CSFA faculty.) The program appealed to a returning GI population that confounded parents and families by refusing to settle down to civilian life, and enrollment at the school boomed in the immediate postwar period. Yet the GI Bill benefits could not last forever, and a concerned board decided MacAgy had gone too far. During a coup in 1950, MacAgy was ousted, and Ernest Mundt was installed in his place. Mundt and his supporters wanted to return CSFA to its prewar focus on commercial arts, arguing that advertising and design were needed if artists were to find jobs in the "real world." When MacAgy was let go, many of his faculty members resigned in protest, and the school's enrollment dropped from approximately 325 students to less than 70. In 1953 the GI Bill was extended to cover the educational needs of Korean War veterans, and the Board of CFSA decided to make it an accredited college. In the fall of 1953, in this turbulent brew of warring pedagogies, Jack Spicer was hired. When asked afterward what he had taught, he replied, "Everything."[42]

The California School of Fine Arts commanded a handsome site high on Chestnut Street above North Beach. The young painters and sculptors Jack met in his classes were a wild bunch. Among them were some of the artists who would turn San Francisco into one of the important international art centers of the 1950s, as the Bay Area became the scene of an exciting confrontation between surrealism and abstract expressionism, which in turn devolved into a new movement of funk assemblage.[43] Their work were "secret," however, since their only audience was themselves. Paintings and sculptures were made, shown, bought, destroyed, thrown out, painted over, all in a short period of time. There was little thought of tomorrow, of preserving the work, or even of documenting it, and no interest in "reputation" beyond the narrow confines of the local scene. (When Wally Hedrick and DeFeo "made it" into the "Sixteen Americans" show, for example, they did not bother to attend.) Spicer was impressed by their integrity, their absolute commitment to art, and their Duchampian indifference to conventional artistic standards. His later thinking about his own work—his refusal to seek copyright, his insistence on small-press and limited editions of his books—owes a great deal to the artists he met at this time in his CSFA classes.

To the painter Wally Hedrick, Spicer seemed "very academic, which at the time seemed strange, especially to visually oriented people" like himself and his painter friends. As Hedrick settled into class, he realized that Jack's bookishness was "mixed in with this completely off the wall surrealist humor and imagination." Nominally, Spicer taught English and drama, in workshops that were strange combinations of group therapy, creative writing, art history, and playwriting. "He taught us how to write a traditional essay, poem, short story. The one I thank him for is he taught me how to take words and to use the library and do research." Although the students didn't realize it until later, Spicer's pedagogy was "revolutionary, verging on the bizarre."[44]

He had thought long and hard about teaching methods, ever since Stuart Loomis had expounded on John Dewey's theories at Berkeley. The painter John Allen Ryan recalled Spicer's first day of class, when he stood, tall and gangly, at the front of the room and announced, "I plan to be my own best student," in a shiny, stodgy black suit, waving big hands. "A charming man. We didn't know this was to be the only suit he ever wore for us!" Trying to find the "natural" interests of the students and entice them into thinking and writing through the lure of popular culture, Spicer found himself re-examining the boundaries between high and low culture. What were the "natural" forms of writing, of textuality, of thinking about poetry? Song lyrics, popular radio shows, movies, traffic signs, cards. One day Spicer came to class with a Tarot deck and invited all to pick a card. (Hedrick picked the "Hanged Man.") "Your assignment," said Spicer, "is to write an interpretation of the card." This forced them to visit the library and read about Tarot's symbolism. The class put on a play—Shakespeare—but Spicer told them they weren't ready for "real" Shakespeare and would have to be content with staging the little "play within a play" in *Hamlet*. As another assignment, Spicer handed out typed copies of his Berkeley poems and his Minnesota poems and asked the class to rewrite them in their own style.

Spicer drew on other forms of popular culture, too. One exercise involved the current spate of science fiction novels and radio dramas, such as those by Norman Corwin, which played into postwar readers' fears and fantasies about the end of the world by describing characters doomed to die from atomic fallout. In a darkened room illuminated only by a bright, flashing strobe light, Spicer told his students to improvise monologues about the nuclear apocalypse. He also flirted daringly with androgyny when he led his students to writing and acting monologues based on Tennessee Williams's *Streetcar Named Desire*. "One week we'd all be Stanley," Hedrick recalled, "and the next week Blanche."[45]

Hedrick and Ryan were part of a large contingent of artists from Pasadena who had congregated around Pasadena Junior College, and were now using GI benefits from the Korean War to go to CSFA. Older than the usual run of students, they gave their new teacher back as good as they got. His confraternity with his students was so complete that it alarmed other members of the faculty. His classes became legendary for the amount of noise and chaos they produced. After one difficult assignment, the class rebelled and conspired overnight to show up for the next class already drunk or high. When Spicer came in he found a case of Rainier Ale on his desk. "Jack scowled ferociously and then burst out laughing, and we all went out to the backyard. Used to be there was a row of plane trees running down it, and a great sward of grass where we sat to paint the Bay at that time. So we all went out there and spent a good afternoon, killing the case," Ryan remembered. "To hell with the assignment!"[46] When Spicer announced a prize for the first "letter to the Editor" by a student to be printed in one of the city's six daily newspapers, he was chagrined when Ryan's was published in the *Chronicle* four days later. Spicer confessed that he had hoped to win the prize himself. He wanted to be his own best student.

Charged with teaching his students history, Spicer came up with an unusual tack, in which the apparent incongruities of history were revealed to possess an arcane, almost secret meaning. Freud, for example, was born in 1856. So was Bernard Shaw. What were people reading in 1856? We know the Crimean War ended in 1856. What were its causes, what were its results? In 1856 Dickens was writing *Little Dorrit*, Melville publishing *The Piazza Tales*. Abolitionism was setting the States on fire. Louis Sullivan and L. Frank Baum were born—weird concordance of two midwestern visionaries. And Heine and Schumann both died: Heine, born in 1810. This involved a further leap into the past, a chance to explore romanticism, the Regency, Blake, Austen, Turner, Lewis and Clark, Napoleon. Spicer and his students were borne back—for the length of a semester—into the past, leap by leap, looking always for the roots of history. This method was to reach its peak in Spicer's later "Fake Novel on the Life of Arthur Rimbaud" (1960), which carefully situates Rimbaud's birth within the presidency of James Buchanan, a historicity that leads to unexpected, sinister, surrealist results.

During this autumn of 1953, a new institution took root in San Francisco. The Poetry Center at San Francisco State College was a natural outgrowth of the poetry festivals Kenneth Rexroth and Madeline Gleason had pioneered in the immediate postwar period, but it took Ruth Witt-Diamant, a woman of unusual force and character, to find it the home and backing it needed to survive and grow. A professor of literature at San Francisco State since 1930, Witt-Diamant conceived of the Poetry Center during a sabbatical visit to her idols, the poet Dylan Thomas and his wife, Caitlin, in Wales. Inaugurated with a reading by W. H. Auden, the Poetry Center quickly became a vital force in Bay Area poetry, presenting local writers and importing the big names of Britain and America to give readings and meet students. In its first few years, the Center had already featured talents as diverse as Theodore Roethke, Muriel Rukeyser, Allen Tate, Stephen Spender, and Louise Bogan.

In a very real sense, Ruth Witt-Diamant was the most powerful figure in the postwar poetry world of San Francisco. Until her departure for a teaching post in Japan in 1961, she wielded enormous influence and direction. A woman of great charm and vision, Witt-Diamant could be autocratic and haughty. To become her assistant, as Robert Duncan did in 1956, required a considerable amount of tact and diplomacy. Eve Triem and Madeline Gleason were quiet women with hidden personae, but Witt-Diamant was flamboyant, given to grand gestures. (Jess recalled that he and Robert used always to bring extra handkerchiefs to any event over which "Ruth Witt" presided—they needed them to stuff in their mouths to prevent their hilarity from bubbling over.[47]) She was "not a high society woman, she was of the middle class. Her husband had died long before" Robert and Jess met her, and her children had grown. After Robert took a job as the assistant director, she and he were constantly butting heads about the direction the Poetry Center should go. "Robert did all of the work, Robert and Ida Hodes [Poetry Center secretary]—and Ruth took all the credit." Witt-Diamant was also something of a connoisseur, and painters like Jess would lend her their paintings, which she would hang in her house on Willard Street for the value of exposure. One disgruntled painter, the late Edward Corbett, asked her for payment eventually and she drew up in shock. "How dare you!" At that time Jess found it difficult to sell any of his work. Only friends, and friends of friends, would buy it, at bargain basement prices. One millionaire—Mr. Roth, of the Matson Shipping Line—wound up with a priceless collection because he was a Marin neighbor. Once Roth asked Robert and Jess to house-sit his mansion while the family went away—but neglected to tell any of the neighbors or the police—a neighbor called the police when she saw these two "odd" figures living in the house, and Jess and Robert had to do some fast talking.[48]

Witt-Diamant often invited prominent visitors to stay at her house on Willard Street. The most famous, and her favorite, had been Dylan Thomas. She prided herself on being a "helper" to the wild men who had made poetry a man's game in the mid-twentieth century.[49] Spicer was polite to Ruth Witt-Diamant and enjoyed meeting some of his idols at her Willard Street salon. Auden's visit in October 1954 brought out the gay community, which had long been aware of Auden's not-so-covert sexual preference—Spicer loved to quote from e.e. cummings.

> Auden & Spender, poetical poyds
> Even whose recti are covered by Lloyds'[50]

He had loved and imitated Auden's great 1930s lyrics since he had first discovered them as a teenager. For Spicer, Auden's greatest achievement was his daring introduction of science and political commitment into a writing already rich with formal beauty. The British poet spoke so highly of *The Lord of the Rings* that Duncan and Jess bought copies of the newly published trilogy. They shared them with Spicer, and Tolkien became part of their common language, like Oz.[51] Another august visitor to the Poetry Center was William Carlos Williams. At Williams's reading, Spicer was seen in a new suit—the only time any of his friends ever saw him in anything new.[52] His admiration for Williams was fueled by Duncan, who regarded the Paterson poet as the only equal to Ezra Pound, and who once named "The Yachts" as his favorite poem of the twentieth century.

The students at the Art Institute learned a lot from Spicer, but they educated him too. They turned him on to drugs and jazz. He had smoked a little marijuana at Berkeley—it helped soothe his nerves and made it easier to try to score in gay bars. Now he indulged more than ever, but presently paranoia set in and he went back to beer. One student blamed Spicer's subsequent prohibition on drugs on his personal experiences during this time. "Jack would say he hated dope, but he meant that he got paranoid when he smoked grass," said John Allen Ryan. "I turned him on a number of times, and he tried. He just got flippy, as some people do—a chemical reaction. So he was against it."[53] As a teenager in Los Angeles during the war years, Spicer had visited jazz clubs, but now he began to frequent them in earnest. His letters of this period are filled with a kind of snappy, hipster/beat "head" talk ("Daddy-O") that makes some of them almost incomprehensible today. At the San Francisco nightclub called the Blackhawk,

Dave Brubeck's Quartet started a long engagement and Spicer became a fixture there for a while, reportedly recording some of his own poetry to Brubeck's jazz backup.[54] "I met Jack Spicer at the Blackhawk," said long-time San Francisco columnist Herb Caen. "He introduced me to Chet Baker there. At least he thought he did. Turned out Chet and I had met long before, and after we shook hands we winked at each other behind Spicer's back—in a friendly way, of course."[55]

Most successfully, his art students turned Spicer on to The Place, an artists' bar in a storefront on Grant Avenue between Filbert and Union streets. Jointly owned by Knute Stiles and Leo Krikorian, who had studied at Black Mountain College in the late 1940s, The Place opened in the autumn of 1953 (and reopened in the spring of 1954). The first event, Stiles remembered, "was Jack Spicer's cacophony band from his class at the Art Institute. They were a very noisy lot—almost drove the customers out really, making noises on the balcony."[56] The Place also mounted small shows of young artists' work, including Jay DeFeo's first.

Stiles and Krikorian used the intimacy of their storefront bar—the placement of furniture, a jukebox musical selection chosen by the customers, the hiring of bartenders from the ranks of their own patrons—to create something new. The anarchic principles Stiles had explored with fellow anarchists and artists at Black Mountain, in New York, and especially in San Francisco challenged America's politically conservative postwar society. It encouraged the use of marijuana, exploring ways to break traditional sex roles, "a greater candor about homosexuality, a greater interest in experiment in heterosexual relations"—including the encouragement of women to "use swear words"—and generally frank conversations on all subjects. The revolution was to be personal; it was to make social ripples before waves. "We arranged it in such a way that there wouldn't be any single-tabled people, that people would all be kind of together. The smallness of The Place actually insured the continuity of the dialogue—it was very hard for anybody to get lost. I think that probably set the tone as a meeting place for 'out groups.' And by 'out groups' I mean poets and painters, of course; but also merchant seamen and taxi drivers and lesbians and queers and revolutionaries and so forth. Actually, of course, it became the hub of what later became known as the Beat Generation. My customers," said Stiles, "were people like Ginsberg and Kerouac."[57]

Perhaps this infusion of Beat energy soured Spicer's mood, for at least in the bar Spicer and Stiles failed to get along. In "A Poem for Dada at The Place, April 1, 1955," Spicer attacks the Dada events of the bar, concluding "you only have the right to piss in the fountain / If you are beautiful." To this Knute Stiles responded, "I had no understanding of Jack's feeling toward Dada, or The Place, until I read the poem, many years later. I really thought that he was a kind of participant and one of the most ardent Dadaists." Did Spicer resent the presence of a competitor in a world he chose to control? Stiles didn't know. "If I sat at the poets' table, very often the other people would just shut up and wouldn't say a word: I was not privy to Spicer's seminar."[58]

Of all his students at CFSA, Spicer became closest to two, Graham Mackintosh and John Ryan. He began a long, loving correspondence with Graham Mackintosh during the latter's tour in the army (in a year and a half—1954–55—Spicer sent Mackintosh at least fifty-three letters and cards[59]) Afterward the two remained close friends. When asked if in fact his relationship with Spicer was an intimate one, Graham Mackintosh said, "Our friendship survived such intimacy."[60] Spicer's letters to Mackintosh mirrored and parodied the Cold War rhetoric of contemporary public life, which bristled with antigay sentiment on both the left and right. For Mackintosh, Spicer invented a newspaper, "Aware America," an echo of anticommunist, countersubversive journals such as *Plain Talk, Counterattack, Firing Line, Spotlight, Red Channels, Aware.* The letters mimic the very public relation between Roy Cohn and David Schine that was being trumpeted in the anti-McCarthy press, in which Cohn, a New York attorney, aide to Senator Joseph McCarthy of Wisconsin, and a closeted homosexual, was being lampooned for his attempts to save the blond, dishy, heterosexual Schine from Korea by securing him a draft exemption or, failing that, a cushy commission.[61] Spicer's letters to Mackintosh are a complex and self-conscious retelling of the Cohn-Schine affair, with himself in the role of Cohn—lover, mother, Cold Warrior, god, rolled up into one.

John Ryan, a young, rangy painter-poet from Pasadena, was a breezier companion, what a later gay generation would call a "fuck buddy." Ryan's father was the agricultural commissioner of Los Angeles County, and his family was close to the family of Lew Burch (agricultural commissioner of Santa Cruz County, and the stepfather of Robert Duncan). While most of the students Spicer met were resolutely heterosexual, John Allen Ryan was gay, or bisexual. "We were the only—well, we didn't use the word 'gay.' We were the two queers." Ingratiating, brash, attractive in a black-Irish kind of way, Ryan moved between the worlds of the poets and the painters, and between the gay and straight worlds, with a lack of diffidence that amused and challenged Jack, who was only three years his elder. They shared a taste for alcohol and the absurd. One afternoon as Spicer and Ryan were drinking in Vesuvio, a North Beach tavern, a man they'd never met called them by name and sat down next to them, saying, "I'm going to shock you." He kept saying so as he nursed his one beer. Then he ate the beer glass. He went downstairs to the bathroom, came back up, bleeding from the mouth, and walked out. Every day brought new experiences of this kind, events without explanation or traceable motives, and Spicer and Ryan reveled in the abrupt, Alice in Wonderland, feel to this Bohemia.[62]

Spicer could unburden himself to Ryan without fear of condemnation. Painfully shy about his body, he loosened up under Ryan's beery minstrations. He confessed his anxieties about the size of his penis to Ryan, who did his best to allay his fears. His small penis, Spicer lamented, was the reason he couldn't take off his clothes in front of anyone, male or female. As a result, the sex he had most often—kneeling before a partially clothed man and performing fellatio on him—wasn't really what he cared for or wanted, but what he felt most comfortable with. His brother had a real penis, and so had his father. What was wrong with him? "Nothing," said Ryan, as soothingly as he could, crossing two fingers behind his back.[63]

They took a trip to Mendocino in April 1955 with the poet Jonathan Williams. There Spicer wrote his poem for Ryan, "Midnight at Bareass Beach," which celebrates, in a covert, coded way, the pleasures of physical and emotional nudity.[64] The two men even invented a private language, the way children do, and formed their own "secret" society, the Interplanetary Services of the Martian Anarchy.[65] Ryan remembered:

Jack's mother lived in L.A., and my parents lived in South Pasadena, so we got into going down there for Christmas every year on the train together, drinking Red Cap Ale, which you could only get on trains in those days. Jack Spicer and I were both fluent in Martian. I was North Martian, and he was South Martian, but we understood what we said perfectly well. On one of those Christmas train trips we were heading south on the train, and Jack had to go take a leak. Jack and I had been conversing in Martian, being quite full of Red Cap Ale, and a guy from another table came over and asked me when Jack went to the head, "Are you fellows Australian?" Jack returned and greeted the man, "Sit ka vassisi von ka, sta'chi que v'ay qray." ("Salut!") That's Southern Martian.

Once the stranger understood what was going on, he bought both Spicer and Ryan another drink. "Eiss! Sa schlein! Ja da lond, nar la loff," they replied: "thank you," in Northern Martian.[66] From this point on, Spicer's poetry is invaded by Martians, like the romances of Edgar Rice Burroughs he'd devoured as a boy, or the contemporary science fiction paperbacks he bought and traded. Slowly the notion took root that "invasion" itself might be a better metaphor for poetry than "inspiration," and "Mars" became a verbal shorthand for a frightening outside force that insinuates itself into human thought and shapes our brains through language. The poet Allen Ginsberg, who met Spicer at this time through John Ryan and Robert Duncan, described their poetic differences succinctly:

He was friendly toward me, but held a different vision of poetry. I think he had a thing that has nothing to do with Ego, messages come through the radio stations of the mind, so to speak, whereas I was thinking of the spontaneous mind. Not actually very different in operation: as a practical matter of composition, it's not very different in method. But at any rate I think he thought that my own method was much too involved with personal statement and ego: it's a legitimate objection. The intention of one's attitude, one's training and meditation, I don't think he was particularly interested in.[67]

Another student at CSFA became more of a conventional boyfriend. A friend both of Ryan and Myrsam Wixman, Allen Joyce was a fixture at George Berthelon's Berkeley salon. A cast in one eye gave him an endearing squint, added character to a handsome face. He was the scion of a well-to-do southern California naval family, and planned to write. Spicer planned to teach him how. Joyce also had the makings of a promising drinking partner. "Giving yourself to poetry," wrote Jack, "is like giving yourself to alcohol—most people can't or are afraid. I've given myself to both. So can you."[68] Frustratingly, Joyce, like Ryan, preferred very young boys to men, so the erotic component to Spicer's affection for Joyce was somewhat muted.[69] Still they became a kind of couple until time and distance broke them up.

Spicer's confraternity with his students reached its high point when he and five painters burst the bonds of academia and founded a commercial gallery. The "6" Gallery opened on Halloween 1954 in the Fillmore Street premises vacated months before by King Ubu, an artists-run space established by Jess, Harry Jacobus, and Robert Duncan that lasted from 1952 to 1953. The "6" were the visual artists Wally Hedrick, David Simpson, Deborah Remington, Hayward King, John Allen Ryan, plus Spicer, who hung his own poems next to the paintings of his confreres for the opening show. Wally Hedrick and Jay DeFeo, who married around this time, were the king and queen of the "6"—wildly talented, boisterous, filled with energy. Spicer, who knew he had no talent for curatorial work, contented himself

Opening of the "6" Gallery, Halloween, 1954. The white squares of paper on the walls are Spicer's poems, which were hung to sell. Few sold. The man leaning over to talk to the shorter woman is Hayward King; the weedy-looking mustached boy in the background is John Allen Ryan. *Photo by Robert Berg (collection of the authors).*

with writing press releases—"propaganda"—and beating the drums among the literati.[70]

He was living a full, almost schizophrenic life—teaching at CSFA, sitting the gallery, drinking at The Place, participating in the "Old Ladies' Bridge Club" in Berkeley on Fridays, keeping in touch with his mother in Los Angeles, attending Mattachine meetings (now in San Francisco), and trying to continue his long-term project, the *Imaginary Elegies*. With such a busy schedule, he had little time for writing.

In a concerted effort to get back in touch with his muse, Spicer joined the poetry workshop Duncan was teaching at San Francisco State in the autumn of 1954. There he made the acquaintance of twenty-one-year-old Michael McClure, newly arrived from Kansas, equally comfortable with the poets of Spicer's generation and the young artists of the "6" Gallery circle. "I was getting poems of mine typed, the earliest poems in *Hymns to St. Geryon*," McClure remembered. "Poems like 'For the Death of a Hundred

Whales,' 'The Breach,' and 'Point Lobos Animism.' I counted all the letter spaces in a line and at the end of each line there'd be a number like '72,' and the next line might say '34,' and the next line might say '15,' because there were fifteen letter spaces. That way, it was possible for a typist to center them correctly. I remember Duncan was amused, because Spicer had seen the manuscript, with the numbers, and thought that it was a poetics of 'magic' that I was doing. He asked Robert what it was."[71] To Jack, McClure's lines, with numbers appended, resembled chemical equations— Uranium 238—or alchemical formulas. McClure's dangerous, dark beauty inspired a joking lasciviousness among Spicer and his gay pals, masking a real, common-sense lust. "How did Mike McClure look with his clothes off?" he wrote to one friend. "I have a theory that poets who use rhyme schemes have no meat."[72]

Also joining Spicer and McClure in Duncan's workshop were Helen Adam and Ida Hodes. Born in 1909, Adam was the oldest of the poets in the workshop. Something of a child prodigy, she had seen her first book published in England while still a young girl in her native Scotland. Stranded with her mother and sister in the United States at the outbreak of World War II, Helen Adam had taken a series of odd jobs (including, or so she claimed, a stint at a heroin factory in Reno) and came to roost in the Bay Area around 1950.[73] Duncan had met her in 1953 and been immediately impressed with her multiple talents. Her poetry, unlike anything else currently being written, struck him with the same force as more up-to-date enthusiasms—Olson, Eigner, Levertov, Creeley. Her writing preserved and gave new life to the traditional ballad form, a haunting, otherworldly blend of rhyme and song. Helen Adam was very different from her friend Ida Hodes, a worldly, energetic woman who had come from Chicago via Big Sur and the Henry Miller crowd to serve Ruth Witt-Diamant loyally at the Poetry Center at San Francisco State. After a reading of Spicer's, Helen enthused about the "marvelous" poem Jack had read—"that beautiful poem about Atlantis." Ida racked her brains but could remember no mention of Atlantis. Pressed, Helen exclaimed, "Oh, Ida, the one called 'Wet Dream.'" "I don't think that was about Atlantis, dear," said Ida dryly.[74] Helen Adam's skill, resourcefulness, and genuine contact with the mystery of poetry inspired Spicer as had no other poets since Duncan and Josephine Miles. He soon turned to the ballad form himself, influenced by Adam's insistence that genuine magic lies trapped within the old forms, waiting to escape.

McClure, Spicer, Adam, Hodes, and others joined Duncan in giving a staged reading of his play *Faust Foutu* at the "6" Gallery in January 1955, an artistic event made scandalous by Duncan's stripping off his clothes to represent the revealed nakedness of the poet. Spicer envied Duncan's success with *Faust Foutu*, and when Duncan announced that he had sent it to the Cambridge Poets' Theater, Spicer went back to his room and began to write his own plays on classical and mythological themes.

On Valentine's Day of 1955 Spicer received a letter from Ernest Mundt, the autocratic Berlin-born director of CSFA. "In view of planned changes," he had been fired.[75] His last day would be June 30. "It escapes me now, the reason Mundt fired Jack, but I'm sure it's lurid," comments Wally Hedrick. "Ernest Mundt knew a lush when he saw one. I never saw Jack drunk when he was teaching, but he's the guy who introduced me to the drinking of Rainier Ale. It was a cheap drunk: at Vesuvio's bar you could get a bottle for 35 cents. All you had to have was $1.05 in your pocket and that was an evening. Rainier was a bit more potent, it seemed, than regular beer, and you don't want to drink more than three bottles."[76] Asked about this matter forty years later, Ernest Mundt denied that Spicer's drinking had lost him his job. Neither was it a sexual liaison with a student, as has sometimes been claimed. Instead, Mundt related this layoff to larger organizational changes in the institution itself.[77] Being fired didn't seem to faze Spicer. His friends became dearer to him, Allen Joyce especially so. He fell in love with Allen only when he knew they would be separated.

The late spring of 1955 saw a dramatic crackdown by Bay Area police on local known homosexuals, or "sex deviants," who were leading suspects in a Berkeley murder case. In this *cause célèbre*, a fourteen-year old schoolgirl, Stephanie Bryan, disappeared on her way home from junior high, and many in Spicer's circle were questioned as to their whereabouts. The attending media circus was still in high gear, mirroring the national atmosphere of fear and suspicion, when, in July, Spicer left San Francisco for New York.[78]

While Spicer left in search of the fame and fortune he had dreamed of, this voyage east had an ironic twist, since while he was gone, the "6" Gallery, which he had helped found, could have given him one clear shot at notoriety. Besides art exhibitions, the "6" Gallery was becoming well known for poetry readings, of which perhaps the most famous—hailed as the "birth of the Beat Generation"—was Allen Ginsberg's public reading of *Howl*, on October 7, 1955, with Jack Kerouac in attendance, and Kenneth Rexroth as M.C. Michael McClure, Gary Snyder, Philip Whalen, and Philip Lamantia also read the same evening. McClure and Wally Hedrick, who organized the event, would have asked Spicer and Duncan to read too, had they been in town. "Spicer's friend John Ryan came that evening," McClure remembered, "and gave me a letter he'd received from Spicer—who had left New York and moved to Boston. It asked someone in San Francisco to help find Spicer a job and the wherewithal to come back home, because he wanted to leave Boston. I read Jack's letter from the stage and it got applause from his friends and fans. It was a practical matter. 'Could anybody help Jack?' This was a request for much needed mutual aid: *Let's get Jack out of Boston, where he's unhappy.* It was a letter of plaint: Help! get me out of here! There were a lot of people there and I thought maybe somebody could help."[79] But no one did. When Spicer, trapped on the East Coast, heard how his letter had been read, he burned to return.

CHAPTER THREE

The Poet in New York (and Boston)

New York let Spicer down. No, it appalled him. "I hate this town," he wrote a month after his arrival. "No sense of abandon here. No head-talk even among heads. People smoke their pot sadly. Nobody loves anybody. Nobody speaks Martian."[1] Arthur Kloth, who was living in Manhattan at the time of Spicer's arrival, tried to show him something of the high life. He took Jack to Jones Beach, the free public beach on Long Island, and noticed how dirty Spicer was—he came out of the ocean "two shades lighter."[2] He had come to New York to escape the claustrophobia of being a big fish in a small pond, and to make his way as a writer. He took a job teaching high school English at a New Jersey prep school but lasted only two weeks. "Unbearable torture," he wrote to John Allen Ryan. "It will be months before I'll be able to look at chicken again."[3] ("Chicken" was 1950s gay slang for "underage boys.") He applied for jobs at museums. And he sought out the bar society of Manhattan—particularly at the San Remo bar, recommended to him by the painter John Button, whom he had known in Berkeley. "Jack enjoyed meeting the crowd at the Remo," Button later wrote. "This was a sort of East Coast version of the Red Lizard [the San Francisco gay bar that both Spicer and Button had frequented in their Berkeley days] except that both the lights and the company were brighter."[4] Button and a second young man, Earl McGrath, were Spicer's entree into the high art—and high camp—circles of Frank O'Hara.

The biographer can read Spicer, the man, not only through his own poems but through glimpses of him—apparitions, ghostly reflections—in the poetry of his contemporaries, those who loved and hated him, in the texts in which his person is reduced to a lexical sign. We could assemble an anthology of these poems—from the "Domestic Scenes" of Duncan (1948) all the way to the poems inspired by his untimely death—and, in this fractured hall of mirrors, watch him flicker. Spicer's miserable months in New York in 1955 are brilliantly condensed into a line or two in Frank O'Hara's "At the Old Place." The poem, which has the incidental historical value of being the very first of O'Hara's celebrated "I-do-this, I-do-that" poems, is dated July 13, 1955.

At The Old Place

Joe is restless and so am I, so restless.
Button's buddy lips frame "LGT TH O P?"
across the bar. "Yes" I cry, for dancing's
my soul delight (Feet! feet!) "Come on!"

Through the streets we skip like swallows.
Howard malingers. (Come on, Howard.) Ashes
malingers. (Come on, J.A.) Dick malingers.
(Come on, Dick.) Alvin darts ahead. (Wait up,
Alvin.) Jack, Earl and Someone don't come.

Down the dark stairs drifts the steaming cha-
cha-cha. Through the urine and smoke we charge
to the door. Wrapped in Ashes' arms I glide.

(It's heaven!) Button lindys with me. (It's
heaven!) Joe's two-steps, too, are incredible,
and then a fast rhumba with Alvin, like skipping
on toothpicks. And the interminable intermissions,

we have them. Jack, Earl and Someone drift
guiltily in. "I knew they were gay
the minute I laid eyes on them!" screams John.
How ashamed they are of us! we hope.[5]

"O'Hara and Spicer were too much alike," recalled Earl McGrath—the "Earl" O'Hara refers to in "At the Old Place." "Their enthusiasm, their interest in the young. Basically, they were both doing the same thing, which was trying to run their friends' lives: what they should be doing, what they should be thinking, reading, writing, so forth and so on. Jack was just a little bit more censorious than Frank—it was always like a pep talk with Frank, you know, but with Jack it was always like a scolding. I was always so worried, I could make the wrong move, I could go the wrong direction, to listen to him. He was a very kind person, but a bit of a crab [laughs]."[6]

A letter from O'Hara to the painter Jasper Johns lists the writings of the new poets, East and West Coasts, and says of Jack Spicer, "He always disappoints me, but others think him very important."[7] Joe LeSueur, Frank O'Hara's roommate and close friend, spoke of their relationship: "Jack rubbed him the wrong way, just as another Jack (Kerouac) did. Frank loved New York, and Jack knew it, yet he was forever complaining about the city to Frank, saying how much nicer S.F. was, and Frank would say why don't you go back then—and of course Jack did, and I don't think Frank ever saw him again."

Both poets died at forty. O'Hara was killed by a beach vehicle at Fire Island a year after Spicer died of alcoholism in San Francisco County General Hospital. LeSueur continued:

Frank represented a very urbane and (to Jack, I believe) a campy kind of poetry, or maybe he felt it was a little effete, I'm not sure; but I do remember Jack not much liking Frank's work. But one must remember that this was the early [actually, mid-] '50s, before Frank wrote most of his important and distinctive poetry. And Frank, though he could see that Jack had talent, wasn't very attracted to his poetry. Then, too, Frank was used to winning over people, and Jack simply would not be won over by him. And as I've suggested, they were a little competitive, Frank representing N.Y. and Jack being the champion of the Bay Area poets.

This might sound terrible to say, and nothing should be made of it, but I do believe that Frank would have been more receptive to Jack's considerable appeal if he (Jack) had not been so physically unattractive. But then of course Jack would have been an entirely different person if he had been good-looking, for certainly his being so abrasive, truculent and even slightly bitter related to his unprepossessing appearance. (That's my opinion, and I may be wrong—it's just a feeling I had at the time.) Jack Spicer and Frank never had it out, never got that unpleasant to each other. They simply rubbed each other the wrong way, that's all.[8]

Landis Everson reported that Spicer intensely disliked the East Coast poets who were their contemporaries. "He called John Ashbery a 'faggot poet.' John's first book was called *Some Trees*, and Jack always made a point of pronouncing it 'Thumb Twees,'" Landis chuckled.[9] Duncan speculated on the Spicer-O'Hara connection in this way: "I keep wondering what would have happened if Spicer and O'Hara really could have talked together. Because Jack's affect seems very much like O'Hara's: both poets absolutely insist on the democratization and anti-snob character of the language. Whereas Robin and"—Duncan's voice and eyebrow archly rising —"I, I suppose, have been snobbish."[10] "Jack was clearly over his head in New York," wrote John Button in his memoir of Spicer. "He couldn't compete for coterie with Allen Ginsberg, Jack Kerouac, William Burroughs, James Agee, Paul Goodman, Wystan Auden, James Schuyler, John Ashbery or Frank O'Hara. . . . [V]ery soon he waxed nostalgic about the Bay Area. He began quoting Heraclitus—a sure sign that he wanted to go back. After some time in Boston, he did."[11] New York, Spicer believed, was Sodom and Gomorrah combined. It corrupted a man the longer he stayed there. Look at Tennessee Williams! *Streetcar* had been a masterpiece, but now, with *Cat on a Hot Tin Roof*, he had pandered to the base interests of the audience and spoiled his artistry. The thought of New York brought out all the most un-likable parts of Spicer—his emotional rigidity, his scorn, and his latent, and hideous, anti-Semitism. When he looked around him and saw the vul-garity, the aggressiveness, and the filth of New York, he blamed, as had many before him, "the Jews." The Jews ran poetry, the theater, big business; they ran the homosexual network; they had even made significant inroads into baseball ownership. It is perhaps no coincidence that Spicer's anti-Semitism and racism become overt directly after his father's death, as if mocking the lapse of his family into liberalism, blasting the liberal specter of "tolerance" with fierce negation. Both Jews and African-Americans be-came useful tropes in his oppositional poetics. In his work, notes the critic Maria Damon, "Jews are materialistic and cannot understand the dissolu-tion of norms. Blacks are all-expansive and boundariless, 'in touch,' at the deepest level, with everything that is 'un.'" Damon continues: "Spicer's tone is one of uneasiness and scorn. One senses a jockeying for one-down on the hierarchy of the oppressed, a rivalry that comes out in bitterness and resentment."[12]

He couldn't go back to Berkeley—indeed, there was hardly a "Berkeley" to go back to, with Robin at Harvard, and Robert and Jess in Mallorca. He applied to Robert Creeley for a job at Black Mountain College, where the poet Charles Olson served as rector: "I'm a lively teacher, inclined to be a lit-tle too far-out for most schools. . . . Please let me know what salary, if any, you people would be able to pay. I don't mind eating raw potatos, but I do need drinking money."[13] No reply. How would Spicer have fared at Black Mountain? "Hard to say," speculated the poet and publisher Jonathan Williams. "Paul Goodman didn't fare very well at BMC. Homophobia blos-soms vigorously in the Blue Ridge mountains. Olson was a nervous nelly when it came to gay men, like an elephant with a mouse."[14] In any case, hear-ing nothing from Black Mountain, Spicer moved to Boston, where Blaser se-cured him a low-level job at the rare book room of the Boston Public Library.

Spicer arrived in the rare book room in December 1955, a month before his thirty-first birthday and six months out of his native California. He was fired less than a year later. No one who worked with him guessed that he was about to become one of America's finest poets.

Jim Devlin, a teenager at the time, worked as a page in rare books, securing and replacing the valuable books from the shelves. He remembered Spicer's haunted face and hunched back, his mouth with too many teeth that gave him a goofy look. Sometimes his dark-blond hair would be so slick with oil he'd resemble the 1930s comic strip character, the Shadow—but the Shadow was elegant and debonair. On Friday nights, quiet nights at the library, Devlin's shift coincided with Spicer's. "We'd bullshit." There were wide gaps between them—the freshman at Boston College, and the man who had taken an advanced degree at UC Berkeley. Although Jim was never invited to his house he knew that Spicer lived in the back—the "wrong side"—of Beacon Hill. His social life was a mystery, although Jim assumed it was nondescript. One Friday night Spicer was reading a book—a biography of a late-nineteenth-early-twentieth-century Episcopalian bishop. "I'm going home to read this," Spicer told Jim, rolling his eyes, "and it will probably be boring." *Bor-r-r-ing*, in a "gay" drawl. He could be affected, thought the boy, but he meant no harm. Spicer was interesting, and from far-off Berkeley, and in the Brahmin atmosphere of the rare book room, his accent and attitude stood out like sore thumbs.

The thing that impressed Devlin most about Spicer is how hard he *tried*. He was always trying to be friendly, although he lacked social skills and his California accent put people off. He was like one of the heavy-weighted rubber clowns that you knock down: he just comes bobbing back up again, smiling and unhurt. Yet behind the Pagliacci grin, Spicer felt mortified by the slights dealt him daily. One night Dick Mullaney came in, the husband of another librarian and a Harvard grad. Trying to be friendly, Spicer gave Mullaney a condensed history of Buffalo Bill. Mullaney nodded politely and left with his wife, and Jim laughed at Spicer's naiveté. "Buffalo Bill, give me a break! What kind of subject is that for an intellectual?" Patiently Spicer explained the importance of the frontier and the West, making it clear that it was okay for intellectuals to talk about the West. Jim felt a little ashamed of his ignorance. "For me the 'West' meant Worcester, Massachusetts!" Spicer was defensive about California but, Jim realized, in Boston you'd have to be.

The director of the rare book room was a scholar named Zoltan Havasty, who had published a scholarly edition of *The Bay Psalm Book*, the oldest book printed in North America. Havasty spent much of his time researching what he hoped would be the definitive life of Columbus, and left the day-to-day operation of his collections to Harriet Swift, curator of Americana and Spicer's immediate boss. Spicer was not happy at his job: Swift saw to that. He and another assistant were pretty obviously homosexuals, and Swift made enough snide remarks about "fairies" for them to guess that their secret identities were no secret from her. Despite their regulation suits and ties, they were sitting ducks.

At the same time, Spicer seemed genuinely interested, in a romantic way, in a fellow librarian called Ellen Oldham. A Vassar graduate, Oldham lived in Cambridge where she cared for a retarded brother. She was a pretty woman, but "fading," and Jack made an "enormous effort to get to know her," recalled John Norton, a page who saw Spicer frequently. " I didn't understand why Jack never could get anywhere with Ellen Oldham. He was definitely putting the make on her, but he got nowhere. She rebuffed him steadily."

Margaret Munsterberg, Swift's assistant, was a kindly version of Harriet Swift. "Miss Swift and Miss Munsterberg took opposite approaches to everything." A poet of sorts herself, Munsterberg could be very nice, in a rigid, Teutonic way. She knew German poetry by heart and would talk to Spicer about Rilke. She lived with her sister, another spinster, and the two sisters called each other by loving diminutives—"Gretelein" and "Irmelein." Her absent-mindedness was well known. The library typewriters could be tipped backward to slide into wells, and one of Swift's great setpieces was her imitation of Munsterberg's dismay when her typewriter wouldn't slide back neatly, like everyone else's—because she had forgotten to push the carriage into position. Munsterberg's otherworldly approach to life's difficulties left Swift bewildered and distinctly sour. Before Spicer came to Boston, an incident occurred that was still being talked about when Jack took his job. A pigeon flew in through one of the great tall windows of the rare book room. When pragmatic Miss Swift suggested they call the custodial department right away, the mystic Miss Munsterberg held up a frail hand and said, "Wait! How do we know that bird is not the Paraclete?" Spicer filed the incident away and made it the central symbol of one of his great poems of the period, "Song for Bird and Myself."

Swift assigned Jack to write a review for *The Boston Public Library Quarterly* of a new two-volume edition of Emily Dickinson's poetry, edited by Thomas J. Johnson.[15] Spicer dutifully turned in his review, but Swift rued her decision to entrust the expensive books to such a slovenly man: when she examined the books after Spicer had returned them, she found them covered with smudges and fingerprints. In the rare book room the books were old, sometimes glistening with oil that got all over people's hands.

But Spicer's hands were habitually dirty: his collars too. He wore the same shiny black suit day after day and Swift noted its reappearance each day with a sigh. He smelled, she told the pages. Once or twice Spicer alluded to being hungover, but Jim Devlin never saw him actually drunk at work, although Swift made remarks to that effect.

Swift "had it in for Spicer from Day One. She was contemptuous of him. And he—was a tortured soul—fragile: If you gave him a whack you'd knock him right over. He didn't stand a chance with Miss Swift." Jim told Jack he wanted to write a play—to take an old play and update it. Impulsively Jack cracked, "Why don't you do *'Tis Pity She's a Whore?*"

Meanwhile, Jack was hard at work, writing poetry. Shyly, yet with a certain fierce pride, he showed the pages a great sheaf of typed poems—between fifty and one hundred, according to one estimate. Devlin showed them to a fellow student at Boston College, pretending he'd written them, and got laughed at for his pains. But John Norton was impressed by one—"'The Inheritance: Palm Sunday,' Spicer's poem about the Crucifixion, knocked me cold."

When the end came, and Spicer was finally fired, no one at the library was surprised. (Spicer later explained that he was dismissed because he had broken the spine of the *Bay Psalm Book*.[16]) He walked down the great marble staircase from the rare book room, passing on his right the gorgeous murals that Puvis de Chavannes had painted on the gallery walls late in the previous century—de Chavannes's vision of "The Holy Grail," Percival, Lancelot, Guinevere, Arthur, luminous and stark, beyond this plane of suits, ties, snickers, and frustration. John Norton believes these great murals must have been in the back of Jack's mind when he wrote his own version of the Arthur legend—*The Holy Grail* (White Rabbit, 1964).[17] Never again would he take a job in a library. A few weeks later, he left Boston, never to return. Never again would he leave his beloved "Pacific Republic."

Spicer had another Boston life, which contrasted sharply with the humiliations of the rare book room. Through Robin Blaser, who was working then in Harvard's Widener Library, he met the crew whose groundbreaking work in poetry became known as the "Boston Renaissance." Thanks to this constellation of writers, Boston was able to compete with New York and San Francisco as a center of postmodern poetics. Spicer shared their interest in

Black Mountain College. In the early 1950s, young poets and artists were drawn to the North Carolina school the way they would later flock to San Francisco. The young poets of Boston were no exception. In Cid Corman's West End Library poetry discussion group, Steve Jonas had steeped himself in Olson and Creeley, and later he introduced Joe Dunn and John Wieners to the "Black Mountain" poets. By the time Spicer met them all, Dunn and Wieners had actually been to Black Mountain in North Carolina and back again. Charles Olson, the brilliant poet and thinker who had overseen the college for six years, had run it into the ground financially, but he had nevertheless created the kind of poetic communitas that Spicer dreamed of. Olson himself was a powerful, if uneven, poet. Duncan had praised his work for years, and in fact he and Jess were both then teaching at Black Mountain. Spicer recalled that when Duncan first recommended Olson's poetry to him in the late 1940s, he hadn't been able to understand Robert's enthusiasm. Only with long, careful study did he finally appreciate Olson's gift.[18] Despite his tumultuous relation to Olson's poetics, he was drawn intellectually to the coherence of his system. Even then he resented the way Duncan gave Olson pride of place in his poetic system, neglecting the important developments of the Berkeley writers themselves.

As it happened, Frank O'Hara was spending the spring semester in Cambridge, working with the Poets' Theater on a Rockefeller Fellowship.[19] John Wieners described a harmonious evening in his Boston apartment— "a dreadful room infested with roaches"—at the beginning of his friendship with Spicer and O'Hara: "We [Wieners and O'Hara] had met Jack Spicer previously at the Harvard Gardens, and while I read my poetry in the humid summer evening of Beacon Hill, the both of them wept through the incipient rain and electric-charged air."[20] Don Allen remembered the friction between Spicer and O'Hara when the three men gathered after a performance of the Poets' Theater in May 1956. Although the performance itself—a double bill of Ionesco's *Bald Soprano*, translated by Allen, and Cocteau's play *Orphée*, translated by O'Hara's friend George Montgomery—had been electrifying, the two poets failed to establish any more of a connection than in New York.[21] This was their last meeting. They never had anything good to say about each other again. Later that summer, Robin Blaser had the temerity to praise O'Hara's poem "The Eyelid Has Its Stains," and Spicer snorted, "Third-hand Rimbaud."[22]

Scholarly himself, Spicer was attracted to those whose lives veered from his own middle-class standards. Yes, he was a bohemian, but he was quite bourgeois compared to Wieners, Dunn, and Jonas, who led lives so louche as to approach a form of magic. Gerrit Lansing has called this group an "occult school."[23] Uniformly charming, witty, and lovable, they sought poetry by following Rimbaud into a systematic derangement of the senses, a regime which left little time or inclination for ordinary jobs or schedules. The most liminal of all was Jonas, who was a gay, black man somewhat older than Spicer, a man who might possibly be turned away from the stuffy rare book room. After leaving Boston, Spicer embarked upon a translation of Lorca's "Ode to Walt Whitman," which he dedicated to Jonas. It was Steve, he explained, "who taught me to use anger (as opposed to angry irony) in a poem."[24] Indeed the poem is filled with an Old Testament rage, and a cold separation of sheep from goats:

> Cocksuckers of all the world, assassins of doves,
> Slaves of women, lapdogs of their dressing tables,
> Opening their flys in parks with a fever of fans
> Or ambushed in the rigid landscapes of poison.
> . . . .
> Let the bewildered, the pure,
> The classical, the appointed, the praying
> Lock the gates of this Bacchanalia.[25]

The "Ode" reveals Spicer's loathing of the chic, visually literate, striking gay men—exemplified by Frank O'Hara—who patrolled New York's avant-garde. Steve Jonas became the anti-O'Hara—the "bewildered," the "appointed, the "pure."

The first black man whom Spicer knew well, Jonas became a poetic inspiration of the highest order. Their identification was luckily mutual, close and sharply observed. For years Spicer had perhaps naively conflated homosexuality and blackness. "Jack wished he'd been born black," a college friend recalled, "then he wouldn't have had to be homosexual. He had to be something, you know, that somebody would kick."[26] Jonas served as an objective correlative of Spicer's longings and fears, the outsider complete. He had even changed his name to redefine the new self he created, like a butterfly emerging from a cocoon. Born plain "Jones," *Jonas* perhaps better reflects all kinds of antinomies—the man in the belly of the great beast, the man chosen by God, the sufferer, the exile. Spicer (who played with the closeness of his own name to "Spider," and who abjured the use of the formal "John Lester Spicer" in favor of the folksy "Jack") was a firm believer in the power and ritual of the name. Jonas, like Spicer, was capable of a neurotic anti-Semitism, and the two men rhapsodized on this theme, their connection becoming a *folie a deux* of spite and spleen, as each dared the other into saying more and more hateful things. This freedom must have had an erotic tinge to it. In one poem-letter recently discovered in the Jonas archives, Spicer developed the "Martian" persona he later used to better ends.

A Gentle Warning from One Martian to Another

Don't tell me they fool you,
These earthmen, pretending
That one nose is better than another,
One heart more whole.
White, black, or yellow
They are Jews.
The dirt they walk on is Jew's dirt.
The earth that swallows them is Jew earth.
The sky that surrounds them is a Jew's sky.
They all smoke cigars when they are fat and are sour
When they are skinny.
They all sell poison to each other in department stores on Washington
   St. and government offices in Moscow, and trade poisoned
   beads with each other in the deepest jungles of the Congo.
   Jews!
They disguise themselves as writers, aviators, homosexuals, garage
   mechanics, Irishmen, and paraplegics. Jews!
They push each other into bed and into gas-ovens trying to make
   distinctions.
Come friend, let us make distinctions.
With these creatures there are no distinctions.
Earthmen, Jewman! Fake noses,
Circumcized hearts. Puke
Of the universe.

Jack Spicer 8/56

Jonas's young friend Joe Dunn met Jack Spicer on a spring afternoon in 1956, in the Harvard Gardens in Boston. Joe Dunn's hair was thick, dark, glossy; his forehead was high and delicate; his large hands curled caressingly in space. His jaw was strong; his mouth a little weak; five o'clock shadow made its appearance early. He was a handsome young man and overwhelmingly dedicated to poetry. Dunn's young wife, Carolyn, was there too. Like Joe, Carolyn was short, with the same thick black hair and large eyes. But quiet and sweet, where Joe was edgy. "They were like twins," commented a friend of the Dunns. "If you saw them you would think they were brother and sister."[27]

On this afternoon in the Gardens, Robert Duncan effected the introductions. Joe had met Robert and Jess a few months before, at Black Mountain College, where he had been a member of Duncan's writing class. The group in Harvard Gardens this afternoon was a large one, but as Dunn later remembered it, "Of all that group, Jack and I seemed to be the ones that went up to the bar to get a shot. Know what I mean? The others just seemed to sit there."

Going up to the bar together, he realized, meant he had "something in common" with Jack Spicer; "that was the first indication." There was an immediate rapport between them. Years later Joe characterized the brief walk to the bar as "that one time when you meet someone that you're just totally comfortable with. Who you've never seen before in your life."

It turned out that Spicer lived near Joe and Carolyn. Every day the two men would meet and talk. Over the course of the next months they became exceedingly close—too close, in Carolyn's opinion. Carolyn Dunn, dark, watchful, newly married, was thrust into a terrible, if conventional, position: suddenly she became a third wheel in her own marriage. For Jack had fallen in love with Joe Dunn. It's almost comical to note how Jack's once-frequent letters to poor Allen Joyce back home dwindled to an obligatory trickle once Joe entered his life. Imagine Carolyn's dismay when Joe found Jack a new apartment, right next to theirs, in the very same building! Don Allen admired Carolyn's longsuffering in the face of Jack's obvious enmity and his habit of dropping in unannounced to talk to Joe at any hour of the day or night.[28] These months were Joe's chance to show Jack Spicer the excitement of Boston and the vitality of its poetics. It was an uphill road, though, for Spicer was already sick of the city, even with Robin Blaser and Jim Felts there and a constant parade of California visitors, including Duncan, Don Allen, and Dick Bratset, a friend from the days of graduate school at Berkeley.

John Wieners and Steve Jonas had been Dunn's closest friends since he was eighteen. "Steve was in the same street and building and area as John Wieners," recalled Dunn. "It was just an incredible summer."[29] But Jack just didn't like Boston. He even thought poorly of Boston's greatest star, the incomparable Ted Williams of the Red Sox, who spent the summer proving what a "lousy team player" he was, ever ready to go for a base on balls even when Boston was one run behind in the ninth inning.[30] Joe redoubled his efforts to impress Jack with Boston's many pleasures. As if to repay Dunn for his effusive hospitality, that summer Spicer wrote *Five Words for Joe Dunn on His 22nd Birthday*. What young writer, straight or gay, wouldn't be flattered by the cold romance of its sentiments?

> Whomever you touch will love you,
> Will feel the cling of His touch upon you
> Like sunlight scattered over an ancient mirror.

Still Spicer wasn't happy. He was always "bemoaning the fact that Boston was so dreadful, that there's no poetry there." This despite the resemblance of the "Boston Renaissance" to the "Berkeley Renaissance" of ten years before that Jack was always harkening back to, when he, Blaser, Duncan, and so many others had filled the UC campus and environs with conferences, publications, feuds, affairs, and most of all poems. In many ways, Joe Dunn found, Spicer could be a "cantankerous" man. Without bothering to read any of John Wieners's poems, Spicer dismissed him completely. "He can't write," he told Joe—in a typically jarring snap judgment. "There's nothing of interest in Wieners."

This was infuriating in its way, and meant to wound, but Joe found ways to pay Jack back. He read him Wieners's poetry "anonymously," pleased when a wide-eyed Spicer responded, "That's *beautiful* writing!" Joe was straight, and Jack was gay, but Joe never thought that this difference in sexual preference caused them any problems. He wondered if Spicer's dislike of Wieners's art stemmed from the flamboyance of Wieners's homosexuality. But Spicer professed to love the work of Steve Jonas, whose gayness was even more open, though Jonas's blackness—in Joe's opinion—complicated the situation. It was all very confusing.

Joe and Carolyn's marriage was a little shaky, and after one quarrel Joe felt he had to get away to clear his head. Spicer arranged for him to stay overnight in Manhattan with Glenn Lewis, an old pal from Berkeley. Trained as a mathematician, Lewis received his M.S. degree in 1950, as did Spicer. Now he was pursuing his Ph.D. at the Braun Institute. In Berkeley Jack had taught him the elements of Tarot, and ever since then Glenn had been throwing the cards himself, drawn to their mystery and science. That night Joe—"attractive, rather slight, wounded"—asked for a reading, and Lewis complied. "I guess I was what you'd call 'inspired,'" Lewis remembered. "I didn't know where the power was coming from. And when I told Joe Dunn what I saw in his cards he turned deathly white." Lewis had never met Dunn before, but he saw a terrible future for him—a self-destructive, problem-ridden future life all laid out in the cards. "It was one of the most striking experiences I've ever had. And after that reading I never threw the Tarot again. I figured that if it's true, it's nothing to fool around with. If not, I was just guessing.—Either way it was scary." In the morning Dunn went back to Boston, and Lewis never saw him again.[31]

In Joe's opinion, Spicer's sparse poetry of the period was an advance on his previous work, and he felt flattered to think he'd played a little part in it. Together they assembled a newsletter to send to their friends ("Carbon paper is cheaper than blood")—the latest developments from Boston, from

Spicer, Dunn, Jonas, Wieners, Blaser. This odd document, a curious blend of acid raillery and low camp, features "Coming Attractions" such as Jonas's "Cock Drill," a campy pun on Pound's then-new "Rock-Drill" cantos, as well as Wieners's "Wieners." The newsletter came with instructions: *Post whatever pages of it poke you in the eye in the most public place you can find— i.e., an art gallery, a bohemian bar, or a lavatory frequented by poets.* It's a very gay text, and its emphasis on collaboration, disjunction, gender politics, and "nonsense" locates it in the midst of postmodern practice. It was received with delight by Robert Duncan during the last faltering days of Black Mountain College.

This small exercise in poetic community did nothing to dispel Spicer's unhappiness. Duncan felt that the basis for Spicer's hostility to both Ashbery and O'Hara was his belief that they were the *eminences grises* behind his rejection by the Cambridge Poets' Theater. Jack, who went to New York and then to Boston in the serious belief that he could succeed with his verse plays, had grown bitter when the Poets' Theater group turned down his *Troilus*, as it had Duncan's own *Faust Foutu*. (Interviewed in 1990, John Ashbery explained that he was out of the country, already establishing himself for his decade in Paris, at the time of Spicer's stay in Boston, and that in any case it was not he who accepted or rejected the plays for the Theater.[32] James Schuyler, another associate of the group, denied ever even having heard of Jack Spicer until the 1980s.[33]) Spicer's misery was probably compounded by the fact that Robin Blaser got along famously with the eastern poets. Living in Boston and working in the Harvard Library, Robin had known the men and women connected with the Poets' Theater there, and in a later trip to Paris had been shown the town by John Ashbery. "I remember how he got me around Paris," he wrote, "including Proust's restaurants and an upstairs room with a grinding, mechanical floor, neon lights and music—and gay-mapping Pere Lachaise." Ashbery sponsored Blaser's work and saw it through publication both in his own magazine, *Locus Solus*, and in *The Paris Review*. But "Jack made Ashbery's work symbolic of everything he disliked, second only to Dylan Thomas—and always referred to *Thumb Twees*."[34] Jack had, of course, opposed Robin's staying in Boston, staying with Jim Felts, and indeed going to Europe at all. Robin, he felt, had somehow been infected by Harvard. He took out his resentment of Robin's taste in mean, passive-aggressive ways. The palatial apartment— which Jonas called "Robin's mausoleum"—that Blaser shared with Felts had an enclosed garden under an atrium, a doorman, and one expensive couch covered in pale gray silk. This couch became Spicer's enemy. He left his dirty socks under it, "spilled" red wine on the dove-gray silk.[35]

On the anniversary of the death of Charlie "Bird" Parker, Joe and Carolyn played one of Parker's Dixieland records over and over in requiem. Hearing that music from the next apartment, Spicer wrote "Song for Bird and Myself," which begins, "I am dissatisfied with my poetry. / I am dissatisfied with my sex life. / I am dissatisfied with the angels I believe in."[36] At an evening at John Wieners's, Dunn fell asleep while Spicer was reading from his new project, the "Journal of Oliver Charming." This hurt Jack, Robin reported to Don Allen. At the same time he felt "quick flashes of dislike from Jack because the few chairs placed me too close to Dunn."[37]

In September when the Boston gang decided to have a poetry reading, Spicer made a handmade postcard that began, "EZRA POUND EATS WORMS. You are invited to a poetry reading where five Boston cats are blowing their poetry REAL Hard." A huge capital "J" stood for the first names of three of the readers—Spicer, Dunn, Wieners—a left-leaning "R" for Robin—a slithery "S" for Steve Jonas. "Nothing has been so good since Bird died." To Don Allen's invitation Jack added an impromptu verse, combining Latin and jazz idioms:

Easy on squeezing
Frost off the pumpkin
J. Spicer fecit
Man, but don't break it.[38]

Blaser later remembered the dismal attendance at the reading: eight people showed up.[39]

If Jack was so dissatisfied, Joe decided, why couldn't they do something about it? To precipitate matters he announced that he and Carolyn were moving to San Francisco. Would Jack join them? It was a calculated risk, almost "a challenge" to Spicer's authority, but this time the challenge worked. Spicer was having trouble writing; he couldn't accept the East; and earning a living was a problem. The three of them flew to San Francisco to live in November 1956. Jack dashed off a letter to Allen Joyce:

It is the middle of a blizzard and I write you important news. I have decided to come back. . . . Start praying for me. Start any magic that is still working, working for me. Inform the pinball machines for me. Write on every lavatory wall: MARTIANS ARE COMING HOME.

This is the most important news since the fall of France.

Love
Jack[40]

During a layover in New York, "bound for a place called Berkeley-San Francisco," Jack wrote to Blaser. "I am staying with a person named Glenn

Lewis who tells me that when he first saw Joe Dunn he thought that he (Joe Dunn) was just exactly the kind of person who would fall in love with me. Shadows are so ironic that their tips extend great distances."[41] Glenn Lewis observed: "Joe had a terribly vulnerable quality. Spicer felt close to Joe. He wanted to be his lover, and in some sense Joe didn't discourage that. He told me, 'I want someone to love me,' and as a matter of fact, this might sound strange, but that night in my apartment I felt that Joe was making a kind of pass at me. I didn't act on it—but I've been kicking myself ever since."[42]

Jack found the time in New York to meet with Donald Allen and discuss his poetry, consigning to Allen all the poems he had ever written that he thought worthy of publication. On the flight west, Jack and Joe enjoyed themselves in the way they knew best. "Jack and I were—you know—social drinkers, and we had quite a trip," Dunn recalled. "We stopped at O'Hare Field [Chicago] for two hours, so we arrived pretty well drunk."[43] Spicer had left San Francisco a year and a half before, on June 30, 1955. Stepping awkwardly off the plane, he was never to return east again.

After he had gone, Robin, gripped by desolation, reproached himself for not having made Jack feel at home in Boston. He wrote to Don Allen that he could do little and had done nothing. "The real wreckage came when I visited Jack's apartment to pick up a couple of Dunn's paintings he's leaving with me—not good, but clearly a poet's hand. Anyway, sacks of garbage: the dirt and the terrible poverty. I could hear him say, 'I have no home.' No one needs to tell me that I could give him one and didn't. Clothes that never did fit, which I'd given him, hung in the closets, half a dozen empty whiskey bottles about and one, a third full, stilll in the refrigerator. The sum of all this is that I shall never forgive myself if anything goes wrong in California. Nothing must happen to him."[44]

CHAPTER FOUR

"The Whole Boon of His Fertility"

*T*he poetry community of San Francisco had changed since June 1955. One era had ended and another had begun. The world Spicer had known was altered forever, and he had his hands full keeping up with the changes caused by the Beat explosion. The group that included Allen Ginsberg and Lawrence Ferlinghetti had generated an extraordinary amount of publicity in connection with their reading at the "6" Gallery in October 1955. To some extent the remainder of Spicer's career can be seen as a reaction to the behemoth that the event gave birth to. "The watershed," said Robert Duncan, "—the entire change in character of a rather set line in San Francisco poets, is really Ginsberg's writing *Howl* and through that period Ferlinghetti's emergence. That had already made a new North Beach. Returning to the City after these events, we [Duncan, Jess, Spicer] were in a sense objects of nostalgia from before. By the time we came back in '56, it was really Allen Ginsberg's city—Allen Ginsberg's and Lawrence Ferlinghetti's city." One consequence of the huge publicity given to the "Beat Generation" was the arrival of swarms of young people from all over the country bent on meeting and emulating the poet-kings of San Francisco. Spicer's relation to these young people was necessarily different from his relations to those he had known before the deluge; they treated him as a mentor, and he was all too conscious of himself as a projection of their fantasies, fears, and ideals.

Looking back on this period, Duncan commented, "The term that later got applied—the 'San Francisco Renaissance'—in the first place shows that someone didn't know what a renaissance was at all. What did it mean?

That we revived the Yukon poets or something? When Spicer and Robin and I were Kantorowicz's students, in poems assuming medieval and Renaissance learning—Miss [Josephine] Miles dubbed us 'the museum poets'—we called ourselves the Berkeley Renaissance. And although we wanted other poets to belong to it, we meant that our poetry was really a Renaissance poetry: that Ficino would come into it; that questions of Dante and Petrarch would underlie it.

"The Berkeley Renaissance is where the *term* 'Renaissance' came from. San Francisco liked the term—but they've never been closer to the Renaissance than looking at pictures."

Robert Duncan had returned to San Francisco before Spicer, arriving during the summer of 1956 to take the post of assistant director of the Poetry Center at San Francisco State College. During Spicer's eastern sojourn, Ruth Witt-Diamant had extended her patronage to the "Beat" writers: among them Ginsberg, Gary Snyder, Michael McClure, and Ferlinghetti. To accommodate the growing interest in their poetry, the center had acquired an off-campus site, at 555 Chestnut Street near North Beach, for some of its readings.

Jack's arrival at the end of 1956, "with no job, and in a funk," raised a new problem for Duncan. Coming up with a job took "connivance" and some creative financing at the Poetry Center, but Duncan "saw the opportunity and landed it. A lesbian gym teacher got an actually insane crush on the poet Eve Triem. She wanted to send Eve what I think might have been as little as $100.00. I don't remember that even then that $100.00 was any great shakes as money. [It was actually $200.00.] She turned to the Poetry Center in despair, and wanted to know how to give it to Eve Triem. So I wrote her a real Boy Scout letter [saying that] her fine feelings for Eve Triem might be best expressed by anonymously giving—because I said she should do it in a most Girl Scout fashion—money for a workshop. Ah! Then I had the money for Jack to give a workshop."[1]

Spicer moved from temporary Berkeley quarters into San Francisco, and Joe and Carolyn Dunn found an apartment in the Polk Street area. Jack wrote to Robin Blaser, bragging that "the return to Berkeley shattered all of my remaining sexual inhibitions and I've gone to bed with more people since I've been here than I usually do in a year. This is a mysterious gift I never expected from California."[2] Yet Robin heard otherwise from Duncan, who had been observing the course of Spicer's affection for Dunn. He wrote to Robin on November 25, 1956: "Jack is in the familiar situation with Dunn isn't he? The agonies are special: the natural irruptions of pleading, hurt, violence, and the patronizing which the cultivations of unjust desire gives rise to. He avoids the stages of reciprocity, of passion. . . . I know Spicer will always be bound to be the guide. What if Dante had led Virgil (invented Virgil in order to lead him) thru Hell? Hell has a guise for such enamourd spirits. But for Purgatory or Heaven one must give oneself up to the first guide—to the Beloved, to Beatrice."[3]

Besides the Beat explosion, the poetic climate of San Francisco had changed in another way while Spicer had been away. With the closing of Black Mountain College in the summer of 1956, the Bay Area became flooded with its former students: poets, musicians, fiction writers, and visual artists. Some of them were drawn to Spicer's bar, The Place, because its owners, Knute Stiles and Leo Krikorian, had attended Black Mountain earlier. Joe Dunn, who had studied at Black Mountain College, introduced Spicer to many "Black Mountaineers," and Duncan, who had taught there, introduced him to the rest. Several of the painters—Tom Field, Paul Alexander, Basil King—became Spicer's new favorites, displacing the "6" Gallery crowd he had once championed fervently. Surrounded by a host of new young men, all more or less committed to the arts, Spicer felt heady, oxygenated. Black Mountain's energy now moved him into huge waves of organization and, eventually, art production, fueled by the raw beauty of these boys from North Carolina.

Spicer offered the following prospectus for his workshop: "This is not a course in technique or 'how to write.' It will be a group exploration of the practices of the new magical school of poetry which is best represented in the work of Lorca, Artaud, Charles Olson and Robert Duncan." Charles Olson's name on this particular list of the "magical school" is an ironic reflection on Olson's famous, then-recent essay "Against Wisdom as Such," with its satiric warning against California poetry as an "école des mages ominous as Ojai."[4] Spicer's interest in Lorca began in the Throckmorton House lectures, when the Puerto Rican scholar Rosario Jimenez gave a full, bilingual reading of many of Lorca's poems and selections from his verse plays. Spicer had begun, in Boston, to translate some of Lorca's work, with a copy of the recent New Directions edition of the *Selected Poems* kept by his bedside.[5] He identified with Lorca, the homosexual, dandy, anti-Fascist martyr. (Antonin Artaud—the insane actor, dramaturg, and poet—represented other parts of his own constantly shifting identity.)

The Public Library agreed to lend a room for the workshop every Tuesday night from mid-February through the end of May. Duncan asked arts editors to publicize it with the hook—or as he called it, the "umpf"—of the title he and Spicer had devised: "'Poetry as Magic' which promises a provocative and alive approach to instruction—and one that appeals to poets."[6] Registration would be limited to fifteen.

"My Poetry Workshop class is to be called—Poetry as Magic," he reported to Robin. "How about sending me some ideas. My main one so far is that Houdini is the figure of the poet and that translation is cheating at poker." He had at least one "idea"—a "questionnaire" prospective workshop members would have to fill out as a sort of audition. It was an extraordinary document, with such queries as "If you had a chance to eliminate three political figures from the world, which would you choose?" and "What insect do you most resemble?" Spicer wrote three original poems, of twelve to sixteen lines apiece, and left blank spaces in key places so that applicants could fill them in as they chose. These poems, actually frames on which poems could be hung, remained unpublished until Robin Blaser included the entire questionnaire among the "Notes and Documents" in his edition of Spicer's *Collected Books.*[7] Applicants were asked to write down the funniest joke they knew and to "Invent a dream in which you appear as a poet." The whole experience of the Magic Workshop was to embody this invented dream.

One by one San Francisco poets enrolled. An in-house report prepared for the Poetry Center states that Spicer picked fifteen members from a roster of fifty applicants.[8] The membership was selected by Spicer, mainly but not exclusively from the results of the questionnaire. Meetings were weekly—Tuesday nights from 7:00 to 10:00. Robin Blaser counted eight persons attending: Helen Adam, Ebbe Borregaard, Robert Duncan, Joseph Kostalevsky, Jack Gilbert, Sue Rosen, Elyce Edelman, and Joe Dunn.[9] But this list is far from complete—George Stanley was certainly one of the most active participants. John Allen Ryan attended, as did Bob Connor, a young classicist at the UC Berkeley.[10] Robert Duncan added two more to the list— James Broughton, the poet and avant-garde filmmaker, and Ida Hodes, who in 1957 was secretary to the Poetry Center.[11] This was the core group, but many others attended just one or two meetings. Like the "round table"

Magic Workshop: [*Clockwise*] Spicer, John Allen Ryan, Joe Dunn, Jack Gilbert, Robert Duncan (back to camera), Helen Adam, and a pair of unidentified participants, at San Francisco Public Library, "Poetry as Magic" workshop, 1957. "This is not a course in technique or 'how to write.'" *Photo by Harry Redl.*

of 2029 Hearst, the upstairs room at the Main Library became the center of all the magic in the city.

One of the first to sign up was Ebbe Borregaard, already famous in a minor way as a poet runaway. His mother had appealed to the newspapers of San Francisco to help them find their missing son. Labeled "the Beatnik Boy" to his chagrin, he was triumphantly declared found, his picture appearing on the front page of the papers.[12] Borregaard had served in Korea and had stumbled onto Black Mountain College in literally its last days—its last three or four days, showing up on the doorstep just as the College was being sold. Now the painter Tom Field dragged him to the Public Library and presented him to Spicer as a kind of gift.[13]

Other workshop participants were native sons and daughters of the city. George Stanley, for example, had intermittently written poetry during his first college year in Salt Lake City and later, in the army, as an enlisted soldier buying chickens for military kitchens in Arkansas. When he was a sophomore at Berkeley, George visited San Francisco's North Beach. "Want me to take you to a *real* Bohemian bar?" whispered an acquaintance at Vesuvio's. George nodded, and followed him up Columbus, where they entered The Place. There he met Joe Dunn. "We both had a classical background, both had taken Latin and Greek." George showed Joe a poem he had written. "He said, 'Oh, Jack's got to see this poem.'" At the Dunns' apartment, Joe introduced George to Carolyn, then to Spicer. "I read 'Pablito,' and Jack was very taken with it and said, 'You know, that's really a very great poem.' And he said, 'Come to the Magic Workshop.'"

George Stanley's relation to Spicer was problematic from the beginning, perhaps because the two were very alike—voluble, argumentative, and passionate about poetry. With Dunn's sponsorship, George didn't have to answer the questionnaire. If he had, said Spicer later, he would not have been selected, because his answers to Spicer's elaborate questions would have been "too elaborate."[14] Thus began a troubled relationship that perpetually veered between love and anger.

Like Joe Dunn, Bob Connor was an Irishman from Massachusetts. Joseph Kostalevsky hailed from Los Angeles. To Jack Gilbert, Spicer was a "nose-thumbing, pinball-loving, jeering, beer-swilling, obscene, bad-mannered, vulgar, slovenly, rowdy, bourgeoisie-baiting, savage-witted, misogynous Ishmael." Yet he was also "shy, gifted, covertly romantic, brilliant, and in love with poetry. He was a person I liked very much, and whose work interested me steadily for years."[15]

Jack's assignments to the poets of the Magic Workshop developed out of his work with the rebellious art students at CSFA. "Jack gave assignments like 'write a poem that should create a universe' or 'write a poem in which the poet becomes a flesh-eating beast,'" remembered George Stanley. Ruth Witt-Diamant's correspondence mentions other assignments: "Write a poem concerning some magic sacrifice" and "Evoke magic spirits."[16] James Broughton recalled:

The pattern was not unusual: an assignment was given for a poem to be written that was to be read aloud at the next meeting. What was unusual were Spicer's assignments. His intention was to shock the group into challenging responses.

The first assignment was safe enough: your personal myth about the Creation. (My contribution to this was the poem "Papa Had A Bird" which appears in *A Long Undressing*.) The second assignment was more unnerving: How would you cook a baby? (I don't know what happened to my recipe.) And they went on from there. My poem in *Hooplas* ["A Farewell to the Household Muse"] was for an assignment on the horrors of home life.[17]

Spicer had brought a great deal of new writing from Boston, which he shared with the group. These poems, flown in from the East, became texts to be studied and inevitably to be imitated. Thus Steve Jonas and Robin Blaser became influential voices within the workshop, and by extension in the San Francisco poetry scene in general. Two poems by Robinson Jeffers, "Local Legend" and "Skunks," were reproduced and handed out, reflecting Spicer's interest in Jeffers, an interest that remained strong through the last days of his life when, granting his first and last interview, he told a local reporter that Jeffers was "a real California poet," with the "same association with the Pacific Coast, as a far shore of the continent and a treacherous sea coast, that the San Francisco poets have had."[18] Spicer and Duncan also encouraged the young poets in the group to attend as many poetry readings as possible. They impressed on the students the importance of two very different writers, both visiting the Bay Area that spring: Robert Lowell and Charles Olson.

The Poetry Center sponsored a reading by Lowell at the San Francisco Museum of Modern Art on March 27, 1957. Afterward, Ruth Witt-Diamant held a reception in her home, one of many she threw over the years to give local poets the chance to recite their work before an important visiting dignitary. Bob Connor read one of his "Magic Workshop" poems to Lowell. "I hated reading it. Actually it wasn't that bad. Fortunately I've lost it, so I don't know. Anyway Lowell said, 'That's obscene! It'll never be published.' Obscene! It showed a complete contempt for other human beings: but it wasn't obscene."[19] Of all the San Francisco poets in Spicer's workshop, Lowell was most charmed and impressed by Helen Adam. He took her poems away with him, promising to find her an East Coast publisher.[20]

Lowell's appearance was a success, but it had not the grand resonance of Charles Olson's visit, his first to San Francisco in many years. Because the "New American Poetry" was then so new, the poetry establishment so firmly in place, and the relations of the junior and senior poets so untested, some events took on a special, undeclared purpose: the testing of wills and the staking of territories. Olson's visit resembled one of St. Paul's to an early, underground, primitive church assembly. He was a figure of phenomenal interest to the experimental writing community of the day. Born in 1910, Olson had revitalized American avant-garde poetry after World War II in much the same way as Ezra Pound had before World War I. He came late to poetry, after a varied career that included minor posts in the U.S. federal government—a past that gave him an aura of authority and knowledge which his great bulk accentuated. Olson's admirers saw his friendship with Ezra Pound—struck up during the older poet's incarceration at St. Elizabeth's Hospital in Washington, D.C.—as a direct poetic lineage, the kind of transfer of kingship about which Kantorowicz had written so often. After an explosive study of Melville, *Call Me Ishmael,* Olson turned his magnificent energies more and more to poetry. His correspondence was compulsive, and he made a great friend of another, younger Harvard man, Robert Creeley, with whom he developed a series of wide-ranging theories and plans to bring poetry and writing in general into the era he dubbed the "post-modern." His manifestoes, especially "Projective Verse" (1950), called for a poetry in which "form is nothing more than an extension of content." He had recently wound up a long association with Black Mountain College, where his poetic theory and practice had inspired dozens of (mostly male) poets, from John Wieners to Robert Creeley to Duncan himself. Duncan had lobbied long and hard with Ruth Witt-Diamant to bring Olson to San Francisco, and he had conceived of an additional lecture series as an opportunity for Olson to recoup some of the financial demands of traveling.

After Black Mountain College closed, Olson wanted its spirit to spread as far as possible. Duncan, who was writing *Medea, Part II: "The Will"* in San Francisco, proposed using the same actors who had performed *Part I* in North Carolina two years before, in an unbroken extension of the project. Black Mountain, Duncan recalled, "would now be Black Mountain Abroad, and there would be a Black Mountain East and a Black Mountain West. So the theater group had come: the six actors that were in the cast had come to do the play here."[21]

Rehearsals for *Medea, Part II* began in a makeshift studio/rehearsal space in the Western Addition, with a cast including Don and Eloise Mixon, and the painter Paul Alexander.[22] Eloise was an actress, poet, and novelist, with abilities that surprised the normally unflappable Duncan. "At Black Mountain," Duncan recalled to Ruth Witt-Diamant, "Eloise Mixon who had not yet written a good poem found she had (as we found she had) natural measure in the syllabic line. Now all my experience in twenty years of writing poetry will not give me natural syllabic measure; in workshop exercises there Eloise's performance was considerably 'better' than my own."[23] She became Robert's "muse," to quote Jess, and his subsequent plays each contained a role for her.[24] Paul Alexander, who played the male lead, came to San Francisco in April 1956, intending to return to school in the fall. When the college closed for good he was stuck on the coast. He knew only Robert Duncan from Black Mountain. When Duncan gave him a few names to look up in San Francisco, Paul had only to call one number, James Keilty's, to find a friend. Another painter, Tom Field, joined Paul in the fall of 1956 and "soon after," wrote Alexander, "the whole group from Black Mountain involved with the theater came to San Francisco."

Duncan invited several of his acquaintances to watch the rehearsals. It was at one of these early rehearsals that Paul Alexander first saw Spicer. Paul had read Jack's unpublished play *Troilus* from a contraband manuscript at Black Mountain, so he knew something about the poet. There was no furniture, so they sat on the floor of the kitchen and talked.[25]

Spicer wrote to Blaser that he'd been watching the *Medea* rehearsals: "What strikes me is how essentially unambitious (almost conservative) they are. [Duncan] bites off even a little bit less than he can chew. It makes me see how overcrowded my 'Troilus' was (it was a mouthful big enough for five plays) and shows me 1) he is a playwright and I'm not 2) he will never do anything to change the theater and I will 3) if I live (he has no danger there)."[26] Rehearsals never jelled, and Duncan's work at the Poetry Center fatigued him. The play was abandoned.

Spicer attended Olson's reading on February 21, 1957, at the Museum of Modern Art.. Even though he was hurt and puzzled by Duncan's increasing attention to the "Black Mountain" circle, Jack couldn't deny the attraction of Olson's ambitious, Whitmanic, gestural poetics. Olson, with his new wife, Betty Kaiser, stayed at Ruth Witt-Diamant's house for two weeks.[27] In a subsequent series of lectures (on February 25, 26, 27, 28, and March 1), he presented his "propositions of projection and composition by field in the light of Alfred North Whitehead's *Process and Reality.*"[28] The poets who attended came largely from Duncan's circle: Richard Duerden, for example, a young poet native to San Francisco, had met Duncan at the Co-Existence Bagel Shop in North Beach, and Duncan had invited him to the Olson presentations.[29]

Position—community politics—was always important to the figures in this world of poetry. There was as well a slightly, comic tinge of animosity between those affiliated with the university and those rebelling from it. Duerden recalled, "Tom Parkinson asked Joan who I was—and I'd been a student of his—and Joan very graciously said, 'He hates you.' Which was *almost* true, I didn't like him." Duerden's account of the gathering suggests a group of bantam roosters worrying about their territory. "I remember Philip Whalen and Jack Spicer making superior comments to each other about me. Michael McClure came up to me and said, 'Where did you come from?' In other words, 'Who the hell are you? How did you get into this all of a sudden?' I had a fight with Whalen, and made some nasty remark. Robert Duncan was very cool towards me for awhile over the way I behaved. And Spicer and I got a little annoyed with each other. Whalen and I got a little annoyed with each other."[30] Another Black Mountain refugee, the prose writer Michael Rumaker, later recalled the same occasion in a memoir:

First time I'd seen Charles since Black Mountain. In full beard, "I feel protected," he said. Informal talk and reading at Duncan's place on Potrero Hill later. Olson expansive at front of the room, jammed with young poets and writers mostly; Duncan seated at his right, holding his body in a quiet position of identification and defense, sharp-voiced and sure, against verbal attacks on Olson and his projective verse stance from Michael McClure and Philip Whalen, fledgling and testing their own voices. Myself squirming with protection but Olson, as usual, quite able to take care of himself.[31]

Duncan was a great organizer, a magician behind the scenes—a Prospero who really enjoyed his powers. A whole host of familiar names was prodded into paying five dollars for the five continuous evenings—Helen Adam, Joe and Carolyn Dunn, Michael and Joanna McClure, the filmmaker Larry Jordan, Ruth Witt-Diamant, Tom Field, Harvey Harmon, James Broughton, the actors Wes Huss, Don and Eloise Mixon, and Erik Weir. Suddenly, Duncan thought, Jack Spicer the teacher was replaced by another Jack, the student "who wants the teacher to recognize his abilities."

For many years afterward, Duncan reproached himself for not preventing what occurred the following evening. Spicer brought his deck of cards, a deck designed by the Theosophist artist Pamela Colman Smith and, sitting at Olson's feet, began to lay them out on the carpet. This would be his moment of triumph! But in fact, it was the biggest *faux pas* Spicer could have made. He wanted to work magic, Duncan knew, and Duncan sympathized with this desire. Yet Spicer was done in by a fact he could not have known, that Olson had foresworn Tarot completely some years back, after a frightening experience in which the cards had eerily, accurately predicted—to the day—the death of his own mother.[32]

One by one he laid the cards on the carpet, under Olson's gaze. Duncan was "already thinking, 'Oh, should I say something to Jack'—but what could I say? I'd already been through this one with Olson. But I had no way of anticipating the shock of it." The huge poet "seized upon a moment of seeing to crush Jack totally. More than that; it would have been the equivalent of his own weight thrown on top of Jack's very crushable form. It was a denunciation of using this 'phony' deck—and did I have the courage to say, 'That's the deck I use?' No, not at all . . . Yet I did know Olson was fanatic about using the Marseilles deck."[33] Later, Spicer revealed that Olson had rebuked him for attempting to "make something happen" in San Francisco through incorrect technique. "Your poetry is bullshit, just like your rituals, just like your cards," Olson allegedly snarled.[34] To this rebuke Spicer responded in "A Postscript for Charles Olson," the last poem of his second book, *Admonitions*:

> If nothing happens it is possible
> To make things happen.
> Human history shows this
> And an ape
> Is likely (presently) to be an angel.[35]

Not only did he use a Tarot deck "corrupt in every term," Duncan recalled, but the very subservience of Spicer's posture, the mock observation of humility before Olson, was a tactic so wrong Duncan could only groan in memory thirty years later. "You don't sit at the feet of somebody who's 6'8"," he concluded. "You've done more than submit. You've removed yourself from their territory."[36] Spicer was doubly humiliated since so many of those present were his own students. In spite of—or perhaps because of—the incident, Spicer sent a copy of his first book to Olson ("I've discovered what I owe to you and hate owing it"[37]), but there's no evidence Olson ever read it. *Admonitions* ends with a poem dedicated to Olson, but it's doubtful Olson ever knew about it. *After Lorca* and *Billy The Kid* were the only books by Spicer found in Olson's library after his death in 1970.[38]

Duncan noted Spicer's strange combination of ingratiation and contempt when faced with a poet whose powers were as great as or greater than his own. And several years later he noted it again, when Spicer's ambitious "Homage to Creeley" failed to gain the favor of Robert Creeley. There were other instances of Duncan negotiating a site within which Spicer could shine, and each time Jack managed to do the exact wrong thing, leaving Robert to pick up the pieces. Perhaps, in fact, Duncan rather enjoyed the spectacle of Spicer's social failures. Or perhaps Duncan, committed to an ideal of high professionalism, enjoyed seeing someone do the wrong thing—unleashing the transgressive impulses he too felt but was forced to delegate to others. Duncan had once suggested to Olson that Spicer replace him as faculty member at Black Mountain. Olson said dismissively, "Well, but Spicer is your enthusiasm."[39]

In New York Donald Allen was busy organizing the contents of the sec-ond issue of the fledgling *Evergreen Review*, published by Grove Press, where he worked as an editor. Spicer's appearance in the magazine marked his first nationwide publication, and characteristically he tried to hide his nervousness under a mask of nonchalance and scorn. His references to "The San Francisco Scene," as the issue was to be called, were double-edged: he called the magazine the "Tannenbaum" Review, the "Upas" Re-view—a form of superstitious magic and a running gag that avoided nam-ing it by its rightful name. By January 14, 1957, he was begging Robin to select exactly the right material—"Would you please immediately (if it means staying up all night) pick ten of my poems . . . and send the list to Don. You know better than I do what I should print."[40] A month later: "Pick up the telephone and inform Don what my ten poems are."[41]

The same ambivalence can be seen in his attitude toward John Wieners's prospective magazine *Measure*. In his letters to Boston, Spicer circled warily about Wieners's potential as an editor, his plusses and minuses. Avoiding the use of Wieners' name wasn't difficult, not when you could call him "Hot Dog," as Jack did. Again he sought Robin's help, to choose from among the poems Jack left with him in Boston for a suitable contribution to *Measure*—"such a littlemaggotish name," he added with a sneer.[42]

Chastened, Spicer returned to the Tuesday night workshop. Duncan, writ-ing to Robin Blaser in Boston, gave some account of the energies aroused there, their natures and directions:

[Jack] has his old genius for stirring up troubled psyche, and an all but defined group of young poets results. Connor, George Stanley, Sue Rosen are devoutly Spicerian. If he had no poems this season he has grandpoems. The heart of the Workshop is a nest of sexual disclosures, loneliness (Denise Levertov wrote *re* Ginsberg: "they cultivate their loneliness. I like wildflowers"), minority (jew, queer), social disease and attack (a contagion ward), and the elegiac alternatives of lament and protest.

An enormous amount of work (a poem each week from most of the group) came out of it. I, myself, sitting in wrote three "assignments" but then defaulted as my assent was withdrawn—particularly at the assignment to write a ritual. Jack's concept was first so entirely *that he be included in one's ritual*; he is that ghastly thing the demagogue who howls at all private (as one's rituals of inclusion and exclusion lie hidden—what Olson attacks in *Against Wisdom as Such* and rightly, my idea if it were to display wisdom) sanctuary. Which culminated in the assignment of last week—for all in the group to write a poem to make Jack write a poem. Stanley, Rosen and Connor all, the true converts of the group, added to the lore of Spicer elegies domestic scenes etc. that you and I have had our share in creating.

Two days later, in a postscript, Robert Duncan added some detail to the Spicer-circle portrait he had painted above. "I went to North Beach where saw first handsome Borregaard (and learned that 18-year-old Sue Rosen wears pancake make-up because a friend of her ex-husband's slashed her face, arms, body) and then in levis etc. Jack, who I left at a pinball machine muttering and cursing among colored lights (after talk in which we heard 'Robert Creeley is a fake,' 'it sounds like *Measure* is being turnd into a *Black Mountain [Review]*,' 'Duncan isn't a Calvinist,' 'Sue Rosen is a witch') ((and later in Jack's accounts I learned that Sue Rosen and Ebbe Borregaard were having an affair.))."[43] Sue Rosen was not the only woman accused of witchcraft because she slept with someone Spicer was attracted to—or perhaps, more to the point, with any young man who was also a poet. Borregaard, described so often in accounts and memories of this period as a "Viking" that the tag became a cliché, was the object of many men's admiration. Spicer was "crusty" and "nasty" to Michael Rumaker, in part because Rumaker was more successful with Borregaard than he—or so Rumaker felt, though Spicer's letters reveal that actually he quite liked both men.[44]

Spicer's love for Joe Dunn was being tested daily and nightly. Not only was Joe still married to the disagreeable Carolyn, but he was becoming more and more attracted to the twin devastations of alcohol and drugs— soft drugs at first, then hard ones. Spicer brought Joe to the "6" Gallery, and Joe responded by joining a group of disreputable men who were burning a piano on its premises as a site-specific, Dada-inspired event. It became hard to separate the inspirations of Dada from the acts of a young man who wanted more and more methamphetamine to keep going in the North Beach world. Jack invited Allen Joyce to the Workshop, but Allen withdrew presently, dispirited at the disproportionate attention Jack was paying to his wild Boston sidekick. Jack hardly noticed.

Perhaps it will be easiest to view the dynamics of the Magic Workshop through the poetic eye of another member of the group. Just as Spicer's panic and desperation in New York float vividly to the surface of O'Hara's "At the Old Place," his growing power and *diabolerie* can be appreciated through Helen Adam's eyes. A section of her play, "Initiation to the Magic Workshop," offers a contemporary, dramatized version of the workshop narrative. The heroine approaches the Main Library on a terrible night, begging for admission to Spicer's class:

> Let me come in. Let me come in.
> There's somebody coming who wears no skin.

> The velvet ones are close at my back.
> And a wolf just crawled through the keyhole crack.
>
> Please let me in, it's cold out here
> Away high up on the dark third floor
> With the ghost of Ginsberg howling low at the door.
> Let me come in
> Under Hecate's wing.

Robert Duncan replies to him:

> Rings on your fingers and bells on your toes,
> If you follow the road Jack Spicer goes.
> Does it lead up, or does it lead down,
> To Jerusalem, or to Hecate's town?
> Though the torch of Heaven he can brandish well.

And James Broughton adds, "There's a glint at his heels of the fires of Hell." When the Initiate responds that she is "not afraid of Jack Spicer's spell," for he has "peeped through the keyhole of the gate of Hell," she is confronted by Spicer himself, proud and demonic. In the ensuing speeches of the other workshop members, Helen Adam's skill is at her peak. The characters slyly allude to their own poetic tropes and images (Borregaard's "wapitis," Joe Dunn's mailboxes and letters, Sue Rosen's scary trees), as well as to their relationship to their master, Jack Spicer. Adam herself appears in the Cassandra role, fretting about the implications of so much power, so much magic, being produced week after week in an earthquake-prone city. "I have a feeling, strong as can be, / That we'll all end up at the bottom of the sea." Duncan orders the Initiate to "quaff fresh blood from a paper cup. / Does Spicer's pathway lead down or up?" These verbal challenges are designed to test the Initiate's resourcefulness and will. The play is thus a version of the quest story.

It's also Adam's queerest work by far, one in which poetry is an unruly and amoral site of sexual and gender transgression. Some of the lines given to the gay characters in the play still have the power to raise eyebrows. Bob Connor tells the Initiate:

> Stain your mouth with forbidden juice
> And chase Jack's dragons round my black berry bush.

(In fact, the real-life Connor recalled, "It never occurred to me, all the time I knew Jack Spicer, that he might be a gay type, or a gay poet, or a gay anything else. I didn't really know Spicer. I liked him. He liked me. He was fond of me. But he didn't include me, I don't think, among his poetical friends."[45]) Allen Joyce, displaced in Spicer's heart—in real life and in the play—by Joe Dunn's heterosexual charm, tells the heroine:

> Forget gay dragons and magic trees
> And learn rough love in Los Angeles.
>
> You will not die, but you'll wish you could
> In the blue-moon bedrooms of Hollywood.

This is dialogue racy enough for one of the "gay twilight" pulp paperbacks of the fifties!

"Initiation is a play of anxiety, of fear, of cruelty, bizarre pain and threat. Spicer: "Here comes a chopper to chop off your head!" Adam understood, even better than Spicer and Duncan themselves, how Spicer had tapped into a floating, primitive, and sadistic unconscious, how, for the space of a semester, he changed a group of fairly ordinary men and women into great mages (or were they monsters?) with supernatural powers. Even the gentle Ida Hodes spits out, "You'll be mouse for my cats, and their claws are sharp." It's a fiendish transformation, and yet the pleasure and rhythm of Adam's invention diffuses the sulfur she so clearly sniffs in the air. Never produced, and apparently never shared with the other poets, "Initiation to the Magic Workshop" captures Jack Spicer at the height of his powers as teacher.[46]

Adam's play was influenced also by her overlapping membership in "The Maidens," a small reading, writing, and social group organized by Robert Duncan simultaneously with Spicer's Magic Workshop. In retrospect it's easy to see "The Maidens" as Duncan's own reaction to the Beat explosion, just as the Magic Workshop and its ensuing developments were Spicer's. Duncan and Jess enrolled the unflappable Helen Adam into "The Maidens," along with the poets James Broughton, Eve Triem, and Madeline Gleason. Members were issued an icon, a svelte Art Nouveau moon goddess figurine rescued from the marble base of a "bar stool" when a local soda fountain was demolished. Broughton said, "This was a most casual and open-ended group of six very different poets (3 men, 3 women) who met once a month for a meal to share their new poems in a congenial atmosphere: It was entirely relaxed and unpolitical."[47] Plays were acted out, picnics planned and held. During a summer visit from Boston, Robin Blaser was elected an honorary member. The Austrian photographer Harry Redl, who documented San Francisco's poetic and artistic life during a year-long visit in 1957, captured the Maidens' essence in a number of charming photographs. Frozen into *commedia dell'arte* postures, the "Maidens" stand

Ida Hodes, Jack Spicer, Ruth Witt-Diamant, Robert Duncan in 1957. The "brains trust" of the Poetry Center at San Francisco State College. *Photo copyright © 1997 by Harry Redl.*

gazing fondly at one another, like a cross between a meeting of the Pre-Raphaelite Brotherhood and the cast of a Noel Coward play.[48] Looking back, the group forged an interesting experiment in cultural subversion, combating the rigid gender stereotypes of the 1950s by exaggerated use of costume, fairy tale, high camp, role-playing, sexual ambiguity, and whimsy. Broughton wrote the play "Mission to Gomorrah" for the group to act out in a meeting the following spring: its very title links the sexual transgression of the Cities of the Plain with Cold War HUAC anxieties. (The 1943 film *Mission to Moscow* had been the subject of much vitriol during congressional investigations into communist influence on Hollywood.) The Maidens left Spicer cold. As Duncan became more femme and fey, Spicer became more butch, or tried to (away from Duncan, Spicer could be quite camp himself). In contrast, Redl's stark photograph of the Poetry Center "brains trust" presents Spicer as blurred, sweaty, spooked by the lens, and flanked by stately Witt-Diamant, Ida Hodes, and Duncan. All four fairly fibrillate with suppressed, twitchy energy.

*

Yet Spicer himself resisted his own workshop's magic. "Jack," said George Stanley, "was not writing at the time. One of the things that the workshop was supposed to do was to make him write again. And it wasn't happening."[49] Duncan also remembered this as a time of grim silence for Jack, who "had to sit all the way through his Magic Workshop without a poem. He was in a terrible condition. He was in a great condition about teaching—because it was like being master magician. But he paid a very heavy penalty, unable to have a poem at all during that period."[50] Spicer had begun the poems that became *After Lorca* in the autumn of 1956, finishing his translation of the "Ode to Walt Whitman" at Christmastime—but after that he was stuck. In an undated letter, Spicer remarked, "I haven't written a line since I started in this penal colony." Later again, in another undated letter, "School has robbed me of the ability to do anything but drink and manage the poetry class. More good poetry is being written here than I can remember (partly due to my class) and I have to stand on the outside. I say never again and mean it."[51]

In the meantime, suspense over *Evergreen Review* and *Measure* had resolved itself. Jack was outraged that Don Allen had finally excluded Robin Blaser from the "San Francisco Scene." Nor was he overjoyed at the selections made from his own poetry. "Seems pretty square to me. Made me want to go out and write sex poems."[52] When the magazine appeared in June, Spicer was predictably disgusted because *Howl* was reprinted in it, the "best-publicized poem in the world." Wieners had had the nerve to reject Spicer's Boston piece, "Poem to the Reader of This Poem," for *Measure* and to ask instead for "Imaginary Elegies," the suite of poems Spicer had written for Robin, which he regarded as his best so far—and far too good for the upstart, know-nothing Wieners, who "only understands Black Mountain poetry and Cole Porter," neither of which Jack liked. (Wieners *did* have enough sense to print Blaser's "The Hunger for Sound," which had become one of Jack's favorites among Robin's poems.)[53] Spicer turned over the work produced in the Magic Workshop to Duncan to be sent for publication in *Measure*. Duncan tried to explain that while, yes, he "liked" the work, he didn't like it enough to sponsor it. He was left with the uncomfortable role of seeming to reject his fellow workshop members while Spicer could revel in seeming a "fellow-martyr with the jeunes."[54]

To avoid worry about his own failure to write, Spicer burst into furious activity. In the spring of 1957, his students saw him everywhere—in the workshop, on the street, in bars, at readings. The Poetry Center sponsored two readings by Spicer this spring: one, with Conrad Pendleton, was held at the Telegraph Hill Neighborhood Association, 555 Chestnut Street, on St. Patrick's Day, with Conrad Pendleton, the other, with Helen Adam, was held on the San Francisco State campus (1600 Holloway Avenue), on April 11. Ruth Witt-Diamant arranged the first reading, perhaps taking a perverse delight in assigning Pendleton, the director of creative writing at Fresno State, to Spicer's care. "Conrad Pendleton" is little known today, and that wasn't even his real name, but a more romantic nom-de-plume than Walter E. Kidd. Kidd/"Pendleton" had published widely and had just produced a book called *Slow Fire of Time*—exactly the kind of mediocre, prizewinning verse Spicer and Duncan detested. But Walter Kidd had a gift for flattery, and his letters to Ruth Witt-Diamant reveal that she was susceptible to even the most outrageous. In his eyes, she was generous, charming, incisive, glowing; his references to her "instructional MAGIC" and her "almost incredibly dynamic Poetry Center program" got him a reading and a chance to hawk copies of *Slow Fire of Time* before, during, and after his appearance. Spicer met Kidd to discuss the upcoming reading in the beginning of February, and wasted little time repeating his appalled findings to the sympathetic Duncan and Ida Hodes.

The reading proved a rout. Spicer, wrote Jack Goodwin, "got hold of him before the reading, and quietly told Mr. [Kidd/Pendleton] that the room in which they were to perform was rather large, and that the lighting was rather strong, and that, really, to make one's expressions carry to the last rows, one ought to put on just a bit of theatrical make-up. The upshot was that finally this poor old man in a gray suit and quiet necktie got up in front of this large audience of literary queens, his features heavily emphasized with lip rouge and eyebrow pencil, and, in a trembling but defiant voice, launched into all this wholesomeness poetry."[55] Afterward Kidd complained angrily about the too-obvious favoritism shown to Spicer on the occasion. Hadn't he offered to supply Duncan with details of his life and bibliography? All ignored—what the audience got instead was a "build-down of seven lines" compared to the "ONE-PAGE EULOGY of Mr. JACK SPICER." Maybe, Kidd wound up lamenting, "maybe my poems are just too god-damn 'square.'"[56]

Kidd/"Pendleton" felt he'd been treated shabbily, but Robert Duncan's introductory notes to Spicer's reading were actually a curious eulogy, telling us more about Duncan's own queasiness with Spicer's work than they do about the work itself.

In his own work, Spicer disturbs. That he continues to do so is his vitality. The abortive, the solitary, the blasphemous, when they are not facetious, produce upheavals in the real. Life throws up the disturbing demand "All is not well"—sign after sign generated of accusation manifest—which it is the daring of Spicer at times in poems to mimic. If you do not allow that life vomits; that the cosmos with its swollen and shrunken stars, its irruptions, vomits—you can refuse to allow only by denying fact. And, in the fullness—the image of God must contain the grotesque. The Creator accuses as he blesses His Creation. That God contains more, that God "contains" is an aesthetic that defines my critical departure from delight in Spicer's work where the uncontain, the isolate, appears and accuses the Creator. All partial voice screams out of very hell, divorced from the good, truths that we can afford neither to deny nor to embrace.[57]

The reading was well attended, with seventy-five people present, including twenty students (who got in for free).

What Spicer read at the Neighborhood Association is unknown, but his second reading, at San Francisco State, was recorded. (The cumbersome reel-to-reel tape now rests in the vaults of the Poetry Center Archive.) In a breezy, light, and somewhat arch voice—sounding just like the actor Tony Randall—Spicer began the reading with "Ars Poetica" and "An Apocalypse for Three Voices," which he introduced by saying, "There's an epigraph—I used to write epigraphs when I was younger." "Now for some less humorous poems," he announced, and the reading continued with "Berkeley in Time of Plague," the "Dancing Ape" poem, "Psychoanalysis: an Elegy," "Dardenella," and the then-recent "The Day Five Thousand Fish Died Along the Charles River." Next came the first four "Imaginary Elegies," but in versions very different than the ones published in *The New American Poetry*.[58] The reading continued with the early "We find the body difficult to speak," and "Troy Poem," the "Sonnet for the Beginning of Winter," the revised version of "A Night in Four Parts," and "Midnight at Bareass Beach." The wild laughter provoked by the last title led Spicer to add acidulously, "Although the title is humorous, the poem isn't." Then the reading concluded with "An Arcadia for Dick Brown," "A Poem for the Reader of the Poem," "Song for the Great Mother," and "Song for Bird and Myself."

Giving readings, leading the workshop, making new friends, encountering Charles Olson, renewing old friendships, mooning over Joe Dunn—Spicer's schedule was a heavy one. The straw that broke his back was his appointment at San Francisco State as an Instructor in Language Arts, at a salary just under $2,500 for the term beginning February 11 and ending

June 30, 1957. The experience was so unpleasant that several of his friends thought he did not remain the whole term teaching, but left abruptly, describing his students as "a bunch of puddings."[59] In fact, he finished the term, but his dissatisfaction was well known to his intimates.

Merle Ellis, later a food writer and columnist for the *San Francisco Chronicle*, was just another ex-GI at San Francisco State in the spring of 1957, dreading the required course the students called "Bonehead English." His teacher was Jack Spicer, and Spicer's encouragement and praise changed the direction of his life.

Jack was the first "real" writer I ever met. What happened was—one of the assignments was to first read a poem—and since it was the 1950s the poet could have been anyone, from Ginsberg to Frost—to first read a poem, *then to evaluate it in the style of the poet.* Well, I wrote mine, and for some reason Jack liked it.

The rest of the class moved onto punctuation or whatever, but Jack gave me another poem in every class—and I'd read it and write a response in the style of that poet. And finally, on one of those assignments, Jack wrote a note: *Merle, with luck— if it is luck—you could be a poet.* Now I didn't become a poet—I make my living writing, but not as a poet. But that note kept me going for a long, long time, and I consider myself lucky to have been his student.[60]

Another student was the musician Pauline Oliveros, just then beginning an important career as composer, performer, and musicologist. Her colorful appearance and eccentric, mannish dress and voice endeared her to Spicer. At first, running through the class roster ("Mitchell?" "Here." "Newman?" "Here." "Oliveros?" "Here") Spicer assumed she was a man and replied, "Thank you, Mr. Oliveros."[61] Spicer's teaching, she recalled, "was very important to me and helped me through writing block. More than that, his teaching opened writing for me." His assignments were linear and progressive. The first was, "Write one sentence which is worth saying." When she responded with "Familiarity breeds attempt," he grinned with amusement. The next assignment was to write a paragraph; then a letter. Oliveros continued her recollections:

I met Robert Duncan around the same time. He was the [Assistant] Director of the Poetry Center at San Francisco State. I was looking for a poet to work with on some songs. Robert presented himself and introduced me to Charles Olson's work. I set two of Robert's poems ("Spider Song" and "The Seal") and a short poem of Olson. Robert was very pleased and we became friends. I was at their home quite often. Through Robert and Jess, I met Helen Adam, Robin Blaser, Robert Creeley and many others.

I attended readings often including Jack's. [In Spicer's classroom] I never observed anything that I could call drunken behaviour. He seemed genuinely interested in helping the students. His approach was creative and novel. I felt comfortable for the first time. I count him has one of my important teachers.

I was aware that Jack was on the self destructive side with his drinking and attitude toward himself. It was hard to understand since he was such a great teacher and poet.[62]

Jack himself was less sanguine about his classroom experience:

Teaching is not the right profession for me—and this factory is even worse than not right. I struggle to survive day by day—and dream at night of the horror of telling people what to do. Is there no place for me on this crud-encrusted planet? Listen in this June and find out.

The poetry class, in contrast, is fine. My poetry reading yesterday was quite a success—if such a thing can be. Duncan and I are closer now than ever. But all this is spoiled by the idiotic necessity of playing God to people whose God one would not wish to be. I haven't written a single poem.[63]

Spicer quietly continued his campaign to get his earlier poetry into print. On Duncan's suggestion he offered the "Imaginary Elegies," his most sustained work to date, to *Poetry Chicago*. A polite letter of refusal came back. Then he approached his old friend Landis Everson for advice on how to break into the big national poetry journals. At this time, Landis Everson was perhaps the most successful (in terms of being published widely) of any of the poets from the late 1940s Berkeley group, with new work in *The Kenyon Review*, *Hudson Review*, *Poetry*, and *Quarterly Review of Literature*. These were the "Eastern magazines" Spicer abhorred, but swallowing a big slice of humble pie he approached Landis. Would Landis read Spicer's poetry and tell him why magazine editors didn't seem to care for it?

Jack was asking me to criticize his poems, as if I were the editor of one of these magazines. Which meant, right away, "I reject your poem because . . . ," which is a set-up. On the other hand, if I didn't offer to do that for him, since he was asking me, I would be a disloyal friend. So I was damned either way. I thought, well, I can't be quite sure how he'll react so I'll go ahead and pretend I'm an editor of *Hudson Review* and he had sent poems in. So I did that. Jack stood up and he was absolutely furious and said, "I didn't expect you to understand," and slammed out.

[Spicer] desperately wanted, as would any artist, to have a public career other than just the small group he was involved with at Berkeley and San Francisco. Jack was ambitious. If you sacrifice your real life and flesh for poetry, and you aren't getting anywhere in poetry, then you can get pretty hysterical. Other younger poets like McClure and Snyder were making quite a name for themselves. Well, we were the original Berkeley Renaissance and what had happened? We weren't living in Berkeley any more and where had the Renaissance gone? It had been drawn out of our hands and these interlopers—probably they weren't even Californians—had come along and were becoming famous.[64]

For bar life, there was mostly The Place, where John Allen Ryan had become a bartender—a job he compared to that of a social director on a cruise ship.[65] Spicer was welcome there. Michael McClure recalled that he enjoyed tracking his own legend through close observation of the men's room walls. "He'd go in, read the new graffiti, and come out smiling to himself. One of them, I remember, was 'Jack Spicer goes down on stranded whales.'"[66] The composer Jack Goodwin observed the North Beach poets nightly at The Place. He remembered Spicer as a "squinting, sneering, adenoidal, hunch-backed Socrates presiding over the nightly poets' table, with George Stanley on his right hand, tossing his locks over one shoulder, and the latest tenderfoot on the left, taking notes."

What made it possible to start a floating poets' symposium in the North Beach bars was that there was no hi-fi, no rock, no disco boom-boom. People could actually sit at a large table and wiseacre back and forth, and be heard. In later years, all they needed to do if they wanted to get rid of the poets was to put in a new jukebox. It was like hefting a crucifix at a vampire, and Spicer would leave in a rage . . .

Spicer affected disapproval of the milieu into which his pupils had drifted. "Head-bohemia," he called it, pleased with his phrase-making gift. The position, of course, turned out to be untenable, because "head-bohemia" was where he chose to spend the remainder of his life; but here was an interesting harbinger of his technique. When he finally got his poet factory going, his system for obtaining raw material was simply to walk up to the current prospect and initiate a sort of flirtation-by-insult. Get the other fellow on the defensive. At this point, one could either tell Spicer to go fuck himself, or else start trying to justify oneself. If one chose the latter course, one was very likely to wind up as a disciple.[67]

Another bartender, John Gibbons ("Jack") Langan, introduced a feature of the bohemian bars of Chicago into The Place. This was "Blabbermouth Night," a kind of Dada free-for-all that became wildly popular in San Francisco.[68] Michael Rumaker described these Monday evening events:

[J]udged by the enthusiasm and applause of the bar audience on the wit and verbal persuasion of the contestant, a magnum of champagne went to the best bullshit artist. (No small feat given the raucous cynics and critics in the crowd, mostly writers, musicians and painters who weren't shy with their boos and catcalls, a fact which kept me a firm spectator.)

I don't recall Robert speaking (if he had, it would have to be a night I missed, since *that* would've been memorable, and I can't imagine him not winning, hands down), or Jack Spicer either, but Spicer was one of the initiators of Blabbermouth Night. His presence was very much in evidence as a kind of director, getting the contestants organized and lined up to speak. I never saw Spicer as excited and actively and socially involved as during those weeknight talk marathons at The Place. Perched on a stool at the packed bar, smiling, looking as if he were enjoying himself (a rare thing for him), he cocked his head and listened in foxy amusement, tossing out encouraging words or hissing loudly along with the rest, at the rant and hilarious exaggerations as each contestant declaimed in loud voice and sweeping gestures from the balcony in the rear.

Jack also enjoyed bestowing the magnum of champagne on the victor in a brief ceremony, shy and laconic in praise, almost embarrassed by his unaccustomed display of pleasure.[69]

On Blabbermouth Night, no reading from text was permitted; it was all extemporaneous public speaking. Up on the balcony, set into the wall, stood a box "like a soap-box," where the contestants stood. If you were terrible, one of the bartenders would play a trumpet, or the crowd would hoot you off by yelling, "Take off your clothes," as they do in the French Quarter during Mardi Gras.[70]

Just too late to attend the "Magic Workshop," Joanne Kyger and her childhood friend Emily ("Nemi") Frost came from Santa Barbara to San Francisco. The two women fell in love with the city's bohemian splendors. "We couldn't stand to be away from North Beach," Nemi remembered, "or each other. We couldn't go through the tunnel[s—Broadway and Stockton, which divided North Beach from the rest of San Francisco]. . . . And we just raced to get back. It was home. It was where everything was happening."[71] North Beach was a small world—three or four blocks, like a toy city dropped at the edge of a larger metropolis. Nemi, Joanne, and their friends Paul Alexander and Tom Field rarely went even to Washington Square Park, which was just a block away—only after the bars had closed at 2:00 A.M., when Joanne would cartwheel around the Park.[72]

Kyger worked and held court at Brentano's Bookstore, meeting poets of all schools, including Spicer, who took her under his wing—the wing of Hecate. One night he added her to a group performance of "Zen singers," inviting Tom Parkinson over from Berkeley to witness their performance at The Place on Blabbermouth Night. In her journal she wrote: "We have rehearsed, whenever we felt like it, such tunes as 'Give me some Zen who are Stout Hearted Zen' and 'When it rains it always rains, Zenies from Heaven.'" When it came time actually to perform, however, the singers demurred "on some grounds or other, probably lack of free beer."[73]

More and more young people, most without the talent and alacrity of Kyger and Frost, flooded the once-quiet streets of North Beach. The police became concerned and assigned a special task force to deal with this invasion. "Officer Bigarani was arresting people for pissing in the street," George Stanley recalled, "and a woman named Wendy [Murphy] was arrested for being barefoot. It was a big scandal: the *Chronicle* was playing it up, you know, 'degeneracy' or whatever. And then thousands of tourists."[74]

Who was "beat"? Who wasn't? The wild, crazy style of the Spicer/Duncan group made many of the Beat poets doubt their seriousness. Joanne Kyger, who met her future husband, Gary Snyder, at The Place, was torn between allegiances to two very different kinds of poetry life. The exclusiveness of Spicer's group of poets, friends, and lovers did not escape the members' own notice. "There were definitely circles within circles," recalled another young poet in the Spicer circle. "There was a sense of 'We are not Beatnik.' We [the poets] all felt like that. Sometimes we'd play it up to the tourists: the tourists came in and they thought we were all Beatniks. It was a big game. There *were* Beatniks out there. The Beatniks were more the followers of Ginsberg—more 'everything is everything else.' We called them 'sloppy thinkers.'"[75]

These young poets tended to despise other artists whose interests and personalities seemed unsympathetic. Nevertheless, the allegiances were ambiguous. George Stanley put the matter succinctly: "If you could consider the group centering around Ferlinghetti, Ginsberg, Corso, and later on, McClure—and still later, the Oregon poets, Whalen, Snyder and Welch—if you consider that one group 'Beatniks,' then the group around Spicer and Duncan were anti-Beatniks. But we *were* all Beatniks; we didn't think we were Beatniks, but we were." Stanley, who spent the summer of 1957 working as a clerk in the Police Department, grew to admire Spicer's ability to hold his own in bar life, and to revere him as a master of poetry. A classic late bloomer, George was making all kinds of discoveries about his own nature—how much he loved to drink; how much he loved writing, friendship, sex with men. "Jack took me under his wing and said, 'Go out and find someone to sleep with.' And I did! [Yet] more important than either the liquor or the possibility of romance was the conversation."[76]

Conversation was held either at The Place—where it was hard to hear—or at the afternoon salon Spicer began holding on the lawn and beach of Aquatic Park. On San Francisco Bay at the foot of Van Ness Avenue, Aquatic Park was backed by the Ghirardelli Chocolate Factory, the Eastman Kodak Co. (demolished in 1987), Fort Mason, and the buildings of Fisherman's Wharf. One major feature of the park is an art deco concrete structure (housing dressing rooms, a maritime museum, and—on the roof—banks of open benches). The westernmost benches were favored by gay sunbathers. Another favorite sunning spot was the small green area between the bocce ball courts, the Sea Scouts pavilion, and the water. Spicer repaired to the park every afternoon with his portable radio, his books, and his newspaper, and his friends and students joined him. This became a ritual for the rest of his life.[77] George Stanley, often in attendance, took note of every signal and dictum from Jack. "He didn't go very often to movies, but we went to see Elizabeth Taylor in *Suddenly Last Summer* and he was deeply morally shocked by the film. It was so explicit about sex, sex without love. He was offended, shocked by this public display of sex and the moral attitudes displayed. He was quite puritanical, yeah. High Romanticism was close to his heart. So, also, particularly, was Lorca's view as expressed in ["Ode to Walt Whitman"] where he just gives it to all the cocksuckers of the world, the attitude that the cocksuckers of the world are destroying the possibility of true love between men."[78]

From out of the past an old college pal entered Spicer's life. Jim Herndon had known Jack Spicer in the late 1940s in Berkeley and both had left in 1950, Herndon for seven years in Europe, and Spicer for two years at the University of Minnesota. "He spent one miserable fucking year [actually two years] in Minnesota and he wrote me *one letter.*" Jack had ferreted out Jim's middle name: Boswell. "So he wrote me this letter, to James Boswell the Seventh, from 'Sam Johnson'—clearly his idol. You could see the grotesqueness, the physical grotesqueness: the great asshole, something like that."

In 1957, Jim Herndon came back to San Francisco, and in succeeding years he became indeed something of a Boswell to Spicer's Johnson—a sardonic Boswell who could match Spicer crack for crack. In Paris Jim had wed a second time. After he and his wife, Fran, returned, Spicer called one day to ask Jim if he had a TV. "I'll be right over, " he said, "the McCarthy hearings are on." (The occasion described here was probably a television rerun. The actual hearings in which Senator Joseph McCarthy of Wisconsin lost political control—the so-called "Army/McCarthy" hearings—occurred earlier in the 1950s.)

Jack came over to spend the day, instructing with an enthusiastic naiveté on the finer points of the hearings, as though neither of the Herndons had ever heard of McCarthy or HUAC. He took to Fran immediately, saying, "You're all right." And she liked Jack, too. They "entranced" each other, Jim thought. Every evening that week the three watched TV, and at the end of the week, as a kind of reward, Jack took the Herndons on a "picturesque tour of North Beach"—his ironic phrase—something he would never have done if he hadn't cared for Fran. Jim felt "happy as a lark."

Jack took them to The Place. During their student days, Jack told him, "If I ever get enough money, I'll be an alcoholic. That's the best life there is." There he was, ten years later, ensconced in a bar, "in charge," a role he relished. The evening ended when Jack took the Herndons to Mike's Pool Hall to play pinball. Fran was assigned to concentrate on the numbers necessary to win the game. "Naturally," she remembered ruefully, "I didn't realize that was my task; that was absolutely the whole reason for being there, right?"[79] Jack introduced the Herndons to his new friend from Boston, his "printer," Joe Dunn, badly wasted from drugs—methedrine, Jim guessed. Still you couldn't help warming up to Joe right away, and Jack was concerned for him. "He loves the little fucker," Herndon thought.[80]

Spicer's love, concern, and helplessness in the face of Joe's drug problem spilled over into the book he was now on fire with—the "translation" work of *After Lorca*. The book purports to be a series of translations "after Lorca," although, as Clayton Eshleman has pointed out, a number of the poems in the book are originals, not versions of Lorca's poems.[81] Interwoven between the poems are letters from Spicer to Lorca, teasing statements of a poetics intended to shock readers and to penetrate the invisible membrane that divides "poetry" and "poetics." The poems are each dedicated to a different person ("A Translation for . . . "). Spicer's comic way of justifying the dedications was "at least you assure yourself of one reader," but the multiple dedications serve—as they do in Frank O'Hara's work—to bring a world of others into the text, to create a community.[82]

Spicer's dedicatees make up a formidable range of muses: several of them were students in his Magic Workshop (Helen Adam, George Stanley, Ebbe Borregaard, Bob Connor); some of them were old friends from Berkeley (Pat Wilson, Donald Allen, Robin Blaser); some were former "boyfriends" (Richard Rummonds, Graham Mackintosh, Allen Joyce). One of them was a child of only three or four, Nate Hardin, the son of his old Berkeley friend, Sam Hardin. Several were new acquaintances, bar poets whom Spicer met at The Place thanks to John Ryan. Some of them were the actors with whom Duncan was working on *Medea Part II*—Erik Weir and Ann Simone. The "postscript" is to Marianne Moore, whom Spicer had not yet met. Bob Connor was offended by the poem dedicated to him: the reference in "The Ballad for Weeping" to whiny dogs made him suspect Spicer was secretly comparing him to one.[83]

After Lorca began a transformation of American poetry that deconstructed syntax in the service of a greater community of language. The kind of link between people and poetry found in the poem "Forest," for example, marks a redefinition of Spicer's poetic practice that spilled over into the rest of the poetic world:

> *Forest (a Translation for Joe Dunn)*
>
> You want me to tell you
> The secret of springtime—
>
> And I relate to that secret
> Like a high-branching firtree
>
> Whose thousand little fingers
>
> I will tell you never, my love,
> Because the river runs slowly
>
> But I shall put into my branching voice
> The ashy sky of your gaze.
>
> Turn me around, brown child
> Be careful of my needles.
>
> Turn me around and around, playing
> At the well-pump of love.
>
> The secret of springtime. How
> I wish I could tell you!

Spicer's friends observe that he used lovers for poems and poems for lovers. And indeed, the poems in *After Lorca* are dedicated both to a real friend and to an abstraction of a friendship, a mood, a memory. This public marriage of people and poetry suggests the metaphysics of his unstated world view, which he explores in a letter to Lorca:

Dear Lorca,
    I would like to make poems out of real objects. The lemon to be a lemon that the reader could cut or taste or squeeze—

The formulation about poetic correspondences that followed became one of his best-known utterances. In poetry "that lemon may become this lemon, or it may even become this piece of seaweed, or this particular color of gray in this ocean. One does not need to imagine that lemon; one needs to discover it." For many of Spicer's early readers, his most attractive poetic practice was the transformation of a very personal emotional experience into a language that allows the experience to come to life and perform on its own. Thus, the *Lorca* letter just quoted from continued:

How easy it is in erotic musings or in the truer imagination of a dream to invent a beautiful boy. How difficult to take a boy in a blue bathing suit that I have watched as casually as a tree and to make him visible in a poem as a tree is visible, not as an image or a picture but as something alive—caught forever in the structure of words. Live moons, live lemons, live boys in bathing suits. The poem is a collage of the real.

But things decay, reason argues. Real things become garbage. The piece of lemon you shellac to the canvas begins to develop mold, the newspaper tells of incredible ancient events in forgotten slang, the boy becomes a grandfather.[84]

Spicer's blurring of the line between poetry and prose may have been a result of his studying of Emily Dickinson's manuscripts in Boston. He wrote about the difficulty in editing her work in terms of its consciousness:

The reason for the difficulty of drawing a line between the poetry and prose in Emily Dickinson's letters may be that she did not wish such a line to be drawn. If large portions of her correspondence are considered not as mere letters—and, indeed, they seldom communicate information, or have much to do with the person to whom they were written—but as experiments in a heightened prose combined with poetry, a new approach to both her letters and her poetry opens up.[85]

In June 1957, Spicer wrote to Blaser:

Since school's been out (for me forever) I've been ignoring my unemployment and translating Lorca. . . . I enclose my eight latest "translations." Transformations might be a better word. Several are originals and most of the rest change the poem vitally. I can't seem to make anybody understand this or what I'm doing. They look blank or ask what the Spanish is for a word that isn't in the Spanish or praise (like Duncan did) an original poem as typically Lorca. What I am trying to do is establish a *tradition*. When I'm through (although I'm sure no one will ever publish them) I'd like someone as good as I am to translate these translations into French (or Pushtu) adding more. Do you understand? No. Nobody does.[86]

His next paragraph was one he would soon contradict. "Anyway, *please, please, please* read these as poems and give me some criticisms of individual lines. I can see why Pound got so angry at the reaction to his 'Propertius.'"

Less than a year later he'd changed his mind about criticism. "You are right," he wrote to Blaser, "that I don't now need your criticisms of individual poems. But I still want them. It's probably from old habit—but it's an awfully old habit. Halfway through *After Lorca* I discovered that I was writing a book instead of a series of poems and individual criticism by anyone suddenly became less important."[87] He went on to explain his new aesthetic of the serial poem. As he described it later, suddenly he realized that his previous efforts at poetry had been futile, because he was writing poems that stood alone. The search for the perfect poem had been meaningless, because "there is no single poem." Poems belong together, in a book; inside a book they talk to each other, make love with each other, interact as words do inside the syntax of a sentence. "Poems should echo and reecho against each other. They should create resonances. They cannot live alone any more than we can." With these bold statements he reinvented his poetry, and abjured his previous writing—except the "Imaginary Elegies," which he viewed as a proto-book. The rest were to be pitied, "beautiful but dumb." From this point on, the closely rhymed, metrically precise poems of Spicer's earlier period disappeared. If poems did not have to stand alone, they didn't have to be beautiful.

Spicer's fallow period was over. Donald Allen arrived to spend the summer of 1957 in San Francisco. He remembered that Jack had a new *Lorca* poem to show him every day at Vesuvio's or The Place. Spicer was drinking only beer, not the ruinous brandy that came later. Beer was enough to celebrate each new poem.[88] Robert Duncan, in a letter to Robin Blaser dated December 19, 1957, described what happened that summer:

Jack's *Lorca* and the whole boon of his fertility since this summer has been a major fundament. Boston seems a good sprouting if not a good sporting ground. *After Lorca* gives perspective and body to the previous work; when Spicer is measured on Spicer what lookd grotesque before takes on lineaments of nature. It's that the *[Imaginary] Elegies* are now protean, for they are propositions of the beauties and conservations of the *Lorca* poems. From the Letter to you in his new *Admonitions* I copied the following:

"Let your way of writing of the moment go along its own paths, explore and retreat but never be fully realized (confined) within the boundaries of one poem. . . . There is really no single poem. . . .
"They cannot live alone any more than we can.
"A poem is never by itself alone."[89]

If, as Jack writes, the doctrine was mine, it has taken this return of the doctrine thru Jack (thru the ease of *After Lorca*, and the proportion given now to the earlier work) for me to receive it. I had, when he read thru the Letter, that *donné*: the epiphanic "I have been waiting to be shown this." That releases something once knotted, at which I have been working.[90]

The energies aroused in the Magic Workshop now carried over into regular poetry meetings every Sunday afternoon. The clientele had expanded, but the leaders in these meetings remained Spicer and Duncan, magisterial figures though still in their thirties, since all the regular and most of the other members of the Sunday group were in their early twenties. Meetings

Sunday afternoon at Joe and Carolyn Dunn's apartment, Jackson Street, San Francisco, 1957.
Photo by Helen Adam.

were held at the apartment of John Wieners and in the newly organized East-West House on California Street, as well as a longer series at the Montgomery Street apartments of George Stanley and Ebbe Borregaard, but the habitués remembered most vividly the ones held during the first year at the Jackson Street apartment of Joe and Carolyn Dunn. James Broughton remembered the circle of poets gathered on Sundays as "those who did not belong to the noisier bandwagon launched by Ginsberg and his crew: Corso, Whalen, Kerouac, Snyder, Kyger, et al. In other words a more disciplined and more lyrically conscious group than the political publicity-busy invaders from the east coast . . . Of course there were mergings and overlaps and we all knew one another."[91] In point of fact Gary Snyder and Joanne Kyger both came to the Sunday meetings, Kyger often enough to become a regular. "Joe asked me if I would come to these meetings, and I went, along with Jerome Mallman and Nemi Frost."[92] (Mallman was a painter and bohemian, a close friend of both Joanne's and Nemi's; he is the "Jerry" of Spicer's *Admonitions*.) There Joe introduced her to John Wieners, who had moved to San Francisco in October 1957, and Joanne struck up an intense friendship with him.

From their homes in North Beach the poets darted through the Broadway tunnel to get to the Dunns' apartment—built under Russian Hill after World War II, the tunnel ties North Beach to Polk Gulch. The Dunns' house was built close to the sidewalk—"It was just one step up," recalled Ebbe Borregaard, "and then—darkness." The painter Tom Field remembered a "dumpy" apartment and the Dunns as "pre-punk, proto-punk." Carolyn Dunn's green makeup made a particularly strong impression.[93] In tiny rooms the group drank red wine from three jelly jars: Nemi and Joanne drank from a saucepan. Inside the refrigerator, in the ice chamber, a soggy picture of Rimbaud stood propped up against the ice. A party atmosphere prevailed, tempered with workshop business.

One afternoon, Wieners introduced Kyger to two friends of his from Black Mountain, Tom Field and Michael Rumaker, who demonstrated the correct way to make martinis of Rhine wine and gin. That was "a famous evening," Kyger recalled. After the meeting, more martinis, then dinner, then through the dark tunnel to North Beach again, and then later, the arrest of George Stanley, Jerome Mallman, and Ebbe Borregaard. Said Michael Rumaker of this event:

On a late Saturday night, Ebbe Borregaard, Joanne Kyger, myself and a couple of others, on our way to Dante's Pool Hall after Vesuvio's closed. Waiting at Broadway and Columbus for the light to change and when it did, starting across when Ebbe, a little ahead of us, gave the finger sign to two guys in a car that almost ran over him. The car pulled over, the two guys got out, turned out to be plainclothesmen in an unmarked car and arrested Ebbe for "lewd behavior," and the person beside him [Stanley]. Joanne and I went down to the Hall of Justice to try to get Ebbe out but we couldn't and he spent the night in jail.[94]

Ida Hodes was called to bail out the young men who, walking into a reading the next day, were greeted as heroes.

Spicer might start the meetings with the heuristic exercises developed in his Magic Workshop of the spring, or during the nights at 2029 Hearst when he first learned magic from Duncan. At the beginning of one meeting he consulted a French-English dictionary, like a pilgrim at an oracle, to determine, "What shall the meeting center on?" The Larousse dictionary opened, as if by spirits, to *metallurgy*. Then Duncan read the poem ("The Question") he'd brought to the workshop, and all were amazed and reconfirmed:

> Does the old alchemist
> speak in metaphor
> of a spiritual splendor?
>
> or does he remember

how that metal is malleable?

. . . .

will the good metal return
to use? gold leaf to the house roof?
our treasure above ground,
sure glow for the eye to see?[95]

One of the participants was Harold Dull, a poet who had studied under Theodore Roethke and Stanley Kunitz at the University of Washington in Seattle.[97] He arrived in San Francisco on Labor Day 1957 with Dora Geissler, who asked her new San Francisco friends to call her Dora Dull, although she and Harold never married. "It was unheard of to find a landlord who would rent an apartment to 2 persons of different genders *and* different names. When my mother threatened to visit, I went to the point of purchasing a gold band from a pawnshop, and that was the end of Dora Geissler."[97] Dora remembered Spicer's extreme physical hesitancy and clumsiness—physical traits that almost certainly accentuated his conception of himself as an outsider: the "Dancing Ape," as he wrote of himself in an early poem.

A 99-cent jug of red wine was passed around as the week's poetry output was read, reviewed, praised and put down. Spicer characteristically preambled that we were too dense to understand his poem so he would accommodate us by reading it three times and allowed no comment until the third reading was completed. Reading the poem always posed a problem because Spicer would find the light too dim to make out the words on the page, although there may well have been sunlight over his shoulder. Jack's hands often balled into fists and when performing maneuvers like lighting a match or lifting a glass he really had to struggle to make his hands accomplish the task. So hanging on to the poem, smoking a cigarette and lighting a match to hold to the paper for light to read by, resulted in astonishing spasms of physical exertion which certainly for me heightened the impact of the poem.[98]

September was also the month of the 11th Annual Arts Festival in North Beach. During this weeklong festival, the Poetry Center sponsored readings at Fugazi Hall, and the poets in Spicer's circle were prominently featured in the programming. Helen Adam led off the featured readers, with her new ballad "Queen o' Crow Castle," with Eve Triem and Jack Gilbert sharing the bill. (Gilbert also wrote, with Gerd Stern, a puppet show about The Place, which Spicer attended and found "very funny. . . . There was a marvelous puppet of Rexroth. If all this sounds a bit inbred—it was.") On Friday night James Broughton read from his new Grove Press book, *True and False Unicorn*. Saturday was a marathon of poets, with daytime readings "by young poets," including Richard Brautigan, Ron Loewinsohn, and

Ebbe Borregaard, and at night a "reading from recent work and poems written for the 'Poetry as Magic' Workshop, conducted by Jack Spicer." Poetry was in the air—Ida Hodes's program notes for the festival reminded all that the "San Francisco Scene" had become a locus of nationwide attention. "These same poets," Spicer and Duncan among them, "are featured in a LP record issued by Grove Press."[99] The energy was tremendous, though Spicer "annoyed everybody" by refusing to go to any of the poetry readings at the "ghastly" Arts Festival. He was pleased the weather was so bad; delighted at the thunderstorm.[100] Soon to come was the extradiagetical event that had the whole town talking, the obscenity trial of Ginsberg's *Howl*.

The Sunday afternoon meetings focused on a number of poetic concerns and forms. Harold Dull's memories, after Spicer's death, grew lyrical:

I would so like to get it down just as it was then, everyone, just as they were, Jack, crosslegged on the floor, Duncan in the plush chair, George Stanley, Joanne Kyger, Ebbe Borregaard, I, to see it just as it was, today, in the clear light of the day. And that room we met in, Joe Dunn's, is still somewhere inside me. I can trace my way back—out of the Broadway tunnel, left, and down . . . and I see that yellowish brown house (or is it grey, blue-grey?), the ground floor window, the brown shade, but when I walk in it's so dark. I know the plush chair Duncan sits in, and the dark wine-stained rug Jack leans forward on, and all the other furniture from the Salvation Army, and all the others, are there, but I can't see anything. And I remember how bugged I used to get when I walked in and saw the shade pulled down in the middle of the day—Can't we have some natural light? I'd say and walk over and snap it up. Or did I? It was always down if I remember right. Was I outvoted? If you pull up that shade we won't have privacy. Anybody walking by can look. Or did somebody just get up and pull it down on me? This is the kind of light we like!! I don't remember. But it is down. But I know they are all there . . . Duncan in that plush easy chair writing the latest installment to the Pindar Poem . . . and Jack bunched over an admonition to a young angel. . . . But I can't see anything in that what's even more hateful to me now minus twelve watts (years) dark bulb and I walk over to snap up the shade. But in the protest that follows, George's eyeglasses are tiny clear lakes . . . and Ebbe's great bushy eyebrows . . . treetops . . . and Joanne's fandango cape or shawl she twirls in a huff about her shoulders—a wisp of cloud . . . and I stop, the top of that next hill I thought I'd be able to see everything from would probably be dark by the time I got to it anyway, and I turn back—out the Broadway tunnel, left, and down. . . . [101]

Joe and Carolyn once left town for a weekend. When the Group's members showed up for the meeting, they found the apartment deserted and locked. No problem. "They had a Sunday meeting anyway," Dunn recalled.

110

"George Stanley or somebody stood on somebody's shoulders and opened up a window and went in and opened the door and had the meeting and then locked the door, closed the window and left." Rather cavalier, but it didn't bother Joe: he thought it kind of fun. From these meetings "all kinds of sparks emerged." Spicer brought in the work of poets he admired and read them aloud. Numbers varied—sometimes only four or five people showed up; sometimes they came "in droves."

In the fall of 1957, Joanne remembered, George Stanley approached her in The Place, and said, "Some people are treating these meetings just like a party." The tone of his voice left no doubt that "some people" included herself. She hadn't been reading her own work at the meetings, that was true. Too shy; too hesitant. It was time to shape up. She assembled her work, got on the cable car over the hill, realized she had forgotten her poems, went back home, found the poems, got on the cable car again, and finally read them at the Dunns'. "Robert Duncan loved them, and I remember Jack Spicer looking very serious-faced and saying, 'Now what do you intend to do?' His commitment to poetry was absolute, right down to the marrow of your bone. This was no light-hearted affair at all. And then after I wrote 'The Maze' poem, which was the first one in *The Tapestry and the Web*." Completed late in 1964, *The Tapestry and the Web* became Kyger's first book.[102]

If Spicer was serious with Kyger, Duncan was coy. "I remember Robert Duncan saying, 'There are a few things I could teach you about the line,' and I said, 'Well, tell me.' 'Oh, I'll tell you next meeting.' So, when everything was over, we were standing in the kitchen, and I said, 'Now tell me.' 'Well, ah . . .' and he really didn't tell me anything at all, as a matter of fact." Joanne laughed, a deep, rich chortle of warmth. "But there was something he did tell me which then made me more interested in the fact that there was something going on which I wasn't quite handling, or could handle in some way—some breath-beat implicit in Creeley's tone, the hanging-article at the end of the breath-line, in the ear, giving this kind of staccato rhythm."[103]

When the twenty-one-year-old David Meltzer began attending the meetings at the Dunns' apartment, he became intoxicated by the dynamic between Spicer, who wanted to "de-rhetorize" poetry, and Duncan, who proposed a rhetorical, lyrical verse. At one session Duncan expounded the rhetoric in Vachel Lindsay's poem about William Jennings Bryan, clarifying the function of rhetoric in the poem; Spicer opposed Duncan's formulations with a poetry that was "much more reductive." Meltzer was one of the people who changed the tenor of the meetings by being there, George Stanley felt. He liked to read long poems. Once during a reading Meltzer announced, "Now I will soon be at an end." James Broughton was present and audibly sighed. David finished the remark, saying, " . . . of Part I." Broughton sighed again.[104]

Another newcomer to the circle was Ron Loewinsohn, then a twenty-one-year-old writer, a student at SF State, studying Chaucer. Like George, he was a native of San Francisco. "The meetings were incredibly useful. They got people writing and kept them writing. They kept the level of excitement and activity up." If the criticism itself was banal, the emotional dynamics made the meetings well worth attending. Loewinsohn admired and envied Spicer's integrity.

Jack would have nothing to do with Ferlinghetti; would not allow his books to be sold in the store [City Lights]; did not take Kerouac or Ginsberg seriously; dealt with all of the Beat Generation people with a kind of contempt, a regal "We are not amused. . . . " At first both Richard Brautigan and I were suspicious of this clique of poets. Once we got to know Jack—felt such respect and affection for him—we became part of this group of people who regularly showed up at that table. Jack's memory was incredible. He would remember particular details, not only of *The Canterbury Tales* but of *The Book of the Duchess*. It had been years since he had studied this work, or the criticism around it, [yet] he had complete command of the literature. And his insights with regard to contemporary literature were often good; often very perverse. Jack would be listening to a transistor in Aquatic Park, and my son, Joe, then a baby, would say, "What's that?" and Jack would reply, "That's Martian." Then he would talk about his radio transmissions from West Mars. Well, West Mars is like Borges' library at Babylon, it contained every book ever written. So that it was a kind of *spiritus mundi*; a "world memory," speaking through the radio, being transmitted. There of course you could have Chaucer and baseball and everything else. Nothing was excluded, except ego. That seems to have been excluded. Interesting.[105]

One bright thread passing through the first year's meetings was the establishment of the White Rabbit Press. After a reading by the poets of the Magic Workshop on June 9, 1957, Spicer suggested to Joe Dunn that he found a press to publish this new writing. The time was right: a job had opened in the Print Department of the Greyhound Bus Company, and Joe was scheduled for an interview with Jack Sutherland, the head of the Print Department, who had attended the Art Institute with Jess and John Allen Ryan. Joe described the interview: "I mentioned that I had some artist friends, and when I said, 'John Ryan' his face fell. He said, 'Do you hang out in North Beach, by any chance?' 'Yes.' I almost blew the job right there."

But he didn't. After a trial period of a few weeks, Joe was in, and Sutherland became helpful. "In fact it was he who I asked if I could use the equipment on Saturdays, at nights, for my own press publication. I had to buy my own paper; my own stock. He introduced me to paper salesmen. Plus I was working 9–5; I was running the press. It was through him the Press got off the ground. And he even, like, fabulously gave me the keys to the company—to the offices on Front Street."[106] Joe Dunn's feverish energy and nose for talent guaranteed a steady, almost monthly, production of worthwhile chapbooks. "From November 1957 to September 1958 he surreptitiously produced ten titles under the White Rabbit imprint. In a uniform format, $5\frac{1}{2}$ x $8\frac{1}{2}$ inches, the books were lithographed from authors' typescripts."[107] *Love, the Poem, the Sea and Other Pieces Examined*, by Steve Jonas, was the first White Rabbit book. Jess designed the cover, and 200 copies were printed, selling for 25 cents apiece.

There have been a number of explanations of the press's name. Jack Spicer was attached to the image of "white rabbit." According to Jim Herndon, Spicer's interest grew from James Thurber's cartoons, which often depict the fruitlessness and anxiety of the rabbit's quest for escape from a cruel world. George Stanley suggested that white rabbits function, as in *Alice in Wonderland*, as messengers, figures of Hermes.[108] Joe Dunn himself considered the origins of the name thirty years later. "I'd been reading Lewis Carroll. And I was also offered an audition in a play called *The White Rabbit*. And I started working for Western Greyhound Lines, and a greyhound chases a rabbit. But I don't know actually if Jack said it, or I said it."[109]

Robert Duncan remembered the day when he made the original drawing for the Press's colophon. "At a meeting with Jack and Joe, Jack was trying to persuade Joe Dunn to call the press 'White Rabbit' and Joe was reluctant—it was Joe's press; he was editor. Joe resisted, and remember it was Jack and Robin Blaser and Joe and Steve Jonas all in Boston who were together; and Joe published Steve's first book. But the decisions were made by Joe; he was editor. *Alice in Wonderland* was Jack's thing, not Joe's."[110]

The most valuable view may be Jack's own, given in a later poem, "Partington Ridge":

> A white rabbit absolutely outlined in whiteness upon
>   a black background
> A ghost
> The most
> We can say or think about it is it stays.

Not as a memory of something that happened or a symbol
     or anything
We loved or respected or was a part of history
Our history
It stays
In a closet we wear like a ring on our fingers
The rabbit
Ghost of them
Most of what we knew.

"They ran through the briers and they ran through the
bushes, and they ran through the brambles where the
rabbits wouldn't go."
     Rabbits don't know what they are.
     Ghosts are very similar. They are frightened and do not
know what they are, but they can go where the rabbits
cannot go. All the way to the heart.[111]

Frequently White Rabbit Press business was conducted during the Sunday afternoon meetings. Together the group assembled *After Lorca* from pages piled throughout the whole length of the apartment. One member with a carrying voice was assigned to read aloud from a long novel on Stalingrad, while others bent to the task. Signatures of smaller White Rabbit books were sewn at the apartment as well (although the ambitious *Lorca* was sent to a binder after the sheaves were assembled.)[112] After one meeting Joe Dunn was so energized he fired off a letter back to Blaser in Boston:

Jack Spicer read your poem Sunday together with Duncan & Everson. Just pure pleasure! All that terror to the reader was quite a shatter to Sunday. Spicer intimated that you call it a whatnot poem. . . . You must get pleasure from being so "outspoken" & Nijinsky & thank you for letting it out. Spicer is delighted no end, Duncan etc. & floored quite a few Sunday. I'm 3 acts, 3 books behind on *Faust Foutu*. I've got the *O'Ryan* poems of Olson on press now and one other book next; & I would love then to do the Robin Blaser book. I've already talked with Jack about this & would like to ask you about considering this format for any poems you'd judge. Or maybe like the whatnot poem I should get a hold of yr. work & ignore your no's? . . . But I won't move till I hear fr. you & get a hold on what Spicer has. I do hope we can do something in the W.R., Robin. Excuse the sketch-y, motel-y note and give my love to Steve. Until later—Joe.[113]

Dunn's exuberant letter illustrates the enthusiasm members felt for the writing they were hearing. Spicer noted in a letter to Blaser: "Joe Dunn seems to be falling to pieces. I haven't seen much of him since I know I can't help. North Beach has swallowed him (the drunk world, not the queer world) and nobody goes after Jonah into that whale. You'll disapprove I know, but we have different ideas about the responsibilities of love."[114]

But Joe was feeling confused and ashamed. His relations with Spicer remained warm, and close; in troubled times Jack was his anchor. Although the younger poets Joe was meeting were not uniformly or even often gay, the great triumvirate were—"and their poems were gay poems." Jack's love for him was no burden; it hardly even touched his consciousness. "No, I didn't feel that, because my friends in Boston—that's my touchstone, that's where I come from—like, John Wieners and Steve [Jonas] are gay; and these were my really good friends, since I was an 18-year-old, when I was discovering that poetry indeed goes beyond English 101." Spicer wrote to Blaser that Joe had been "rejected by the Army (as a Queer) and is beginning to resemble Mike McClure."[115] Jack would always love him, but he was "shocked, devastated" by Joe's increasing dependence on methedrine and liquor. Joe's addictive personality mirrored Jack's, perhaps intensifying Jack's revulsion as he watched his young friend's self-destruction. Even White Rabbit Press, a project that had brought them even closer, staggered on for only one more year, due to an increasing dependence on drugs.[116]

On one Sunday afternoon Gary Snyder read his then-new *Myths and Texts* at a meeting at George Stanley's apartment. "Jack Spicer sat on the table and Gary sat underneath the table, and read, Spicer sitting on top of him." Joanne laughed. "Jack decided Snyder's poetry was all right. The thing was that you would read your poems and Jack Spicer would tell you if they were all right or no."[117] At another meeting Snyder introduced Naim, a young Moslem from Lucknow with an M.A. in Urdu literature. Naim recited from Rumi's *Diwani Shamsi Tabriz*, which everyone found "stimulating." He also gave an example of the "same poem sung as a song, chanted as a poem, and recited in ordinary voice, to show three possible modes of delivery" and reported on the readings in India—"all night long with 5000 people listening and 4 or 5 poets trading off."[118]

The electricity of the Sunday meetings was heightened by unexpected alliances between poets of junior and senior orders. Duncan and Spicer had gingerly introduced their old Berkeley friend Landis Everson into the Sunday free-for-all. Everson's initial appearance, reading older poetry, had fallen flat. But in August 1958 he caught fire with the younger poets, especially with Ebbe Borregaard, who pronounced his new sequence of

"Resemblances" beautiful. Duncan was especially gratified, because he had celebrated Everson's beauty and wealth years before in *The Venice Poem*.[119]

George Stanley recalled that the Sunday meetings began with

a reading, followed by "ordered" criticism. I think we [the young poets] could expect what we considered more of a fair hearing from Duncan than from Spicer. Duncan was much more willing to allow the possibility of there being something there, and Spicer was much more willing to allow for the possibility of there being nothing there, just "shit!" Spicer was a harder judge, but Duncan and Spicer *were* the judges. After you read a poem, they spoke first; if they didn't have anything to say, even those who were talking again—myself, Ebbe, Harold, Joanne, and even maybe Joe Dunn and John Wieners—were a bit more attentive.

If people that Spicer didn't know came to the meetings, they were "*Chronicle* reporters." Among them were two bearded men who brought beer with them. When they attended Spicer got into "a mood so foul you might as well not be having a meeting," not because Spicer was displeased at not being recognized—but because he felt that "they were there fundamentally to exploit art."

The less inexperienced poets tended to imitate the senior poets' work.

We were all imitative. Joanne had written a poem in which she had unconsciously reproduced rhythms of Duncan's poetry, and Duncan said a significant thing: "If you want to consciously imitate my work, that's fine, but don't be so lax that you find yourself unconsciously lapsing into another person's voice." That could have been applied to any of us. It did make it kind of hard to write poetry if you were trying not to imitate at the same time Spicer, Creeley, Duncan, Olson. . . . This was not a *kaffeeklatsch*; this was not a meeting of people sitting around being courteous to each other. This was a meeting where your life was on the line. Your poem was on the line, and that was your life that week. And if you read your poem and Spicer said, "Oh shit!" or "You can get that published in . . ."—some magazine Spicer had contempt for—it wasn't really very nice.

There weren't any grudges. If Spicer thought your poem was shit, that didn't mean that he thought you were shit. I remember one time saying to Spicer that I hadn't written any poems for three weeks and I felt very bad, and he said, "Wait until it's three years."

"Rarely was there much disagreement," Stanley recalled. "Duncan didn't very often disagree with Spicer. It's just that Duncan was more willing to talk in a more generally literary sense about the poem, whereas Spicer rarely was interested in talking about that. Either Aquatic Park, or a bar, might be a place for the serious discussion of literature. The poetry meeting was definitely not a place for such a discussion. It was more like a bull ring."[120]

*

The Sunday meetings attracted a variegated group of men and women, but why were no more women writing than Joanne Kyger? The reason was partly financial, since the women who were likely to contribute were busy supporting their men. Dora Geissler recalled:

I didn't read anything at Joe Dunn's. I was Harold [Dull]'s woman. It was sort of like—There wasn't room for me to write, too. There were women in the group, but only Joanne did any writing. Nemi [Frost] went to the poetry meetings, too, but she wasn't a writer. It was the group that went. Joanne and Nemi and I were very good friends. We were so different we weren't competitive. Nor were we feminists. We all enjoyed the company of gay men, probably for similar reasons. For me, coming to San Francisco and meeting gay men was a wonderful experience, because I had just been through that season in my life where you're seen as a sex object, and in Seattle, I would try to talk to people and think they were interested in my mind, and they just wanted to get in my pants? That was always so disappointing to me, and then when I met gay men in San Francisco, and realized, "They're interested in my ideas," I was just overjoyed! I knew my gay friends enjoyed my company for me alone, not as someone to fuck. That was a very comfortable place for me to be then. Feminism really hadn't been invented then to any extent, and most women were uninteresting to me. They would talk about the house, and clothes, and I was never interested in makeup, clothes, the things that they talked about that didn't interest me. The world of ideas and poetry and politics that gay friends would talk to me about, why, that's where I felt at home.[121]

In mid-March 1958, after quitting his post as assistant director of the Poetry Center, Robert Duncan moved with Jess to Stinson Beach, a small town in Marin County just north of San Francisco. Thereafter he attended the Sunday meetings less frequently. Spicer continued in the senior role the two poets had hitherto played, but some felt a diminution in the quality of the meetings. "The most marvelous energy was when both Robert and Jack were there," Harold said. "It was a real difference when Robert wasn't there anymore; his absence was very noticeable. They'd talk to each other in their different styles; they'd criticize each other; but not always opposed forces in their purposes. Sometimes supportive. I don't remember sparks flying," Dull continued, adding that Duncan sometimes wrote during the sessions, which added to his legend. "I remember him working on the Pindar poem."[122] After Duncan's move, even Jack felt that the "Sunday afternoon era will pass now."[123] Yet the meetings had built a momentum, and a reputation, and they continued for years.

CHAPTER FIVE

Honey in the Groin

On September 30, 1957, Jack Spicer wrote to Don Allen, "I have some new poems, a rash, and a lover."[1] The lover was Russell FitzGerald, who had cruised Spicer during the *Howl* trial, where both were spectators.[2] By the time the trial ended on September 9, Jack was pretty much his. Russell FitzGerald was twenty-three; his skin was fair, his hair the shade of red the French call *feuilles mortes*. In some photographs he eerily resembles the young Spicer. Born in Bucks County and newly arrived from Philadelphia, he wanted to become a painter. In fact, he wanted everything—the consolations of Roman Catholicism (he was a recent convert), the depths of Beat bohemia, the experience of radical art, and love in all shapes and sizes. Like Spicer, FitzGerald was six feet tall, although Spicer hunched and stooped so habitually most people thought him a much smaller man. When they were together Russell seemed to tower over him.

Russell FitzGerald kept a diary, which serves as a major document of this period because of the scope and depth of its scrutiny. The diary reflects Russell's piquant mixture of intense idealism and dry cynicism. Want to intrigue an older man further? Mention a past romance—mention your only previous white boyfriend, a man you're fleeing from, one who yet haunts you still like the very Hound of Heaven: "September 29—spent 24 hours with Spicer. The morning talk didn't run down until 2 in the afternoon and then instead of going to hear Brother Antoninus I talked about Chuck and how I thought I was really feeling very guilty and was dishonest about the whole thing." Who knows how the affair would have played itself out, except that soon Russell fell in love himself, and with—of all things—a

Russell FitzGerald. "Why don't you paint and shut your mouth and I'll kiss it." *Courtesy Dora FitzGerald.*

Beatnik! Thus began a triangle that tormented both Russell and Jack for many months and informed the art of both men.

The unlikely object of Russell's attentions was the surrealist poet Bob Kaufman, who was a few months younger than Spicer. Kaufman was the son of a black, Catholic mother and a German Jewish father.[3] He carried his anarchist politics and taste for public bravado through the streets and bars, cafes and parks of North Beach. Eventually he published several books of his allusive, nightmarish poetry, among them *Solitudes Crowded with Loneliness* and *The Ancient Rain*. "Well, what's he like?" Russell asked. "He's negro. Been married, had a child, drinks too much. He does not work and does not want to. Can amuse even those who dislike his popularity. Alive as only negroes are. Spiteful to those he cons. Speaks with a peculiarly clear pronunciation—beautiful vowels. The voice and the skin: like milk chocolate. Bad teeth, stains. Growing a silly beard. Living in the same clothes for weeks; sleeping anywhere. Says he has to sleep with chicks to avoid sleeping with men." But what was in him, that Russell should love him so? "He has a fire about him that seems to come from a knowledge of life's ugliness and a passionate commitment to human dignity. Dignity that will pay any price to stay free. He stands and walks with such natural grace that even, slumping, he's beautiful. There is reason to believe that he's attracted."

By October Russell was "making goo goo eyes for hours" at this "hilarious and heartbreaking beautiful animal."[4] He envisioned a series of enormous pictures called "The Stations of the Cross," with Kaufman as the black Christ, and in the months that followed his desire continued to seesaw between Kaufman and Spicer. He'd hooked Spicer, and felt a very strong affection for him. But the sex they had wasn't as good as the sex he wanted to have with Bob Kaufman. Before long Russell's open, erotic pursuit of Kaufman became common knowledge, and even something of a scandal in the North Beach of 1957.

The meeting of Jack Spicer and Russell FitzGerald came shortly after Spicer had completed his breakthrough work, *After Lorca*. Russell felt the excitement: "October 19—nothing done. Last night I wanted to read 'Letters to Lorca,' the completed manuscript of which [Spicer] was carrying from bar to bar and repeating how happy he was and how beautiful they were. Was it only my shyness at asking or did I want to be asked to read them not out of too deep respect for a writer's privacy, but out of mere self-centered distraction?" Next day Russell bumped into Jack on the way to North Beach and the two turned into a bar, the Anxious Asp.[5] Jack talked dejectedly about his former love, "Mac" (the artist Graham Mackintosh), while Russell waxed eloquent on Kaufman. And then Russell finally got to read some of the *After Lorca* manuscript. Its honesty and "guts" overwhelmed him; still he couldn't stop wondering, "How have I come to admire guts?" The beauty of the work haunted him, showing up his own "small meanness" and the paltriness of anything he might achieve with his painting. Truth and art, love and death, all were forced upon his mind; he wanted to cry "as though I had suddenly lost something and turned around to find it not only gone but utterly unwanted." Twice he wrote, "Jack Spicer, I hate you."

At the same time Russell's passion for Bob Kaufman was growing, in one horrible pleading scene after another. No matter how frenziedly he threw himself into making art, he couldn't stop thinking about Kaufman. Painting the "Stations of the Cross," he would "wake up in the middle of a brushstroke saying his name, pressing my lips behind his ear"—in fantasy, of course, since Bob remained teasingly out of reach.[6] How, Russell asked himself, could he rescue himself from this flood of torment? Or should he abandon himself to his fate? "It's foolish," Jack advised, "to play checkers when everyone else is playing chess." *But he'd always been a fool.* He was twenty-three. "Especially when you're perfectly capable of playing chess as well as the others." *Yes,* Russell thought. *And my sneaky checker game wrecks the game for everyone else.* He had reached the state of self-loathing. *Is it possible to play the game and still not hurt people? No.*

The alternative? Worse.

Jack was spoiling for a fight. When Russell refused to quarrel, Jack "flipped" or pretended to. On Halloween, just for fun, Russell showed up at The Place in full drag and Jack was furious—"not only furious, but embarrassed, personally embarrassed," reported a witness, "and then ever more angry because of his embarrassment."[7] Jack's moods were as erratic as Russell's own, and he could be highly irrational—he accused Russell of painting the picture "Some Funny Valentine" as a curse on him. In some ways they were evenly enough matched. "November 25—'What wouldn't I give for a good chess game right now?' said Jack, and I said, 'What wouldn't I give for some pink paper airplanes right now?' Then we both agreed; [we would give up] everything except art."

Jack proposed that they live together, but Russell demurred, feeling that it wouldn't be fair to Jack. He avoided the Sunday afternoon poetry meetings, where Jack was reading aloud from his new, ongoing project *Admonitions.* "Non-plussed" by the language and customs of North Beach, especially its erotic and possessive storms, Russell thought about returning to Philadelphia. As autumn trailed into winter, the situation grew more uncomfortable. Spicer would be eating lunch with Russell, engaging him on the high questions of art and love they both enjoyed discussing, and then Bob would walk by the restaurant. Russell would spy him passing the window and feel a "rabbit punch in the stomach." *Horrible to find that a response so violent should have become automatic.* And Russell would look at Jack and see the hurt in his eyes. His obsession was destroying them both. He must get out of town before something terrible happened. "December 14—the bus ticket is purchased and my suitcase and portfolio are ready at the terminal. It—something—is over. I'll never be twenty-four in North Beach again, I'll never be stupid about the same things. I love Jack. We have had a good time. I love Bob. We have had no time at all." Russell left for New York. "If—*if*—you come back," Jack told him, without much hope, "we will play bridge." But pragmatically Jack expected that he would lose Russell to the excitements of the East Coast.

Always careful with money, Jack wrote to Robin Blaser in Boston begging him to sell more copies of *After Lorca*, claiming to be living upon their sale. He sent a long list of people to whom he'd sent complimentary copies. The list was composed entirely of diminutives and nicknames—a form of superstitious magic, as though curtailing the names of the great would bring them down to size, thus: "Bob Creeley/Bob Lowell/Wynnie Auden/Bill Williams/Chuckles Olson" and so on down to "Laurie Riding/Hildy Doolittle/Edie Sitwell/Bubbles Cocteau/Tom Eliot/Sal Dali/Alice Ginsberg/Clytemnestra Jeffers," the great artists renamed as strippers, or gangsters.[8]

Drained of his savings by Russell's profligacy, Spicer returned to the University of California to work part-time in the linguistics department under the direction of his former mentor, David Reed. After that, until eighteen months before his death, Spicer's place of employment was in Berkeley at the University, while most of his evenings he spent in San Francisco. Though he also took charge of seminars for Reed as well as helping in other departments, Spicer's job was primarily to help Reed research a Pacific States atlas of American dialects.[9] "He used various forms that asked questions about language," recalled a fellow poet. "He used to ask people, 'What do *you* say: a "couch," a "sofa," a "Chesterfield," a "divan"?'"[10]

Spicer wrote "For Kids" late at night in Joanne Kyger's apartment on Columbus ("above LaRocca's"), after an evening at The Place, using Kyger's scratchy-nibbed fountain pen, dripping ink.

> Boom, boom, boom
> Under
> No moon.
> Henry Clay,
> Who
> Will
> Scream like a gong?

The holograph looks markedly different than Spicer's other manuscripts, which were written in pencil, in a childish, round hand. The poem belongs to the series of short, often cryptic poems ("For Joe," "For Russ," etc.) that make up the volume published as *Admonitions*. John Wieners had given Kyger the nickname "Kids" (sometimes "Miss Kids") after her habit of bursting into a bar or party and exclaiming, "Kids, I got an idea!" or "Kids! Let's go out!" This poem, "obscure late-night writing," in Kyger's words, reverberated in her consciousness for over thirty years, though "where he got the 'Henry Clay' from I'll never know."[11] By now Jack's composition of a poem had become a fixed practice: the length of his poems was determined by the dimensions of the blank piece of paper on which he wrote, a nearly-square, lined page from a school notebook.

At one of the Sunday meetings Duncan wondered out loud whether Spicer's new *Admonitions* wasn't in fact a retread, a "tendency to formulation," of *After Lorca* of the summer before. "There is a static rhetorical position in the imperative mode," he wrote worriedly to Robin Blaser. And the younger poets, he added—Stanley, Borregaard, Dunn, "Harold Doll"—all seemed to be copying Jack's most hieratic characteristics. Duncan's own "musical development" had fewer followers.[12] But Spicer pressed on with it. Through Myrsam Wixman, he met a young student of Russian history and language at Berkeley named Bob Judson. The son of a ranchman in Riverside (southern California), Judson was tall, slender, wiry, sharp-nosed, blue-eyed, with a noticeably cute backside and a charming inability to hold his liquor. He had the glamor and down-home charm of a TV cowboy. Endearing also was his nickname, "Toughy," and the pleasure of correcting his belief that, since he was studying it at Cal, he knew all about the Bolshevik Revolution.[13] For him Spicer wrote:

> I could not invent a better skeleton
> That you could
> Like a pumpkin on wet Halloween
> Flicker into.[14]

In late January 1958, the poet Denise Levertov, making her first trip to California, came to San Francisco with her husband, the novelist Mitchell Goodman. She was the guest of the Poetry Center for a reading arranged by Robert Duncan. As with Olson's visit the previous year, Duncan had found it necessary to finance Levertov's appearance through private subscription, since the Poetry Center could offer her only $25. A wide variety of San Francisco poets subscribed to help pay her fees—Joe Dunn, for example, gave $5, Ferlinghetti $4, Broughton $2, George Stanley $6, Ruth Witt-Diamant a confidential subscription of $5, and so on until $150 was raised in total.[15]

White Rabbit Press, under Joe Dunn, had produced a book of Lever-tov's, *Five Poems*, and was about to publish Helen Adam's book *Queen O' Crow Castle*. A party was held in Mill Valley, north of San Francisco in Marin County, to honor the two women poets. "The Mill Valley party was arranged by me," recalled James Broughton, "to welcome Denise Levertov who had just arrived from Mexico. I had known her there and this was my gesture to introduce her to the local poets."[16] Jack Spicer, who admired Levertov's writing, was one of a number of poets asked to read at the soiree in her honor. He, who often used misogyny as part of a Surrealist-derived shock technique, bombarded the audience with a poem from his own current project, "For Joe," from *Admonitions*.

> People who don't like the smell of faggot vomit
> Will never understand why men don't like women
> Won't see why those never to be forgotten thighs
> Of Helen (say) will move us into screams of laughter.
> Parody (what we don't want) is the whole thing.
> Don't deliver us any mail today, mailman.
> Send us no letters. The female genital organ is
>   hideous. We
> Do not want to be moved.
> Forgive us. Give us
> A single example of the fact that nature is imperfect.
> Men ought to love men
> (And do)
> As the man said
> It's
> Rosemary for remembrance.[17]

Jack tore into the poem with "extraordinary venom," Duncan recalled. All present felt implicated in Spicer's misogyny—Helen Adam dreamed about the occurrence and told Duncan her dream. She was working as a bike messenger, knocking on office doors, delivering messages. Each door opened and Helen produced an envelope, handing it over and saying, "I'm sorry, but I'm a woman."[18]

This is a poem capable of endless interpretation. Michael Davidson, for example, reads it as a demonstration of "absurd logic," in which Spicer "parodies and entertains at the same time":

However hostile to women, Spicer's poem is hardly a celebration of homosexuality. His misogyny is linked to a profound sexual ambivalence, expressed in its most violent form in the poem's opening lines. Nor does the poem address heterosexuality in ways that might moderate or qualify his attitude about women. Rather, he offers the most extreme version of sexual preference: either "faggot vomit" or the "hideous" vagina. Spicer implies that acknowledging one's homosexuality involves adopting several corollary attitudes about women as well as about fellow gays.

Davidson also sees the poem in its specific historical context, as a test of "group loyalty against a outsider."[19] It is also a manifesto on the future of the community, as well as a query into the transmission of communication. "Don't deliver us any mail today, mailman. / Send us no letters" is a particularly apt admonition in a poem "For Joe" Dunn, since Joe had been a mailman in his Boston days. Indeed, much of his poetry from this period—like Spicer's own—draws power from themes of dead letters, misfired communications, and mystic and mundane correspondences. The poem also implicates "Joe" as a homosexual—an extreme example of wishful thinking on Jack's part. In the introductory letter to *Admonitions*, Spicer tells Joe that "the poem I wrote *for* you gives the most distorted reflection in the whole promenade. Mirror makers know the secret—one does not make a mirror to resemble a person, one brings a person to the mirror."[20]

Perhaps the key line in the poem is "Parody (what we don't want) is the whole thing." Davidson has pointed out that "For Joe" seems to be some kind of message to Robert Duncan, who helped organize the Mill Valley reception for Levertov and Adam. It interrogates Duncan's recent poetic practice, at least the part that stemmed from his involvement in "The Maidens." It's possible, then, to read "For Joe" as a defense of Helen Adam, an objection to Duncan's exploitation of her as a woman, of using her as a "fag hag"—pretending to like her, but exploiting her womanhood as some kind of disguise one can slip into and out of for art's sake. Spicer brings the mirror up close to Duncan's determined assumption of ultra-high camp, drag personae, and the sexual ambivalence underlying the "Maidens" project. Who are the men who "don't like women," who find the "female sexual organ hideous"? Parody à la "The Maidens" is "what we don't want." "We do not want to be moved" into "screams of laughter," which was the basis for the Maidens' foray into gender confusion.

Several years passed before Levertov countered Spicer's misogyny with a poem of her own, "Hypocrite Women," published in *O Taste and See*. The relevant lines are: "And if at Mill Valley perched in the trees / the sweet rain drifting through western air / a white sweating bull of a poet told us // our cunts are ugly—why didn't we / admit we thought so too? (And / what shame? They are not for the eye!)."[21] In 1964 Spicer closed the circle when he quoted from "Hypocrite Women" in a poem from *Language*: "Sable

Some of the Maidens: Jess, Madeline Gleason, Robert Duncan, Robin Blaser, James Broughton. This photo probably dates from Blaser's flying vacation to San Francisco from Boston in the summer of 1957, when he was named an honorary "Maiden." *Photo by Helen Adam.*

arrested a fine comb. / It is not for the ears. Hearing / Merely prevents progress. Take a step back and view the sentence."[22]

Denise Levertov explained her part in the affair:

Actually that party in Mill Valley was the only time I met Jack Spicer, as far as I recall.

I have read things by him that I thought were good, but my personal impression of him was that incorporated in my poem, "Hypocrite Women." I thought it was extraordinarily ill-mannered of him to recite an anti-woman poem at a party where Helen Adam and I, two women, were the guests of honor—& I have never revised this opinion.

So for my poem, what I meant was that women (at that pre-Feminist, or at least pre-late-20th-century-Feminist period) might also think that genitalia were not pretty, visually—but their *function* was not visual anyway, so why should they be. I said "hypocrite" because the thought was one not commonly admitted. I later came to see how much of women's self-deprecation came from macho male attitudes. That occasion was also my first exposure to homosexual males as a group—I had, & have continued to have, individual homosexual friends but I find homosexual males & lesbians uncongenial in groups, when they reinforce each other's sexism towards heterosexuals.[23]

126

Years later, Spicer praised both Levertov and Adam in his Vancouver Lectures.[24] According to James Broughton, Spicer's behavior in Mill Valley reflected "his contempt for me and my friends, and his disgust for Duncan's devotion to me and to [Madeline] Gleason. Spicer did of course his utmost to insult everyone, not only the ladies, but coruscating me for not serving better liquor and refreshments. Jack was always the insulting devil's advocate, unfriendly with truth. Ultimately I avoided contact with him to avoid the daggers of his tongue."[25]

Early in 1958 White Rabbit Press published George Stanley's *The Love Root* and Ebbe Borregaard's *The Wapitis*, and the two poets were scheduled to read together at the Poetry Center. Jack agreed to write a set of program notes for Stanley's reading, and Robert Duncan consented to perform a similar service for Borregaard. Jack cast his essay in the form of a letter, like the essays on poetics concealed as letters to and from Lorca in *After Lorca:*

GEORGE STANLEY by JACK SPICER

Dear George,

I'm afraid I won't be able to write your program notes for you. In the process of trying to write them I have discovered how much I dislike program notes. You may, however, publish this letter of apology.

I can think of nothing to say about your poetry that would be of interest to you or your audience. What you will be reading to them is the result of only a year of effort—a year in which you discovered that wit could be combined with pathos, that a short poem can suggest the event it celebrates, and that you have a fine voice. This is, although I don't expect you to believe me, a great deal to discover in one year.

It would perhaps be unfair of me to suggest to you, who have beaten me so often at Scrabble, that you have too many words, or, as one who has listened with delight to you subvert a conversation, that you are too quick to hit the nail on the head. These are, for the moment, amiable vices and ones which, if they are pushed far enough, can themselves become style. Nor can I, with any degree of honesty, object to the fact that the subject matter of all your poems is erotic. You were interested in the erotic this year.

As for hinting that there are other houses of poetry that you might enter, you know about them as well as I do. You will enter some of them and burn down others. There will be, I leave this to you as both a threat and a promise, other years.

> Love,
> Jack[26]

This mixture of intimacy and "threat" would continue to characterize Spicer's mature writing on the nature of poetry.

*

It was at this time that Spicer first met Robert Creeley, from whom he'd borrowed the title to his book *After Lorca*. A letter from Duncan to Robin Blaser told a happy tale of Spicer's first exposure to Creeley:

Robert Creeley and his new wife and child spent the first part of the week with us; left this morning. After (last night) a triumphant reading. Only Denny [Denise Levertov]'s and Charles [Olson]'s equal that beauty. And Jack was completely won, shaking as he does with the recognition. He would exceed us, you and me, now if he could in affirming Creeley's place in our constellation. Jack hadn't, as we both knew, and tried to argue, read the work at all. And was the more nakedly exposed to the reality. Hadn't he been prepared too by his own achievement in *After Lorca*? It was reciprocal; Creeley had liked *After Lorca* and meeting him was fascinated by Spicer.[27]

Although the meeting was brief, it made a strong impression. "Creeley is interested in your work," Robert wrote, a day later, from Stinson Beach, Gregorian chants playing on his phonograph. "W[ou]ld you write to him now that you've heard his reading and changed your opinion to a conviction?" Robert hoped that Jack would now play a role in *The Black Mountain Review*, under Creeley's editorship. The *Review* was the "only field edited by an intelligence that's solid." Jack should send everything to Creeley—he, Duncan, did. Send the *Admonitions*. Creeley was a wonderful editor, insisted Duncan, both for what he used in the *Review* and for what he didn't.[28]

From April through August 1956, Creeley had lived in San Francisco and become involved not only with the Beat writers, but with Kenneth Rexroth and his third wife, Marthe Larsen. Creeley and Larsen became romantically involved and attempted an elopement that was foreshortened by Rexroth's wrath. Spicer had been living in Boston at the time and had sympathized vicariously with the young lovers. He subsequently used the triangle in various configurations within his writing, eventually culminating in the drama of *The Holy Grail*. But in the spring of 1958, alone in his Leavenworth Street apartment, he incorporated them in "The Tower of Babel," a detective story, the classic genre form of guilt and absolution.[29]

Like many intellectuals, Spicer found his enjoyment of mystery and detective stories a guilty pleasure, but he loved the genre, particularly the hard-boiled novels of Dashiell Hammett and Raymond Chandler (both still writing in 1958, although Hammett had long since ceased to publish). "There was a bookstore on the corner at the north side of campus [UC Berkeley] where they had a detective story collection. They kept track of those that you'd read—you got to mark your initials—and Spicer would just read one after another," said Blaser. Other Berkeley students have indicated that Spicer met "1/2 of Ellery Queen" at a literary soiree in the late 1940s.[30] ("Ellery Queen" was the pseudonym of two cousins, Frederic Dannay and Manfred B. Lee, who wrote a successful series of detective novels from 1929 through the early 1970s.) When other poets scoffed at Spicer's interest in the detective genre, Spicer replied, "Well, William Butler Yeats, that's the way he relaxed."[31] Even at the end of his life, when he tired of almost everything, he was still reading detective stories. Another fan of the genre was the poet W. H. Auden, whom Spicer had met in October 1954 at the home of Ruth Witt-Diamant.[32] Spicer has the antihero of his detective story, the poet J. J. Ralston, give his name in chapter 1 as "W. H. Auden," perhaps as a tip of the hat to Auden's famous defense of the detective story, "The Guilty Vicarage," in which Auden argued the fictional sleuth is really the priest of the twentieth century, restoring order out of chaos.

Prose fiction was not a new genre for Spicer. He had published a minimalist story, "The Scrollwork in the Casket," in a student magazine. On the eve of his trip east he had written enthusiastically about his plans to the poet Jonathan Williams: "I'm full of short stories and poems waiting to be written (including a series of Runyonesque stories written in head language about the gay-head scene in S.F.[33] He had advised Charles Olson to read *After Lorca* as though it were a novel, and in a later letter he recommended Joe Dunn's *Better Dream House*—a "lovely screwy kind of Dada novel."[34] Apparently the possibilities offered by the novel were still fresh in his mind. Perhaps, too, he was inspired by *Queer Catholic*, the *roman à clef* Russell FitzGerald was attempting in New York, in which he was to figure as one of the chief characters.

In spite of his well-known reluctance to sully his work in the marketplace, Spicer felt no qualms about trying to obtain remuneration for this novel. This was going to be his meal-ticket. In fact, Spicer was becoming willing in general to "cash in" on the widespread public interest in the San Francisco Renaissance, as Duncan suggested in a letter to Blaser:

The utter corruption of the scene now is "career," is the lurking opportunity. It would seem fantastic to the Grove Press editors who must in a sense feel they are taking a flyer (with Ginsberg the one sure fine *thing*) if they saw what a SUCCESS this anthology ["The San Francisco Scene," *Evergreen Review* no. 2] seems to poor Spicer and to Rexroth. It's a bandwagon of every interest but the creative. Thus Jack is full of plans to capitalize on the success of poetry, i.e the LIFE magazine article, the

Grove Press thing, and the issue of MEASURE, but he is "unable" to write poems. Performance, entertainment, effect are paramount. And process, source, necessity unimportant.[35]

Once he had achieved the poetry of *After Lorca*, Spicer felt even fewer inhibitions about "capitalizing" on the perceived "success of poetry."

The novel proceeded apace. His friend, Grove Press editor Don Allen, was let in on it from its early stages. Said Allen of this work: "The novel seems to have been a project [Jack] started on in early 1958. By late spring he seems to have sent me two chapters, which I delivered to a literary agent. By July Jack wanted the chapters returned to him so that he could revise them before [Robert] Duncan typed the whole MS. As late as January of 1959 I wrote asking about the novel but learned nothing more. And I don't recall much about the novel, except that it was supposed to be a mystery and that Rexroth was caricatured in it."[36] Kenneth Rexroth is indeed caricatured in the novel, as the pompous windbag Arthur Slingbot, but his relationships interested Spicer beyond caricature. The heroine, Madelaine Cross, was based on Spicer's idea of Marthe Larsen, Rexroth's long-suffering wife. Marthe's/Madelaine's embrace both of the Rexroth and the Creeley figures symbolized a balance between traditional Berkeley values and the new iconoclasm of the Beat movement; both Spicer and his alter ego Ralston craved this balance, which they could not achieve.

In the novel, an "academic poet," Jim Ralston, has returned to San Francisco after ten years of exile in Boston. His marriage is collapsing, and his writing has gone flat. Once an active member of the Berkeley Renaissance, he has been lured back by sensational media accounts of the San Francisco scene, in the hope of recharging his batteries. Shaken and vulnerable, Ralston exhibits "the frightened running of a child that had been given a bloody nose by an angel or a quarterback," as he gingerly attempts to renew old ties with his Berkeley past. He is invited to a dinner party by Madelaine Cross, once the muse of the Berkeley Renaissance, now the wife of San Francisco's loudest poetry shaman, Arthur Slingbot, whose erudition, enthusiasm, "radical chic," and talent are as infuriating as they are admirable.

Set into an essentially comic story is an account of the long, unsettling after-dinner entertainment of Mr. Hashiwara, a Zen monk: an intricate parable of guilt, redemption, suffering, castration, incest, rape, murder, "rage and anger." "I have a sick tiger inside me," says a merchant in the tale, and so did Jack Spicer. The San Francisco poetry renaissance stirred up complex feelings in him. In the wake of the *Howl* trial, San Francisco was giddy with excitement and ambition. "You don't know how thrilling it is," Madelaine says. "It's like having a party in the middle of an anthology." Spicer was wearily ambivalent, however. In employing the metaphor of the tower of Babel to describe what was transpiring, he explicitly excluded phallicity ("there was nothing sexual about his dream") so that nothing remained but language and will—and, of course, phallicity. Ralston's return to the Bay Area, and his search for "a new kind of poetry," amount to an unavailing quest in search of an unreal Grail. Only his erotic involvement with Madelaine and his tentative exchange of powers with Rue Talcott bring palpable pleasure, and these relationships have more pricks than kicks.

More than most writers, Spicer was painfully aware that people are symbols, constructions of a hundred more or less interlocking nets of desire, language, convention, and use. While Madelaine is a wife, muse, mother, hostess, girlfriend, heroine, and "prose writer," she also becomes a symbol of an enviable freedom from all these roles when surprisingly, later in the novel, she takes centerstage and assumes a vivid role of her own in the detective "plot." Spicer came to see the Kenneth Rexroth/Marthe Larsen/Robert Creeley triangle as a modern version of the Arthur/Gwenivere/Lancelot story in the Camelot legend, which reflected his own feeling of expulsion from a lost Berkeley paradise. Madelaine's rueful, jaded monologues are sketches for those of Gwenivere in the fourth book of Spicer's later *The Holy Grail.*

Spicer based the character of Washington Jones, a black bohemian arrested and jailed by racist police for a crime he may not have committed, on his impressions of Steve Jonas and Bob Kaufman. As Washington Jones lies languishing in jail, natty, brilliant, inured to police state racism, Jonas has become similarly enmeshed in a tragicomic, nightmarish trial of his own in Boston, leading to a conviction for mail fraud, and Kaufman was well on his way to becoming, as he sometimes claimed, the "most arrested" man in San Francisco.

Just as Russell FitzGerald attempted to fictionalize his relation to Spicer in his novel *Queer Catholic,* Spicer used the detective novel to recreate his first vision of FitzGerald. Ralston goes to a North Beach bar called The Birdcage, where he meets a number of young Beat writers and painters, including the sullen, mercurial Rue Talcott. Rue insults Ralston's poetry and then presents him with a poem of his own, lodged in the mouth of a live fish. The hallucinatory, cubist precision of detail underlines the beatific vision:

First came the hands (as memory Picasso-like tried to reproduce in flat space the movement of his impression), this enormous hands, and then the beer glass that the hands were carrying, a different, larger beer glass than those used at The Birdcage (logic told him that it must have been the beer glass that located his attention to the hands—but no, the hands came first). Framed behind the hands and the beer glass, subsidiary for the moment, was the rest of the body, elongated and gangling, a face in which he saw mainly curves and thinness—and youth, of course, he must be only eighteen or nineteen but that came behind the rest of it in the picture, a corduroy jacket, huge faded khaki pants that came not quite to his ankles and yet (he had no belt) were two sizes too large for him at the waist. He was looking at Ralston too, curiously, as if he were surprised that he too was making a permanent recording of his impressions. There was no element of sexual attraction, Ralston thought, in this exchange of, what was it, recognitions, not even of the unidentified erotic which can pass, unexpected and meaningless, between any two creatures like a bolt of heat lightning in the summer sky. It was merely—no, Ralston did not understand it then and remembering it later he still did not, would not, understand it.[37]

Rue's entrance is underscored, almost like a film, by an "alto sax . . . doing a solo about cowboy movies."

The novel begins with ease and fluency, and continues with great flair through 167 pages. Eventually, however, "the poetry simply drew him away from the prose length. Jack cooked up the notion that he would do a detective story," Blaser reported. "It would give him a kind of ground. And it would both protect the poetry—leave it free—and then he could have this wonderful time with something he loved anyway, the detective story. So he worked at it, and of course as you read it, it really is a part of his work, and as splendid as that is, it would have had the same difficulty for a wide audience as his poetry had at that time." In fact the novel became a kind of spiritual memoir for Spicer, in which he faced up to the hurricane of Beat energy that swept San Francisco and left the Berkeley intellectuals envious, inspired, and secretly horny. Blaser speculated: "I think the detective story would have become as complex finally—for all the original plan of its being a kind of scam—it would have become as complicated as the 'Textbook of Poetry.'"[38]

Although Russell and Jack were apart, their relationship continued. Russell paid a duty call on his mother in Denver, and Jack sent him a handwritten copy of his "Imaginary Elegies" there as a kind of wistful Christmas present. He remembered Jack's "delightful mask of satire and merciless needling, covering kindness." By January 1958, Jack had sent Russell a sheaf of letters, inscribed with love, and a copy of *After Lorca*. When Russell opened the book in Philadelphia he was swamped with a complex longing. One of the poems in *After Lorca* is directly informed by Russell's place of residence: in "Buster Keaton's Ride," where one of the characters talks about the "lights in Philadelphia." Russell's emotions while reading this plea can only be imagined. Whether he wanted to be or not, he was homesick for San Francisco, and for the man he considered its greatest writer—"The towers lighted in the fog-threatened night. The wet grass in Aquatic Park and Irish coffee, and other things . . . O Jack, dear friend and lover."[39]

In his diary he held imaginary conversations with Jack, and hurled into them all the things he wished he had been able to say in person. *I think*, he told Jack on March 1, *you are confused about your feelings for me by the presence in them of sex. It was only, as you say, irrelevant. The excellences which we esteemed in each other were only called to our attention by this element which, tastelessly attached, as it is, to social and age relationships, should have concerned us not at all.* He was so young and Jack was so old! Imagine writing a book called *Admonitions*, didn't that reveal an avuncular frame of mind? Russell read the poem called "For Russ":

> For Russ
>
> Christ,
> You'd think it would all be
> Pretty simple.
> This tree will never grow. This bush
> Has no branches. No
> I love you. Yet.
> I wonder how our mouths will look in twenty five years
> When we say yet.[40]

He reached for his diary to answer the questions he saw in the poem. "There are no branches, because the seed and fruit are all passed by as useless forms to friendship which is received whole or not at all and which may change but can not grow." In the diary he expressed his qualms about the relationship, in which sexual matters complicated a friendship he would prefer to conduct free of sex. The following day, March 2, brought another upsetting letter from Jack, the "Beloved Pedagogue." Jack was troubled. So was Russell. "I have to play flagellante with Jack too? Can't any of these things be what they can—static—instead of wrecking themselves by straining to move?"

None of Russell's letters to Jack have survived, but at least one of Jack's from this period has been preserved. In it he alluded to his poem "For Russ,"—the "yet or not yet" allusion—while making what was for him an astonishingly explicit promise.

Dear Russ,

Is it love (yet or not yet) love you want or something for the scrapbook? I mean scrapbook in the ultimate sense?

When I first read the letter I imagined a whole new sentence—"I don't mean a new paediea."

Eating cotton fills your mouth with cotton.

I think we were like planets that passed closer to each other than any astronomer could imagine once in an intergalactic year and now occasionally touch (relatively) in outer orbits. I am afraid of you.

Fill your mouth with cotton and I will fill mine with words.

Why don't you paint and shut your mouth and I'll kiss it.

Jack[41]

Later Russell was to describe Jack's appeals of early 1958 as "magician's letters" that beckoned "like a road back west."[42]

By March 26, Russell was reading Kerouac's new novel *The Subterraneans* and had begun a novel of his own, which he called at various times *Wanderland* and *Queer Catholic*, envisioning it as a blend of Kerouac's hot bohemianism and the cool, "merciless" prose surface Mary McCarthy was using in *The Groves of Academe* and *The Company She Keeps*.[43] But he didn't get very far. The novel kept dissolving into masturbatory fantasies of Kaufman:

O the gentleness of the first caresses my lips would trace up the spine of your burning cock, the coolness of my tongue around its bursting head. I want to watch your stomach tremble while my teeth just touch the head's flaring edges; then feel your ankles lock across my spine and your cold fingers explore my ears while my tongue strangles a gag and the doors of my throat spout saliva. I want to feel your nails rake my back, your teeth pull my hair, while my tongue streams juices down the tiny sluices of your clenched balls and covers the nap of your wiry hair with sticky dew. . . . My heart hears yours change gait while my kisses unlock your ass, stuffed with laughter and crying joy.[44]

In April Russell returned to San Francisco. Abandoning his reservations of the fall, he moved into the Leavenworth Street apartment with Jack, the two of them sharing an old-fashioned Murphy bed that, when not in use, swung back into the wall and was concealed, poetically, by a full-size mirror. This honeymoon period was fruitful for Spicer's poetry and for Russell's painting, as the work of the two men interacted in a way that might almost be called collaboration. For example, Spicer began planning a book on Tarot, while Russell designed a Tarot deck, later to be reproduced in a printed edition of one hundred copies. (The book on Tarot was never finished, but a tantalizing outline remains.)[45]

Russell viewed himself as a sinner, a criminal, a torturer, and a killer. "I have sucked over fifty different cocks since last Easter," he confessed. "And left forty obligations unfulfilled, rather than vomit at Mass. I have tortured what I hated in myself in my friends until their collapses revealed it. I have practiced a ritual ingratitude toward every thing I love."[46] Russell's diary recorded details of his practical indebtedness to Spicer. "June 10—Still no job, Jack's money still steadily receiving . . . just walking on hot pavements." "June 11—I owe Jack $200 at the end of the week. He must have foreseen this when he issued his invitation" to return to San Francisco. "'Free enterprise' he called us." Such largesse was worth the strain of having his own emotional ups and downs mirrored in Jack's: "Jack echoes my depression like an amplifying cave, hours after I'm OK." Spicer's feelings for Russell were more complex. With him in mind he composed *Billy The Kid*, an experiment in extending the lyric modes of *Lorca* and *Admonitions* to include a disjunctive narrative of the Old West.

> Billy The Kid
> I love you
> Billy The Kid
> I back anything you say
> And there was the desert
> And the mouth of the river
> Billy The Kid
> (In spite of your death notices)
> There is honey in the groin
> Billy[47]

Arthur Penn's *The Left-Handed Gun*, written by Gore Vidal and starring Paul Newman, was a Spicer favorite at the time and may have been the immediate occasion for his homoerotic and tensely romantic treatment of the famous youthful killer.[48] Jack continued to attend the Sunday meetings at Joe Dunn's and tested *Billy The Kid* there as he had read *After Lorca* the winter before.[49]

Throughout the spring of 1958 while Spicer was writing *Billy The Kid*, FitzGerald began a parallel project. "June 14—Jack wrote a mixture of prose and poetry about Billy the Kid today while I started my first Billy. Why shouldn't I love Billy?" A marriage of tensions existed between the works and within the friendship. As FitzGerald noted in his diary:

June 19—I say Vermeer is responsible for making his unknown light appear and Jack says that the light wanted to be seen and Vermeer was smart enough to recognize it when it first haltingly appeared on his canvas and [to] allow it.

June 27—Jack's body looks small; stretched out on the couch, face turned away. His little belly goes up and down beneath his belt. Someday that will stop. Someday all that warmth and those shaky hands will turn off like a light bulb. In some satin-cushioned box that motionless body will break open beneath its clothing. A damp mud fall from those bones. Those bones become finally dust themselves.[50]

Spicer went to the hospital for an embarrassing operation—removal of anal warts. In a macabre, joking mood, Russell asked Jack what he wanted him to place on his grave, and Jack told him: green onions. And Russell promised that, wherever he was, he'd come back and put green onions on Jack's grave.

At this time, Duncan and Jess were entertaining the poet Louis Zukofsky, his wife Celia, and their son Paul (touted as child prodigy as a violinist) at Stinson Beach. Zukofsky was in town as an eleventh-hour replacement for the ailing, depressed Theodore Roethke at San Francisco State, teaching a summer workshop set up by the Poetry Center. Several of the central fig-ures of the Spicer group attended Zukofsky's workshop—Kyger, Borre-gaard, and Stanley among them.

Duncan had invited Zukofsky and his family to spend every weekend with him, but plans had to be changed, since Paul was carsick during the ride to and from Stinson Beach, and Celia and Louis Zukofsky had their feet pressed against the floorboards the entire ride—Stinson's scenic curves and heights and hairpin turns scared them out of their wits.[51] Sev-eral attempts on Duncan's part to get Zukofsky and family together with Spicer led to the latter's mournful poem "Conspiracy" (in *A Book of Music*): "A violin which is following me / / In how many distant cities are they lis-tening / To its slack-jawed music? This / Slack-jawed music? / Each of the thousand people playing it. / It follows me like someone that hates me."[52] Spicer recommended to Russell FitzGerald Zukofsky's poem (in *Some Time*) on William Carlos Williams as the best work done on his favorite poet. Zukofsky's portrait of Williams as "Billy / The kid," who "shoots / to / kill," undoubtedly found its way into Spicer's handling of the same sub-ject.[53] In later years, Spicer was to exhibit a deep familiarity with Zukofsky's poetry.

*

The "honeymoon" period inspired Jack to a level of productivity he had never before experienced. By summer's end, he had finished *A Book of Music*—a "ravishing performance" that forced Duncan to acknowledge that Spicer was not limited to the epistolary/"imperative" mode of *After Lorca* and *Admonitions*.[54] The long drought was over. *Billy The Kid*, the detective novel, and the Tarot scheme all continued while Russell painted and sketched in the next room. One evening Jack brought Russell over to south Berkeley to meet the members of his bridge group; Russell drew quick sketches of all present.[55] Russell and Jack had dinner at Joanne Kyger's house—Russell showing his drawings, Spicer reading from his work and drinking a gallon of wine, and teasing her about her passion for Gary Snyder: "When you're tired of him, Joanne, may I have him?"[56] It was an idyllic time for Spicer. Jim Herndon remembered Spicer and Russell walking over to visit on the afternoon of the Fourth of July.

On the 4th of July, you don't go see *Waiting for Godot*, you go to the fireworks! Russell brought a little pot. I don't think Fran ever smoked any—but [Jack] smoked a little of it. Not Jack's scene at all, but he was doing it, and we rode down to the Marina in the car. [This was] one of the few times I ever saw Jack actually what you would call normal, ordinary, chemical "happy." I drove down with Jay [one of two sons], who was about two or three, and Jack was being Jay's "uncle," and Jack and Russell were sitting in the back seat holding hands, like teenagers. It killed me. I thought, "Poor fucker, he's really happy." Naturally it didn't last, his being happy, because Russell lit out like everybody else.[57]

The relationship could only have proceeded on an even keel just so long as its third party, Bob Kaufman, had remained out of town. But when Kaufman returned, in mid-July 1958, Jack "flipped." The delicate balance was upset, and once again Jack found himself on the short end of Russell's affections. Russell recalled, "Jack at the end of an argument says 'I am not in love with you, but I suppose I would be if I had to.' I think "It means the same thing," and fall asleep." When he woke he told Spicer that he felt as though he were "hanging over some frightful abyss," knowing that Kaufman was somewhere nearby and not being able to possess him. That same night, July 15, they went out to the bars and Russell saw Bob for the first time in months.

"Kiss me," Kaufman said, and Russell obeyed, while Jack looked on appalled. In disgust and weariness he said, "I'll see you later," and wished Russell luck. "Bob and I played cat and mouse as before," Russell wrote some weeks later, "only this time his interest was as intense as on the last nights of last year. He managed to pass out. I took him to the Colombo Hotel and sucked his big cock at about five in the morning. I went to work hungover and upset. I felt disgusted. Even the smell on my hands seemed sickening." This marked the first time Russell was able to seduce Bob Kaufman, and even Jack, miserable as he was, seemed impressed by the results of Russell's persistence. Russell wrote in his diary that Jack felt his

actually making it with Kaufman was the best thing that could have happened. Yet from then on he became progressively more and more irrational about everything we said and did. He staged grotesque scenes in bars—insisting wild-eyed that if I didn't go to bed immediately I'd be absent from tomorrow's work.

Jack was "put down" at the Sunday [poetry meeting]. We talked. He suggested that I move, temporarily. I moved to the Colombo for a week of room service, then came back to the Entella. Meanwhile ("back at the ranch?") in the midst of pursuing Kaufman and watching Jack's friendship alienate itself I met Floyd [Froschauer] who promptly fell in love and began planning "our home together."[58]

Russell tried to put a brave face on the debacle. "It is not ununderstandable that I have not painted for almost a month. 'The Mysteries' wait as does 'The Dance of Death.' I've spent a week making love to Floyd and slowly realizing how much Jack and I have lost. I began to suspect it was deliberate. What, after all, would it have been like for Jack had we stayed together: he becoming more and more dependent and I struggling more ruthlessly for independence."[59]

That Russell could have so betrayed him sexually, while accepting his financial aid with such equanimity, disappointed Jack deeply. That he'd betrayed him with Bob Kaufman, of all people, made Jack wild with outrage. "Bob Kaufman!" Duncan cried gleefully years later. "Half-Jew and half-black! Was he the cause or effect of Spicer's rage?"[60]

A full year after Russell seduced Kaufman, Jack continued to nurse his resentment against them both. When Kaufman's "Abominist Manifesto" was published in the Beatnik magazine *Beatitude* (1959), Spicer scrawled the word "Nigger" after the article, and left it at Russell's for the casual browser to find. Later Kaufman indeed saw the annotation and had the savoir-faire to laugh. ("But not much," reported Russell.)[61] Russell later told Robin Blaser that Spicer had written *Fifteen False Propositions Against God* in the period after kicking him out of the Leavenworth Street apartment.

The young novelist Nick Diaman, new to San Francisco, provided a close-up look at relations between Jack Spicer and Russell Fitzgerald after their breakup:

Jack would attack Russell on religious grounds, Russell being Roman Catholic and Jack identifying himself as a Calvinist Protestant. Or Jack would dismiss Russell's comments on poetry, telling him that painters were only qualified to discuss art and only other poets were qualified to discuss poetry. When I asked Russell what was behind their arguments, he told me that they had been lovers and that when they had broken up, Jack wrote *Fifteen False Propositions Against God* and nailed the poem to Russell's door.[62]

At first neither Jack nor Russell was aware that the symbiosis of their work had continued past the breakup of their affair. But it became clear when Jack read the *Propositions* to Russell, calling them a "rosary of lies." As he spoke the words both men realized that Russell's series of paintings called *The Mysteries of the Most Holy Rosary*—"Still Lifes, Bottles & Eggs on a Table," as Russell characterized this series to Robin Blaser—had been Jack's unconscious inspiration for the *Propositions*.[63] It was as though their minds had become so fused that neither departure nor betrayal could separate them.

CHAPTER SIX

"The Hell of Personal Relations"

*T*he "Dharma Committee" was a loose clique of writers and artists organized around the central community event of the fall of 1958, Duncan's writing workshop, "Basic Techniques in Poetry." On August 25 the Poetry Center's Ida Hodes issued a press release announcing the Workshop, and the following month found her processing applications and mailing them back and forth to Stinson Beach for Robert's yea or nay.[1]

While the auditions for Duncan's workshop were proceeding, Ida Hodes's desk at the Poetry Center was "a mess" as she tried to organize a book fair to be held later in the month, to which she was inviting small presses, local magazines, bookstores, and publishers. She secured a pair of locked cases for display at the fair and begged Jess and Robert Duncan for "treasures" to fill them "What about some of Jess's Morgenstern with illustrations? It would be l-ove-r-l-y!"[2] She approached Joe Dunn, who replied that he was "most happy" she had thought of asking White Rabbit Press to her fair. Spicer gave Dunn some suggestions of a high-tech kind: to include a loud "or soft" speaker and a tape recording of poems that would sound off every half hour. Jack also wanted George Stanley to design and install a "White Rabbit corner."[3]

The poet Jack Anderson recalled this book fair and its White Rabbit booth in a review/essay he wrote almost twenty years later on the publication of Spicer's *Collected Books*. A young man from Milwaukee, newly arrived in the Bay Area, Anderson was a graduate student at Berkeley in 1958 and joined its literary magazine *Occident*, in which Spicer himself had published poems and essays ten years before. Anderson wrote:

Soon after I moved to the region, there was a book fair in a tent on Fisherman's Wharf, and one Saturday afternoon my job was to superintend *Occident*'s exhibit. At the next table were representatives of the White Rabbit Press, the influential small press Spicer founded with Joe Dunn. Spicer himself came by and started talking. Though jolly, he was also disconcerting. Academically trained, he despised pedantry and university bureaucracy and warned me against becoming the most hated literary creature of the period, an "academic poet."

I kept seeing him around town, that hulking bearlike man who looked as though he ought to say, "dese," "dem," and "dose," but who instead had a beautifully cultivated speaking voice. He even came to a few of my poetry readings, just as he went to hear lots of young poets read. When that happened, the poet was usually thrown into a state of elation and panic, wondering, "What do you suppose Spicer thinks of my work? Does that expression on his face mean anything in particular?"

Anderson's perspective is an interesting one, because he was an outsider looking in on a circle of more privileged poets, themselves a band of iconoclasts: "There was a circle of younger poets around Spicer. I was never part of that group. To begin with, I was too shy and too uncertain of myself artistically. Moreover, I was too uncertain of myself sexually—and it was obvious, except perhaps to the hopelessly innocent, that Spicer and several of his associates were gay."[4]

Later in the Berkeley semester, Anderson's friend Diane Wakoski, and several other poets from Thom Gunn's writing class at Cal, gave a reading in San Francisco for the Poetry Center's North Beach extension, organized by Gunn and by Ruth Witt-Diamant. Nearly forty years later, Wakoski remembered the occasion well, since it was her first encounter with Jack Spicer. "The old wooden building was sparse and plain," she wrote, "and people sat on folding chairs. The room probably held about fifty people at most, and that night there were probably only about twenty-five people in attendance.

Perhaps a few more. In my memory Helen Adam was there, memorable with her red cheeks, Salvation Army-style clothes, and probably propping up her bicycle inside the door. Perhaps because I was the only woman listed on the program, I was put in the middle of the program. What I remember is that Jack Spicer became a very noisy member of the audience (part of what he was valued for, I later found out), making sure each poet knew which poems were appreciated and which were rejected or ignored. And of course what I remember after this almost forty years is that he cheered and stamped and whistled when I read some of my poems. Clearly, I was chosen; I was the best. And that's what I felt. That I had debuted into the literary world and been chosen. Jack Spicer was the king-maker, the chooser, Plato's Philosopher King. I was so desperate then; there was nothing in my life but poetry, and people seemed to sense that vulnerability and not resent the good things that happened to me at that period in my life. And to have been chosen by this man who rejected so *many*, well that meant something! Right after the reading Ruth Witt said to me (and to none of the other poets, oh I was so smug, little white-footed Diane) "We have to invite you back to read again." And she did, the following year. So, I was an inaugurated poet before I graduated from Berkeley and left my California life behind to live and work and write poetry in New York City. And I believe I owe it all to Jack Spicer.

Wakoski couldn't often afford the fifty cents it took to get from Berkeley to San Francisco and back on the F train, but she subsequently went to a poetry meeting, and there was "dismissed as quickly and as thoroughly as I had been accepted at the poetry reading" when her comments about another poet were "clobbered" by Spicer. "In retrospect, I think I mixed up poetry and ideas about poetry. If he didn't like my ideas about poetry, surely he couldn't like my poetry?" This glimpse of Spicer's mean side failed to dissuade her that he was, as she put it, the "Lion King" who had made her "a little Diane Lion King" for one night and gave her a career.[5]

During this period the long-standing enmity Jess felt for Spicer relaxed briefly. The diaspora of 1955 (with Jess and Duncan in Europe and at Black Mountain, and Spicer in New York and Boston) meant that Jess had seen nothing of Jack. Because Jess did not travel with Duncan on the latter's occasional jaunts to Boston, he and Spicer did not encounter each other again until the winter of 1956–57.

The poetry of *After Lorca* and *Billy The Kid* moved Jess to rescind some of his opposition to Spicer. He agreed to illustrate both books, primarily as a favor to Joe Dunn, who had thrown himself into the White Rabbit business, and only secondarily to establish relations with Spicer. But when Joe started getting into heavy drugs, White Rabbit ended. Enkidu Surrogate, a press operated briefly by Duncan, published both *Billy The Kid* and Duncan's *Faust Foutu*, which had been planned as part of a second series of White Rabbit books. Joe had actually taken money from subscribers, which he spent instead on drugs. His own book *The Better Dream House* had to wait ten years for publication, until after Graham Mackintosh had taken over the printing of White Rabbit books.[6]

One weekend Jack brought Russell FitzGerald to Stinson Beach. Jess never saw Jack so happy as he was with Russell that weekend. Afterward Russell wrote Jess an "extremely lengthy" letter suggesting a collaboration, an idea Jess found as unappealing as the pushiness of its expression. At this time Jack began learning to draw, little crayon drawings that Jess thought showed some talent.[7] At this time, too, Jack began to think of himself as an authority on painting—a connoisseur of painting, like Duncan, Jess, and Blaser, and such was the authority of his opinion that several young painters began to believe him and to trust in his judgment.

Two books with very different purposes convey the energy of the young poets of 1958. Joanne Kyger's *The Dharma Committee* (1986) is a kind of scrapbook of memories, published to mark both the passage of three decades since the Sunday poetry meetings and the beginning of a conference devoted to Spicer's work; while N. A. Diaman's *Second Crossing* (1982) is a gay-lib novel that uses the poetry scene as a backdrop for romance. Nick Diaman had grown up in the San Joaquin Valley. New to the bohemian world of North Beach, he had been introduced to the group by George Stanley after a casual meeting at the Coffee Gallery.[8] At The Place, Diaman met "a rather plain-looking man with a receding hairline, light brown hair combed straight back, in his early thirties then, quiet, introspective, sitting hunched over the beer or ale he was drinking." This was Jack Spicer. "He didn't even turn his head to acknowledge my presence when we were introduced."[9] *Second Crossing* is a short novel with a wealth of biographical references to the poetry scene in San Francisco in the late fifties. The hero, Jason Mellis, is young, lonely, ambitious, rebellious, and gay. He arrives in San Francisco in the autumn of 1958 looking for the poetry scene he's read about in *Evergreen Review* and, to quote the book jacket, "experiences a period of intense change and surprising self-discovery as he comes to terms with his emerging sexuality." The style is gushy—"Being in San Francisco and a part of this scene is one of the most exciting things that's ever happened to me!" Although some real names are used in the book (David Meltzer, Graham Mackintosh, Helen Adam), they crisscross with quite transparent fictional names. Thus Spicer appears as "Jack Spencer" and Duncan as "Robert Dawson." George Stanley is "Greg Stafford"; Ebbe Borregaard is the Viking "Aric Lindblom." The real star of the book is Mariann Ryder, young, wild, hip, talented, the center of aesthetic and erotic attention.

In *The Dharma Committee*, Joanne Kyger reproduced entries from a journal she kept in the 1950s while attending Duncan's workshop in "Basic Techniques in Poetry." On October 13, 1958, she wrote:

At Joe Dunn's poetry reading yesterday (The White Rabbit Press) no one came except Nemi [Frost], Jerome [Mallman], Tom Field and I. So we drank ale and used the hoola-hoop, also practiced Zen lotus positions and took Dada photographs.

George Stanley and Joanne Kyger—king and queen of the "Dharma Committee"—were the most talented of all the new writers Spicer came to know in San Francisco and celebrated in his second book, *Admonitions. Photo by Helen Adam.*

Then we ran to the Bread and Wine Mission, but on passing The Place, Shiela ran out and said, "Leo [Krikorian] will buy a bottle of champagne if you come in." We did and he did (very small). Then he bought drinks for the house, and then a large gallon of wine. Joe gave him a life membership to the White Rabbit Press publications which Leo (drunk) tore up before he read.

Then Carolyn, Tom and I went to the Bread and Wine Mission for dinner and heard Bob Kaufman read poems: "Jesus was fucking Mary, etc." The young minister watching with usual face—concentrated interest. These are famous times I am sure.[10]

Duncan came to class high on Martinis on October 8, which Joanne found a relief because she was bored by his strictures on vowels and consonants. That night the Dharma Committee was formed, an ad hoc organization

The painter Harry Jacobus lounges behind Joanne Kyger in this Stinson Beach scene from June 1959. *Photo by Tom Field, courtesy Joanne Kyger.*

with a laissez-faire attitude and a set of jokey rules. ("All members must be depraved once a week.") The Dharma Committee sometimes met at the Bread and Wine Mission, on the southwest corner of Grant and Greenwich, for the free spaghetti dinners, and for the poetry readings that were a frequent feature. Joanne read her work on a bill with Gary Snyder, Richard Brautigan, and Ebbe Borregaard. It was the first reading, Borregaard remembered, where any of them made money: five dollars. On the way out, an old man approached him and said, in an Italian accent, "I don't understand what you were saying—but I sure liked the music." "I think that kept me going for another couple of years." On the night of the reading, she was nervous and exhilarated, "totally stoned," and Spicer had to come to her apartment to pick her up.[11] Within a year or two, Joanne Kyger and Gary Snyder were to be married in Japan. Their alliance may be construed as a link between the Spicer-Duncan group and the hardcore Beat writers, since Snyder had been one of the readers at the archetypal "Beat" event, the "6" Gallery reading of October 1955.

Dora Geissler remembered the excitement of the period:

We were all kind of refugees. You know that youthful state, where your head is just popping with ideas all the time, and you want somebody to share them with? I remember going for a walk with my brother once, and sharing my ideas with him, and—he didn't get it. We'd all had that experience where we would go and talk with somebody, and nothing happened. Then we all met in San Francisco and [imitates sounds of fireworks]! It just felt like sparking, all the time, so it was a real high. The whole was so much greater than its parts, so that when we left the group, we felt so diminished that we couldn't bear to separate from each other. That's when we got into these long all-nighters, where we'd wind up back at somebody's house, to eat and drink some more, and then we'd all fall down. Joanne called it "heaping"—we would all put on extra clothes, and sleep like little logs, end to end. Then we would wind up back in the bar the next day. We just couldn't bear not to be with each other.[12]

Dora noted the pleasing pathos of becoming a "Spicer-ite" at this juncture:

Failure to attend the nightly bar scene was not far from treason and might result in ostracism. Naturally, keeping up fabulous conversations seven nights a week— there were also the Aquatic Park afternoons, remember—was impossible, resulting in several evenings a week where everyone would glumly stare at each other pining for the good old days when the Beach was exciting. Of course, that excitement was only a catalyst away, who may arrive any minute, or would have to wait till the next night or so when the chemistry shifted.

We enjoyed a variety of diversions in addition to our endless talking to each other: acting outrageous to entice tourists to keep buying us beer, baiting victims Jack thought should be bugged for crimes like publishing their poems, or singing with great gusto in various modes. Musical comedy, Zen, Baroque, and electronic were our more successful singing styles.

At this point, Jack declared that we were just too foolish to be dealt with as a group and would henceforth refuse to sit at a table with us. He called us the Kindergarten. We had, however, permission to join him at the bar as long as we approached him singly. I enjoyed doing that, because Jack was kind and accommodating at those times.[13]

Nick Diaman spent many autumn and winter nights at the poets' table at The Place.

The people I was most likely to find there were Jack, George, Joanne, Ebbe and Russell. When Joe and Carolyn Dunn split up, Carolyn returned to Boston and Joe disappeared for awhile. Harold and Dora . . . lived in the country where Dora was teaching and visited frequently. Jack Moore, a psych student at U.C. Berkeley, was there a lot on weekends. Poet Bruce Boyd made frequent appearances after his arrival from Venice, California. Others came and went.[14]

Carolyn Dunn's return east didn't distress Spicer. He had never cared for her, not since the early Boston days. She was always cleaning! Spicer's Boston poem "Song for the Great Mother" is an insidious, misogynistic portrait of Carolyn, here called "Mrs. Doom," whose broom is so thorough it sweeps away all love, all meaning, from the poet's universe.[15] No wonder Spicer disliked her! His apartment in San Francisco was as slovenly as he. The white shirts and ties he wore, as befit his image of himself as a professional linguist, went unwashed for days, his socks, too. He wore shirts and socks until they were stiff, as though starched. When they grew too stiff, he'd stop by the nearby Army-Navy store and buy more. Thriftily he stuffed the old ones in his closet. "You opened the door," Dora Geissler recalled, "and the stench was incredible, because his closet was totally jam-packed with socks, underwear and shirts that were beyond the pale." In the closet also were stored row upon row of empty brandy bottles. During his "honeymoon," Russell FitzGerald had tried to keep the apartment orderly, but now he was gone and the confusion grew. For an ashtray, Spicer used the open carriage of his manual typewriter, which was heaped with butts and ashes. He continued to depend on others to type his work, penciled in his childlike hand.

Marianne Moore came to read for the Poetry Center. There was some confusion over her directional mike, which Ruth Witt-Diamant mistakenly adjusted straight up so that Moore gave her reading without being heard.[16] Nevertheless, her visit was a success, and Spicer sat in the front row to observe his heroine closer.

"I get all kinds of things from California," wrote Moore to Witt-Diamant, who had been her hostess in San Francisco. "Today a poem *to* me from Jack Spicer." This was "Radar," the last poem in *After Lorca*, which bears the dedication, "A Postscript for Marianne Moore." Spicer was touched and pleased by the postcard she wrote him from Brooklyn Heights, which read, "The cure for loneliness is solitude." He might not have been so pleased had he known that Moore culled this aperçu from her own current project, an essay of advice for teenagers called "If I Were Sixteen Today."[17]

What drew Spicer to "Brooklyn's Poet Laureate"? Her passion for baseball, George Stanley conjectured.[18] Moore confided to Ruth Witt-Diamant,

"["Radar"] has a strange atmosphere and I am asked all sorts of questions. The better the writer, the less time he wastes on visitors, perhaps."[19] A few years later, Marianne Moore was asked to review Donald Allen's *New American Poetry* for the *New York Herald Tribune*. She found the volume, as a whole, raddled with the "diction of drug-vendors and victims, sex addicts and civic parasites," but wrote thoughtfully and well of Spicer's contribution, the "Imaginary Elegies," saying, "Jack Spicer is not indifferent to T. S. Eliot and is not hackneyed, his specialty being the firefly flash of insight, lightening with dry detachment, as here:

> Poetry, almost blind like a camera
> Is alive in sight only for a second. Click,

the accents suiting the sense."[20] A year later she reprinted her comments in her own selection of her work in prose and poetry, *A Marianne Moore Reader.*

Thus at least two lines of Jack's work sneaked their way into unsuspecting library shelves all over the country. In general, however, his campaign to impress the aging modernists with the poetry of *After Lorca* was only a qualified success at best: no response came from "Laurie Riding," "Hildy Doolitle," "Tom Eliot," "Ez Pound," "Edie Sitwell," "Bubbles Cocteau," or any of the other "70 year olds" that he loved and feared at the same time. And although his success with Marianne Moore was only a qualified one too, he believed it to have been whole, and that perhaps was enough.

In November Jack abandoned his filthy Leavenworth Street apartment and moved across the bay to Berkeley to share a flat with Myrsam Wixman at 2532 Benvenue, close to his work on the Berkeley campus. An imaginative cook, Wixman made his own fortune cookies with saucy fortunes inside ("You will die on bridge"), and once he served nutria to Allen Joyce and Spicer—"white rabbit" on a larger scale, perhaps. "They said it looked like a boiled baby." Wixman spent the day attending lectures and making notes on them for a lecture notes firm he worked for, and would meet Spicer in the evenings at Robbie's cafeteria nearby. "It was a flat with two bedrooms," Wixman recalled.

I used the living room as a bedroom. And Max [Deskin, another friend] and Spicer had their own bedrooms. Max's bedroom opened on the kitchen, Jack's was next to the bathroom. I don't remember what time Jack got up. I got up quite early, went to one or two lectures, took the notes, went to the Lecture Notes Office, typed them up and gave them to the editor. And came back the next day for the editorial conference. Stopped in at Robbie's, at 3 or 4, and Spicer would be there already or he would come in after me. And we had mutual friends, and I'd be sitting there with them, or Jack would be sitting there with them, and we'd spend an hour, drinking a couple of pitchers of beer with 2 or 3 or 4 or 5 other people.

Depressed, Spicer spent his days off lying on top of his bed in his underwear. It was at this time, too, that Spicer met a female friend of Wixman's who became a true Beat heroine, though her adventure is little remembered today. This was Wendy Murphy, a young Berkeley bohemian from Hollywood, a "tiny little tyke with blue eyes, kind of doll-like." On a sortie to North Beach with friends, Murphy encountered the infamous Officer Bigarini—notorious for his persecution of bohemians—and, because she was wearing sandals and parts of her bare feet were visible, he arrested her at Grant and Columbus entering The Co-Existence Bagel Shop. "After she got to the station, she grabbed a typewriter and dropped it on Officer Bigarini's foot," Wixman recalled. "He complained that he had been injured, and she was charged with malicious mischief and vandalism, because the typewriter had been damaged." Since he was 230 pounds and she 85 pounds, Bigarini vs. Murphy attracted much press attention of a sympathetic sort, and although she was convicted and put on probation, her case focused attention on the rough treatment metered out by Bigarini to the "beatniks." Her trial, coming so soon after the prosecution of Ginsberg's *Howl*, made her, for a few weeks, into a media star, and Spicer enjoyed both the comedy and the pathos of her situation. It was exactly like a scene from *The Tower of Babel*.[21]

Without Spicer in San Francisco, Russell FitzGerald found North Beach bleak and inhospitable. For a week he had nothing to eat but oatmeal, nowhere to go but back to bed. When George Stanley offered a room in "his ménage," he accepted with alacrity. And so Russell moved deeper into Dharma society, in the new apartment with George Stanley, Ronald Primack, and a fourth tenant, the Zen poet Bruce Boyd.

Bruce Boyd was a San Francisco native. Born in 1928, he was older than the other poets in the flat, and had studied philosophy at Berkeley from 1948 through 1953—years during which he fell under Spicer's influence. Later he credited Spicer with giving him "the idea of writing poetry" when they'd first met at Berkeley, but he waited a few years before trying to write seriously. To Spicer and Duncan he expressed gratitude for giving him the "*impetus* to poetry, which is *therapeia*."[22] Boyd was a frequent visitor to the Bay Area, but his home was in Venice, the oceanside district of Los Angeles that was the Beat capital of southern California. Boyd "was one of those persons," an observer recalled, "that have a funny way of talking that drives people crazy. He would digress in peculiar ways—and he was into Zen Buddhism, which Jack hated." At a poetry meeting in March 1959, Boyd

gave a long introduction to his poem, which was already "bad manners." You weren't supposed to say anything. The biographical circumstances of the production of the poem were a matter of absolute disinterest. The only thing of interest was the poem itself—which you, probably, didn't have much to do with.

Boyd went on at great length about how he'd taken peyote and had visions. Spicer hated drugs—so Bruce really set up the scene as badly as he possibly could. Then he announced that he would read this poem, "Some Apotropeia instead of an Alba"—and everybody present recognized that somebody had struck it rich and had written an absolutely authentic poem. That was certainly one of the great poems written during that period.[23]

When Boyd moved from Bancroft Way in Berkeley to San Francisco to be closer to Robert Duncan's new workshop, he set up a zendo on the roof of his new living space. The apartment was "completely devoid of anything whatsoever. No furniture—hardly—at all," Primack recalled, "except Bruce Boyd's zendo furniture. We slept on the floor."[24] Russell wrote in his dairy on November 24 that he had begun to accept whatever "a creative and pagan society" might bring, including

a weekend of talk and alcohol at PAX, The Place, [Coffee] Gallery and [Bread and Wine] Mission. Pills with Joanne which were somehow depressing. George gives me a copy of his COCK POEMS (1 to 5). [Gary] Snyder reads the wrong selections from his great MYTHS & TEXTS. George throws his love at con-boys; the pills, the poetry, the wine end at Paul Naden's party where, spellbound, we watch B. Siedar enchant a tiny child in footie pajamas, and sing choruses of disgust at his wife who dances with a faggot.[25]

He spent Thanksgiving at The Place, eating its free Thanksgiving dinner and suffering through some "rather nasty conversations with Spicer. I guess he must go on in his world of gambling, teaching, and exploiting; making magic, telling people what he thinks they ought to be told, and using everything to feed the economy of poetry." The entry for December 10 recorded more of the same:

Four days of work, drink and sleeplessness, resonant dreams. I cock tease Jack Moore. Joanne sleeps with me but she is drunk and hysterical and I am impotent. The Feast of the Immaculate Conception. Finally this morning I could not go to work in that bloodsucker: The Emporium. What has been driving me? I am in a state of exhilaration and pain—like love.[26]

December 15 is a red-letter day: "A long weekend ends quietly on Sunday night. Thursday started everything or IT, as we say, when Jack Moore drove Joanne, George and I to Mt. Tamalpais at 3 A.M. A scene of importance; tender and hysterical." The Dharma Committee elected Russell its "Bodhisattva of the Week," and Joanne wrote in the Committee Newsletter: "George Stanley, Russ FitzGerald, Jack Moore, Joanne Kyger have found a new way to look at stars. It is flat on your back drunk on Mt. Tamalpais with a rip in the seat of your leotards at 3:30 A.M. with Kirby Doyle raging down the streets of Sausalito because he cannot think of a hideous enough death for afore mentioned members of the Dharma Committee. . . . It has been suggested by Robert Duncan that we all write Cock Poems for the next class. Splendid!"[27] "Saturday," Russell wrote:

IT reached a still higher pitch. Around the right-bower table at the Coffee Gallery with Joanne only tangent at another, IT received Bobby Kaufman and held him through long duels with Spicer. I broke glass and cut two small cuts in one hand (the right). I showed him the neat drops of blood and he sucked the wound fiercely in an accidental privacy that our public sometimes drops. He drew and held the admiration of everyone in the Gallery with one of his freewheeling monologues denouncing the faggot table. IT maintained the awful pitch even through a night of scotch and discussions with Jack Moore on the values psycho-science had no right to define. On through dawn to George's where Spicer tried a few more choice weapons ("When are you going to get a permanent job?" "Isn't it time for Mass?") Five hours of daylight sleep. Mercifully deserted Beach. No jazz, no people, no Joanne.—At the Bagel Shop under George's definition of Bob as a saint, "it is only necessary to know they are alive and, occasionally, share with them some appropriate ritual."[28]

As 1958 passed into 1959 Jack kissed Russell on New Year's Eve and wished him good luck. Both had drifted into new relationships, but Russell was one of the few old boyfriends Spicer did not quickly forget. They were the ant and grasshopper of Grant Avenue: while Spicer believed in work, Russell had no firm convictions on any subject whatsoever. On January 4, 1959, he wrote, "Eight days of incredible intercourse and complete neglect of all responsibilities. A week living outside of my life. Sleeping on floors with 'everybody.' Amusements only anchored by an hour of poetry when Duncan reads the second half of *The Opening of the Field*, or a short surprise of serious and drunken conversation about our 'relationships.'"[29]

On January 22, FitzGerald recorded the conclusion of the poetry seminars at the San Francisco Public Library, which both Spicer and Duncan had used through 1957 and 1958 to collect a new group of poets in the City. "Duncan's final workshop class ended in explosions. Joanne & George read the *Carola* letters and were interrupted when Jack handed Duncan the crucial page (unread) and Duncan moved a match toward it. George rescued it and refused to allow insult to halt the reading and proceeded to finish the all but crucial page. Later long discussions by Joanne & Jack & Duncan of magic forces. Jack remains puzzled at George's satisfaction. Duncan confesses his reaction was fear. The new force intended to free those who have been nursed by the Magi made a clear appearance." The two years of continuous poetry experience served as the field of training for most of the Spicer/Duncan circle of young writers.

"The Hilarity of the Desperation of Being on the Edge—this is how the Fall of 1958 recollects itself to me," Kyger wrote years later. "The invention of the Dharma Committee was in response to a need in myself to bridge the gap between our Spicer group and the world of the Beat writer, with all its attendant publicity. [Kerouac's novel] *The Dharma Bums* had just been published. And although the Dharma Committee was a parody of the Boy Scout Zen guys, it was a flag waving attempt at attention."[30]

John Wieners was much on the new scene. He and his boyfriend Dana Duerke had driven to San Francisco from Boston in a new, cherry-red convertible, and Wieners's lovable nature and charming, frank weakness had endeared him to all he met. His first book, *The Hotel Wentley Poems*, had appeared from the fledgling Auerhahn Press, its stark lyricism impressing the Spicer group.[31] Since Wieners lived and played in the Polk Gulch area of San Francisco, just over Nob and Russian Hills from North Beach, he'd became a semi-regular at the Sunday poetry meetings. Wieners and his friend, the painter Bob LaVigne, didn't drink as much as most of the regulars—they were more into drugs, and this marked them off to a certain extent.[32] So did Wieners's loyalty to the poetic principles he had learned while a student at Black Mountain College, in which he had enrolled after an early meeting with Charles Olson in Boston in 1954. But soon the drugs and the devotion to Olson became alarming new trends among the young poets in the Spicer circle.

Duncan had long been urging the Poetry Center to sponsor a reading by Wieners, and Spicer had been equally vocal in behalf of Harold Dull's work. In late June 1959, the two poets read together in a program they shared with Celeste Turner Wright, a surprised and altogether nonexperimental writer. Wieners was at the very height of his considerable talents— two days before he had dashed off one of his most haunting poems, "Act Two (for Marlene Dietrich)." The reading inspired Spicer to write one of his infrequent essays, comparing the great modernists who were his heroes to

Jack Spicer with the "Head of Spicer" at Robin Blaser's apartment, late 1950s. *Photo by Robert Berg (collection of the authors).*

the younger poets whom he was still teaching. It's interesting not only for his specific comments on the writing of Dull and Wieners, but for his vision of what poetry can do:

Harold Dull first began writing under the direction of Roethke and Kunitz at the University of Washington. There he learned to write good academic verse, one piece of which was published in *New World Writing*. A little less than two years ago he came to San Francisco. In a remarkably short time he shed most of the careful habits he had learned and began writing poetry. A book of his, *Bird Poems*, was published by White Rabbit Press last fall. He now lives on the North California coast where his wife [*sic*] Dora teaches school and he drives the school bus.

Dull's poetry is entirely concerned with his own identity. Objects and living things are taken into it and shaken into patterns like pieces of celluloid in a kaliedo-scope [*sic*]. But only the mirrors are there, waiting, observing each other through these observances. The result is a savage and beautiful concentration of *self*.

This could be boring to a reader on the outside of this self, but in Dull's case it is almost never. He has both intelligence and good sense in technique (mirror arranging) and has been able to learn (an extraordinary thing in North Beach!) from the technique of other poets.

Dull forms an interesting contrast with Wieners. They have, in my opinion, a roughly equal chance of emerging as poets—in the sense that Pound, Moore, and Williams are poets—and so may be fairly compared. Wieners lacks any sense of identity in his poems (even, surprisingly, in the most personal). He throws his self out into the world, to include or embrace the world, rather at times like Tar Baby gone mad. Bright colored bits of reality stick to him. There is not the least sense of the dance of the poet's identity within the poem. Yet the poetry that results is as valid as Dull's, the poems as beautiful.

What I am trying to indicate is that neither the ways of Dull or of Wieners is enough. And yet, except for the three 70 year old poets I have mentioned and Robert Duncan, nowhere in American or British poetry have I seen the two combining.[33]

During the reading, Wieners's frankness in sexual matters dismayed many in the audience, even his champion Robert Duncan—who was "not shocked into realization of an estranged view of the world but embarrassed for the reader." In Duncan's view, Wieners had striven for the *derangement* of a "Catullus or a Villon," but he was too weak both as poet and as reader to carry it off.[34] In his characteristically lyrical, druggy style Wieners wrote, "Just say that I am still trying to find my poetics in this city of troubled spirits. Old ghosts float in with the night fog and tides. They possess us. Not men under the moon, but sitting out our time in the sun. Rhythm and blues in the afternoon. Let this be the form of my life. And what of that I manage to get on the paper will be my poem."[35] Within a year Wieners was incarcerated in a Massachusetts hospital, suffering from mental and emotional depression. His future visits to the Bay Area, including a triumphant appearance at the 1965 Berkeley Poetry Conference, were brief. In middle age, in his native Boston, he looked back and, in response to a question, he would say that "Never a day goes by without my thinking of San Francisco." The poems he wrote in response to Spicer's death are some of his loveliest ("Hotel Blues," "Ballade").[36]

Spicer said that drugs had "killed" Wieners and were threatening the other, most talented members of his circle. There's so much mention of "valo" in *The Dharma Committee* that Kyger felt the need to explain: "Valo, by the way, was the insidious cotton from a nose inhaler sold in various nefarious drug stores, recently banned in San Quentin. It caused a lot of doubt about the existence of things, like George Stanley and myself." Eating a little bit of this cotton left people feeling uniquely inspired and able to stay up all night effortlessly; they would talk and chatter nonstop. "Jack hated that," Stanley remembered. Once a few members of the Committee played a childish trick on Spicer, and dropped a little piece of valo into his beer at The Place. Soon Spicer was chattering as quickly and inanely as any of them. No one let on. "Spicer never-endingly and scathingly condemned dope." He claimed that the typical marijuana experience was having your Uncle Al tell a joke so marvelously funny it would leave your sides in stitches "while at the same time you knew old Uncle Al had no sense of humor."[37] Drugs, for Spicer, were a crime against poetry. "What is The Main Theme of The Poem?" he wrote, in an exercise notebook:

> Where is the person that was in the poem you wrote him?
> He is out in the field taking drugs through his leg(s) or his arm(s).
> What harm
> Was there? I could almost
> Break a walnut in two with my fingers.[38]

The drug use of the "Dharma Commitee" was another of the seemingly impassable gaps between Spicer's poetic vision and the hungry hedonism of the Beats. As writers like Joanne, George, Joe Dunn, John Wieners, and Russell moved into deeper intimacy with drugs, Spicer felt them slipping away from poetry's truth and life and order. And there were social consequences just as disturbing. Ida Hodes, the blameless secretary of the Poetry Center, lent her apartment one evening to the regular poetry meeting. Immediately afterward, a pair of FBI agents knocked on her door, gained entry, and interrogated her on her knowledge of the young poets—Joe Dunn, George Stanley, John Wieners—with whom she was associating.[39] Not only was the criminological apparatus watching Spicer's group, but the drug underworld was too. At least one of Spicer's readings was disrupted by a crowd of junkies angry with Spicer for allegedly having "snitched" to the police about Joe's habit.[40]

Years later, Joe Dunn recalled that he and Spicer, on one of their walks together in San Francisco, had stumbled onto the filming of a Hollywood movie, Alfred Hitchcock's *Vertigo*. A recent viewing on television convinced Joe that he and Spicer are visible on the fringe of a crowd scene, staring at Kim Novak. When it was suggested that *Vertigo*, a tumultuous romance of obsession and recovered memory, is a fitting analogue for Spicer's own relationship with him, he paused and chuckled. "You might say so. I remember how we goggled at the stars, it all seemed so freaky. Jack said, 'You never know what you might find when you walk through this city.' It's a great picture." He coughed and said, "Not a bad film for us to make our debut in."[41]

*

Into this drugged city, in the fall of 1958, came a young man who seemed *clean*—a young man who embodied all that Spicer held most precious about his native land—a young man from America's heartland, a man with whom he fell in love almost at once. This was James Alexander, of Fort Wayne, Indiana. Spicer made him the focus of not only *Apollo Sends Seven Nursery Rhymes to James Alexander* but also much of his longest work, *The Heads of the Town Up to the Aether.*

For Jim Alexander, the two signal events of 1958 were high school graduation and his discovery of Rimbaud's *Illuminations* and *A Season in Hell.* In time he came to feel that he himself was the reincarnation of the French symbolist poet, and that Spicer was the reincarnation of Verlaine. The strength of his belief impressed Spicer: it was flattering, it was momentous, and it might just possibly be true. In the young Hoosier Jack Spicer saw enormous poetic gifts and ability. Many scoffed at the teenager's claims, but Spicer gave him the compliment of taking him seriously.

After graduation, Jim spent the summer working on Long Island with his brother, the painter Paul Alexander, who was resting after the disappointing rehearsals of *Medea, Part II* in San Francisco. Paul told Jim that Olson respected Rimbaud; this approbation from one of his older brother's teachers confirmed Jim's own growing feeling. In the fall of 1958, the brothers drove to San Francisco.[42] They took an apartment in the "Monkey Block," where Jim found a passage from *Illuminations* scrawled on the wall above his bed: "I have strung garlands from steeple to steeple, golden chains from star to star, and I dance." He also found that, without even trying, he could write in Rimbaud's spidery handwriting. He wondered if these were mystic signs that he had been fated to come to San Francisco and discover a past life as Rimbaud.

Spicer, cross-legged on Joe Dunn's floor, met Jim at one of the Sunday afternoon meetings. It was not a meeting out of a romance. Jack looked "pretty much like a bum—diskempt, middle-aged," Jim thought. But Spicer was attracted. He gave the boy a signed copy of *After Lorca*—step one in a familiar courtship ritual. With Spicer, Alexander attended a session of Duncan's "Basic" class at the Main Library with Spicer; he began to study the work of Olson, Duncan, and Creeley. He began writing seriously and finished the main body of a long piece he called *The Jack Rabbit Poem.* By Christmas the Alexander brothers were back under their parents' roof in Fort Wayne, where Jim finished *The Jack Rabbit Poem* and sent it to Spicer.

The poem "just blew Jack away," Dora Geissler recalled. At last he'd met

James Alexander. "'Jim loves me,' the Right said. 'Jim loves me,' the Left said. But the Frank Terrors were busy at being born and said nothing" (*A Fake Novel About the Life of Arthur Rimbaud*). *Photo by Helen Adam.*

a man on his own wavelength, Jack raved. "Jim wrote *my thoughts* and sent them to me."[43] The magical boy from Fort Wayne became the Muse personified, and not only a Muse but a great writer himself. Stefan George had had his Maximin, but James Alexander was a Maximin with genius. The fact that the magical boy had entitled his poem *The Jack Rabbit Poem*—without either *Jack* Spicer or his White *Rabbit* Press in mind—gave further credence to his strongly held belief that larger forces, such as those displayed in reincarnation, linked him and Spicer in a preordained bond.

from The Jack Rabbit Poem

> why ju leave, Jack, Jack Rabbit, that train
> speed unough to make um wonder at

> at your black art from start
> to where they marvel, query, where
>
>   it was say
> Timbuctu, the sands of
> and negro dark
> and negro dark
> attracted
>
> didn't know what vague
> unexact, act, unexact, not
> by fact by
> outside faculties but
>
> Jack, Jack Rabbit, - not
> a-void
>
>   b
> you got to know when
> to lay low to lay off even
> when it's idea
>
> stay, Jack, with, stave the
> pangs, stay
> out of bland slush or
> thorn jungle:
> stones sand and, nil. - Don't
>
> listen to em Jack
> with their mouths shut idle
>
> you go straight mad eating silence[44]

Jim Alexander acknowledged,

There was for me a certain mystery about my relationship to Jack Spicer which had to do with the Rimbaud theme that permeated Jack's poetry. This relationship between Jack and I does seem to reinforce the plausibility of reincarnation. But it also might be interpreted as a devious plan to mislead people from the truth—a construing of similarities to hatch some plot or other, the purpose of which is to mislead some people from the truth. So I am very circumspect about what interpretation is to be placed on the signs and indications that Jack and I were indeed acquaintances less than a century before in the respective personages of Paul Verlaine and Arthur Rimbaud. And I'm even more concerned about the significance of such a consideration. It would seem on the surface to be little more than self-aggrandizement, yet I think the times are such that a knowledge of former incarnations can be helpful and sustaining. On the other hand, they—mysterious indications—may contribute to the phenomena of self-delusion.[45]

Spicer fell in love with both the boy and his work. He championed *The Jack Rabbit Poem*, declaring to one and all that Jim had written one of the very few "dictated poems." It was almost as though Spicer had invented Jim. He altered his conception of Rue Talcott, the "love interest" in the ongoing detective novel, to make him less like Russell FitzGerald and more like James Alexander.

"His poems have something to them even I can see, sort of a combination of wild French stuff and the Wild West."

"I'm afraid I don't understand."

"Well it's hard to explain without making it sound corny. Freight trains and angels and small Southern jails and denunciations of the letters of the alphabet. . . . Oh, he got [the poetry] out of tin cans. I mean he'd steal paperbacks from drugstores—maybe comic books first but then paperbacks and then good paperbacks and he heard about Dante and Whitman and Rimbaud and then he invented a Dante and a Whitman and a Rimbaud of his own—all out of tin cans. Shit, I make him sound better than he is, I know that. But he's pretty good."[46]

Spicer told Gail Chugg, another young writer, that if he read Alexander's poem carefully, he would see that "all of *The Heads of the Town* came out of that work." Chugg continued: "I asked him why he sought out young writers and educated them and cared for them very deeply, and he said, 'The new can only come through the young. When they get older they have ways of blocking poetry out.' He paid attention to the young because they discovered things for him. He said one time, 'All gay writers over twenty-five identify with Verlaine.'"[47]

Many of Spicer's letters of this period contain a courtly reinvention of romance. In this period Spicer's correspondence had a distinctly public character.[48] Spicer used Jim's absence to begin a series of letters to Indiana. He kept copies of the letters, which he shared with his fellow writers as happily as he shared his poetry. When he was a house guest of Duncan and Jess at Stinson Beach, for example, he wrote the following letter to Jim Alexander in Fort Wayne, which was actually addressed to a "James" of Spicer's own invention.

Dear James,

Went down to Duncan and Jess's Friday to read them the letters.

Their house is built mainly of Oz books, a grate to burn wood, a second story for guests, paintings, poems, and miscellaneous objects of kindly magic. Cats. It is a place where I am proud (we are proud) to read the letters.

It is a postoffice.

I had not realized how little alone one is in a post-office. Before I had merely posted the letters and wondered.

It is possible if you have the humility to create a household and the sense to

159

tread on all pieces of bad magic as soon as they appear to create a postoffice. It is as mechanical as Christmas.

Late at night (we drank a gallon of wine and talked about the worlds that had to be included into our poetry—Duncan wanted me to send Creeley the letters because Creeley, he said, needed the letters—and I went to bed upstairs with George MacDonald's *Lilith*. I had to piss and walked down the outside stairs and saw (or heard but I think I saw) the ocean and the moonless stars that filled the sky so full of light I understood size for the first time. They seemed, while I was pissing away the last of the wine and the conversation, a part of the postoffice too.

This I promise—that if you come back to California I will show you where they send letters—all of them, the poems and the ocean. The invisible

Love
Jack[49]

Writing *Apollo Sends Seven Nursury Rhymes to James Alexander* and *The Heads of the Town Up to the Aether*, Spicer maintained a distinction between the formal "James" and the familiar, intimate "Jim," as though there were two people—one, the muse of his own invention, and the other, the boy he allowed himself to love. Spicer sent Jim a package to Fort Wayne, a copy of his new sequence, *The Red Wheelbarrow*, in tribute. Later he recalled the result in the wistful "Several Years' Love," the aftermath of his failed romances with both Russell and Jim:

> The other'd written me a letter
> In which he said I'd written better.

But that was in the future. For now, Jim Alexander was Spicer's tonic. Spicer has often been thought of as an essentially "urban" poet, especially in contrast to many of his San Francisco contemporaries such as Lew Welch, Gary Snyder, and Philip Whalen. His work shares many of the urban concerns (the cultural buzz, the surrealist charge of great cities, the blur of faces) we see in the Boston Renaissance poetry of Wieners, Jonas, Joe Dunn, and Edward Marshall. Yet at the same time Spicer had a great love of the wild California landscape, which manifested itself throughout the remainder of his career and culminated in his vision of the "Pacific Republic."

Harold Dull and Dora Geissler relocated to Annapolis in September 1958, dramatically expanding the borders of Spicer's tiny North Beach–Polk Gulch–Berkeley enclave. For two years the Dulls lived in Sonoma County, some ninety miles north of San Francisco. The first year Dora taught in a one-room schoolhouse, and Harold drove a school bus in the tiny settlement of Annapolis. Their house stood on a hillside in open country, with animal trails terracing slopes, corral fencing here and there to contain flocks and herds, and the conifer forest spread in patches or broad woods over the low mountains of the littoral. The Dulls' exodus enraged Jack, who accused them of betraying the cause, as Dora remembered. "We certainly could never again expect to be part of the scene we were deserting. I tried to argue that we were expanding the possibilities, that now all our San Francisco friends would have a country retreat as an added option." But Jack was "scornful and urged others not to give comfort to us traitors. If we really cared we would be living in town."[50]

George Stanley visited the traitors in the spring of 1959 and found in the Annapolis hills the inspiration for a new long poem, *Tete Rouge*. Since the Magic Workshop and the subsequent master classes of Duncan and Louis Zukofsky, he had been dissatisfied with his work, which he later characterized as "attempting to imitate Creeley and Zukofsky and Spicer all at once." The sheep trails of Annapolis served as a new source of imagery. The result was Stanley's version of a *"poème à clef*. All of the people in the poem stand for various people: myself, Ronnie [Primack], Harold, Dora, they're all there in the poem. Stan Persky thought that Tete Rouge was him, but no. Everyone was wondering, 'Who was Tete Rouge supposed to be?'—'Was it Jack?'—'Was it Stan Persky?' It isn't anybody. It's a character who comes out of Parkman's *The Oregon Trail*."[51]

Despite the high-flown sentiments of his letters to Jim (and to "James"), Spicer was still seeing Russell on a regular basis, although the romance had been leached out of their friendship. In his diary Russell described the enforced separation between Spicer and Jim. "Jack sleeps in my arms without sex. He reads a marvelous new work. A correspondence with James (& Jim) Alexander. The people who should understand it, who should discover it's there—form making beginnings & endings—don't. Ebbe Borregaard hits the personal and George Stanley stabs at the political. The art goes on blooming like hell above."[52] Meanwhile Spicer stayed in the City, working in Berkeley. The desertion of the Dulls was still a sore spot.[53] On a visit to Berkeley, Duncan spotted Jack and wrote a long letter to Robin Blaser about the experience. (Robin was still living in Boston with Jim Felts and working at Harvard's Widener library.) Duncan's letter, dated February 28, 1959, throws light on the possessive and demanding nature of Spicer's relations in friendship, his needs as a poet, and his understanding of honesty and truth in every kind of situation.

Dear Robin,

I saw Spicer in Berkeley last Tuesday—where now he is not only on that research grant but also teaching a class as instructor in the English Department. And
prodded him about your writing you hadn't heard from him. I hadn't thot there
would actually be anything back of his not corresponding, but he has wound himself up on the idea you are guilty against *Poetry* on two counts—the major one, that
you live with Felts (which Spicer has long nursed as Felts is *bad* for you, etc.) and
the second and immediate one that you are going to Europe (instead of coming
back here . . .) but Spicer said if you were sincere etc. you would live somewhere
like New Orleans without any money (Spicer has recently been receiving letters
from an anonymous admirer in New Orleans: who writes for instance that Spicer is
the only poet besides himself who knows what love is—which it turns out is loneliness and longing for love). His resistance was such that he set himself against the
possibility that your new poems were what I said they were. Deeper—there is the
defense of longing for love against the practice of love. There was the current in
Jack's discussion too that you had betrayed friendship (deserted San Francisco
(Jack Spicer) for Europe; and Jack Spicer the friend for Jim Felts the false friend) . . .
well, I have, as I pointed out to Jack, been fairly un*poet* or anti-poet myself if going
to Europe and not being in San Francisco counts. (And Jack, when [Duncan's *The
Opening of*] *The Field* was completed said: 'When are you moving back from Stinson
Beach now?') I didn't go further and say straight out that if there *were* any alternative proposed to me between Jack and the way I live I would not be confused. . . .

It seemed to me in Boston that Jack posed himself as a "problem" in order to
make a contest in which you would be deserting Jim for Jack. . . .

You can never satisfy Jack's requirements: it's for Jack to satisfy yours.

love,
Robert[54]

The following week, on the first day of March, Russell met Jack in
Berkeley; they went mushroom hunting with Kyger and Stanley, drank
rum, sang, and consumed a mushroom dinner with too much wine. Then
"disgracefully disheveled and turned on," they went to a reading by Duncan at the Poetry Center.[55] A few days later Ruth Witt-Diamant threw a late
supper for the visiting British poet Stephen Spender, who wanted to meet
"the young poets of San Francisco." She had asked Jack to assemble some
for her—Stanley, Borregaard, Dunn, Duerden, the Dulls, "Kyger, etc., and
if there is anyone you think I left out who ought to come would you be my
voice and ask them to come along?"[56] John Wieners attended and added to
his legend by boasting afterward of oral sex in a taxi with Spender.

Was Jack showing Russell copies of his letters to Jim to underline just
how completely Jim had taken over Russell's function as muse? Jack had
written that he'd gone to bed with "Lilith"—only a novel, but enough to
draw Russell's anxious attention. "Jack Spicer loans me *Lilith* & shows in a

conversation with Bruce [Boyd] how right he is about history and how accurate his conception of Christianity is. 'It's either the most monstrous lie ever perpetrated or it's true.'" Thus FitzGerald's diary entry for March 19, 1959. MacDonald's *Lilith*, one of the strangest novels ever written, is a classic in fantasy literature. Its hero spends so long in a deserted library that he is drawn into another, more primitive and violent world, where he meets and is humbled by a series of archetypal humans, gods, and beasts. Its shivers and epiphanies form one of the bases for Spicer's masterpiece, *The Heads of the Town Up to the Aether*, which he would begin at the close of the year.

In the meantime it was the peripatetic Stephen Spender whose presence in the Bay Area gave Spicer a troubling scare. The "Bread and Wine" Mission on Grant Avenue, led by the young minister Pierre DeLattre, had been for a year or more one of the centers of the San Francisco Renaissance. *Everyone* had read there—all but Jack, who disdained its connection to Christianity and DeLattre's ecumenical enthusiasm. He refused all invitations until DeLattre cannily said, "Gosh, Jack, I really feel bad about that, because *Stephen Spender* is going to be here and I'd really love to have him hear you." Whereupon Jack, seeing another chance to impress a hero of his youth, agreed to read. On the night of the reading, by a bank of six candles, Spicer read a few poems and then, as Spender slipped into the audience, Spicer asked for more light. More candles were lit. Still, he said, he could not see the poem. The overhead flood lights were thrown on full blast. And the reading was abandoned because he couldn't see any words on the page. "He had to be led out like a blind man," DeLattre recalled. "Jack Spicer was so terrified that he went psychologically blind." This was the onset of a recurring, puzzling vision problem which was to make giving readings increasingly problematic; his public readings became rarer and rarer, each one an occasion of agonistic suspense. In moving closer to a poetry without voice, he was now seized by the poet's ultimate nightmare, when the page goes blank, the words themselves taken from one. Though Spicer's poetry had long been fueled by tropes of blindness, the poetry about to appear would be filled with "blinking" and "squinting," objects disappearing and reappearing, the instability (or infidelity) and treachery of words, characters, signifiers. Of course, he blew it with Stephen Spender.[57]

Jim Alexander hitchhiked back from Indiana to San Francisco and stayed with Tom Field till he could locate his own apartment. Another Black Mountain refugee, the painter Bill McNeill, found Jim a job. Laid off after two weeks, Jim wrangled a post at a Berkeley bookstore. At lunch breaks he met Spicer at Robbie's Cafeteria on Telegraph Avenue ("I don't recall as he actually ate anything. He said the food was of poor quality"), and at night frequented the North Beach bars where Jack had established himself as a central figure.[58] He was an object of much curiosity in the Spicer *kreis*, for Jack had seen to it that "the magic of Jimmy Alexander coming to San Francisco was billed in such a way that when he arrived, everybody was sure that a god had arrived!"

Like Jack, Russell found Jim Alexander almost bewilderingly attractive. In his diary, he wrote at length of the emotional detail surrounding the life of the community at the time.

James Alexander. You open to me in an all night conversation at Cassandra [a hangout on Grant Avenue] and again at an all night party above the Mission. I dream in DeLattre's sofabed of loving you and wake to find your body gradually responding. At the end of almost two hours I discover, thanks to a knock on the door & the sunlight, that the body my love has almost penetrated is not your own. Shock, disgust and despair. You and George & I and the Dulls & Jack Spicer at Gino & Carlo's. We attempt to use you. You change us by breaking bottles and glasses at George's face. In your absence Jack asks why you did it. I answer I don't know. 'Then I hope he spits out the whole Beach!' 'What if it's only part of it?' 'Then I'll start throwing things!' 'If you do, *you* might *kill* someone.' '*That's right!*' I leave & after searching for you & finding Jack and the others I investigate Bob Kaufman's party. The police are still there. I wander down Greenwich Street and weep in the doorway. The walk home seems endless. Jack returns with the Dulls for the expected impromptu dinner. They discuss Jack's *Nursery Rimes for James Alexander.* I read them and find that Jack has supplied the omission that Duncan found in Jim's poems: between the syllables Jack has managed: Love.[59]

As Spicer's estimation of James Alexander reached its zenith, he pushed his work everywhere he could. When Donald Allen asked for suggestions for his projected anthology of new American poets, Jack recommended Jim alone. "Black Mountain by descent (brother went there) and is probably the only new poet on the horizon. Partly the fault of the horizon."[60] Although in general Spicer respected Allen's selection of the writers he was assembling, this reply has the ring of a plug to it. (Don remained grateful that Alexander was the only poet Spicer so pushed onto him. At the opposite extreme was the peripatetic Allen Ginsberg, who tried constantly to intercede for his Beat pals.)[61]

Jack's next step was to feature his writing in his new magazine, which he called *J.* The idea of a new magazine had been bruited about in North Beach poetry circles for some time, and the successful launch of *Beatitude*, edited by (among others) none other than Bob Kaufman, made Spicer envious, scornful, and competitive. Finally he announced that "The first issue of J will appear in the early part of September. J will be a 16-page mimeographed flyer very much like Beatitude. It will sell for the same price or lower."[62] He was so poky about beginning it that one poet wrote, "Jack Spicer will never get his magazine out, he is lazy & listless and just won't."[63] It took the assistance of Fran Herndon to get "J" going. The initial "J" stood for several people, including Spicer himself and Jim Alexander, but the name came from a misunderstanding of the name of Jim and Fran Herndon's younger son. Spicer thought the boy had been named "J" after his father, Jim; the boy's name was actually Jay. Through 1959 J occupied most of Spicer's energies. Though Spicer did not design the magazine specifically as a showcase for Jim Alexander, it's worth noting that he abandoned it when Jim betrayed him.

These years were times of special closeness for the Herndon family and Jack Spicer. Fran would make an elaborate lunch and off they would go to Giants games at Seals Stadium and, later, at Candlestick Park. Jim and Jack knew every team, all the players, all their statistics. Sometimes they would go to a bar and watch basketball on television, with Jack as a kind of color commentator, issuing a series of hilarious caustic comments. Not only was Jim Herndon beginning to write seriously, but Fran was beginning to paint, working in close consultation with Spicer. Jack acted as godfather for the Herndon's infant son and became practically a member of the family. He obviously enjoyed the intimacy of this group, as well as the chance to exploit Fran's secretarial labor and her fine eye.[64]

From the beginning Spicer personally selected the work for J, often soliciting it from the authors before random submissions were taken. In San Francisco, a box for contributions was kept on the bar, first at The Place and later at Mr. Otis's bar on Green Street. All subsequent *Spicerkreis* publications followed this pattern, with the submissions box placed in Gino & Carlo's bar. Larry Eigner's work, however, was solicited. Impressed by Duncan's dedication to Eigner's work, Spicer got his address from Don Allen and wrote to Swampscott, Massachusetts, to ask for poems for J. Recalled Eigner: "Spicer told me he wanted a magazine that came out of a box, like Duchamp's collection of his multiples. A magazine you could bring to a desert island. He said he didn't mind that my poems didn't come from out of a box, because they came from out of a chair." (A victim of cerebral palsy, Eigner had been in a wheelchair all of his life.) "He asked me if I knew Josephine Miles, and the idea amused me, like a branch of Poets in Wheelchairs Anonymous. He said, 'Don't get defensive, I just thought you might have *bumped into each other* somewhere,' and his sardonic humor I found refreshing."[65]

The first issue of *J* opened with James Alexander's *The Jack Rabbit Poem* and contained material by several poets to whom Spicer had written poems or letters in *Admonitions*: Joe Dunn, Richard Brautigan, Robert Duncan, Harvey Harmon, and Robin Blaser. Duncan's contribution was "Dream Data," the opening of his "Sequence of Poems for H.D.'s Birthday." Spicer wrote to Don Allen: "J is being sold in the Piss Pot [the Paint Pot] and the Hoof and Mouth [the Cloven Hoof], both Grant Avenue non-bookstores that don't charge anything for handling it. We only print 300 copies and they sell out soon. At two bits why shouldn't they? I keep ten copies for my own—one of which I'll always send you. For extras tell people to send me a dollar and I'll send them a copy if I like their letter. 50 cents west of the Mississippi and East of Mount Diabolo. It's me being me. . . . New York contributors are not forbidden but quotaed."[66]

With the second issue began the serialization of George Stanley's *Tete Rouge*, which ran through issue 5. Issue 2 also contained a contribution by Jess. Robert Duncan's presentation was "A Letter" (entitled in *J* "Dear Carpenter"); both this poem and "Dream Data" appeared later in his volume *Roots and Branches*.[67] Spicer included his own "Epilog for Jim" in *J*2.

*J*3, with a cover by Russell FitzGerald, opened with "Some Apotropeia instead of an Alba," Bruce Boyd's long poem. In addition, issue 3 contained the poetry of Ron Loewinsohn and a sports story by James Herndon, introducing him to Spicer-circle readers. The rest of the world did not become aware of Herndon's work until much later when Simon and Schuster published his first books, *The Way It Spozed To Be, How To Survive In Your Native Land,* and *Sorrowless Times.*

The fourth issue of *J* presented Robert Duncan's remaining poems in "A Sequence of Poems for H.D.'s Birthday"[68]—which contains a note, "finish[e]d October 24, 1959," thus dating the issue of the magazine within a month or so. (October 1959 also marked the publication of Spicer's third book, *Billy The Kid*, illustrated by Jess.) After the H.D. poems three short poems by Richard Brautigan appeared on a single page. Another page also contained poems: one by the editor, Donald Allen, one by the poet and painter John Allen Ryan, and this one ("Jacob") by Spicer:

> He had sent his family across the river.
> The wives, the heavy oxen—paraphernalia
> Of many years of clever living.

The water flowed past them. All that evening
Jacob was wrestling in the arms of a stranger.
It was not unexpected. By midnight
They had explored each other's strength and every hour
                was a tender repetition.
At dawn the angel tried to free himself and Jacob
Held him with one last burst of strength, screaming.
After that there had never been an angel. Lucky Jacob
Limped across the river, thinking of his wives and oxen.[69]

"Jacob" displays the kind of exotic sexual imagination often associated with a Spicerean non-sexual event. The poem is probably really about property: "Lucky Jacob / Limped across the river, thinking of his wives and oxen." It illustrates one feature always present in Spicer's writing when sex is a subject—an almost imperceptible connection of what is going on to every possible implication it may have. This particular event, which Spicer's wit makes (or sees as) comic, is terrifying as well. Sex with angels is a private act.

It didn't take long for Spicer to grow weary of the labor of *J*. From the beginning he had wanted it to be a magazine with a perverse editorial viewpoint: an agonistically "amateur" magazine, as opposed to the despised university reviews with their inbreeding and their vaunted professionalism. To this end, Spicer advertised for the poet who had never before written anything in his or her life, for everyone, he professed, has one good poem in them. "If J is going to be a little magazine I don't give a damn about editing it," he wrote, defining a "little magazine" as one that "prints poetry (or prose or drawings) by friends or friends of friends of the editor. My friends (and the friends of my friends) are good poets but, with some notable exceptions (mainly so far in J2), they have ceased to surprise (Diaghilev's word to Cocteau A S T O N I S H) me." Thus the homemade pages of *J* reflect the private, local, populist inspirations of Spicer's politics, as well as the "funk-junk-assemblage" art scene in which he and Fran Herndon were participating. There are some awful individual poems, but it didn't seem to matter. When well-known poets tried to submit their work, Jack had Fran write back "really vile letters, and he made me sign them. 'Stick this poetry up your ass!' I had to say. I can't believe I did it. But I did."[70]

Spicer's search for buried Caesars led to some results that might have been expected. Nick Diaman wrote some poems under a pseudonym, sneaked them into the cigar box at The Place, and was elated to find one published in *J*. He tried to deflate Spicer by pointing out the hoax, but to

Jack it only proved his original point. Three poems, indeed, scattered throughout the run of *J*, written by Spicer himself, were published as if by "Mary Murphy," the Hollywood starlet whose enduring claim to fame is her role opposite Brando in the biker romance *The Wild One* (1954). "What're you rebelling *against*, Johnny?" "Whaddya got?"

At the time Spicer was publishing *J*, painting was flourishing, with the Black Mountain painters (Tom Field, Paul Alexander, Knute Stiles), the artists associated with the Six Gallery and King Ubu Gallery (Wally Hedrick, Jess, Harry Jacobus, Jay DeFeo), and such disparate spirits as Bruce Conner and Nemi Frost, making pictures and objects that were seen and talked about in North Beach and the rest of the Bay Area. Robert Duncan was writing the early sections of *Roots and Branches*. Helen Adam was writing her *San Francisco's Burning!* and reading it in intimate settings around the City. In Spicer's own group, this was the time of Jack's *Apollo Sends Seven Nursury Rhymes to James Alexander*, George Stanley's *Tete Rouge*, Harold Dull's *The Schoolbus* and *The Tree*, and Ebbe Borregaard's *October 7th Poem*. John Wieners's *The Hotel Wentley Poems* had recently been published, as well as work by Michael McClure, Gary Snyder, Philip Whalen, Lew Welch, and Richard Duerden—whose *Foot* magazine was appearing in its first two issues. The new poetry was on a threshold of "arrival," since Donald Allen was negotiating with the poets to be represented in the anthology *The New American Poetry, 1945–1960*, which would make their work a commonplace in the writing of the English-speaking world. In this rich movement San Francisco played a leading role. But Spicer panicked every time one of his "children" left him.

At that time, Joanne Kyger was living in East-West House, a Zen commune on California Street. With Gary Snyder, Lew Welch, and Philip Whalen, she formed a group that functioned independently from other writers' circles, especially in its Buddhist emphasis. Spicer was always sardonic about these writers, and once introduced Joanne to another woman as the "Alger Hiss of Zen Buddhism."[71] Joanne spoke of Gary Snyder's courtship of her, and about their friends: "Lew Welch comes from Chicago. His marriage is just broken up so he seeks out his old friends—and new ways—and he hangs up his wedding ring on this nail in Gary Snyder's shack and starts driving a cab in North Beach, hangs out with Nemi Frost and myself. He looked at my poetry, and I remember Gary Snyder saying, 'He's not interested in your poetry, he just wants to go to bed with you!'"[72] Snyder had already returned to Japan to continue his Buddhist studies, and Joanne planned to join him there. After Snyder sailed for Japan, Russell FitzGerald wrote in his diary that Joanne was whimpering, "I feel bad! I suddenly realized that no matter how much I stamped my foot I couldn't change what was happening. I couldn't make that ship move back."[73] Kyger's departure for Japan was the first of several desertions, as Spicer saw them, by talented writers leaving San Francisco for elsewhere—Siberia, in Jack's mind.

George Stanley noted that for Spicer "the geographies of elsewhere really didn't exist. The further away you got from San Francisco the more the real and the imaginary mixed and so you had New York—the symbol of wickedness—and you had Oz. I think of one of Jack's little plays ["Buster Keaton Rides Again"] in *After Lorca*, something like 'the lights of Philadelphia twinkled in the distance'—those places just didn't exist. He always advised people to go to Mexico rather than Europe. He'd say, 'If you're looking for a foreign country, Mexico is the most foreign country there is.'"[74] Poets and writers from other parts of the country hardly seemed to exist for him, either, except as enemies and/or mirages. He told Harold and Dora, for example, that he didn't believe in the existence of the Beat poet Diane Di Prima, whose work Kenneth Rexroth was recommending—her very name, he said, was too preposterous to be real. She was to be referred to only by her initials; thereafter they joked about the imaginary, chimerical "DDP"—a Fata Morgana of the East.[75]

The jokes and hoaxes multiplied. *Search* was a digest-sized magazine, like *Fate*, sold at drugstore newsstands near to the copies of *Fantasy & Science Fiction* and *Amazing Wonder Stories*. Its contributors wrote earnest, pseudoscientific articles on life after death, psychical research, Houdini, "pyramidology," Conan Doyle, true and false mediumship, Stonehenge, Martians, protoplasm, UFOs—a whole cornucopia of "the unexplained." A regular feature was "It Happened to Me," first person accounts by readers of unusual occurrences. In the August 1959 issue of *Search*, George Stanley published a hilariously deadpan account, an allegory of his first meetings with Spicer at The Place and Aquatic Park:

One of my favorite pleasures as a young boy was playing on the beach. I always liked the more secluded beaches and would often walk several miles to reach one particular spot called North Beach. This little beach was cut off by steep cliffs and probably only a very young boy would risk the dangerous climb down. But the place fascinated me and I would go there often. My favorite game was listening to sea shells and trying to make words out of the whispery sounds. I was never alone on the beach however, for there was an old gentleman called Jack Spicer who seemed to be there most of the time. He was a most kindly person, but because of his unusual way of living, Mr. Spicer was considered a crank. But he was very smart (he told me that at one time he could speak thirteen languages including Esperanto) and could make very funny remarks. Once he said he wrote letters to dead men, and I think he was serious.

Abruptly, the story shifts to a grim discovery scene, when the young boy George discovers the old man dead on the beach. "When it's someone you know, the shock is almost too great . . . like going too close to a buzzsaw or almost falling out a window." After bringing a cop back to the body, George vomits, and some "nasty dreams" ensue. Years pass, during which the boy avoids North Beach. "The place had changed and now the very walls were black." All of this prologue serves as a set-up for some spooky hijinks familiar to *Search* readers—ambiguous scenes of half-recognition (the boy, now grown up, sees an old gentleman in a "beat cafe" who looks just like "the corpse on the beach." This apparition disappears suddenly.

At home that night I thought over the incident again, and in an idle way picked up an old sea shell that I had collected from North Beach years ago. Unconsciously I placed it to my ear, but there was no echo. No murmur. Then in a voice very clear and sharp someone or something said, Luke XVI: 26. I looked inside the shell but there was nothing. I placed it to my ear again and the echo had returned. It was just another seashell. I then recalled the words that had been spoken and dashed to the public library for a bible. The passage reads: "Between us and you there is a great gulf fixed; so that they which would pass from hence to you cannot; neither can they pass to us, that would come from thence." I never used to believe in ghosts, but now I have seen one.[76]

Stanley brilliantly spoofs the plodding, polite persistence of *Search*'s house style, but only incidentally. His aim was deeper than parody: to interrogate Spicer's own magic-making by placing it in another, tawdrier context. If ghosts are as banal as these, what sense in talking to them, writing them letters? Like any practical joke, the "Great Gulf" piece reveals the anger with which it was made: in this case, an Oedipal anger that jumps out from behind the props—the seashell and the Bible verse—to produce an embarrassed discomfiture. Into the great gulf between Spicer and his students words continued to rain like arrows. George himself would be the next to earn Spicer's enmity by leaving San Francisco for New York.

Spicer's relations with those outside his geographic circle were often very odd. His books, and the publications he edited or influenced—*J* and *Open Space*, as well as the publications of White Rabbit Press—were supposed not to be distributed outside the Bay Area.[77] Spicer felt they should belong exclusively to what Robert Duncan called "orders of Poetry," which located his groups, his personal influence, at the center of the valid. His motive was less personal than professional—if this concept had any meaning in relation to this eccentric man. For Spicer, poetry flourished in certain conditions, and only in those conditions; it reflected personal states of being, which in turn had to be illuminated by a kind of poetic worthiness—the truth of the person—before the poetry could be acceptable. Otherwise the poetry could not be good. Poetry had to be made in the favored circumstances of the San Francisco region. All other places, and persons loyal to them, suffered by comparison.

There were departures, but there were always new arrivals. The teenaged Stan Persky arrived in San Francisco from Chicago. He was stationed at Treasure Island, in the middle of the Bay, serving in the Navy. An enthusiast of the evolving literature of the Beat era, he had read Kerouac's *On the Road* and Ginsberg's *Howl* and had already established contact by mail with Jack Kerouac, Gregory Corso, and Allen Ginsberg in New York, with Irving Rosenthal, editor of *The Chicago Review*, and with Ron Loewinsohn, then living in Los Angeles. Because he was still a minor, he could not get into the bars of San Francisco, so he frequented The Coexistence Bagel Shop, where he devoured the new poetry along with the bagels, played chess with strangers, and met Bob Kaufman, the jazz musician Bob Siedar, and the extraordinary Mad Alex, a black man who sat in the corner window "and talked a kind of schizophrenic/surrealistic language, which I was assuming made sense if only I could understand it." On Monday nights he would get a free spaghetti dinner, with wine, at the Bread and Wine Mission. Ginsberg came to town to read there, and Stan finally met him in person after their long-distance correspondence. He met Don Allen, who introduced him to Rosalind Constable, from *Time* magazine, as part of "what was new." He found himself quoted in *Time* in the context of Constable's tour of the Beat world.[78]

One afternoon Stan was walking along the rail tracks in Aquatic Park and saw a man walking toward him—slightly tubby, walking slowly on what are known in baseball as "piano legs." The man passed, with an exchange of looks. Stan was being "cruised" but he didn't know it yet. A short while later, he attended a reading and recognized the reader, Jack Spicer, as the man from Aquatic Park. Still in the camp of Ginsberg, Snyder, and Whalen, Stan didn't care much for what he heard. Out of a brown paper bag Spicer produced a copy of *After Lorca* and gave it to the sailor, pointing out the cover price and insisting he rarely gave out books for free. Stan wrote:

In retrospect, I didn't realize any of it at the time: all this was probably sexual come-on of a mild sort (I do know Jack had sexual desire for me, as a result of later experiences). I wasn't exactly pre-sexual, but I obviously had no idea that an older man could desire a younger one—oh, to be so dumb once more!—obviously I thot that the way sex worked was that young men the same age desired each other, even tho that meant, horror of horrors, being 'queer.' Before getting to San Francisco, I remember a warning by Ron Loewinsohn—that the poets associated with the White Rabbit were queer—I don't know how explicitly Loewinsohn made the point, maybe only hinted, but anyway this "warning," given what I knew about myself, added a bit of attraction to these White Rabbits.

Somewhere I met George Stanley and it was he who invited me to the Sunday afternoon poetry meetings. At either the first or second meeting I attended I produced a long poem, imitative of Snyder, (whose "manly" treatment of nature was what I was poetically enamored of at the moment), entitled "Jackknife Poem" (the pun on Jack was unintentional), in which I taped together several sheets of paper on which it was written so that it could be unfolded (like a jackknife? there was a lot of this *objet* consciousness, as I recall). I read aloud this very long poem. There was considerable debate among the people present about whether it "was" "a poem." (What I learned from all those meetings, by the way, was that there was such a thing in the world as "a poem" and it didn't have much to do with "excite-ment," either of personal adventure or colloquial language, and it was after I learned that by a process of osmosis that I fell in love with *After Lorca* and the rest.) One person present was Ebbe Borregaard, who was an imposing and somewhat frightening creature. Anyway, after a lot of debate, Spicer said, "Read it again" and a howl of protest went up, particularly from Ebbe at the thought of having to endure this lengthy amateurish effort. (I had never heard of the idea of "reading something again.") And, indeed, I did read it again, the whole damn thing, unfolding all that paper. I think the final verdict was that it was "a good, bad poem" (a category of judgment I had never heard of before, but would eventually become familiar with—a good, bad poem, of course, is much better than a bad (or chickenshit) good poem (many of which, in Jack's view, Duncan wrote). Thus my introduction to the strange and marvelous world, the boulevard of broken dreams, *etc.*[79]

In this world Spicer "was the master." Stan continued:

Duncan was on the scene, but he was more distant. You'd see how the group came to recognize somebody having written an authentic poem. Something had changed reality—with one of those poems. So you'd not only learn the language of it, but at a certain point, the combination of the learning how to recognize what was going on as well as think in poetry, at that point you actually had true responses of your own in all this. That is, the poem and you could respond to it.

Spicer's line was essentially that the poem was some kind of dictated process, that it had a magical character, and that the poet was an instrument played upon by something else. Later on I saw that that was a way that Spicer had of explaining something, a way of getting a narrative to come, how he thought poetry worked. I was never sure whether he actually believed that, but since he kept saying it, well— maybe he did believe it? In any case, his purity was very apparent. This guy was living as a poet, and for no other reason, as far as I could tell: he lived to write these poems. These poets were quite a bit different from those performance-oriented poets, the ones who were more involved with display—Ginsberg, McClure, Ferlinghetti. These were poets who thought that all of that was shuck—sloppy, sentimental. There was a more classical line among these people, it seemed to me.

Well-educated himself, Spicer discouraged Stan from university life, warning against the "bad, gray" English department, and suggesting that he write imaginary lives of the French symbolist poets. Stan had never heard of the French symbolist poets, but "anyway, I wrote their lives and they were, immediately again, recognized as authentic. This was *for real*— I'd magically hit upon something."[80]

It was wonderful to be nineteen. The Sunday afternoon poetry meetings were the absolutely central moment of everything; everything else was the detritus of having to be alive (we used to live for poems the way writers today live for calls from their agents). I used to torment my elders, after the meetings, as we were rolling down the hill (the meetings I remember best were at George Stanley's apartment on Montgomery; but there was also a hill to come tripping down when they were held at East-West House on California), I would compose and recite oral poetry—poems that would never be written down, that would evaporate into the San Francisco air—one of those acts of child genius sadism that leaves those even a mere ten years older, and already losing the mindless courage of youth, gasping with envy.[81]

Harold Dull and Dora Geissler returned to San Francisco for the summer of 1959, renting an apartment on Fillmore Street in the Marina district, where one or two of the Sunday afternoon poetry meetings were held. Spicer's love for Jim Alexander was put to its final test when Dora and Russell FitzGerald both became attracted to the young Hoosier and concocted an elaborate, almost incredible plot to stymie the relationship between Jim and Spicer. Once Russell realized that Jim had a crush on the earthy, sensual Dora, he sensed a way to turn the situation to his advantage.

First Russell explained to Dora how unkind and disagreeable Jack had been to him ever since *l'affaire* Kaufman. Dora listened with fascination. From the moment she'd met Russell—or even before, from the moment she'd smelled him—she'd been in love with him. "He smelled like flowers, and I was hooked." In the quarrel between Jack and Russell, she took Russell's side as she always had, acting as an accomplice, aiding and abetting his schemes and his boy-chasing. Now Russell told her to seduce Jim, in order to remove him further from Jack; since it pleased Russell, Dora was glad to comply. She wasn't a professional heartbreaker; she merely did what Russell commanded. She was his "soldier." In any case she didn't think Spicer really was in love—he loved the idea of Jimmy more than the actual person.[82]

She was also fascinated by James Alexander's astonishing beauty, in that first season after his return from Fort Wayne. Their affair soon became an open secret in North Beach—it *had* to be open, otherwise Spicer wouldn't be hurt by it, and yet it couldn't be flagrant enough to risk her "marriage" to Harold. "If I had one man attached to me," she explained, "that would keep the other men off. I didn't want to have everybody wanting a piece of the action—So by having a man, then you could be more private, and then I could just have my gay friends, and not have to be pursued as a free agent. So I used [Harold] as my cover; but I guess I didn't feel any great disloyalty to him, because I was doing what Russell was asking me to do; and, after all, Russell was my true love, right?" It came to the point where Jim showed Dora an apartment, a love nest, he had made ready for her, with a bed, a lawn chair, and a loaf of bread. At that point she disabused him—she was not in love with him, she would not live with him. She was already living with one man, Harold, and in love with another, Russell. There wasn't room for Jim. Nobody took her romance with Russell very seriously, because there wasn't a straight bone in his body. But she continued to love and obey him above all others.

In September 1959, the Dulls returned to the Point Stewart area of Sonoma County for the new scholastic year, to a Pomo Indian rancheria a few miles from Annapolis known as the "Kashia reservation." They lived in a three-room house attached to a one-room school, where Harold taught ten Indian children, in grades one through eight. Dora commuted the few miles to the Annapolis school where she continued to teach, and to pine for Russell.

George Stanley registered for his senior year at Berkeley, mindful of Spicer's repeated admonition: "Drop out! Drop out! If you're going to be a poet, drop out of the university." After buying his books, spending a morning standing in the registrar's lines, and taking the F train back to San Francisco, George went to a restaurant for a sandwich and a Coke. At that moment Jack's advice hit him, hard. He went back to Berkeley immediately and "reversed the whole procedure, got my money refunded for the books. I was proud I could tell Jack 'I dropped out, like you were telling me to!' It was the right thing to do, at the time." Eleven years later, after Spicer's death, George completed his final year.

But in 1959, instead of returning to Berkeley, he began another poem— *The Pony Express Riders*, for Jim Alexander. The polished poem demonstrated Stanley's continuing absorption in western and country scenes, and concluded his "first phase" as poet in San Francisco. "I had misunderstood, I think, what Flaubert was trying to do in *Madame Bovary*. What I thought he was trying to do was to reproduce the phenomenal world by language so that the language itself became a transparent thing. I attempted to do this by writing these very minimal poems in which the poem would kind of bring through an image that wouldn't change. Some of the time an idealistic project but it was my own apprenticeship to what to do, and it was one of the things that Spicer advised—I think Spicer got this idea from Baudelaire—which was to write with a minimal vocabulary. That idea was being talked about. So that was what I tried to do then."[83] Russell FitzGerald's diary, November 17, 1959, later described the effect of these poems: "Last night Robert Duncan read Stanley. *The Pony Express Rider* poems. The last he read very right. They were part of a story he made of poems whose authors and titles he did not announce and whose quality or value he described as 'better than I now write.'"[84]

When Jack discovered that Jim had been sleeping with Dora, there was no explosion, only a slow deflation of his hopes. The excitement that surrounded Jim's descent on North Beach had become, by the fall of 1959, only a memory. As George Stanley said, "The bloom was off! After Jim became involved with Dora, Jack began to figure the young poets as a circle of corrupt decadents. It came to the point where Jack was accusing all of us of attempting to corrupt Jim." Wearily, Jack renamed the incestuous crowd the "Goop." In a later poem he elaborated: "The goop is an international criminal organization / that talks to each other, makes passes at each other, sings to each other, clings to each other, is as absolutely alien to each other as a / stone in Australia."[85] "We were a bunch of people who were crass and had no real interest in poetry," Stanley said, with obvious resignation.[86]

With Jim Alexander in the hands of the "Goop," Spicer decided to end *J*. The fifth and final issue opened with "1942," a meditation on family and death by Richard Brautigan, and included a pair of linked poems by

Richard Duerden. Duerden had responded to Spicer's request for a poem for *J*: days afterward he reconsidered and submitted a second version. *J5* printed both, each signed as if they were quite different, which indeed they were. "I never look back," Duerden said. "I find it distasteful. The art of my life is like driving on the freeway. I go from place to place, never revise."[87]

"*J* is in trouble," Jack told Don Allen. "I'm now in the position where I have to manage both the editing and the circulation which I can't. Will give it up (probably with 5) rather than surrender to the Ferlinghettos"—that is, to bookstore owners who charge a handling fee for books placed on consignment. "The awful thing is that new (good) material keeps pouring in. What an awful world. *J* dies and *Evergreen Review* keeps going. Culture vs. poetry."[88] Fran Herndon and Jack collected some artwork for a projected sixth issue of *J*, but got no further than that.[89] Instead, the sixth issue was edited by George Stanley, and other derivatives followed.[90] The bloom was off.

"I didn't do this to be mean to Jack," averred Dora. "I knew that there was no way that Jimmy wanted Jack! See—Russell always kind of preferred straight men, it seems to me. No. There was never any problem between me and Spicer. We were always very, very dear friends."[91] Recollections converge on a text and slip away, accurate or not. What one sees is a collage of bored evenings at The Place or Mr. Otis's bar, a petulant Spicer, conversation about a Hitchcock movie, a rumor about Dora Dull enticing Jim Alexander to bed or vice versa. Rain plays against the bar's plate glass window and Jack Spicer slouches down Grant Avenue toward Mike's Pool Hall to play pinball, wet and angry, muttering his oft-mumbled, "It's a bad night."

After its dedicatory poem, *The Heads of the Town Up to the Aether* opens with "Several Years' Love," a recollection of Spicer's feelings for the two men he then most recently loved. The lovers, of course, are Russell FitzGerald and Jim Alexander.[92]

> Two loves I had. One rang a bell
> Connected on both sides with hell
>
> The other'd written me a letter
> In which he said I've written better
>
> They pushed their cocks in many places
> And I'm not certain of their faces
>
> Or which I kissed or which I didn't
> Or which or both of them I hadn't.[93]

In Spicer's "Epilog for Jim," magic is locked in the shadows of buzzards' wings above the poet as he acts out his "betrayal" by Jim Alexander.

> The buzzards wheeling in the sky are Thanksgiving
> Making their own patterns
> There in the sky where they have left us.
> It is hot down here where they have left us
> On the hill or in the city. The hell
> Of personal relations.
> It is like a knot in the air. Their wings free
> Is there (our) shadows.[94]

Nevertheless, Spicer continued to use the figure of Jim Alexander inside his poetry. His greatest work waited for the destruction of their intimacy to appear, radically transformed.

Another loss, of a different kind, cast gray shadows over the season for Spicer—the dissolution of his weekly bridge club. He remained a regular right up until the sudden demise of the Friday night games. Jess Sawyer remembered him arriving with copies of *J* to share with the group. "He seemed to be issuing a copy of this almost every week or two—it couldn't have been that often, but I actually had the feeling there would be one of them available every time we went to one of the meetings of the bridge club. The journal was typed, the pages colored by hand: rather thin, fascicle, celebrating *J*. Wilben Holther endeared himself to Jack by reading these things completely very soon and the moment they next met, at the next meeting, he would always be asking questions and saying how marvelous something was, how much he had enjoyed this and that. This encouraged Jack—so we all got copies of *J*."[95] Spicer's lives in Berkeley and San Francisco were so separate that probably few of his friends in North Beach would have known who Holther was, but Wilben Holther had received a dedicated poem in Spicer's *After Lorca*, as had at least a half dozen others from his Berkeley life. The second issue of *J*, in fact, contained a contribution by Wilben Holther, "Lament for Otto de Fey."[96]

The "Old Ladies' Bridge Club" meetings at the North Berkeley home of George Berthelon contributed immeasurably to Spicer's conception of what today we might call a gay community. George Stanley speculated on the values two such different men as Spicer and Berthelon shared: "These were guys who were non-ghettoizing homosexuals. There was a sort of connection between these non-ghettoizing homosexuals and a kind of class consciousness. George Berthelon, when I mentioned he had nice geraniums growing in his garden, said, 'I'm so glad, I'm really glad you

called them "geraniums." I hate people who call them "pelargoniums."'
They shared a feisty, anti-bourgeois, anti-traditional-homosexual attitude:
'We suck cock: take it or leave it!'"[97] In the "Old Ladies' Bridge Club" the
social dimensions of homosexuality were tested, refined, expanded. Out of
all Spicer's circles in the late 1950s, this one was perhaps the clearest lineal
descendant of the "Berkeley Renaissance" group of ten years before. Although many of Spicer's gay classmates had dispersed to other parts of the
country and abroad, those in Berkeley kept the faith, forming a sort of support group of mutual sustenance in their resistance to conventional mores,
and a network of gossip, job leads, gamesmanship, and sex advice. The
years made them more cynical. But for Spicer the ideal of a homosexual
community still burned bright. The third week of April 1960 changed all
that, for it brought the death of George Berthelon.

Jess Sawyer described Berthelon's death with rich memory. "It was alcohol, I suppose, that was involved. He had a strep throat, and decided to
drink quite a bit late one afternoon. He got sick to his stomach and I believe managed to suffocate somehow or other."[98] "He could have been
saved," said Myrsam Wixman. "He went to a famous East Bay doctor
whose specialty was rectal gonorrhea—a gay doctor, his clients were
mostly queens. The doctor may not have taken Berthelon's complaint—
made over the telephone from work—seriously. [He] saw Berthelon in his
office and gave him a cursory exam, diagnosed a cold or flu, and sent him
home with aspirin-and-rest-and-fluids advice, [made] no throat culture.
. . . It was galloping strep. Had he been diagnosed and subjected to rigorous treatment he might have survived. Finally George ran upstairs to
Wilben Holther and his last words were, 'I can't breathe,' and then he
died."[99] "I was sitting in 'Mr. Otis's with Jack Spicer that night," George
Stanley recalled. "George Berthelon's death I recall as being a very sad
night." Russell FitzGerald was in the same bar that night and watched
Spicer's devastation when he learned of the tragedy. Berthelon had been
Spicer's father confessor, his lover, his confidante, his friend. In his diary
Russell wrote, "Last night George Berthelon's death touched George (S.)
and I almost as much as if he were one of our own generation."[100]

Jim Alexander described the Spicer circle of 1958–59 with nostalgia:

Jack brought a sense of awe to the reader, though at times he was too busy being
clever. His best works, in my opinion, were his early works. Jack himself often remarked this quality in others, such as the French novelist Raymond Radiguet. As
for me, I had pretty much stopped writing—for Jack—after *The Jack Rabbit Poem*.

In all I think it was a very enriching experience for me, meeting so many new

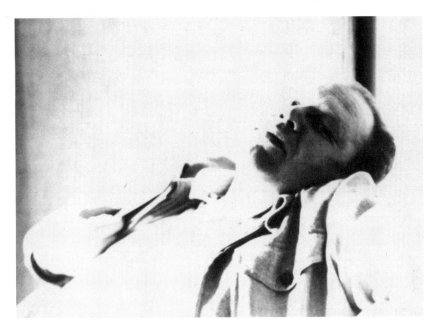

Jack Spicer. "It is hot down here where they have left us / On the hill or in the city." *Photo by Edgar Austin (collection of the authors).*

personalities, many of whom were close friends over the years or at least day by day acquaintances. There was a shared feeling of the importance of the arts, and among the writers was a certain reverence for poetry. Poetry evoked something for us of cosmic significance. We were exhilarated and carried away by this and thought we were surely the cleverest and most knowledgeable people on earth.[101]

1960 served as a watershed for the Spicer circle. The Dulls, Stan Persky, Joanne Kyger, George Stanley, Russell FitzGerald—all left North Beach for a while, at the decade's end, to return for another long season in the first half of the 1960s. The Dulls traveled in Spain and other parts of Europe; Duncan and Jess were in Stinson Beach; Joanne Kyger, Gary Snyder, Bill McNeill, Allen Ginsberg, and Peter Orlovsky explored Japan and India. These leavetakings confounded Spicer: he could not understand any poet leaving San Francisco, and he could be cutting when he felt wounded or ignored.

For the members of the group, this was a time of artistic evolution. For Spicer, it was a time of great loss, as he watched the departure of so many poets, the collapse of his dreams for James Alexander, the death of the bridge club, and the farewell to Berthelon. He began to drink, solemnly, somberly, like some grave ritual that could have only one end.

CHAPTER SEVEN

Heads of the Town

*L*ate in 1959, Robin Blaser returned to the Bay Area from Boston. From this point on, he acted as the linchpin of the Spicer/Duncan group, his presence holding together the elements of an increasingly complex set of forces, as relations between Spicer and Duncan began to unravel around him alarmingly. For almost fifteen years he had been close to both Spicer and Duncan in a warm and mutually loving friendship. Yet as soon as he arrived, cracks in the entente began to appear. The next six years were uneasy ones for Robin Blaser; he found himself thrust into the role of peacemaker while attempting to revitalize his own writing. His poetic production, or at least his poetic publication, had been small in the 1950s. Of all the poets that Don Allen gathered into *The New American Poetry*, Robin might have published the least. The reason was partly his perfectionism; but this need to be "perfect" stemmed, again at least in part, from his sense of standing in the shadows of two mighty, and vociferous, giants.

In Boston and at Harvard, Robin had broken away from the crippling weight of Spicer and Duncan's influence, and he had found a new constellation of poets, only to be stymied when, one by one, they were lured away to San Francisco by Spicer. "I could have killed him!" he laughed years later. "Jack stole my entire scene, left me with nothin'!"[1] Without John Wieners, Joe Dunn, and Edward Marshall to amuse him, Robin befriended the Gloucester poet Charles Olson, establishing an enduring bond that would last until Olson's death in 1970.[2] Duncan, who had earlier "discovered" the poet himself, was skeptical of Blaser's intimacy with Olson.

Spicer was wary and tentative. After his Tarot humiliation at Olson's hands, he was afraid of Olson, like a burnt child who shuns the fire. Thus the wobbly triangle of Duncan/Spicer/Blaser was actually a rhomboid, with a hidden point rarely referred to.

Robin established himself and Jim Felts in Pacific Heights, a luxurious neighborhood of San Francisco, while Felts continued his medical studies. Soon Robin took a job in the order department of San Francisco State College [now University] Library, working with the sardonic and alcoholic Robert Berg. Ruth Witt-Diamant asked Robin to read at the Poetry Center, but he declined politely. He had no intention, he told her, of entering into the politics of poetry in San Francisco. It would take him at least a year to "know where I stand in poetry in this area. In the meantime, I prefer to work quietly."[3]

In fact, around the time of Blaser's arrival, late in November, new energies began to swirl. First came a new series of weekly meetings. Compared to the fluid roll call of the Sunday afternoon meetings at the Dunns', membership was sharply curtailed; it was limited to Spicer, Blaser, Herndon, and Landis Everson. All had been students at Berkeley in the late 1940s, and in retrospect, the inclusion of Everson and Herndon in Spicer's new, 1960-model workshop seems to signify an attempt to recreate the halcyon days of the Berkeley Renaissance of ten years before. The new circle met usually at Blaser's apartment, but sometimes at the Herndons' house on Russian Hill, above North Beach. Herndon remembered Everson's presence at the meetings with enjoyment, but Robert Duncan, who was pointedly *not* invited, thought that the inclusion of Everson was "fruitless." Landis, thought Duncan, "was just an elegant writer for *Kenyon Review*," and Blaser and Spicer were foolishly trying to make him "real."

"What Spicer was looking for," Duncan continued, "was a poetic fate; and interestingly enough, he saw true addiction to baseball as a fate, and the end product of that—this *Kreis*—as a design for fate." The pressure on Everson to excel was severe, as Jim Herndon observed at first hand. Jack's "hidden agenda" was, Herndon felt, "for him and Robin to attack Landis for being a phony asshole because Landis had been, back at Berkeley, one of their prime candidates. Jack had Robin totally on his side—Robin, to give him credit, was always on Jack's side, even when Jack pissed him off so he could hardly stand it—and the purpose for getting Robin to attack Landis was to tell Landis to straighten out, stop this chickenshit, popular, bullshit poetry he was writing: get back to the old thing we know you can do!" And there was yet another item on Jack's "hidden agenda" that Herndon spotted. "It gave him something to do between eight and eleven every night, because he didn't want to go to the bars earlier."[4]

Duncan's contemptuous attitude toward Landis Everson may be read as resentment at not being invited to participate himself. He had, in fact, been "disinvited." Robert's move to Stinson Beach had put an end to much of his involvement in the San Francisco scene, and perhaps it was impractical to expect him to attend many meetings, but to be shunned entirely was a different story! In his unpublished notes written toward an introduction to a projected Spicer bibliography, Duncan's hurt and rejection were still palpable, fifteen years afterward. It was an exclusion beyond his understanding, one that struck deeply at his sense of the shared history of the Renaissance that he, Spicer, and Blaser had created together. From the exclusion of this period can be dated Duncan's gradual distrust of Blaser and his alienation from Spicer, which waxed and waned over the next five years, until Spicer's death served as a giant full stop or exclamation point.

Yet the bad feeling between Spicer and Duncan had existed before Robin's return to the Bay Area, though it had been considerably masked by their shared excitements in writing, teaching, and publishing. Spicer was envious first of Duncan's happiness with Jess, and then envious of Duncan's increasing fame and popularity, spiked by the forthcoming publication of *The Opening of the Field*, which would have a national distribution. (Ironic, since, as we have seen, Duncan had scorned Spicer's detective novel and condemned *his* lust for Mammon.) On Duncan's side, he thoroughly disliked what he termed Spicer's "Puritanism," his rigid condemnation of Duncan's honest efforts to obtain a wider audience for his poetry. Robert had been rankled, too, at Spicer's antipathy toward the "Maidens" experiments.

In addition, there was just so much of Jack that *Jess* could take. The break came after Jess and Robert invited Robin and Jim Felts for a visit to Stinson Beach—Robin had hinted that it was a tremendously important occasion for them, their anniversary, Jim's birthday, or the like, and Jess made the offer to invite them. Robert returned after spending some time at the bars in San Francisco with Jack and told Jess, rather sheepishly, "Oh, Jack's coming too." Jack had just about invited himself. Jess's eyes grew wide. He stepped back and demanded to know how to get hold of Jack. Robert produced a phone number, and Jess walked down to the pay phone at the grocery store—because he didn't have a phone. "Jack," he said, "don't come here any more."[5]

The writing group continued quietly without Duncan who, although stung, maintained a surface civility toward Spicer and Blaser. Herndon was working on a novel and read a chapter a week. Robin began the poems of *Cups*, while Spicer began the poems that became "Homage to Creeley."[6] By February 1960 he could write to Stinson Beach in triumph to announce its near-completion.

> . . . Writing it has (so far) been the most thrilling and spooky poetic experience I've had—including *After Lorca*. The title of the whole is "Homage to Creeley." The 1st part (which you have) is titled "for Cegeste" (your help has been invaluable), the 2nd (which is finished) "for the Princess," the 3rd (3 of the 10 done) "for Heurtebise." Will send you and Jess all the moment I'm through. Hope to see you alone one of the next times you're in town. The neutral sources through which we correspond wouldn't be unhappy to see a minor nuclear war (fireworks) between us major powers.
>
> We ought to be able to misunderstand on our own.
>
> Love,
> Jack[7]

"Spooky"? It was during the writing of "Homage" that Spicer announced to Blaser that he had been writing his poetry through "dictation." He was no longer "in charge" of his writing—some outer force was using him as a trance medium. For Spicer, dictation was a release from the responsibility of authorial intention and all it denotes. No longer was his "personality" to intrude. The days of dedicated poems were over. The spirits that wrote the new poems hardly knew the boys Spicer loved. The morning after he wrote "Dillinger," he stumbled across a copy of the *San Francisco Chronicle*, and discovered that the last of Dillinger's gang had been shot down in a barber shop.[8] He became convinced that he was in touch with—and perhaps had been in touch with for years—a great "Outside" force, as powerful and omniscient as the spirits that visited Blake and attended the seances of William and Georgie Yeats, or those who wrote the "Sonnets to Orpheus" through Rilke. He was now a radio, picking up transmissions from "ghosts."

Fran Herndon was skeptical about Spicer's Orphic notions. "He went through the whole period where he said his poems were dictated. That's when he was doing *Heads of the Town*." Given his state of mind at the time, she added, it was highly possible that he believed what he said. Fran hesitated. "I'm sure Jim Herndon would never agree with that. He thought it was another Jack *con*, that Jack was just saying that because he doesn't want to explain why he would walk through the [Broadway] Tunnel and go home at two or three in the morning and write these poems. What I see it as is a truly creative period in which the imagination works, these poems come out and he has visions and no one understands why he has them. Alcoholism certainly plays a part in all of this at some point, but how much

I really don't know. But I do think Jack wrote most of his work when he was drunk. Or pretty drunk." Fran acknowledged that she found it hard to accept Jack's idea of dictated poetry because his erudition and opinion were so much a part of the finished product.[9]

Blaser was undergoing a similar strange experience—a kind of elation mixed with a vast emptiness—which manifested itself in *Cups*. The book begins with two men—identifiable as Blaser himself and Jack Spicer—sitting in a tree. Are they birds or poets or both?

> The clown of dignity sits in a tree
> The clown of games hangs there too.
> Which is which or where they go—
> the point is to make others see
> that two men in a tree is clearly
> the same thing as poetry.

It concludes with images of death and ritual mutilation of these hapless bird figures, feathered bodies slashed "in triangular parts" by Amor, posing as a geometer:

> When reassembled
> they hung in that tree,
> their genitals placed
> where their heads should be.[10]

Cups can be read as a fantasia of dismemberment, cannibalism, violent expulsion, excretion, death, and desire. Blaser's birds are not only helpless victims; they are also murderous birds of prey. Even their shit can kill, as the narrating subject of "The Park" relates:

> Jessie Whitehead told me they sometimes choose a tree
> and kill it, they so mire the branches[11]

The figure of the aviary was in the air in the winter of 1959–60 (when Alfred Hitchcock began *Psycho*) but it had been a mainstay of the poetry of the Berkeley Renaissance long before that anxious winter. The figure of birds sprang up, full-blown, when Robin Blaser first told his name to Spicer and Duncan. Instantly the poet was a bird, and the other poets birds too. The trope was in full feather in 1951 when Spicer wrote:

> The robin and the thrush have taken wing.
> The sparrow stays. He sings a dismal song
> And eats the seed uncovered in the snow.
> An ugly bird, call him the heart's agony.
> "Sonnet for the Beginning of Winter"[12]

And, in the "Imaginary Elegies," "Believe the birds." Robin had come to San Francisco to rebuild a nest among these amoral, magisterial birds. The next six years were a terrible, wonderful time for him.

Spicer's friendship with Jim and Fran Herndon was at its closest while he was writing "Homage to Creeley." From the very first evening they had spent time together, Jack seemed to see something unusual, vivid in Fran that she had not seen herself. It was as if he were creating a person, the way he created a poem, out of the raw materials she presented, and for a long time she did not know what it was he wanted her to be. Fran was mystified but elated by a power that Jack saw hidden inside her demure, polite social persona. He knew before she did that she would never be completely satisfied with the roles of mother and housewife.

When Jack scrutinized her, as if envisioning in his mind's eye a new and somehow different person, she began thinking: there must be some off-moments from being a mother—and during those moments what do I do? "I remember clearly discussing school with him. And out of the alternatives I mentioned, he zeroed in on the Art Institute." (In 1960, the California School of Fine Arts was changing its name to the San Francisco Art Institute, but it remained basically the same institution.)

She began to drop two-year-old Jay off at a nursery school in North Beach, and walk up the hill to the Art Institute on Chestnut. She was quietly astonished at this turn of events, but already Jack was "a very powerful figure in my life. His opinions were crucial."

In the evenings Spicer came by the Herndons'—sometimes three or four times a week, sometimes every night. Fran felt herself waiting for his visit, convinced of the link between the lithographs she was creating and the poems that were pouring out of him. He was never present while she worked on her graphics, and she never saw him writing, but somehow the results of their private endeavors meshed in a way that seemed perfect to them both. "Sometimes it was reaching, but he knew that there was some connection in [my] work and what he was writing. It was as if at times it was prophetic (I mean, he would never have expected that to happen)—and he was just ecstatic when he could see that connection. At times it surprised *me*, because I had no inkling of the poems that were preceding or coming after those lithos. He saw it as not in any way illustrating the poems, but just an interaction of some kind." This experience lasted no longer than four or five months. "It was a magic process."[13] She loved the

James Herndon and Fran Herndon in 1958, shortly after their
return from Europe. Jim Herndon's middle name was
"Boswell,"—a fact Spicer was quick to take advantage of. *Photos
courtesy of Fran Herndon.*

litho stone she used, its perfect smoothness and porousness, its absorption
of acid. Never again, she recollected, did she achieve what she achieved
with the lithos for "Homage to Creeley." "Somehow when the poems were
finished, that's when it was over, really."

Yet sometimes, for his own mysterious purposes, Jack created tension
between the Herndons. One evening Jack mentioned, apparently casually,
the name of a woman Fran knew as a friend of Jim's—just a friend. From
the context, Fran immediately realized that the woman had actually been
Jim's lover. Upset, she tried to hold back the tears: that Jim had not been
honest was painful. "Then Jack read his poems to us. It was exactly the
right moment. Certainly he had all my attention because I wanted to get
away from the pain. Jim did, too; Jim didn't want to focus on that unhappy
moment. So we were absolutely the greatest audience Jack could possibly
have had that evening." And later, Fran realized that Jack's apparent *faux
pas* had not been accidental after all. He had wanted to create a context for
the poetry, and Jim's girlfriend was a handy pretext.

Fran Herndon became Spicer's closest collaborator: "He saw in me something greater than I saw in myself—*I think*." *Photos courtesy of Fran Herndon.*

To know [Jack], to see him every day and to read his poetry, I am sure was essential to my deep love for his work. I saw more in Jack's poetry by knowing him, and seeing him every day. Most of the people I met later who were poets were really through Jack, going to the poetry readings. I made sure I got to the readings because by then I was very caught up in them. I felt [poetry] essential to my work, and I was very serious about my work then.

You could set your watch on his arrival at a bar, or his arrival at our house, and his arrival at Aquatic Park. I never knew him to be late. The only appointment I ever missed with him was when Jay was seriously ill. I left Jack a note even that day, that I wouldn't be there when he came to lunch. And he was very upset that day, very disoriented. But the thing he mentioned to me, the first thing he mentioned to me was the fact I'd written him such a cogent note. It was reassuring to him. I told him why I wasn't there, where I was going, and what was wrong.

So I was this very steady person in his life. I was always there for him. In the end I could not maintain what he was asking of me. It was a source of great guilt for me when he died. It was only normal. He was somebody very important in my life. He saw in me something greater than I saw in myself—*I think*.[14]

Spicer's growing estrangement from Robert Duncan had a practical consequence—he had no one to type his manuscripts. Spicer entrusted the bulk of the book to Fran Herndon and to a new acquaintance, Gail Chugg. Gail Chugg, born in Utah in 1927, was active in North Beach poetry circles at the time and, in later life, was to become a well-known Shakespearean actor, a founder of the Berkeley Stage Company. He now became Jack Spicer's "secretary."

Spicer and Chugg became close, meeting daily to discuss problems that arose in preparing the poems for publication. When not working together, the two lounged around the beach at Aquatic Park, backs to the sea, boy-watching. "There was a boy up there sunning, in swimming trunks. . . . I would say about sixteen to eighteen. This kid looked old-fashioned, like photographs of boys—not boys, young laboring men—before the War. He looked nakeder than, say, the kind of man who flaunts his strength, or his beauty, or his body. He was a beautiful kid. But a very special kind of kid . . . and Jack said, 'I'm going to write a poem for him tonight.'"[15]

"Homage to Creeley" now became the first of four sequences in a longer work, which Spicer called *The Heads of the Town Up to the Aether* after a lost Gnostic text he saw referred to in the English translation (1960) of *The Secret Books of the Egyptian Gnostics*, by the Parisian Egyptologist Jean Doresse.[16] Each poem in "Homage" itself received its own ghostly prose footnote, which together Spicer called "Explanatory Notes." The poems of "Homage to Creeley"—minus their "Explanatory Notes," and still without a title—were finished by mid-March 1960. During that month Russell FitzGerald attempted to organize a reading of them at the studio he was sharing with the painter Nemi Frost. But Jack complained that the arrangements made by the improvident Russell were "inadequate . . . too indefinite," and postponed the reading. Russell felt rebuffed. "There is nothing to say," he told his diary. "Maybe 'goodbye.' 'You're insane' would do, if 'insane' meant anything. Perhaps 'goodbye' is what he wants. If so, he has it."[17]

Spicer moved back to San Francisco from Berkeley and lived in a basement apartment nearly, if not quite, under a Bank of America vault at California Street and Van Ness Avenue in "Polk Gulch," a district of hardcore hustling mixed with less intense but very gay pastimes. Nearby, on the western slope of Nob Hill, was The Handle Bar, a gay bar serving a Polk Street clientele and tourists. The bar appears in the "Explanatory Notes" to the third poem: "'I like it better in L.A. because there're more men and they're prettier,' someone said at The Handlebar tonight."[18]

Typing the book, Gail confided to its author that he found one of the poems—"Elegy"—highly threatening. "Whispers / Get out of hell—/ You big poet / We soldiers from hell's country / Here / Safe as you are / You write poetry / For dead persons." "That's your most frightening poem," he told Jack. But Jack disagreed. The most frightening, he replied, was "Magic."[19]

> Strange, I had words for dinner
> Stranger, I had words for dinner
> Stranger, strange, do you believe me?
>
> Honestly, I had your heart for supper
> Honesty has had your heart for supper
> Honesty honestly are your pain.
>
> I burned the bones of it
> And the letters of it
> And the numbers of it
> That go 1, 2, 3, 4, 5, 6, 7
> And so far.
>
> Stranger, I had bones for dinner
> Stranger, I had bones for dinner
> Stranger, stranger, strange, did you believe me.[20]

"When 'Magic' came," Jack confessed, "I was terrified."[21] The whole of "Homage to Creeley" is studded with allusions and quotes from Spicer's favorite writers: these were the "furniture in the room" which the Martians came in and rearranged. Nursery rhymes, spells and incantations, folk and pop music, medieval riddles, bardic incantations, drinking songs, stage directions, radio jingles: these were the materials of the weird science fiction landscape Spicer's poetry now pushed him into headlong, dreaming. In a novel he admired, Alfred Bester's *The Demolished Man* (1951–53), a group of empaths ("empers") who can read men's minds successfully prevents crime by serving as police. A criminal mastermind manages to commit a murder, in full range of the empers, by memorizing an advertising jingle so catchy it forces all other thought out:

> Eight, sir; seven, sir;
> Six, sir; five, sir;
> Four, sir; three, sir;
> Two, sir; one!
> Tenser, said the Tensor.
> Tenser, said the Tensor.
> Tension, apprehension,
> And dissention have begun.[22]

Bester's influence is transparent in Spicer's poem, the catchiness, the counting, the subtle shiftings of suffix and meaning (from "tenser" to "Tensor" in Bester, from "honesty to "honestly" in Spicer), the maniacal repetition beyond rational thought. The whole of *The Heads of the Town* would become an invocation to the *Unheimlich*, to Freud's sense of the "Uncanny."

In a two-story Victorian apartment at 1713 Buchanan Street in Japan Town, Ebbe Borregaard had organized a gallery and with a Barnum touch he called it "Borregaard's Museum."[23] There in mid-April 1960 Spicer read "Homage to Creeley" for the first time. Poets thronged into the small whitewashed rooms to hear the thirty short pieces. Among those present were Blaser, George Stanley, Harold Dull, Helen Adam, Landis Everson, Jim Alexander, Philip Whalen, Ron Loewinsohn, and Edward Marshall— like "giving a party in the middle of an anthology," as Madelaine says in Spicer's novel of the San Francisco Renaissance. Spicer read the poem through twice, then broke for an intermission and returned to read it a third time. His listeners were touched and thrilled by his new work, almost speechless, but they disappointed Jack by having little intelligent comment or reaction.[24]

No one was more impressed than Harold Dull and Dora Geissler, who were about to leave for a two-year stay in Europe. The Dulls were pooling their salaries for the projected trip, and money was tight. Nevertheless, they decided to print "Homage to Creeley" themselves, using the mimeograph machine on the Pomo Indian reservation where they lived. They had printed twenty-five copies before Spicer realized that the text was only the beginning of a larger work, a work that kept coming from a mysterious, threatening Outside, and flowered into *The Heads of the Town Up to the Aether.*

The publication, in April 1960, of Donald Allen's anthology *The New American Poets 1945–60* marked the beginning of another split in the poetry circle, as those who were excluded felt hurt, jealous of those who had been included, and betrayed by their sponsors. When George Stanley saw a copy of the book, he tried to keep a stiff upper lip, but confessed in a letter to Joanne Kyger (who had also been excluded) that

I realized how I really wanted to be in it, not because it is good, but because it is somehow lonely not to be. I wish I had sent them Flowers, etc. instead of the 2nd rate things I did, so I cd be even rightly angry at Don Allen . . . but it's only his personal dislike for me that saved me from having those things in there . . . that and

Jack's and Robert's not writing him or Robin when they were making it up. It's fine to think you're above that & your poetry is real (wh. it is) but when you see all the names you feel like Enoch Soames. . . . It should be some consolation that there are other real poets left you (among them you & Jim)—but!²⁵

Spicer's own feelings about the anthology were muted. In it he was represented by the first four "Imaginary Elegies": mightn't something like *Billy the Kid* or "Homage to Creeley" have been more representative of what he was doing now? On the other hand he was grateful for the attention, although, in the years to come, his ferocity and insistence on dictation put off many young poets who had come to San Francisco to meet the original of the warm personality they imagined as the author of the "Elegies." Inclusion in another anthology published shortly afterward satisfied Spicer on another score. This was the elaborate, two-volume *The Californians* (1961), edited by Robert Pearsall and Ursula Spier Erickson, a historically based survey of California writing from the time of the Native peoples to the Beat Generation, which included not only poems, but diaries, excerpts from novels, travel writing, political manifestos, and so on. Thus Spicer found himself contextualized not only through the work of his immediate peers (Ferlinghetti, Rumaker, Everson, Kerouac, Broughton, Ginsberg, Miles, Gleason, Rexroth), but in the company of novelists (Henry Miller, Isherwood, Huxley, Gavin Lambert, Saroyan, Steinbeck, John Fante, and James M. Cain) and, taking the long view, poets and writers of previous generations—George Sterling, John Muir, Jack London, Vachel Lindsay, Helen Hunt Jackson, Bret Harte, Ina Coolbrith, Ambrose Bierce, Robinson Jeffers, and Meridel Le Sueur. It was this approach Spicer favored enough to imitate when he and Blaser planned his own anthology later in the 1960s.²⁶

To the young poets in his circle Spicer now poured out his scorn for the way both Blaser and Duncan seemed to "bow and scrape" to Donald Allen, now that he had made them "famous" through *The New American Poetry*, thus fanning the flames of discontent. "Duncan used to despise Don, and now he thinks he's a fine man doing great things for poetry." In June 1960 the Poetry Center sponsored a reading by John Crowe Ransom, the poet who had earned Duncan's enmity in the 1940s by rejecting his work from *The Kenyon Review* after Duncan's declaration of homosexuality. The San Francisco poets stayed away from the reading en masse, but perversely Spicer attended and praised Ransom as senile but perfect. Spicer also resented the fact that Duncan, on his infrequent trips to San Francisco from Stinson Beach, now failed to look him up regularly, preferring the company of Robin and of Lawrence Ferlinghetti, whose City Lights Books had

printed a volume of Duncan's *Selected Poems.*[27] Shortly afterward Ferlinghetti himself added fuel to the fire by asking if he could reprint one of
Spicer's poems in the *Beatitude Anthology* he planned. (Spicer's work had
appeared twice, a month apart, in the then-new *Beatitude* magazine the
year before—his "15 False Propositions" in issue 3, and the "Epithalamium" collaboration in issue 6.) "Under no circumstances may you publish my poem," Jack fired back.[28] These contretemps led directly to the
most amusing poem of "Homage to Creeley," the bitchy "Ferlinghetti."[29]
Spicer opens the work with an echo of the pop/jazz of the day, "Be bop de
beep," which he uses to parody Ferlinghetti's talent and practice in poetry;
the attempted *coup de grace* is delivered in the "explanatory note": "Ferlinghetti is a nonsense syllable invented by The Poet." This comment is
striking not so much for its hostility to what Spicer took to be a minor poetic ability, or for its distaste for an individual, as for the confidence behind
the remark itself, the surety that he, Spicer, could make such a statement
about a well-known contemporary. In such matters he was often fearless,
perhaps foolhardy.

Within a matter of weeks George Stanley had decamped and moved,
with Russell FitzGerald, to New York, where he discovered the Cedar bar
and Frank O'Hara, and Greenwich Village, where he met the avant-garde
circle published by LeRoi Jones and Diane Di Prima in *The Floating Bear.*
When George left for New York, Jack wrote him a "brusque" letter. George
"wrote back to him a complaint saying, 'I thought we were friends.' He
wrote me back and said, 'We've never been friends.' He said, 'I respect
your poetry, and you've been a wonderful conversation companion, but
we've never been friends.' Most of my life with Spicer, it seems, was spent
arguing."[30]

Together with Blaser, Spicer hit upon the idea of running a college of their
own. While he waged war on the university system, Berkeley had nurtured
him; now he was discovering that, ironically, he and others had implanted
in the younger poets a too-complete disdain of higher learning. "The Acad-
emy was a temptation to us in our youth," he wrote to Duncan, "but I have
not met one moderately intelligent or talented person under thirty who
has been so tempted. The danger is George's initial reaction: 'I don't want
to learn anything about modern French poetry.' (He took French in high
school.) Or Ebbe's 'Why should I want to learn anything about mythology? I have Graves' book at home.' . . . I quote the reaction of the two

most educated members of that generation then I remember how we learned and listened from Kantorowicz and weep."[31] In early May Robin asked Duncan and Jess to participate in "Black Mountain College in Exile"—later to be called "White Rabbit College." As Robin and Jack envisioned the curriculum, all courses would be taught not only by but for writers and painters. Duncan would teach mythology; Jess, modern painting; Spicer, Elizabethan poetry; and Blaser, French poetry (beginning with Artaud). Would Robert and Jess agree to lecture once a week, from June 15 through September?[32] Duncan would be surprised, perhaps dismayed, by their impudence in appropriating the memory of Black Mountain College, when neither of them had studied or taught there. Olson would have to be applied to for his permission. But "the name would not permit us to goof," Jack wrote. "The past should be remembered."[33]

That summer Robert and Jess were busy with other projects (and in any case living in Stinson Beach made them chary of commitments in the City), but the idea kept brewing. In August Robin called Philip Whalen and asked him to teach a course on Buddhism. He also asked Jess to sound out his friend Harry Jacobus about teaching a painting course.[34] Blaser spent the fall and winter of 1960 not only working in the library of San Francisco State but leading its "Workshop for Practicing Poets," yet he continued to make plans for the college. Years later he described the project in detail. "We were to organize a White Rabbit College at Ebbe Borregaard's Museum—but Ebbe objected. Anyhow, Pauline Oliveros was to teach music, Jess Collins painting, Spicer was to give a course in 'poetry and politics' and another in Old English. I was to teach French and 'the history of Troy.' Duncan was to teach 'God lore.' Duncan wanted money; Spicer opposed money; Ebbe wanted to make up contracts. Only Duncan's course, and an Oliveros concert, were ever done."[35]

Duncan's course was held at Borregaard's Museum from December 15, 1960, through January 26, 1961. For seven consecutive Thursday evenings he spoke with Coleridgean authority and eclecticism on "The History of Poetry"—his personal map of the twentieth century, which began with *The Waste Land*, Zukofsky, *Paterson*, Rexroth, Ginsberg, projective verse, Patchen, his beloved H.D. and her *War Trilogy*, and ran all the way through to Creeley and Levertov. These lectures were given with a bite and fervor that made his audiences regret no other courses were to be given.[36] But at this point Duncan and Borregaard quarreled, in a series of open letters, over the future and function of the museum—Duncan objecting to Borregaard's plans for a retrospective show of "New Art" that would

In happier times—Jess, Ebbe Borregaard, and Jack Spicer on the deck of the Drew House, Stinson Beach. *Photo by Joanne Kyger.*

gather the work of Tom Field, Jess, Harry Jacobus, Jorge Fick, and other painters, without taking into proper account the different origins of the painters. Ebbe fired back defending himself from Duncan's scorn.[37] Paul Alexander recalled that

Ebbe printed up some sort of statement about what was going to happen, with this and that, and so on and so on, and he included some people and excluded other people and made everybody very angry with him. Jack came over to my studio in kind of a rage, and Nemi [Frost, who, like Paul, had been excluded from Ebbe's prospectus for the "New Art" show] was there; and Jack used Nemi and me as a sounding board for him to form a response, a denunciation of Ebbe's plans. I remember that evening as a lot of fun, actually. I'd never seen Jack at work before. How he stormed around!

Jack wrote to Ebbe: "Dear Mr. Beauregard: Since you sent me a copy of your open letter, I presume you wish me to respond. My response is that Duncan is a learned and creative whore and you, while being whore, are neither learned nor creative. Sincerely . . ."[38] "That, of course," Alexander continued, "was the end of the school. Duncan of course also had to write a public denunciation, so that was the end of it. Rabbit Mountain never got off at all. That was what Jack wanted to call the school: 'Rabbit Mountain.'"[39] Thus for the immediate group around Spicer, the reality of the university idea was realized only in the bar-university.

In the meantime a figure of importance to the original Black Mountain poets had arrived in San Francisco. Cid Corman, the editor of one of the seminal journals, *Origin*, had been living in Europe and Japan for six years, and his presence in San Francisco created no little stir. Not only had Corman been close to Olson and Creeley; he had done much to promote the poetry of Louis Zukofsky, and in Kyoto the previous year had published *"A" (1-12)*. Now he was staying at East-West House, the co-op on California Street that was the site of the last of the Sunday poetry meetings. Lew Welch was living there, Lenore Kandel too—a regular Beat contingent.

Although Corman and Spicer had been aware of each other's work for years, they had never met. Their connection had been made on the East Coast, when Spicer had befriended the young black poet Steve Jonas, part of the Boston Gang. Spicer had dedicated his translation of Lorca's "Ode to Walt Whitman" to Jonas because, he told Robin, it was "Steve who taught me to use anger (as opposed to angry irony)" in a poem. When Jonas was younger—only twenty-one—he had joined Cid Corman's very early West End Library poetry discussion group in Boston, and through Corman the entire Black Mountain–Boston connection had begun.

One afternoon, at East-West House, Corman gave a reading of selected sections of Zukofsky's *"A"* to a small gathering. "Jack came," Corman recalled,

clearly boozed up already—on the stout side—with Robin steering him. They sat on the rug as did most: I sat in a chair (as always). I read the first movement, "A"-11 and largely from "A"-12, the most complex and longest segment of the poem. (The work was virtually unknown anywhere as yet.) When I finished—maybe 45–60 minutes, I entertained comments and questions. Jack was the first to respond, VERY critically. He felt I was skimping—that LZ had written some very hard-to-follow poetry and I made it all seem easier/simpler than it was. To some extent, of course, he was right: I was trying to bring listeners into the work, not scare them off. JS had a quicker mind—to poetry—than most and he was exceptional. Anyhow, I read, at his prompting, "A"-7—The wooden horses highly structured and much worked section. (The choice was mine, the instigation his.) A hard piece to read, but I had prepared for ANY case and read it well. Jack applauded: he was satisfied. Robin and I felt friendly at once in talk afterwards—JS was in his own head—and he apologized quietly for Jack's state, etc. Only much later, after his death, when his collected poems appeared (so well edited by RB) and his letters with RD, did I begin to appreciate what he was into. It isnt my kind of poetry, if you will, but it breaks open possibilities—an intelligence of poetry.

I used to see him around North Beach—invariably soused—and alone—but we never meshed. I doubt if he read ORIGIN much. And I was in SF only till 1962 —before returning to Kyoto—which has really been my home for some 32 years or more.[40]

In January 1961, on "Friday the 13th"—according to Borregaard's publicity announcement—Jack Spicer gave a reading at Borregaard's Museum that included his new long poem, *The Heads of the Town Up to the Aether.* Robert Berg, no partisan of Spicer's, was in the audience. Since their student days at Berkeley, he had seen an aura of malevolence around Spicer, enhanced, he felt, by his assumption that poetry justified bad behavior. Berg was one of many who found themselves awash in Spicer's wake and resented his undisguised hostility toward them. He was a victim, as well, of Spicer's anti-Semitism. For example, in two letters at least, Jack referred to Berg as "Mr. Bug" and a "fat semitic gelding."[41] "Spicer's face," he now wrote in his infamous diary, "is etched in character lines, each one filled with dirt, like the spine of a prawn."[42]

Berg's diary recorded this version of Spicer's reading:

Myrsam Wixman and the Alans (Joyce and Hislop) came to dinner before Spicer's reading. M. forgot the Parmesan for the spaghetti alfredo, but I fell off the wagon and skipped dinner. Ebbe Borregaard's Museum is above the Minakin restaurant in the Western Addition. We sat on benches (Parkinsons, Herndons, Duncan, the wasted John Button, Landis Everson—in from Stinson Beach to have his scalp massaged, Max in his trenchcoat, the notorious Wendy Murphy). Spicer, wearing his baseball rooters cap, read about Rimbaud until he decided that the naked electric bulb above him was inadequate, at which point the chorus (Robin) seated behind him took over.[43]

For several years surrounding the writing and publishing of *The Heads of the Town Up to the Aether* one popular ballad was a central Spicer reference—"The Battle of New Orleans," as recorded by Johnny Horton. As background for the first reading of the poem, Robin Blaser sought out and bought this record that Jack so loved. The plan was for Robin to sit behind Spicer for the first section, "Homage to Creeley"—as a kind of "ghost" voice to the poem—and read the "Explanatory Notes" after each poem was read, while the Horton record played throughout.[44] But before the reading, Jack went to dinner at Gail Chugg's apartment on Sonoma Alley and got rapidly drunk—"piss-your-pants terrified," Chugg recalled. "Robin had to go in and read for him. It's rather interesting because Jack has that early thing about you have to get back to the voice, and yet he was petrified—apparently—about reading his own poetry."[45] Though Spicer tended—particularly toward the end of his life—to appear drunk at important occasions, presenting *The Heads of the Town Up to the Aether*—by far his most ambitious work—was definitely an occasion for terror. Robin Blaser continued the story. After "Homage to Creeley," Jack was "too drunk to go on after this effort and, though there were protests from the floor, I finished the reading of the 'Rimbaud Novel' and the 'Textbook of Poetry.' Thus Jack read only 'Homage' that evening."[46]

Spicer's fellow poets could not praise *The Heads of the Town* highly enough. Robert Duncan wrote him on April 28, 1961, after examining the complete text:

Jess says to tell you in answer to your once saying about that telegram that you wouldn't forgive him until he crawld to you, that he is crawling all the way on his bloody knees to your station of the cross.

It's your beautiful *Textbook of Poetry* that lifts this head into the Aether. For me it comes like *The Structure of Rime* comes to me writing, maybe out of the aether.

Yes, I realize there is an active correspondence with letters of the *Structure*. But how, too, *Textbook* breaks with drafts of light down thru cloudland, the many-imaged stuff—sudden floods over the world I thought most mine to show it, yes—as you announce it must be Astonishd. Es-stone-ishd! *"You"*? The speech of this part of the work is so common (commune) that I am most Jack or most Jack is I—alike as two telephones. Where "you" is talking.

And Jess who most loves the truth of nonsense hasn't rejoiced so since *After Lorca*. My sense of this gnostic work now is: *Homage to Creeley*, written by the poet, by Jack Spicer, by ghosts (Heurtebise), ghostwritten (for Creeley, Cocteau by the poet and Jack Spicer), and interruptions.

Rimbaud (written by the counterfeiting and whitemailing offices of higher poetry. Arriving as always after it was written, forwarded from where it was sent) . . .

(We are sitting at lunch and Jess breaks out: "God, is the whole younger generation like this?"—how the mind will go back to a large dog shitting on one's Italian rug!) "One's prayer rug!" Jess cries.

"The wires in the rose are beautiful"

"And the gradual lack of the beautiful, the lock of the door before him, a new Eurydice . . ."

Jess praises: "He wears the clothing wherein he walks naked."

"(Eros, Amor, feely love, starlight)" these are radiant lines for me. And all the passage—"Only by beginning not to be a soul." "A sole worshipper. And the flesh is important as it rubs into itself your soleness."

what "my grandmother left in the bedroom when she died in the living room," and the whole instruction: "to mess around. To totally destroy the pieces. to build around them."

Where Jess, a painter, kept the grandmother chewing on the pieces of the puzzle "the only way to cause an alliance between the dead and the living"—

I was moved at the reading, Jack, what the text brings is the ground for discovery. You have brought the matter so close to my heart (where matter and spirit seem to find a harmony in not being a soul—is that it? but surrounded by these atmospheres of the soul's sentiment) that I am confused, feeling it all *mine*, and carried beyond my envy.

We searched for this textbook among gnostic remains. The Textbook of Poetry remains.

love,
Robert[47]

The 'most publicized poetry event of January 1961 was not Spicer's appearance at Borregaard's Museum but the "Tribute to Kenneth Patchen" held on January 29th at the Marines Memorial Theater in downtown San Francisco. Patchen, born in the Midwest and a graduate of the University of Wisconsin, had long been a Bay Area resident and had long been troubled by a variety of crippling back ailments. To help pay the bills for his latest surgery, the Actors Workshop invited a variety of San Francisco businessmen, poets, professors, columnists, and entertainers to participate in a benefit to honor the ailing poet and painter. The organizing committee formed a peculiar cross-section of San Francisco arts, old and new, with many of the established poets (Josephine Miles, Madeline Gleason, Thomas Parkinson) chipping in alongside their younger counterparts, the mainstays of Don Allen's New American Poetry. The poets who read from Patchen's work onstage in front of Bob LaVigne's bright stage curtain included Michael (here "Mike") McClure, Philip Whalen, Kenneth Rexroth, and James Broughton. Ferlinghetti read a poem of his own; jazz bands played, sopranos warbled art songs and Hoagy Carmichael numbers. Helen Adam and Ida Hodes sang and danced in a little musical. Helen recalled that Rexroth, who was acting as emcee, came offstage just before her appearance and screamed with rage about having to appear with a "faggot tap dancer." Rexroth's chilling and alarming vehemence impressed Helen strongly, but the joke was that the dancer turned out to be married, with a family, in San Jose.[48] In the face of his long-standing contempt for emcee Rexroth, it is a surprise that Spicer agreed to let his name be used among the committee members and in the show's advertising and press releases.[49] Spicer and Rexroth had long been feuding, as Jack Goodwin recalled:

Knowing Rexroth's paranoia about communists, queers, Standard Oil, and Roman Catholicism, Spicer used to like to bandy bitcheries with Rexroth. I mentioned this young drunk painter, Charlie Walker, a tall, rangy, cherubic, golden blond item who always wore a powder-blue lamb's wool sweater. At the end of a reading, Spicer piloted him up and introduced him to Rexroth, who took the beamish boy's hand and shook it, making various avuncular remarks, which, as it happened, went on to some length, and all this time the hand-shaking continued, Finally Charlie Walker, unable to resist the opportunity of pleasing Spicer, said quietly, "You can let go of my hand now." Rexroth turned vermilion. They crowed about that at the bars for weeks after.

So Rexroth's recognition of Spicer tended to have qualifying clauses tacked on . . . "*Whatever else* Jack Spicer may be, he is a poet of some stature."[50]

The drinking continued and escalated. At the bars of Green Street, Spicer appeared on a predictable schedule, advancing with the years from ten to eleven o'clock. Eight bars, each with its own attractions, lined the block of Green Street from Columbus to Grant. The Cellar had been good for the jazz-and-poetry performances of the Rexroth days almost a decade before, and the Green Valley, at the eastern end (510 Green), was a good daytime place, with an inexpensive restaurant, where Spicer watched ball-games on TV. In between were such almost unused bars as the Montclair, on one corner of Jasper Place, and the Columbus Cafe, which attracted elderly Italian men, remnants of an earlier North Beach population.

When the Spicer circle shifted to Green Street in 1960–61, Mr. Otis was the first bar to catch its favor. This was the bar of Spicer's *Heads of the Town* period. Then the "scene" was Katie's. Then it was Gino & Carlo's and—against Spicer's approval—The Anxious Asp, a beer-and-wine bar with a loud jukebox and an ethnically mixed clientele, partly gay, with many passers-by without roots in the community.

At Katie's there were poetry occasions: readings and meetings where magazines and group affairs were discussed and organized. There were pool occasions, and the lively social life of the bar's crowded evenings. Katie herself was a toddling, footsore lady with a mass of gray hair flopping on her head, a loud and strident voice from Sicily by way of New Orleans. Her estranged husband, Silvio Canciatore, meat chef at Alfred's restaurant nearby, quietly played pinball on Katie's machines, smiling broadly when he won against his soon-to-be-former wife. Spicer often played beside him.

For the remaining years of Spicer's life, his circle frequented Gino & Carlo's. George Stanley once said of an artist, "Oh well, he's as far away from us as The Coffee Gallery," meaning a great distance, though in fact The Coffee Gallery was less than a block away from Gino & Carlo's, just around the corner of Grant and Green.[51] The front half of Gino & Carlo's was a narrow cave: dimly lit, with a telephone booth by the door. A wall ran along the east side, indented by a scattering of amusement machines and two small tables for drinkers. In the early 1960s, a jukebox, a cigarette machine, and a pinball machine crowded the table drinkers into each other. One table (sometimes both) was "the poets' table." On one wall stood a dime-store black mail box for contributions to the various publications alive in those years.

Across from this area was a long bar with wide backbar and work area for two bartenders. Winter or rainy nights could be very slow, but business was usually brisk. Two pool tables occupied the squared space of the back room, and beyond them were the bathrooms. A door at the back led to the kitchen and storeroom, with an entrance to the basement, a dirt-floored cellar where less-fortunates sometimes spent a night or lived awhile between more fixed arrangements. Over the years there were great feasts at Gino & Carlo's, from pasta al pesto on St. Patrick's Day to the jumbles of free food—maybe even free drink—with holiday sports on television. Christmas and New Year's Day were pageants of memorable hangover hysteria, food, drink, sports, and noise equally proportioned in a festivity that made Gino's into a world of its own and kept everything else outside.

Some called Gino & Carlo's "Jack Spicer's living room." But the bar was a busy place and the poets' presence was but one vein of many gleaming in the house. Some customers had no idea people connected with the arts gathered in the bar at all. In the morning especially, when Genovese scavengers ("garbage collectors" in San Francisco) occupied many of the stools at the bar, drinking after a night's work, there was little in the bar to suggest formal "poetry." For some, though, perhaps a hundred in two generations, Gino & Carlo's served as an art bar perhaps matched only by such institutions as McSorley's, the San Remo, or The Cedar in downtown New York.

The young Lew Ellingham had spent his twenties in an inhibiting relationship with an Ivy League professor who paid his bills and took him through Europe in the summers. Finally, taking risks, he found a job as a clerk in a Bay Area steamship company, with the intention of becoming a writer (poet, even), conducting a sex and love life that was not a dependency, and making his own way financially and emotionally. In the summer of 1961, he met Gail Chugg, who was living on Telegraph Hill with Jim Liberman. Jim and Gail had white-collar jobs, lived rather prosperously, and drank a good deal in the Green Street bars. To Liberman's distress, Ellingham fell in love with Chugg, and Chugg with Ellingham. The painter Bill McNeill took over Lew's tiny apartment, and he moved with Gail to 4 Harwood Alley, where Nemi Frost had lived (and nearly lost her life at the hands of a deranged lover), and where Paul Alexander had also lived briefly. The week before Gail and Lew moved in, the apartment had been host for a masque by Robert Duncan, acted by Paul Alexander and friends of both Duncan and himself.[52]

Lewis Ellingham. *Photo by Helen Adam.*

Chugg introduced Ellingham to Creeley's *For Love*, Olson's *The Distances* and *The Maximus Poems*, and editor Donald M. Allen's *The New American Poetry, 1945–1960*. These were the big books and names one must know or learn immediately. Chugg also knew the little presses and magazines; he had a complete set of *J*, and most of the White Rabbit productions, including *After Lorca*. Chugg presented the lore of the writing with each new book: with Duncan's then very recent *The Opening of the Field*, for example, came the knowledge that he had written most of the "Pindar" poem while sitting at The Coffee Gallery at a poetry reading or while a participant at the Sunday afternoon meetings.

The next big event of the community was a theatrical one, the musical version of *San Francisco's Burning!*[53] Helen Adam was a delightful and delighted Scotswoman who ebulliently amused, worried, mystified, impressed, and trifled in wonders. The play she wrote with her sister, Pat, figured the occult and the unlikely as well as the very ordinary in a parade of common folk and stock characters. In private performances, Helen Adam had already made the role of "The Worm Queen" her own. On two semi-private occasions (one on Halloween 1960) at Borregaard's Museum in Japan Town, Helen and her sister presented the lyrics they had composed as a grand ballad of mystery and death. Now their play had been made into a musical—music by Warner Jepson, direction by Kermit Sheets. It was performed at The Playhouse, at Beach and Hyde streets, near Aquatic Park in San Francisco. Gail Chugg played a leading role, that of "Neal Narcissus," a part originally offered to, and rebuffed by, Robin Blaser.

Opening night was December 17, 1961. Blaser and Lew Ellingham attended the opening together. Lew did not know Robin well; his relations, in fact, with all serious writers were fragile. The following afternoon he wrote a prose-poem, one of "six essays" that were collectively, he imagined, a serious work of poetry:

It was a December evening, not particularly chilly, when I arrived early to meet a friend for a drink before attending the opening of a play. The theater stands near San Francisco's bay-front, as does the bar where my friend and I were to meet. A promenade runs along the small beach by the theater and at one end a long pier extends over the water, which this evening was calm, exceedingly so. Only a slight undulation unstilled the mirror which stretched toward Marin County and the Golden Gate. Lights, yellow and white, marked the great bridge, the highways approaching it, and the towns on the land opposite me. I set out along the pier, testing the breeze and the distance of a passing ship. It was refreshing, a forgotten experience revived.

This prose poem, and five others, served as Ellingham's entry into the literary life of the Spicer circle. He gave copies of the "Essays on Six Subjects" to Spicer and Robin Blaser, and shortly after he received a telephone call from Blaser: "Wonderful! Will you join me for a drink at Gino's?" Robin rarely went there, never alone or for no reason. This, then, was Lew's initiation into the group at a new level.

While *San Francisco's Burning!* became a hit, running successfully for six months, it was a bittersweet triumph for the Adam sisters. They had lost a bit of control as their play was turned into a musical by The Playhouse theatrical group, ruled by Kermit Sheets and his close friend (and sometime lover), the poet James Broughton. Robert Duncan denounced the new production in a lengthy piece, eventually published in *Roots and Branches* as "What Happend: Prelude," which condemned "Mr Fair Speech and his cousin, By-Ends" (Broughton and Sheets) for luring the Adam sisters from the paths their original genius had led them to, in the interest of making a play that "anticipates What-the-Audience-Wants."[54] Since Duncan had already attacked Broughton in print in 1958, a new affront from him came as no surprise.[55] The consequences, though, were painful ones for Helen

Adam. Duncan's accusations of selling out must have stung, even though they were ostensibly limited to the Broughton/Sheets combine. Helen knew quite well that she had, perhaps, sacrificed a piece of her integrity in order to achieve the success she so needed and wanted.[56] As Adam scholar Kristin Prevallet has written,

This cross-fire in which Helen was forced to prove her loyalty to both Broughton and Duncan simultaneously could not have been easy. This period of her life was further complicated by her getting fired from the filing job she had held for ten years, as well as what she perceived to be the failure of the "composer" of *San Francisco's Burning* to create the music that perfectly corresponded to her vision. Partly as a consequence of this stress, in January of 1962, at the age of 53, she was hospitalized for several months where she received four shock treatments to heal her of thoughts of suicide.[57]

Gail Chugg—caught between his life as an actor, his affection for both Adam sisters, and the poets who reserved opinion on this development in their lives—could only regret the schism. His role in *San Francisco's Burning!* was especially vulnerable to Duncan's attack for changes in the text. "Jack, of course, would not have come to *San Francisco's Burning!*—he wouldn't have anything to do with it," Gail said. "Jack really did not like the theater, had no use for it whatsoever. Yet he told me he had an unfinished play, *Troilus*. I tried to talk him into letting me read it, but he wouldn't. He told me he thought Chaucer's *Troilus and Criseyde* the greatest poem in English. We later did a production of Shakespeare's *Troilus and Cressida*, and I was playing Ulysses. I asked Jack, 'What, as an actor, should I know about Ulysses?' And he gave me very, very good advice. 'You've got to remember that they've been trapped on that plain for years—deep, deep sexual frustration. And rage, in a man.' By God, as an actor, that played!"[58]

In early 1962 Stan Persky had returned from European duty with the U.S. Navy, anxious to reestablish himself in the Spicer circle. His manic energy and flood of schemes amused some and alienated others, those who maliciously dubbed him "Sammy Glick," after the Hollywood hack antihero of Budd Schulberg's 1941 novel *What Makes Sammy Run?* To Ellingham and Chugg, Persky proposed a new magazine, and thus was born *M* in the spring of 1962. Ellingham was then twenty-nine years old, Chugg was thirty-five, Persky twenty-one. From the very start much went wrong, largely from confusion of the lesser ranks about the goings-on of the major ranks. The inexperience of the three editors accounted, too, for difficulties; but even so, there was no lack of manuscripts to publish. In fact the resulting magazine grew larger than tradition—which called for a slim product, frequently issued, and modeled on Spicer's *J*—by now required of the editors.

They solicited work from all the bright lights in the Spicer-Duncan circle, then committed an enormous solecism, or "fuck-up," as Persky said later.[59] First they rejected Robert Duncan's "What Happend: Prelude," and then, in a fast motion supposed to equalize the impact of this daring step, they also rejected poems by Spicer as "inadequate." For years Stan, Gail, and Lew berated themselves for missing the chance of publishing these poems, particularly since one poem they all remembered—was it called "Spider's Dance"? "Spiders and Cobwebs"?—it seemed to have been lost forever. In 1990 Kevin Killian unearthed the poem, "Spider Song," from the Spicer papers in the Bancroft Library at Berkeley. Like many of Spicer's poems during the 1959–61 period, it is addressed to a "Jim" who in many ways resembles the young poet James Alexander but who is really a complex of mixed signs of desire, intention, loss and possibility.

> The spider is awake in the eyebrows of sense.
> The famous spider famed in song and story.
> Even the thought of him makes my eyeballs cold. He
>   tells one to wait
> It is his season.
> Even his web, which he built, is still at
>   the window
> Jim, don't we love one another enough not to
>   like spiders
> To keep their names off the banisters of our senses
> Impersonal de-
> Personed like our love
> We smash their web.

The rejection resulted in a letter from Spicer that shows off Spicer's own particular style of vituperation, just as "What Happend: Prelude" shows off Duncan's. The anti-Semitism which had faded from his poetry since the unfortunate "Jew salesmen in amethyst pajamas" of *Billy The Kid* now resurfaced in the heat of anger.

Dear Lew:

With your usual honesty and courage you did not tell me that the name of the magazine is now to be White Rabbit Review. You left it for Gail, who sweeps up for you, to tell George. I presume that it is Sammy Glick's notion that I will be silent because my two poems were rejected. Or perhaps Sammy thinks that feuding with two major poets (one dead) will get him more publicity or a chance to sell out for a better price than feuding with one. Perhaps it will. Poetry is becoming like his father's used car business, or whatever it is, more every day.

I simply remind you as a sort of last poetic warning that a rabbit is a totem animal. He does not belong to your clan or Sammy's clan. He belongs to a clan which though de-populated has enough of the dead to still support us.

Rabbit people are the only ones who can steal rabbits. George, although his plum-colored volume does not really belong to the White Rabbit series, would have the right to die trying; Sammy, and you and Gail as his schiksas, do not have the right to try.[60]

Gail was the one hurt the most by this letter, since Spicer had Jim Liberman type it up and deliver it—Liberman, Gail's former lover, whom he had broken with to live with Lew, and who hated Lew in consequence. The night the letter arrived, Gail left the apartment, upset, and found Spicer on Grant Avenue. "Jack," Gail pleaded, "I had nothing to do with this."

Jack ignored the plea.[61]

M was something of a family magazine which presented a few quite fine poems, informed by romanticism, and a valuable translation, Jim Herndon's rendering of Heinrich von Kleist's *On the Marionette Theatre*. Stan Persky contributed a moving poem called "Lake," which he had composed while in the U.S. Navy in Italy.[62] George Stanley's poem, "The Death of Orpheus," was much discussed. Its mid-poem line, "with dark gold but his legs where white and female," contained an apparent error—an extra "h" in what should be "were white and female." Stanley had copied the poem several times and the "where" always appeared. Therefore the typo was accepted, as magic, or as something closely resembling the idea of dictation to which Spicer, and thus his circle in some degree, was so sensitive.[63] M's first issue also contained Robin Blaser's *The Faerie Queene*, third part of his long lifework *The Holy Forest*.[64]

Some months later, the second issue of M was published. It was visually more attractive than the first, for while both were mimeographed on ordinary $8\frac{1}{2} \times 11"$ typing paper, the second issue used various colored papers to set off special groups of poems. It contained a book-length poem by Ebbe Borregaard, *October 7th Poem*, which never appeared elsewhere. This was the time several people have called "the magazine wars."[65] Richard Duerden was editing *Foot*; with Ron Loewinsohn he was also editing *The Rivoli Review*, produced from Duerden's apartment on Rivoli Street in the

Haight-Ashbury district. Loewinsohn and Richard Brautigan soon produced another magazine, *Change*. Magazines had in fact become trendy. George Stanley produced a magazine called *The Capitalist Bloodsucker-N*; Larry Fagin, just arrived on the scene, produced several tiny issues of *Horus*—actually another vehicle for the irrepressible Persky, who signed Fagin's name as editor as a joke, and filled the issues with parodies of Duncan, Spicer, and so on.[66] "Everybody seemed to have access to a mimeograph machine," remembered Ron Loewinsohn. "You could then put out your own magazine. This was marvelous: it meant instant publication, instant reaction from people."[67] And then, like the other little magazines, *M* came to an end. Only in 1964 did Stan Persky's *Open Space* take up the publishing necessary to the circle and its friends.

Robert Duncan returned with Jess to San Francisco from Stinson Beach in the spring of 1961, six weeks after the first public reading of *The Heads of the Town*. In his next book, *Lament for the Makers*, Spicer made his relation to Duncan's poetics one of the central themes and motifs. *Lament for the Makers* is a slight book, with neither the length nor the ambition of *The Heads of the Town* or the three books that followed. An air of enervation, even exhaustion permeates the voices that drift in and out of its few pages: mad voices, looking for referents and finding few. Composed in May 1961, *Lament* was the second book Gail Chugg typed for Spicer, who made a great show of ignoring Gail's part in the *M* debacle in order to have some fair copies of his work.

The atmosphere of *Lament for the Makers* is that of arid soil, all that was left after Spicer gave everything he had in him as poet to the creation of *The Heads of the Town*.[68] In the last line of *Heads*—"Now the things that are for Jim are coming to an end, I see nothing beyond it"—Spicer revealed that, in Gail Chugg's words, he "had taken the risk he would never write a poem again. He had expended everything in *Heads of the Town*. A lot of sorrow in it, and part of the fright in it, is waiting for it to come."[69] The void Spicer faced became the field of *Lament*. Its occasion—and in a sense, the subject of the poem—was the "no-place" the previous long, great poem had left Spicer in.

The first line of "Dover Beach," *Lament*'s opening poem—"tabula rasa / A clean table"—points directly at the void Spicer was facing.[70] Spicer's relations with his peers in the art, Duncan in particular, were deteriorating; by May 1961—a month after the Borregaard's Museum/"creative whore" affair—the break was nearly complete. Soured indeed the relationship had become. The poem continues, "Damn it all, Robert Duncan, there is only one bordello,"[71] a line formed from Ezra Pound's on Robert Browning in Pound's "Canto II" about Browning's poem *Sordello*. The bordello, of course, is the whorehouse always so close to the temple of pure art in Spicer's mind. Spicer had undertaken a double task, to pick himself up from the swept fields of an exhaustion of poetry, and to demonstrate that he alone consistently served poetry among his friends (notably Duncan, as once best poet). Spicer's turn on Pound's lines implicating Duncan was deemed too nasty to print by cooler heads, who persuaded him to change the "Duncan" back to "Browning" for its first publication.

Lament for the Makers is threaded with allusions. We get a variation of Lewis Carroll's Mock Turtle's song—"Pope, Pope, Pope of the evening / Beautiful Pope. Help / Me as sheer ghost. I / Would like to write a poem as long as the hat of my nephew, as wide as is spoiled by writing / Crash"— which is also a reference to Spicer's own poetry, "I would like to write a poem as long as California," in his "Psychoanalysis: An Elegy."[72] By the time we come to the book's second poem, "The Birds," we have arrived at "A penny . . . for the old guy" (Eliot's dedication to "The Hollow Men") and "Asmodeus" (a Jewish devil god). From Duncan's *The Opening of the Field* Spicer took the figures of the birds and the worm of "The Ballad of Mrs. Noah," turning the original gentle cartoons into figures of horror. In Graham Mackintosh's edition, this poem is illustrated by an invisible bird. At first the page facing the poem seems blank, though in fact, very faintly etched, white on white, is a tiny V-shape—a bird—hollow air. The poem ends, "As we define them they dis- / appear."

Then follows a striking poem, "The Birth of Venus," a partial deconstruction of Ralston's dream of poetry in the detective novel Spicer had now abandoned with so much else:

> Everything destroyed must be thrown away
> If it were even an emotion
> The seashell would be fake. Camp
> Moving in nothing.
> Camp partly as the homosexuals mean it as private
>   sorrow
> And partly as others mean it—lighting fire for food
> Neither, I said, seawater
> Gives nothing.
> The birth of Venus happened when she was ready to be
>   born, the sea water did not mind her, and more

> important, there was a beach, not a breach in
> the universe but an actual fucking beach that was
> ready to receive her
> Shell and all.
> Love and food of[73]

The title poem continues with an imagery of distant drifting timbers "in the ghost of moonlight"—logs that reverberate, like a backpacker's memory by an isolated lake. A sense of loss—"the sound that is not really a sound at all."

Then the brutal ending, for which Gail Chugg gave an account of its genesis. "Spicer was reading a great thick book, a bound volume. He handed me the book and pointed out one section. I read it and handed it back. It became the 'Postscript' for *Lament for the Makers*." The story, worthy of Mafiosi, is of D. H. Lawrence's wife, Frieda, who—after she had suffered the theft of her husband's ashes—decided to have them mixed into a huge mass of concrete weighing over a ton. "So I fixed it," she said.[74] To Spicer, a predictable vulgarity. Frieda Lawrence was only representative of the kind of person who always erred away from the good because error was the certain fate of mankind. In later years, Spicer came to regard *Lament* as his "least successful book," a failed attempt to capture the voice of the Scottish poet William Dunbar (1460–1530) as he had let the voice of Lorca run through him four years before.[75]

Joe Dunn had gone into methedrine so deeply that White Rabbit had been suspended; this, in Jack's view, was intolerable. Somebody must take over, and Jack volunteered Graham Mackintosh.[76] A small trade school had taught Joe everything he needed to know in a few weeks, and *he'd* become a printer: why not Graham?[77]

As he had with *The Heads of the Town*, Spicer threw himself into the printing of *Lament for the Makers* with the enthusiasm of ignorance. Its first edition of 125 copies was the first production of the "new" White Rabbit Press. Although in the years that followed Spicer turned over more and more of the technical work to Mackintosh, with this book he got himself very involved, to Graham's amusement and sometimes his exasperation. Spicer knew nothing about cars, but, as he boasted to Graham, he did know how to fix a radio. One day, he explained, his radio fell off his refrigerator and began playing again, and now he firmly believed he could fix radios. Got a radio broken? "Give it to me, I'll fix it—I'll take it home, put it on the refrigerator, and knock it off." This was partially his own joke at his ineptness with machinery, but in Graham's view it was a paradigm for Jack's divine ignorance.

When we were doing *Lament For the Makers*, Jack typed a whole bunch of mimeograph stencils. And I said, "We're *not* going to mimeograph."
He said, "That's all right, but the mimeograph stencil provides much better copy." Now what that meant I don't know. But here he'd typed those mimeograph stencils, which were totally useless. It seemed to me as huge an inductive leap for him to think that those were useful as the kind of inductive leap he could do about understanding what Einstein was all about. . . . It's funny. The technical: of all blind spots really *the* classic blind spot.[78]

To underline *Lament*'s theme of whoredom and sellout, Spicer had Graham reproduce the "acknowledgments" page from Duncan's *The Opening of the Field* as his own, replete with its list of the important "Eastern" magazines Duncan had published in. He was taking no prisoners. *Lament for the Makers* remains one of Spicer's most enigmatic and disturbing compositions, and set the tone for his future dealings with Robert Duncan. With the publication of the book, Spicer was able to reify his own myth: he was the poet who cared nothing for fame, while Duncan was the once-promising hack who lusted after publicity and riches. The irony, of course, is that a part of Spicer reveled in publicity himself. "Who was it says that Spicer hated publicity?" retorted a skeptical Herb Caen, for many years a daily columnist for the *San Francisco Chronicle* and *Examiner.* "He was one of my very best sources. I remember the young poet who came to the City and changed his name . . . his name was Kenneth and there were already Rexroth and Patchen and others . . . he changed his first name and the joke was he should have changed his last, which was something like 'Fool'?" [This was Harold Dull.] "Spicer gave me that item. You could always count on him for some tip about the crazy poetry world: usually, it was aimed to hurt the Beats. No, he loved to find his name in my column. Who doesn't?"[79]

"California is an independent state—but I'll demonstrate that in art,"[80] Spicer told Don Allen, with the air of one making a formal prospectus. Spicer caught on with neither the established nor the "New American" poets of the East Coast. In New York, Don Allen took over a poetry class for the ailing Louise Bogan, and read aloud one of Spicer's poems to the young people assembled there. Afterward Bogan was "aghast" to find out what had been read in the name of poetry.[81]
Spicer's letters to Blaser in the late 1950s are full of demands that Robin

quit his job at the Widener—or it would ruin his poetry. Harvard's approbation of others in the San Francisco writing community could rouse
Spicer to heights of vitriol. Bob Kaufman was invited by Harvard to read
his work in March 1960; Spicer had resented Kaufman for years because of
his success with Russell FitzGerald where he, Jack, had failed, so Kaufman
plus Harvard was a combination especially hard to take. He called Kaufman a "spade," to which Kaufman replied, "I'm not a spade, I'm a metaphysical spook." Disgusted, Spicer added, "I've heard of professional nig-
gers—but you're the first amateur."[82]

How racist was Spicer? Opinions vary. "LeRoi Jones [later, Amiri Baraka]
was visiting San Francisco and unbelievably he and Jack got along very
well," Ron Loewinsohn remembered. "Just at that point, [Jones was] making the turn into becoming a real black nationalist. This was, again, one of
Jack's sort of perverse things—everyone expected Jack to beat up on LeRoi
verbally. LeRoi's a really clever, personable [person], and one of the most
charming people in the world. Partly Jack fell for this charm. Also, it was
the delicious pleasure of having all the people who were expecting Jack to
'take on' this East Coast, popular writer—Jack made friends with him instead. Jack was always looking to [do] the thing you were not expecting."[83]
The encounter took place during Jones's tour of the West Coast in the autumn of 1961—during the time Spicer was preparing to begin *The Holy
Grail.* Baraka confirmed this meeting, adding, "I didn't know Spicer was a
card-carrying racist—and took him at face value. He said nothing to me to
indicate anything else—which was best for both of us!"[84]

A few years later a young poet drinking with Spicer and George Stanley
at Gino & Carlo's heard Spicer make "about as lame a remark as I've heard
before or since." It began with a "round of anti-Semitism," and after a Jewish patron protested, Spicer leaned over scornfully and said, "Don't feel
bad—this isn't Auschwitz, you know."[85] Liberal inhibitions on the expression of such attitudes were weaker in the era following World War II than
they became a generation later, and Jim Herndon defended Spicer using
the following argument:

It's not possible to think of Jack Spicer as being anti-Semitic, or anti-black, or anti-
female. He was telling the Jews to come off it. And the blacks to come off it. And, I
suppose, ladies to come off it. And join the fucking human race, in language I
think he probably knew as little about as any human that ever lived. But he wanted
to. I guess that's what I'd say. There was everybody being wonderful about blacks,
and blacks were wonderful, and Jack'd say, "No, these fucking blacks ain't no
good! They're assholes. They'll come in the goddamn bar and ruin the bar. 'Cause

they'll always be fucking around and trying to make a dime off you, conning you."
The same thing about Jews, and the false political movements.[86]

Larry Fagin, a student at San Francisco State and a young poet, first saw
Spicer coming out of Robbie's Cafeteria in Berkeley. "That big head, that
slumpy gait. I remember his white socks—no one wore white socks with a
suit, I thought, *How marvelously tacky and perfect.*" Larry had begun to
work as a translator, editor, and writer in avant-garde European publications, after the death of his fiancée, a young German woman. David
Meltzer introduced Larry to Stan Persky, who suggested that he show up in
Gino & Carlo's some evening. One evening at sunset he sat in Gino's reading the Robinson *Chaucer* when Spicer came in, sat down, and noticed the
young man deep in his book. In his sometimes hesitant, stammered
speech, Spicer asked, "Whaaa—t you reading?"

He sounded like a hick, Fagin decided. Very guarded, Fagin said only,
"*Troilus.*"

"Read something," suggested Spicer.

Fagin took the challenge. "I began to read and, sitting across from me,
closing his eyes, nodding, Jack picked it up and began reciting along
with me, for almost one and a half columns, from memory. It was mind-
boggling. I was actually in awe. That very moment at the table when he
picked up on that Chaucer, I said, 'This guy!' It was like finding a Master,
like being under a Buddhist *rinpoche.*"[87]

Bill Brodecky had followed Larry Fagin from Weisbaden, where their
families were associated with the American military occupation, to the
University of Arizona. Now they were both in San Francisco, where Bill intended to pursue painting. "Although Jack was constitutionally built in
such a way that poetry was the only thing he really understood in the
world," said Brodecky, "he held painting in high regard." Tom Field was the
"reigning king" of painting in the North Beach scene, "followed closely by
Paul Alexander and Fran Herndon."

Jack had gotten Fran painting. One time I'd bought some linen to paint on. She
said, "Oh Bill, you ought to be painting on cardboard." It just went right through
me. I never quite forgave her for that. I felt like saying, "Fran, just because *you*
started painting last year for the first time in your life doesn't mean everybody
did." My grandmother was a painter. I'd been around painting all my life. But Fran
was a product of Jack Spicer's Pygmalion complex.

Tom Field decidedly was not. Tom had been at Black Mountain—Paul too.
Field was brilliant, really, an inspired painter. But he was a drunk, and already the
energy was going out of what he was doing. I found him already referring to his
own history: "Pacific Transport," the "Kerouac Painting," "Genji" and "Valencia"

Bar life, North Beach, 1962, at the Anxious Asp: painters Nemi Frost and Tom Field. *Photo by Robert Berg, courtesy of John Allen Ryan.*

were all works of history, although only two or three years old. When I got here [San Francisco], Field's "Pacific Transport" had just been done. It was a *buzzzz*. It was *terribly* exciting.[88]

Bill Brodecky was certainly right about the reputation of this work, the excitement surrounding it, though in fact it was painted in 1958. "Of course *I* naturally, being me, just as I preferred Robin Blaser's poetry to anybody else's, preferred Paul Alexander's painting to Tom's. I think Paul is extremely gifted. Tom's painting, while wonderful, was a little too airy for my taste. Paul had thick sensuality and gorgeous, drooling color. But Jack simply laid down the law that Tom was the best painter in North Beach." Spicer's Protestant soul, bleached from constant scrubbing, found a resonance in Field's variation on 1950s action painting, the firm, strong brush strokes, the shocking juxtapositions of color and form. Spicer liked the ambiguity behind such big gestures, the suggestions of ethereal revelation grounded in experience, as he approved of the classic work of Vermeer, Mantegna, Velazquez. Does Spicer's preference of Field—gay North Beach's answer to Willem De Kooning—over Alexander indicate, as well, something of his own "homophobic" machismo?

"It was the intelligence of [Field's painting] that Jack liked," Bill

212

Brodecky said firmly. "He had a good eye for painting. Not like Robin's, who has a towering genius as far as eye-for-painting goes. Jack didn't have that, but he had an eye for a certain thing in painting nobody else had: he could spot the spiritual weakness in a painting. For example, Jack hated 'Genji' of course: it's a gorgeous painting, but a little rotten at the core. Just a tiny bit. Whereas 'Pacific Transport' is steel right to the core."[89]

Bill Brodecky stayed with Larry Fagin at a hotel at 444 Columbus, in "one little room—right across the street from Gino's," Bill added pointedly. "On the first night, Larry took me into Katie's [a bar and the new center of the Spicer circle]. This was one of the most exciting periods of my life.

When Larry called me at one of my temporary jobs and said, "I need to see you." I knew immediately he had read my diaries and knew I was gay. I was petrified [that he would respond with hostility]. But at the same time I was sort of exempt from terror because *he* was in the wrong, snooping in my stuff. I knew he was scared to death. He came down, and he said, "Well, you know, I knew," and I said, "No, you didn't."

It frustrated him that he didn't have an easier access to it, but, see, it was wonderful when he found out I was gay.[90]

Fagin discussed homosexuality in the Spicer scene. "Stan Persky, who was deciding what his sexual life was going to be like, took me to one of those Turk Street dens of iniquity. At the time, in the Tenderloin [district of San Francisco], there were a few gay hang-outs. I remember him taking me to a downstairs scene where, oh my God! It was like a huge several-thousand-square-feet of belly-to-belly men. In flaming red—it was like being in hell! Persky was just delighted, delighted with the frightening aspect of it. That was my initiation into a homosexual social scene.

If I would simply have translated most of the homosexual syndrome into a hetero-sexual syndrome I would have probably been a lot more clear about it. Less confused. In other words, this guy = a girl, right? That would have been real simple. Yet it wasn't that easy. There was no point of reference, even though I knew about homosexuality to a degree. Brodecky was a big help because I saw from his side the timidity and fear and also gentleness and the true human emotions in that. I guess I was sort of keen on George [Stanley] a little bit too so I totally thought [his love affair with Bill] was great. I was very sympathetic with Bill's scene because he had suffered all those years. He came from a very difficult family situation. His mother was very strict and aggressive and he was suffering terribly with that. His brother knew he was gay. He and I used to talk about it. But there was nothing we could do about it, no way we could accommodate Bill, make him feel comfortable. I loved

Bill dearly. I wasn't thinking "I'll use Bill as a bridge into learning about this gay scene" at all. In fact I was so interested in the literary end of it, I kept pushing aside the gay thing. Not easy to do: every other reference was to cock size or to something.[91] There were times I did feel outnumbered, but I said, "Great, why not?" I was one of the very few heterosexuals on that scene. I was so sympathetic with Brodecky, and I met George, and of course I loved George because he was so tremendously helpful and generous to me at the time. He might have had a little crush on me, in fact we went to bed once—nothing serious. He was one of the first people I'd met whose mind completely dazzled me; and sincere. I was a little frightened of somebody like Jack who did not make himself emotionally available without a lot of prerequisites. Whereas I didn't have that awe of George Stanley, who seemed like a slightly older brother, with Jack like a father. Persky was the one active figure I could identify with—a character like Leo Gorcey of *The Dead End Kids*. So I would check him out, follow his lead a lot.[92]

Bill Brodecky met Jack Spicer on the street going into Katie's. In the doorway Spicer pointed and said, "Isn't that the moon?" As Brodecky recalled,

I said, "Gee, I didn't even notice." And he said, "Oh, you're heartless." He was disappointed. It was obvious that I wasn't Jack's type of young man. I wasn't the masculine type he usually went for. The guys he fell for were usually straight. But I wasn't attracted to Jack: I didn't care.

Being straight, Larry had difficult access to that scene. Sure enough, one day, Larry and I were in bed—we shared this big double bed, *small* double bed. He said to me, "Jack doesn't like you." You see, I was this ornament of Larry's, and because Jack wasn't interested in me, I was failing him in regard to Jack.

"What do you mean, he doesn't like me?"

Larry said, "Jack says you have no sense of humor." So I was failing Larry, you see. Jack was a marvelous conversationalist; could talk about anything. Although I was always a little afraid of Jack. I was afraid I bored him, and you know when you're afraid you bore someone, you bore them. I don't think Jack thought I was very bright.[93]

Bill had first met George Stanley in The Anxious Asp. Stanley, diabolical in dark glasses, rather frightened Bill. His bare one-room apartment was devoid of the sensual, "and yet it was magical for me. George was a fascinating person: terribly intelligent, of course; but somehow he wasn't intimidating. I was very touched by his feeling for me; and flattered, of course. I mean I was flattered to the point where I almost shriveled up and blew away!" Yet everyone was glad for George that Bill had entered his life. Jack was the "only fly in the ointment"—because he wasn't bowled over by Bill the way everyone else seemed to be. But eventually Jack was won over too.

After his return from New York, George Stanley's relationship with Spicer was a much less dependent one than it had been earlier. Spicer's

Bar life, North Beach, 1962, at The Anxious Asp: poets George Stanley and Larry Fagin, with painter Tom Field. *Photo by Robert Berg, courtesy of John Allen Ryan.*

cold letter ("You and I are not friends") had cured him to a certain extent and made him wary of Spicer's power. George's love affair with Bill Brodecky—a household of his own with another, with its own rules—in 1962 was a move away from the older poet, although it was an arrangement that Jack approved of. Yet the differences between Spicer and Stanley sometimes grew into an active hostility—nasty banter publicly, ungenerous comments privately. Once George and Jack decided to go to the movies—a film special to them both, *The Testament of Orpheus* (1960), Jean Cocteau's sequel to his own *Orphée* of ten years before. Spicer had finished work on *The Heads of the Town Up to the Aether*—his own massive revisioning of Cocteau; and George had written "The Death of Orpheus" during his year-long stay in New York, now ended. George took it on himself to invite Fagin and then went further and told Bill Brodecky to come along too. Why not—he was, after all, his boyfriend! But for Jack two was company, four definitely a crowd. "Oh, Jesus," he said to George, "I didn't want to make this a *theater party.*"[94]

Jack's ongoing, passive-aggressive hostility toward Stanley received indirect acknowledgment in Spicer's writing of 1962–64. For example, *The Holy Grail*, "The Book of Galahad" 2, contains the lines, "George / Said to me that the only thing he thought was important in chess was the killing of the other king. I had accused him of lack of imagination."[95] An untitled poem in the "Thing Language" section of *Language*, beginning "the metallurgical analysis of the stone that was my heart . . . ," contains the line, "Silicon, as George would be the first to tell you, is not metal."[96] "Love Poems" 4 refers unsympathetically to the work of Robert Duncan, George Stanley, and Harold Dull. The poem draws upon the authority of Charles Olson, from his essay, "Against Wisdom as Such," written to scourge Robert Duncan for his pursuit of wisdom when poetry is the question always for the poet.[97]

> "If you don't believe in a god, don't quote him,"
>   Valéry once said when he was about ready to give
>   up poetry. The purposefull suspension of dis-
>   belief has about the chance of a snowball in hell.
> Lamias maybe, or succubi but they are about as real in
>   California as night-crawlers
> Gods or stars or totems are not game-animals.
>   Snark-hunting
>   is not like discussing baseball.
> Against wisdom as such. Such
> Tired wisdoms as the game-hunters develop
> Shooting Zeus, Alpha Centauri, wolf with the same toy gun.
> It is deadly hard to worship god, star, and totem. Deadly
>   easy
> To use them like worn-out condoms spattered by your own
>   gleeful, crass, and unworshiping
> Wisdom[98]

"Zeus, Alpha Centauri, wolf" are the "god, star, totem" Spicer revered, and believed others "used." George Stanley recognized immediately that Spicer had taken Olson's phrase "against wisdom as such" to mount a triple attack on "me and Duncan and Harold Dull, for having our own 'gleeful, crass, unworshipful wisdom.' He was attacking my poems in *Beyond Love*, and Harold's poems in *The Star Year*, and Duncan's poems. I'm not sure which book Duncan was writing at the time, it may have been *Bending the Bow*—poems a great deal mythological."[99]

Bill Brodecky remembered another occasion in which the artistic differences between Stanley and Spicer erupted in the middle of an ordinary dinner:

Jack was over for dinner. I had done this painting while playing the early Judy [Garland] records over and over: it was action, broad brush abstract. A fairly large painting, of a young girl with her mouth open, and down in front of her was this little box. At dinner everything Jack said infuriated George. George would contradict, and tell Jack to go to Hell—the typical reaction of somebody breaking away from authority. I took Jack out to the studio to show him some new things, and this painting Jack liked. He smiled. And he said, "There's just one thing I wish you would do—write the word 'RADIO' on that box in front of her."

And George said, "No! He will not do anything of the kind. And don't suggest things like that." To me it meant if you're going to have a spade, call it a spade; Jack's aesthetic always. If there's a hint something's there, you name it. You drag it up and you identify it. It meant more of that to me than it meant that he was proselytizing for his idea of poet as radio, which is what George, understandably, heard.[100]

"Jack was a priest," Robert Duncan said.

So is Robin a priest. So am I a priest. Because words were themselves some kind of thing that we administered. "Priest" is the right word. All of us understood, and talked about it when we came across the medieval studies, that the priest did not qualify the Mass—the poem is the Mass. The priest can be an idiot!

The priest, as a matter of fact, since the priest is administering the Mass, not receiving it, can then be in a state of sin and it doesn't make any difference at all. That's how we saw the poem. I don't think Jack ever made that error.[101]

The idea of the poet as priest whose spiritual condition makes no difference to the quality of an art work he presides over is perhaps the essence of "dictation"—how and whether one can correctly "hear" the poem as it comes from wherever poems come from.

Spicer's circle was expected to respect such views. Exceptions were made only by Spicer himself; others invited a charge—seriously intended—of heresy or worse if one attempted to interpret Spicer's intentions for him by acting in his name, or by opposing him even in small ways. Don Allen was cautioned to be seriously selective about giving *J* to others. That copies of the magazine went to New York at all probably was not known to Spicer's Bay Area protégés: it would be uncharacteristic of Spicer to admit to doing business with "outsiders."

Robert Duncan and Lew Ellingham touched upon the themes of Spicer and games, Spicer and homosexuality, Spicer and a circle of followers as poets and friends. Ellingham was fond of using the German term, *Kreis*—circle—in recognition of the poet Stefan George's association with the poetic (and mostly homosexual) circle of which George was more than first among equals: the *George Kreis*. Concerning this Robert Duncan said. "It wasn't a *Spicer Kreis*. Once we look at these figures we find out that the *Spicer Kreis* has trouble [cohering] because it wants to have power, and I am the one who deprived it of its power. My interest in other things deprived it of its power. I remember coming into Gino & Carlo's one night, and coming in George Stanley grabbed me and said, 'Well, now you're here.' And I said, 'You mean so that you can have the necessary four homo-sexuals, George, to run your little magic circle? No way!' I said." Duncan chuckled. "That was what I was unforgiven for, that I was not in the neces-sary circle—only there like I was anywhere else.

"Had I been, there would have been a formidable amount of psychic power going in the *Kreis*. It would not just have been a circle."

Duncan referred to the presence of women and heterosexuals in the cir-cle. "Joanne Kyger was read out in these same years, although I think most of that seemed to have been coming from some spiff that Persky and Blaser had with the idea of Joanne. Yet Jack was cooperative with it." Although Kyger remained a principal of Spicer-influenced publications and society, as much after as before her years in Japan, there was indeed a homosexual drift to the inner group by the 1960s to a point nearing exclusiveness.

"Jack the poet, the one looking for powers, draws on women poets as major powers in the same sense he does on men poets. But for his *Kreis*—which is not the whole of poetry at all, but is a circle of magic intensifica-tion—he needed a monosexual circle of witches. I'm convinced they also had to be alcoholic, which I wasn't going to be; they had to be fervent spectators of baseball—think about it. If you go to the poems, baseball is as serious as politics." Harold Dull wasn't interested in baseball—but, Duncan observed, "Everybody in the *Kreis* in some sense *wasn't* in it."

Everybody was guilty of not being the full ticket. Remember, I wasn't interested in baseball; I wouldn't have gotten further in the *Kreis*. Harold Dull, for example, I think went deep into Spicer's work and drew on it very fully—and he was never of the *Kreis*, since he wasn't interested in baseball, nor was he homosexual.

I think it was essential to be homosexual in the *Kreis*, although [it was] only in the definition of the *Kreis*—to reiterate it—[that] I ever thought the gay thing was important. When it came to writing, and the reality of a person, and the recogni-tion a person was close to it, Jack had no trouble recognizing that Jim Herndon was close to him and that he was close to Herndon. So he didn't think in terms of straight and gay. He could only despise gays who presumed that that was some kind of reality.

The reason that the question of "gay" didn't come up [as special in Spicer's rou-tine thought] is that this *Kreis* that Spicer was forming was a magic circle, so the gays outside didn't signify. But clearly Jack kept gay company. His bridge club was not a part of his *Kreis*: a bridge table is an interesting table, he saw bridge as a magic game, he thought of bridge as a trap—and the players were gay. But if we got to the baseball games, the players aren't gay.

Sexuality is so charged with magic I think all Jack's life he could only conceive of it as an operated magic that brought one into this trap . . .

218

—the trap of love. Robert Duncan's remarks were intuitive, drawing from a framework of memory orchestrating feelings about a man whose life and work were very important to him. "I experienced an essentiality or a reality in Spicer's work, as I did in Olson's, that I really didn't find elsewhere among my peers."[102]

CHAPTER EIGHT

The Holy Grail

*T*he *Holy Grail* (1961–62) represents a return to the scale of *The Heads of the Town* after the brief shriek of *Lament for the Makers*. Formally, however, it is quite different than either. In *The Holy Grail* Spicer inaugurates a new formula for the serial poem—a series of seven sections—which he repeated in his last two books. If *The Heads of the Town* takes its tripartite structure from Dante, *The Holy Grail* plays on associations with the number seven in mythology—the seven ages of man, the seven heroes of antiquity, etc. It offers a dream world, a dream of history and perception. George Stanley said that Spicer was "trying to turn time sidewise so that consecutive events superimposed." All history and mythology occur at once, as in *Finnegans Wake*: the atom bomb and the death of Marilyn Monroe coexist in the same world as Merlin and Lancelot,

to see it all happening now—not anything so specific as to tell the story of the Holy Grail for the present, because that's exactly what he doesn't do in the poem, but simply to bring to life Perceval and Arthur and Merlin in their humanness in the contemporary landscape.

In Spicer the Grail, was a different thing depending upon who was searching for it. Galahad, who found it, took it away, and used it for his own personal reasons. Galahad is the subverter of the Order of the Round Table. All is reversed in Spicer: the cup drinks our lives. I don't have a systematic understanding of the way Spicer, in his poem, reinterpreted text that already had a traditional orthodox [theological] interpretation. But he was determinedly unorthodox. Spicer really rejected intellectual disposition for its own sake. He wouldn't allow it to go on! He'd get up and play the pinball machine.[1]

Questioned after his 1965 reading of *The Holy Grail* in Vancouver, Spicer estimated that the poem had taken seven months to write. Perhaps, then, it was begun in late 1961 or early 1962 (his dating was sometimes elastic). In any case, its opening was clearly linked to the minor poem "Lessons in Love: I," which was published under Spicer's name in the first issue of "Larry Fagin's" magazine *Horus*.

Lessons in Love: I

Everyone is named Tony.

This tiny, minimalist joke of a poem might well be the seed of the Arthurian matter of *The Holy Grail*, for two Tonies open two of its books, those of Gawain and Lancelot.[2] The first "Tony" is Tony Sherrod, of Knoxville, Tennessee, and the second is Tony Aste, one of the "Jets"— Spicer's nickname for a group of young men who arrived in North Beach in the spring of 1962, when the then-fresh musical, *West Side Story*, was still playing in the theaters. The Jets worked odd jobs around town, *when* they worked—car park, restaurant work, such things. Their boyishness was a certain winner in the homosexual community of North Beach; while accepting such easy laurels, the Jets were firm in accepting every challenge to their early manhood. Calling this pack of straight youth the Jets was a complicated game of undercutting their masculinity. Spicer had seen the original Bernstein/Robbins/Sondheim/Laurents musical in New York and marveled at the sly way its homosexual creators had subverted a band of singing, dancing Broadway chorus boys and turned them into a threatening stormcloud of heterosexuality. Calling the 1962 North Beach arrivals the "Jets" did the same thing, but in reverse. Spicer's "essay" "Homosexuality and Marxism" was addressed to these men; the essay first appeared in George Stanley's magazine, *Capitalist Bloodsucker-N* (1962).

Of the Jets, Tony Aste shone the brightest. He was a handsome, lanky loner from Salt Lake City, passionate, resourceful, and self-sufficient. Tony Aste made friends easily, and Jack began pursuing him as if by reflex. He was tougher than the boys Spicer normally favored, who were "emotionally nakeder," in Gail Chugg's words, and by and large gentler than most of the kids around North Beach. Tony Aste was a special case: Jack treated him like a peer—he was to Spicer what Neal Cassidy was to Kerouac, a talespinner, whose stories of his rough childhood and youth were always startling and sometimes poetic. He served as the embodiment of a vision, a muse.

He told Spicer he had been sent to reform school where, on the first day, he was beaten unconscious three times and fucked eight times.

I was so busted up they put me to bed for three weeks. I swore that when I got out I was gonna do the beating and I was gonna do the fucking or they were going to have to kill me. And I did. And if somebody got too hard to handle I had a couple of younger kids who would lay down for the guards and the guards would take care of him.

I was in high school and a bunch of us took off up Emigration Canyon. My buddy's girl was pissed off at him about something so he had to come without her and after we had been up there for awhile and got the fire going and belted a few beers, my girl got mad at me and went off to make out with another guy. Me and my buddy were both madder than hell and said, "Fuck 'em," and took off down the road and tried to hitch a ride but nobody would stop. My buddy started yelling at them, "Stop, you chickenshit sons-of-bitches!" and he says to me, "First one that stops, let's drag him out of the car and beat the shit out of him." But three more came around the curve and don't stop so he starts yelling, "Bastards!" and picks up a rock and whangs it at the next one that comes down and we both pick up the biggest boulders we can find and heave them and they still just keep on going and we're getting madder and madder so I said to him, "Shit! I tell you what: you lie down in the road like you been hurt or had an accident and when they stop and get out to help you, we'll both jump 'em."

So he says "OK" and we see the lights flashing into the hills from a car coming down and he lays down in the middle of the road and the car came around the curve and ran right over him and kept on going down the hill without stopping and he was smeared all over the fucking road deader than hell and I started screaming and then I stopped because I wasn't me any more and I could hear the guys from the campground yelling and running down the road and I wasn't me anymore of a sudden I was a deer and I tore off up into the scrub to get away from the people and the blood and I stayed up there in the top of the mountains for a long time and I thought like a deer and I was very close to the mountains and that's all I remember I was a deer.

Tony was found six days later, at five in the morning, lying on his belly lapping the water from a swimming pool of one of the wealthy homes that were then beginning to climb up the Wasatch foothills.[3]

Spicer doted on Tony Aste, loved his expansive tales: in one such story, he and a teenage friend from San Francisco, a partly American Indian orphan, "Link," blew the doors off the Mormon Temple in Salt Lake City.[4] In San Francisco, he and fellow Jet Bill Roberts drove their pickup truck up and down the hills of North Beach, stopping the car in the middle of the street long enough to go into the store for a bottle of wine.[5] Before long, as Dora Geissler put it, "Jack was chasing Tony Aste's ass all over North Beach."[6] The fact that Tony was a wanderer qualified everything he did and set the pattern for all his actions. It also qualified everyone's expectations of him. As a result, he could live confidently in a condition of permanent adolescence. In his wild *jeunesse* and tales of nomadic rambles across America, Tony must have triggered Spicer's fantasies of his father's vagabond, pre-Dorothy, youth.

Early after his arrival in North Beach in the spring of 1962, Tony Aste befriended Richard Brautigan, opened an affair with Virginia—Ginny— Richard's girlfriend, then married her. By Brautigan Ginny had had one child, Ianthe; with Tony Aste there were more. The Tony/Virginia/Dick triangle was very much on Spicer's mind when he wrote *The Holy Grail*, but sitting behind it was very much, still, the Creeley/Marthe Larsen/Kenneth Rexroth triangle which had so fermented Spicer's imagination since he first heard of it in Boston, and which had already inspired his detective novel and "Homage to Creeley."

Not surprisingly, one consequence of Tony's elopement with Virginia was a new closeness between Spicer and Richard Brautigan. Spicer admired Brautigan's poetry and had published it in *J*. At this time, Brautigan was wrestling through the writing of his first "novel," which became *Trout Fishing in America*. He brought it to Spicer page by page, and the two men revised it as though it were a long serial poem. (Later, Blaser would perform a similar service for Brautigan's novel *In Watermelon Sugar*.[7]) Brautigan dedicated *Trout Fishing in America* to Ron Loewinsohn and Jack Spicer. Loewinsohn speculated on the reasons for the double dedication. "Me, I think, just friendship; and Jack, editing, help, whatever he did. Jack was absolutely fascinated with *Trout Fishing*, and spent a lot of time with Richard talking about it." Spicer may have recommended cuts; this was rumored in the community at the time. "Anytime you [could] get Richard to accept criticism [was] an unbelievable accomplishment. He [was] so defensive, and so guarded; and Jack was able to get him to make changes. Whatever he did he deserved some sort of Henry Kissinger award."[8]

Jack told Gail Chugg, "Brautigan's written a great poem! . . . I just got through reading the whole thing. It's called *Trout Fishing in America*."[9] Not only did Spicer champion *Trout Fishing in America*; he arranged for Brautigan to read the novel in public, over two consecutive nights in a San Francisco church (at the corner of Market, 16th, and Noe Streets). In a caustic letter written in December 1956, Robert Duncan sharply criticized Brautigan's early poetry and urged him to attend the upcoming "Magic Workshop" that Spicer would administer in the spring of 1957. "I suggest that before you think of reading you go into the open Forum of your contemporaries."[10] It is uncertain whether Brautigan took Duncan's advice—certainly he was never a regular member—and thus the date of his meeting Spicer has probably been lost, but their friendship was firm by 1958, when Jack wrote "For Dick" in *Admonitions*:

> Look
> Innocence in important
> It has meaning
> Look
> It can give us
> Hope against the very winds that we batter against it.[11]

During the composition of *The Holy Grail*, Spicer was engaged with Fran Herndon on her current project, the "sports" collages that made up her enduring achievement in art. The lithographs for Jack's "Homage to Creeley" were, of course, black and white; in the collages she burst into color as though entering a paradise of revealed myth and truth. Across town Jess was creating a similar series of "paste-ups," like Herndon ripping and slicing up visual images and rearranging them onto canvas. Fran chose the humble pages of *Sports Illustrated* for her materials, painting over and under these images and achieving a rich, often misty glaze. The subjects of this series were sports-world versions of betrayal, tragedy, and loss, such as the trade of Y. A. Tittle for Lou Cordelione by the San Francisco 49ers; the first Liston-Patterson heavyweight fight; the scandalous death of the boxer Benny "the Kid" Paret. Take the haunting "Ghost Riders": Herndon's brushstrokes transform the photographed horses straining for the finish line into wraithlike creatures, like Kandinsky's horses, not "real" beasts but expressionistic, ephemeral, vivid animals, closer to unicorns. Perspective is flattened: foreground and background keep switching, giving the collages a watery, dreamlike quality removed from Jess's ornate, precise surrealism.[12]

With Fran Herndon's work in collage and Tony Aste's physical beauty inspiring him, Spicer was drawn further into the Grail material by Ariel Parkinson's illustration for one of his earlier "Lorca" poems:

Dear Ariel,

Naturally I can't thank you enough for the picture. The figures of the bull and the boy start emerging in the morning sun (opposite where the picture hangs) and start fading into jasmine in late afternoon. Beautiful.

That Gawain poem your show inspired has become a part of a long Holy Grail poem which I am about half through (27 poems in 4 books already). I intend to give you the original manuscript of it when it finished.

Love, Thankful Love
Jack

"The drawing Jack mentions," wrote Ariel Parkinson, "was made for 'The Ballad of the Little Girl Who Invented the Universe' [*After Lorca*, 1957]. It had been in a solo exhibition of my paintings and drawings in the big east gallery of the San Francisco Museum of Modern Art in 1962. When the exhibition closed, I gave it to him."[13] Fran Herndon also began work on a "Grail Series" of her own, working in woodcuts, etching, and collage to create companion pieces to Spicer's Percival, Lancelot, Guinevere, and his memorable "Fool Killer."[14]

Is *The Holy Grail* a poetic *roman a clèf*? Spicer told Graham Mackintosh that he appears in *The Holy Grail* as Lancelot.[15] Larry Fagin, who had confided in Spicer his sorrow—his fiancée had been electrocuted in Germany when a toaster fell into her bathtub—was somehow not surprised when he found this tragedy transmuted into the Book of Gwenivere. Spicer had already written a novel that figured Kenneth Rexroth as a modern Arthur, and Robert Creeley as a modern Lancelot, with Marthe Rexroth as Gwenivere. Again, the hunt for the Grail is also a kind of superelaborate detective story. Fagin came to associate Spicer with a Raymond Chandler character, his ritualistic determination, his lonely Polk Gulch haunts—" down these mean streets a man must go," and Robin Blaser has spoken of the influence of Spicer's unfinished detective novel on the mysteries of *The Holy Grail*.[16] This is not surprising, since as he worked further on the narrative of the Grail, Spicer found himself writing about idealists in all periods of history, including his own. Songs of the Spanish Civil War combine intimate and martial qualities with a sympathetic politics of the Left:

> Wir sind die Moorsoldaten
> Und siehen mit dem Spaten
> Ins Moor.

For those coming of age during and after the Second World War, especially within the years between the end of the Russian Alliance and the growth of the McCarthy era, a chorus of the above International Brigade classic will be familiar. For the veterans then attending school, university life often revolved around a social celebration of left-leaning politics in bars and student living rooms. Some students, or their teachers, may even have served in Spain as Loyalist soldiers—the above song comes from an anthem of the Ernst Thälmann Brigade of anti-Nazi Germans fighting Franco forces. Spicer chose the quatrain translated by Jim Herndon as

> Wherever the eye looks
> Moor and heath all around
> No bird-song quickens us
> Oak-trees stand bare and crooked.[17]

Another German line used in the *The Holy Grail*, in the voice of Merlin, comes out as "Homeland you are mine again."[18] (The rest of the poem's occasional Teutonic intrusions/explosions are apparent inventions of the *Diktat*/Poet—almost-nonsense, after a fashion.) But idealism is inevitably stained by reality: as the critic Peter Riley has pointed out in his study of the seven books of *The Holy Grail*, the poem moves from the self to the world to "total failure" and death.[19]

At this point Spicer's world in North Beach was enjoying new excitements. Stan Persky returned to San Francisco in 1961, the Dulls and George Stanley in 1962. Russell FitzGerald soon came back from Philadelphia and New York. The world Spicer and Duncan had shared in the 1957–60 period had become, both socially and artistically, partly a matter of history, partly something the participants wished to restore. As though to mark the end of an era, Ruth Witt-Diamant resigned her post as director of the Poetry Center, to take up a teaching job in Japan. She was replaced at the Poetry Center by the playwright and poet James Schevill. New young people now arrived on the scene, with no memories of Grant Avenue, or The Place. For them, the feeling of the street was buoyant, in the bars, the parks, and at the beach, within the society of Spicer and his friends, throughout the quarter generally. Elvis had been a long-accepted figure—the Beatles stood at the threshold. John F. Kennedy's patriotism seemed fresh compared to Eisenhower's, but daily life was increasingly apolitical, reckless, and searching. Written in the spring of 1962 amid a new cultural shift, Robert Duncan's three Dante sonnets, which commemorate friendships in decline, have a special flavor of impending age, of nostalgia.

After the publication of *Lament for the Makers*, projected, it would seem, almost as a sustained insult to Duncan's reputation, Spicer little expected Duncan to show any forgiveness. But in early 1962, Duncan made an unusual sortie into North Beach to show the Dante sonnets to Spicer. The third "Dante" sonnet especially warmed the hearts of the group around Spicer for its accessible beauty and remembrance of a golden era sometime not too long ago.

Sonnet 3: From Dante's Sixth Sonnet

Robin, it would be a great thing if you, me, and Jack Spicer
Were taken up in a sorcery with our mortal heads so turnd
That life dimmd in the light of that fairy ship
The Golden Vanity or *The Revolving Lure.*

Whose sails ride before music as if it were our will,
Having no memory of ourselves but the poets we were
In certain verses that had such a semblance or charm
Our lusts and loves confused in one

Lord or Magician of Amor's likeness.
And that we might have ever at our call
Those youth we have celebrated to play Eros
And erased to lament in the passing of things.

And to weave themes forever of Love.
And that each might be glad
To be so far abroad from what he was.[20]

"[Spicer and Duncan] were really scrapping with each other," said Stan Persky. "They respected each other, saw themselves as comrades, colleagues, companions in the enterprise of the serial poem. They had invented it, and they saw themselves as staying close to it. I remember Duncan bringing [the Dante poems] around to the bars; I remember Jack going outside and handing me those poems so I could read them by the light of the neon sign outside some bar. They're gorgeous, beautiful poems, and Spicer thought they were beautiful poems. Then Duncan, of course, having gone to the trouble of getting Jack to accept those poems, immediately stormed at Jack's acceptance of them and said, 'I knew he was going to like those poems! He doesn't like other poems—'"[21] Yet Duncan had gone to the bother and pain of a trip to North Beach to prove something to Jack. Their sense of community was never breached.

Still, during the summer, dissent ripened to a glorious vintage. A letter from Duncan to Spicer in June 1962 revealed a new phase of deterioration in their relations.

Dear Jack,
   Here are the few poems since the *Set of Romantic Hymns*. The only one written in the East is the *Thank You For Love*, that may be an occasional verse for I wrote it in response to Creeley's book. It's because of a fealty I would not break that now when my work can so little please, I mean to send it to you: that in your opposition, the power of your demand is kept over me. I don't mean your directives from North Beach—tho I must mean those directives in part for "North Beach" you reveal as our Glastonbury—but the orders of the imagination: this set of the first

seven of the grail poems. Forgotten, "a ship of singing women" must have given me recall of the Wynken-Blynken-and-Nod boat (not of women but of child Dutch sailors) that came into the H.D. Book. And now, this morning re-reading your grail poems, I realized I had "missed the boat"—the other boat, the barque of fey singers: after the little boat of dreams, the *"bateau de lueurs reméne par un mousse"* Breton calls it in a poem I am translating in commission I've accepted.

Lewis Brown tells me your aversion extends to Jess, and with another tale Harry Jacobus relates of being deliberately confused with Jess, the rumour would seem to be true. I understand and must go on working under the charge of how compromised my poetry is: the onus is not unjust. I have, after all, only to compare the immediacy of these grail poems and my own habits. But where, if that is the charge, Harry's work and Jess's is despised or mistrusted, the charge is unjust, you've lost sight.

Yet, as with Kenneth Rexroth after his attack on Marianne Moore as a "fascist," tho I accept and even determine the separation as a truth of things, there remains the fact that it is a separation in friendship. I'm not talking now about a separation in poetry—Rexroth no longer operates as poet—and you and I do. And besides, the wench is dead. But I am talking about the offense against inner orders of a household (as the truth of Marianne Moore was and is an inner order; and the truth of Jess's art and spirit is an inner order),

Robert[22]

Spicer now "refused to read any of Duncan's work or have anything to do with Duncan," said Ron Loewinsohn. "The person reading poetry, for Jack, had to be as devoted to poetry as a person writing it. That's one of the reasons for some of the things that sound so goofy. Somebody offered Philip Whalen $10 to read at a poetry festival, and Jack said, 'I'll offer him $11 not to read.' I agreed with him completely, but—I was young!"[23] *Foot* magazine asked Spicer to contribute some of his work, but had to be content with this letter instead, to which Loewinsohn alluded:

I am not submitting the poetry I promised to the magazine. One of the three editors of your magazine is participating in the San Francisco State College Poetry Festival.

This editor (who will receive ten dollars for his participation) is as aware as I am or you are that 1) SF State College would like to turn all poets into cable cars. 2) A poet is not a cable car. 3) If a poet is gradually becoming a cable car he is gradually ceasing to be a poet. 4) He is telling others, who are too young to know better, that there is no difference between cable cars and poetry. 5) Poetry in a funny and metaphysical sense of the word is a Union and making it or yourself (which happens first) into a cable car is scabbing on the Union which can't be broken but sure as hell can be scabbed upon. 6) Everyone who ignores these instructions ends up on KPFA or writing for the Examiner.

If it is a question of financial need, I would be very glad to give this editor eleven dollars not to read in the festival.

Jack Spicer[24]

Spicer became so identified with this letter to *Foot* that his obituary quoted from its comparison of poets to cable cars. Philip Whalen was stung and nonplussed by Spicer's criticism, though in later years, mellowed by Zen abbotry, he dismissed Spicer as "unpleasant to everyone."[25] But in April 1962, in response to Spicer's abuse, he wrote the dark, threatening "For Jack Spicer," a retelling of the Bible story of Daniel in the lions' den, explaining later to Kyger that "I am tired of Jack Spicer complaining to his friends about me, considering I don't hardly know him, so I made this poem for him so that he'd have something specific to complain about and I could feel that I deserved whatever idiot complaints he might make in the future."[26] From Whalen's poem:

> I said to the lion, "All right, go ahead."
> He filled his belly and went to sing on the mountain
>
> What's the score now? He's
> Hungry again.
>
> Darius hopes for the best
>
> His grandson will perish.[27]

For a few summer months in 1962 Katie's was the center of the Spicer bar activity, and the group's poetry events were a series of readings from a table in the bar. A Spicer-circle author presented work against a more or less stilled room of people, while the hush of activity without words came from the pool tables in the back room. Patrons looked on, some interested, some bored, from the bar or seated at tables. The cash register rang; a jar of Polish sausages was opened; a customer ordered a drink refreshed.

At such a reading Lew Ellingham publicly misread a poem of Duncan's, incurring his wrath, though Lew believed that since he was drunk the circumstances were too unserious to merit much anger. He was simply, he thought, a willing puppet of Spicer's nightly play, and Duncan but a distant, if revered name. When Lew invited Duncan to read at Katie's, he knew Duncan would refuse, for the troubles of the Spicer-Duncan relationship were known to everyone in Spicer's group.

June 12, 1962

Dear Jack,

I won't be reading at the Bourbon Street series. I couldn't finally stomach co-operating with Mr Allingham [sic]. Altho he's prettier than Mr Schevill, and North Beach is more authentic a locale than the Poetry Center—he don't write better than his Poetry Center counterpart. But all I said in reply to Allingham's somehow inevitably school-marmish letter (he's as infallible at putting it wrong as Ruth

Witt-Diamant) was *No*. While I delight in putting down a solidly insensitive ass like Schevill, it's only too clear Allingham is nonsolid and sensitive. Shakey, I think, rather than fluid, as far as the nonsolids go. . . .

Robert[28]

Insofar as possible, during the summer Spicer and Duncan kept their distance from one another. For Duncan it was a peaceful summer in most respects, untouched by Spicer's malice. Larry Fagin saw that "Robin Blaser seemed at the time more like a divine messenger between Duncan—who was sort of like the exiled queen mother or something—and Jack—who was always Merlin."[29]

A Merlin unraveling. Arthur Kloth, a New Yorker for the past ten years, spent a week in July visiting old friends from Berkeley. In his sister's car he drove to California Street to Spicer's basement apartment on the fourth of July, Jack's favorite holiday. Spicer jumped into the car, flashing yellow teeth stained by tobacco. Banked in solid fog, Arthur and Jack maneuvered to the Marina for the annual fireworks show. "They could have had fireworks all night long, and you couldn't have seen them." Afterwards a dejected Spicer directed Arthur on a guided tour of the gay and bohemian bars in North Beach, winding up drunk and despondent on Green Street where, to Arthur's dismay, Spicer entered into a drunken argument, a "yelling spree," with the equally drunk Alan Watts. Finally the two Berkeley chums took off to a party in the Berkeley Hills, given by Allen Joyce and Alan Hislop, and were promptly eighty-sixed from its panoramic views of fog. "I'm writing *The Holy Grail*, 'The Book of the Death of Arthur,'" Spicer told Kloth. "And you're Arthur."[30]

In Europe Harold and Dora Dull had shown Stan Persky a maunscript of Robin Blaser's then-unpublished *Cups*. Impressed, Stan had written an appreciative letter to Robin, but the two had not yet met. On a cold, rainy night, Persky was sitting in an almost deserted bar, wondering out loud about the reclusive, elegant Robin Blaser. Robin never came down to the bar, Spicer assured him. Cocky, ambitious, confident, Stan bet Jack a quarter he could get Robin to come down to meet him. It was "a quarter Jack was happy to lose because he wanted to get Blaser to come down to the bar so *he'd* have somebody to talk to." Jack, in fact, gave Stan the nickel to make the call. "I announced that I had come to town, was twenty-one years old, and I wanted to meet him. I had read his poems and was down here in the bar with Jack Spicer and George Stanley. 'Why don't you come down here and have a drink like a regular guy?'" And Blaser came down and had a drink like a regular guy. Presently Persky realized he'd be more than "willing to have an affair with Robin Blaser. I was attracted to the elegant-looking poet who wrote great poems—I don't know how sexually attracted to him [I was]." Robin had magic, a "style of magicality in the name of art."[31]

The two began a serious affair. Sometimes Blaser visited Stan at Union Street, but more often Stan was invited to Robin's fabulous apartment on Clay and Baker Street. Once Robin invited George Stanley and Bill Brodecky to lunch there—"it was like going to have lunch with the Queen," Bill remembered. "*That* exciting, that high. I had never had such high-class attention in my life and I was just in Seventh Heaven." Examining the thoughtfully decorated rooms further, Bill noticed that amid the Spanish arabesques of the upper plaster walls "there was one band, sort of muted purple, up near the ceiling. To me that has always symbolized Robin, that thin, attenuatedly elegant band of purple."[32]

Still Stan could not decide. He was living on Union Street with Lew Ellingham and Tony Aste, the man he (Stan) loved. (Tony sat up one night pulling the lash on a gun, the clicking sound, repeated regularly for some time, threatening in the still darkness.) "Everybody was in love with Tony Aste," Stan recalled.

I did recognize the difference between what I felt for Tony Aste—hopeless love—and what I felt for Blaser—which was something else: a lot of admiration, respect, a love for his work and who he was, his uniqueness and all that. But it didn't have that kind of sexual charge and Blaser himself recognized that.

I doubt if *he* was hopelessly in love, because I was pretty easy to get. I remember Robin saying, "You're in love with Tony Aste." So I don't feel particularly guilty about the complexity of my motivations, because his were as complex as mine were. I was an active participant in my own seduction in this situation *vis-à-vis* Robin, and was calculatedly enough making some of this happen. I remember him coming up to Union Street, and somehow we got ourselves into some kind of awkward sex kind of stuff, and he invited me over to have dinner at Clay Street. I remember him making *filet mignon* stuffed with truffles: a "big deal" evening.

I thought that this was all marvelous, this presentation of coherent worlds. Blaser was showing me, teaching me a whole sensibility, different from Spicer's; and yet again they were somehow united.[33]

No social event presided over by the Red and White Queens of *Alice* could rival the entertainment inadvertently prepared by Robin Blaser for the reception of Spicer's *The Holy Grail*. The first reading, perhaps, of this book of poems can be dated—August 28, 1962. Robin Blaser remembered the poems were finished that very day. (Marilyn Monroe's death, which enters into the poem, was on August 5.) So confused and disoriented became the atmospheres and personalities of this event that several witnesses denied any reading took place. Others remembered a beginning; others acknowledged the possibility of a complete reading.[34] The reason for such confusion will become apparent shortly.

The occasion of the reading was a dinner party given by Robin Blaser to celebrate the arrival of two visual artists, painter John Button and his boyfriend, the sculptor Scott Burton. John Button, a native San Franciscan, had known the poets of the Berkeley Renaissance in the late 1940s. He made his home and career in New York, but had kept in touch with all. When he had been in UC Hospital two years previously for a serious cancer operation, Spicer had come to visit him with a bottle of brandy clenched in a brown paper bag.[35] Button and Burton—whose mother, romantically enough, worked as a social secretary in Jacqueline Kennedy's White House—stayed now at the home of Gerry Fabian, a longtime acquaintance of Spicer's and a friend of Button's for many years. Fabian, Button, Burton, Duncan, and Jess all came to the dinner at Robin's apartment at Clay and Baker Streets with its ornamented stucco and tall French windows. On the phonograph Robin played, over and over, Henry Mancini's "Moon River," the theme from Blake Edwards's film of *Breakfast at Tiffany's*—"in honor of Scott Burton," Gerald Fabian remembered, "who was a character out of a Capote novel himself." The dinner went without incident, although the promised after-dinner entertainment must have given rise to one or two premonitions.

It was a warm summer night. Robin changed the record on the phonograph to *The Faerie Queene*, Henry Purcell's music on Arthurian themes.[36] These musical selections were a preparation for Spicer's reading of *The Holy Grail*, in the same spirit Blaser had played a recording of the American folk-pop ballad "The Battle of New Orleans" to accompany the reading of *The Heads of the Town Up to the Aether* the year before. As *The Faerie Queene* played, Spicer entered the apartment, drunk. He staggered over to the phonograph and switched off the record.[37] Robin was disheartened to see that Jack had brought along some uninvited guests, among them his future roommate, the young clarinetist Ron Primack. Robin had worked hard to orchestrate a reunion of Duncan and Spicer; and all seemed for naught. Spicer, fresh from the new, important poem, lavished ample reserves of ridicule and contempt on everything that caught his glance in the rich setting, both from the exhaustion involved in the writing, and in the spirit of

Robin Blaser, domestic scene. "The riches of art." *Photo by Robert Berg (collection of the authors).*

competition with his peers present—Duncan and Blaser—and his small army of youthful admirers at his back.

Shouldn't Blaser have expected a fiasco? Stan Persky suggested this: "Obviously Robin had gotten overexcited by John Button being in town. He hoped everybody would like each other."[38] Button's memoir dealt only obliquely with the evening: "Robin Blaser had a poetry reading in his apartment. Jack was the guest of honor. But Jack had become even more perverse and difficult then. He wouldn't allow anyone else to read, and he refused to read himself."[39] Years later, Robin said that Spicer reacted "negatively to the atmosphere"—intensely so. He sneered at Robin's paintings— by Jess and Tom Field, among others—a strange outburst, for Jack had always held these painters in high regard. The rooms were fine, the address good—too fine, too good, for the Spicer/North Beach aesthetic. Where was the bohemian shambles, the improvisation? In Blaser's apartment Spicer's puritanical, unluxuried middle-classness showed itself, and he never tired of joking about Robin's enjoyment of luxury; he was more circumspect about Duncan's and Jess's interest in the same, feeling that their collections came from an interest in the subjects of their books, paintings, and artifacts more than from their value as objects. Robin remembered the dinner guests not wanting a reading, which condemned it to failure.

The atmosphere became increasingly painful. Spicer attacked Duncan for championing the new poetry coming out of Vancouver. Duncan felt stung by this, since his visits to Vancouver had done much, perhaps inadvertently, to promote Spicer's own reputation there too. Gerry Fabian remembered "Jess Collins's pain. I remember feeling it too." Fabian spoke of "the romantic glow with which Robin surrounded John and Scott's newfound affair."[40] Jess remembered that "the whole event was terrible from beginning to end." As a latecomer to the Berkeley Renaissance, Jess had never met John Button, and neither Button nor Burton impressed him terribly. But when Spicer came in after dinner, it was just too much. "I just left," he says. "Robert tried to get me to stay, saying it would hurt Robin's feelings if we left, but I said, 'I just don't care any more,' and I got up and went out." Blaser remembered Jess leaving the apartment and being urged on the street to return. Jess recalled the bus routes he took to get to his home in the Mission District from Telegraph Hill in 1962. "Robert stayed awhile then left too."[41] Bill Brodecky, present with George Stanley, recalled no reading, remembering only his dislike for the New York couple, who seemed to him pretentious.[42] In short, any hope that "everybody would like each other" was soon scattered. Neither Stan Persky nor Ron Primack, both of whom Robert Duncan recollected were guests, even remembered attending—or crashing—though both accepted the possibility they might have.[43] Blaser later resolved this confusion of memories: "Jack read the poems to me that night in the bedroom; we were alone." A private, or nonpublic reading became a general memory. The poem seems to have been in progress in these happenings, its birth occurring through one reality after another.

Robert Duncan called the event "gruesome. Jess and I were invited over to hear Jack read, and Jack brought the gang around; we had sort of been guaranteed that the gang wouldn't be there. Jess couldn't stand them by that time, and they were bad boys as ever. Primack and Persky and George Stanley and Jack Spicer." Duncan told this with less-than-resigned exasperation, even twenty-odd years after the event. "They were really like nasty boys. I think Jess would never take anybody's guarantee again that somebody wouldn't be somewhere when we were; by that time he'd banned Jack's name."[44] The next day Duncan wrote to Blaser about the party:

Dear Robin,

This morning, still worn thin from the Spicer scene, I most regret that we didn't anticipate the whole thing and take our leave before the gang arrived. But in the future do send us a telegram when plans for the evening change. I've sat thru the last evening of knowing sneers at Tom's painting or Vancouver poets—and that after managing some sixteen years of Spicer venom against Stein or Pound (could anything have been worse than his humors at the Pound meetings in 1949?)—yes, it all seems worse now, unbearable, painful without relief. The spectacle of George Stanley's toadying does not improve the show. I am glad that the play *[Adam's Way]*'s to be done at the subscription series, for that will surely mean that Jack won't attend.

There must be explanations to Tom Parkinson for I cannot endure the idea of a dinner with Jack's charming and elegant company—I'll have to leave Creeley to that exposure and in a selfish interest in my own pleasure go to Hilde Burton's with Jess for dinner.

You had oddly enuf then an evening that was a turning point. August 28th, 1962 terminated my friendship of any kind with a long suffered friend—the idea of Spicer is preferable to the actual presence—

Robert[45]

A fellow librarian, Blanche Jantzen, had offered Blaser $3,000 to spend as he pleased; he suggested that she help support the arts instead, recommending three projects: (1) for Donald Allen, to help launch his publishing venture, the Four Seasons Foundation; (2) for the Peacock Gallery, an exhibition space that would show the artists, among others, close to the Spicer circle; (3) a donation of $1,000 to the Auerhahn Society (a nonprofit corporation set up to receive tax-deductible donations for this purpose) to publish *The Heads of the Town Up to the Aether*.[46]

The Auerhahn Press was a small, high-quality printing firm run by Andrew Hoyem and David Haselwood, whose relationship with Spicer quickly turned stormy. "When Dave Haselwood was publishing *Heads of the Town Up to the Aether*, Jack was as close to insane as I ever saw him," Dora Geissler recalled. "He was convinced that Dave was out to destroy him, ruining his poetry and killing any possibility of future writing."[47] Spicer increasingly manifested the paranoia of an advancing alcoholic, as well as the toll taken by the stress of his fanatical dedication to his work. A younger poet remembered this as a harrowing time for Spicer, a man agitated by his own weakness, disturbed that he had compromised his own integrity to achieve the fame he both wanted and reviled.[48]

Spicer was also tormented by a thorny copyright question. *The Heads of the Town Up to the Aether* was Spicer's first copyrighted book, but he was opposed to a writer's ownership of his works. *Any* copyright ownership was an abuse, in Spicer's view.[49] Gail Chugg, who typed the book, reviewed these events from his own perspective: "If it is true that Jack *was forced* to accede to a *copyright*—it may explain his nastiness and craziness—Jack, who could savage a friend for copping out, was quite capable of damning himself for such a transgression. It could easily have driven him to an unself-forgiving near-psychosis." Spicer's position against copyright was a political and artistic commitment of the highest order, and the frozen, sullen behavior he exhibited during the conflict was, thought Chugg, the rage he felt at himself—"only incidentally did his self-hatred include others."[50]

Jack asked Fran Herndon to publish her lithos to "Homage to Creeley" alongside his text. In addition, Spicer embellished each of one hundred copies of the limited edition with an original crayon drawing of his own as frontispiece. With the book in production, Fran accompanied Jack to the Auerhahn offices both as an artist and chaperone. Hoyem and Haselwood were grateful that Fran could mediate between them and their abrasive author. "In the end, when the book was finally finished and Jack was signing them and drawing these cute little pictures, they actually asked me—I wouldn't want you ever to repeat this, though I'm putting it on tape—to ask him to wash his hands. Can you imagine suggesting that to Jack?" And Fran laughed and laughed.[51]

The book, when issued, didn't "do" as well as everyone hoped. Some of the blame for its poor distribution must be ascribed to Spicer himself, though in September, Robin complained to Hoyem and Haselwood that Auerhahn wasn't doing enough to promote the book.[52] As part of his ongoing feud with Ferlinghetti, he refused to let City Lights carry the book. In addition, Dave Haselwood wrote in a letter to a puzzled patron, "some of [Jack's] minions alienated Discovery [Bookstore]—which means that only N.Y. bookstores and a few others scattered around the country carry it."[53]

Evidence of Auerhahn's attempts to promote *Heads'* sale remains in the press's files. Requests for review copies were handled speedily.[54] Enough of an advertising push was made to lure many prominent figures of postmodern poetry to order a copy—James Laughlin, publisher of New Directions, the poet Gerrit Lansing, Cid Corman among them.[55] Even Donald Hall, at the University of Michigan, was sent a copy in hopes that he would mention it in his radio program on the BBC.[56] One bookseller, entering into the promotional spirit, suggested a snappy nickname (*Heads Up!*) for Spicer's more cumbersome title, but this annoyed Spicer and the idea was quietly dropped.[57] A surprising inquiry from Rizzoli was made in October—were the Italian rights free to print *The Heads of the Town* in Milan? (They were, but Rizzoli finally declined the opportunity.)[58]

One story completes the circus of Spicer's relationship to Auerhahn, a story with a charm particularly Spicer's in its oddity. Spicer invited Hoyem and Haselwood to hear him read his poems. Hoyem remembers that "Spicer seemed to be relatively sober, but he became maudlin and tearful during the course of the reading, apparently overcome by sentiments encoded in the writings." Before the reading, Jack asked what Haselwood would like to hear. *After Lorca* was Dave's favorite of Spicer's books, and Jack read it from beginning to end. Haselwood said of this occasion "that Spicer was capable of making such a gesture is the point of the story. And that such hardened characters as poets and publishers *can* touch each other, beyond words or politics, is what makes life bearable in the rather snippy world of artists."[59]

Although Spicer had dedicated—by means of the notion of a *homage*—the first part of *Heads of the Town* to Robert Creeley, he apparently failed to send him a copy. Some seven months after its publication, Creeley wrote to Auerhahn from Vancouver, where he was then teaching, sending his check for three dollars and asking for a copy. He'd seen the book in San Francisco, he wrote, but hadn't bought a copy then, on the "vague understanding" that *Heads* would be distributed up North. It was a "very wild" book, he added, both on "Jack's part, certainly, and your printing too."[60] Spicer had told Gail Chugg that the reason he had called the opening section of the poem "Homage to Creeley" was "because he made it possible to write short poems" in contemporary times.[61] Advised of this, Duncan sighed. "Jack admired Creeley, and I think he wanted, I think he felt—no! It's much sadder than that—(now a *homage*, remember, is not something you do expect a reply to)—I think Jack thought it was sort of a secret magic, that Creeley would be close to him. [But after the publication of the book] he never heard from him." Duncan hesitated, remembering Jack's puzzled disappointment, his own excuses for Creeley's silence. "I dodged it, saying, 'Oh well, Creeley's very busy.' It was the greatest blow to Jack."

Was Spicer's seeming neglect to have *Heads* sent to Creeley an oversight? Carelessness? Deliberate omission? "Bob told me he couldn't make anything of it. Again—both of those [Olson and Creeley]—I've never been able to fathom and didn't try. You can't ask somebody who says he didn't make anything of something *what they didn't make anything of!*" Duncan continued, "So Jack drew a complete blank: and did what I do with complete blanks, put 'em away. But Olson always had just the impression that this just showed that Dunk [Duncan] is capable of being enthusiastic about things all on his own when they won't work out."[62]

Or perhaps Spicer did send Creeley the original, mimeographed edition of *Homage to Creeley*—the version Harold and Dora Dull ran off on the Kashia Reservation in the spring of 1960. This would be consistent with Creeley's recollection of having been in Guatemala at the time he would have been sent the poem. Perhaps the flimsy stapled poem was lost in the mails—just like an episode out of "A Fake Novel!" And perhaps, the sting of Creeley's imagined rejection still painful, Spicer cut him off the complimentary list when Auerhahn issued *The Heads of the Town Up to the Aether* thirty months later.

Though Duncan recalled that Creeley couldn't understand Spicer's "Homage" to him, Creeley himself reflected in a letter to Lew Ellingham in the spring of 1983:

I'd taken Jack's "Homage to Creeley" as his play on the syntactical/almost "pronominal"/authorial patterns of my writing to that time (i.e., in poetry particularly). What I could or wanted to "authorize" in that way. So I read his work as a run-through on those presumptions, from a clear base in language preoccupations. I didn't think he was following me into whatever "romantic" condition(s). Ah well. But I did take it as an interest in what I was doing, and as a non-bullshit (in that respect) "homage." In short, I was honored and impressed.[63]

Creeley added that "In any case, I don't recall any dilemmas such as Robert and your conversation suggests (?)." Creeley referred to his "apparently opaque statement. I meant simply Jack's attention to (and play on my attention to) the AGENCY of the speaker. Who's 'authorizing' the words—the construct of the authority—etc. etc."[64] All this, in fact, seems not too far from Chugg's summary of Spicer's view that Creeley "made it possible to write short poems." Spicer's responses to connections with important writers tended to proceed at dual levels, expressing both the emotional hurt that Duncan alludes to and the professional understanding that Creeley suggests.

Contemporary critical response of *The Heads of the Town* was spare, and unenlightened. When books of poetry were sent to the San Francisco *Chronicle* for review, it was the newspaper's practice to forward them to the Poetry Center, and apparently no one there cared for Spicer's work. On radio station KPFA Kenneth Rexroth is said to have reviewed *Heads* with the statement that it had a couple of "funny old jokes" in it. "He liked the one about the sheepherder and the virgin wool," Gail Chugg recalled. (The note to the fifth "Homage to Creeley" poem is "virgin wool is defined as wool made from the coat of any sheep that can run faster than the sheepherder.")[65] And the Vancouver poet George Bowering gave the book a puzzled review in the "poetry newsletter" *Tish*:

When I was in San Francisco this last summer I kept hearing from the young North Beach and Berkeley poets that Jack Spicer was the best poet in the United States. I think that either they live too close to him or that I have too much distance. I see this book as a kind of Spicerian commonplace book wherein San Franciscans will learn some more about the thoughts of Jack Spicer; but I think it's too esoteric for this reader at this time.[66]

Within a few years, the distance narrowed, as Spicer made two voyages to Vancouver, and George Bowering, like other Canadian poets, came to acknowledge Spicer as a master. In the meantime Spicer remained a prophet without honor even in his own country.

The next conflict between Duncan and Spicer was not long in coming. Duncan was busy with a new play, *Adam's Way*. As was his custom, he wrote the play while the actors were assembled and the work was in progress, literally in rehearsal. Several close to Spicer's group were actors in the play, among them Helen Adam and Robin Blaser; Paul Alexander, Ida Hodes, Lew and Deneen Peckinpah Brown. The painter Tom Field took the part of Pook in rehearsals, although he shipped out before the opening of the play. The performance took place on October 1, 1962, at The Tape Music Center in San Francisco, a small place adequate for theater *in camera*. "I still have Duncan's sets for *Adam's Way*," Robin remembered. "Jess borrowed Paul Alexander's watercolors and drew a sort of fantasy of Helen Adam and of me wandering through that weird world of *Adam's Way*."[67] Duncan felt comfortable with his cast, his "little group of friends" as he described them in the program notes.

Blaser later recalled: "In San Francisco the 'bad feeling' dated from the *Adam's Way* performance at the Tape Music Center when Spicer, manipulating his magic by opposition, again from North Beach, arranged to have that play picketed."[68] "Dear Joanne," Stan Persky wrote, "Harold & me are going to Duncan's dress rehearsal of a play about Adam & Eve and the sun and moon and Atlantis and woman all that usual shit he writes about when he aint got no poem." From the end of the bar, Spicer growled that *Adam's Way* was "early Swinburne," the worst thing he'd written in ten years—whether he'd read it or not no one could say. "Even the charming Blaser, who's in it, does bar parodies of "mind and moon" on pernodded occasions." If the dress rehearsal failed to please, Stan, Harold and George planned to picket the opening, hoping to offend the rich Pharisees in attendance.[69]

"Persky carried a sign," Blaser recalled ruefully,

and so did Stanley, saying "Fuck Duncan, Fuck Jess, Fuck Chi-Chi!" The police arrived and were going to arrest Stanley and Persky—in those days dirty words weren't allowed in public. I remember talking to a policeman with my face completely covered with that lizard's mask, which was actually a sequined rather armpit-smelling evening vest that I wrapped around my face in order to look like a lizard.

Duncan was tempted to give them the works. But by the time the conversation went along, why the police let them go, and the play went on. In the meantime, of course, Jack was sitting down there in Gino & Carlo's playing the opposition magic still—"to be contrary to," to use Blakean terms.[70]

In "Image-Nation 5," Blaser gave this heightened, or tightened account of the same incident:

> George divided the city East
> and West of Van Ness to the West
> the soufflé makers, to the East
> the men of a 'truer' language
> letters arrived proving everyone
> else was 'evil' signs went up:
> 'Fuck chi-chi' the police came
> I asked the author not to press charges
> Fuck, I said, is a young word
> I had stepped out of my part
> in the play as an Atlantean lizard—
> my face swathed in a sequin bodice—
> her perfumed sweat clinging
> to the words I spoke through
> the glittering cloth—trousers
> sewn of kitchen-foil scales
> the play was about interstices
> and the players who wanted
> the movement
> of visible
> and invisible worlds
> they are a commotion
> of one form[71]

"Jack began to try really to divide people," Blaser said. "In some sense he meant to divide by way of a poetics: but of course that worked out as a division by persons. So that the North Beach scene would be a separate scene *from*. And this did, I think, put enormous pressure on people's loyalties, in one way or another."

After these proceedings of theater encasing theater, Spicer's isolation from his two Berkeley peers seemed complete—though it was not, in fact, so. Blaser's own position was ambivalent. He felt hemmed in at every side, by Duncan's estrangement from Spicer's bar life, and by attacks from *les jeunes* that painted him as a would-be Duncan. He wrote to Jess, giving "samples" of the "vicious, pointless" barbs he was receiving from Stanley and Persky: "George: 'You are deeply middle-aged.' Stan: 'I'll sleep with you anytime . . . the rest of you stinks.'" It was Jack, of course, behind this barbaric sniping, Jack who must have felt that Robin and Duncan had joined the Establishment, sold out. "Jack is reduced to lying or he's gone completely Kook."[72] For Duncan and Jess, the estrangement was to remain sealed.

October 11, 1962

Dearest Robin,

Your note to Jess confirmed our dread that the swarming fever of trumpt up existence in Spicer's sphere would break against you. I found, after I had made the gesture of having something to do with them again (my going to go to see Jack in his lair and make an obeisance just before going East this spring), that I had been quite happy in avoiding the lot entirely. Yet I know it can be of no such simple thing for you (well, it wasn't and isn't a simple thing for me) but a grievous recognition to come to: How much Spicer and George and the gang want to hurt and humiliate the spirit in one. In the root meaning of *evil*, Spicer is evil, for he writes even to acquire power *over* souls around him, and would use poetry to intimidate, usurping the place of one's inner *daimon*. Certainly he will use friendship to bind and command. It was finally seeing this this way, that made me realize I really couldn't deal with it. I can only avoid it. It was such bliss in the course of *Adam's Way* to revel in the directions and predilections of my spirit without having to fight the shadow battle thru it all against the Puritans of Gino and Carlos. And I did manage pretty well to go ahead generously in my rhetoric without trying to save face.

> what soul
> isn't in default?
> can you afford not to make
> the magical study
> which happiness is?

We do have to, Robin, ask ourselves where our happiness lies—again and again to recognize and return to the things we love. Or else it is all a field of lies. And against Olson's lovely radiance, these mean souls would thrive.[73]

For the printing of *The Holy Grail*, Spicer returned to White Rabbit, counting on his telepathic connection to Graham Mackintosh to avoid the storms of Auerhahn. Graham produced a red, white, and black cover, after toying with a version in purple and yellow—royal colors for a magisterial book, colors that upset Spicer.

The colors were personal to him. There are only two colors, red and black. There's the white paper, which represents purity of the soul. There's the black ink, and the type, which represents certain forces which are at work, evil forces. Black/evil forces. And the red, which is allowable, because it's Christ's blood.

It's a metaphor that goes back to Gutenberg. "We have Christ's blood, we have evil—the black type—that's all we can get to show on the white purity of this paper, which is the purity of the soul." It wasn't that Jack believed in Jesus Christ, or believed in the Devil, or believed in the purity of the soul. But it was a convention, that sounded right. Jack would not allow any deviation.[74]

Jack had also, in the opinion of his friends, become obsessed with conspiracy. Leaving a movie just as the bus to North Beach passed, rather late at night, Spicer described the cabal between theater owners and the bus authority that allowed a third partner in "the fix"—the taxi companies—to then profit from the arrangement. This was Jack at his most elegant and absurd. Sometimes, as in the beautiful poems of his "Graphemics" in *Language* where he invoked a simple observation of "Indian signs" and "sundials" to suggest the relations of chance, Spicer's concern with determination was very lovely. On the other hand, as in the case of "The Fix," his poetic seemed sometimes at the verge of paranoic raving.

"The Fix" takes the Black Sox scandal of 1921 as the precursor to all following machinations. Spicer quotes the famous childish challenge, "Say it ain't so, Joe," so full of perplexed naiveté in the face of adult guilt and betrayal, as "Say it isn't true Joe." George Stanley said, "In baseball the owners were the enemy, Horace Stoneham of the Giants, and Walter O'Malley of the Dodgers: in 1962 Jack Spicer became convinced that the National League pennant had been fixed."[75]

> This is an ode to Horace Stoneham and Walter O'Malley.
> Rottenness.
> Who has driven me away from baseball like a fast car. Say
> It isn't true Joe.
> This is an ode to John Wieners and Auerhahn Press
> Who have driven me away from poetry like a fast car. Say
> It isn't true Joe. The fix
> Has the same place in junkie talk or real talk
> It is the position
> They've got you in.
> The Giants will have a National League playoff. Duncan
> Will read his poems in Seattle.
> Money (I forgot the story but the little boy after it all was
>   over came up to Shoeless
> Joe Jackson) Say it isn't true Joe.

I have seen the best poets and baseball players of our
    generation caught in the complete and contemptible
    whoredom of capitalist society
Jack Johnson
At last shaded the sun from his eyes
                .A fix
You become fixtures like light
Balls. Drug
Habit
Walter O'Malley, Horace Stoneham, do you suppose
    somebody fixed Pindar and the Olympic Games?[76]

"This is an ode to John Wieners and Auerhahn Press," announces the poem, "who have driven me away from poetry like a fast car." In October 1962 Spicer was displeased with Wieners since the long-delayed *Measure* 3, "The City," had not appeared until that summer. He had been leery of submitting his work to Wieners, but he had gone ahead and done it anyhow on Robin's say-so. Wieners's poverty and drug problems had delayed the appearance of "The City" for a full four years, and Spicer must have been appalled to find his 1955 poem "Central Park West" in its table of contents. Now that he had begun thinking of his poems as books, there literally wasn't a place for a single orphan poem like "Central Park West." Between them Auerhahn and Wieners were driving him away from poetry like a fast car. The "Fix" material has a curious textual history. When Spicer posted the first "Fix" poem on the wall of Gino & Carlo's, Lew Ellingham copied it onto a brown paper bag, which Gail Chugg preserved among his souvenirs, returning it twenty years later as a token of their long friendship. In October 1997 Fran Herndon, delving in an old file cabinet in her basement, uncovered five additional poems in this abortive "Fix" sequence, the most substantive such discovery in many years. "Countess Death," Spicer wrote, "give me Some life in this little plain we live in from start to finish/ Let me slit their throats and smash their heads on the/ Stone."

For some time Jess had been making a series of illustrations to a long-planned edition of Robin's poems. (Despite a large amount of fine work completed within the previous decade, Blaser had yet to publish his first book.) Arrangements had been made with Auerhahn to handle the printing, and here trouble arose—Spicer's animosity toward Auerhahn was as strong as ever, and seemed to infect Robin with impatience too. Finally the tension was so strong that, in an "act of rage and despair," and without first informing Jess, Blaser withdrew his book. Duncan accosted Blaser and charged him with a cavalier disregard of Jess's feelings. Robin hastened to apologize, and broached the possibility of finding another publisher for the book, including Jess's "necessary and beautiful" pictures for it, but the apology came too late. Hurt and baffled, Jess announced that he had decided to "pass" on publishing his collaboration in any future edition of Robin's poems. Ironically, at this very time, Duncan and Jess were themselves immersed in their own quarrel with Auerhahn, which led to withdrawal of their *Book of Resemblances* from its auspices.[77]

Duncan and Jess saw this fiasco as another of Robin's "capitulations" to Jack, but Robin denied it. He acknowledged to Jess that he'd been "selfish" in not warning Jess beforehand of his intentions, but insisted that his love for Jack was over. Practical drawbacks to the Auerhahn plan were what made him break his contract, he wrote. In addition, his anguish over the continuing torments from the younger poets had devasated him and rendered him helpless to proceed. "You cannot know," he told Jess, "what George's 'poems' said—I was a gargoyle spitting shit—a womanish soufflee maker." As he sat listening to these insults, he could only believe "that I had opened a window and an unknown Malice had thrown the contents of a slop jar in my face."[78] Blaser's relations with the Duncan household were balanced on a thin edge of anger and loyalties. A letter from Duncan makes it clear that Jack Spicer, and Spicer's circle, continued to play an important role in Blaser's life—to Duncan's distress:

Dear Robin,

It was good to have a note from you with the payment on the painting. If there is a time when you want to see us, we will be delighted to see you—three ring signal on bell, or best, a post card telling us you may come by. Your responsiveness has always meant a lot to us—and then, too, we miss a certain Blaser flavor that adheres to recognitions we've had thru your eyes.

But George Stanley's observation that you were going to have to make a choice between "North Beach" and us has proved most true. You've suffered I think because you've tried to keep a loyalty that does not fit. The damnable thing about loyalties, Robin, is that they falsify actual response and choice. "North Beach" is not just a crowd that you have for some years now preferred to see to us, but an idea of poetry that has in this same period proved clearly to be entirely other and even alien to mine, and an idea of how to live that is hostile to ours. For a long time you yourself brought us the increasing evidence of the separation in the ways with news of each ridicule and rejection my work met in Spicerian circles. At the point at which you read a new poem (just after your being under disapproval for participating in *Adam's Way*) which you told us was splendid enough to reinstate you in their eyes and *never considered it important or interesting for us to read*, the separation was wide enough to be taken for granted.

I did not and do not write for the approval or disapproval of North Beach. I think I was most acutely conscious of this when they "liked" the third Dante sonnet.

It is harder to realize that an audience is false when they reject a work. Except that friends do not make a cause out of what they do not like.

Mustn't we be missd like something of the past, once a part of your daily life, that has been let go as you develop in your own direction? When you write you seem unhappy at the thought of us, as if we had been wrongd in being "wrong": but the choice might be accepted without incurring the judgment. I would have friendship include that possibility.

love,
Robert[79]

CHAPTER NINE

The Long Silence

*R*on Primack had been on and off the scene for several years. With Los Angeles, Europe, the Juilliard School, and a failed marriage behind him, Primack was "pretty loose"—as he later described himself—when he first arrived in San Francisco in 1958, aged twenty-one. John Allen Ryan, the bartender at The Place, remembered, "Knute Stiles and I picked Ron up the first night he was in town. He stayed with Knute the first night, then with me."[1] Knute Stiles remembered Primack's arrival differently. "Ronnie Primack presented me with credentials which turned out to be fake, to the effect that he was twenty-one at midnight. I set him up with a pitcher of beer and introduced him to everyone—that was his entree. Later he told me I had introduced him to dope and homosexuality, and so forth—as a seventeen-year-old. I had no knowledge at the time that I was introducing him to anything. I wouldn't say he was a virtuoso, but I didn't get the impression that he was somebody I was initiating to anything. He seemed to be—a perfectly willing kind of partner."[2]

How did he find North Beach and the Spicer group so quickly? Ron Primack recalled, "I was lucky enough to stumble into The Place. Zero connections. And of course Knute gave me free drinks; I was pretty good-looking then." Ron laughed in his rich, tense, generous voice. Young and straight in a world of gay artists, Primack hadn't "the slightest interest in male bodies." He felt disturbed and fascinated at the same time by what we now might call the male gaze. The theatricality of the scene intrigued him: "There seemed to be something very important going on, very unusual to me. . . . Everybody had enormous human gestures. There were just one or

Ron Primack. "When the taxi does not move it does not move / Burn it as quick as you can."
Photo by Robert Berg, courtesy of John Allen Ryan.

two people coming in, becoming very eloquent and stylish. Soon the bar changed, though," Ron went on, "from being kind of arias and duets, to choruses—the gestures started to grow. From those arias and duets followed great choruses of people. It was just like a mad opera. One guy drank strawberry beer with a carnation in it. And Joanne Kyger had her leg in a cast." George Stanley introduced Ron to Spicer, at the table at The Place. "Harold and Dora Dull were there—a lot of excitement." The jukebox in The Place was a thing of legend. "They were playing 'Beowulf,' and things like *Carmina Burana*, stuff like that, that'd get you all hot. The Place was really rocking."[3]

Though he "could hardly stutter a word out," Ron began to write, and his first poem he wrote with others. "We were sitting around the table, and [Spicer] was there that day. Line poems were one of the little exercises people did then, and this was just one of them." Two friends were getting married, and the roommates wrote a poem together—"Epithalamium"—as a gift.[4] (This marriage broke up soon after, George Stanley recalled.)[5] Russell FitzGerald found some heavy parchment-like paper and copied out the

poem in his exquisite calligraphy. Five lines were Spicer's: "heart of a
mouse / We / they and us / bless / your doorways."[6]

At the Sunday meeting, the "Epithalamium" was tried out, first by one
writer, then another. Nobody could read it correctly. "Just as it was about to
be abandoned," Stan Persky wrote, "John Wieners volunteered to try it—
and suddenly, in his flute-like voice, everyone heard its delicacy, music,
wit, especially as Wieners got to the final lines: 'Oh do / be, do be /do be /
mine,' hearing the exact play of the jazz sensibility of 'doobie/doobie/doo-
bie.' Suddenly 'heard,' there was a spontaneous burst of enthusiasm, the
sure measure that always greeted a 'real poem.'"[7]

"I moved in with Jack," Ron recalled, "in '62." This was the period following
The Holy Grail, the full year and more before Spicer began *Language*, and the
only long interruption in Jack's final five years of writing. As he and Ron
Primack began living together, there were intense, unusual features about
their connection, for Spicer experienced his next poem through Ron, even
while the creation and achievement were distinctly Ron Primack's own.
Ron had an unusual gift for intimacy, coupled with a native sharpness free
of overintellectualizing. Slightly older than the Jets, he shared their freewheeling lifestyle and the boyishness of their appeal—he was a mellower
Tony Aste, not quite as dangerous and more reflective. Robin was one of
many who envied Spicer's luck in "landing" Ron Primack as a roommate.
"The hottest little box Jack ever had was Ronnie—beloved Ronnie Primack. I mean, Ronnie was—I have never been so tempted in my life! Ronnie would sit on a staircase just as you were about to go up, just offering
you *everything*, especially between his legs. And there wasn't a mean bone
in his body."[8]

Jack and Ronnie shared Jack's basement flat in the apartment building
at 1650 California Street, near the Bank of America branch at Van Ness and
California. "You had to walk down the hall to the bathroom and the show-
ers. It was a two-room apartment, connected by a small hallway. In one
room, as you entered, was a kitchen. And to the right was the bedroom."
Sometimes the kitchen was warm with sun from its one window. Under
the bedroom window was the bed they shared. The green velour of an
overstuffed easy chair, worn through in patches, showed the stuffing and
springs. Along the bedroom floor, like dominoes, stood volumes of history
and philosophy checked out on long-term loans from the UC Berkeley library. On a small table stood Jack's typewriter, its carriage and keys gray

with heaped cigarette ashes. There was no telephone and no window-shade, only a piece of cloth tacked up against the window, which looked out onto the parking lot nearby. All night long people knocked at the door—people from the bar, visitors for Jack. But neither Jack nor Ronnie got up to admit them; in the morning the door was covered with messages. Sometimes Spicer's pals ducked through the parking lot and tried to get his attention by tapping on the bedroom window.

Above the bed hung a painting of an orange centipede. A second cloth concealed the closet door, and to that cloth Jack had pinned a frayed hang-ing he called "Uncle Louie." Despite its down-home name, "Uncle Louie" was a gaudy piece of Orientalism, the representation of a pharoah sur-rounded by lines of hieroglyphs and Egyptian figures, created in Cairo dur-ing World War II by women artisans. The piece hung four feet long, and eighteen inches wide, and in Ron's words, "it looks like it's worth a million dollars, but of course it's not. It's just a commercial piece of appliqué."[9]

Jack woke late in the morning, shaking from the previous night's hang-over and the previous night's poem. He would move the makeshift win-dowshade to check on the weather, pad to the kitchen for some instant cof-fee, then douse it with brandy. After two or three cups, the trembling hands could hold the morning paper, and more serious reading followed. After a nap, it was already two o'clock, time for his daily walk to Aquatic Park with his cheap leather-covered radio, usually accompanied by Ron.

They would stop first at the Bait & Tackle Shop at Polk and North Point, which catered to customers who came to fish from Aquatic Park pier, or to sail from Fisherman's Wharf. Jack would buy a submarine sand-wich on a French roll, a six-pack of Budweiser or Falstaff, and a pack of Camels or Lucky Strikes. In this period Jack sometimes affected a pipe, and once bought Ron a pipe as a gift. Once at Aquatic Park, a few short blocks farther on, "we'd sit around and he'd get his about-$4.50 transistor radio going, and have the baseball games when they were playing. Often he'd walk down the street with the thing to his ear, catching some bit of infor-mation, the news, whatnot. And he always had something going about the weather; he could tell what it was going to be like, even though it was changing constantly." Ron eventually got a job as a typist at a dress manu-facturer's, because Jack, he realized, "could not afford me not to be work-ing." After that, he had to beg off from the afternoons in Aquatic Park.[10]

Jack himself rarely went to work—David Reed, he told Ron, let him do as he pleased. According to Ron, Spicer was paid around $350 a month. Paid monthly, he exchanged all his money for five dollar bills and brought them home to the jacket in his closet that served as his bank. He liked the handiness and convenience of five-dollar bills—"he could drink and get home in a taxicab with it—share one—walk if necessary—for five dollars," for a tall glass of brandy and water cost about sixty or seventy cents. He was as frugal as Ron was profligate.

"He always bought his brandy in the same place, at Weinstein's on Polk Street, and he always bought a quart," Ron remembered. "He used to say that all brandy was the same, that they just poured it out in different bottles." Jack's special discovery was "Charmaine." This $3.98 bargain brand was, he claimed, the *exact same brandy* that Macy's department store sold for seventeen dollars a bottle. Another treat he loved was apple brandy; and on special occasions, Ron bought him a bottle of Courvoisier. James Broughton, who visited Spicer, remembered that he "was devoted to brandy, and he insisted on the best brandy. Otherwise he was indifferent to niceties. He was invariably rumpled and even unkempt. Though he cared little for good cooking, his sharp tongue was always ready to bite."[11]

On their way home from Aquatic Park, Ron and Jack "would stop at one of the little markets on Polk Street and get vegetables for a sandwich. Jack would read or take a nap. And continue to drink, only now he switched to brandy-and-water. Jack would have liked to become very domestic, to have seen us triumph in a man-and-wife kind of sense. But you know it wasn't in the cards."

Lew Ellingham asked Primack, "How did Jack deal with the fact that you wouldn't sleep with him, physically?"

"Well, I did sleep with him," Ron answered. "We slept together. Jack's sexual life was pretty uninteresting. I mean he didn't have many demands. It wasn't that important. That's just a frank admission on my part. If there was some very great sophisticated scene—sexual scene—I don't even know what that would have meant to him, anyhow. It was sort of irrelevant anyhow. I don't think he was interested in any wild crazy sexual thing. But in companionship, friendship. There was never any real reason that Jack and I should have been together, there was never any one single reason like I can think of in other relationships of mine, where I could figure that out. There was not every reason in the world to point to, towards our relationship, to even make sense, no matter how you looked at it."[12]

Out again in the evenings, Jack went to the bars, about ten, sometimes in a cab, but usually walking to North Beach through the Broadway Tunnel to Katie's "Bourbon Street," with its great mural of a youthful Dante espying Beatrice at the Ponte Santa Trinità, his future poetry a gleam in his eye.[13] "When we used to go there," Ron added, "[Katie's] was always dark, and really interesting. Every tobacco in the universe was sold there; every kind of cigarette known to man." Katie's had a short but vivid life, ending when her rent was substantially raised and Katie moved her bar off the block though still nearby. The new bar became an "opera bar" (the jukebox music) and *de facto* gay bar. Katie very much wanted Spicer to come to her new bar, going to the length of buying a life-size charcoal drawing of Robert Duncan reading, which was the work of Peter LeBlanc, a local artist. Thwarted: Spicer did not drink in bars decorated for him. Now there would be only one bar for the Spicer circle: Gino & Carlo's. "Jack drank slowly. He might have five or six drinks. And if he had a dollar, a dollar and a half, two dollars at the end of the night, he had a taxicab. He needed quarters to play pinball, but quite often he'd win pinball, and that would be $5: I mean that would make it right there. He made most of his money at Katie's. It seemed those machines were good for him."[14]

While Ron Primack believed that Spicer played pinball to make money, Graham Mackintosh thought it unlikely Spicer made much money that way. Said Graham, "It cost him money. It might have put an extra $10 in his pocket every so often." It cost ten cents to play a game. "If you won a game, you could get a dime back. Fifty games: five dollars. We played at Mike's, because Mike's was one of the few places that didn't try to get out of paying off—the bartender would just come by and look, and if the games were there, he'd reach under [the machine] and erase them by pushing a button, and give you the five, seven, ten dollars. I actually won that big. Jack never did."

"Is there any skill in the game?"

"Yeah, there was—a low-key finesse skill. It has to do with how hard you hit the ball. It would tilt very easily."[15]

During this period, Spicer was proofing galleys for the Auerhahn edition of *The Heads of the Town Up to the Aether*, but otherwise he was "between books" the way some people find themselves between jobs. In their relationship Ron found the voice he needed to write his book of poems—*The Late Major Horace Bell of the Los Angeles Rangers*. Jack, who wasn't writing at all, was listening to, listening for, Ron's writing. "He was extremely magnanimous, generous. Jack could explain to me how to find out poetry. You have to open up some area of your life, to find out where poetry is, and he was acute enough, perceptive enough, to know that."[16] When writers' block took hold of Ron, preventing progress on his poem, Spicer offered some cryptic advice, a line from his own poem in "A Fake Novel about the

Life of Arthur Rimbaud": "When the taxi does not move it does not move /
Burn it as quick as you can."[17]

"More than anything else, Jack and I shared a romantic attachment to
California, particularly southern California. He knew pretty much everything about California. The Mulholland incident attracted him, and the
corruption of Los Angeles. And he knew pretty much what would turn me
on. He knew ghosts impressed me—the ghostly history of southern California. So he just sort of said, 'Well, this is something to look at.' He was
very casual about it. Something I might look into. Just to start reading
about all this. And 'I'll give you some books you can start with.' So I did,
and the poem kind of popped out of the reading."

The adventures in the mid-nineteenth-century gold fields—and
demise at the hands of authority—of southern California desperado
Joachin Murietta matched in many ways those of the Spicer favorite, Billy
the Kid. Spicer offered Ron Horace Bell's 1881 memoir *Reminiscences of a
Ranger*, which details Bell's lengthy pursuit of Murietta, and mythologizes
him by recounting the "many legends of his appearances in many places
at once."[18] Hunter and hunted square off in Primack's poem, *The Late
Major Horace Bell*. "That was how I found out how poetry can start off.
'Cause until then I didn't understand, I couldn't really figure out, that it
was process."

> Murietta had momentum
> Where and what he was doing
> > was already begun as our lives
> > are begun with horseshit
> This horseshit persists.
> The business of Murietta is a shattering
> > of painted masks.
>
> Who will say that your head
> > is made of pictures of the dead?
>
> Each mask is recalled
> What was given as your face
> > appears and reappears as the same wave
>
> As Murietta appears and reappears
> > in the map of California
> > your figure follows the procession
> Marches until strongholds become

"I didn't want to know too much. I always had this feeling, that Jack—
he didn't say this, but I always knew—that he liked that. He always liked

some ignorance. And I was afraid to ask too many questions. Because I thought it might ruin things; things might turn out in my favor as a poet simply out of ignorance."[19] And so Spicer, while writing nothing himself, experienced the release of the outside voices when *The Late Major Bell* was being written.

Lake Elizabeth

There were the usual stories
of puzzling clues.

With Don Pico came the advent of Christianity

For Bernstein (a Jew) there was always a caricature.

But for Pico I suspect God
   and the fact that he had
    seen a movie on the crusades.

As Gaudier Bryzeska might have said:
"The Planes show where the demon swims."
          Ron Primack, *The Late Major Horace Bell*
               of the Los Angeles Rangers[20]

It was not Spicer's poem, but it issued from the same "outside." The ghosts proceeded laterally as though Spicer's writing was on an invisible screen. There was no longer any text, only the work produced by others: Ron Primack's book, Fran Herndon's sports collages. "I was on the take, you know," Ron said, "getting my poem. Jack was providing me with this way into the poem. I was just going along with it like that. I wasn't aware of Jack's troubles and the things that were disturbing him." Jack urged Ron to go to the university—unusual advice from a man to whom the idea of a university had become anathema.[21]

Spicer presented Graham Mackintosh with the manuscript of *The Late Major Horace Bell* and regarded its eventual publication as part of the natural course of things. Mackintosh recalled, "I said, 'Who [wrote] this?' He said, 'Ronnie Primack.'" Graham let out a groan, and Spicer reassured him of its worth. "I said, 'OK.'" Then I said to Ronnie Primack, 'Well, we'll be doing this book. What do you think about it?' He said, 'Maybe it should have some drawings in it,' or something like that. It was at that level." For Graham knew little about Ron Primack, not even that he played the clarinet. "I went up to his apartment one time, when he was living with Jack, and I said, 'My goodness, what are you doing?' He said, 'I'm putting new pads on it.' I said, 'You are? What do you know about clarinets?' He picked it up and did *Rhapsody in Blue* as well as I've ever heard it. Then it turns out he's been with the Boston Pops at the age of ten, played in"—Graham flourished imaginatively—"the La Scala Orchestra, all this kind of stuff."

"It was a fun little book to do," Graham continued, "and I still read those poems with pleasure. Sort of lyric."[22] Mackintosh's then-wife, Cathy, did the artwork. The yellows on the book cover, redolent of southern California themes, have not faded, nor has the fold-out map inside. The map is wonderful in its simplicity though the subject is Los Angeles and its environs: Visalia is drawn where Santa Barbara might be; and there are quaint places, like Lake Elizabeth and Banning, and wavy lines for the Los Angeles and Santa Ana rivers (places in the book), all making the country look as if someone had drawn it from a hilltop. Tulare is there, where Murietta was killed. And Venice, which appears in the text as if it were the Italian city as much as the Californian.

One day Lew Ellingham was in Polk Gulch and decided to visit Jack, who turned out to be not only at home but even receiving guests. On the double bed he shared with Ron, under the oblong painting of a red centipede, Spicer sat squint-eyed, hunched forward over crossed legs, close to a wall, the lighting dim. Ellingham recalled later that Ron was wearing gold-yellow, Jack crimson. Recovering from an illness, Jack seemed very happy with the pint of Courvoisier Lew brought him, making slighting remarks about Robin, who had recently passed by with a less expensive offering: the usual disparaging comment about Robin's "wealth" (which consisted in having a rather ordinary job).

Ellingham had quit his job, and his life was now centered in North Beach, in his affair with Gail Chugg, in a routine where unemployment insurance, daily and nightly drinking, and endless conversation pushed around the hands of the clock. One evening a sequence of angry, drunken challenges ended in a fight with Gail at their front door, until a neighbor called the police. In a waterfront hospital Gail received fifteen stitches for a cut Lew had given him with what later humorists said was a Purex bottle. Lew was arrested and jailed for felonious assault with a deadly weapon with intent to kill. When Gail refused to press charges, Lew was released onto the streets, unshaven, dirty, blood-smeared. In broad daylight he hid behind a post until he saw a taxi stop nearby, waiting for a traffic signal to change. He jumped in: "North Beach, Katie's bar—Green Street."

Jack Spicer, to whom Lew told his woes, said only, "I am not a support-ive person." His statement, though, was not true; Jack was at his best pre-cisely in such a situation (he had functioned with great ability and sympa-thy in other affairs of this kind). Once Gail and Lew decided again to live together, Jack told me, "I'm not surprised. It had to go one way or another. That kind of situation moves things." It did, but not for long. Gail left to marry a woman, Eliza Pietsch, with whom he worked at his theater.

At the time of the Cuban missile crisis, October 1962, a few members of the group joined a big rally in the Civic Center area, in front of San Francisco's City Hall. It was a short walk into the square from Polk Street where the actor Sterling Hayden lamented, "I've been doing this all my life and it seems there's no end to it." The event was somber. Said Jack, very nervous—he carried a lot of physical fear—"Khrushchev can't back down and neither can Kennedy." They all believed that, but Spicer's increasing fears and paranoid fantasies, fueled both by drinking and by the experi-ence of Cold War tensions over three decades, were more extreme than most. "He was in bad shape when we met on the F train during the Bay of Pigs crisis," recalled Gerry Fabian. "Of course everyone was terrified, but for some reason I didn't think the missiles were going to come over the pole just yet! Jack was trembling, totally paranoid, and said, 'You better start putting pans of water under your bed.' 'I beg your pardon?' 'You bet-ter start saving water.' He was quite sure that the Russians were going to attack in full force."[23]

Late in the fall or sometime in the winter months of 1962–63, Tony Aste was driving Spicer home one evening from the North Beach bars via the Broadway Tunnel in an old car—Tony always had some old car—and an accident occurred. Jack was badly hurt, and from this moment on his drinking increased to stifle the pain that lingered far past the terrible in-jury. He was terrified of cars and had long dreaded an accident. In the late 1940s, while Spicer was driving down from Berkeley to Los Angeles as a passenger in Robert Berg's car, there had been a minor crash, from which Jack had escaped with only minor cuts and bruises, but he refused to drive with Berg ever again.[24] His poetry, like George Oppen's, sees cars as the twentieth-century equivalent of monsters. In "Car Song" he wrote: "We pin our puns on the windshield like / We crossed each crossing in hell's despite." In "To Be Inscribed on a Painting" (also in "Homage to Creeley"), he wrote:

> The fate of the car
> And the fate of the ride
> Is only a bridegroom
> Without a bride[25]

In Spicer's writing, malevolent automobiles with minds of their own (and car radios) fling themselves across a landscape littered with wrong turns and disastrous collisions, presaging the spectacular universe of J. G. (*Crash*) Ballard. He saw the real crash as his punishment for loving the driver, Tony Aste. Ron Primack was at home on California Street when Jack limped, bloody and frantic, into their apartment. His ribs were broken, he claimed: he was going to die. He demanded that Ron call the Herndons, the way a frightened child would call for his parents. Ron obliged, and Jim drove over in the middle of the night. Down Polk, down Ivy, the car sped to Emergency Public Health, where the doctors examined Jack, taped him up, and ordered him not to move—and never to drink again. Jim Herndon remembered the doctor's ominous words: "You drink any more, you've had it, it's over," and Jack's cavalier retort: "Oh fuck! They don't know nothing."[26]

Released from the emergency room, Jack returned to the California Street apartment. When Fran came by to visit, she discovered to her dismay that Jack was still in great physical pain, unable to fend for himself, and Ron rather haplessly was hoping that Band-Aids would cure Jack's cracked ribs. Impetuously, she took Spicer in to stay with her family while he convalesced, while Ron lived in the California Street apartment without him.[27] It was a hasty invitation Fran came to regret. Though the Herndons and Spicer could not have been closer friends, Spicer's emotional dependency took a sharp turn toward the infantile. Ron seemed strangely uninterested in visiting Jack at the Herndons'. "That's about when we split up," Ron recalled.[28]

For the first time, Fran came face-to-face with Jack's alcoholism. As he begged her to fetch him some brandy, his hands shook. Whitefaced he told her he *had* to have it.

And that was when I was aware, absolutely, that he had, really, a serious problem. He did that testing constantly with me: "How much do you love me?" "Do you love me enough to treat, to get—" After the accident, when he came, he was actually like a child. I felt he was in competition with little Jack [her son].

He wanted me to get him a seat for the toilet so that he wouldn't have to get down so far when he had to go to the bathroom. It was like, get a potty chair for me, really. You know—help him down on the seat.

He became petulant, frightened when she left the house and he was alone.

"And in my dilemma about what to do I called a doctor friend of mine, who came to the house." She told the doctor that something was wrong: the shaky hands, the heavy drinking. Maybe there were internal injuries? The doctor recommended admitting Jack to San Francisco County General for *delirium tremens*. "Jack never forgave him, and he never forgave me, for that. He thought we really had betrayed him. After that Jack and I were never the same again."

Their collaboration on the *Sports Illustrated* collages abruptly ended. Jack accused Fran of telling her "doctor friend" he had been hallucinating: but she hadn't mentioned hallucinations—she didn't believe Jack had the DTs. She had told the doctor that she didn't know what was wrong. She thought Jack might have internal injuries and made it clear that she wanted to get him into a hospital. Jack refused to go with the doctor to San Francisco General. Jim backed Fran up and insisted Jack follow doctor's orders, even if it meant returning to the hospital. But after his cracked ribs were taped, he failed to return to the Herndons'. He was miffed. After that, Jack behaved differently toward Fran. He would drop by for dinner occasionally, but the inspired camaraderie was gone. Fran, too, felt put off. "I think at that point I made a choice. I think definitely *I* made a choice, to create some distance between Jack and me."[29]

Instead Spicer repaired to the Francisco Street apartment of Dora and Harold Dull, recently returned to the city after nearly two years in Europe. In March 1962, still in love with Russell, Dora had given birth to Harold's twin daughters on the Spanish island of Ibiza, and the family returned to California in the summer. Dull's poem of this time, *The Wood Climb Down Out Of*, is bleak and broken, in a tentativeness that hesitates before a rich landscape and parallels the poet's sense of broken possibilities "as if seven years / we have lived / like this / tried / nothing but / to cross / and climb down / to the sea."[30]

It was not a happy household. Dora was secretly making plans to leave Harold. Spicer was a difficult guest, as he fretted, convalesced, and waited in vain to hear from Ron Primack. He abandoned all thoughts of his own writing. He was a "former poet," he announced. Dora's twins screamed and chased beer cans and made such a nuisance Jack couldn't follow the ball games. (He called them "Gertrude and Alice.")[31] Convinced that Ron was in anguish worrying about him, Jack insisted that Dora make frequent trips to the phone booth on the corner, to call around town and track Ron down. His conversation, once far-ranging and sprightly, was limited now to descriptions of his acute distress, caused by the "knitting of the bones," and to brave declarations of Ron's devotion. Dora wasn't convinced that Ron cared very much—he certainly wasn't available, never came round. She poured Jack brandy and listened to his woes as he listened to hers.

"He asked me to marry him so he could get properly looked after and devote his energies entirely to writing. I figured I should probably do so but wondered whether he wouldn't be bothered by my babies, the twins I had brought back from Spain."[32] Dora saw clearly that the car crash was a physical manifestation of a extreme emotional collapse:

His mind, his spirit, was as injured as his body was. Had he been emotionally and spiritually strong, then he could have fended for himself with his cracked ribs, but it was like his soul had cracked, too. Because he *knew* that Ronnie didn't really love him, and that he was gone, and you know, he sort of saw his life falling apart. I don't know where he was with the teaching job, but the idea that—You see, that was one of the things about those books, why he went so weird about those, because the necessity to make money to live on, and how could the book make money, and if the book couldn't make money, then he had to go teach again, and to go and teach was like—like entering some warped zone where you're not even you, where you just chop out this chunk of your life in order to do something that you can't relate to at all. And so, I think, in his desire to see if he couldn't have a book that could make money, and yet knowing that it couldn't, and needing to work. I think he knew *The Heads of the Town* wouldn't be a financial success, but in the back of his head there was the thought that—as an alternative way of making money. Yet he was always putting down Ferlinghetti for making money off poetry, and the rule was that one must never make a penny off poetry. That was a very strict rule. Yet, if you don't, and if you want to spend your life writing poetry, then where the hell is the money going to come from? Because he couldn't figure that one out, I think that's what made him so angry and so crazy with people. He didn't really pose that question out loud, but that was the dilemma he was stuck with.

It was at that point that he thought I should marry him. I should get rid of my kids and marry him instead. He was so crazy, and so in need, so needful of being taken care of, that I mean he couldn't possibly share me with my babies. He lived in a world of magic, so it was okay to say things that are completely illogical. If I had given away my babies, I could have taken care of him.

He knew I wasn't married to Harold, he knew that I was only with Harold because I had told Harold that I was going to leave him at my convenience, not his. I just said, "Sorry, Jack—the kids are part of me." And I think I agreed to it, as long as the kids could be there, too. And he said, "No, only you—not the kids." I said, "Well, no deal then."

Jack was, you know, almost incompetent about looking after himself, to a level that you only really see with mental patients who are untended. So you could see, this man really meant it when he wanted to be taken care of. He really wasn't competent about things like that. I mean, sometimes in Life we make certain compromises, and that was one of the compromises, that in order to have his magicianship, or whatever, then the tradeoff was that he couldn't really allow his mind to get into these practical details. But that also points out where he really needed somebody. And that even that, you know, his proposal seemed preposterous and illogical, if you were that needy, you might just do that. I remember, you know, Jack limping for weeks, because the sole of his shoe was loose and flapping. This would go on for weeks, he would lift his foot with this flapping sole, before he would break down and get himself another five-dollar pair of shoes.[33]

By the winter of 1962–63, Jim Liberman had moved into the rust-colored clapboard Drew House in Stinson Beach, the house where Duncan and Jess had lived for years during the writing of *The Opening of the Field*. Ron retreated there after breaking off with Spicer: Jack angrily accused him of deserting a sinking ship. A small upstairs, reached by an outside staircase, attached an attic room to the living room below, with its low ceiling and fireplace and splash of windows toward the sea. A glassed porch (covered outside by a huge bougainvillea, darkening the room), a small kitchen and bedroom and a tiny deck made up the rest of the floor. A laundry room connected directly garden and basement. The cottage is close by the road, the sloping roof rising almost from the pavement's surface; along the garden is a fence tall enough to hide the base of a lemon tree, other vegetation, and a bench. The view extends forty miles over the sea from the living room, deck, attic, and garden. For several months Ron found rest at Stinson Beach, where Tom Field and John Allen Ryan were also living with Liberman. Ron would run along the Matt Davis Trail, emerging on a vista of open land above the sea. One day Helen Adam came up for a party. "She'd just come down from the mountain and snakes, she said, had been draped all over her. She said the snakes fly above the grass. As you walk on top there, they wrap themselves around your legs and arms. Helen scared me to death."[34]

In Stinson Beach Ron encountered other residents, among them two friends of Spicer's—the poet Landis Everson and his companion, the painter Bob Harvey. "Jack liked that relationship a lot. Because they adopted a little boy [Bob Harvey's son by a former marriage]. I think Jack would have liked that he and I were like that. That I was cooking meals and that we adopted a child and that we lived in a house like that—he would have liked that. Jack admired Landis and Bob."[35]

A bizarre episode ended Ron's Drew House residency. Jim Liberman was arrested and convicted for possession of stolen merchandise—the antiques that decorated the house.[36] After the fracas both Tom Field and John Allen Ryan returned to San Francisco, going to sea as soon as possible.[37] Shortly thereafter, Ron gave a reading from *The Late Major Horace Bell of the*

Los Angeles Rangers at the Herndons' apartment on Russian Hill. On the book's appearance, Blaser sought unsuccessfully to see it reviewed in the *Chronicle*, along with Spicer's *Heads of the Town*. But his efforts came to naught, possibly because Spicer and/or Primack had so alienated the poetry establishment with what one potential reviewer called their "distinct antipathy" toward proper channels.[38] Soon afterward Ron left for New York for a long stay, and Jack finally moved out of Harold and Dora's apartment. "Jack stayed until he was better, until he realized Ronnie had just plain left, and was ready to make it on his own again. I remember eating a quart of yogurt upon his departure to somehow deal with my exasperation and relief."[39] By July 1963 Spicer had left the basement apartment at 1650 California, where he had written most of *The Heads of the Town* and all of *The Holy Grail*, and moved around the corner to another dingy apartment, this time at 1420 Polk Street.

At Halloween time in 1964, Spicer commemorated his life with Ron Primack in a poem. Jack and Ron went to visit Harold Dull and Ila Hinton at the Drew House in Stinson Beach and stayed in the detached garage below the old garden. The poem unites Jack's premonitions that love's end and his own stalked him—whether or not in terms that "love is a metaphor"—and, in its own way, acknowledges that what has gone before is now behind him. He was finally over the painful breakup.

> Like a scared rabbit running over and over again his tracks
>   in the snow
> We spent this Halloween together, forty miles apart.
> The tracks are there and the rabbit's feeling of death is
>   there. And the children no longer masquerading
>   themselves as ghosts but as businessmen, yelled
>   "Trick or treat," maybe even in Stinson
> The tracks in the snow and rabbit's motion which writes
>   it is quite legible. The children
> Not even pretending to be souls of the dead are not.
>   Forty miles. Nothing really restored
> We
> And the dead are not really on the frozen field. (The
>   children don't even wear masks) This
> Is another poem about the death of John F. Kennedy.[40]

A further succession of young male poets passing through Spicer's life distracted him from the long silence that had begun with the completion of *The Holy Grail* in August 1962 and did not end until the first poems of *Language* appeared to him in November 1963. By the time Ron Primack left him, Spicer was already involved in helping other young writers learn about poetry. Harris Schiff, for example, "went out to San Francisco to become a poet. I was a student at Antioch, studying with Judson Jerome, and I hated the whole English department there, and I decided to go to San Francisco where everything was theoretically still happening. I remember telling Jerome I was going to drop out and go to San Francisco to see if I could really become a poet, a poet apart from the academic system and the university structure. And he said, 'You would know the answer to that if you just thought about it for five minutes.'"[41]

By March 1963 Schiff had come to San Francisco, where the photographer/painter Steve Lowi sent him to Gino & Carlo's one night to meet Jack Spicer. He was nineteen, with "no idea of the whole context he was working in, all the different enmities. My idea of the universe was that everybody loved everybody, and especially in the world of poetry. The idea that there were people who would spit on the ground if the other party walked by—like, for example, Robert Duncan and Jack maybe, I had no idea about that. Duncan was in *The New American Poetry*, Jack was in *The New American Poetry*, and the New American Poetry must be one great, happy family of geniuses."[42] Harris, under Jack's wing, was in for a long series of hard shocks.

For Spicer and Duncan were now openly warring. To LeRoi Jones Duncan wrote an impassioned letter defending himself against the charges of the "Spicerian elite." Since the Allen anthology (1960), wrote Duncan, "there's been a long growing antipathy back of this: Spicer has accused me of 'whoring'—by which he means reading at universities, printing in Poetry magazine and The Nation, and, further then, writing in order for such markets." In New York, Jones felt himself similarly abused by the O'Hara-LeSueur circle: Duncan saw the two "scenes," Spicer's and O'Hara's, as homosexual cabals threatened by mavericks. "As I get it there is a good deal of feeling on the part of Jack—and of George too here—that I have deserted ranks. And along with this an intense rivalry posed of Spicer the authentic versus Duncan the fraud. (Olson having been put into the Spicer disposall in the beginning of all this.)"[43]

The venom Duncan was feeling from the North Beach crew had begun to give him the willies. By the spring of 1963, he was convinced that Spicer and his group were placing curses on him. In *Change*, a single-issue magazine published by Richard Brautigan and Ron Loewinsohn, Duncan printed a piece that reflected his fears. "A Part-Sequence for Change," an apotropaic poem, was written to ward off the "bad magic" of the Spicer cabal.[44]

1

If they had cursed the man,
dried back the water in the spring
by boiling water in a frying pan
until the thirsty sun
feard for the song that he once sang
and burned to sing,

over them the cursed image,
over them the blackened thing.

2

I shall draw back
and among my sacred objects
gather the animal power back,
the force that in solitude
works in me its leases,
the night-bird's voice
in the day's verses.

The flame in the body of the lamp
fumes upon the surface of the glass.
The boy I was watches
not without fear
black places in the darkening room
where animal faces
appear and pass away

and reappear.

3

Estranged. Deeply estranged.
Fish caught in no net,
hand at the harp without strings
striking the dark air for music,
to go by.

Deeply estranged.
For I have been let go from what
I felt in the music.
I have been deserted by the words spoken
in the rapture of being deserted,

the writhing and
therein thriving catch of fishes
raised by the Fisher out of my solitude
into the acclaiming throng without me.

But say they take this song up

and in the threads of their voices
these words appear (mine) (theirs).
Estranged. Deeply estranged.

Once more the young days of the year
find out the invisible ranges
and break from the tree
changes and turnings of the heart,

the swarm of too many buds
for melody

and the ascendancy of the shadow
in the blossoming mass.
                              Nov. 1962–March 1963[45]

The poet David Bromige, newly arrived in the Bay Area from Canada, had met Duncan in Vancouver several years before. He now joined others—Hilde and David Burton, Ebbe and Joy Borregaard—in a weekly soiree at the Berkeley home of Jo Fredman Stewart, who had known Duncan and Spicer during the days of 2029 Hearst and the birth of the Renaissance. Bromige recalled, "Robert would go there, and hold court, and read his latest work. Now that I think about it, perhaps this was a recent event, and was taking the place of the Spicer-Duncan-and-acolyte alliance that had lasted some years and then come to that screeching halt." At these weekly meetings Duncan generally read from his new *H.D. Book*, but at one session "A Part-Sequence for Change" was read. Afterward a puzzled Bromige walked with Duncan to the bus stop and asked him about the poem he'd just read. The cursed image? The blackened thing? What was the portent of the boiling water/frying pan image?

And he said, [imitating Duncan as high-pitched, querulous] "What? Don't you know? Would you boil water in a frying pan?" I said, "Well, no," but I felt, as quite often with Robert, displaced in the head. But then he went on in a footnote. "Well," he said, "I wouldn't put it past them that that's what they're doing over there, Spicer and those people. I think they're putting curses on me, they're practicing black magic, and that would be one form of black magic." Well, I wanted to know more, naturally, and I said, "Why would they want to do that to you?" And he said, [again querulous voice] "Oh, I don't want to go into it. It's horrible." Robert loved to gossip, and he loved to talk about himself; but I guess it was just too painful to relive in the telling.[46]

The alliances were continually shifting, as Blaser continued to shuttle diplomatically between Spicer and Duncan. Because of his attendance at the Sunday poetry meetings, Persky and Robert Duncan had known each other on friendly terms once, before the *Adam's Way* protest. "And of course I was kind of *enfant terrible*. Duncan had reason to think that I had insulted him [due to the *Adam's Way* protest]. So there was this business of delicately reintroducing me into the Duncan-Jess household. Robin and I would be invited to dinner, and at this point I began to see this wonderful world of Duncan and Jess—again, another way of making life fully devoted to art. Duncan and Jess would celebrate the riches of art, whereas Spicer's way was a bleak, lonely, painful thing, to get to true poetry."[47] But Duncan, at least, did not take to Stan and was not shy of letting Robin know about it:

June 8, 1963—

Dear Robin,

It is clear, at least, that you make it a condition of accepting invitations at all that Stan Persky also be invited and that, being aware that we do not enjoy Persky's company and being thoughtful of us as friends, you make it an added condition that we not be embarrassed by being invited at the same time. "I was perfectly clear," you write, "that I did not want the embarrassment of an invitation which would be impossible for either of you." O.K. But you are evidently not clear on the patent fact that it is you, Robin, who make the conditions of embarrassment which you "do not want." And that you have set up a formula of total acceptance of Stan Persky and total rejection of Jess and me. In the simple principle which you have devised for social relations: I will go nowhere without Stan Persky + I will, in friendship's name, spare Robert and Jess the displeasure of Stan's company—is hidden, barely, the meaning I will go nowhere where Robert and Jess are present. "Without placing blame, expectations, or whatever upon anyone . . ." How nice of you! To save me the blame of my not liking Persky? To save Persky some blame? It is you who have made the present situation and imposed its laws. . . .

Well, I think you can at least simplify your present pressures by giving up the problem of how "to find a way to see the two of us." It is a delusion that you do not want what you so patently insist upon. As long as seeing us is a problem, we would not cheat upon the principle that has excluded us by seeing you in Persky's absence. When you are ready to see us again openly and fairly, without this mess of conditions, then we will be glad indeed. But let friendship mean what is open, fair and glad. We'll keep our faith in that and not take this present state of double-think to be friendship.[48]

But in little more than half a year Duncan would be participating in the Persky-edited magazine *Open Space*. Perhaps this fact comments on the importance of their work in poetry to the people of this scene. They were never far apart, however much they seemed to be. Still, the injuries were real enough, the anger unpleasant. In due course, his affair with Persky ended Blaser's seventeen-year connection with Jim Felts, which had survived from their Berkeley student days in the 1940s.[49]

*

Harris Schiff stood up to Spicer's most exacting scrutiny. "He must have thought I was pretty funny, this 'poet' showing up; but he had them all the time. He said, 'You're the latest arrival on the Underground Railroad.' He had this theory about an Underground Railroad that went from the East Coast to the West Coast, liberating all the poor slaves in New York. 'So you're a poet, huh? Bring me everything you've written.' I was eighteen years old and looked it; or younger, really naive. So, yeah, I brought him everything I'd written, which was not that much." In 1963 Xerox machines weren't on every corner, but Harris brought in his poems to Gino & Carlo's, then waited.

And waited. "I would go back to the bar, and he hadn't read 'em yet. And finally, he had read them, and he told me, 'None of these are any good.' He had a beautiful smile, and I'm sure he said that with that smile. 'They could be good. But you're always trying to fix them up, and put a catchy ending on them; you're always interfering.'" Spicer explained to Harris that a poet had to be like a radio receiver, and just receive messages. The poet had to learn how to recognize when a transmission was coming in, and when it had stopped. That was the poem. It didn't necessarily have a catchy ending, or a fancy ending, or make sense. The poet's jobs were to recognize when a transmission was coming in, to start writing, and to recognize when it was over. And that was it: that was the task of a poet.

Disappointed by Spicer's reception—Harris had figured that Jack would "just say, 'These are great, let's publish all of them, I'll tell you how to do it, I'll tell you who to see'"—he nevertheless tried to learn the lessons the older man had to offer. He was given assignments on how to become a poet. First of all, to read Cocteau's play *Orpheus*, and to see his film version, which was handily playing at a nearby art cinema. Next to drive down Route 1 to Big Sur and check it out. (In the spring of 1947 Spicer had himself traveled to Big Sur and Partington Ridge, hoping to write a novel there.) "I wrote a poem down there, which I was excited about, and I brought it back. He said, 'This is—you got it.' That was after months, many months, of first him telling me, 'No. This is bullshit here, these are no good.' Still whenever I saw him it would be, 'Well, are you writing anything? What do you have? Bring it to me.'" Soon it was baseball season, and in an old Plymouth Harris drove Spicer out to Candlestick Park, where the lessons continued. "Baseball was right there with *Orpheus*, for Jack, as part of the transmission. It still is for me, and for a lot of other poets. It's just a beautiful game: beautiful to watch, always. It always is informative, the way the players appear

against the background of the game; what happens to the individuals
within the background of the game, and how the game just always goes on
even as the individuals fade away. When it went out of our lives, it was definitely a bleak time, a difficult time. There was nothing else quite like it—
till the baseball season came again."[50]

Harris was joined for the summer by a high school friend, Lewis Warsh,
who remembered being shown a copy of *The Heads of the Town*, then ush-
ered into Gino & Carlo's on his first night in San Francisco.

It was a very depressing bar. There was a table in the back, and there were these
guys at the bar sitting there looking really depressed. There were no women there,
except for Jamie MacInnis. Harold Dull was there. George Stanley was there. And
of course Larry Fagin was there—he seemed like the only person who was at all
cheerful. I didn't know what to make of it. I was thinking, "Poetry? Poetry scene?
Is this it?" I didn't feel happy in this bar. And then Jack came in.

I guess my arrival had been spoken of by another young poet: we were the
"Blackheads," Spicer's name for us [Warsh, Schiff, Steve Lowi, a nickname paralleling the "Jets" of a previous year, and the "Jesuits" of 1964]. The "Blackheads"—
again a little anti-Semitism maybe? So he knew who I was. I remember he came in,
wearing a seedy sports jacket and a white T-shirt and baggy pants and loafers with
white socks. He was thirty-eight years old—and he seemed ancient. Spicer would
come back after his ball game and there would be this morose group of people. It
seemed that if one opened one's mouth one was at risk.

Spicer asked the eighteen-year-old Warsh what he did, and as soon as he
replied, "I'm a writer," he saw their faces close down, knew he'd made a
mistake. Went home kicking himself for not replying, "I'm a poet." He had
failed a crucial test. But soon he felt comfortable enough to begin "going to
Aquatic Park on Sunday afternoons where Spicer held court. The summer
that the Chicago Cubs had eight managers. Moe Grabowski was pitcher for
the Cubs I guess, not a very good one, and Spicer called me 'Moe Grabowski.'" Spicer's nicknames, usually affectionate, often carried an ominous
edge, and this one carried a flash of psychic insight. How on earth, wondered Lewis, had Spicer known what he had told no one in San Francisco,
that the Warsh family name had been shortened way back when from
"Warshowsky"? Warsh and Schiff tried hard for the glamor of bisexual
chic, but it didn't take. "Harris and I were both *adventurous* types, and we
later turned out to be *heterosexual* types." The poetry scene was awash with
drama: the impending split between the Dulls; a pregnancy scare for a
young woman poet; the suicide threat of one of the artists. At summer's
end, Warsh drove back to New York with Steve Lowi, much seasoned.
Warsh would return, for (to quote from *The Holy Grail*) "in spite of all this

horseshit, this uncomfortable music" kept happening. In a depressing bar in North Beach, some of the most challenging and emotional poetry of its time was being written.[51]

During this summer Robert Duncan solidified his ties with the burgeoning poetry scene in Vancouver. From July 24 through August 16, the University of British Columbia sponsored the Vancouver Poetry Conference. Besides Duncan, the conference featured Olson, Creeley, Ginsberg, Whalen, Levertov, and the fine Canadian poet Margaret Avison.

Duncan had "discovered" Vancouver in 1959, when Ellen Tallman learned that the San Francisco poet had accepted an invitation to read in Seattle, at the University of Washington. Ellen had become Mrs. Warren Tallman, but in the late 1940s she was Ellen King, attending Berkeley with Duncan and Spicer. Now she extended Robert an invitation to Vancouver, where her energetic husband was a professor at the University of British Columbia. On December 12, 1959, Duncan read in the basement of the Tallmans' home, at 2527 West Thirty-Seventh. Forty people each paid fifty cents to hear him read. He was astonished and revitalized by their interest in new poetry. In the spring of 1961, the Fine Arts Group of UBC sponsored the first Vancouver Festival, and this time paid Duncan $200.00 to come and speak—plus $125 plane fare. This was considered an excellent wage, and again both poet and overflow audience delighted each other. A few months later Robert returned to Vancouver to give three lectures—a group of enterprising students, baffled in their attempts to understand the New American Poetry, as they met weekly to read Don Allen's anthology, invited him to be their Virgil. Duncan's residency "laid the groundwork," said Warren Tallman, "for Jack Spicer and Robin Blaser," for one of his lectures was a precis of the paths taken by the Berkeley Renaissance members. "But basically for Robert that was times past; he was talking even more about Charles Olson, Robert Creeley, Denise Levertov. He was very waspish about Allen Ginsberg; that whole line was being drawn up: but we didn't *know* that." In 1963 the Vancouver Conference brought all these notable spirits together for the first time, and in this conference the seeds were sown for the Berkeley Poetry Conference of 1965, at which Jack Spicer made his last public appearances. In the meantime, said Tallman, a "Spicer legend" was being built in Vancouver.[52]

In San Francisco, Harris Schiff received his next assignment from Spicer. Harris' parents were visiting the City, and driving back East with him by way of British Columbia. Jack told him to ditch the parents and to attend the Vancouver Festival, to track down Robert Creeley and get him to introduce him to Duncan.

Jack told me, "I would like you to find Robert Duncan and tell him that I have sent you with a question for him and that would he please send an answer back with you." And the question was, "What is the difference between poetry and cable cars?" So [in Vancouver] I met Robert at a party. Everybody was drunk, I believe, including me. I said, "Jack Spicer sent me up here to ask you a question, and would you let me know what your answer is." He said, "Oh yeah?" I said, "Yeah. Jack wanted me to ask you if you would tell him what the difference is between poetry and cable cars." And Duncan really got really pissed off and just said, "*Fuck* you. Get out of here, you little creep."

And Jack just thought it was a funny thing to do. Which it was, you know? But . . . maybe he assumed I knew something more than I did about people's works and the differences between them. I was just flipped out. I actually felt really hurt, because I felt really used. I didn't know *what* was going on, I had no idea what kind of dispute on basic poetics was going on there. He was appalled, actually, that I was not treated well.

Only after Spicer's death did Harris come to feel that the cable-car prank might have been a retaliation by Spicer for not having been invited to participate in the Vancouver Conference. "Now that I've grown up in the literary world, I can imagine what his feelings were. I had no idea what was going on at the time."[53] Warren and Ellen Tallman drove down to San Francisco after the Vancouver Conference, sharing the driving with the young Canadian poets Fred Wah and Pauline Butling in "late August 1963," Wah recalled. "We were on our way to Albuquerque to start grad school (with Creeley), and we met Jack and Stan Persky and George Stanley (maybe Harold Dull was there and not Stan, my memory's a little vague). It was a glorious evening and Jack was asking a few questions about the Vancouver show and George was kind of North Beachey territorial (though I was knocked out to meet the author of *Tete Rouge*, a favorite of mine at the time). Jack smiled and was quite pleasant; I think Warren actually did most of the talking. Most of my sense of Spicer as a person is from listening to Warren, Creeley, and Olson talk about him. I never met Spicer again."[54]

In the summer of 1963 Lew Ellingham had found interesting new work as a book editor for the Sierra Club. His new roommate, Armando Navarro, just returned from the U.S. Army after two years as a draftee, was a native of San Antonio. Latinly heterosexual, he was the focus of a good deal of homosexual longing, some of it extravagant. His vanity was not offended, but girls were distinctly his interest and he had many. Also recently returned to San Francisco was Russell FitzGerald, wild and reckless as ever. His heavy drinking and his predilection for black strangers—sometimes policemen, sometimes extortionists—were bringing him closer and closer to the bad end his mother predicted for him. Everywhere he looked for relief from the suicide he felt sure awaited him.

"One afternoon," Armando recalled, "Russell came over with a big, nasty black guy—you know—the kind that just got out of San Quentin? I was at home by myself, on the bed we used as a couch. I was watching a W. C. Fields festival on TV, every afternoon a new one. Russell came in and asked for [Ellingham] and I said, 'No, not here.' You have to remember, I'm real naive then too. They're sitting there watching TV. I look over and Russell's sucking this guy off. I was shocked! I'd never seen anything like that. I didn't know what to say so I said 'Russell! That's really bad manners! Use the bedroom!'"[55] The apartment was bedlam. Everyone drank a lot, and Armando endlessly played a record of the film score of *Black Orpheus*, the celebration of the Rio de Janeiro *mardi gras*. On top of this Ellingham's former protector arrived, an Ivy League university professor who had decided to spend the summer in San Francisco instead of in Europe. Almost every night Lew's academic friend entertained a small crowd at Katie's new "opera bar" and restaurant. A movable feast, the party would journey along Grant Avenue and Green Street, perhaps ending at someone's apartment. In August Lew decided to hold a dinner party, inviting his academic friend from New England, his barber, George Stanley, Spicer, Don Allen—then at the height of his editorial fame—Armando Navarro, Bill Brodecky, others too. Russell FitzGerald, a fine cook, prepared an entree of curried chicken; the liquor buffet was substantial.

The dinner turned out to be the launching pad for an unlikely event—Russell's elopement with Dora Dull. Russell disguised his anxiety with strenuous, elaborate preparation of the food. In his nervousness he carelessly passed an arm or hand against a cactus plant, and Bill used bandaging tape to extract the quills from Russell's flesh.

For some reason, Don Allen became angry during the evening. Uncounted insults, slights, and injuries were taken for granted at parties in those times, and once Ellingham had provoked him severely by disparaging the work of Grove Press author John Rechy (*City of Night*). In retaliation, Allen pulled the chair out from under him as he was about to sit down. Another time someone let it slip that Allen was regarded as San

Harold and Dora Dull, and their twin girls, at Washington Square Park in North Beach, spring 1963. *Courtesy of Dora FitzGerald.*

Francisco's answer to the witty, icy film star Clifton Webb. Late in the party Russell took Ellingham aside, to ask if he had any money. Lew had a $20 bill and two single dollars. He gave Russell the two singles, not wanting to have nothing at all left, explaining to Russell that "This is the drinking money." Dora went home in the morning, gave Harold his orange juice, then decamped with her daughters. Only the next day, when Harold Dull came looking for Dora and their twins and his car, pushing by into the apartment when Ellingham answered the door, did he realize something out of the ordinary had occurred. Harold was left without clues for some time—weeks perhaps—of the escaping couple's adventures, and he searched the Bay Area for what he had lost. Friends said he came looking for signs of baby clothes hanging out at mutual acquaintances' dwellings in Stinson Beach: such was his uncertainty and frustration. In time he followed them to New York, to no avail. Since Harold and Dora had never married, he had no claim. The break was complete.

Russell and Dora went to Denver, to his mother, who had promised him an inheritance once he married. "When he, in fact, showed up with me, she was absolutely furious, made us sleep in separate rooms, and I had to witness her practically seducing her son, you know, on the floor of the living room. It was really awful. Her promises about all the things she would give him if he got married were out the window. She wanted to be his number one." Eventually the FitzGeralds established a base in New York on the Lower East Side (Dora working for the welfare department, Russell at his painting and occasional writing). There was no word from Spicer. Dora had grown up in New York, and for love she lived now among the cockroaches and squalor that she had promised herself she would never return to. Russell was "happy as a clam" on the Lower East Side, where there were black men galore. "One was just more charming than the next for Russell. He just couldn't get enough of them. There were always black men spirited into the corners of the apartment. So that period was a pretty productive one for him. I thought it was pretty horrible, but he would say, 'Dora, these are the best years of our lives!' And I would say, 'Not for me, they ain't.' Sure enough, for him, it was—he was speaking the truth for himself because, I think that probably was the best time—as good as it ever got for him." In the spring of 1970 the FitzGeralds moved to Vancouver, where Russell died ten years later, bloated and broken.[56]

Since the days of *San Francisco's Burning!* the Adam sisters and Lew Ellingham had been close friends. Helen and Pat lived with Isabelle, their invalid mother, on 17th Street, in the Haight-Ashbury district, near Golden Gate Park. The sisters sometimes bicycled in the park with Ellingham or climbed in Sutro Forest for its rustle of eucalyptus and views of the sea and city. Sometimes the sisters were hostesses at dinners or parties at their apartment, amid an incredible collection of books, objects, and art in a Victorian wonderland, with plenty of wine with dinner. Actors, friends from North Beach, writers, filmmakers, painters were the guests. A typical dinner was ample and Scottish—great plates of food, with several desserts to follow: cake, piles of ice cream, orange yogurt on top of pears; then port and brandy. The dark, book-lined walls were decorated with curiosities collected at thrift stores when *art nouveau* candlesticks and bookends could be bought for less than a dollar. Vigil lights and bay candles burned at table and in window. Over the years Helen had developed a wide arena of friendships, as she wrote ballads in traditional Scots metric, reading them to always enthusiastic audiences, private and public, small and large. Her close friendships with James Broughton, Duncan and Jess, Madeline Gleason, and other poets and artists in the community—and her open, direct way of accepting this popularity—were attractively augmented by the easy access young and old had to her life.

With Helen, Lew drove to Stinson Beach one sunny afternoon. His new editorial job promised the financial freedom he needed to follow his wish to write in a seaside village. Stinson Beach is divided into two parts, houses on the hillside, and beachside houses. The hillside seemed the only part of the resort that was quiet enough, and beautiful enough with its wide views, to serve his tastes. Soon they decided upon the vacant Drew House. By September 1, 1963, Ellingham was established in this Hansel-and-Gretel cottage, which is celebrated in several poems in *The Opening of the Field*. Sitting in the garden, Lew could trace first the lines in Duncan's book and then the settings they described. "The purple briar-rose" was there, and "pampas grass" lined the road, which forked uphill above the house, then made a circuit and returned by the cottage and garden again. "Structure of Rime" (XIII) also recreates this garden and its landscape, the "Mountain" that falls to the ocean here, the "rigorous trees that take on the swirl visible of the coast winds and the outcroppings, the upraised and bare granites."[57] Ellingham walked with friends along the long beach at night and saw all this, the lights of the city of San Francisco glittering to the south, low over the ocean far to the right of the shadings of blackness the view offers on fogless nights.

In the autumn of 1963 Helen Adam and Bill McNeill presented a movie they had made after a great deal of work and experiment. The film was shown at the Peacock Gallery, an establishment funded by $1,000 allocated by Robin Blaser from monies given him for projects of this kind. The gallery, at Laguna and Union, was a comfortable space. Its rooms, with fine carpets and soft antique chairs, displayed the paintings of artists chosen by Blaser, who wrote the essay for the exhibition catalogue. "This show is intended to involve," he wrote. "It is large, over sixty pieces, extravagant, insistent upon the importance of imagination. . . . I have wanted to insist upon the image in this show of paintings. The marvelous we had lost came back."[58] Some of the painters were from Black Mountain, others from the university at Berkeley. All had settled in the Bay Area and were living and working in a network of friendships. The show included Jess Collins, Harry Jacobus, Lyn Brockway, Tom Field, Paul Alexander, and Fran Herndon and ran from October 12 through November 23, 1963. To end the show *Daydream of Darkness* was premiered.

Daydream of Darkness was Bill McNeill's film of Helen Adam's fairy-tale ballad. For a year they shot footage throughout the City, at the ocean and in parks, in the interiors of apartments of friends and their own. The film progressed, spontaneously, without a preconceived script: Adam wrote the poem and McNeill produced and directed it. Then came the editing, which the two auteurs did in collaboration. "What was [Helen's] great thing?" Bill McNeill asked, shortly before his death. "When you put your hand over your cup, when you wouldn't want any more, what was that term? What's the Scots term for 'a bit more?'—A 'dopple' more! Just a 'dopple.' Eighteen dopples later, you went 'Aaaagh!' And another bottle of wine was brought out. She loved champagne too—she lived!" As McNeill recalled the premiere of the film, he grew excited, sharing memories of the Peacock Gallery—the arabesques of the rugs, the squares of the paintings on the walls, the washes of wine flowing for the festive evening. "It was going to be a big art-gallery trip and all that sort of jazz—the most important thing in the world. We were all going to 'arrive'—all going to be world-famous! We were going to do another scene! And Kennedy got shot that morning [12:30 P.M. November 22]."[59]

Don Allen suggested that the showing be canceled as a gesture toward propriety in this time of national mourning—and anyhow, would anyone come in such circumstances? But Helen refused. Paul Alexander recalled that the showing was well attended, but eclipsed by the assassination. "None of us were TV viewers used to letting the networks tell us what to feel and how to react. We still went to the forums to talk [events] over."[60] "It was horrible because we were just going crazy because of the Kennedy thing," remembered Nemi Frost. "They should have canceled. No one could concentrate. There was no place to sit so we were put on our knees, cursing and shrieking."[61]

If Spicer was in love during his long period of silence, it was with the young poet Harris Schiff. Schiff remembered:

You were asking me about being a straight guy in a gay community. There was heterosexuality around that scene. At Gino & Carlo's it was, yeah, more gay than not (we didn't have the term 'gay' at that time). I didn't feel that uncomfortable with it: I was kind of a cockteaser, really. To some degree, that was my relationship with Jack. It wasn't really fair to him. On the other hand, he was fair with me. He never really—But you know, it was like, I loved him, he loved me; I was scared of going to bed with him. . . .

I feel funny saying all this stuff, but why not? . . . It's just true, it's history. I don't really see the point of talking about it, exactly, but what the fuck! I mean, Jack kind of advised me about love. I had married—I was in a relationship with a woman I didn't love. I married her. He wouldn't say to me, "Harris, what are you doing? You don't love Anne." Instead, he would make a statement that just implied everything and it was up to you to figure it out. "You can live with someone you don't love for five years, and then that'll be the end of it. Five years tops. You figure it out, kid."

Jack had this beautiful smile, as I say. He was a center, you know, he was someone who made people feel good, so like when you went to Aquatic Park in the afternoon, and if Jack wasn't there, *forget* it, it wasn't the same.

Jack was very gentle. He was very caring. He was a beautiful guy. He was very tender. He respected people's boundaries really tremendously. He had a tremendous respect for who I was and for what . . . he never pushed me. I was a really naive kid, and he was very careful with me, he was very encouraging.

I disappeared for awhile, I took a lot of drugs at a certain point there, and got kind of crazy for awhile, from the methedrine that was around at that time.

I didn't see him—for months; I was really nuts, you know? And I went to see him, when I had finally recovered enough to talk about it. He said, "Well, where have you been?" I said, "I've been insane." And he said, "Oh, you don't really know what that means." And I told him about some of the experiences I'd been through, and he said, "Yeah. You *have* been insane!" I told him that I'd been taking methedrine and he said, "Don't do meth. Take heroin if you have to do something like that. You can have a good time with that, but don't take methedrine." There were a lot of casualties already from methedrine. It was really—San Francisco was just flooded with it at that time.

He never read me out or anything [for taking drugs]. I was just an innocent, you know? I didn't know what was going on, with a lot of things, especially the backbiting, infighting about the best formula, who knows the best formula. I was really the vessel for the Grail or whatever. It was a question of being pure.

Oh, God, I hope I haven't embarrassed myself, these things I'm saying: but what the fuck. Jack didn't have the mannerisms of other people on the gay scene there who were queens, shrill, effeminate, affected . . . Jack was just kind of serene.—No, Jack was drunk! Jack was pickled! What other wisdom did Jack teach me? He taught me how to piss in the sink. He lived on Polk Street, in a dark, pretty dark apartment, with the bathroom down the hall. But there was a sink. And you know, at a certain point, when I was going down the hall, he said, "Just pee in the sink, just turn on the cold water and pee in the sink." Which, you know, was wisdom I've used many times since.

He drank when he got up in the morning. Brandy with water. He got this brand, I think it was "President," he said it was from Magnin's, and it was a pretty good brandy, and he always had a bottle of brandy with him. Alcohol killed him. It's pretty funny for him to be reading people out of his life for using drugs, because he was drunk. And smoked Kools. I smoked Kools, too, and I drank the brandy. I couldn't really drink that much, but I drank as much as I could. The brandy was my drink, too. Whatever he did, I did, too—pretty much. He'd stay at Gino & Carlo's almost every night till two in the morning, when it closed, and then he'd walk home through the Broadway Tunnel. And I would often walk him home, and stop over for a drink, another drink. And then I would eventually go on to Fillmore & O'Farrell, where I lived, which wasn't very far. Just over the hill. You know, I—I'm just trying to—

Life is strange. I'm pretty much solidly a heterosexual person; I lust after women,

I love women. I sometimes wonder if I had been able to be Jack's lover how it would have changed our lives. But I wasn't able to do that. I was only able to, you know, kiss him sometimes, be close to him, be his student, this young poet that he taught some of his wisdom to. But he really needed that person, too. Really needed love. Didn't have it, and everything kind of closed in on him. He was drinking—he drank so much. You know, it was just a steady amount of drinking. Brandy and beer. And then there were all these wars: all these wars about who was the purest. And all these people who seemed to be—you know, it's so ironic, that now he's dead, and everybody admires him, even in the wake of his work there are still all these different people claiming to be the purest. The poetry business, it's inexplicable how much feuding and fighting and hatred and intensity there is about it now. I think that's what the baseball image was—you needed a scorecard to tell the players, and then some, and you need a whole sporting establishment, and columnists, to tell you what's going on. The baseball just kind of informed the poetry.

I knew about these things, but they were grown-up stuff, and I was just a kid. I was just trying to get it right as to how to write the poems, and to write some good ones. Then all these drugs came into the picture and changed everything. I ultimately went East to try to pick up the pieces, which I eventually did, you know? But just shortly after I got there [summer of 1965], the phone rang, I got a call, to tell me Jack was dead.[62]

In the fall of 1963, Allen Ginsberg returned from the excitement of the Vancouver Poetry Conference to visit friends in San Francisco where, during the period from 1953 through October 1956, he had written many of his most beautiful and enduring poems. His relationship to Spicer was a fairly distant one, though friendly on Ginsberg's side. Now he sought out Jack Spicer at the Poets' Table in Gino & Carlo's "to reconnect."[63]

Ginsberg had first met Spicer in the spring of 1955, at the apartment of Robert Duncan. The venerable sage of Paterson, New Jersey, had agreed to write an introduction to Ginsberg's book of early poems, *Empty Mirror*, and Ginsberg had brought Williams's text to Duncan's apartment for him to examine. Jack Spicer was visiting too, and Ginsberg retained a "strong visual image" of their meeting in the warm, dark rooms Duncan shared with Jess Collins.

During Spicer's New York/Boston period, Ginsberg had remained in San Francisco, where he wrote *Howl and Other Poems* in a sustained cadenza of energy and vatic spirits. Following his reading at the Six Gallery, the publication of *Howl*, and the resulting trial for obscenity, Ginsberg became a poet of international notoriety. With Gregory Corso, he left the Bay Area in October 1956, for "Mexico, and Europe, then back to New York," thus narrowly avoiding a collision with Spicer when the latter returned to

San Francisco in November 1956. For a long time the two poets remained in separate orbits, as Ginsberg's wanderlust took him to places Spicer never dreamed of going, and his fame grew and grew. Ginsberg had, in fact, stolen some of Spicer's thunder: in a letter to Robin Blaser, Spicer commanded him to "read Ginzberg's *Howl* and see if you think it the crap I do. Only people like us have the right to attack it."[64] Ginsberg's open homosexuality, his obscenity, his defiant mix of symbolist, biblical and surrealist energies—the poetic elements of *Howl* had been the personal property of the Berkeley Renaissance, and Ginsberg had somehow swooped down into San Francisco while its natives' backs were turned and filched them. "You see," said Warren Tallman, "Allen did an unforgiveable thing—he had gone to Berkeley in the mid-fifties, and stolen the show. Then *none* of them [the poets of the Berkeley Renaissance] liked him."[65]

In the spring and summer of 1959, Ginsberg returned to the Bay Area to give readings, to participate in early LSD experiments, and to co-found the Beat magazine *Beatitude*. Stan Persky met him in this period, after some initial correspondence. Following Ginsberg's Berkeley reading in June 1959, a huge party was thrown by a woman Russell FitzGerald dubbed the "Transvylvanian Countess" in his diary. Spicer was in attendance, and Russell's diary describes Ginsberg bowing down before the seated Jack. (Stan remembered it as a playful simulation of a blowjob, which may have further alienated the awkward, repressed Spicer.) Who was the "Transylvanian Countess?" Thirty-one years later Ginsberg identified her as "a very well-known patron of the arts, later known as Panna Grady, who later turned up as a great friend of John Wieners and Charles Olson and William Burroughs and myself and many others, in New York City and later in London, in 1967. She lived in London for awhile, and now lives in the South of France, married to Philip O'Connor (*The Memoirs of a Public Baby*)."[66] The party was held at the house the countess and her sister had rented in Berkeley—a big, open-style (Wright or Maybeck-designed) Berkeley house. At her party Stan Persky sat on the steps of the staircase, hypnotized, as Ginsberg recited the last section of Hart Crane's *The Bridge*, aiming each line directly into Stan's eyes in a seductive, charming, and funny manner.

Poets in attendance were Gary Snyder, Stephen Spender, Spicer, and Peter Orlovsky. "The latter removed their clothes," George Stanley recalled, "and somebody sucked somebody's cock, but, thank god, I don't remember who."[67] ["That was me," Ginsberg recalled. "I intuited in Spicer a jingly-jangly fear, under all the defense, a fierce *Manjusri*, almost a demon, guarding him from the world, and I offered my mouth to him. I saw in his eyes the desire, the recoil, the fear, and he bolted. Plus I was drunk. Some party."]⁶⁸ During this period Ginsberg and Orlovsky showed up for some of the Sunday afternoon poetry meetings at East-West House—stellar company, polite on the sofa, while James Alexander recited the whole of *The Jack Rabbit Poem*.

That was in 1959. Four years later, Ginsberg returned, after years in India, via the Vancouver Conference where, after hearing Denise Levertov's account of her Mill Valley ordeal, he announced to all that he wanted to head to San Francisco to "cheer up Jack Spicer." Spicer abhorred the playfulness and whimsy of Ginsberg's Buddhism and never missed a chance to mock it. At Gino & Carlo's someone stepped on his scarf and Jack looked down, then said, "Pardon me, you're stepping on my karma."⁶⁹ In *The Collected Books of Jack Spicer*, Blaser noted the web of poetic rivalry that bound Spicer unwillingly to the vastly more famous Ginsberg: "Allen arrived at Jack's table in Gino & Carlo's Bar and said he'd come to save Jack's soul. Jack replied that he'd better watch it or he'd become a cult leader rather than a poet."⁷⁰

Later Ginsberg said he thought it "not very likely" that he issued such a challenge during his 1963 meeting with Jack. "Well, maybe, but I think it was more jocular. I wasn't coming up to him and saying, "I'm going to save your soul." I hope nobody's taking that as a serious challenge dialogue. Basically, I went there to kind of reconnect with him, because I respected him. I didn't understand his poetry, but I understood his influence on a lot of young poets. I didn't understand his circle at all. I just wanted to be friendly, and check in."⁷¹ This was the last sustained meeting between Spicer and Ginsberg. Yet Spicer's obsession with Ginsberg's great success and easy command of the big, professional world of poetry, and his inability to deal with Ginsberg's poetics, continued to color his world. His very last poem tries to sum up all that he felt about Ginsberg, a spectacle too great for even the single-minded poet of dictation to ignore.

But now, finally, there was new activity on his own horizon—the year of *Open Space*.

CHAPTER TEN

Crisis

*J*anuary 1, 1964. The *Open Space* year. Once regular meetings had connected the poets, but none had been held in a year. Those who had been close had scattered. This lack of a formal poetry network bothered Stan Persky who, by the last years of Spicer's life, had become his amanuensis and strongest supporter. Every night he saw Spicer in Gino & Carlo's, unhappy, querulous, his writing a thing of the past. For the year to come, the magazine *Open Space* provided a nexus of the poetic interests of Spicer's community and inspired Spicer himself to resume his own writing.

The magazine gave "open space" to a specified list of writers and artists whose work would be printed without censorship or constraint, and the project became a kind of reunion for many in the Spicer group. Among the participants were Blaser, Duncan, Adam, Kyger, Stanley, Borregaard, Dull, Ellingham, and Spicer. The magazine was committed to a timeframe of only one year, an echo of the limit that Duncan, Jess, and Harry Jacobus had placed on San Francisco's King Ubu Gallery in 1953.[1] One year, and fifteen issues.

Not only poets but painters were dragooned into the magazine. Bill Mc-Neill, for example, was bullied into the *Open Space* project after Stan Persky accused him of "not contributing to the community." Outraged, Mc-Neill repaired to his studio, and in one night executed 150 paintings of irises on gold leaf. The next evening he accosted Persky in the bar, bestowed the picture on him, and said, "Fuck it! Shove these up your ass!" These paintings were inserted in *Open Space* 3, glued to an $8\frac{1}{2} \times 11$" page if they were smaller than this standard format size. McNeill later created another set of flower pictures—poppies, for issue 7, in fragile mono-prints.[2] Bill Wheeler, in the May issue (5), made a rather abstract engraving of Spicer, for which he defrayed costs as well. Robert Berg presented photos, doctored sometimes to collage, as in two displaying "poets talking like statues." Covers and drawings were made from random objects—the cover for issue 6 from a Christmas card made by Helen Adam. The list of artists who contributed is extensive: Armando Navarro, Bill Brodecky, Harry Jacobus, Robert Duncan, Fran Herndon, besides those already mentioned. For each copy of *Open Space* 7 Ken Botto made individual illustrations of "Gino's bar," above a poem by Joanne Kyger, and facing McNeill's gouache poppies.[3]

Even Jess agreed to participate, no small coup considering his bad feeling toward Spicer. Why did he give his consent? "Because I didn't consider that Spicer had anything to do with that!" Jess replied. "I liked Stan Persky—he had a lot of energy and intelligence. We [Jess and Robert] were both satisfied with the job he did."[4] Jess participated wholeheartedly, while about half the text of Duncan's book, *Bending the Bow*, first appeared in the magazine. All of Blaser's current work, too—"The Moth Poem," "The Holy Forest," and the early *Image-Nations* series—found their way into *Open Space* issues. And in a real sense, *Open Space* kept Jack Spicer alive in 1964—its very regularity helped to provide a rhythm in which to situate his final two books. He composed almost the entirety of *Language* for *Open Space*, beginning with "Thing Language"—his first poem since the "Fix" series of October 1962.

> This ocean, humiliating in its disguises.
> Tougher than anything.
> No one listens to poetry. The ocean
> Does not mean to be listened to. A drop
> Or crash of water. It means
> Nothing.
> It
> Is bread and butter
> Pepper and salt. The death
> That young men hope for. Aimlessly
> It pounds the shore. White and aimless signals. No
> One listens to poetry.[5]

Open Space was printed cheaply, thanks to the junk-mail house of Merchandising Methods, where Stan Persky worked, as did Ebbe Borregaard, Bill Brodecky, Gail Chugg, and James Alexander. In a nearby law office Helen Adam found temporary employment and joined the others at lunch hour in South Park, a seedy, oval area concealed from the main streets by housing and businesses in Rincon Hill near the terminus of the Bay Bridge. With so many poets and artists working there, the warehouse was an "insane place," Stan remembered, blessed by its "saints," a large number of Mexican women who stuffed envelopes.

In the front of the junk-mail office Stan typed the submissions on an electric typewriter boasting plastic ribbons that produced exceptionally clean, sharp copy. "Then there was a kind of device to make a plastic plate on which you could print this. I could run these off. Then Mike's kid [Lee], or Mike [Kummer, the business printer] would come in on Saturday and run the whole thing off. I would do all the collating, usually by hand. I paid the company for the cost of the materials—paper, time; but they did everything else, a favor to me after hours."[6] Out of this furious concentration of energy came *Open Space*. Because of it 1964 became, in George Stanley's words, the "last great year. '64 looked back to the great years we had had in the '50s. And even through 1964, Spicer was raging at everybody."[7]

One cool sunny morning, Stan brought copies of the "#0/Prospectus" issue of *Open Space* to the Drew House at Stinson Beach, which Lew Ellingham now shared with Paul Alexander and Paul's cat, Albert Pinkham Ryder. On the deck, sunlight caught the withered remains of the climbing Belle of Portugal rose that had struggled up to the second story from the garden. Stan and Jack looked at each other as the issues were distributed to the small company in the living room and on the porch. Spicer, by a nod, pronounced the magazine acceptable.

By evening George Stanley and Ellingham were drinking in the front room before the fire. Jack, Stan, Paul, Robin Blaser, Helen and Pat Adam, Bill Brodecky, Paul—other guests may have been in the room or were displaced through the house, town or beach—out walking. George's comment on Spicer's new poem—which was to become the first poem in his penultimate book—was "No one listens to poetry!" George mimicked Jack's petulant sneer, the mimicry mocking Spicer's irritability and pessimism. Yet a tender, even romantic vulnerability surrounded the first issue of the poets' new vehicle. This one, they felt, would be run right—not like *M* or the rush of magazine-war throwaways. Jack would have his hand in it; Stan Persky now knew more and understood better. The group was in safe hands. *Language* could continue.

*

In February 1964, Richard Duerden proposed a recreation of the Berkeley Renaissance in the form of a reading by Duncan, Spicer, Blaser, and others. *Open Space* had again drawn these poets into a common cause and renewed the possibility of retrieving their friendship from the mire of recrimination. (Duncan had agreed to recommend Blaser's work to the Guggenheim Foundation the previous month.)[8]

Duncan wrote that he would back the reading 100 percent: it would be giving something to the community of Bay Area poets. Spicer suggested a round table—both to recall the great round table at 2029 Hearst and to assure the audience that no one poet would sit at its head. Duncan agreed, adding pragmatically that a round table would "take care of smoking and ashtrays, for one thing, a worry when you rent an auditorium you want to use again." The proposed reunion forced Duncan to rethink the whole great Berkeley Renaissance he had helped to pioneer almost twenty years before. He suggested asking Landis Everson and Thomas Parkinson to read, even if their contributions to such a recreation would be problematical—and even the despised Leonard Wolf ("it wld be instructive to the young and innocent of mind that we once were conversant with the poet of *Hamadryad Hunted*"). Robin, Jack, and he must work out in correspondence what they meant to show their audience. "I am curious myself as to what we think we were doing—and here what does Parkinson think . . . or Landis think was going on? And what do we think was going on?"[9] Although nothing came immediately of the round-table proposal, the long shadows of the Berkeley Renaissance were to draw closer and closer around Jack Spicer in the eighteen months before his death.

Lew Ellingham celebrated his thirty-first birthday at Stinson Beach with a party, with the weekend group present at its usual fullness. The day was fine if cool. The solarium was set for an early evening dinner of mussels steamed in white wine, with melted garlic butter and French bread. At dinner Helen Adam recited "I Love My Love," a combined song and incantation that ended with a sinister stage-whisper: "In through the keyhole, elvish bright, came creeping a single hair. / Softly, softly, it stroked his lips, on his eyelids traced a sign. / 'I love my love with a capital Z. I mark him Zero and mine. / Ha! Ha! / I mark him Zero and mine.' / The hair rushed in. He struggled and tore. . . . "[10] Candles flickered on the bunched picnic tables brought together and covered with bedsheets to accommodate the assembled diners/listeners. By the window dividing the solarium from the living room Jack Spicer tacked up a poem:

> The log in the fire
> Asks a lot
> When it is lighted
> Or knot
>
> Timber comes
> From seas mainly
> Sometimes burns green
> -Ly
>
> When it is lighted
> The knot
> Burns like a joke
> With the color of smoke
>
> Save us, with birthdays, whatever is in the
>   fire or not in the fire, immortal
> We cannot be
> A chimney tree
> Or give grace to what's mere-
> Ly fatal.[11]

The birthday party occurred in late February, and the poem appeared in the March issue of *Open Space* (3).

Ellingham's name appears twice in the first "Morphemics" poem in *Language*. When Spicer spoke of "twins / At the same business" as waves and particles (in physical theories of light) he alluded to the fact that Ellingham was a twin. Less direct were his allusions of *"thanatos"* and "dry in August," drawn from the romantic, dark vision of Robinson Jeffers and his settings for lyrics and narratives in the Big Sur country, and particular favorites of Lew.

> Morphemes in section
> Lew, you and I know how love and death matter
> Matter as wave and particle—twins
> At the same business.
> No excuse for them. Lew, thanatos and agape have no
>   business being there.
> What is needed is hill country. Dry in August Dead grass
>   leading to mountains you can climb onto
> Or stop
> Morphemes in section
> Dead grass. The total excuse for love and death[12]

Spicer insisted that *Open Space* should not leave the city limits of San

Francisco: no subscribers, no libraries, no contributors, outside the Bay Area. Persky agreed. "I thought all of those rules were true and necessary to maintain the purity of the art."[13] Some issues were smuggled out nevertheless—the "Underground Railroad" worked both ways.

From the days of the 1950s' Sunday poetry meetings, Stan Persky had found four of the younger poets especially promising. Now in 1964 they were reassembled, almost literally from the corners of the globe. Joanne Kyger was ending her marriage to Gary Snyder—after four years in the Orient, Kyger returned to the United States to continue her project of adopting the myths of Penelope, Odysseus, and the suitors in *The Tapestry and the Web*. Harold Dull came back from New York City where his efforts to salvage something from his life with Dora (now married to Russell FitzGerald) led to disappointment with the East Coast in general. Ebbe Borregaard surfaced from hibernation in a private life, again to make poetry—*Sketches for 13 Sonnets* emerged in springtime, fluent in a contemporary near-Elizabethan language. In April George Stanley, Kyger, Dull, and Borregaard appeared together in *Open Space*, as "the White Hopes." Later the novelist Samuel R. Delany recalled how *physically* apt this description was.

You *must* describe Ebbe, Joanne and Harold physically—that is, physically as they were at the time. Otherwise, the meaning/irony of the term will be lost on most readers. The fact is—even in 1969, when I knew them all together—the three of them were simply the *blondest* people I'd ever seen! Having all three in a room at once (and I think all three of them came to some party [I gave] that year) was an experience between a particularly crazed Nordic invasion and an atomic fireball carrying on—in the most pleasantly joking way, of course—in your own living room! But you must give some indication of that towering, tripartite, Scandinavian *whiteness* (among, let's face it, a lot of smaller, darker, browner people, the Italians, Catholics, etc. among you, yea unto Link and Bob Kaufman.)[14]

During this time Spicer's reputation was slowly growing. Don Allen's anthology *The New American Poetry* continued to sell in surprisingly respectable numbers, and the publication of *The Heads of the Town Up to the Aether* and *The Holy Grail* added to the curiosity many felt about the writer of the "Imaginary Elegies." Inquiries began to trickle in. From New York wrote the poet Robert Kelly who, having first been introduced to Spicer's work by the poets Diane Wakoski and George Stanley, asked Spicer for permission to include *Billy The Kid* and two books of *The Holy Grail* in the anthology which Kelly would co-edit with Paris Leary, *A Controversy of*

Poets: An Anthology of Contemporary American Poets. Spicer agreed, writing in a brief contributor's note, "Am by trade a research linguist."[15] Kelly recalled, "People told me 'He'll tear you apart if you don't allow him to select his own poems,' but he was mild as a lamb: 'Do what you like, and thanks for asking.'"[16] Another letter came from the poet and lecturer Lawrence Lipton, who wrote from Venice, California, describing his plans for a UCLA class in "West Coast writing," to be held in the autumn of 1964, featuring "field trips to the homes of writers in all parts" of California. Would Auerhahn provide the home address of Jack Spicer?[17] In a certain whimsical mood Jack might have welcomed a busload of UCLA students into his shabby Polk Street apartment. There were, of course, many interiors in a community so varied:

> I hear a banging on the door of the night
> Buzz, buzz; buzz, buzz; buzz, buzz
> If you open the door does it let in light?
> Buzz, buzz, buzz, buzz; buzz, buzzz.
>
> If the day appears like a yellow raft
> Meow, meow; meow, meoww
> Is it really on top of a yellow giraffe
> Meow, meow, meow, meow. Meow, meow[18]

"His mind never went," Blaser asserted. "In the sense that he knew the 'areas' he could defend his mind. That was in terms of the poetry. When the delirium tremens started—'buzz, buzz, buzz, buzz, buzz'—he just simply put that into the poem."[19]

In a lighter sense "buzz" flavored the social life of the winter and spring of this new-magazine year. The season of birthdays was just begun. In May Paul Alexander's and Robin Blaser's (both Taurians) provided the opportunity for a grand gathering at Stinson Beach. There were stacked bottles of California champagne, trays of food, and a delicious springtime at the oceanside to savor. The atmosphere was pagan. From a deck one could scan the ocean over the housetops of the village, a wide view. Robin read by a plate glass window across which they'd strung a grid of hefty threads with baubles pendant to prevent recurrence of an accident that had happened earlier in the morning, a bird stunned by flying against the pane, potential breakfast for Paul's cat. Soon to come was the evening's birthday party. With lemons and flowers from the garden they arranged a support for Bill Brodecky's table decorations, masses of white candles clumped on driftwood bases. The afternoon stretched into an evening and tomorrow where people slept in houses of friends of the group as well as the Drew cottage, the glitter of ocean or splash of stars equally forbearing.

Art, society, and the rites of Taurus were served. But it turned out to be an expensive party—the wine bought in North Beach cost the next month's rent at the cottage, which caused sufficient crisis for Ellingham to leave Stinson Beach the following month. Harold Dull and Ila Hinton then moved to Stinson and Ellingham to Ila's Telegraph Hill apartment at 16 Edith Street, an enclave à la North Beach. From his residence at the Drew House came Harold Dull's *The Star Year.* Each move seemed to play its part in the making of a larger project that these people had set about to do.

Privately Helen Adam was nursing doubts about her ability to survive in the world. For years Adam had protected her mystic powers by taking low-level clerical jobs where she would not have to think about the things of this world. Yet Adam's mysticism and otherworldliness existed side-by-side, uncomfortably, with a drive to become famous and adored. She had held high hopes after meeting Robert Lowell, during his 1957 visit to the Magic Workshop poets. He had, after all, enjoyed her class reading so much he took away her poems with him and promised to find her a publisher. Back in Boston in 1959 an embarrassed Robert Lowell remembered her sheaf of poems with guilt and unease. "They really have, I think, all the charm and originality I felt in them two years ago," he wrote. But their "goodness," he felt, really needed her voice to show them off to best effect. "They'd be a smash on records, but I have no connections in that world."[20] Her ballad-opera *San Francisco's Burning!* had been a huge success, but once the run was over, the money ran out too. By January 1964 her finances were wearing thin. "I am finding it hard to find jobs which require no business skills, and to keep them when I do find them," she wrote in January to James Schevill, the director of the Poetry Center. "I have just lost the little selling job I had over Xmas, because I made too many mistakes adding up the sales taxes." She planned a new version of her musical, which she dreamed of seeing launched on Broadway, using traditional folk music in the public domain to which she would match her lyrics, but the research required what was most precious to her—time. Helen Adam was almost fifty-five years old.

Then she met the man who became her "angel." He was the poet James Merrill. He encouraged her to apply to the Ingram Merrill Foundation in New York, which made grants to poets with specific projects and a severe lack of funds. All through the first half of 1964, she waited for news of her application. She made fifty dollars from her Poetry Center appearance, but otherwise money was extremely tight in the Adam household. In June she squared her shoulders and applied for another clerical job, this one in the library at San Francisco State. At the end of the month she heard the incredible news—the Ingram Merrill Foundation had awarded her four thousand dollars to continue work on *San Francisco's Burning!* "It is almost unbelievable good luck," she exulted, in a letter of thanks to one whose name she had used as a reference. "I can't tell you how much I appreciate your generous kindness."[21] She and her sister moved to New York, to the West 82nd Street apartment they occupied until Pat Adam's death in 1987.

Spicer's own crisis came in March 1964 when he was fired from his job at UC Berkeley. This was the time of his own "Deadly Desert," a reference to the Oz books which pops up in the "Intermissions" section of *Language*.[22] "As far as I could see," said Harris Schiff, "they dealt Jack the final blow, really one of the fatal blows, when they let him go as an instructor. That really did it for him. That was when he lost his will to live."[23] Fran Herndon had never known Jack when he wasn't working at Berkeley, and she and Jim had perhaps the closest view of Jack's shock and despair. Jim Herndon recalled that

Jack used to go over to Berkeley every morning, get there at ten or eleven. I don't think he did a hell of a lot of work. So what? Jack got paid for three or four hours a day—nothing, but he needed to have somewhere to go. I'll say this—I'll never think otherwise—he was in good shape then. He came home from Berkeley, took a nap and [in the evening went to the] bar and drank. Shit, there are a thousand guys who do that every day and live to be eighty. You know, he contributed to that linguistics department, there's no question about it. Probably not a whole lot, they could have gotten along without him, but Reed could have kept him. That job was important to him. When he left it, he just sat there and drank.[24]

He had been working for David Reed on the "Linguistic Atlas of the Pacific States" (which included, Reed said, "later, Nevada too") from 1957 until he was dismissed in the spring of 1964, on the grounds that the atlas project was "no longer viable. This was before computers—because we had so much information we had no way of analyzing it." Reed returned his funding to the University Administration, letting Spicer go as his (only) staff member. When asked if he had dissolved the project in order to "get rid of Jack," since he reactivated it a year later with new employees, Reed said, "That would be too strong. But I wasn't getting anything I could use from him. The problem was largely in the project itself." He denied that Spicer's drinking, his homosexuality, or any other personal matter entered into his calculations. "In those days I drank a good deal myself." He had been told about Spicer's homosexuality along the way of their relationship, adding that, on an occasion late in Jack's life, when Jack was a dinner guest at the Reeds' home, Mrs. Reed had noticed "how good [Spicer was] with the children."[25]

Not sure what to believe about Spicer's termination at Berkeley, Robin Blaser called David Reed and learned the truth, that Jack had been fired—"eased out." At the same time, Reed attempted to find him other work at Stanford University in Palo Alto. Considering the hours he kept, and his physical condition, Robin considered such a job impossible. "He was becoming physically," Robin hesitated, "weaker and weaker."[26] Jack was experiencing "real panic" trying to maneuver his way into Stanford, and Fran became Spicer's phone contact for work since, except for his brief stay in Berkeley upon returning from Boston, Spicer had no telephone during the last ten years of his life. After his first interview at Stanford, Jack talked to Fran, angry about the disdain shown him by even the linguistics department secretaries. The suit he had worn to the interview had been clean and pressed, but it was impossible for him to exude the well-fed bourgeois aura Stanford expected from its staff. He was, Fran realized, like *a tramp*. She would see him on Polk Street with the whole seat of his pants out. "And the ridiculous thing is I would go and buy him pants."[27]

Nemi Frost noticed the same thing at Aquatic Park, where Jack spent his afternoons with a sixpack of Rainier Ale, a copy of the *Chronicle*, and his portable radio. Always, at ten to four, he had to leave because that was the time for the Polk Street bus. As Nemi followed, she couldn't help but see his pants were split from waist to waist. "No underwear or anything, of course. And then he gets on the bus and I thought, 'O Jack!' I thought, *Dare I say anything? No! I don't.*"[28]

Berkeley's security and its concomitant routine had freed Jack to receive the Martian transmissions. "That's one thing Jack believed in," Jim Herndon said dryly.

Do the same thing every day. Eat the same thing for dinner on Tuesday as last Tuesday. Get to the bar on time and go home at a certain time. When something stopped he was very upset, and the loss of the job killed him.

Jack would insist on coming over to Fran's place every Wednesday or whatever, at a certain time, and having a certain thing to eat, certain things to drink—of course that's pretty fucking convenient, besides opening up to poetry, you know? The routine had to be a routine which Jack also happened to like—and which put a lot of other people to trouble.

[One] could easily call Jack a very selfish son-of-a-bitch. His little self-contained life you could describe, if you want, as nutty, or obsessive, but his things about the real world were never nutty. I think they were always right.[29]

When Reed fired him from the Linguistic Atlas project, Spicer's self-contained world turned sour, and on Fran Herndon's advice, he applied for help at Mt. Zion Hospital's Psychiatric Services. In light of his previous experience with psychiatry, this was indeed a radical step.[30] Jobless, broke, with no word yet from Stanford, Jack moved through the intake process in a daze, meeting with a doctor once or twice to come to terms with his depression. Yet Jack would not admit to Fran that his alcoholism had become too much to cope with. "He never said to me, 'I'm an alcoholic. I have a drinking problem.' Never. I finally asked him if he would go to therapy. I said, 'I don't know how else to help you.' He agreed to go. We arranged for him to go to Mount Zion."[31]

This was in March. Spicer was put on the waiting list for regular analysis with a private doctor. Arguing that his personality was too domineering, he rejected the group therapy offered him, which would have materialized sooner. Meanwhile he waited for news from Stanford. Fran Herndon continued to work on Spicer's behalf, even though it sometimes seemed to her that he did not deserve it. At Christmastime he had come to the house one evening to review a portrait Fran had done of him. "He was getting more and more drunk, you know, and he hated the portrait. He told me so. What he was saying was, 'You've changed and it's no longer magical for me. Here is this portrait and it's nothing like the other paintings you've done. The magic is gone.' He said, 'It appalls me.' Something really very cutting. I got very angry at Jack.—Oh, he really meant it," Fran continued. "I had made him 'heroic,' Jim said, and Jack couldn't *stand* it."[32]

In a panic, Spicer tried to think of further financial resources. He decided to swallow his pride and try to make up with Lawrence Ferlinghetti, the owner of City Lights Books. For years Spicer had refused to allow any of his books to be sold at City Lights, but now, faced with ruin, he was grasping for straws.

Lawrence Ferlinghetti was Robert Duncan's age, six years older than Spicer. Much involved in contemporary French letters, he was one of the first to understand the potential of paperback books—already standard in France—and, in purchasing a bookstore, had chosen one with an anarchist background. Ferlinghetti bought City Lights from Peter Marin, a Bay Area anarchist well known to Spicer in Berkeley circles. Marin's family included such celebrities of the Left as Carlo Tresca and Elizabeth Gurley Flynn.[33] These were shared images for Spicer and Ferlinghetti, and Jack felt that Ferlinghetti should have been more responsive to an economic/utopian business attitude than he was (however much he may have been). "To Spicer," wrote Alistair Johnston, "Ferlinghetti represented the worst aspects of the commercialization of poetry. Spicer thought [Ferlinghetti] was a facile poet, exploitative of others, and behind a 'bleeding-heart liberal' façade lurked a capitalist bookmonger who profited by selling what Spicer thought should be freely disseminated."[34]

Suspicious of Ferlinghetti's involvement in the publication of *Howl*, Spicer believed that Ferlinghetti's notoriety, and Ginsberg's by extension, stemmed from the publisher's mania for publicity. It was part of "the fix," Jack snickered, and told George Stanley that, in order to create a scandal, Ferlinghetti had arranged with the printers in England to wrap the boxes in proofs of the poems so that the word "cocksucker" would appear on the outside of the boxes, making it more likely that the books would be seized for obscenity.[35]

David Meltzer remarked, "You couldn't be in North Beach at that time and have any relationship with Jack and Joanne and Ebbe—his various bars—without being caught in the barbed-wire flak of bitchery."[36] About the issue behind the bitchery, however, no one has offered more than surmise. One unconfirmed rumor was that the feud was grounded in personal dislike, that Spicer had been enraged when City Lights Books bought White Rabbit books from Joe Dunn, which allowed Joe to maintain his methedrine habit, and that this had enraged Spicer. Graham Mackintosh, however, came to believe other than emotional considerations were involved:

Jack always maintained that the bottom level of anything, personal, social, astrological, whatever, was economic. That Ferlinghetti was making money—and let's face it, Ferlinghetti *wasn't* making money off small press books. He was making it off other kinds of books and his location and a few other things. He was ripping off small presses only inadvertently. City Lights was a paperback bookstore in a great location. It became sort of a cultural focal point: you know, Gary Snyder would have a note up on the wall, "you see somebody, call me, Gary Snyder." A kid coming in from Nebraska would revel in little notes like that.[37]

Probably no enterprise could have met Spicer's expectations. His beliefs

and ideas about business seemed to shimmer somewhere between delusion and idealism, as befit the son of a man who had boasted of knowing
Rosa Luxemburg.[38] Jack's capitulation to Ferlinghetti and City Lights at this
juncture in his life—he, Jack Spicer, who once had told Ariel Parkinson
"Castro si, Ferlinghetti no!"—was a telling sign of his desperation over
money.[39]

Ferlinghetti never understood why he loomed so large in Spicer's psychic life. "I don't think I ever had a complete conversation with him in my
life," he said in November 1990. City Lights did sell White Rabbit books,
but he had other sources besides Spicer for them. About the rumor that
Spicer had burned White Rabbit books in the store, Ferlinghetti swore,
"Not as far as I know! I never heard anything like that." In 1960 Ferlinghetti
edited an issue of the magazine *Beatitude* (17). "I had a lot of fun putting
that together. We gave a lot of poets false names—Allen Ginsberg, for example, became Allen 'Ginsboig'—and false quotations. At the front of that,
you know, it says, 'You are all a beat generation'—Gertrude Stein in conversation with Jack Kerouac." Among the "false quotations" in *Beatitude* 17 is
one attributed to Jack Spicer—"When I hear the word 'Ferlinghetti' I reach
for my gun." "Oh, I made that one up," Ferlinghetti said, faintly amused. He
was not familiar with Spicer's poem "Ferlinghetti," nor its notorious line,
"Ferlinghetti is a nonsense syllable invented by the poet." Once more,
Spicer's barbs failed to hit their target in any appreciable way. "Why would
anyone want to publish a biography of Spicer?" Ferlinghetti added with apparent bewilderment. "He's almost forgotten nowadays, isn't he?"[40]

In May 1964 David Reed called Fran with what appeared to be good
news—despite the odds stacked against him, Jack had landed the job at
Stanford. "I walked over to Jack's place on Polk Street to tell him. Jack just
clutched me by the shoulders—I'll never forget that. Hugged me. I felt
such an awful feeling because I knew he would never do that job."[41]

Spicer's new job at Stanford was as a research assistant for a think tank,
funded by the Carnegie Corporation, called the Institute for Mathematical
Studies in the Social Sciences. With what mixture of bitterness and self-
loathing, and strange pride, did Spicer arrange with Graham Mackintosh
to feature the cover of *Language* (July-September 1951) on the first edition
jacket of his own book with the same name. In this issue of the journal
Language, Spicer's only professional publication had appeared while he
was still studying at Minnesota. On the cover of the book *Language*, the
name "Jack Spicer," in a huge muddy scrawl of maroon, almost obliterates

the prim linkage of "David W. Reed and John L. Spicer." It was his way of telling Reed, "I don't need you any more; I am a poet." But at Stanford, Spicer's skills were used to prepare a series of lessons in sentential logic to be given to sixth-graders via the IBM computer. Each student sat at a booth with an image projector, a monitor screen, a light pen, and a pair of earphones and listened to stories, poems, riddles, and language-related "games," while response was monitored to accelerate learning. Spicer joined a battery of "writers, teachers, linguists, mathematicians, reading experts, curriculum experts, psychologists, artists, computer programmers and computer technicians" in developing this early experiment in so-called "computer-assisted instruction."[42]

In the summer Jack received a letter from Dr. Harry Z. Coren. Twenty-seven and "relatively green," Coren had just come to San Francisco after his first year of residency in Cleveland, for the beginning of his out-patient psychiatry training. He saw twelve to sixteen patients a week, and Spicer was the first homosexual of either sex he had ever treated. By the time Spicer began meeting with Coren, on July 15, he was "already feeling much better."

Coren's office was in a fairly new building, modernist, blocky, economically built, weakly ornamented. A stairwell brought patients from Divisadero Street past plain, pastel, two-toned walls to a bank of two rows of four chairs each in the small waiting space. The doctor's office, cool, small, adequate, was around an 'L' a short distance away. Sessions were weekly, in the afternoons at first. The fee was on a sliding scale, geared to Jack's miniscule income. Originally charged five dollars a visit, he later was able to negotiate down to four dollars. He offered at first to pay for each session as they came. Afraid that bills would pile up, getting him into "a jam," Spicer nevertheless adopted the laissez-faire policy that the clinic seemed to encourage. For both analysand and analyst, this policy eventually proved a mistake, for even at four dollars Jack often forgot to pay, or couldn't afford to, and over the next six months his bill soared to three figures. This huge sum hung over Jack's head like the sword of Damocles and eventually his shame became one of the factors in abandoning the analysis.[43]

Inspired by the success of *Open Space* in re-energizing the Spicer and Duncan writing circles, the painters and visual artists associated with them decided to launch a similar gallery project—a gallery planned to run for a year, like King Ubu, that would hold twelve monthly group shows. Paul Alexander, Bill Brodecky, and Larry Fagin opened the gallery in June,

1964. "I wanted a name which denoted activity," recalled Alexander, "and we tried out various words and George came up with the word 'buzz' and I thought, 'That's perfect.'—We didn't even want to use the word 'gallery.' We just called it 'Buzz,' period. Of course everyone always called it 'Buzz Gallery' anyway whether we did or not." Spicer refused to attend, boycotted the shows even of the artists he loved best. "One of the reasons he was angry with us," Paul remembered, "is that he assumed we had stolen his word. His 'Buzz' poem *was* prominent at the time, but it's a word in the public domain."[44] Paul, trained at Black Mountain, had tried the artistic life in both New York and San Francisco, and concluded:

The idealistic artists' life of North Beach was in every way more attractive to me than the commercial make-it world my New York friends were so excited about. I loved the clear light, seacoast compactness of San Francisco and the easy-going, exciting combination of living and people in North Beach. Jack Spicer was of course the center for the poets and since so many of my friends were his poets I saw a lot of him. I don't think I would have otherwise because we didn't have much to say to each other. He was very defensive around me, probably because he thought I would disapprove of his interest in Jim [Alexander, Paul's brother]. To Jack I was an "international faggot." I don't think this attitude hurt me but it was always disappointing that he would blackball events that I sponsored.

"I guess we did become closer as time went on," Paul continued, "and once we even went to bed together (both very drunk, but not *that* drunk). Of course we loved the same people. I needed the nightly gatherings at the bars and when this began to fade so did my trust and hope. As long as there was a group of artists to talk to and identify with life was secure. When Jack died that scene was over and I've never enjoyed bar life again."[45] For some—perhaps for most of Spicer's intimates—what Paul Alexander has said summarized their experiences with North Beach life.

Buzz, a mixture of artists' living space and exhibition rooms, peripheral to any other San Francisco art scene, showed Tom Field, Nemi Frost, Ernie Edwards (collages), Fran Herndon, Jess, Harry Jacobus, Bill Wheeler, Knute Stiles, Bill McNeill, Bill Brodecky, and Paul himself; its announcements—posters—were printed by Graham Mackintosh. There was a "poet's show," with photos by Helen Adam, drawings by Robert Duncan, and many *things*. Spicer never set foot in it.

In mid-September the terms of Jack's Stanford job altered, and he had to make the transition from part-time to full-time work. Bus and train schedules forced him to wake up at 6:30 in the morning and return home after 6:30 at night. What was the job? "Doing something he wasn't interested in," he told Coren. His set routines collapsed around him like a circus tent with a broken pole. Among other things, his lack of freedom meant that the afternoon sessions with Dr. Coren had to be canceled. Rather than terminating analysis, the doctor offered instead a twice-monthly evening appointment. "And then," Coren recalled, "very quickly, within a week or so, *that* changed. He had what he called a crisis. He had called and wanted to see me and we arranged an emergency session. He was thinking about quitting his job, wasn't sure whether that was correct, or maybe was some response to the therapy. . . . At one point he became confused, down there [Stanford in Palo Alto] on campus and wondered what he was doing there, kind of lost touch with himself for a few seconds. He was again feeling suicidal at that point." His health was manifestly in crisis. During September, Spicer was in the throes of a persistent anxiety, "a minor dissociative state." Dr. Coren noted that Spicer had returned to a twenty-hour week by September 15, 1964: "I have a sense that over the summer [Spicer's situation] wasn't quite as intense; he started full time, and it became intolerable; and then he cut it back, and that lasted until the grant ran out . . . on February 28th of 1965."[46]

Dr. Coren noticed that Spicer had a slight tremor; his posture was faulty and he slumped a lot. In general he was unkempt. "He would wear a suit if he had something special to go to, but most often he didn't bathe. Too often, he would smell. His fingernails were dirty—he had tobacco-stained fingers." The analyst's impression was that, beyond being too "depressed" to clean himself up, Spicer was challenging society's standards by presenting a dirty front to the world.

He discussed it in terms of cleaning up his closet. Sometimes some potatoes on a shelf would begin to sprout and it would go on for weeks or months before he finally would toss them out. He'd put up mushrooms or tomatoes to marinate and they'd gone bad and he had to toss them out. He would go through phases of sometimes taking care of himself and his surroundings, so to speak, and at other times just feeling that they don't count.

He was an interesting man. And he cared about whether I liked him or not. He would entertain me with jokes. That was a way of keeping away from something too upsetting to himself. He was different from me. I don't think that [friendship] would have arisen. I never viewed him as a friend. He was an older person . . . and in a different stage of life, and in a different field.

And a different sexual preference, too. To a young psychiatrist in 1965, the salient thing about Spicer was that he was a homosexual, and more or less openly so. "First of all," said Dr. Coren, "[Spicer] felt a strong feeling about being put at a disadvantage because of homosexuality by the world at large. . . . The other thing is that he had some anxiety and concerns about why he was homosexual: What did it mean that he didn't get married at thirty-five like his dad?"[47] Spicer's anxiety over his failure to marry was reflected in his public statements at this time on the great poets he admired who *did* marry: Yeats and Jeffers. In the "Vancouver Lectures" of June 1965 he alluded to the case of Yeats, who married when he was forty and was careful to marry a "rich wife." Interviewed the following month, at the Berkeley Poetry Conference, he told Tové Neville that Robinson Jeffers was "'a real California poet' and added, as an aside, that during a time when you had to be a Stalinist to be a poet, Jeffers was anti-Stalin. However, 'he had a rich wife and could afford it.'"[48] The fantasy of a "rich wife" was clearly on his mind in his last days: a woman wealthy enough to support him while he did the work that he needed to do. Yet, as he admitted to his analyst, no woman had interested him sexually or romantically for many years, though he had tried several times so to interest himself.[49]

Again and again he had felt the strains of being different from those around him, and suffered under those in power. He had been unlucky.

The homosexuality . . . not getting a Ph.D. Not signing the Loyalty Oath. He equated it "to having green hair or being a Jew. It didn't automatically disqualify you, but it did count against you." There was a lot of feeling about authority that came up; and lots of anger; and submitting and not submitting; and a lot having to do with whether you play ball with society, or don't; and "if you try to, sometimes even then you can't. And so what's the use of even trying?" So there was a lot of that conflict still going on in his life.

He didn't like being put down for [his homosexuality] or having it held against him, and in that regard his comment about "green hair or a Jew" is an unconscious way of putting me on his spot forcefully, you know, to make me feel exactly what it was for him. It was also humorous. He had a lot of humor. One of the ways he would handle issues would be to joke and keep me at bay with that, and entertain me; it was very important to him.

Once I went out to get him [Spicer] in the waiting room; he was heavily engaged in conversation with a woman and I had to get his attention. He came in and said, "That's the wife of a friend of mine. She comes here also."[50]

This was Fran Herndon, of course, who was also in therapy. "Jack thought I was going for him. Isn't that interesting?" One day he met her on the street and announced the latest discovery he'd made in analysis about his past. "I left my grandmother dead on the couch," he told an astonished Fran, then asked her, "Where did you leave *your* grandmother?"[51]

294

Said Dr. Coren, "There was a lot of feeling of anger at society and other people—at society in general about allowing poets to be poets or taking care of them. At the same time it was his own conflict also. He would have liked to have exploited his poetry and made money out of it; at the same time he felt that would hinder him as a poet. He thought Duncan was a better poet than he was, but that 'Robert became a whore. He's still a better poet, but he's not writing as well as before.'"

Spicer continued to express anxiety about his future, his finances, his career. To sympathetic Dr. Coren he sketched castles in the air. If there was only a way he could exploit his poetry without breaking his principles, how the money would roll in! He was almost there: if he could only hang on a little while longer, it would happen of its own accord. It was like waiting for a grandmother to die who was going to leave you money, he said. Already, he noticed, people were beginning to react to him with some deference. "He was now forty; he felt that he was entitled to somewhat more, and that if he could just manage, somehow or other it would come to him rather than having to sell himself out for it, in ways that were OK, such as reading his own lectures.

"He did not deceive himself easily about who he was and what he was," continued Dr. Coren. "There were times he was confused about certain things, go back and forth and back and forth on issues; not being clear to himself. Some people are very superficial in giving rationalizations for why they're doing something—I didn't have that feeling with Spicer. He was willing to call a spade a spade as well as he could see it. He was often quite harsh with himself. Sometimes he wished he could feel some things more deeply than he did at the time. Sometimes situations would occur and he knew they were important to him and yet [he] would be dismissing them—he didn't feel upset or concerned; he felt he should have." Asked if he perceived Spicer as a manipulator or a controller, Coren replied, "No. No. Maybe because he had the latitude to express what he wanted to; felt safe. Also he handled me, as he put it, not as a friend or someone important to him, but someone 'out there,' whom he could leave at any time he wanted to. So to that extent we kept a certain amount of distance." Coren went on:

He noticed, after the first couple of sessions with me, that at times he was carrying on a dialogue with me about some issue he was going to talk about, had talked about, or was continuing, a thought on his mind. It's a sign of anxiety and preoccupation with the issues that had come up or were about to come up—What was interesting is that when he was writing poetry that wouldn't bother him. Yet when he was trying to work on his job, he would find himself distracted, often, and think about these dialogues.

There was something else he also said: If he tried to make a poem do something, he would invariably mess it up. Yeah, he put it like this: "Poetry is really dictated to you. And when you get in its way, that is, when you think it would be nice to include this because it's timely or such, you mess up the poem." He said, "Of course the poem uses the past and things, but if you try to improve it, it doesn't."[52]

Spicer was notably sensitive to "the human crisis": it framed his vision of the world in existential terms. Spicer's life had been a series of humiliations, major and minor, and in therapy some of them began to surface. Holt's birth, when Jack was three, had been in itself a kind of displacement. In response Jack had developed great reservoirs of rage. His anger could be formidable, and Jack himself worried about it, about his heredity, about his guilt. "One of the things he talked about was that his dad had once lost control of his anger and, at least the way it was related to him, had almost killed his stepfather. I know of one incident—I don't know when it was—that Jack Spicer once hit his brother with a brick on the head." Those who knew Jack remembered displays, always—and horrendously—verbal, of just such strong feelings. In therapy Jack rehearsed the teenage scenario of many gay adolescents, humiliation by a gym teacher. This one criticized Jack unmercifully for his poor coordination. In a way, he said, it would have been easier to have a wooden leg; something that would explain why you couldn't do the things that the other kids could do.

Even his dentist—"that ass!"—humiliated him by telling him he had been brushing his teeth "all wrong," even though he had no cavities. To Dr. Coren he reported that after such a lecture, "he had stopped brushing them entirely. He had been criticized for something that in fact he must have been doing well enough because he didn't have any problem." The doctor knew well enough that he, too, was another authority figure, and asked about Jack's feelings toward him. "Well," Jack replied, "all fathers, dentists and psychiatrists are lumped together. But at this point I don't feel any anger at you, *yet*.'"[53]

As a young man Jack's awkwardness and ugliness caused him a great deal of anguish. "It was more than his being gay," said a Berkeley classmate. "He was like a Neanderthal man, and there was nobody who was interested in Neanderthal, at that point. Maybe he could have found someone now, since guys have gone kinkier."[54] "He's so ugly he doesn't deserve to have sex," said another Berkeley quipster.[55] In Palo Alto his boss was giving him mixed signals. "Why haven't you moved to Palo Alto?" he'd say, and

Jack would get the distinct impression he'd be treated a lot better if he did, or that if he did move the job would continue. Finally, in January, he announced, "I might be able to move in April," and the boss turned around and said, "Too bad your job will be over in February."⁵⁶

Coren noted Spicer's social concerns:

He was concerned throughout with society issues, it seems to me. He was the first person to talk to me about the Vietnam War. He was very sensitive to the idea of society making people do things counter to what he thought people should be free to choose. That troubled him. I mean I think it was his personal experience, that way, also. But that did trouble him. So I remember he came in and talked about it—I think the bombing had started, one of the escalation points about which at that point I wasn't very sensitive. Later on I became sensitive to it, partly because of Mr. Spicer's talking about it. He was quite upset about it.

He talked about the job and how he felt in Palo Alto [when he was moved from part-time to full-time employment]—how it was, whether he was losing his mind, or what? He came in and talked about that and whether he should quit or not. What that would mean . . . would things get worse for him? . . .

Spicer continued a few days later on—this is now the 8th of February of '65—on could he make use of his poetry commercially; and he talked about this conflict in using his poetry for money. [Coren reads from his notes.] He's frightened. If he considers poetry to come from a part of himself that feels so foreign he wonders if he's schizophrenic. And he wonders "Can he feel this gulf within himself?" [A long pause.] Yeah, he was also, in regard to this, the idea of selling himself out, or what he does do for other people, there was an example about "Should he go to bed with a woman for his analyst?"—that thought occurred to him. It was right in connection with that Spicer wonders whether he should send his poetry to *The Nation*.⁵⁷

By the last week of April 1965 Dr. Coren had begun to register a lot of resistance from his patient. Jack had "fairly strong feelings about not wanting to come." Dr. Coren went out of town to attend some professional meetings during the first part of May, but he reminded Jack of their next appointment, on the evening of May 10. Spicer failed to show. A few nights later, on the 14th, Coren called the number he had listed as a contact, "and a woman answered"—Fran Herndon, of course. Would Jack be coming to therapy the following Monday? he asked. "Didn't he let you know?" Fran said. "Jack left tonight for Vancouver; he might not be back for several months."

Did Spicer profit by these sessions? Dr. Coren noted that during the therapy Spicer quit using Miltowns, a "minor tranquilizer"; the drug was a predecessor of Librium and Valium. Fresh from the last poem of *Language*, Jack told him that:

he felt he would be freer to talk about poetry [now]; he was somewhat afraid that therapy might interfere, if he talked too much about it. His feeling was that poetry is dictated to him from the outside. He particularly felt that strong[ly] since he did the poems *After Lorca* in '57. At that point he felt as if Lorca was actually writing the poems through him, that he sort of translated some of the poems. And he made a comment which wasn't clear to me at that point: There are times he doesn't recognize himself in what he said in the poems; he's surprised at what he says. That was different than in dreams. Which is interesting to me, because usually you think of dreams as being also closer to the creative process or primary experience. But he does recognize himself in dreams. That's why he doesn't feel that the poems just come from another part of his own mind. Much more different. Then in fact he talked about himself as John Spicer, the person, and Jack Spicer, the poet. He says a compliment to his poetry is like saying to someone "You have a famous brother."[58]

A number of young writers from New York joined the Spicer circle this year. Because all had some college education and two of them came from Catholic homes, they became known as "the Jesuits." Andy Cole and Tom Wallace, both from Brooklyn Catholic backgrounds, came onto the scene. They were soon joined by Larry Kearney, also from Brooklyn.

Kearney had known Andy Cole at the State University of New York at Binghamton. There Kearney had become interested in the work of Duncan and Spicer from reading Don Allen's anthology, and from listening to the poets' recorded voices on the Evergreen LP "San Francisco Poets Reading," the companion record to the 1957 *Evergreen Review* issue of "The San Francisco Scene." He listened to it a lot when drunk—to Duncan's oracular "This Place Rumord to Have Been Sodom," and Spicer's insistent, edgy "Psychoanalysis: An Elegy." Playing the record became sort of an obsession. And he was restless at school. He called Cole and Wallace, who were staying at Nemi Frost's apartment at Grant and Union. There was no more room at that inn, but if he was really serious about coming, they promised to look for a place for the three of them. He hung up the phone, committed already.

The morning Kearney arrived in San Francisco he took a cab to North Beach and walked into the first bar he saw, an inconspicuous place in the middle of the block. As it happened, the bar was Gino & Carlo's. Larry checked into the Swiss-American Hotel, opposite Mike's Pool Parlor on Broadway; hung out with his Binghamton friends at Nemi's; tried a couple of the bars everyone talked about. Life was pleasant. At Nemi's he met Tom Field, Stan Persky, and Gary Snyder. Joanne Kyger lived across the hall. Larry had never seen apartments decorated so dramatically as these, with plants, pictures, and mirrors everywhere. He felt far from Brooklyn. Stan gave him a copy of the latest *Open Space*—he thought it arcane and somewhat frivolous: but within a few weeks his poems would be appearing in the next issues. He was being drawn into a world of poetry and bohemia for which Binghamton had not prepared him.

Then, one night in Gino's, he met Jack Spicer. Larry was sitting at a table by the jukebox when Jack came into the bar, talking with Graham Mackintosh and two others, and Larry joined the conversation. Spicer was charming. The next day, after Larry learned who he had been talking to, his interest deepened. He was twenty-one years old.

After two weeks Larry moved, with Andy and Tom, into an apartment at 1156 Kearny Street—a grim place, but a handy location some two blocks from the Green Street bars. Larry first took a job repairing ovens in Daly City. Another job, at Architectural Models, on Brannan Street, south of Market, lasted three-and-one-half months.[59] The days were all the same: the drinking was pretty heavy, and the bars conveniently located. San Francisco was hot and hazy in April 1964. The gang spent a lot of time drinking on the roof of Nemi's building. "It took me awhile to get my balance," Larry remembered. "I don't know if I ever got it, to tell you the truth."

At Gino & Carlo's Spicer and Kearney developed "a funny relationship. Jack was capable of great intimacy, a kind of kids' thing of being understood at the level of the in-joke, the remark that means one thing to two people at the table, but something quite special to a third person at the table. He had a very expressive face and when he was talking to you he would project an intimate concern over what you were thinking or saying. He gave me a copy of *Billy The Kid* and said, 'I think you're ready for this now.'" Spicer told Larry that he, not Helen Adam, had been the true winner of the Ingram-Merrill Award; that he, in a grand act of pity for one even needier than himself, had had it "transferred" to Adam.[60] Kearney believed Jack and was suitably impressed by his generosity. But the fantasy spun by Spicer was not created solely to seduce Kearney: it was also a desperate man's dream of rescue from the poverty, humiliation, and excess that were plunging him closer and closer to the edge.

Soon baseball season was upon them, and Jack and the "Jesuits" took Nemi Frost to Candlestick Park for her first ballgame. Frost recalled:

Before we got to the ballpark, we had to drive miles out of the way to a certain deli where Jack got a certain submarine sandwich. I couldn't believe it. Right in the ballpark you can get beer and hot dogs, but Jack said, "You never want to eat that garbage at the ballpark. It's a—" I don't think they had the expression "ripoff" then, but you know . . .

So our seats are in the bleachers, right? We were the only white faces up there, or just about. Andy and Kearney and [Nemi's boyfriend] Tom Wallace. Then me and then Jack. And next to Jack were his famous Rainier ales, right?

Between innings, Tom Wallace saw someone he knew and ran up to say "Hi" to him, and Larry and Andy were off someplace. Jack opened his sixteen-ounce Green Death in the hot sun, where it had been sitting for an hour, ready to explode.

Whzzz! Old Faithful! All over, all over these tough blacks; it went everywhere. It wouldn't stop, it went on and on and on! Tom Wallace looked down and saw it happening and he decided to stay up and talk to his friend. I said, "Thanks a lot!" One guy pulls out a knife—he didn't do anything, but he was just like—*really.*

Spicer pretended that it was, like, not even happening. Either he didn't care, or he cared so much that he pretended it didn't happen. He didn't do anything to stop it. He just sat there on the bench. Spraying. Forever . . . It was just amazing that we didn't get murdered. Everyone was saying, "You motherfucker—you goddamn honky"—ohhh—and Jack was totally oblivious. That was my first baseball game.[61]

Kearney, too, remembered this dangerous game. "He could have gotten us killed."[62]

Jack's activities were becoming increasingly curtailed. He stopped reading anything other than mysteries, science fiction, books on chess and bridge, and the *Chronicle*, though once Larry noticed him perusing a paperback copy of Norman Mailer's *Superman at the Supermarket.* He went occasionally to poetry events, such as the well-publicized, well-attended reading at Fugazi Hall, on Friday, June 12, 1964. During the reading, which the poets called "Freeway," Jack kept up a nonstop, fairly quiet patter poking fun at the readers: Philip Whalen, Lew Welch, and Gary Snyder. He continued to go to Gino's, and to Aquatic Park. Every time Larry went to the park, he saw Jack there, sitting in the sun, proud of being able to tell the time of day by the shadows the sun cast next to him on the grass.

When Kearney first came to North Beach, there was much discussion of the "Pacific Nation," which was to become a concept of importance during the rest of Spicer's life. Desperate to salvage something from the noises of consumerism, strident capitalism, and vulgarity, Jack had proposed a "Pacific British Commonwealth formed from the Tehachapi Mountains all the way up the coast to northern Canada and perhaps even Alaska" that "would not include Los Angeles." The new nation would be an entity of healthily unlikeminded peoples in a geographically stunning, western-toned, desperately real fantasy of landscapes and economies adequate and undemanding, *Pacific* in all aspects of this notion.[63] Harold Dull published a poem on this subject summarizing its aims:

Pacific Nation

Our entry in the World Almanac
PACIFIC NATION Area: Not available.
No way has yet been found to measure
both the parts visible and the invisible.
Population: Likewise. A mere handful
and/or legion. *Language*: Poetry.
Capital: San Francisco was once thought
to be but I doubt it now. *Principal*
Product: Poetry. *Longest Rivers*: Yes.
Highest Mountains: Yes. *Deepest Lakes*:
Yes. *System of Government*: No. Or at
least no one likes to think there is.
Religion: Likewise. *Additional*
Information: See IMAGINATION. See JACK
SPICER. See FOG. See OIL SPILLS. See
LONELINESS[64]

Spicer told Robert Kelly he was a member "of the California Republican Army which hopes by violent means to reestablish an independent California which will ally itself with France and China."[65] Maps of the Pacific Nation were being drawn up. There was jockeying for important positions in the new government—who would be Secretary of State? Who Culture Minister? Kearney found it all "pretty boring."[66] He found Spicer's connection to Philip K. Dick more interesting: when Larry brought Jack a copy of Dick's novel *Counter Clockwise World*, Spicer said bashfully, "I know Phil Dick!"[67] Dick's novel begins with a scene right out of Spicer's later poetry—a man approaches a hot dog vendor at Aquatic Park and receives a slip of paper that reads "HOT DOG." There was a strange confluence in the work of the two writers, since Spicer's theories of dictation, of the "Outside," resemble Dick's later vision of VALIS to a remarkable degree. VALIS, Dick's acronym for the "Vast Active Living Intelligence System" that permeates our universe without mercy, only unintelligible revelation, is as scary as anything in Spicer.[68] (The "Pacific Nation" itself is anticipated in references to the "PSA" [Pacific States of America] in Dick's 1962 novel *The Man in the High Castle*.)

Larry Kearney was straight, and Spicer was openly gay, "but I never really had a strong sexual take on him. He never made any sexual overtures to me at all, ever. He did in print, but personally he kept it at 'good friends.'" In print? Soon after they met, Jack began to write his "Love Poems" to Larry, printing them in *Open Space*. ("Love Poems" were complete by August, five months since their meeting.) Larry was flattered, but uncomfortable too: "The assumption was that I was yet another young literary hustler from the East Coast looking to make it big. I was cast in a mold that didn't fit. I wasn't hustling anybody for anything. I had no problem with Jack on the sexuality. What set me on edge was the clubbiness of the scene, the bitchiness, particularly in the position I was in, because I was a newcomer."

He was embarrassed when his role in Spicer's life became a matter of public scrutiny and innuendo. The incident began with Spicer's own crotchety "Protestant Letter" to the editor, published in *Open Space*:

Dear Stan Persky [I add the last name because I am sick of the tea-party first-name business, my fault as well as yours, as if Open Space were a Turkish Bath of the imagination]:

The only poem that interested me in the whole July issue (including my own) was the rhymed poem called "Underwier" about halfway through the issue. Though the signature to it is given as Lew Ellingham, he tells me that the authors, in tandem, were you, Ron Primack, and Jim Alexander. The poem seems to me better than anything the three of you have written in the last two years and I wonder why you did not give your names to it.

Something happened. It isn't happening often enough now and I wonder if the accusation against Open Space is not that it is too homosexual but that it is too homogenous. Like cartons of milk. . . .

I am, nonetheless, submitting poems to this August issue and will continue to even if things get worse.

Sincerely yours
—Jack Spicer

Was the magazine "too homosexual"? By refocusing on art, Spicer perhaps saved the magazine from the hostility of the half of its contributors who were in fact heterosexual. He was an ideal figure to raise the problem since he uniquely enjoyed the confidence of the entire contributor/readership. Spicer's complaint about the course of the magazine piqued Stan. He was caught between three masters who would have discomfited any editor: his lover, Robin Blaser, who sought an artistic décor; Jack Spicer, who had served as Stan's teacher and promoter for many years; and Robert Duncan, who felt the magazine was useful in preserving the peace of the group. In addition, the contributors as a whole wanted to see the magazine continue, and strengthen. Because Stan knew that no one was actually prepared to consider an alternative to the magazine, he was able to reply to Spicer:

Dear Jack,

. . . Trying to figure out how to be fair to you is hard, who have so often used unfairness for your way. Even in my dreams you confuse me by two of you: Dirty Jack and Radiant Jack. In one part I come into your room, your back to me, I see your elbows in the holes of your shirt, the oily glass, the back of you looms up big as a ship, and you growl and tell me to give it up. In Radiant Jack you yourself come to the warehouse where we're working, wearing clean sports-clothes, and you have tickets to the ballgame for me. It isn't that you've given little or withheld too much—only last week you led me to a new friend, among the dead, where one has more luck with friendship than here—but it seems to me you want a world small enough so that wherever you spit you'll hit something, a world you can control. Though you've often shown how you can serve poetry, more and more often now it seems to exclude the music, paintings, statues, objects, adventures, I want in my rooms, my life—and the world isn't fixed.

You complain about my support of what I'm drawn to, and I'll try to amend slanted reporting, yet I've seen you play Colonel Tom Parker building up an Elvis Presley when you wanted to engineer and insure a sympathetic reading for someone who attracted you.

—Stan Persky[69]

The "Elvis" reference hurt Kearney and put Jack on the defensive. Pressed, he described his relation to Larry as purely avuncular: he said, as Kearney recalled, that "when young people come to town, they feel that they've been invited to a fancy dinner party and they don't know what to wear."[70] Yet Spicer was indeed in love with Kearney. George Stanley later commented, "Kearney was almost an image of the way Jack looked as a teenager—it was literally a *Doppelgänger*—with a big head and yet having prematurely a kind of alcoholic pinkness to his complexion. I don't think Jack ever expected anyone like that to turn up, but once Kearney turned up, it was inevitable that Jack would fall in love with him."[71] Everyone in the circle knew that the "Love Poems" in *Language* were dedicated to Larry, although technically they remain anonymous.[72] Kearney mused:

What Jack responded to in me—what he recognized and perhaps what other people recognized, but didn't respect—was my fear. Jack was possessed by fear and was acting in the face of it. I think Jack picked that up very fast in me. I know I picked it up in him. He seemed to understand exactly what [my fears] took out of me and what level of control I was maintaining. Even in those nine poems [the "Love Poems"]—Jack said something about "I see you cowering in the corner."[73]

I felt, many times, that even if the conversation was going around the table, we were talking to each other underneath that conversation. There were a lot of emotional fears and attitudes that were shared automatically as a general approach to the world. I think that's what it was. I loved Jack very much. Personally Jack was very important to me. What he's left me, though, is relatively impersonal, and much more important.[74]

Another of Spicer's poems in *Language* stemmed from Lew Ellingham's work for the Sierra Club, where he was editing a book *(Not Man Apart)* with a text of poems by Robinson Jeffers, surrounded by the images of well-known photographers who had worked in Big Sur—Ansel Adams, Edward Weston, and so forth. The bleak, romantic vision of Jeffers flavored North Beach for awhile, and Jack said that his poem reflected a Gino & Carlo's conversation he had had with Ellingham one evening just before he wrote it.

A redwood forest is not invisible at night. The blackness covers it but it covers the blackness.

If they had turned Jeffers into a parking lot death would have been eliminated and birth also. The lights shine 24 hours a day on a parking lot.

True conversation is the effort of the artist and the private man to keep things true. Trees and the cliffs in Big Sur breathe in the dark. Jeffers knew the pain of their breath and the pain was the death of a first-born baby breathing.

Death is not final. Only parking lots.[75]

In the autumn of 1964, Ellingham arranged a meeting between David Brower—then executive director of the Sierra Club—and Spicer and Blaser. They had dinner at Nick's, an Italian seafood restaurant in Spicer's neighborhood at Polk and Sutter.

In the wake of Ellingham's work on *Not Man Apart*, Spicer and Blaser had proposed a project to Brower on California poetry, related both to Spicer's "language map" work at Berkeley and to the earlier Pearsall-Erickson anthology *The Californians*. They planned an ambitious and innovative anthology, covering three stages of California poetry. The first was nineteenth-century Frontier poetry, including that of the earlier Spanish period and probably ending with the Carmel group of Jeffers, Mary Austin, and Lincoln Steffens. The second period took California poetry through the Second World War, with Rexroth perched on the dividing line, and the third focused on the postwar period. The idea was to cover the state, not just southern and northern California, but rural areas as well (Mary Austin might represent the Owens Valley, for example; Jeffers, Big Sur); and not only "literature" would be included, but epehemera and historical texts (gold-rush newspapers, letters, Spanish sources, and even Indian legends). It would create a grid covering both time and place, like the Regional Atlas Spicer had spent so many years working on. Nothing ever came of this; Brower was never given a text. Blaser recalled, "We were working on the anthology of California poetry, and—Jack didn't do anything. That was so unlike Jack. I was grabbing books, trying to read the most God awful stuff, and we were going to make maps—there may be bits and pieces of this God-awful project left someplace or another. But he couldn't do anything. He would *do* awful things one way or another, and then there was no feeling about it. None. There was no engagement at all. It didn't matter at all."[76]

Much of the excitement of North Beach (as the Spicer circle understood it) came from the life flowing in the streets and bars and the habitats of its citizens. Lew Ellingham's column in *Open Space* gave a dramatic picture of life—and crime—in Gino & Carlo's bar:

Arriving in Gino's one evening about mid-month, Donato, one of the bar owners and then on duty behind the bar, called me over to say with some excitement, "Did you hear about the hold up?"

"No."

Joe, a retired bar owner and cook, the only other customer in the place at the moment, said, "Yeah, to us an' Jack Spice. He come in, the man, he once had a tab here, an' Jack an' somebody else (Gary Snyder) was at the table. He had a gun an' the other guy went away an' Jack got up for the first time I see him polite when he say, 'Now look, I've only gotten three hours sleep every night this week and I have to get up at 6:30 to go to Stanford' an' Jack walks for the door but the gun's still at his back up his coat. Then the guy turns on Donato an' say 'How much cash are you insured for?' an' Donato say, 'We don't have insurance,' an' he say to me with the gun, 'How much money do you have?' an' I say I'm drinking on tab here, I'm broke. So they all go away."

I saw Jack the next night and asked him about the incident. Jack said, "You mean the water pistol?" We spoke of the would-be offender, someone known to us both. Then en route to the pin-ball machine, where every conversation ends, Jack concluded, "Oh well, you know how crazy he is."[77]

By the summer months of 1964, the monthly issues of *Open Space* were ripe with many tastes, with poets such as Michael McClure, Joanne Kyger, and Richard Duerden, as well as Harold Dull and Larry Fagin, Larry Kearney and Jamie MacInnis, mixtures of the new and old.[78] Charles Olson's essay, "Against Wisdom as Such," again raised its head in *Open Space* 8. Stan Persky reprinted Olson's essay to give a focus to the debate over "wisdom" and "poetry" that concerned the circle of poets now publishing in the magazine. In issue 8, too, was work by Jim Alexander. Four years before, Spicer's "love poem"—*The Heads of the Town Up to the Aether*—had been directed toward him. This time Spicer's "Love Poems" were aimed at Larry Kearney, another example of Jack's hopeless but beautifully worked fabric of "words, loves."

George Stanley continued to live with Bill Brodecky, but by the end of 1964 he was in love with Armando Navarro, despite the limits Armando's heterosexuality imposed on the relation. Spicer could not accept this new attraction, nor George's acceptance and celebration of a new popular mindlessness which such phenomena as the Beatles and Bob Dylan implied. Spicer "absolutely hated the jukebox," George recalled, "especially when music like the Beatles began to come in. The Beatles really were the end for Spicer. He hated their kind of soupy romanticism, which made the things people talked about seem irrelevant—religion and politics. The hippie thing just sort of wiped all that with a paintbrush with rainbow paint on it."[79]

As suggested by a poem in *Book of Magazine Verse*—"The Beatles, devoid of form and color, but full of images."—Spicer was hostile to the Beatles, for breaking up conversations in bars with electric guitars on jukeboxes and for representing a consumerist culture forced upon a defenseless population by exploiters with neither conscience nor taste (Spicer's view). All of his group—except him—adored the Beatles. Joanne Kyger, newly returned from Japan, where Beatlemania had not yet hit, had only the vaguest idea of which Beatle was which, but dragooned Spicer and Richard Brautigan into collaborating on a fan letter.[80] To further annoy Jack, George Stanley and Larry Fagin developed a routine, so that whenever the jukebox played "If I Fell," the love theme from *A Hard Day's Night*, they would act it out in American Sign Language.[81]

George's life with Bill Brodecky did not survive his new experiments toward love and situation; they had been together three years when it ended early in 1965. George's poems of this period, later collected into his volume *Beyond Love*, were based on Classical themes and his passion for Armando; both the poetry and the passion drew down Spicer's wrath. "He didn't like the poems at all! There was a real difference of opinion there: Duncan thought my translation of *Orpheus in the Underworld* [from the *Georgics* of Virgil] was wonderful. And someone asked Spicer—I was too timorous to ask myself—'What did you think of that poem?' And he said, 'That *poem* made me never want to *hear about* Orpheus and Eurydice again!'"[82]

Inside the September issue of *Open Space* a drawing by Jess serves as a kind of internal cover, or door, into and within the magazine. Hidden, almost, is a Latin 9—IX—suggestive of mysteries yet undisclosed. (Undisclosed, too, was the issue itself. Stan Persky distributed very few copies of this issue to prevent collectors from assembling whole runs of the magazine for later sale. Only the contributors to the particular issue and a few friends therefore were given this number.) By the final issues of the magazine, at the end of 1964, Stan Persky had widened the circle of writers and artists. Along with the regular contributors the entire community became involved, reflecting, perhaps, the changes that were taking place at the Spicer table at Gino & Carlo's bar, where the balance began to lean toward the affairs of youthful and heterosexual players in the games of love and writing.

When *Open Space* was announced Ron Loewinsohn, for example, was "suspicious of the whole enterprise. I thought it was another in-groupy thing: everybody talking to each other by their first names." So even though Persky put his name on the list of people to receive free copies of the magazine, and offered him "open space" to publish anything he might produce during the year of 1964—the skeptical Loewinsohn decided to have nothing to do with the project. "I was very righteous and sort of turned my back on the whole thing." In early 1964 Loewinsohn left San Francisco on a four-month tour with his wife, Joan, and his travels brought him to Albuquerque, where he met with Robert Creeley.

Together the poets discussed the literary situation in San Francisco, including the *Open Space* project. Creeley advised Loewinsohn to drop his skepticism and welcome the support of a serious critical community, advancing his own Black Mountain experience as an example. On his return to San Francisco Loewinsohn began to give Persky the sections of his current project, the long poem *The Step*, as he wrote them. "It was tremendously useful to be writing a long poem and to be able to publish it in progress, and able to get instant feedback on it. Part of that book is 'Lots of Lakes,' which is dedicated to Jack Spicer. It takes off on Jack's poem about 'Death is not final. Only parking lots.' ['Lots of Lakes'] is a kind of parody, but also a *hommage* to Jack, and to a certain extent to George Stanley also. Jack told me when that issue of *Open Space* came out, that George Stanley came to the bar and said, 'Did you see what Ron did to us?'" Here Loewinsohn mimicked Stanley's laugh.[83]

This was a world, too, that loved its jokes. Not even so august a figure as Don Allen was spared. The cover of *Open Space* 11 displayed a photo of an emperor penguin, which stands "about three feet eight inches tall"; the photo was overlaid with a motto saying, "The Penguin Anthology of Contemporary American Verse, edited by Donald M. Allen." Persky would not have expected Allen to like this spoof of the new Penguin *Anthology* he had edited with Robert Creeley; nor would Persky have cared whether Allen liked it or not. There were few sacred cows. Spicer portrayed as foibles— or perhaps as more sinister—Blaser's reputed elegance and Duncan's alleged self-aggrandizing in myth and thought. Lesser victims of Jack's spite

"Jack Spicer," etching by Ariel. *Courtesy of the artist.*

or contempt were beyond the pale: they wrote or studied "verse," not poetry. The jokes were often cruel, the minions blindly faithful. Their purpose—as a circle—was to forge, and reforge, a world bonded by ardent belief and tempered by the humor of people living in the easy styles of a
bohemian community. Humor, in fact, was a rich resource for Jack, and for
many within the circle, saving both from the worst taints of fanaticism.

What were the alternatives to "the big, gray" English departments of estab-
lishmentarian orthodoxy? Persky suggested that Spicer may have found
one fundamental to the vocation of making poetry:

Spicer was always grousing about one thing or another. But the main thing was
that he spoke with absolute authority. As he delivered some statement about how
the poetic world operated, it was delivered with an authenticity nobody else had.
What was built into the authenticity of those statements: "Poetry is important."
"This is to be paid attention to." "This is serious." "This is a realm of being and existence and meaning beyond what is visible in the ordinary world." He proposed
that there was a secret meaning to the world, and poetry revealed it. All this stuff
that you did, like listen to ballgames or get your ass wet because the grass leaked
through the *Chronicle*, all that was a part of life. But the secret meaning of life was
there were ways of being true to poetry, and you had to live so that you were true
to poetry. He provided a model for your life, and seemed to do it with great rigor,

although to anybody who didn't know him he would seem to be an ungainly person who hung out in bars and the park, younger people around him. But the main thing was, this poetry stuff was for real. You practice it honestly or falsely, and Spicer advocated you practice it honestly. There were constant examples of those who had taken false roads, fallen off to various hells of their own devising. Duncan came in for criticism by Spicer.

Its nature? "Well," said Persky, "that Duncan had ceased to write real poems."[84]

Spicer was a voracious reader. Gail Chugg recalled hearing him talk about "the James Bond novels, Robert Heinlein's *The Green Hills of Earth*, John Horne Burns's *The Gallery* [Spicer saying to Chugg, "It's marvelous when that dead soldier comes in"], Walter A. Miller's *A Canticle for Leibowitz* [Spicer remarking on the wonder of the ending with the birth of the girl child]."[85] Graham Mackintosh and Larry Fagin both recalled Spicer's praise of Alfred Bester, whose career in the 1950s included two important novels, *The Demolished Man* and *The Stars My Destination*, and several collections of stories, including Spicer's favorite, *The Dark Side of the Earth*.[86] Other writers read by Spicer include the southern California novelists Erle Stanley Gardner, creator of Perry Mason, and John Fante, the then-little-known social realist and author of *Ask the Dust* and *Wait until Spring, Bandini*.[87] In a letter written to Blaser in 1956 Jack advised Barbellion's *Journal of a Disappointed Man* ("Marvellous and would be special food for your poetry"), and "for sheer bitchy fun," Angus Wilson's then-new novel *Anglo-Saxon Attitudes*.[88] Among his contemporaries, he ranked Duncan's and Blaser's poetry high, and told George Stanley he thought Thomas Merton's poetry "really good." He also loved Hart Crane's "Chaplinesque." About Olson, George recalled, Spicer was up and down. He thought *The Maximus Poems* "bullshit," but "recognized that Olson at times wrote a good poem, like "Let the Dead Now Prey Upon Us.""[89] Later, Spicer told Kearney that Charles Olson was the "best poet in the country," and in a drunken argument in Gino & Carlo's insisted to Jamie MacInnis that Lawrence's *Birds, Beasts and Flowers* was the best book of poetry written in the twentieth century, and that "The Ship of Death" was the century's single greatest poem.[90]

Month by month, Spicer's isolation—professional isolation, social anger—became more pronounced. He seemed to cultivate it as if it were a small, prosperously vivid garden. Graham Mackintosh offered to publish Larry's poetry, against Jack's advice. "You're not ready to publish," Jack said flatly. "If you do, I'll never again read anything you write." Kearney thought and responded, "Well, I'm sorry about that. But I'm going to publish a

book." There was silence; then Jack chuckled and said, "We'll still be goddamn good friends."

Though Graham Mackintosh was nominally the publisher of White Rabbit Press, most of the circle realized that Spicer was the gray eminence, the
ultimate arbiter. Had his threat to stop the publication of Larry's book been
a real one, the book might never have appeared. Paul Alexander recalled
that Spicer stopped the publication of at least one White Rabbit book:

Graham had arranged with Nemi and James Keilty to bring out a book of one of
James Keilty's short one-act plays. Nemi did five, or maybe ten illustrations. She
did a lot. They were quite fine. It was all well underway before Spicer heard about
it, and he just squelched it right away, right then and there. Graham's work was
broken up, and the play was unpublished, and Nemi's drawings were unpublished. I don't know what Keilty thought about it, but Nemi just shrugged it off.
"C'est la guerre"—"that's just the way it is." Of course, Spicer wasn't objecting to
Nemi's drawings, he was objecting to James Keilty's play. Probably the main reason
is that he hadn't been in at the ground floor, but certainly he didn't approve of the
writing. That was a terribly destructive thing Jack did.[91]

A few weeks after *Fifteen Poems* appeared, Larry was sitting at the bar in
Gino's and Jack said, "There are two real poems in your book. I'm not
going to tell you which ones they are." This was, realized Larry, Spicer's
way of burying the hatchet. Kearney reflected:

His investigations were always into whether or not you were one of the Enlightened. He was very concerned about that. You *can* assume that there are people who
are in touch with poetry. They're not necessarily *above* anyone else. If Jack was aristocratic, it was a spiritual aristocracy, that was, pretty much, I guess, Calvinist. You
were marked.

When it came down to it, if "poetry" was there, Jack would disregard any of
that. I would be fairly certain that he had a certain measure of contempt for the
popularization of the Eastern tradition. Any body of knowledge or revealed wisdom Jack would pick what seemed true or important. The rest of it: the hell with
it. It didn't matter. To actually attach yourself to a whole body of thought didn't
seem to be in his emotional make-up.

All Jack's prejudices were right on the surface. As far as I'm concerned they
were essentially trivial. If somebody came into the bar and was just too loud or
played the jukebox he was a "New York Beatnik." It didn't matter where they came
from. Spicer was concerned about getting the poetry down in as accurate a form as
possible. I think everything he did he did to facilitate the transmission. He found a
form that was reasonably adequate, at least as much as it could be, to what he was
doing. One of the things I took from exposure to Jack was my own conviction that
there isn't anything but content.[92]

By urgings and leaps the message got across.

Spicer's affection for Larry Kearney, the feeling that prompted the "Love Poems" of *Language*, was darkened, or perhaps deepened, by Kearney's own deep attachment to the poet Jamie MacInnis. The daughter of a legendary trial lawyer, MacInnis was a woman of deep poise, moving with ease between the worlds of the upper class and the bohemian Beat. Among the habitués of Gino & Carlo's, she stood out: her shining young health, beautiful bone structure, precise speech, and fine skin were a reproach to the pasty male drinkers she mixed with. She was stylish, outspoken, and lovely. Under the lights of the bar, her brown hair glowed with red and blonde tints; her Irish eyes were sparkling and green. She had been a student at the Convent of the Sacred Heart in Pacific Heights, had had crushes on curates, had feared and admired the nuns there. By the time her relationship to Spicer began, MacInnis had already met, married, and left Alvin Light, a sculptor who taught at the Art Institute, and had borne a daughter, Lulu Light. She was extravagantly talented as a poet.

To Spicer she brought an intensity and religious feeling that attracted and repelled him. When they met, she offered herself to him in a direct, almost Iphigenia-like way, and he retreated, appalled. Dora FitzGerald remembered her habit of waiting on his doorstep, until all hours of the night, hoping for another glimpse of her hero.[93] For several years she had coped with his sexual rejection in a time-honored way, by flinging herself after the younger men in his circle, one after another, no matter their sexual preference. So strong was her will, and so striking her beauty, that she succeeded with even the most unlikely. Now it was Kearney's turn.

Larry Kearney first saw MacInnis across the barroom at Gino & Carlo's, a few weeks after his arrival in San Francisco in the spring of 1964. "I was sitting at the table and Jamie had her back to me, sitting at the bar. There was a shock of recognition. I asked Jack who that was: he grimaced, very painfully, and said something like, 'That's Jamie MacInnis and if you fall in love with her I'm going to throw up.'"

"He was quite clear about her," Larry remembered; yet in fact, Jack's feelings toward Jamie MacInnis were decidedly mixed. He was intrigued by her wealth and confidence, her roots in the colorful California history he loved. She resembled his early love, Kate Mulholland, to the extent that the fathers of both women wielded great powers in California society, law, and finance. And Jamie had an added allure—a gift for poetry that rivaled that of his very best disciples. Like Helen Adam, she was a female Sagittarius, with some of the magic, talent, and restlessness of Adam. On the other hand, MacInnis's adventurous sexuality disturbed and alienated Spicer at the same time that it attracted him. Her taste for competition and rivalry led to some curious versions of that old figure, the romantic triangle.

Despite Spicer's threats, Kearney did fall in love with MacInnis, and almost at once. They had little in common; even their tastes in fiction and poetry were decidedly different. Jamie had only recently returned from a long stay in New York, where she'd lived with Larry Fagin. Although Jack had warned Fagin against MacInnis, claiming that she was evil and incapable of love, the besotted Fagin had ignored him, abandoning San Francisco for the East Village with Jamie the previous summer. The couple amicably shared a flat with another exile, Ron Primack, on Avenue C at 8th in the East Village. Harold Dull, who had followed Dora and Russell FitzGerald to the Lower East Side after their elopement in 1962, was still lingering in New York, and Fagin and MacInnis stayed with Harold through the winter of 1963–64. On their return to San Francisco, and to Spicer's table at Gino's, their romance ended. Jack could now point to Fagin's heartbreak and use him "as an example of somebody [Jamie] had sort of walked over," Fagin said. "But Jack loved Jamie's poetry. Jamie was the first woman on the scene since Joanne Kyger that had any currency as an artist, as a poet."

Kearney ignored Jack's imprecations against Jamie much as Fagin had. Like Dumas's Armand, he knew that his liaison with this woman—the Marguerite of North Beach, with some of Marguerite's incipient sickness— would offend his "father," but he had fallen in love. He looked forward to meeting Jamie's daughter, Lulu, who lived with Alvin Light and his new wife. Together Jamie and Larry watched as Lulu rode the carousel at Golden Gate Park, and Larry felt oddly joined to them both. He understood Jamie's diffidence about her own motherhood; she didn't feel like a fit mother; and he wasn't ready to be a father; it was as though they were kids, playing at being a family, but with a real baby who could be conveniently lodged elsewhere once the merry-go-round came to a halt. On a regular basis, a check would arrive in Jamie's mailbox from her father's law firm, and once a week her mother's maid came by with sacks of groceries. The love affair between Larry and Jamie enraged Spicer, who would leave the bar pointedly when they walked in. At the same time, the couple began to find the homosexual cabal trying, an "impossible situation." Kearney recalled that in a Polk Street bar, while he looked on, Jamie provoked Stan Persky by mocking Robin Blaser's affected elegance. "Stan said, 'How would you like it if we took you out in the alley and gang-raped you?' She said, 'Oh dear, do you really consider yourselves a gang?' That was the general feeling."

In the last analysis, Jack's melancholia prevailed against his rage and bitterness. Larry's love for Jamie was no unforgivable sin, "just—as far as he was concerned—one more proof that something was fucked up in men's minds. His general position was that I was a babe in the woods, and that she was taking advantage of me. It's part of his mythology. As far as Jack was concerned Jamie hexed the pinball machine just by being there. He said she was a witch," Larry said. Jamie's clarity, the pith of her quick intelligence, the accuracy of her aim in jokes and witticisms, the turns of her poems, all created an aura of powers hidden but potential. Her style was flavored with an erotic musk, threatening to the shy, gay, and vulnerable Jack Spicer. In any case Jack felt a degree of responsibility as art master and duenna, and was alert to possible disturbances in the magic rhythms of the situations he devised and proposed.

Kearney saw how Jamie affected Jack. "Jamie was a sexual threat to Jack. She made heterosexual advances at him and scared the shit out of him." One evening, at Jamie's apartment on Geary near Kaiser Hospital, Jack read some of his new work. He was reading in public less and less often now, since his hysterical night-blindness, or the panic of his surroundings, gave him a good deal of trouble. Jamie made him so uncomfortable that he finally put down his manuscript and left.[94]

Cruelty was in the air. "All social intercourse at that time," recalled David Bromige, "with anyone who had any involvement in the aesthetic world might well have this Beat flavor to it, the put-on, that what was being said in fact was the opposite of what was meant; that people might be playing 'Get the Guest,' or 'Get the Guy from the Midwest,' as they do in [Albee's] *Virginia Woolf*, you know, from the same time period. That's the sensibility of that time, though it's very easy to forget that now. A lot of cruelty. It was a theater of cruelty."[95] Richard and Suzanne Duerden threw a party in their big two-story flat in the Haight where, with Ron Loewinsohn, Duerden published a little magazine called *The Rivoli Review* during what Ron called "the mimeograph magazine wars."[96] Duerden didn't invite Spicer "because he wouldn't have come." That didn't prevent Spicer from seeing it as a snub. At Gino & Carlo's Jack said, "Why didn't you invite me?" "It would have been very rhetorical," Duerden replied, and Spicer growled in return.[97]

At the party Larry and Jamie stood close together in the Duerdens' living room. Jamie pointed out Robert Duncan, who had been one of Larry's heroes since college, both from his battered record of the "San Francisco Poets Reading" and from the City Lights *Selected Poems*. Larry, a "relative kid," was thrilled, but Duncan dashed his hopes by giving both young people the cold shoulder. "He kind of looked at us and said, 'Who are *you*? The *Pepsi Generation*?' and walked out of the room."[98]

Kearney recalled a rash of spiteful remarks. "Jack was given to a lot of high-flown pronouncements about who he was going to abandon and cast into the outer darkness; pronouncements like 'The best thing anybody could do for Jamie is throw acid in her face: she'll never write anything good until her physical beauty is gone.'"[99]

Larry Fagin added:

And then there was Jamie; Jamie was extremely guarded, [but] she didn't want competition from anyone.

She didn't have self-confidence; she always put down her poetry. At the same time she was definitely in love with Jack Spicer in a very real, honest, direct way. She was very tentative, but very smart, certainly very tentative about her poetry. Jack was somewhat encouraging to her. But I don't think he actually totally took her under his wing because he saw that corruptive thing in her, too. Although she wasn't addicted at the time except that she drank a lot.[100]

The final issues of *Open Space* became a site on which Spicer, Kearney, Fagin, and MacInnis herself inscribed a poetry filled with desire and longing. This is "Ducks for Grownups," by MacInnis:

> In the rain the white ducks
> picked up or took
> all the moonlight that was meant for water.
> No swans were needed. Ducks
> in the dark take all the light from the sky
> and all the underwater light
> and float between
> and dare you.[101]

In a long poem, *Procris and Cephalus*, Fagin wrote:

> Poor fool, moving among men
> in the middle of becoming men
> Your heart keeps
> The Time she tells.
> Time piece of fool's gold
> tell men how she moves
> through the fair
> the forest and shadows
> sewn in pure air[102]

Larry Kearney, in *For Jamie*, wrote:

Because I have
loved you as much as
I can,
I have reached a limit;
at the garden wall.
Gardens have boundaries
and some idea
of perfection. The stone corner
like a dark chair
is an idea of autumn. And
still stone. A man's
garden shows how he
dresses his children.
Little people. This
is no garden of mine;
I drag enough
wherever I go,
the way my twilights
still flicker
in the light from the furnace.
I don't want it. Gardens
lie about terror. The idea
of Eden, with a gate,
lies about love.
Gardens with well-paved paths,
for cripples; gardens
with purple, profuse, for
sneaky geometricians.
I'm as sick of my
past as yours. I've
loved you as much as I
can. Bent there,
trailing ivy.[103]

The most oblique tribute to Jamie was Spicer's own, which became "Graphemics #5" when it was printed in *Language*. Jack and Jamie occasionally walked or took cabs or drove with others through the Broadway tunnel after Gino & Carlo's bar closed at 2 A.M.

You turn red and green like a traffic light. And in
    between them orange—a real courting color. Neither
The pedestrian or the driver knows whether he is going
    to hit the other. Orange
Being a courting color
Doesn't last long. The pedestrian

And the driver go back to the red and green colors of
    their existence. Unhit
Or hit (it hardly matters.)
When we walked through the Broadway tunnel I showed you
    signs above green lights which said "ON A RED LIGHT
    STOP YOUR CAR AND TURN OFF YOUR IGNITION."
    On an orange light—
But there was not an orange light
In the whole tunnel.[104]

CHAPTER ELEVEN

"The Chill in My Bones"

*T*he year of *Open Space* had ended, but those who thought Spicer might relapse into silence were confounded, for in January 1965, without a pause, the opening poems of the *Book of Magazine Verse* came to him after the last poems of *Language*. When T. S. Eliot died that month, Spicer was moved, and spoke to Larry Kearney of his admiration for *Four Quartets* and their attempt "to move into the dark, which was very important to him." Despite the "Canto for Ezra Pound," which he and Duncan and others had written in 1948, Spicer had never cared as much for Pound as he had for Eliot. Pound, he felt, lacked Eliot's courage—never went into the dark.[1] The deaths that January of both Eliot and Churchill were two more signs that an old world was passing, and he evoked their presences in the beginning of *Magazine Verse*. One world was dying: what new world would be born? In another country Spicer found a community of writers who appreciated his work, and the promise of a new career.

In February 1965 he boarded a plane to Vancouver, his first flight since a westbound jet had brought him and Joe Dunn to San Francisco nine years before. He had been invited to give a reading at the University of British Columbia, by the energetic expatriate professor Warren Tallman, on behalf of the Vancouver Poetry Society.[2]

For years Tallman had been inviting the New American poets to give readings on campus for an annual Festival of Contemporary Arts. (This is the "festival" of Spicer's later "Poems for the Vancouver Festival.") Duncan and W. D. Snodgrass had inaugurated the Festival in February 1961, and in successive Februarys Creeley and Ferlinghetti, Ed Dorn, and Michael McClure had each come north for this event. Beyond poetry, the Festival was filled with dance, music, architecture, fine arts, film, "you name it," Warren Tallman remembered.

This year Tallman asked Spicer and Lew Welch to come up and read from their work. Apprehensively he picked up a shattered Jack at the airport. Getting into the car, Jack asked, "Can we stop and get something to drink?"—his hands shaking uncontrollably. At the liquor store, Tallman offered to deal with the salesclerk, but "Jack refused to let me do the transaction. That was peculiar to, consistent with Jack now." He wore an invisible sign that read *do not touch me. Do not interfere with my physical activity.* So Warren stood back and let Jack complete the painful ritual of digging the bill out of his pocket and placing it in the clerk's hands. Once he had a few drinks inside him, he was steady and charming, ready to try to be nice to Lew Welch. Out of respect for the Tallmans, Spicer and Welch, no admirers of each other's work, made a concerted effort to maintain courtesy, but strain developed. "Lew was in a great, motor-mouth mood. He was drinking, too, and a walking anxiety case about his reading. He needed to talk. Jack and Lew got along rather well, considering; surprisingly so." Yet once in a while Jack would grimace over his shoulder with a pleading look that said, *Won't this guy ever shut up?*

The reading at UBC to an enthusiastic audience of three hundred, mostly students, was a great success. The room was jammed: even the cloakrooms behind the room were jammed with students—some of them interested in poetry, but many more "just caught onto the excitement." "Mid-February was the perfect time of the year," Tallman said, "to hold this Festival, because it's the worst time of the year: the students hate their profs, the profs hate their students, and the students don't want to study anyway. They more or less deserted their classes and went to the readings *en masse.*"[3] As Warren introduced Jack to the crowd, he remembered Blaser's admonitions. There might be a few problems with Jack, Robin had told the Tallmans. He might want to drink, and his nervousness might leave him high and dry in the middle of his reading. "Jack frequently blanked out visually, was not able to see the page. In time past he had had Robin step in and finish the reading for him." But no catastrophe occurred—the reading went well. Twenty-five-year-old Gladys Hindmarch was one of those who attended. "He gave an absolutely smashing reading. I've heard many a good reader: Olson at his very best, and Ginsberg doing the *Sunflower Sutra* in a way I've never heard on tape or elsewhere. This was just different, yet absolutely marvelous. It might have been the best reading I've ever been to in my life." At these noon hour readings, free lunches in brown paper bags were distributed, and normally the reading was plagued with the continuous rattle of paper. Seven minutes before the next period began, a buzzer would sound, and the resultant shuffle would terminate the reading. Not this time. "It was absolutely silent. Even when the buzzer went, they just stayed silent, let him finish what he was doing. Then we stood up and cheered. It was just terrific. Everybody knew they were in the presence of something really magical at that reading."[4]

The cheering amused Spicer, but of more interest was the appreciation given him by the local writers. "When you say 'poets' in Vancouver at that time, what you mean is about eight or ten poets. There were the downtown poets and the campus poets—the *Tish* poets and the UBC poets. There were also all their friends, their girlfriends, their boyfriends, their pals. They all knew about Jack, they'd been *waiting* to hear Jack Spicer read." Indeed, Spicer's visit united, if only temporarily, a number of disparate schools of poets, each with its own history, traditions, and agenda. The "downtown" poets, more Beat-influenced, were also more conversant with the visual arts than their campus counterparts. Both groups suffered in the shadow of the East: poets, even experimental poets of the large urban centers of Toronto and Montreal had the same sneering, majestic attitude toward Vancouver that New Yorkers had toward San Franciscans. Now, longing to burst from its "provincial" cocoon, Vancouver was ready for a messenger. This is not to say that Spicer was a unanimous success. The "downtown" poet Maxine Gadd, for one, spoke for several when she recalled Lew Welch as far nicer and sweeter than Spicer, who struck her from the first as a man "who disliked women."[5]

Jack proved to be a friendly, easy-going houseguest, with a few crotchets. The only way he slept at night, he said, was by reading detective novels until he dozed off. Once he prevailed upon Warren to take him to a downtown bookstore so he could get some of Ross Macdonald's latest private eye novels. At night he would take a bottle of brandy to his room, and curl up with Chandler or Macdonald. "We'd been warned, of course, that he could be a problem; but he wasn't at all."[6] Ellen Tallman saw the visit from a different angle. "I think," she said,

that Jack was annoyed by Lew being there. I don't think that Lew was exactly a favorite person. But Jack also was a person who liked to be there by himself. He liked the attention. And he gave good attention to everybody, to our children, and our cats. He was like a real member of the household. He *was* very bossy about cooking things. He would say, "You're *not* making rice without consommé in it? Put chicken broth in it!" He'd be quite bossy, and I'd say, "Jack, I'm sure I cook more than you ever do!" I mean, he had a few standards, that he probably learned from Robin. He'd say, "No, no, no! You listen to me!"

He was wonderful to have around, actually. He was extremely appreciative, and writing. It was wonderful to watch him. He would sit in the sun, with his glass, or cup, of brandy-and-milk, writing his baseball poems, which he'd read to us at night.[7]

Once back in the States, Spicer's emotional level wavered. On the one hand, his trip had been a success; he had read without night blindness, and the audience loved him. He had had a financial success, too—he had been paid a hundred dollars and had his airfare covered. "He felt really good," reported his analyst, "because it all seemed to fit within the confines of what he felt was appropriate to himself."[8] On the other hand, Jack's paranoia, fueled by alcohol, was on the upswing. Larry Kearney noticed that Spicer now "misread situations as a matter of course. Anybody who came into the bar in a threatening manner had a knife. 'Did you see the knife?' 'Did you see the gun?'" If a fight threatened, Jack would run into the big, boxy wooden telephone booth to protect himself. "He was always getting into tense difficulties."

His anxieties about being a passenger in a car returned: the memory of Tony Aste's accident in the Broadway Tunnel was again potent. One night Larry was driving him home from Gino's "and he was terrified." Tom Wallace, also a passenger, was urging Larry to drive faster, and although Larry had no intention of speeding, even the possibility traumatized Jack. "He just couldn't stand it," Larry recalled. "He said, *I know you've got tight control, but I've got to get out. I've got to get out.* So I dropped him around the corner."[9]

Larry Kearney saw Spicer from a variety of perspectives. Surveying poems of his own that had been written over a decade, Kearney noticed the role of alcohol, not in a qualitatively degenerative sense but simply as an independent factor.

A lot of the poems are specifically alcoholic poems. I'm not saying the poetry is alcoholic; I'm saying the objects, the surroundings are. The weird thing is that, for people who are trying to make contact or correspondence with something outside, and are getting into a more accessible state as receivers of such information, using alcohol as a tool, what happens is that alcohol isolates you more and more. All your energy is going into making the contact and gradually you're shrinking, so that you end up at the bottom of your personality. You're merely a consciousness and there's nothing more. It has no distinguishing characteristics.

"You don't notice," Larry continued, "you just wake up and there it is. You know there are certain things you wouldn't do if you want to stay alive and that's about it."

Spicer knew he was dying, Kearney decided later.

I think a lot of his terror when he was doing *Magazine Verse* came from his sense that maybe he was working in the dark with nothing but his brain. That scared him. When Jack started the "Sporting News" poems he showed me two of them. He wanted to know whether I thought the catcher's voice was real, whether he was being conned.

I told Jack I didn't really know. I personally think that this doubt was alcoholic and that Jack was not sure that he was really *hearing*. That's what at base his concern was. The voice was there and he was putting it down, but he didn't feel secure with it. Jack felt, or understood, that information/poetry frequently came in distorted—he felt willfully distorted—forms. His view, I think, was that you never really knew who was talking to you or what the message was. It could be play: hosts playing.

Spicer could not have sought help for his alcoholism, Kearney believed, for "up to a certain point, the alcohol permits us an openness and a disregard and an occasional intuitive jump. His progression into the poetry was completely tied up with his progression into alcoholism—he really couldn't separate them from one another."[10]

In February 1965 Lew Ellingham combined his own birthday party with the first reading for Robin Blaser's *The Moth Poem*. The event took place in his tony apartment on Edith Street, on Russian Hill. A huge punch bowl on the open porch was sentinel to the diminutive inner sanctum of three rooms, one the kitchen. On the porch, too, and also on the floors above and below, were cabanas for toilets. Everything was made of wood, painted a flaking white. Ida Hodes lived upstairs; otherwise the tenants, who had lived in these $40-per-month units for years, were unknown to the group.

Houseplants decorated the porch. Tubs of bamboo and pots of begonias clustered by a table with fifty glasses borrowed from The Capri bar, for the vodka and champagne punch with floating quince blossoms that fell by chance from the branches spread above it. A screen door from Figone's Hardware was used to drain the water from the massive cauldron of spaghetti, while the sauce of meatballs and oozing tomato concoctions simmered in vast skillets. Gallons of red and white table wines took up the slack as the punch disappeared, and then the guests were served Robin

Blaser's reading. Robin read from a corner of the living room, by a north-facing window with a small view of Angel Island in San Francisco Bay, by a cluster of flickering gold candles, to guests seated on the available seating and spread over the floor. Others were in the kitchen, bedroom, on the open porch. Nemi Frost sat with her skirt fanned over the floor, resting against a bookshelf. Jack Spicer, stooped and smiling, found his square to squat on by the plywood surface that served as a studio couch. The room was quiet. Robin read the poem through twice without pause, his reading style chiseled, urbane, intellectual, yet warmly emotional. Next day Elling-ham made the sharp ascent of Russian Hill, hungover, on a brilliant morning, to leave the stubs of Robin's gold candles by his door.

A month or so later, in late March or early April, Lew Ellingham saw Jack Spicer for the last time at a poetry meeting, this one at George Stanley's and Bill Brodecky's Polk Street apartment, near the corner of Filbert, under Russian Hill. Six to ten people were present, including Len Frazer, a University of Chicago dropout and the subject/object of the love poems Lew had invited him to hear. Frazer was straight, the lover of a woman from Janis Joplin's circle, and he worked at the Anxious Asp with Elling-ham and Stan Persky. Ellingham read "Hem," and "The Orchid." The ho-moerotic concerns of both poems provoked a charge of sentimentality from Harold Dull, countered by a correction from Spicer. "It really takes another homosexual," Jack said, "to understand this kind of thing, to really grasp it." A short time later Lew sold his set of *Open Space* to the Bancroft Collection at UC Berkeley for a hundred dollars, to go to New York. He boarded the Greyhound at the station, lovesick, lonely, and broke, waiting for the bus to leave. He saw a friend wandering up and down the aisle, obviously looking for him to say goodbye, but Lew didn't hail him and left without saying anything. He'd pre-bought tickets for sandwiches at the bus reststops along the way, the fare eighty dollars, his "food package" another ten. He was to stay in New York for a year, during which time Spicer died.

At 1420 Polk Street, without visible means of income, Spicer continued to eke out an existence. Stan Persky was trying to assume more and more control over Spicer's finances, to set up his business affairs in an orderly fashion. It's likely that Jack's mother, still living and working in Los Angeles, supplied him with money now on a regular basis. One of the great losses of his job in Berkeley was the drying up of his library privileges, so no longer were his floors covered with scholarly books borrowed on indefinite loan. Instead a single row of paperbacks (science fiction, chess books, computer science) lined the windowsill.

The printing of *Language* was next on his agenda. Lew Ellingham had made a typescript from the issues of *Open Space* and from Spicer's handwritten versions of final poems that did not appear in the magazine; Graham Mackintosh was set to work printing the book for White Rabbit Press. The pressing question remained: how to insure the circulation and promotion of Spicer's other books, given his peculiar limitations on its flow? At this point Auerhahn's publication of *The Heads of the Town* reasserted itself as a sore point. In April 1965 Persky wrote formally to Dave Haselwood and Andrew Hoyem to inquire about the remaining copies of the 1962 volume. Although Dave Haselwood remembered Stan Persky arriving at the Auerhahn shop and demanding the surrender of the remaining copies of *The Heads of the Town Up to the Aether*, Persky's letter is a formal offer to buy, for two hundred dollars, the 300–350 copies of the book that remained in stock.[11]

Jack's Berkeley friends Sam Hardin and Bill Cartwright, who owned a Berkeley bookstore called Shakespeare and Company, came to the rescue and offered Jack a job. Not much of a job, but it paid. He would be a clerk, advising customers on the best books in stock. Jack came into work on time, but quit during his try-out period, still in the middle of discussions as to his duties. He had thought of a new scheme—computer-based?—for organizing the stock of the bookstore, but Hardin and Cartwright demurred. "Okay," Jack said with a weary smile. "So long."[12]

The poetry meetings in San Francisco staggered on, but with a new sense of anger and misunderstanding among the poets, reflected in a contemporary letter written by Stan Persky to Joanne Kyger after one such meeting, his "report on last night's fiasco." [In this letter "D" and "M" are pseudonyms.]

Things did seem okay, as Ernie Edwards opened by reading the 4th in a series of sleep poems, the work again was good, and Jack & Robin had the same enthused response to this poem that we had had to the first 3.

But this time it was D. Just as we had heard it the 3rd time, D arrived, late, & somebody said, "Read it again so D can hear it," & that started it—D, it became clear in a minute, had been drinking all day; he's about the worst, most distasteful man I know when drunk, sort of in the Lew Ellingham class—and everything comes—a slowing down in time to a drunken pace, haggling, hairsplitting and a belligerence directed at everyone, starting with Ronnie [Primack], whom you have the same reaction to at times. So D decided he had to re-read each person's poem—dragging it out, taking over—

George read—the first poem in 4 months—it wasn't bad—holding back, but shit if you don't get a poem for months then you get what you can—however, there was more to contend with than the poem: 1) George being haughty & absolutely above response, & determined to keep straightening his vest and show us he's as important/as good as/as difficult as Jack & Robin, which he ain't—2) D putting the poem down too hard, but he's too drunk to even listen so it just comes out as animus—3) George asks Ronnie to read it cause he wants to hear another voice and D says, "Why him! For Christ's sake he's the worst reader here—just mumbles, can't speak . . . "—You can imagine what kind of scene that set—& [Larry] Fagin bored & letting us know by private droning conversations in the corner—his display of disgust—what kind of help is that to the poet?

Larry Kearney then read—already the thing was hopeless—beyond saving— poems wooden in their emotion, pat, controlled—& after reasonable kind of comment in the face of it—D had to read them aloud—stumbling, stopping in the middle to interpolate, staggering until I had to get up & take them out of his hand & put a stop to it. It wound up with Ronnie reading another good poem in his series that nobody heard—& then M—a one-night stand faggot whom George brought—read 2 long poems in honor of his recent turn-on to LSD & Buddhism & life-is-so-too-lovuhlee—

Thus completing the debacle, and we poured out, numbed, disgusted, disturbed.

Compared to the fresh young faces in Vancouver, the San Francisco scene seemed grimy, hateful. Scenes like this one strengthened Spicer's tentative decision to leave California. "Before Jack's second trip to Vancouver," recalled Harold Dull, "he was at the end of this period of just casting everything off, that was very sick and turning off a lot of people. Then he went to Canada. He had this new growth, new start."

Spicer sought the constant renewal of his community of artists. Harold Dull recognized the importance of continual rebirth. "This was certainly central to Jack, this waiting for 'new blood.'" At the time of Spicer's death, "There was a sense of the scene's demise in North Beach. The 'flower children' came and everybody started going over to the Haight[-Ashbury district]. Like this was denying Jack his source of 'new blood.' I mean in the sense of a drying up at that time, too. The Beach was no longer the center of the City; the Haight-Ashbury had started—drugs, psychedelic art. It was just anathema to what we were doing. This scene had been built up and 'new blood' should keep coming into it and we just wanted to see it keep growing and flowering, and suddenly, historically, something had come up in which people could not be serious about poetry anymore."[13]

Robin Blaser talked once about sources in his writing, emphasizing the points of meeting and differences in relation to the work of Spicer, Duncan, and himself. He paraphrased a line of thought Duncan had once produced: "If you want to understand Olson, you have to know Melville; if you want to understand Spicer and Blaser, you've got to know Hawthorne."[14]

Poe was left out, I think unfortunately. But then "If you want to understand me [i.e., Duncan], you've got to know Emerson." Now, in that code is a very, very interesting little map of poetic directions. Involved here, at some point or another, it seems to me, is an important division. When I did "The Practice of Outside" I was trying to answer that.

I began the essay not wanting to reduce Jack simply to the little events of himself—the risks taken that cost him his life—and [in any case] he never saw himself as simply himself. He saw himself as always divided. There's the scene at the end of that wonderful John Granger piece. Granger says, "He knew God by division."[15]

I didn't think that I had ever known a poet who was so little understood by his contemporaries. In that I must take my own guilt—for example, the alienation I felt from *The Holy Grail* was very, very great. Where now, and after the work I've done, it seems to me to be one of the great key books of this issue of the Outside, the alien. When I say he was very little understood by his contemporaries, I have in mind such things as Duncan's footnote in the *Audit* essay on *Les Chimères* where he writes that Spicer chose death over life, which seems to me really entirely beside the point. That isn't at all what Spicer chose.[16]

Robert himself had indicated to me once that he was very, very distrustful [of dictation] because it reminded him of Cocteau: the business of the dictation machine didn't give enough power to the poet. Then further, I had the hostility of the Black Mountain people to Spicer's work, which really dates from the poem in *Admonitions* written against Denise Levertov. On the whole Olson wouldn't read Spicer, at all, even though I sent the material. It was his policy that [Spicer's work] was absolutely against women. And of course the image of the world winds up to be a woman in "Causal Mythology,"—imagine what kind of thing was going on in the imagination there!

Blaser referred to a passage in Olson's essay-lecture, his presentation at the 1965 Berkeley Poetry Conference, which conjures a bizarre assault, explicitly sexual, by "the father of all the gods" upon "the spirit of the world, anima mundi."[17]

Blaser advanced a summary of responses to Spicer's work:

Then the other Black Mountain people began to understand Spicer as Orphic. At one point I received a note from somebody or other—I think it was Jack Clarke—saying that one thing that had to be stopped was the "Orphic." Now by the "Orphic," of course, they meant something rather close to what Robert Duncan had in mind, the choice of death over life. All of those seem to me, in a very complex fashion, to be very, very apart from what it was that Jack actually was trying to do.

I'm not going to deny that Jack was an alcoholic, nor am I going to say that the alcoholic danger came forward and simply took him. My point is that the work he was doing was so much involved in this divided world, in order to repose an outside that could either be dark or light, good or evil, et cetera, that in the work of it, he got caught. What I'm trying to say is that one can set up a condition of practice that can endanger you. It is the ultimate risk. The alcoholism was a very neat companion to that.

My own approach [in "The Practice of Outside"] was to put together the Structuralists and Phenomenologists in order to argue the issue of perception in Spicer. Because of its depth and intelligence, Spicer's perception is terrifying. He remains unsafe when a lot of people can run around writing little love poems where you at least have—however sad you are—you've got the assurance that, there you are! Well, by the time you get into structures that are speaking the meaning of the world and you're interrogating the whole damn thing, you may very well be in danger of being there.[18]

Blaser spoke to Ellingham about the points where Robert Duncan, Robin Blaser, and Jack Spicer met as artists, and divided.

If you look at that lovely essay of Duncan's in *The New American Poetry* where he argues about the traditionalist;[19] if you look at the *Chimères* essay in *Audit*—there indeed you get that sense of how marvelously Duncan sits, how comfortably and magnificently he sits within a sense of language as being back behind you. Whereas on the other hand you get this increased textuality in Spicer; it comes out in his study of linguistics. The text is there and it can sometimes be sick as sick can be. It can be like cubist painting where you can't get through the fucking frame. There isn't a vision; there's no way. There's a total materialization of language.

Here he gave an example of what he meant in Spicer's work, the first line in "Love Poems" number 6 in *Language*: "Sable arrested a fine comb."[20] He continued, "What's involved here is very fundamental opposition that has everything to do with time/space in [Spicer's] poems."

Ellingham suggested, "If Duncan sees language behind him, as his reinforcement, and Spicer language in front of him, as his possibility, it's like science fiction in a way. I assume, now, that for Jack there's *no* form behind him, that he's giving form to the formless?"

"Well, Duncan is continuous," Robin Blaser replied,

a continuous voice in poetry; where Spicer has to do with direction, with a break. Language doesn't do what it should do. Language doesn't appear to be God's voice at all. If it is, then it requires a tension of opposition, of difference, of outside and inside, so that one recognizes again a form; the forms are very broken. It seems to me that Spicer's work has taken upon itself magnificently the actual, what do you want to call it? The crisis of meaning? A condition of disbelief? It seems to me that Spicer, with a greater sophistication than anybody—I mean, you don't sit around worrying about the death of God if the word "God" has somehow fallen into the street, all the contents are loose and running about! In the gutters! Crisis is present and the transcendent, as such, is very, very much in question. "You know those lines that Spicer so liked from [Rilke's] "The First Duino Elegy," *"Wer, wenn ich schriee, hörte mich denn aus der Engel Ordnungen?"* "Who, if I cried, would hear me among the angelic orders?"[21] There, that whole sense of being crushed by the angel; the overwhelming nature of it, so that you get a differently poised vision. You get one that has to work with the end of something at the same time; then, you're trying to shape it again.

Blaser disagreed with Robert Duncan's view that Spicer needed a cult of sex or sexuality as magic to be practiced within a homosexual circle ("the *Kreis*") as a means toward poetry:

I think one can make too great a point of the tie of Spicer, Duncan, and Blaser because we were homosexual. I very much object to separating the homosexual poetry out as though somehow it lacked an information that a heterosexual poetry had. That's just sheer nonsense. I'm terribly uneasy at the sense of setting the homosexual apart, as though it were some kind of specialization. I not only do not believe it, but I think the twofold vision remains the same for all of us, with the great variety that lets us go on writing love poems for the rest of our lives, and struggling to get a little bit beyond the twofold vision, just one's self and one's attraction. I'm hardly going to explain drinking—and alcoholism—by the guilt of homosexuality. Don't think Spicer spent much of his energy on the *guilt* of it. He certainly knew the despair of relationship and wrote most terrifyingly of it.

By 1965 the issue [of Calvinism in American letters] had been posed in the wrong terms. One is no longer within the Calvinist-Puritan tradition at all. One is now caught in the entire wreckage of whatever that tradition was. I thought that [the question of Spicer's relation to Calvinism in literature] was posed in such a way that there was not an answer to it.

We do know that Spicer had mixed Methodist/Presbyterian background in his youth. He took theology seriously: had read a very considerable amount, not only of Calvin—*The Institutes*—but very carefully in Luther, because he enjoyed Luther's language and, you know, Jack had rather good German. One of the first exciting courses we took—Robert didn't take this—was Hawthorne. Hawthorne and Melville. Melville's magnificent subject is, really, the breakdown of [the Calvinist tradition]. It's being in the midst of this, without being able to let it go, and at the same time—you need interrogators; Spicer was an interrogator, rather than an asserter.

So theology was extremely important. All of us took a great deal of interest in it, not only because we were interested in the beginnings of American literature, but because we did have ties to earlier American literature. Then of course a lot of material we were taking came out of theology. All of the stuff with Kantorowicz, where we did the Byzantinology course, had to do with the nature of theology and its difference from the theology of the West. The stuff in *The King's Two Bodies* [Ernst Kantorowicz's final major book, the research for which served as his lecture material for the Berkeley Renaissance poets] is fundamentally involved in theological structures, translated, then, into active forms in the world.

In addition to that, we had other courses from Kantorowicz. One was in Byzantinology and then that had an extension into a graduate course—Spicer and Duncan took it, and it was our last text, called "Constantine Porphyogenitus"—and its subject was, "How to Approach the Byzantine Emperor." So the three poets have a common interest in ritual, in theology which, I suppose, should be differentiated from things like theogony. All that is very, very important. Spicer is so American that he is going to be interested in the Calvinist thing.

Here conversation turned to religion and magic.

Religion is a permanent characteristic of human nature. And—when you put it abstractly—its fundamental aspect is the way you are bound to the world. I would argue that being bound to the world is always very large indeed. It's the stars and the sky and so on, and it plays itself out in poetic language over and over again, whether you're attached to one, to any system or not.

It seems to me that magic's means is frequently, in fact always, by way of language; that it is an active relationship to the Outside. Magic is a way of constantly redefining and keeping alive the subject/object relationship. It can be quite dangerous.

It has no parameters, because it insists that whatever is going on is alive and doesn't fall into definition or completion, but is most frequently incomplete and a system in which one is always tied to the largeness, to the awe of, to the *incomprehensibility* of. Language is the instrument by which you play the notes of Inside and Outside. You have sound, and symbol; you can have painting, and architecture, and sculpture, and music and dance—all of which are language. The three people you're talking about all are after words-as-such. And words complicate because words both determine and make indeterminate.

It's also very Theosophical. In Duncan's *Adam's Way*, for example, he used the term "interstices." So at one point Helen Adam and I are going down on our hands up against an invisible wall. There are voices on the other side of the wall that we can barely hear, and not hear clearly. You need not identify the invisible with death, but certainly it seems to me rather fundamental that whatever one wants to say the invisible is, you're going to deal with the nature of death in it. In philosophical terms the invisible can be taken as simply that on which everything is founded. That all visibility is founded upon the invisible.

We get very confused in modern thought, with Foucault arguing that our sense of invisibility now has to do with three great ranges, taken out of the movement of modern thought, as it becomes a vast kind of materialization. He calls them Labor, Life, and Language. So that you've got Labor as that vast economic system, which is invisible, and maybe centuries-old in the form in which it takes we have to articulate our way into to make a living. You've got Life, its vast invisible form, of which we're a visible moment. And Language—as Foucault would point out—it's both *older* than we are, and always *other* than we are. Robert knew it magnificently; Spicer knew it with a kind of terror at times. Spicer marvelously set it up so that we would build the Outside again, that we wouldn't let it all fall into psyche, and into subject.

That becomes very dangerous business. You're very much endangered when you give yourself over entirely to working the vastness. With that marvelous passage I so like to quote of Victor Hugo's, "Every man has his Patmos"—St. John's place of exile. It's just as well in response to this to remain in *ordinary* thought, in *ordinary* consciousness, in *ordinary* feelings, because otherwise you go to the edge. And there, the ways of the marvelous meet you. As Hugo says in that great passage, "Forever you are somehow touched with the dark."

Robert Duncan was touched by the dark as much as Spicer, in many, many ways. And certainly I am touched by the dark. It is a part of the spiritual discipline of what it is to be a poet. Not all poets take poetry to be a spiritual discipline. I'm taking Spicer's own description of it: invisibility is then filled with a vast vocabulary that is, that can be ancient, and then of course is also modern. Because we have to be in our own time as well as being as old as what we are. Then, at that point, *in* comes that vast vocabulary of the invisible, which can be gnostic—if that's the way you've been working—which can be Biblical—that has to do with the vocabulary of the invisible which then, as it edges toward visibilities, tends to tell marvelous stories. And the vocabulary of it, it seems to me, is on the whole, permanent. It makes myth fundamental.

Calvinism supposes over and over again a dualism. Even the greater part of Luther does the same thing—and I did research this carefully: this is to argue the absolute otherness of God. Which is to say, the absolute otherness of complete meaning, of absolute meaning. It divides the world in such a way that you have a dualism: a godhead, and the created world, separate from Him. One may trace this throughout Jack. He was fascinated by it; he knew a lot about it; he is, essentially, quarreling with it. In order to find *not* dualism, finally—though he kept, it's true, feeling the world as dualistic in some way—he so modernizes it that it becomes modern condition rather than Calvinistic condition. And then the search is to find the way in which we are dealing with—what? with contraries, with opposites; not, simply, with dualism.

Spicer's blasphemy, in fact, is directed against that thought which would protect the purity of God.[22]

Spicer abruptly terminated analysis and again left the country. On May 17, 1965, Larry Kearney took Spicer to the bus terminal to meet Robin and Stan. The three were traveling to Vancouver, where Warren Tallman had arranged a joint reading for the poets at the New Design Gallery. Jack was nervous and upset, afraid that the police might board the bus and find him with a bottle of brandy—forbidden on interstate buses. "At every bus stop," Blaser sighed, "I had to find a tavern to get him a drink. I said, Jack, let me buy a pinch bottle, and he said, 'No, no, that's illegal.' He was paranoid about all that. It was absolutely ghastly. So we would get off and you know, it was a pee stop, and thank God for America and the fact that it drinks! I always could find a tavern, and we'd drag Jack in, he'd get a quickie, and then we'd get back on the bus. And when we got there, they wouldn't let us in. Stan looked terrible, I looked terrible, and Jack was ah! So we were stopped and taken off the bus and not allowed to come into the country."[23]

In Kerrisdale, Karen Tallman was at home when the RCMP called, asking if it were true that her parents were expecting the three disreputable, drunk bus passengers being held in custody. Her parents were out, but Karen quickly sketched together a story good enough to get the poets released and poured back onto the bus. At the age of eleven-and-a-half, almost twelve, her years of experience with American poets had inured her to their drunken mishaps.

Karen had lived in Vancouver since she was three, but still was very much an American girl in a foreign city, a factor that enhanced her natural bent toward the outsider. "Our family was decidedly an American family living in Kerrisdale. The people who didn't mow their lawn. The eccentrics." Among their neighbors, the Tallmans' reputation was a slightly scandalous one: when Karen was nine, her home became the quake center of the Vancouver Poetry Conference. The family picked Allen Ginsberg up from the airport: he'd come straight from India, redolent of incense and gowned in saffron swami robes. "Charles Olson was staying with us—it was wonderful. And exciting as hell for us kids—nobody told us to go to bed!" Her room had two beds in it, and every morning she woke early to find out who had taken the other one during the night.

The poets, preoccupied with "their own mouths and thoughts," were not always easy with children, as Karen had learned over the years. Spicer was the exception. He was ghastly in appearance, yet wonderful at the same time, like something out of a fairy story. The time and attention he showered on her, and on her younger brother, Ken, came as an exhilarating surprise. "He was quite aware of what we were doing, and he was also into teasing us about whatever was going on. He knew what school assignments were coming, things like that, and was on our case about what we were going to do about them." He was not her idea of a family man, but it was clear that he enjoyed family life.

At the kitchen table—a piece of plywood hooked into a wall with constantly chipping plaster—Jack sat and *shook* a lot; he shook the plaster, breaking it from the wall. The voraciously fat Greedy-guts, Karen's cat, sat on the windowsill observing him closely. "He had this sort of torture game: the cat and he tortured each other, in and out of the window, opening and

Jack Spicer, clowning around to amuse the kids, Karen and Ken Tallman, in Vancouver in the spring of 1965. Bloated, puffy, sick—but "good." Photographed by Karen Tallman with her Brownie camera. *Photo courtesy of Warren Tallman.*

closing, opening and closing, and Jack always sat right by the window where Greedy-guts came in and out, a game they played."

He loved his brandy and orange juice, drinking upwards of a bottle of brandy a day. Every week Ellen Tallman drove to the Liquor Control Board and bought a case of brandy, hauling it into the back room of the house, so that Jack would not complain. Because he hated the Beatles, he wouldn't allow Karen or Ken to play their records loud. And, he added, Bob Dylan had a horrible voice. Karen and Ken were outraged, and argued right back. But these were "scraps—playful scraps." As much as he drank, Jack was not wild—not wild the way Karen thought of Olson, or Ed Dorn, or Creeley.

331

When Jack drank, the brandy made him mellow and more interested in the children as people. What was frightening was getting to love him and at the same time having to watch him fall apart. He was shaky, sick-looking —obviously "failing." It was hard to judge his age: he was so young and so ancient. He was like a—chameleon, Karen decided. He wasn't young and cute like their other tenant, Dennis Wheeler, but she loved him just as strongly—not a crush, like she had on Dennis—she loved him because he was good.[24]

Stan and Robin were staying at the home of the local writer Gladys Hindmarch. Older and wiser, she saw the cruder side of Spicer's alcoholism one morning, having driven to the Tallmans' with her houseguests in tow.

I was pouring coffee, and I was trying to find out if people wanted more, or didn't want more. but Jack just kept talking. So I poured his coffee, too, then put the pot back on the stove. Half a minute later there's this enormous noise, and Spicer stood up and hit the lampshade off the light right above the table, absolutely furious at me, Because, it turns out, what he had in his coffee cup was brandy, and he didn't want coffee, and I had poured a bunch of hot coffee on top of his brandy. He was enraged; Stan and Robin had to come to my defense. I actually think he was embarrassed by his own anger, at a certain point in it; but he really was mad. Really mad at me, and I felt really quite—I mean it was just like so—sort of alcoholic behavior, but it was a true mistake!

Gladys Hindmarch smiled and said, "Jack was interested in several of the young men who were around. And one of these would be Dennis Wheeler. Another would be Rick Byrne, and another would be my brother-in-law, Neap Hoover. And Jack was interested, whether the people were heterosexual or homosexual."[25]

Neap Hoover, a thin, tall anthropology student, married to Gladys's sister Leni, was in and out of the Tallman house continually, as was tall, lean, dark-haired Dennis Wheeler, with his astonishing blue eyes. Dennis Wheeler—the "Dennis" of Spicer's "Ten Poems for Downbeat"—had been one of Ellen's students—her favorite student, and she was a woman who lost her heart easily. He was "a young guy who was interested in the arts and he died at a very early age," Stan recalled.[26] Out of a deep well of love, Jack came quickly to need the affection of these men. Gladys Hindmarch speculated that for Jack "it would be something like having sort of like twenty- or nineteen-year-old *angels* about, having them in and out. . . ."[27] When Jack was introduced to Philip, the year-old son of Neap and Leni, he immediately began talking Martian to him, making wriggly faces, deadpan, like Buster Keaton.[28]

Dennis Wheeler was "one of the magical figures," Warren Tallman recalled, who wrote poetry, made films, studied earth architecture in New Mexico.

One reason that he is so vivid to so many people is that he died of leukemia, probably contracted from chemo treatments he was given for a bronchial condition, when he was twelve years old, before they knew radiation was deadly then. In his twenties [Wheeler died just before his thirtieth birthday], the leukemia surfaced, and it's pretty clear that that was what triggered it. Dennis is one of the fallen heroes of the town, one of the tragic heroes. He also was a great love of Karen's. You see, he was the Older Man [laughs].

Dennis was tremendously active in Vancouver in all of the circles. Very, very on to Jack's poetry, very, very on to Duncan, and he knew the Berkeley scene also. Persky and Blaser and Spicer were all interested in him semi-erotically, as with Neap Hoover also. Although there was nothing overt about this, it was just kind of there. Well, Karen didn't have a crush on Jack, she just loved him.[29]

During their stay, Gladys volunteered to drive the three San Francisco poets around to meet some of the interesting younger writers. One morning they drove up along the North Shore to Horseshoe Bay, to pay a call on Judith Copithorne, who lived in a unique, Japanese-style house of only five hundred square feet—a kind of fairy tale house, half pagoda, half modernist fantasy.[30] The Tallmans took Spicer to visit other friends outside the poetry circle too, and he warmed to the Epsteins: Norman, a technical engineer from Toronto, and Marilyn, an enlightened, left-wing, Jewish intellectual from New York City. The Epsteins identified themselves as "intellectual anarchists," and though they were indifferent to poetry and had skipped Spicer's lectures, "we visited and all got drunk and were singing old labor songs, which both Norman and Jack knew. These old labor songs which he'd learned in L.A., living in the hotel with his mother and dad. He was very much working-class oriented in his sympathies."[31]

And at home Karen and Ken got Spicer hooked on network television. For years he had watched his ballgames and other sporting events on TV, usually in one bar or another, but in Vancouver he discovered the whole zany panoply of sixties programming. He developed a fondness for *Peyton Place* and other soapy serials—the contemporary equivalents of "Our Gal Sunday," "Mary Noble, Backstage Wife," and the other radio programs he had followed with his mother, father, and brother during the Depression. In addition, there were televised election debates, which featured Prime Minister John Diefenbaker. "Jack was fascinated by John Diefenbaker, who was the Prairies' lawyer. He loved Diefenbaker, the old-style populist politician, who had this tremendous rhetoric, and who also had a variety of palsy of some kind, so he always was slightly shaking when he talked." Warren Tallman laughed. "Jack felt immediate affinity with this guy, and he thought Diefenbaker was really great."

Spicer had mapped out a publicity campaign for the gallery reading. "This was the kind of penny-ante project he dearly loved," Warren decided. "To have that poster just right, and to have it distributed to the right people. We're talking about maybe ten dollars in expense, but he took great pains to get that right."

At the door to the New Design Gallery Warren handed out mimeographed announcements for a series of lectures to be held at his home— Spicer's "Vancouver Lectures," as they came to be known. Three lectures, five dollars for the series, two dollars individual admission. The audience was familiar with this type of lecture series, as Duncan and Creeley had each offered them in the past, again at the Tallmans' home. As the reading was about to begin, Jack ran out of brandy and pleaded with Warren to run out and buy him some. There was a liquor store a block away, so in the nick of time, Warren was there and back, sneaking in the back door with another pint. "As soon as he saw that bottle of brandy he felt a lot better. It was his insurance. It was not a craving for alcohol, it was a craving for comfort, and steadiness."[32]

The New Design Gallery reading was organized primarily as a showcase for the serial poem, and secondarily for Robin, whose stately, vibrant readings of The Moth Poem and Cups began the evening. Spicer read briefly from Billy The Kid.[33] He stumbled a few times, but in Vancouver these lapses did not throw him as badly as at home. Still the worry was there. "Would his vision blank out?" Warren fretted. "Was he going to stumble on a word and have the whole structure collapse on him? We were worried, because we'd been warned." Hung in the gallery space was a show of large canvases—"big, big-bellied pregnant women"—by a local painter, Joy Long. Spicer's figure at the podium, hunched over and nervous, surrounded by these huge Amazonian earth mothers, left an indelible image.[34]

After the intermission Robin read The Park, and Persky gave an animated, comic account of the Lives of the French Symbolist Poets. To conclude the evening, Robin read The Moth Poem again. He recalled: "It then became very clear not only was Jack going to stay to talk to people—but he did not want me there any longer. He wanted it to be his scene."[35] Spicer was also annoyed with Stan Persky and made his displeasure known. The reason was the publication of *Language*, which appeared during this month. Jack "thought that Stan didn't proofread it properly; you could see it just wrenching to Jack to have any mistake in his book at all. Stan and Graham put it together from the manuscript in San Francisco, and then Graham sent it up to Vancouver. When the package was cut open, and the book opened, Jack was in a state about it. Now, it may be that Stan was not at fault at all, I don't know," Tallman recalled. "But he blamed Stan. He said, 'Persky said he was going to do it, but he hasn't done it at all. It's a complete mess.' There weren't that many mistakes, but there was a whole passage left out, which bothered Jack, and there were mistakes in some of the lines."[36] And so, Robin sighed, "and so we got on the bus."[37]

Gail Chugg's account of his own work with Spicer on two earlier books revealed that Spicer was casual about errors, not from indifference, but as part of a plan. Persky recalled, "I would say, 'Jack, it looks to me like you misspelled this word—' and he said, 'Well, it doesn't matter.'" But Spicer would brook no alteration in his text, since he "had this great theory that allowed him not to have to do any more after he'd gotten the poem. Mistakes in the poem really didn't affect it—I assumed some of them were drunken mistakes."

Graham Mackintosh touched upon the circumstances and implications of Spicer's theories of dictation. "Just as a practical matter, Jack said he wrote early in the morning but, having been a long-time drinker, I think what happened was he'd be of a certain blood-alcohol count, which would allow him to pass out for about five hours. Which would bring it around to approximately seven in the morning. Which was the time he would do most of his writing. Then he'd go back to sleep, and sort of pass back out. You could say 'dictation,' but I think 'twilight images' were forming in his mind. I don't know about the whole dictation thing"—Mackintosh's voice now was a whisper—"I know a lot of things that were supposed to be dictation were printer's errors."[38]

By the final two years of Jack's life, Stan was watching Spicer's production closely. In addition, both Duncan and Blaser were regularly supplied copies of his texts, for close and experienced readings; others as well would look at this work. Persky added, "People want to make some big deal out of them [Spicer's mistakes]. I don't think there's any big deal to be had."[39] In Jack's view the dictation process not only did not require, but did not allow, alteration of textual matters. This could lead to unexpected results, such as the doubled poem, found in both "Two Poems for *The Nation*" and "Six Poems for *Poetry (Chicago)*." "Jack didn't know that was repeated," Robin says, "until he brought it to me and read the poems twice."[40] Graham Mackintosh's view of the matter was a simple one. "Jack was amused by chance. I think he liked happenstance." If there are mystical sources for Jack's work, Mackintosh looked to subtle sources in Spicer's life, including his heavy drinking, combined with a very highly developed sense of playfulness, for the poetry's origins.[41]

The question of *what* dictation is carried a lot of interest for the writers who were Jack's friends, peers, or both. But many in North Beach were content with the notion that Spicer's Martian voices were best left unanalyzed, that they were play—John Ryan made a tape with Spicer and himself talking a Martian language—and that too close scrutiny would violate the fragile structure that was called both "poetry" and "North Beach."

"Dedication to the poem [was Spicer's] religion," said Stan. "People are always saying Spicer is a Calvinist—but Spicer's religion was poetry. The poem itself, and the practice of poetry, is the whole religion. In Blaser's case, the poet explicitly has a priestly function. In Spicer's case you don't get any goodies at all for being a poet. You just have to endure being a poet, so to speak."

When reminded that several poems in *The Book of Magazine Verse* mention God quite explicitly, Persky added, "I don't assume, by virtue of Spicer saying that he has seen God-—that he thought that he had seen God. That was just something that went into poetry. There's no 'I' in poetry. When he said *I* had seen God, it's just the poem talking. The poem has seen God."[42]

The events known as Spicer's Vancouver Lectures took place in Warren and Ellen Tallman's home beginning on Saturday, June 13, 1965. "Jack set up these three evenings in which he went through *The Holy Grail* and so on." Robin Blaser described them. "There were three lectures in which Jack Spicer gives the first real description of his poetics."[43] Spicer had, certainly, talked about his poetic concerns before, notably in *After Lorca*'s letters and the letter to Robin Blaser in *Admonitions*,[44] and in a symposium, "The Poet and Poetry,"[45] published in *One Night Stand and Other Poems*. But the Vancouver lectures have special value, informing the difficult ideas of his later poetics—dictation and the serial poem.

Tallman noted Spicer's pleasure at the series. "All the money was given to Jack. And he was also selling various books of his that were in print. He was very pleased that the overall fee netted him about a hundred or a hundred and fifty dollars. He *really liked* having received that money." He was also feeling pleased that the poets of Vancouver accepted without question his status as one of the major American poets; these writers, who had already welcomed Olson, Duncan, Creeley, Levertov, and Ginsberg to their city, showed him pride of place by arranging these lectures for him. Again the technical arrangements had to be just so, even though the lectures were held not in a public theater or auditorium but the Tallmans' living room. Canadian poet George Bowering remembers that he spoke from behind a snaky Medusa of microphone wires and cords.[46] Instead of having just an ordinary lamp, Jack insisted on having blazing, intense light to read by.

He began by explaining his theories of dictation, illustrating his points with a reading of the "Textbook of Poetry," the last book of *The Heads of the Town Up to the Aether*. "I don't think that messages are for the poet any more than the radio program is for the radio set. And I think that the radio set doesn't really worry about whether anyone's listening to it or not, and neither does the poet." To an audience for whom "self-expression" and the poetics of voice were central tenets of poetry, this lecture came as confounding and exciting news.

The young people sat on the floor, or sprawled upon the chairs, and up the staircase. Dennis Wheeler sat close to his girlfriend, Sherry Sandwell. But not only the young paid attention. Among the poets gathered in the Tallmans' living room was one skeptic, Vancouver Island poet Dorothy Livesay, who cast a cold eye on the glow Spicer's presence was bringing to the community. Spicer, she felt, was a dangerous influence. "She was very hostile to what Jack was doing," Tallman recalled. "But she wrote him a letter which he liked. He took it as a compliment, that she was saying, *Don't seduce our youth*. She didn't mean it sexually, or altogether sexually; she meant that a cult was forming, and Jack took this as a perfect compliment." "[Livesay is] on almost every tape asking questions," commented Gladys Hindmarch. "At one point Spicer says something about clearing out; you know, like how do you sort of clear a space, what do you do, you clear a space, sort of as if he was telling her to leave. But there was no way—she was *there*. If you hear sort of a somewhat caustic comment, in a middle-aged woman's voice, it's Dorothy Livesay. She really wasn't being given her due. Here's all these young poets and nobody's paying any attention to her and they were certainly paying all their attention to Jack. But to give her credit, she came and listened and participated anyway, as a poet there, not as a person who was then going to try to persuade another way. She was just pretty good, and asked a number of questions, and she wrote one of her best books, *The Unquiet Bed*, shortly after the lectures."[47] Livesay, one of Canada's foremost modernists, was "keenly interested in Spicer's use of serialiam," she wrote later, and took to heart Spicer's suggestions that "one should practice going to sleep with an idea or a word in mind and then waking up to find it could become a poem."[48] Her own poem "Making the Poem" brilliantly encapsulates all of the major points Spicer made during his three talks, and develops them in a nonlinear, spiraling way:

> I wake:
> it's middle of night, danger
> is the poem. Here
> it's been waiting, counting,
> am I
> ready?[49]

Spicer's second lecture was, he announced, on the development of the serial poem, with a reading of *The Holy Grail* as an example, but beyond explaining why the famous long poems of the twentieth century are not serial poems, the lecture became a further examination of dictation: the book dictated as an outgrowth of the dictated single poem, with numerous tips to young writers just beginning. "I wasted quite a great deal of time trying to write perfect little poems, and I sort of resent the time I wasted. My advice for somebody like Dennis, who's starting out, would be to try the most complicated things and fall flat on your ass doing it. If you want to be dignified, there's no reason to be a poet. It's the most undignified thing in the world, other than the person who hands out towels in the Turkish bath."

Blaser summarized his views on the Vancouver Lectures: "One of the things that is most interesting is that it's the place in which Jack tried to make distinctions, and he winds up setting himself apart—poetically—both from Robert Duncan and Robert Creeley. And—which I think would seem curious to the Black Mountain crowd—identified himself closer to Charles Olson."[50] This question was of special interest to Blaser, who wrote on Charles Olson as a foundation of contemporary thought. "Language," Robin said,

is what is fundamentally important to Spicer and to which he is so sensitive—he is so misunderstood in his own context, and in part by me, until I worked very hard: language had to be poised in the middle—between things, and among things. It did *not* belong either to Jack or to the Outside. The Outside spoke into it and Jack spoke into it. Now, the loss of the Outside, for Spicer, was so extreme at one point that he chose to pose the Outside as dictating in so that he himself got lost. It was the Inside that no longer sang itself freely and surely. Not the Outside. The Outside came in with all the terror that the Outside is.

Spicer's language, properly understood, is a chiasmatic language, a language that is the thing between you and everything else. Because otherwise, what have you got? You've got the entirely subjective poet or you've got the entirely objective poet, both of them total phonies, as far as I'm concerned. It's an older language that accounts for Spicer's interest in earlier verse, returning to a language before it became transparent and was entirely tied, either to modern science, so that it referred transparently to a world described objectively, or it was entirely subjective and belonged to the world of psychology, anthropology, and sociology. Instead Jack posed a language that had to be the instrument between and among these things. I think the reason that he chose to join himself to Olson in those last weeks was the sense that Olson had, where the poet is among things, not in charge of them. This is where he is not Romantic. Because Spicer did not think he was in charge of, but that he was among things. There is a world out there. One of the grand things about Spicer is that he always reaffirms that world. But that world can be terrifying. And violent. And not always protective of the little man or woman.[51]

George Stanley built upon Blaser's point that Jack Spicer's late poetry displayed something other than "total despair." "The poems for the *Book of Magazine Verse* are as great as anything else he ever wrote, maybe greater. Maybe that's the best he ever wrote. When I look into it I like the *openings* towards politics, the Church, and Trotsky; the *openings* toward religion and Pope John. It's a book that's very open to all sorts of instances and movements."[52]

Louise Fitzhugh's novel *Harriet the Spy*, then a new book, tells the story of a young New York misfit, child of professionals, who declares a lonely revenge on her peers by compiling copious dossiers on all the classmates, teachers, relatives who live more fully than she. This was Karen Tallman's favorite book. In emulation of Harriet, she had organized a cadre of sixth grade girls as spies, with notebooks and sometimes blatant curiosity about the mysterious adult world. Karen's special target was Spicer, since he was the most enigmatic man she knew. Although Karen had been told his lectures were for adults, she sat on the stairs outside and took notes. During the lecture on *The Holy Grail*, he kept talking about "metaphor," which she could not understand, so her notes became more copious. The next day she asked him for more detail about "metaphor," and he sent her off with a reading list of some terribly difficult material, texts almost impossible for her to get through, but she persisted, thumbing through, making notes, copying out poems as though the more labor-intensive her study, the closer she'd get to her goal, the secret of Jack Spicer. "He certainly was the most mysterious, and also, simultaneously, probably the most accessible of the writers that came through." She needed desperately to know "what he was about, what he was talking about—and why all these people were coming to listen to this. Not that I thought they shouldn't be listening to him—but it was curious that people were so . . . entranced, almost."[53]

Spicer's third lecture had only a tentative topic, the difficulties of being inside the process of receiving a poem. As Peter Gizzi has pointed out, this lecture announces itself as an act of high risk: Spicer creating a theater of the imagination in which a poem is captured in the very act of escaping from the body of the poet. A reading of the incomplete *Book of Magazine Verse* is given. The lecture is structured like a trial, in which Spicer repeatedly accuses his audience of not believing his sincerity about dictation. It's quite exciting, like an old melodrama, or the impassioned testimony of HUAC witnesses, or the memoirs of Whittaker Chambers. "I don't care if you don't [believe me]," Spicer swore. "It doesn't matter a good goddamn to me. But I just want to say for the record that I do believe it, that there is something *jenseits* [German: "other world"] that has nothing to do with me whatsoever, and this I believe."[54]

Warren Tallman recalled Jack's emotional state:

Jack always had a drink at that time, so I assume he had a brandy-and-water, although often for occasions like that he'd switch to beer. For the other people, beer was available to everyone. It was relaxed. People could move, could walk out into the kitchen if they wanted to get something. These were people young enough so that their bones, etc. [laughs]—so most of them were sitting on the floor. It was quite crowded. I remember people were quite close, and Jack liked that for some reason, to have them right immediate there. That is, he was able to feel the audience very much present.

By the time of the lectures, Jack was eating regularly, so the booze moved into the background, in a sense. Jack could get drunk—he was certainly drunk in Berkeley, really gone. But usually it didn't affect his brain that way; he talked on in a lucid way. And he was feeling good: he felt as if he was talking to the right crowd. He was elated by both the young men and the young women in the audience, not as sexual objects. He wasn't trying to make anybody, for instance; he just felt very drawn to them, almost in a motherly way. He was not grumpy at all, he was very accommodating. If asked a dumb question, he would answer seriously.[55]

Spicer's popularity in B.C. had a direct, concrete result. The chair of the Simon Fraser University English department, a linguist named Ron Baker, offered him a teaching job, even though Baker knew about Spicer's alcoholism.[56] Warren Tallman verified the offer. "Ron Baker, who had taught at

UBC, was very high in Canadian academic circles. Ron, knowing Jack as a linguist, and knowing that the poets in town, all of whom he knew, were actively interested in this man Spicer, invited Jack to come teach here, in September 1965. The plan had been that Jack return in September and starting teaching linguistics, poetry, whatever, at Simon Fraser University."

Jack's death changed all that; but then Baker turned to Blaser instead. Wasn't Robin a linguist too, and a librarian on top of it? He had been in Harvard's Widener in the late 1950s; for the past several years he had worked at the library of San Francisco State. And Robin was a poet too, and a good friend of Spicer's. "So, by one of those miracles of a place starting up, Robin was hired to teach, and Robin began to start teaching in September of 1966."[57] Thus, although excluded by Spicer from his lecture series, Blaser and Persky came in a roundabout way to emigrate to Canada eighteen months later. Others came too—George Stanley, Russell and Dora FitzGerald.

The *Book of Magazine Verse*, which was not published until after Spicer's death, was perhaps his most quixotic project. In the spring of 1965 he submitted two sets of poems for *Book of Magazine Verse* to the editors of *The Nation* (Denise Levertov) and *Poetry (Chicago)* (Henry Rago). Neither submission was accepted. Persky denied that the altercation between Spicer and Levertov years before influenced her refusal to print Spicer's work. "No. It was fairly innocent. She wanted to print it but she had too much stuff—she was overcommitted."[58] In a sense, however, Spicer's application to Levertov represented a full-circle turn to the events of 1957–58, as did his application to *Poetry* magazine, for in late summer 1957 he had indeed sent his *Imaginary Elegies* to *Poetry*, on Robert Duncan's suggestion, despite his qualms about their length and homosexual content.[59] Predictably, they'd been rejected. Had they been taken, Spicer's career might have been very different, but hardly as adventurous. His oppositional poetics could not have stood the shock.

At about the same time, Spicer submitted poems to the Vancouver poetry newsletter *Tish*. They would almost certainly have been accepted, but they were lost in the mail and received in British Columbia only after his death. George Bowering, one of the founders of *Tish*, described his relationship with Spicer: "First time I ever met Spicer was in Gino's, summer 1962. This was sitting at the bar. I went there with Ellen Tallman and, I think, Blaser, wch is a strange place to imagine Robin, but I was spending the summer fooling around with Tony [Aste] and [Bill] Roberts and the weird Salt Lake connection, living in a Maybeck house, in Berkeley near the campus. On introduction, Jack turned to me and asked if we used a lot of dope in Vancouver; I always remember that as a kind of dumb remark; but I have often made dumb remarks on first talking to people, including my wife."[60]

Bowering told several anecdotes about Jack Spicer in Canada:

I was at the lectures, as you guessed, and that is me called "George" [on the tapes]. I missed the Blaser-Persky reading at the New Design Gallery by one day, because in 1965 I was living in Calgary, and had just driven into Vancouver, so I made it in time for the Vancouver Lectures and then drove to Mexico. But there was also this convention going on, the Learneds, wch is our version of what you people have called the MLA [Modern Language Association] Convention. For some reason we went to a party given by the Ryerson Press, at that time a professional Toronto publisher of poetry, and Jack was there, in a terrible whitish seersucker suit, lookt as if he got it at the Salvation Army thrift shop and slept in it. Took a walk after that & pissed in some UBC horticultural bushes and then away for the real stuff [there had been no liquor, and perhaps little interesting conversation, at the publisher's party].

Jack liked going to see the Vancouver Mounties, Pacific Coast League team when he was here, used to sit along the first base side and shout so loud, you could hear him all over Little Mountain; I carry on that tradition, same park now, but us poets sit in section 9 along the third base line. I always like to remember I went to the ball park with Jack, but I don't think I really did."[61]

"What always amazed me," Bowering said elsewhere in his letter, "was that Jack, who lookt like such a big degenerate southern sheriff guy in pictures, was so small, so short." In fact, many people who got to know the six-foot-tall Spicer late in life remembered him as a stooped, bloated man of forty, who looked sixty. "His hair straight back with water, clipped off at back, freckly or wenny face, and that wonderful voice that comes over so well on the tapes, and even shows up in the transcripts. Spicer was an odd person for us, because we had lots of prior visits from Duncan here, and were used to his arty talk as the standard of SF poets, and there was Jack with his homey metaphors and baseball lingo, which I loved."[62]

Baseball was even then threatened by the spectre of professionalism, so a 7–8,000 seat stadium like Stadium Park, home of the Mounties, appealed to Spicer more than cavernous, windy Candlestick Park in San Francisco. The first of his "Seven Poems for the Vancouver Festival" shows what the experience of this community meant to Jack Spicer and how he wished to give this meaning to others.

Start with a baseball diamond high
In the Runcible Mountain wilderness. Blocked
   everywhere by stubborn lumber. Where even
   the ocean cannot reach its coastline for
   the lumber of islands or the river its mouth.
A perfect diamond with a right field, center field,
   left field of felled logs spreading vaguely
   outward. Four sides each
Facet of the diamond.
We shall build our city backwards from each
   baseline extending like a square ray from
   each distance—you from the first-base line,
   you from behind the second baseman, you from
   behind the short stop, you from the third-
   baseline.
We shall clear the trees back, the lumber of our pasts
   and futures back, because we are on a diamond,
   because it is our diamond
Pushed forward from.
And our city shall stand as the lumber rots and
   Runcible mountain crumbles, and the ocean,
   eating all of islands, comes to meet us.[63]

CHAPTER TWELVE

Last Summer

*H*arold Dull met Jack's plane on his return from Vancouver and was struck by how *tall* Jack seemed, as though Vancouver had released some of the care he habitually wore on his shoulders. Dull was anxious to show Jack his current project, a book finally published in 1967 as *The Star Year*—its opening poem had appeared in the *Open Space* "White Hope" issue as "Venus and the Moon." *The Star Year*, a record of discovery of stars in life and sky, celebrates the beginning of his new life at the Drew House with Ila Hinton. A piece of mail awaited Spicer on his return to San Francisco—Henry Rago's letter rejecting his work for *Poetry* magazine.[1] He shrugged it off: it would make great copy for the projected *Book of Magazine Verse*, his last essay into abjection and negation.

"Why," he asked, "didn't anyone tell me how wonderful television is?" This made Larry Kearney smile, but Jack's new drinking habit worried him: Spicer was now drinking brandy with half-and-half, cream and milk, which meant liver pain.[2] The euphoria of Vancouver lessened, day by day, to a kind of explosion of feeling regarding the upcoming Berkeley Poetry Conference, to which he had been invited. On the one hand, Spicer shared Duncan's feelings of accomplishment; it was gratifying indeed to be asked back to Berkeley as an honored guest, as opposed to the inglorious banishment—as he thought of it now—of 1950. And to be invited was a step up from the Vancouver Conference of 1963, to which he had not been invited. On the other hand, at the Berkeley Conference he would be only one of a number of voices, and he feared that the assembled masses would canonize Charles Olson, leaving his own poetics in the shade. He determined to attend the conference, give his reading and one last lecture, and return to Vancouver, shut at last of his damned California.

The Berkeley Poetry Conference was organized by Richard Baker, who worked in UC's University Extension. Baker planned an assembly that would continue the gathering of the poetry tribes who had congregated in Vancouver two years before. The conference serves as a break in San Francisco's poetry scene almost as notable as the reading and publishing of Allen Ginsberg's *Howl* had been a decade earlier.

Dozens of lectures and readings were planned and given. Charles Olson flew in from the Spoleto Festival, with John Wieners among his entourage. Gary Snyder, LeRoi Jones, Robert Creeley, and Robert Duncan were to give large lectures and readings. (As it turned out, LeRoi Jones canceled his appearance, due to an increased interest in Black Nationalism, and Ed Dorn was hastily drafted to take his place.) Allen Ginsberg—fresh from being crowned "Kraj Majales" ("King of the May") by the cheering students of Prague—was poised for an enormous sensation.

From Detroit a band of young poets approached the Berkeley Conference in the hope of meeting their own personal heroes. These poets, members of the collective known as the Detroit Artists' Workshop, published a magazine called *Work*, and set out to cover the Berkeley Conference in a big way. Robin Eichele was a devotee of Duncan. John Sinclair admired Olson and LeRoi Jones. Magdalena Arndt went west to see Creeley. Her photographs of the Conference participants were published in *Work* 2, dedicated to the memory of Spicer. (It is odd, considering Spicer's alleged misogyny, how many of the finest photographs of him were made by women!—Kyger, Adam, Tové Neville, Arndt, even Karen Tallman's Brownie snapshots.) The Detroit poets passed out copies of the first issue of the magazine, which contained George Tysh's very positive response to Spicer's *The Holy Grail*. Later the word spread around Detroit that Spicer and his circle, far from being pleased at such recognition, were "pissed off" at the presumption Tysh had shown in reviewing the book at all. "Who the Hell is he?" it was said, was their common attitude—he was an outsider, a Detroit writer.[3]

From Vancouver Warren and Ellen Tallman descended to rent a house on Tamalpais Street, in the Berkeley Hills, for the duration of the Conference. A huge dog, Licorice, came with the house, and the Tallmans wound up taking him everywhere in the car. Robert Creeley stayed with them, with his then-wife Bobbie Louise Hawkins, displacing an irate Charles

Olson. "We had told Charles that he could stay with us that summer, but before he got there, Bob and Bobbie moved in. I loved the Creeleys, but I didn't love them together at that point. They were just not about to—they just wouldn't move out! So I got a place for Charles to stay at Barbara Joseph's—the friend who helped Robert and Jess buy their house—and her husband Jorge Fick, the painter." When she went to pick up Charles at the airport, she told him she had arranged a more convenient place, one with fewer stairs, for him, and that Barbara would wait on him, drive him around, cook for him, everything he wanted, everything Ellen would be too busy to provide. "But he didn't forgive me for that. He said he was disappointed I would let him down in this way." The Creeleys, she argued, were fighting too much to be kicked out. "They're throwing each other, and their luggage, down the stairs, and I can't do a thing with them!" Olson would not listen. It was her job, he insisted, to bring the Creeleys to heel, and her job to cater to him.[4] But women in general were not given much to do at the Conference, except to host parties, take photos, have sex with the poets, and make up the majority of the audience.

Karen Tallman liked the new house in Berkeley, where she shared a bedroom on the top floor with her brother, and with Kirsten Creeley. Kirsten's beauty unnerved her. "I was a frumpy twelve, and she a *glorious* fourteen." She felt very much divided, for part of the time she had to spend with her grandparents, Ellen's parents, who were well-off and straitlaced, and the other part of the time she awaited the arrival of all the poets she had gotten to know in Vancouver—Olson, Ginsberg, Duncan, and most of all, Jack Spicer. Because he had lived with them in Vancouver, Karen thought, it felt strange to have him living in San Francisco and not in the Tamalpais house in Berkeley. They did not see him often. He told her he was looking forward to the end of the summer, when her family would drive him back to Vancouver and he would start his new life with them all.[5] Some of the Vancouver writers Spicer had met were also in attendance at the Tallmans': Dennis Wheeler, Gladys Hindmarch, and Neap Hoover. The conference program listed a special reading: "New Vancouver Poets, organized by Jack Spicer," to counterpoint the reading of "New Bay Area Poets, organized by Gary Snyder." These little listings document how far Spicer's predilections had swung away from "organizing" San Francisco poets and toward the north. Yet he participated only reluctantly in this conference, which he imagined to be Robert's invention. In Vancouver Neap Hoover had asked him what he thought the Berkeley Conference would be like. "Oh," Jack groaned, "it's gonna be the All-Star game."[6]

By this time Spicer had made contempt a personal style. On a bus in North Beach, he met up with an old acquaintance, Knut Stiles, once the owner of The Place. "I remember Spicer saying 'Oh, Olson is coming to the University, all the poets are going to read, and they're going to have a big seminar over there.' And I would say, 'Who?' and he'd say, 'Well, everybody but Phil Whalen; Whalen refused because they offered more money to Michael McClure.'" Stiles expressed surprise at this: weren't Whalen and McClure "kind of equals?" and added that he liked Whalen's work. Spicer's response was flip. "Yes, that's what's wrong with both of you, you're really just intellectuals."[7]

At the Tamalpais house, the long-bruited reunion of the Berkeley Renaissance principals was finally held. Karen was delighted to welcome Spicer to the rented house. She noticed now how unsteady he was, how aged—in just a few weeks, he seemed so much older. The steep stone stairs of the house might have defeated him, but Karen volunteered to be his leaning post. They climbed one step at a time, all the way to the top, his whole weight on her young shoulders, as though he were a very old man, his big barrel-chest hunched like Quasimodo. Licorice panted by her side. "How's Greedy-guts?" Jack grunted. "Good, Jack, good," she reassured him, thinking to herself, *But you're not, are you?*[8] Warren's trusty home-recording equipment was brought into play, and hours of conversation were taped featuring Spicer, Duncan, and Blaser, with Stan Persky acting as a sort of emcee. Listening to them talk was an audience of familiar faces: Ellen, who had attended Berkeley in the late forties, and Don Allen, as well as Jo Fredman, Hilde Burton, and others from their magical, long-gone student days. Freed temporarily from the in-fighting and squabbles that had depleted their energies, the three poets read from their student work, told old jokes, reminisced, drank, and smoked.[9] It was a family affair, as opposed to the public re-creation of the old Round Table proposed a year before.

At the Berkeley Poetry Conference, Spicer was to lecture on "Poetry and Politics," and separately, to read *The Holy Grail*. "Spicer opposed the entire thing, though he did his part," Blaser remembered. "He spent his time in North Beach telling everybody not to attend. And of course neither Stan Persky nor George Stanley attended." Both these writers actually did play parts at the Conference, but it is interesting that Robin refused memory of them—though he lived with Stan Persky and read at Berkeley with George Stanley—suggesting how much this stress of divided loyalties was already taking its toll. Spicer's view was that, to use Blaser's words, "The whole thing was 'a terrible set-up,' everything was 'wrong.'" It was Jack's typical magic by way of opposition." A terrible set-up, "and *bad* poetry: one shouldn't participate, not listen to it. We never got any very good answers about why it was he was going through his part of it. Both for the reading and the lecture Don Allen and I would collect him, bring him over [to Berkeley], because he was extremely shaky, he was to be dead in less than a month."[10]

Larry Kearney remembered Spicer's worry about the upcoming lecture. "Poetry and Politics" was to be given at 10:30 in the morning, on July 14, 1965, in California Hall on the Berkeley campus. "Jack was in a panic about it, for days before."[11] Forty or fifty people attended, and some who had not seen Spicer in a while were shocked at his haggard appearance. Thomas Parkinson turned to George Stanley and exclaimed, "What can we do about Jack?" George said, "Get him a job." Parkinson shook his head. "I got him a job at the California School of Fine Arts, for God's sake!"[12] Jack spotted Jo Fredman sitting in the back row with Duncan and asked her to sit with him in the front, but she declined (since her job on campus necessitated leaving early). Instead she pointed to Kate Mulholland, who would be his shoulder to lean on. "It was evident that he was depressed, subdued, and, I guess, scared."[13] Spicer's lecture was "rambling and occasionally incoherent; there wasn't a hell of a lot there," for "by that time he was pretty much always drunk." (But Blaser defended "Poetry and Politics," saying, "It was an extremely interesting lecture, I think more useful now than it was then. Because one can understand it so much better.") The questions loosened him up, Larry recalled. At the end he came into his own when a man stood and quoted Allen Ginsberg as having said, "Love is a political stance." Jack "just shuffled and said, 'Well, I guess Allen can make it that way, but I've never been able to.'"[14] In the audience, still beautiful and striking, sat Julia Cooley Altrocchi, Spicer's first landlady at Berkeley, serene in a hat trimmed with a blue heron feather, loyal to her boarder to the end.[15]

Robin Blaser's own contribution to the Conference was a reading of his translation of Gerard de Nerval's *Les Chimères*. Duncan introduced the reading with a carefully written speech, which Robin remembered well. "The introduction was meant to do me in and unnerved me entirely. I was in shock. I don't know how I managed to go ahead and do my reading."[16]

The atmosphere surrounding the Conference excited the younger poets, who saw for the first time their heroes of the East and West Coasts meeting and talking. At a party Blaser showed Larry Fagin the then-new *Lunch Poems* of Frank O'Hara, and Fagin also met the young poet Ted Berrigan, who read from his *Sonnets*. In Gino & Carlo's Fagin looked to the left and saw Spicer, and to the right he saw Charles Olson. It seemed to him a time of exciting fermentation, unification, energy.[17]

Spicer attended no events other than his own. Blaser and Persky went to all. Spicer stayed in Gino & Carlo's, across the Bay in San Francisco, appearing to be only casually interested in what was happening in Berkeley, but deceiving no one. He had to know exactly what had happened each day, who had shown up, what was the gossip, who was making a success, who a failure. Persky and Stanley told him much, and poets came across the Bridge to meet him and seek him out. From his table, Spicer heard all about the Conference: the Olson lecture that had everyone talking (was Olson drunk and raving, as Duncan felt, or brilliantly Dionysian, as Blaser claimed?) Though Spicer feared Charles Olson, he felt sorry for him as well, for Olson's wild drinking and pill binges concealed his panic from a recent tragedy: the year before, his wife, Betty Kaiser, had been killed in a car accident; Spicer, who never really recovered from his own car accident, identified with Olson's terror and loss. Beyond that, he had genuinely liked Betty when he met her in San Francisco in 1957. Had Duncan really told Hilde Burton, while watching Blaser onstage with Olson, "He's up there telling Olson how good he is"?[18] Had Ginsberg actually kissed Josephine Miles on the mouth?[19] What were the parties like? Kate Mulholland and Gerald Hurley held a huge bash at their house on Etna Street, with the "more decorous" poets sitting in the living room, and the "wild crew"— Peter Orlovsky, Bob and Bobbie Creeley, Olson and Suzanne Mowatt— dancing in the barn.[20] Propped up against the wall at Gino's, Spicer signed the petition circulating among the Conference poets which condemned the "immoral acts committed by the United States Government in Vietnam," adding plaintively, "I just wish I knew what language the Vietnamese we are killing or protecting spoke."[21]

Remembering how "happy" Jack Spicer had been in Vancouver, Harold Dull acknowledged that he believed "Spicer was coming down just for a short time. He was planning to go back to Vancouver. I think it was his intention to go back." Harold then told a story about his own involvement with the Berkeley Conference.

I had a funny thing going at the Poetry Conference. I had been asked to give a reading and I had been asked to read with Ed Sanders. They had certain classes of readings. There was the Big Advertised Readings—Duncan, his reading was incredible; Jack's, and Charles's—and a second kind of order—and George Stanley was reading there, in that second order. Then I was reading with Ed Sanders and for some reason I felt—it really was stupid—but I felt I wasn't being given the consideration that I should have—that I should have the same billing as George. It's one of the things I've regretted all my life, that I didn't read there at that time, that I was stand-offish. I really did feel that—a "white hope" inner-core group, the young ones there, George and I, Ebbe Borregaard and Joanne Kyger—real validity.[22]

Thus aspirations surged within this community even while its central event was about to unfold, the death of Jack Spicer.

When the Conference was over, Ellen Tallman felt exhausted, and Karen quite blue. She missed her father's young poet friends who had been sleeping all over the house—Neap Hoover, Gladys Hindmarch, and her beloved Dennis Wheeler. But soon she was cheerful again. She and Ken had skateboards—the new fad among the young, the big, boxy old-fashioned skateboards that were like stretchers on wheels—and they revved them up and down the Berkeley hills, barely avoiding cars, and suffering the inevitable scraped knees and bruises. "Skateboard summer," she afterward thought of it. Jack came over now and then, sometimes staying overnight, sleeping on the floor when he'd had too much to drink. He looked awfully sick. Did the older people around think he looked as sick as she did? Karen couldn't tell. No one said anything. They all talked as if Jack would be driving back with them to Vancouver when the summer was over. Karen's grandparents, Ellen's parents, lived in Piedmont, a wealthy East Bay suburb, "—and they were a whole ordeal to be dealt with by us. My grandfather had me taking sailing lessons on one of those lakes along the freeway there, below Berkeley, which I despised, because it was so uncool, all these preppy rich kids doing these things. I was traveling between two totally different worlds. We had to be careful with our grandparents, so they wouldn't know quite how wild life at the house in Berkeley was. They would have been freaked out." The Kings had read about the Berkeley Conference and shaken their heads at the lavish treatment afforded to Allen Ginsberg. "If we had let slip by accident that he'd been staying with us, they would have been horrified." But keeping secrets was well within Karen Tallman's scope. Like her heroine, Harriet the Spy, Karen knew how to play things close to the chest when adults were involved. Adults weren't all that interested in what kids had to say anyway. Only Jack was.[23]

Spicer maintained contact with young people, the newly arriving in North Beach and his new acquaintances in Canada. Again he heard from Sister Mary Norbert Korte, a Dominican nun he had met at the Berkeley Conference. He wrote her, thanking her for her poems, ending with, "Pray

Jack Spicer and Sister Mary Norbert Korte, after his reading of "The Holy Grail" at the Berkeley Poetry Conference. "The communion of hearing each other's songs is what John XXIII died for. It's not a real communion until you can hear them at night and I can hear them in the daytime." The photographer Tové Neville sent this photo to Spicer as he lay dying in SF General, in "hopes he will get well soon." *Courtesy of Holt V. Spicer.*

for me. I can't."[24] Each "season" brought a new population to North Beach. Spicer dedicated one of the very last poems of the *Book of Magazine Verse* "for Huntz," Hunce Voelcker, then a young writer newly arrived in San Francisco.[25] In a story published in 1973 about his attachment to Jack Spicer, Voelcker remembered

that summer in the bar in 1965 the Rolling Stones sang *Satisfaction* on the jukebox in the bar. Sometimes the Poet sat his back to jukebox with his chair against it and it was silhouetted by the lights behind him and their shapes. The Giants did not win again today it's two years since now still they cannot win. At two o'clock at closing time the Poet would go home to poetry. Often he made poetry when he went home. They said good-night to him. They saw him sometimes in Aquatic Park in afternoons. . . . They saw him often at the bar.

Hunce is the phonetic spelling for the German "Hans," the Poet said, Hans, German for the English, John; John, God is gracious; John, Giovanni, Juan, Johann, Johannes, Ivan, Jack, the Poet said. Verlaine was only twenty-seven at that time.

351

Your name came up twice in a poem last night, the Poet said.

Poetry's for poets baseball is for everyone the Poet said at least John thought the Poet said.[26]

Hunce Voelker's boyfriend was a teenager of American Indian extraction whose name was Luther T. Cupp. Like Tony Aste, Cupp had survived a terrible childhood, in and out of mental hospitals and orphanages, a deserting soldier for a father, a mother and grandmother who beat him and locked him in a closet, but he'd emerged from the closet in a big way. Cupp's schooling was understandably spotty, and he was a wild child, but stunning, with long black hair and a nice body—"grungily handsome," according to one friend, and flirtatious and attentive to poets. In another of his half-affectionate, half-sardonic gestures, Spicer nicknamed him "Link," and afterward Cupp went by the name "Link Martin." Link enjoyed local fame in these years as actor and writer as well as participant in many adventures, sexual and emotional, involving members of the Spicer-generated community. With *Open Space* fresh in his mind Link made plans for his own magazine, called *Cow*, and he asked Spicer for advice on everything. How old was he when he became involved with Spicer: fifteen, sixteen, seventeen? Estimates vary; no one knows; for Link himself was not sure of his own age. He was Spicer's final Rimbaud, but a Rimbaud marked by an inexhaustible need for love and reassurance. He was simple and affectionate, in the nude he was spectacular, "his equipment just like frightening," and he came on like gangbusters.[27] According to Hunce Voelcker, and another witness who knew Link well, the writer Samuel R. Delany, Link presently became Jack's lover.[28] As with Fran Herndon, Spicer was attracted to Link partly because of his Indian blood; he found a Lawrencian comfort in communion with another of his "tribe," for he still claimed to be part Blackfoot himself. Plans for *Cow* moved forward, and the first issue was scheduled to appear before Spicer's departure from San Francisco, late in the summer. (When it did appear, it was laden with notices of Spicer's death.) A later friend of Link's, the poet Paul Mariah, reported that Link came to rue being known as the "boy who killed Spicer." A cruel piece of gossip reached Link's ears, that someone had called him Spicer's own "Death Car Girl"—a reference to Frank O'Hara's tag for Ruth Kligman, the painter who had been a passenger when Jackson Pollock's convertible crashed in the Hamptons, causing his death. Link was "pissed off," reported Mariah, who then reflected, "But you know, he kind of gloried in it too."[29]

Meanwhile, Jack continued to take the bus down to Aquatic Park in the summer afternoons, and memoirs of this last summer emphasize his haunted, but still powerful, mind.[30] He was still capable of giving sound advice on poetry and living. Larry Fagin brought some science fiction poems for his approval—a measure of Fagin's increasing confidence in himself as a poet, since heretofore he had not read his work aloud to Spicer—at least not at Aquatic Park. Spicer listened, nodded his approval, and commented, "Don't pun on pressure points."[31] But Lewis Warsh, returned to the Bay Area for the summer to attend the Berkeley Conference, recalled a prophetic afternoon: "I remember being at Aquatic Park with him two months before he died and he couldn't get up. He put his hand on my shoulder and pulled himself up. I wasn't thinking about him dying. But when I got back to New York and heard he had died I wasn't surprised."[32] Stan Persky recalled the Aquatic Park experience in detail:

The grass was always wet when we went down to Aquatic Park on Saturday, lots of times, spread out the green sheets [sports and business pages] of the *Chronicle*, and sat on this paper and pretended that you weren't going to get wet. Spicer had a little radio, and he'd listen to the baseball game, which he never really listened to but kept track of the score with. And you always brought books with you, like E. M. Forster's *Howards End*; or Spicer thought that *Brighton Rock* by Graham Greene was a novel that ought to be read; and Tolkien. *The Lord of the Rings* didn't show up in the poetry as importantly as Lear and Carroll, but at the time it seemed important.

You always brought a book down to the park, which you never got to read, like you never got to listen to the ball game. You ended up gossiping and talking. Spicer was there, and other people would show up—a social circle. Spicer was, for me, the magnet.[33]

At night he showed up, as usual, at the bar. His old friend Mary Rice Moore recalled meeting Spicer at Gino & Carlo's just at this period. She stared at how old and fat he had grown. "I thought he was just fat. 'We'll have to do something about that!' I thought, being a possessive lady and still so unaware of his alcoholism or anything." She kept seeing through this bloated, cranky wreck to the young, smiling man with whom she had shared a Minneapolis rooming house all those years back, the man she had loved. He had been cursed, she thought, by his idea of himself as the "dancing ape," and now, at age forty, he had made it come true.[34]

For the Herndons, Spicer's death lasted almost three years, from the auto accident of autumn 1962 to the final days. "At the end," recalled Fran Herndon, "Jack probably was just eating a sandwich a day. He was, as you know, getting more and more remiss in hygiene and getting himself dressed—his clothes were going. It seems in my mind now a pretty rapid decline. My general feeling is—no one wanted him around. [Yet] when I tried to get therapy for him I'm sure people thought I was interfering. There were those who thought he should just be allowed to drink himself to death."

Asked if he was already being discussed in those terms, Fran replied, "Oh definitely. He was going to die. Definitely. And he was expelling people one by one. In the end, in his drunken state, where he was so drunk he could hardly lift the bottle, and he was pouring it and it ran down his mouth, I think really it was disgusting even to Jim. Because Jack was filled with self-pity, Jim felt, and that was one of the things Jim couldn't stand. And Jack would just not stop drinking. He just increased more and more."[35]

It was difficult for Jack's friends to believe that he planned seriously on taking the job offered him at Simon Fraser University; it was hard to imagine even that Ron Baker had offered him one. Larry Kearney said flatly, "If the poets in Vancouver, and the college administrators, thought that Jack was able to work in a university, then they must have been blind." Said Jim Herndon, "Jack couldn't have handled a job like that. There was no way Jack could be—or wanted to be—a professor or anything like that. And welfare was no good. He'd have to have somewhere to go. Not as a poet-in-residence: I remember him losing his temper and saying, 'If they think I'm going to be like Allen Ginsberg and fly around and sleep in people's houses and eat their meals, they're crazy.' You know, 'I'd rather die,' and he probably would."[36] The "fame" of poets was much on his mind, and his last poems reflect his lifelong struggle between the allure of celebrity and the honor of obscurity. At the Berkeley Conference, Richard Moore had started filming what eventually became a multipart series for public television: hour-long cinema verité episodes, each featuring a different "great American poet." The series eventually featured O'Hara, Anne Sexton, Zukofsky, Duncan, Wieners, Olson, Ed Dorn, and many others—but not Spicer. Oh well—what was public TV anyhow, just a station that always seemed to be showing the American flag and playing the National Anthem:

> I can't stand to see them shimmering in the impossible music of
>   the Star Spangled Banner. No
> One accepts this system better than poets. Their hurts healed
>   for a few dollars.
> Hunt
> The right animal. I can't. The poetry

Of the absurd comes through San Francisco television. Directly
   connected with moon-rockets.
If this is dictation, it is driving
Me wild.[37]

Spicer's final poem summed up his views about Allen Ginsberg, whose recent poem "Kraj Majales" described his recent travels in Czechoslovakia where, after being received hugely by the students of Prague, he was expelled by the Czech government. Ginsberg had become an international "Beatnik/hippie" celebrity, bearded, a "guru," a poet in a grand and popular sense. The Communist government of Czechoslovakia was then reputed to be especially repressive in a Stalinist sense. That Ginsberg was allowed to visit the country at all was considered remarkable in the West.

At least we both know shitty the world is. You
   wearing a beard as a mask to disguise it. I
   wearing my tired smile. I don't see how you
   do it. One hundred thousand university
   students marching with you. Toward
A necessity which is not love but is a name.
King of the May. A title not chosen for dancing.
   The police
Civil but obstinate. If they'd attacked
The kind of love (not sex but love), you gave
   the one hundred thousand students I'd have been
   very glad. And loved the policemen. Why
Fight the combine of your heart and my heart or
   anybody's heart. People are starving.[38]

Spicer's wrath at Ginsberg wryly masked his own pleasure in the three or four university students who had traveled from Vancouver to him—toward a "necessity which is not love but a name." He, too, had played King of the May, on a smaller scale, of course, but with some of the same feelings of triumph.

"I think Jack knew," sighed Harold Dull, "that he wasn't going back up to Vancouver, that he'd come back here to die. There was a definite sense of farewells. He came to stay with us at Stinson Beach for a few days. We had conversations during that time too. He was so very, very positive in a kind of 'good-bye' sense, the way he was talking about what I was doing in the new poems that I had written and was reading to him at that time. Sort of like support/good-bye: I had a sense he was saying good-bye."[39]

To Robin Blaser, Jack Spicer's heavy drinking seemed of recent date. "Seriously—two or three years. It's quite curious. Because all of us drank;

most of us still do—and Jack had always done some and on the whole, of my early memories of him, he could suck a bottle of beer for an entire evening. I can remember the first time I went to pick him up about noon, something like '62, I would think—we were going to Berkeley together—I realized he'd been drinking before I arrived. That was the first time I knew he had been laying it on heavy in the morning. It wasn't that he wasn't eating at all. But he would have difficulty when he came to dinner. He wouldn't eat the vegetables. He would eat the meat, but he wouldn't eat any of the other things. You'd say, 'Can I get you some—?' and 'No, no, no!' It was a very quick downhill path."[40]

On the last day of July 1965 Spicer collapsed in the elevator of his building on the way home, drunk, from a long sunny afternoon at Aquatic Park. He was found unconscious in the elevator of his building a few hours after collapsing there. He had his dinner in his hand: a chicken sandwich. When the elevator doors rolled open, another tenant of the building saw his befouled body, oozing with excrement and vomit, and ran to the landlady, who called the police. Ambulance sirens roared up and down Van Ness Avenue all the way to San Francisco General Hospital, in the Mission. In the confusion Spicer remained unidentified.[41]

In the poverty ward of General, Spicer lived on, in deep coma, while his friends wondered what had become of him. He carried no identification in his torn, patched suit. It was several days later that Robin Blaser discovered, having called several hospitals, that the man at General was Jack Spicer. He was near death. Blaser alerted the Herndons, and Jim went crosstown to the hospital, where he found a distraught Robin arguing with hospital personnel. "The doctor, a young guy, was saying, 'What are you concerned about? This is some fucking old common alcoholic drunk. The sonofabitch is going to die in a while anyway.' And Robin took the doctor by the shirt, really grabbed him, and said, 'You're talking about a major poet.' Gave him a long lecture. Robin would have just torn the guy apart. 'We're going to have trouble here,' I thought. 'If the doctor gets tough, I'll get tough. Robin got tough, what the fuck!'" The upshot? "The doctor wheeled Jack into a better room and gave him a little more attention."[42]

But the prognosis was grave. Spicer was jaundiced and in a prehepatic coma with complications—thrombophlebitis, and a urinary tract infection. His gastrointestinal tract was bleeding, and he had pneumonia.[43] The strange thing was that, after initial treatment to detoxify his blood, Spicer's condition improved for some time. He became aware of who and where he was, and he recognized his visitors, and tried to speak. Robin said later,

As far as I can judge, he hadn't really lost his mind in the hospital. He was desperately trying to speak what had happened. It was that the extreme of the alcoholic condition separated his mind from his vocal cords. It was very clear that he was having real delirium tremens in the hospital when he was looking at corners where he saw things clearly. He could not speak—what they were—because he was garbled. The only time he brought down that incredible garble was the point at which he broke, and with a terrible struggle, shitting in his pants [a hospital diaper] and everything else, to speak those sensible words to me: *My vocabulary did this to me. Your love will let you go on.*[44]

In the three weeks that it took Spicer to die, the news spread of his condition to North Beach, San Francisco, and the rest of the California arts community. Many visitors braved the long bus ride all the way to the Inner Mission, where the grim hospital was located. In Berkeley, at the Tamalpais house, Warren and Ellen Tallman told their children that Jack was ill. "It was very disturbing," recalled Karen. "At first I didn't realize how serious if was, I don't know if others realized how serious it was. But I remember just wondering if he was well enough to come back when we left, in August." She decided to do her part to save him. I was a shrine-building kind of child, so I had a lot of shrines for Jack. In this magical house in Berkeley, up high in the hills, there were lovely, exotic plants, wild strawberries and things, and this very steep hill we had to climb up to the house, that had ledges along the way, so I had all these shrines on all these ledges that were supposed to take care of Jack. I was a quite obsessive kid, I was. Tied in with that, of course, the unfortunate sense of responsibility for trying to keep him—get him healthy, which was not working."[45]

Warren Tallman remembered those days:

Jack said, "I was trapped inside my own vocabulary," and then he told Robin, "You will be saved by love." Well, by "trapped inside my vocabulary" the sense that I get is that he was trapped also partly inside his own banishments—he was just not going to give Olson the time of day. And by that time he was not going to give Duncan the time of day either, and he was not giving Ginsberg the time of day. All the time, sneakingly, he would say, "You have to understand, these are great poets," but he'd say it [laughter] very grudgingly. He didn't want to have anything to do with them, but at Berkeley he said, there's a sense, because—He knew he was in bad shape, he knew his own drinking, and he was—you see, when he left for Berkeley, he was very healthy, and everybody said, "Jack, you look great." But he started—he picked up drinking again, and no food, and that just went right down crash. Just eating a peanut butter sandwich. . . .[46]

Graham Mackintosh described his experience in the hospital room. "I only went one day. It was too painful for me to be involved with the corpus demise—that's all it was. He did say one thing: 'Will you give me a ride home?' and I heard Fagin, I think it was, say, 'No, Jack, you're in a hospital—don't you understand you're in a hospital?' That was like the only words that came out of him in sequence. The rest was hallucinating. He was irretrievably over the edge."[47]

Kate Mulholland, whom Spicer had loved and lost while still a young man, offered another remembrance of Spicer. A week before he died, she went over to the hospital one day to see him. The yellow roses she had sent stood by the bedside as she entered the room; no one was around. "Oh God, he was in the last throes! There was sweat all over him, he was having these high fevers that would kill him. I think of hypothermia, where it goes up and down; it just gets out of control—he was just drenched. I thought he was comatose, but then these eyes opened up—something looking at you from a great distance—and he said, 'What have you been doing with yourself?' I said, 'Oh Jack, you know, being a housewife,' I said, 'and raising three kids. It keeps me busy.' He kind of raised up his head and said, 'Well, that's more than most of us have done,' and then he sank back and that's all he said."[48]

Other friends from across the Bay, who had not seen him in a long time, had no idea of his state. "We were in Berkeley," Mary Rice recalled, "and he was over there and he was in a different scene, and we weren't in it, unless we'd go over and see him." Sam Hardin dropped by the ward with a bottle of wine. The doctor said, "One more drop and he's dead!" So then Sam knew what the scene was. Word quickly spread in Berkeley of Jack's decline.[49]

When Spicer was dying, Robin used sometimes to drop by Robert and Jess's house after a visit to the hospital. Sometimes he would look terrible, his face drawn and his movements tense. To Jess it was obvious he was in a kind of anguish. He would say, after a difficult visit, "God, why am I doing this?" And despite Jess's hatred of Spicer he told Robin that if he (Robin) stopped visiting he would never forgive himself. Robin took sustenance from this.[50] On August 6 Duncan wrote to a friend, "At the beginning of this week Spicer was taken to the S.F. General Hospital in a coma with complications of pneumonia, critical hepatitis, and a blood clot in the leg. Wednesday he recognized and talked with those who visited him but by yesterday (Thursday) he was in coma again. If he dies—and there is that possibility according to the hospital—it will come as a major loss for that group surrounding him who have been dependent upon him for their identities."[51]

Fran Herndon caught the sensitivity of Jack Spicer's relation to Nemi Frost, celebrated in the community for her well-told tales of people's lives. "Jack asked Nemi if she had any of the latest gossip—he couldn't even say 'gossip,' he said 'glossip.' She knew what he meant because they shared gossip together." Fran remembered something about her own relations with Jack Spicer: the "testing" of friendship(s). Jack asked Fran to get him "some solid food," adding, "but of course you won't." She went to the appropriate person on duty to ask and was told, "You must be joking! Mr. Spicer can't even swallow his own sputum, let alone eat solid foods." Fran was of course dismayed.[52]

Larry Kearney visited him (once with Jamie MacInnis), twice a week, in the hospital ward. The waiting room was always full of poets and writers, and inside, Spicer was relearning his alphabet. He could not sit up by himself, but nurses and visitors propped him up with pillows. Once, as Joanne Kyger entered the ward in a pensive, quiet mood, Spicer's arm, fixed in a splint and studded with plastic tubes, seemed to rise from his body. Joanne jumped back. Later, she confided her immediate fear, that Jack had been going to hit her.[53] Nurses had tacked up Herb Caen's column of Monday, August 9, to the gray institutional wall above his bed: "Jack Spicer, one of the best of S.F.'s New Wave poets, is in S.F. General—broke and broken after a bad fall—but he'll make it physically and artistically."[54] A flurry of get-well cards lay unopened on the nightstand, from Russell FitzGerald in New York, from John Button in Maine, from the Herndons who had left on an already scheduled camping trip.

Warren Tallman remembered that when Spicer

was in the hospital in San Francisco, and was in and out of this coma, Karen visited him, and at one point Jack talked to her. The doctors were very weird, because they said, "Well, he's in a coma, and he doesn't know anything you're saying." I just didn't believe it. At one point, he told Karen that he'd had a dream in which Greedy-guts was at the window. And this was simply a straight flashback to what had actually happened in the kitchen [of the Tallmans' home in Vancouver] because Jack was playing this game with Greedy-guts, the cat, not letting him in, opening the window a crack, so that Greedy-guts was trying to get in, and Karen, of course, wanted to let him in, and Jack [laughs] was giving her an education on what a cat's rights were, and what a cat's rights weren't! At the hospital, when she visited him, he came out of his coma and spoke to her, said he'd been dreaming of Greedy-guts.[55]

But Karen said, "I never got to see him in the hospital. I'm not sure why we weren't taken in, because Ken and I used to wait in the car when Ellen and

Warren went in to visit him. I suspect it was for him that we weren't taken in, because he was feeling so lousy, and I think everyone was feeling spooked and horrified at what was happening. Warren remembered it differently, but we kids were not allowed in the hospital room. I wish I had been, actually, because it—there was—yeah, I would have liked to have seen him."[56]

Another member of the group, Deneen Brown, sent notes to Robert Duncan reporting the progress of Jack Spicer's illness.[57] Two tiny cards remained in Duncan's personal files. The first says, "Jack was very lucid Friday night—it's probably worth going over. He'd like to see you I'm sure, Robert. If you'd like a ride let me know. Love, Deneen," adding her telephone number. Duncan did in fact make a visit, in response to this advice, but when he walked into the room, Spicer was in a coma. "The last time I saw Jack, he was clutched like that," Duncan said, gesturing fiercely, crunching his body as if in a fetal position, somewhat inhibited by the chair in which he sat. "I realized the fist is just clenched, 'I will not open to life, I'm not going to be born again.' It was strange indeed, but no wonder Jack and I were to become very vivid poles—for me the more light the better, including anything went round." Duncan did not stay longer.[58] The final note from Deneen reads, "Tuesday. Dear Robert, Jack died at 3 o'clock this morning. Stan asked me to drop a note by to you. Love, Deneen," to which Duncan added his initials and the date, August 17, 1965.[59] One witness who visited Duncan shortly after Jack's death reported that he was "raving! 'Jack Spicer was unmitigatedly evil! He was possessed by the Devil.'"[60] And though in later years Duncan softened toward Spicer, and again acknowledged him as one of the kings of poetry, he remained sardonic, skeptical even, certainly about Robin's propensity for attendance at the deathbeds of the great, for in five years Robin was among those present at the death, in New York, of Charles Olson.[61]

The painter Paul Alexander wrote, "The last year of Jack's life was very sad—he didn't want to die—but on his death bed in San Francisco General he looked radiant—when he would recognize a visitor his smile glowed; it was the last communication I had, that deep smile with no irony around the edges."[62]

Stan Persky had given his name, and Robin's, to the doctors at San Francisco General as a contact in case Spicer's condition changed, or if any decision had to be made. The doctors kept them informed from day to day.

Stan somehow had the notion that Jack's coma would last indefinitely. Other people could die; but somehow it did not quite occur to him that it was possible for Jack Spicer to die. "I was all of twenty-four. Young people just have weird ideas about reality." One morning before sunrise, he had just gotten to work at Merchandising Methods when the doctor phoned and told him that Spicer had died. Slowly Stan replaced the phone on the receiver. Ebbe Borregaard had just come to work, and Stan said, "Well, I'm taking off—I'm through for the day." Stan remembered being impressed that Jack Spicer *could* die, "that there really were great powers in the world. I remember feeling—I don't know what to call it—almost a *thrill* in the face of this amazing event. I must have, what? called Robin? I can't remember what happened after that. Eventually we all must have ended up in the bar."[63]

"You know what I did when the hospital phoned?" Robin Blaser said. "It's shameful, but true. I knew what it was and I said, 'Oh, I'm terribly sorry, you'll have to call this number,' and it was Stan's number at the warehouse. I couldn't," Robin continued. "I thought, 'I can't receive this information.' So—I'm ashamed—now, I hope I would, but—I just couldn't bear it. I knew what it was about. The hospital wouldn't call me up otherwise. So, then, of course the phone call came to me. I was sitting there waiting because I knew what it was about."[64]

It was up to Robin to call Jack's mother in Los Angeles, where Dorothy Spicer was still working as manager of the Amhearst Apartments. In turn, she called Holt, Jack's younger brother, telling him that Jack had fallen down a flight of stairs and been killed. (Holt said, "I later found out that was not the truth, but it seemed to be the cover story for the rest of the family.")[65] Mother and son arrived in San Francisco to consult with Robin about funeral arrangements, and to examine Jack's effects at the Polk Street apartment; Robin and Don Allen were appointed executors to Jack's estate.[66]

Because Spicer's family was known to most of Jack's friends only from accounts of his annual visits to Los Angeles to see his mother at Christmas, many were curious about the family that had produced such a brilliant, flawed figure. Stan Persky's impression of Jack's mother and brother was simply that "They had no idea that Jack was important to these people; they didn't have any idea who he was or anything—it was obvious."[67] Fran Herndon looked back and said, "It was very hard to determine what his mother was like from what Jack would say about her. Jack made his usual visit to L.A. at Christmas. He anticipated he was not going to find it pleasant, it was going to be rather boring, but it was a duty trip. He would play bridge or whatever . . . with her. A game. And take her a bottle of Scotch. He would stay about a week—four or five days usually. He would go almost every Christmas. The story Jack always gave people," Fran continued, "was that his mother destroyed his father, who was an old Wobbly, and made him into some lower-middle-class nothing by forcing him into this hotel business. He held his mother responsible for his father's degradation. He saw it as degradation. Because, after all, it's pretty romantic to think of his father as a Wobbly."[68]

Holt Spicer had not seen his brother in some years. He, like Jack, had attended the University of Redlands and there had made his mark as a brilliant debater, winning the National Debate Tournament two years running in the early 1950s. At St. Joseph's College in Springfield, Missouri, he had been the Director of Forensics since 1952, becoming Dean of the College of Arts and Letters as well. Before his marriage, he and Jack had arranged a hasty rendezvous at the Bakersfield train station; "we got a six-pack of Red Cap ale and drove around Bakersfield and sang some songs and told some tall tales." Inspecting Holt's fianceé, Marion, Jack had quipped, à la Groucho Marx, "Everybody told me you were such a nice girl, I'm so happy it isn't true."[69] In the specialized world of intercollegiate debate, Holt was a highly respected figure; both brothers were brilliant talkers, but at the funeral, Holt was understandably subdued and quiet, so Jack's friends saw only the non-Bohemian, nonpoet. Fran Herndon watched the Spicers closely:

Holt was obviously the son who did well in Dorothy's eyes, the model child, who did what his mother expected of him. Jack was a mystery she never quite figured out. He always asked her difficult questions and she never really had the answers. The brother was very gracious in thanking me for the portrait and for all the things that I had done for Jack. They were very grateful that I had included him in our family and that I had done all these things for him. His brother looked just like a middle-class, middle-aged, respectable citizen. A very nice man. None of Jack's mystery about him at all.[70]

To the San Francisco mourners, used to thinking of Jack as hero and genius, however unsung, and practically without family or even ordinary antecedents (the time was one of heroic structures), Jack's family came as a surprise, a reminder that not all of the United States was like San Francisco. Jack's alcoholism and homosexuality, hidden from his family while he was alive, were revealed at his death, and both matters, Holt said, were revelations to him (however, in the case of homosexuality, not a surprise).[71]

At the funeral home, Holt recalled Jack's wishes for cremation. "Jack was very opposed to funerals, morticians, the morticians' lobby, etcetera, and on numerous occasions made it known that he wanted to be buried as cheaply as the laws of California would allow. He definitely wanted to be cremated and he did not want any formal funeral or any marking."[72] Robin bowed to the family's request. "It was all very sad," Blaser said. "I didn't know what to do there at the funeral home. They chose a common drawer. I didn't feel I could say, well, let me pay for a separate thing. And then the funeral man said, well, do you want to go and see him? And I turned, and the family didn't want to."[73] But there was a wake, at the Allen Street apartment Robin shared with Stan, from which *Open Space* had been issued.

Josephine Miles, Spicer's first teacher in poetry, called Robin to express her sympathies, as did Charles Olson, to whom Spicer had dedicated his "postcript" to *Admonitions* (1958). Somehow Robin kept thinking Duncan would call. But "Duncan didn't. He arrived at the door—because I gave, you know, a little wake, and people just piled up. I remember running to get tin cans and stuff and so on because the roses just lined the hallway. People brought flowers and gifts and drawings, things I'd never seen, it was quite magical. Anyway Duncan arrives and Duncan says, 'Jess doesn't like parties.' Then he came in and proceeded to neck with someone in the kitchen while the Spicer family was there, which in those days was—"[74]

"When I arrived in San Francisco with my mother," Holt remembered, "I was very favorably impressed with Robin Blaser and Don Allen and other of Jack's friends I met at the time. Obviously I was aware that Jack was a writer and a poet. Either he or mother—I think probably mother—had sent me some of his work, at an early stage. We were treated very kindly by all of Jack's friends and it made me feel good to know that there were many people who really cared about him and his work."[75]

Larry Kearney's description of the wake expressed others' impressions too. "It was an extremely drunken event." Larry paused. "Well, for some of us it was."[76]

Later Ebbe Borregaard wrote with anger about "Robin Blaser's noodle on Spicer that languich killd him."

It's like saying of Charlie Bird that music killd him. If you wanna get cute you can say language did it, but wasn't it the 19th century? And nursery rimes, and his idiot friends?

I am absolved! For I am only a fool. His idiot intellectual friends were truthfully irresponsible! I want to feel I have transcended their curse. Maybe it's only my kind of arrogance.

What of them who abuse the temple? Alcohol or drugs what's the dif? Money or mental laziness? Jesus Christ wld beat it out of them all. If I only cld ring them bells agen! And if Spicer was there and it was jazz all our names wld be one.[77]

In New York Russell FitzGerald heard the news of Spicer's death and left the house he shared with Dora and her twins. He walked around the corner to the neighborhood bar on First Avenue and there pondered his promise to place green onions on Jack's grave. Without a grave, how could his promise be kept? His thoughts turned to *Sabus*, the opera he was writing, and the pressing problem of how to introduce the St. Sebastian character in modern terms. Suddenly Spicer spoke, loud and clear, "Christ," he told Russell, "he's a nigger cop!" *Eureka!*[78]

Across town Helen Adam was saddened by the news of Jack's death. She had loved his work, and liked and admired him as a person. Philosophic reflections helped her to bear up. "I think he is a tragic loss to poetry," she wrote to friends in California. "But he must have come to the end of his Karma in this incarnation, & was able to throw aside his body while still young & go on with all sorts of accumulated power to something new & I am sure, splendid!"[79] Steve Jonas issued a bizarre statement blaming Spicer's death on his failure to investigate the lessons of history, particularly the sinister implications of the National Banking Act of 1862 and the establishment of the Federal Reserve Bank in 1913. Jonas sent his opinions in a round robin letter to Gerrit Lansing, Robert Duncan, John Wieners, Charles Olson, Robin Blaser, and Robert Kelly, urging them to "bring order in our heads and set our Hearts to Sinceritas," by exposing the machinations of foreign money brokers wherever they occurred.[80]

After Spicer's death, Don Allen found that he would be walking down the street and in the distance he would see Spicer's unmistakable figure shambling toward him. He would think, "Oh, there's Jack," but of course it wasn't. Don Allen recalled opening the trunk, with Robin, the battered trunk Jack had hauled from hotel room to flat, all through San Francisco and Berkeley. Inside, atop a pile of manuscripts, notebooks and souvenirs, perched a bright Zuni fetish, pointed in the direction of Robert Duncan's home on Potrero Hill, a voodoo reaching from beyond the grave.[81]

Jim Devlin, who had been a page as a teenager in the rare book room at the Boston Public Library, was a grown man when he heard of Spicer's death. A professor of English at the State University of New York at Oneonta, he was on hand when Brother Antoninus came to the campus to read his work, and he mentioned to the old man that he had known Spicer as a boy. "He—died," rumbled Antoninus in his gruff stentorian basso. "Died? How did he die?" Devlin asked, amazed. Antoninus shrugged. "He—died," he repeated, *basso profundo.*[82]

George Bowering wrote: "In 1965 it was pretty well settled, I took it, that Jack was going to move here [to Vancouver], the assumption (spoken) that if he didn't, SF would kill him. The idea I got, just before I left town, was that Jack would go down to the 1965 Berkeley Poetry Festival (which followed 63 Vancouver and 64 Buffalo), and then get his stuff, and move up here. After the *Lectures* etc here, Angela and I drove to Mexico, and it was there that I heard of his death from two editors of *Coyote's Journal* who came to visit." His letter continues, "that summer [1965] I was writing my book *Baseball* which is partly about Jack and dedicated to him. I had finisht the first 5/9 of it before going to Mexico, and finisht it after I heard of his death, and so of course that gets in there too."[83]

Dr. Harry Coren, Spicer's psychiatrist, had not seen him in months when a colleague mentioned he had seen his obituary in the San Francisco *Chronicle*. Regretting that he had not done more—Dr. Coren nevertheless believed that alcoholism was not the thrust of the therapy. "My sense was that he [Spicer] was depressed. Not suicidal, but unhappy, and wanted to talk to somebody about it. He used alcohol to feel more comfortable. As a tranquilizer. He had some concerns about it from time to time. I think he felt he couldn't do any better."[84]

A month or two after Jack's death, Dorothy Spicer retired and moved from Los Angeles to Springfield, Missouri, where Holt and his wife lived. She had stayed on in California so much longer than she had intended. After her husband's death in 1951, she had "stayed in California," Holt said, "mainly to be close to Jack, and to be of help."[85] Their quiet, attenuated relationship might have been the most important of all Jack's famous "loves," but Dorothy Spicer died in 1980, fifteen years after her gifted son, and we shall never really know.

Les Chimères

*C*ompetition and cooperation characterized the early poetic relations within the Berkeley Renaissance structure—notably those of Duncan, Blaser, and Spicer. Spicer's death opened a new phase for the survivors of this complex. An essential leg of the triad had disappeared, causing radical wobble. Since this artistic and emotional edifice was already engaged in internecine struggle, it was but a small turn for the remaining participants to focus angers upon each other. The difficulties between Blaser and Duncan had already begun with Robin's presentation of *Les Chimères* at the Berkeley Conference.

For months afterward, Duncan and Blaser exchanged their respective translations of Gerard de Nerval, as well as letters about them. Duncan's translations were published in *Audit*, along with his critique of Blaser's work and the correspondence between the two poets on the topic. Blaser admitted, "I must say I really found myself unable to hold my own in that because I didn't really know how to articulate what our real difference was." Asked whether the issue was that it was a "version" rather than a "translation," Robin answered,

Yes. From Robert's point of view, that very, very much reduced and changed its meaning. Which, of course, I would not agree to. There is a fundamental thing involved. The word "translation" itself, in my use of it there, was an adaptation by me from Pound's sense of translation and from a statement of translation by Jess, who used to describe his translations of illustrations into painting. From the very beginning [Blaser's Nerval work] was meant to have a musical relationship to the French text, because I found that copying lines and substituting rhythms falsified. Probably one of the best places to look at this very important issue is in *Caterpillar*, an issue where Gerrit Lansing takes up the two translations. [Blaser chuckled.] Lansing talks about the problem of translating the *Rubaiyat* and compares Duncan's to Robert Graves's version and mine to Fitzgerald's. Which is quite amusing; rather witty, as a matter of fact.[1]

Lansing urged his readers to accept Duncan as a far finer poet than Graves, and also acknowledged Duncan's willingness to admit where Blaser's poems have power.[2] He also clearly found Blaser's work more satisfactory than Duncan's. In turn, Blaser attempted fairness to Duncan by admitting that the exposition Robert Duncan accomplished in the *Audit* article *contra* Blaser's work was "crushing."[3]

Robert Duncan began an explanation with Lew Ellingham of the same events. "Robin's production in the early Berkeley period was very much that of a follower of Spicer and myself. I really think that's always been one of the elements that makes it hard for Blaser to face Spicer and myself—he puts himself in that position, of course."

"By the time he gets to the difficulties with *Les Chimères*, I think he feels he has to pay a very high price," Ellingham remarked.

"Yeah," Duncan agreed, "and that his teacher's giving him a B- or a something; might be giving him an A, which I practically do."

"He pays high tribute to you in that controversy," Ellingham added. "He admits you beat him."

"What one wants to know is why did he arrange the controversy? Because it started with letters of mine asking him what he was doing and why did he call it a translation. Because I wasn't so dumb. I wrote, 'I too know that Ezra Pound did this thing on Propertius, and I greatly admired the trip that Lowell does in *Imitations*, but here you call these *translations*!' That's what got me," Duncan decided. "But it also got me to translating them myself."

Ellingham said, "Well, I think Robin was just caught emotionally by surprise, that's all."

Duncan declared, "Spicer was the first poet I'd met who was real in the sense that I mean by poet. We were sitting around hoping Robin would turn out to be. The importance of the manuscripts that began coming from Boston was that maybe Robin would turn out to be a poet. He kept trying."

Ellingham asked Duncan, "On the whole, are you pleased with what's happened in Blaser's career?"

"Oh, I wish he didn't have a superego bigger than something sitting on top him," Duncan reflected. "It does seem to me that the authoritative position of teaching is—He's really destroyed by the need for status, something neither Jack nor I were bothered by at all. But he's not de-stroyed as a poet! It's just that we've got so damn few poems, and maybe that's where it is."

"Was he always slow as a writer?" asked Ellingham.

"Perfectionist. That's almost not the same as 'slow,' but how many you permit—how many are permitted at all."

Duncan later discussed the interrelationships of the three Berkeley Renaissance poets as an entity:

Through the period of my writing *The Opening of the Field* and, pointedly enough, through about several months after Robin's arrival in the West [from Boston]—Jack was completely taking me as a kind of master of what he would then do. So he's almost in a filial relation, generation-wise; and our Stinson Beach house became a kind of sanctum for him. But both Jess and I noticed—and I could remember from a lot of things before—we were wary of Jack's activities of adopting parents and breaking them up.

Duncan jumped from this to Jack's later behavior in San Francisco:

It's not only that he's going to ask Fran, "Let's get rid of Jim," but meanwhile he separated Jim from Fran. *He* isn't going to get rid of Jim. *Fran* is. Now he's got two. And this is the pattern that Robin himself would repeat, remember, when he really got Jack and me separated, then he had Jack. Not only was he in between, but he had the only access to me that Jack would ever have and he had the only access to Jack that I would have. That was the favored role. But Jack would play that very gladly. He would be the sympathizer between two people, and he never did get to play that role with Jess, [who] read that role out completely.

Part of Jess's vehemence was that he had attended the poetry conference/writ-ers' conference meetings where in 1949 Jack was attacking *The Venice Poem* and Robin was defending it. So Jess responded, had a primitive response of anger to-ward Jack—and yet only in the sense of domestic things. And he was also cautious about "Would Jack be attacking Robert again?" That was very much in his mind.

Jess saw that thing as an attack on me. I think I told you that I much *wanted* that attack on me, that I was shocked when I read Spicer's letters [in the late 1970s, preparing for the writing of the Preface to Donald Allen's edition of Jack Spicer's single poems, *One Night Stand*]. I wouldn't *allow* Jack to have a different opinion of *The Venice Poem*.

Even though Spicer began to accept this poem, Duncan needed Spicer's resistance to his writing in the crucial years of development this poem embraced. Spicer was initially

opposed to the closing of the poem, in his Puritan frenzy was saying "false" and his usual thing, [but] now he was writing me within six months, and in *my* Puritan frenzy I refused to read it. So one of the bonding things—if I think of a way in which I was always closer to Jack than Robin would be—was first we were both

Protestant, and second we were both Oz book readers. But the Protestant thing switched off in no time—the Calvinist/Protestant thing—*we* understood. And Robin, a Roman Catholic, a kind of classicist, sees it [the disputes coming from Spicer's criticism] in terms of Gnostic heresies—but Calvinists don't think that this news is a Gnostic heresy. It's only Catholics and Jews who have Gnostic heresies, because Protestantism is the arch-heresy.[4]

One significant element was the competition between Blaser and Duncan for the affections of Jack Spicer; another was the importance of strife for all three.

Stan Persky recounted the tale of Spicer and Robin Blaser meeting on the occasion of Blaser's completing his *Les Chimères*. The time was early summer 1965. "They weren't talking to each other at that point, and in fact Robin was afraid I was going to loan Jack money or something like that. He was all prepared to be incensed about that. We had argued about it."

Spicer was notoriously correct about money, and very cautious. The occasion would have had to be one of great emergency—not inconceivable at this time in Jack's life, of course—even to produce the thought in his friends' minds. Usually he was quite circumspect about money, his financial systems so buried that it is not even possible to state exactly how he managed to live in the period after Berkeley fired him.

Stan continued, "Robin was angry that I would be betraying him, taking Jack's side in this spat they were having. They just weren't talking to each other." Such disputes had grown so common few even attempted to explain them.

Things were falling apart for Jack. I wasn't loaning him money, as it turned out, nor was I planning to. Anyhow, we were then living at 24 Allen Street. Blaser was writing this very difficult poem, and he had enormous doubts about this particular translation of Nerval. When Robin came to the end of it, I said, "It's a good poem; why don't you let Jack Spicer hear this poem?" And Robin immediately agreed, even though both Spicer and Blaser were spending a lot of time announcing to other people they weren't speaking to each other, and they indeed weren't, always saying bad things. I went down to Aquatic Park the next day and I said, "Jack, Robin has finished his poem and wants you to come up to the house and hear this poem." Jack didn't bat an eye: "No question about it!" And he arrived at 24 Allen Street as though nothing had happened.

I think Spicer was feeling kind of ill. He went back and took a nap and our white cat, Tim, slept on Spicer's chest, slept in this little alcove there, surrounded by books, and after his little nap, he got up, went into the kitchen—there were these redwood chairs with dark maroon or reddish color velour—around this table and Blaser read the poem. Spicer said, "Wonder-full," and then he said, "I wish I had written that"; and that was it. It was all validated and Blaser knew his poem was OK.

When Duncan's reaction to *Les Chimères* developed into the *Audit* essay, Robin felt betrayed. Stan saw Robin in great pain. "Duncan had done this terrible, unfair, stupid thing." Robin was in "agony. Mental agony," Stan qualified. "Enraged, feeling that Duncan had stabbed him in the back. He also felt Duncan was *wrong*. Duncan also made some subsequent translations of Nerval—quite wooden, those particular translations. I don't know what Duncan's motivation was in this."[5]

The alliance of the three Berkeley poets seemed to be a triumvirate of two and a half, in Duncan's mind, with Robin being the half. After Spicer's death, Duncan expected Robin to try to rise to Spicer's position; he hoped that Blaser would take Spicer's place once this poet was dead. It didn't work out. Before the *Chimères* affair, Duncan's presumptions of superiority had amused Blaser. Bill Brodecky remembered a dinner during which Robin related a conversation earlier that day with Duncan. "Of course," Duncan had said, "my genius is greater than yours." And Robin had laughed at such a typically Duncan statement.[6] But there was little laughter over the Nerval translations.

The poetry community of Spicer, Duncan, and Blaser glittered with an almost hallucinatory intensity, filled with wounded feelings and grand, hieratic gestures. The poetry responded to, and of course participated in this field of ritualism. In "The Faerie Queene," Blaser wrote:

> The dismemberment happens
> like rain against the sidewalk
>
> I piss
> into the roots of my love
> where words break true

Blaser has spoken of the "triangular imagination" shared by himself and his two Berkeley peers. We all know the Freudian side effects of triangulation—the forced, shifting identification into father, mother, child. Blaser's own great personal beauty created a vortex, a hole out of which a certain madness, a *folie*, was given its head. His epic-length *The Holy Forest* continually recasts the relation of language and person into that of a deeply wounded relation to words themselves. "The words drink us up," advises "Image Nation #5." "We," the rootless subjects of this discourse, are constantly being consumed or subsumed by an outside force, to become its objects, in part precisely because we are so delectable, tempting. In "Image-Nation #9":

> sometimes the harp pierces the body
> and a man only hangs on the strings

> we have eaten ourselves luxurious and
> careless

No wonder the boundaries between word and person blur and the "radical stage of syntax" (Kristeva) shows itself for the first time:

> this language
>
> which is coloured, takes in slime, is
> some centre where one is helpless
> even to oneself
>> "My Dear," *The Moth Poem*

"This language" is "coloured," tied into sexuality in any number of different ways; it "takes in slime" not only because it takes in everything, but because it's oral and anal at once; it's a center without the reassurance that word usually denotes, a center of the unbearable. After Spicer's death, Duncan drew off his velvet gloves to excoriate Blaser's Nerval translation. These were the final, terrifying peristaltic convulsions by which San Francisco at last expelled, excreted, Robin Blaser, with jet propulsion, out of the States and into Vancouver. Kristeva: "Writing causes the subject who ventures in it to confront an archaic authority, on the nether side of the proper Name." Blaser, *Syntax*:

> it is true you can get art
> out of anything as it comes to be
> the backside of itself
>> "Diary, April 11, 1981," *Syntax*

How does the distinguished become the abhorred? To be beautiful is to be vulnerable, then despised; to be admired is to be humiliated; to give off sexual magnetism is to provide spoor for one's enemies. One notes how often Blaser is "stunned," "astonished," in every one of his "marvelouses" a victim steps forth proudly out of the shadows of the repressed. Blaser's survival and triumph as a poet was to make a ritual of his repeated defilement by his "parents," Spicer and Duncan, and to allow the castration/translation to take place. As Maria Montez said, in *Cobra Woman*: "Geef me the cobarah chewel." Blaser:

> Attis ran to the wooded pastures
> of the weavers of gold, the shadowy place, where as if a
> bee stung his brain, he took a flint knife and let the
> weight of his cock and balls from from him, so
>
> when she felt her limbs lose their manhood, still with

fresh blood spotting the ground, she grabbed the drum
with snowy hands, beating the polished hide with soft
fingers, she rose to sing to her companions
"The Translator: A Tale"

Jim Herndon examined the evidence of Jack Spicer's relations with his two friends in poetry, Robert Duncan and Robin Blaser, commenting:

I can remember really having a hard time reading *The Venice Poem*, and asking Jack about it. "Shit," said Jack, "it really is a great poem, he's just not talking your language." It was always clear to Jack that he and Duncan were the greatest poets in the world, and he never forgot old Duncan. Jack used to try to get people to get Duncan to come up to Gino & Carlo's and sit there in the bar. He wanted Duncan to come up there and sit in Gino & Carlo's and Duncan and Jack and everybody would engage in this debate: "the invisible world" *versus*, in the same way they had talked years back in Berkeley. But that was no longer Duncan's style. Jack missed that a lot. I don't think Jack felt he had any peers except for Robert and, later on probably, Robin.

Jack missed Duncan's intelligence. There's no question that's what Jack was trying to do, the same way Duncan was trying to get Robin to respond. And maybe have some fun! Argue about something, and maybe actually get something serious done, which in the atmosphere of Berkeley they apparently did. He wanted Robert to enter into a little political-poetical debate. And they'd have a lot of fun. Jack was really disappointed. Oh, that's what Jack wanted! Same as Duncan wanted with Robin.

Duncan acted with Jack just like Robin acted with Duncan. Just got outraged and said "Fuck you," and rolled up and got afraid. Duncan misunderstood [Jack's baiting] in the same way that Robin misunderstood Duncan's attack, which was an attack, there's no doubt about it."

Asked whether Spicer thought he had the right to give Duncan an A or a B-, Herndon replied,

No. Jack would have flunked Duncan, right? But not because Duncan wasn't his equal: because he was on the wrong path. As if Jack was teaching physics and Duncan was writing an essay about anthropology. There was a way, and another way. This way is the real way, and that is a false trail.

Jack was afraid that his little coterie of guys would escape and go out into the world—talk about white rabbits!—go out into the world and get eaten up. Jack was always afraid—he talked endlessly about it—if these guys read *Time* magazine, they'd be fucked. "They'll think they're smarter than *Time* magazine, but they're not. Because nobody is. Dangerous." So all these guys like Stan and George and Ronnie and doubtless Fran, and me—were in danger if they left his circumscribed limits: which could actually take up their whole fucking twenty-four-hour day— where they could go eat, where they could go drink.

By the time of Gino & Carlo's, Duncan was The Evil One. That's what Jack thought, anyway. Jack wanted to circumscribe all these cats' activities, like Stan and George. Because they would be in danger if they got an influence from the outside world, it would eat them up. Do you remember when Robin wrote that translation of Nerval—and Duncan pooh-poohed it, and haw-hawed it, wrote his own rather childish translation? Robin, of course, got insane with fury, right?

Duncan and Jess used to come up to our place all the time to talk to Fran. Duncan was saying all the time, "What's Robin mad about? We could have a great thing here. We'd all get in a New York magazine"—Duncan had it all planned out. What Duncan really wanted to do was have a nice little exchange argument, like the Paris cafés or something, and publish all their ideas in all the journals and magazines and have a lot of fun with it. Yet Robin was just insane with rage. I think the same thing happened with Jack and Duncan. Jack was writing all those letters, and getting Persky and people like that to picket Duncan's play—Jack hadn't read the play, and those guys did everything Jack said and thought it was fun. Jack wasn't mad at Duncan, he didn't hate Duncan. I never heard him say a word against Duncan's actual poetry, ever.[7]

In this Jim Herndon might have been carried beyond his purpose, for Jack Spicer loudly and explicitly said much against Robert Duncan's poetry. Under this kind of attack, though, existed respect and friendship.

Robert Duncan, when asked whether he, Blaser, and Spicer were "priests," agreed vehemently—especially since priests need not be worthy of their office and the sacraments. Or as Duncan put it, "The priest can be an idiot!" To this also he said, "Robin Blaser can get pretty goddamn priestly! I think now my priestliness is disappearing because I've decided I'm going to be a basilisk with another tenure"—Duncan smiled—"and no longer will there be a priestly tone. There'll just be a very loud voice and the *malocchio* [evil eye] fixed upon any presumptuous soul who tries to nibble crackers or get drunk on wine, right? With no blood in sight!"[8]

Robin Blaser put these matters—the connections of these poets and peers—in his own way: "The characteristics shared are, it seems to me, in some sense the incredible importance and power of poetry and language as an instrument in the world. That seems to me to be shared, and it seems to me in some part to have been learned around Robert." Referring to the early Berkeley years, Blaser continued,

Jack brings Robert to me with poems. Duncan's recognition of Spicer was immediate. What I'm trying to say is that the ties should be given as much value as these divisions. The divisions are extremely important to what I would call a triangular imagination. I do not think Duncan shared that triangle. I think Duncan sees himself as singularly alone, perhaps, in this.

I myself have a strong sense that Spicer's own way, and I in my own, maintained a kind of vision of the poetic as always working with three voices.

Duncan wrote me in the middle of the *Les Chimères* battle—in the *Audit* essay—where he wrote and said, "Opposition is true friendship," quoting Blake from *The Marriage of Heaven and Hell*, but I mean it also to move in some sense for Jack. That what is involved is an attitude, or stance, towards language. Do you think language is behind you, or do you think of it as in front of you? Now, if you do think of it as behind you, this marvelously holds on to the entire tradition of the sacred, of the origin of the language as actually being there. If you think of it, instead, as being in front of you—which I believe Spicer did—there was an incredible task, once again to shape a world and it was adrift from what had been happening.[9]

A marriage of heaven and hell indeed seems apt for the bonding of these three spirits: Duncan—"with language behind him"—and Spicer—"with language in front of him"—and all three poets united "in a vision of the poetic."

As Robin Blaser insisted, in Spicer's poetic meaning not dualism but simultaneous presence of light and dark married in a single enterprise was the learning that rendered his life. In addition, Spicer's admiration of popular culture, moving with and parallel to his ordinary training in literature, provided a peculiar strength to his community. Certainly his own work gained by such attachments. By participating easily and even enthusiastically in broad aspects of the democratic culture of his time, from science-fiction and detective-story reader to gamesman to sports fan to bar patron, he drew upon vitalities rich in the popular energies of a whole people. Add to this the interplay of his intelligence and his concern, and the result was Jack's circle in North Beach through at least a decade.

After these three came a poetic diaspora. That no ongoing artistic community survived Jack Spicer's death has much to do with Spicer's personality itself. For Jack's social skills were the principal agency of bonding for this group, especially so for those new to, marginal to, or inexperienced in art, poetic or otherwise. Though the bond began with Robert Duncan in the workshops of 1957 and 1958, Duncan in time withdrew, finding domesticity and the comfort of approving friends more to his taste than the street life of North Beach. Robin Blaser had entered the lists later and hesitantly, careful in his distancing from this world of streets and bars; his were the towers of high Romance. Thus the king dies, the catalyst is removed, the knights and damsels wander.

The inner courtyard far afield: Washington Square. Lombardy poplars at its center, the lawns spreading to the corners of a city block, benches, paths, border shrubbery; the park cut through by Columbus Avenue, its view from the Transamerica Pyramid to Mount Tamalpais in Marin County. Low, unassuming buildings surround the park, except where its northern edge is dominated by the paired steeples and façade of Saints Peter and Paul Church, center of Italian Catholic life in San Francisco.

Engraved—and gold-embossed—on the lintels of the church's entries are the opening two lines of "The Paradiso" of Dante's *Divine Comedy: "la gloria di colui che tutto muove per l'universo penetra e risplende,"* "the glory of Him who moves all penetrates and shines through the universe." Once Gail Chugg and Lew Ellingham were walking in the park and Gail asked Lew, "Do you know the line that follows those two over the church's doors?"

"No."

"'In una parte più è meno altrove,' 'In one part more and in another less.' That's the difference between the Church and poetry." In the small urban park—Washington Square—a center of North Beach life. Today there are more likely to be Chinese than Italian people sitting in the sun on benches, walking along the paths, though the young from wherever else seem the same—and so many of them. Early in the morning, as sunlight climbs down the church belltowers and over the facings of buildings and trees, gulls circle the lawn, rising from rest, a last look for food, and are gone. Old people make a group in one corner of the park slowly moving through the paces of *t'ai chi ch'uan,* the graceful exercising descended from martial arts training. Mornings hold hope, are never hot in San Francisco.

Notes

Prologue (pp. ix–xiv)

1. Jack Spicer, "Imaginary Elegies I–VI," *One Night Stand & Other Poems*, ed. Donald Allen (San Francisco: Grey Fox Press, 1980), pp. 45–54; hereafter abbreviated as *ONS*.

2. Jack Spicer, "The Poet and Poetry—A Symposium," *Occident* (Berkeley, Fall 1949); reprinted in *ONS*, pp. 90–92.

3. Blackfoot ancestry: Myrsam Wixman, interviewed by Lewis Ellingham; Fran Herndon, interviewed by Kevin Killian; Holt Spicer, Jack's brother, doubted the family legend of Indian blood (Lewis Ellingham/Holt V. Spicer Statement). Mary Baker Eddy: Dora FitzGerald, "A Jack Memoir" (unpublished essay) and "Jack as Coyote," *Ironwood* 28 (Tucson, Fall 1986), p. 147. Father a Wobbly: James Herndon, interviewed by Lewis Ellingham. Anarchism and contempt for liberalism: Robin Blaser, interviewed by Lewis Ellingham; James Herndon, interviewed by Lewis Ellingham; Jack Spicer, "Poetry and Politics," lecture given July 14, 1965, at the Berkeley Poetry Conference, published in *The House that Jack Built: The Collected Lectures of Jack Spicer*, ed. Peter Gizzi (Wesleyan University Press, 1998).

4. Robin Blaser, interviewed by Lewis Ellingham; Dora FitzGerald, "A Jack Memoir."

5. James Herndon interviewed by Lewis Ellingham.

6. Bill Brodecky, interviewed by Lewis Ellingham: "As a person Jack was pretty impossible. He was a terrible liar. He pretended to know all about gourmet food and yet when he died he was eating peanut butter out of filthy utensils. He didn't want people to know what a failure he was in those areas. He was ashamed of it."

7. *Mandorla 1*, published in Mexico City, featured three poems ("Orfeo," "La cancion de un prisionero," and "Guerrea en la jungla") from Spicer's *A Book of Music*, translated into Spanish by Laura Guzman and Alfonso D'Aquino. Eliot Weinberger's anthology *Una antologia de la poesie notreamericana desde 1950* includes translations of "Thing Language," "Love Poems," and "Graphemics" (from Spicer's 1965 volume *Language*). Thanks to Roberto Tejada, editor of *Mandorla*, for pointing these out. *Billy The Kid*, *The Holy Grail*, and *Language*, translated by Joseph Guglielmi, Jacques Roubaud, and Jean-Pierre Faye, were published in French in 1976 (a separate edition of Guglielmi's *Billy the Kid* appeared in 1990), while *Lament for the Makers* (*Lamentation pour les créateurs*),

translated by Sydney Levy and Jean-Jacques Viton, was published by Format Americain in 1994. Thanks to Claude Royet-Journoud for these citations.

1. Prodigy Gone Wrong (pp. 1–33)

1. J. F. Goodwin, "Spicer and All the Poets, (or *After Spicer*)," *Hanging Loose* 58, p. 32.

2. "The Book of Percival" 4 (from *The Holy Grail*, 1962), *The Collected Books of Jack Spicer*, ed. Robin Blaser (Santa Barbara: Black Sparrow Press, 1975), p. 192; referred to hereafter as *CB*.

3. Jess Collins, interviewed by Kevin Killian, November 4, 1990. Later, in the mid-fifties, Jess (born Burgess Collins in Long Beach, California, in 1923) dropped his surname and slowly became recognized as one of the greatest international painters and collagists. We refer to him as "Jess" throughout the remainder of this text, though some quoted references to "Jess Collins" also appear.

4. Harry Z. Coren, interviewed by Lewis Ellingham, 1987.

5. Holt V. Spicer, interviewed by Lewis Ellingham. Much of the information about Spicer's early life in this chapter is taken from this interview, 1983.

6. Kate Mulholland, interviewed by Lewis Ellingham, 1984.

7. Spicer's reading was recalled by Gerald M. Ackerman, interviewed by Kevin Killian, November 6, 1991.

8. Aldous Huxley to Jack Spicer, July 3, 1941, Bancroft Library, University of California, Berkeley.

9. Ariel Parkinson, interviewed by Lewis Ellingham and Kevin Killian, June 22, 1991.

10. Holt V. Spicer, interviewed by Lewis Ellingham, 1983.

11. Tové Neville, "Jack Spicer: Impressions from an 'Estranged' Poet," (San Francisco *Chronicle*, Sunday, August 29, 1965). This article, published shortly after Spicer's death, contains the only interview of JS we have been able to locate.

12. Andy Cole, interviewed by Lewis Ellingham, 1983.

13. Myrsam Wixman, interviewed by Lewis Ellingham, 1982. Myrsam Wixman was a fellow student and friend of the Berkeley Renaissance poets. Spicer's letters to Wixman have been published in *Mirage* 2 (San Francisco, 1986), ed. Bruce Boone.

14. Its first chapter was printed as "The Wasps," in *To* 3/4 (Philadelphia, Penn., April 1994), pp. 69–94, ed. Kevin Killian.

15. Holt V. Spicer, interviewed by Lewis Ellingham, 1983.

16. Robin Blaser, interviewed by Lewis Ellingham, 1983.

17. Robin Blaser, interviewed by Kevin Killian, May 22, 1992.

18. Josephine Miles, interviewed by Eloise Toxey, Berkeley Oral History Project interviews, p. 17, Bancroft Library, University of California, Berkeley.

19. Ariel Parkinson, interviewed by Lewis Ellingham and Kevin Killian, June 22, 1991.

20. Robert Duncan, interviewed by Eloise Tovey, Berkeley Oral History Project interviews, p. 24, Bancroft Library, University of California, Berkeley.

21. *Collected Poems 1945–1946* was published after Spicer's death by Oyez/White Rabbit Press.

22. Linda Hamalian, *A Life of Kenneth Rexroth* (New York: Norton, 1991), p. 149.

23. Leonard Wolf, interviewed by Kevin Killian, January 11, 1994.

24. See Robert Duncan, "The Homosexual in Society," *Politics* 1 (New York, August

1944), p. 210, ed. Dwight MacDonald; revised and much expanded in *Jimmy & Lucy's House of K* 3 (Berkeley, Calif., January 1985), pp. 51–69.

25. Robin Blaser, interviewed by Lewis Ellingham, 1982.

26. For more information on the "Berkeley Renaissance" and its links to the larger and later poetry movement called "The San Francisco Renaissance," which includes the Beat and Black Mountain infusions, see Michael Davidson's book *The San Francisco Renaissance: Poetics and Community at Mid-century* (Cambridge: Cambridge University Press, 1989).

27. Robert Duncan, interviewed by Lewis Ellingham, 1983.

28. Janie O'Neill, telephone interview with Kevin Killian, April 5, 1993.

29. Robert Duncan, "Jack Spicer complains . . . ," Robert Duncan archive, Poetry/Rare Books Collection, State University of New York at Buffalo. Thanks to Josephine Fredman Stewart for providing this poem to us.

30. Robert Duncan, Josephine Frankel [Fredman Stewart], Fred Fredman, Hugh O'Neill, Jack Spicer, *A Canto for Ezra Pound*, Charles Olson papers, University of Connecticut, Storrs, Library.

31. Spicer, "Miller: Remember to Remember," *Occident* (Berkeley, Fall 1947), pp. 44–45.

32. James Schevill gives an interesting account of Bern Porter's life in *Where to Go, What to Do, When You Are Bern Porter* (Gardiner, Maine: Tilbury House, 1992).

33. Bern Porter, letter to Kevin Killian, February 13, 1997.

34. Robert Duncan, interviewed by Eloise Tovey, Berkeley Oral History Project interviews, p. 36, Bancroft Library, University of California, Berkeley.

35. "A Heron for Mrs. Altrocchi," *One Night Stand & Other Poems*, ed. Donald Allen (San Francisco: Grey Fox Press, 1980), p. 17; hereafter *ONS*. Background on Julia Altrocchi was supplied by Thomas and Ariel Parkinson, interviewed by Lewis Ellingham and Kevin Killian, June 22, 1991, and by Gerald Fabian, interviewed by Kevin Killian, September 19, 1993.

36. Josephine [Fredman] Stewart, interviewed by Kevin Killian, March 8, 1992.

37. Ariel Parkinson, interviewed by Lewis Ellingham and Kevin Killian, June 22, 1991.

38. Ariel Parkinson, letter to Lewis Ellingham and Kevin Killian, June 25, 1991.

39. Thomas Parkinson, interviewed by Lewis Ellingham and Kevin Killian, June 22, 1991.

40. Wayne Burns, interviewed by Kevin Killian, April 27, 1993.

41. Ekbert Faas, *Young Robert Duncan: Portrait of the Poet as Homosexual in Society* (Santa Barbara: Black Sparrow Press, 1983), pp. 274–78.

42. Ariel Parkinson, interviewed by Lewis Ellingham and Kevin Killian, June 22, 1991.

43. Mary Morehart, "The Morehart Hoax," *Bed* 4: Flaming Tales of True Romance (Vancouver, B.C., 1976).

44. Letter, Jack Spicer to Robert Duncan, "Fall of 1946," Robert Duncan papers, Bancroft Library, University of California, Berkeley. Forster at the tea party, miffed, perhaps, that some—like Blaser—confused him with the author of the Hornblower novels, and exasperated in any case that no one had anything to ask him about save for his long-ago memories of Mary Butts, a woman he disliked, finally offered, "She had red hair." Robin Blaser, telephone conversation with Kevin Killian, August 1997.

45. *Richard II*, Act IV, Scene 1, ll. 280–86.

46. Robin Blaser, interviewed by Lewis Ellingham, 1983.

47. Thomas Parkinson, interviewed by Lewis Ellingham and Kevin Killian, June 22, 1991.

48. Josephine [Fredman] Stewart, interviewed by Kevin Killian, March 8, 1992.

49. See Duncan's autobiographical annotations to several of Spicer's letters to him, published in *ACTS 6*, "A Book of Correspondences for Jack Spicer" (San Francisco, 1987), pp. 5–12, ed. David Levi Strauss and Benjamin Hollander.

50. Gerald M. Ackerman, interviewed by Kevin Killian, November 6, 1991.

51. Gerald M. Ackerman, letter to Kevin Killian, August 8, 1992.

52. Thom Gunn, in conversation with Kevin Killian, February 28, 1992.

53. Robin Blaser, interviewed by Lewis Ellingham, 1983.

54. Sam Hardin, interviewed by Kevin Killian, January 23, 1993.

55. Roy Harvey Pearce, *The Savages of America: A Study of the Indian and the Idea of Civilization* (Baltimore: Johns Hopkins Press, 1953). Blaser and Spicer are credited (p. xiii) with "bibliographic assistance."

56. Roy Harvey Pearce, interviewed by Kevin Killian, July 31, 1994.

57. Stuart Loomis, interviewed by Kevin Killian, July 9, 1995.

58. Jack Spicer, "The Poet and Poetry—A Symposium," *ONS*, pp. 90–92. Originally published in the Berkeley magazine *Occident* (Fall 1949).

59. Gerald M. Ackerman, interviewed by Kevin Killian, November 6, 1991.

60. Myrsam Wixman, interviewed by Kevin Killian, April 2, 1994.

61. Donald M. Allen, interviewed by Kevin Killian, November 1990. Donald Allen, the future editor and publisher, would in time edit the "San Francisco Scene" issue of *Evergreen Review* and the massive anthology *The New American Poetry 1945–60* (hereafter *NAP*), publications that gave Spicer his first nationwide recognition. To other Berkeley students, Jack just seemed like a mess. A letter has survived, which reads in part: "I'll call Bill's home as soon as I arrive, but I fully expect that you will not have returned by then. But, come that day, we'll hie us off to some secluded nook and catch up on the latest campus scuttle-butt. First on the list would seem to be the subject of your coming novel, JACK SPICER: PRODIGY GONE WRONG." Donald F. Snepp to Roland C. Ball, Jr., August 25, 1948.

62. Ekbert Faas, *Young Robert Duncan: Portrait of the Poet as Homosexual in Society* (Santa Barbara: Black Sparrow Press, 1983), pp. 274–80. Faas tells the most comprehensive tale of the collapse of the Writers' Conference, though his findings have been disputed by some of the surviving witnesses.

63. Richard Montague, the brilliant, unstable mathematician, who died at a tragically young age, was the model for the eponymous character in Samuel R. Delany's novel *The Mad Man* (New York: Richard Kasak Books, 1993).

64. Robert Duncan, interviewed by Eloise Tovey, Berkeley Oral History Project interviews, pp. 19–20, Bancroft Library, University of California, Berkeley.

65. Thomas Parkinson, interviewed by Lewis Ellingham and Kevin Killian, June 22, 1991.

66. Kate Mulholland, interviewed by Lewis Ellingham, 1984. The collapse of the San Francisquito Dam (1928), a part of the aqueduct project, which killed 450 people and caused extensive damage in property, is also a part of the Mulholland legacy. Mulholland Drive in Los Angeles is named for the family. Roman Polanski's film *Chinatown* tells a version of the Owens Valley/Los Angeles corruption story, in addition to which Catherine ("Kate") Mulholland published an account of these events in *The Owensmouth Baby* (California State University Northridge Libraries, 1987).

67. Sam Hardin, interviewed by Kevin Killian, January 31, 1993.

68. Kate Mulholland, interviewed by Lewis Ellingham, 1984.

69. Don Allen, interviewed by Kevin Killian, October 15, 1990.

70. Harry Z. Coren, interviewed by Lewis Ellingham, 1987.

71. Gerald M. Ackerman, interviewed by Kevin Killian, November 6, 1991.

72. This account is drawn from interviews with Landis Everson (1983), Kate Mulholland (1984), and Jim Townsend (1991).

73. The poem was published in *ONS* as "Orpheus' Song to Apollo," p. 22.

74. Jack Spicer to Richard Rummonds, letter from 1953, in *Some Things from Jack* (Verona: Plain Wrapper Press), 1972.

75. Landis Everson, interviewed by Lewis Ellingham, 1983.

76. Robert Duncan, interviewed by Lewis Ellingham, 1983. This view is regularly repeated by persons who knew Spicer in the 1940s.

77. *Carnal Matters*, Alexander Goodman, "The Battle between the Poets and the Painters" (Washington, D.C.: Guild Press, 1969), pp. 71–72. Haimsohn sent Lewis Ellingham a copy of this book, written for the pulp market, with handwritten notations identifying the fictionally disguised characters by the actual names of the persons who were the characters' models.

78. Edward Halsey Foster, *Jack Spicer* (Boise, Idaho: Boise State University, 1991), pp. 15–16.

79. The following information is drawn from Lewis Ellingham's interviews with Jim Herndon (1982), and Kevin Killian's interviews with Sam Hardin (January 31, 1993) and Glenn Lewis (January 3, 1991).

80. Minnette Lehmann, interviewed by Kevin Killian, May 5, 1991.

81. Sam Hardin, interviewed by Kevin Killian, January 31, 1993.

82. Ibid. See also Jim Herndon's recollections printed at the end of *CB*.

83. Gaby Onderwyzer [Stuart], interviewed by Kevin Killian, December 17, 1993.

84. "The Dancing Ape," in a revised version, was published in *ONS*.

85. Robin Blaser, interviewed by Lewis Ellingham, 1983.

86. Ellen [King] Tallman, interviewed by Kevin Killian, July 3, 1991.

87. Lewis Ellingham contacted the leader of the American Civil Liberties Union legal defense effort in this affair, Ernest Besig—now retired—who remembered Jack Spicer as "a minor figure in the fight" (telephone conversation, October 25, 1984) and explained the details of the loyalty oath problem as they would have affected Spicer. Two oaths were involved, the first a requirement (1950) by the Regents of the University of California specifically directed to faculty and specifically providing that no faculty member be "a member of the Communist Party." This oath was declared unconstitutional by the State Supreme Court in 1952 in action brought by Professor Tolman of the Psychology department at Berkeley. However, by then a new legal obstacle had been created by a member of the State Assembly, known after its sponsor as the Levering Act. This made it unlawful for any state employee to advocate the violent overthrow of constitutional government, both state and national. By putting the matter in a more positive way, directing those who signed the oath only to uphold the already understood provisions of existing constitutional law, as Professor Parkinson observes, the oath was rendered more palatable to faculty. The same seems true concerning the more general aim of the law, affecting all state employees instead of just university faculty. Besig said, "Professor Tolman succeeded against the University Oath in the courts in 1952." This, however, "had no bearing on the Levering Act challenges, the first of which was made by San Francisco State College teachers and lost, the second succeeding [1968]. Grounds in both cases were the 'too broad' writing of the law, singling out 'special groups.'"

Professor David Reed, from the late 1940s through the 1960s a member of the University of California faculty, in the English department until 1965 and thereafter head of the linguistics department, explained his understanding of the legal situation as that given above, confirming Parkinson's and Besig's assessments in detail. Reed remembered specifically the Levering Act language as requiring state employees to sign a disclaimer of membership in any organization advocating "force, violence or other illegal acts" in the overthrow of the U.S. or California governments.

88. Josephine Miles, interviewed by Eloise Toxey, Berkeley Oral History Project interviews, p. 20, Bancroft Library, University of California, Berkeley.

2. After Berkeley (pp. 34–62)

1. Jack Spicer, undated letter to Robin Blaser from 1950 or 1951, in the possession of Mr. Blaser.

2. Sam Hardin, interviewed by Kevin Killian, January 31, 1993.

3. Mary Rice Moore to Lewis Ellingham (phone interview), September 17, 1984. Other details are drawn from Kevin Killian's interview with Mary Rice Moore on June 23, 1991.

4. Jim Herndon, interviewed by Lewis Ellingham, 1982.

5. Jack Spicer, letter to Robert Duncan, Fall 1950, as published in *ACTS* 6, "A Book of Correspondences for Jack Spicer" (San Francisco, 1987), pp. 9–12, ed. David Levi Strauss and Benjamin Hollander.

6. "Jack Spicer Section: 'Lines Excised from "Imaginary Elegies" (1957–8)'" *Lyric&* 2 (San Francisco, July 1993), pp. 85–89. For an account of the making of *Imaginary Elegies I–IV*, see Kevin Killian, "Under the Influence: Jack Spicer, Robin Blaser and the Revision of 'Imaginary Elegies,' 1957," *Exact Change Year Book 1* (Boston, February 1995), pp. 133–34.

7. Harry Z. Coren, interviewed by Lewis Ellingham, 1987.

8. Arthur Kloth, interviewed by Kevin Killian, November 4, 1990.

9. Spicer, "Train Song for Gary," *ONS*, p. 57. The other poem inspired by Bottone's absence is "Sonnet for the Beginning of Winter" (*ONS*, p. 58): "The robin and the thrush have taken wing. / The sparrow stays. He sings a dismal song / And eats the seed uncovered in the snow. / An ugly bird, call him the heart's agony."

10. Mary Rice Moore interviews, 1984, 1991.

11. Jim Herndon, interviewed by Lewis Ellingham, 1982.

12. Myrsam Wixman, interviewed by Lewis Ellingham, 1982.

13. Mary Rice Moore, interviewed by Kevin Killian, June 23, 1991.

14. Gary Bottone to Lewis Ellingham, January 11, 1984.

15. Jess Collins, interviewed by Kevin Killian, November 18, 1990.

16. Thomas Parkinson, interviewed by Lewis Ellingham and Kevin Killian, June 22, 1991.

17. Jack Spicer, *Some Things from Jack* (Verona: Plain Wrapper Press), 1972.

18. Earl McGrath, interviewed by Kevin Killian, September 21, 1991.

19. Wally Hedrick, interviewed by Kevin Killian, August 27, 1996.

20. This incident is described in Gerald Ackerman's unpublished memoirs of the Berkeley period.

21. Gerald Fabian, interviewed by Kevin Killian, September 19, 1993.

22. Lewis Ellingham/Jess Sawyer Statement, pp. 1ff.

23. Robert Duncan, interviewed by Lewis Ellingham, 1983.

24. Lewis Ellingham/Jess Sawyer Statement, pp. 3–4.

25. Myrsam Wixman, interviewed by Lewis Ellingham. Spicer's letters to Wixman have been published in *Mirage* 2 (San Francisco, 1986), ed. Bruce Boone.

26. Lewis Ellingham/Jess Sawyer Statement, pp. 7–8.

27. Jess Sawyer, in an aside to Lewis Ellingham when they met to discuss the tape made on the bridge club, mentioned Spicer's conversational references to anal warts as the probable cause of Wilben Holther's concern; see *CB*, p. 59, where Spicer comments on this condition in writing by way of an answer to a Robert Duncan workshop questionnaire (answer III-2).

28. Lewis Ellingham/Jess Sawyer Statement, pp. 9–10.

29. Myrsam Wixman, interviewed by Lewis Ellingham, 1982.

30. Richard Bratset, interviewed by Kevin Killian, October 3, 1993. Robert Berg's diaries are in the possession of Vince Fernandez of San Francisco.

31. Robin Blaser, interviewed by Kevin Killian, May 22, 1992. Blaser gave a similar version of this incident in "A Correspondence," *The Capilano Review*, ser. 2, no. 22 (Spring 1997), pp. 43–53.

32. Rodger Streitmatter, *Unspeakable: The Rise of the Gay and Lesbian Press in America* (Boston: Faber and Faber, 1995), pp. 17–50. Who exactly came up with the idea of "One"? Streitmatter credits Dale Jennings, but other sources say it was Spicer's Berkeley friend John Button.

33. See John D'Emilio, *Sexual Politics, Sexual Practices* (Chicago: University of Chicago Press, 1983), pp. 67–72.

34. Robin Blaser, interviewed by Kevin Killian, May 22, 1992.

35. Myrsam Wixman, interviewed by Lewis Ellingham, April 17, 1997.

36. Robin Blaser, interviewed by Kevin Killian, May 22, 1992.

37. Myrsam Wixman, interviewed by Lewis Ellingham, April 17 and June 5, 1997.

38. Stuart Timmons, *The Trouble with Harry Hay: Founder of the Modern Gay Movement* (Boston: Alyson Publications, 1990), pp. 175–80.

39. Spicer, "Three Marxist Essays," *ONS*, p. 88.

40. Robin Blaser, interviewed by Lewis Ellingham, 1983.

41. Thomas Parkinson, interviewed by Lewis Ellingham, 1982.

42. Richard Candida Smith, *Utopia and Dissent: Art, Poetry and Politics in California* (Berkeley: University of California Press, 1995). See especially pp. 67–137, which provide an extensive overview of the ideological struggle behind the supporters of Douglas MacAgy and Ernest Mundt, successive directors of CSFA.

43. Rebecca Solnit, *Secret Exhibition: Six California Artists of the Cold War* (San Francisco: City Lights, 1990).

44. Wally Hedrick, interviewed by Kevin Killian, August 27, 1995.

45. Ibid.

46. John Allen Ryan, interviewed by Kevin Killian, May 31, 1992.

47. Jess, interviewed by Kevin Killian, November 4, 1990.

48. Ibid.

49. Richard Duerden, conversation with Lewis Ellingham, May 11, 1983.

50. According to Gerald M. Ackerman, interviewed by Kevin Killian, November 6, 1991, Spicer quoted this quip so often that Ackerman thought he had written it himself. Thanks to Gerrit Lansing for spotting the reference.

51. Jess, interviewed by Kevin Killian, November 4, 1990.

52. Michael McClure, interviewed by Kevin Killian, July 19, 1992.

53. John Allen Ryan, interviewed by Lewis Ellingham.

54. The Spicer/Brubeck tapes have vanished, but were played during the opening of the "6" Gallery and at several associated benefits. Columnist Herb Caen wrote, "Several young ladies with long blonde hair and leather sandals, several young men with bare chests and beards gathered in circle, listening intently to record of avant garde poem,

recited against background of polytonal music. . . . The recording was poet Jack Spicer reading, with music by the Dave Brubeck trio" (Herb Caen, San Francisco *Examiner*, Sunday, September 26, 1954). Thanks to Jack Foley for bringing this to our attention.

55. Herb Caen, interviewed by Kevin Killian, 1992.

56. Knute Stiles, interviewed by Lewis Ellingham, 1982.

57. Knute Stiles, interviewed by Lewis Ellingham; *ONS*, p. 64.

58. Knute Stiles, interviewed by Lewis Ellingham, 1982.

59. The Spicer-Mackintosh correspondence begins at the time when Mackintosh was stationed at Fort Ord, near Monterey, California, and has been published in part (approximately half the letters and cards from Spicer to Mackintosh) in *Caterpillar* 10 (1970).

60. Lewis Ellingham, "Spicer Project Notebook" 5, entry for August 24, 1984, p. 7.

61. For an examination of the Cohn-Schine affair, see Richard Gid Powers, *Not Without Honor: The History of American Anticommunism* (New York: Free Press, 1995), pp. 263–70.

62. John Allen Ryan, interviewed by Lewis Ellingham, 1982.

63. John Allen Ryan to Kevin Killian, May 31, 1992.

64. Williams's brief memoir of his association with Spicer was published as "Dear Spicer," in *ACTS* 6, "A Book of Correspondences for Jack Spicer" (San Francisco, 1987), p. 44, ed. David Levi Strauss and Benjamin Hollander.

65. J. F. Goodwin, "Spicer and All the Poets (or *After Spicer*)," *Hanging Loose* 58, p. 33.

66. John Allen Ryan to Kevin Killian, May 31, 1992.

67. Allen Ginsberg, interviewed by Kevin Killian, October 16, 1990.

68. Spicer's letters to Allen Joyce are published in Jack Spicer, "'Kennst du Das Land?' Jack Spicer's Letters to Allen Joyce," ed. Bruce Boone, *Sulfur* 10 (Los Angeles, 1984), pp. 136–53.

69. Myrsam Wixman, interviewed by Kevin Killian, April 2, 1994.

70. For a detailed picture of the "6" Gallery, see *Lyrical Vision: the 6 Gallery 1954–1957* (Davis, Calif.: Natsoulas-Novelozo Gallery, 1990), the catalogue to a 1990 retrospective of work shown at the 6 during its heyday.

71. Michael McClure, interviewed by Kevin Killian, July 19, 1992. An edited version of this interview, titled, "An Empire of Signs: Jack Spicer," was published in McClure's book *Lighting the Corners On Art, Nature and the Visionary: Essays and Interviews* (Albuquerque: An American Poetry Book, 1993), pp. 113–28.

72. Letter to Allen Joyce, *Sulfur* 10, p. 151. His letters to John Allen Ryan, as yet unpublished, contain similar allusions.

73. Wesley Day (interviewed by Kevin Killian, October 25, 1991) supplied many details of Helen Adam's life.

74. Part III of Spicer's "A Night in Four Parts" is titled "Wet Dream." This anecdote is told by Duncan, Blaser, and Spicer on the "Summer Days" tape, a recorded conversation made during the Berkeley Poetry Conference in 1965, and preserved in the Rare Book Collection at Simon Fraser University Library in Burnaby, B.C.

75. Ernest Mundt to Jack Spicer, February 14, 1954, Artists' Files, San Francisco Art Institute.

76. Wally Hedrick, interviewed by Kevin Killian, August 27, 1995.

77. Ernest Mundt, interviewed by Kevin Killian, telephone conversation, September 1991.

78. Stephanie Bryan disappeared April 28, 1955; in the autumn police arrested a suspect, Burton Abbott, whose wife and mother-in-law led them to his trail. He was executed in March 1957, although many thought he was innocent. His case, like that of

Caryl Chessman, led to public protests and the eventual overturn of the death penalty in California. See Keith Walker, *A Trail of Corn: A True Mystery* (Santa Rosa, Calif.: Golden Door Press, 1995). The Bois Berk papers at the San Francisco Gay and Lesbian Historical Society reveal further details of police persecution of Berkeley homosexuals in the months before Abbott's arrest.

79. Michael McClure, interviewed by Kevin Killian, July 19, 1992.

3. The Poet in New York (and Boston) (pp. 63–77)

1. Jack Spicer to John Allen Ryan, August 17, 1955.
2. Arthur Kloth, interviewed by Kevin Killian, November 4, 1990.
3. Jack Spicer to John Allen Ryan, October 7, 1955.
4. John Button, "Some Memories" (1980), *No Apologies 2* (Spring 1984), p. 30.
5. "At the Old Place," *The Collected Poems of Frank O'Hara*, ed. Donald Allen (New York: Alfred A. Knopf, 1979).
6. Earl McGrath, interviewed by Kevin Killian, September 21, 1991.
7. Frank O'Hara to Jasper Johns, July 15, 1959.
8. Joe LeSueur to Lewis Ellingham, June 27, 1983.
9. Landis Everson, interviewed by Lewis Ellingham, 1982.
10. Robert Duncan, interviewed by Lewis Ellingham, 1983.
11. John Button, "Some Memories," p. 30.
12. Maria Damon, *The Dark End of the Street: Margins in American Vanguard Poetry* (Minneapolis, University of Minnesota Press, 1993), p. 165. The whole of Chapter 4 in *Dark End*, "Dirty Jokes and Angels: Jack Spicer and Robert Duncan Writing the Gay Community" (pp. 142–201), is a fine essay on "poetry as social practice."
13. Jack Spicer to Robert Creeley, August 12, 1955, Robert Creeley archive, Washington University Libraries, St. Louis.
14. Jonathan Williams to Kevin Killian, June 19, 1991.
15. See John L. Spicer, "The Poems of Emily Dickinson," *Boston Public Library Quarterly* (July 1956), pp. 135–43. Spicer wrote two other brief notices for the *BPLQ*: one on "Wimpfeling's Adolescentia, 1505" (January 1957) and one on "The Legend of St. Meinrad, 1567" (July 1957). These appeared after he had left Boston and the library and returned to San Francisco.
16. See, for example, *CB*, p. 352.
17. This account of Spicer's job at the Boston Public Library draws upon information supplied by James Devlin, interviewed by Kevin Killian, November 26, 1990, and John Norton, interviewed by Kevin Killian, November 11, 1990.
18. Duncan and Spicer discuss Charles Olson's influence on the so-called "Summer Days" tape, a recorded conversation made during the Berkeley Poetry Conference in 1965, preserved in the Rare Book Collection at Simon Fraser University Library in Burnaby, B.C.
19. For O'Hara's stay in Boston, see Brad Gooch, *City Poet: The Life and Times of Frank O'Hara* (New York, Alfred A. Knopf, 1993), pp. 272–81.
20. John Wieners, "Chop-House Memories" (May 1968), in *Cultural Affairs in Boston: Poetry & Prose 1956–1985*, ed. Raymond Foye (Santa Rosa: Black Sparrow Press, 1988), p. 80.
21. Donald Allen, interviewed by Kevin Killian, October 15, 1990.
22. Robin Blaser and Jack Spicer, "A Dialogue between Eastern Poetry and Western Poetry" (unpublished), Bancroft Library, University of California in Berkeley.

23. Gerrit Lansing, "Tribute to Steve Jonas," *Little Caesar* 10 (Los Angeles, 1980), p. 115.

24. "Jack Spicer: Letters to Robin Blaser: 1955–1958," ed. Lori Chamberlain & Terry Ludwar, *line* 9 (Simon Fraser University, Spring 1987), p. 37.

25. "Ode for Walt Whitman, a Translation for Steve Jonas," *CB*, p. 31.

26. Jim Herndon, interviewed by Lewis Ellingham, 1982. With Hayward King, the black painter who was one of the original six of the "6" Gallery, Spicer's relation was a formal one.

27. Nemi Frost, interviewed by Kevin Killian, August 7, 1993.

28. N. A. Diaman, "Memories of Jack Spicer at the Poets' Table," pp. 9–11.

29. Joe Dunn, interviewed by Lewis Ellingham, 1986.

30. Spicer's contempt for Ted Williams can be heard in the discussion following the third of his "Vancouver Lectures" (June 1965).

31. Glenn Lewis, interviewed by Kevin Killian, January 3, 1991.

32. John Ashbery, interviewed by Kevin Killian, September 13, 1990.

33. James Schuyler, interviewed by Kevin Killian, February 12, 1989.

34. Robin Blaser to Kevin Killian, November 20, 1990.

35. Robin Blaser, interviewed by Kevin Killian, May 22, 1992.

36. *ONS*, pp. 77–80.

37. Robin Blaser to Donald Allen, November 12, 1956, Archive for New Poetry, Mandeville Department of Special Collections, University of California at San Diego.

38. Postcard from Jack Spicer to Donald Allen, September 1956, Bancroft Library, University of California, Berkeley.

39. *CB*, p. 352.

40. "Jack Spicer's Letters to Allen Joyce," ed. Bruce Boone, *Sulfur* 10 (Los Angeles, 1984), pp. 152–53.

41. "Letters to Robin Blaser," in *line* 9, p. 32; Lewis observes that Spicer's reference to a "person named Glenn Lewis" is certainly ambiguous and probably ironic, since Blaser had known Lewis in Berkeley in the late forties.

42. Glenn Lewis, interviewed by Kevin Killian, January 3, 1991.

43. Joe Dunn, interviewed by Lewis Ellingham, 1986.

44. Robin Blaser to Donald Allen, November 12, 1956, Donald Allen papers, Archive for New Poetry, Mandeville Department of Special Collections, University of California, San Diego.

4. "The Whole Boon of His Fertility" (pp. 79–117)

1. The poet Eve Triem (1902–93) was an occasional participant in the SF poetry activities of the 1950s and a friend of other poets—she appears, for example, in *Literary San Francisco*, p. 167, in a photograph of a literary evening at Kenneth Rexroth's also showing Jack Spicer, James Broughton, Philip Lamantia, Ida Hodes, and others of the time and scene. Her selected poetry, 1937–1983, appeared under the title *New as a Wave* (Seattle: Dragon Gate Press, 1984). For Robert Duncan's statements see Lewis Ellingham/Robert Duncan Interview (I), pp. 3–7; in a letter by Duncan to Blaser, November 28, 1956, Duncan gives Spicer's fee as $200 (Bancroft Library, University of California, Berkeley). Almost six months before the Workshop, in a letter to Spicer, June 7, 1956, Duncan remarks, "the income from the Workshop . . . is not enuf to keep a monkey in peanuts." The complications caused by the anonymity of this gift almost prevented San Francisco State from accepting the money, and the Workshop plan was

in jeopardy for a few weeks. See Poetry Center files, esp. H. E. Brakebill to Ruth Witt-Diamant, December 17, 1956, Bancroft Library, University of California, Berkeley for details.

2. Spicer, "Letters to Robin Blaser, 1955–1958," *line* 9 (Simon Fraser University, Spring 1978), p. 35.

3. Duncan/Blaser correspondence, Bancroft Library, University of California, Berkeley.

4. Charles Olson, "Against Wisdom as Such," *Human Universe and Other Essays,* ed. Donald Allen (New York: Grove Press, 1967), p. 67.

5. *The Selected Poems of Federico Garcia Lorca,* ed. Francisco Garcia Lorca and Donald M. Allen (New York: New Directions, 1955).

6. Robert Duncan to Miss Mincer, January 25, 1957, files of the Poetry Center at San Francisco State University.

7. The master mimeo of the questionnaire remains in the files of the Poetry Center at San Francisco State University.

8. Ruth Witt-Diamant/Robert Duncan, "Poetry Center Report, June 1957," p. 5, files of the Poetry Center at San Francisco State University. Bancroft Library, University of California, Berkeley.

9. *CB,* p. 353.

10. John Allen Ryan, interviewed by Lewis Ellingham, p. 31; Bob Connor, interviewed by Lewis Ellingham, p. 25. In the Poetry Center archives at San Francisco State two Harry Redl photos exist, one of which shows a young blond painter, Charlie Walker, among the participants of the Magic Workshop.

11. Lewis Ellingham/Robert Duncan interview (I), pp. 7–8.

12. J. F. Goodwin, "Spicer and All the Poets (or *After Spicer*)," *Hanging Loose* 58.

13. Tom Field, interviewed by Christopher Wagstaff, March 18 and 25, 1986. "Interview with Tom Field" was published in conjunction with the Tom Field memorial retrospective at San Francisco's 871 Fine Arts Gallery in the autumn of 1996.

14. Geroge Stanley, interviewed by Lewis Ellingham, 1982. "Pablito at the Corrida," from a selection made many years later, is the first poem to survive in Stanley's *You* (Vancouver, B.C.: New Star, 1974).

15. Jack Gilbert, "Respects to Spicer," *The Gator* (San Francisco State College), May 3, 1966.

16. Ruth Witt-Diamant to Luther Nichols (of the San Francisco *Examiner*), May 28, 1957, from the Poetry Center files at the Bancroft Library, University of California, Berkeley.

17. James Broughton to Kevin Killian, October 1, 1990. "A Farewell to the Household Muse," which has as a dedication "For Jack Spicer on the opening of his magic poetry circle," is dated "Spring 1957." The poem was first published in *Odes and Occasions* (South San Francisco: Manroot, 1977), p. 19.

18. Tové Neville, "Impressions From an 'Estranged' Poet," San Francisco *Chronicle,* August 29, 1965, p. 33.

19. Lewis Ellingham/Bob Connor interview, pp. 26–27.

20. Robert Lowell to Ruth Witt-Diamant, March 30, 1959, Poetry Center files, Bancroft Library, University of California, Berkeley.

21. Lewis Ellingham/Robert Duncan interview (II), p. 67.

22. "Western Addition": a neighborhood in San Francisco, just west of Van Ness Avenue and extending to Masonic Avenue, which was developed in Victorian times and is now largely occupied by Japan Town, the black ghetto of the Fillmore district and a reclaiming "gentry."

Notes

23. Robert Duncan to Ruth Witt-Diamant, June 16, 1958, files of the Poetry at Center at San Francisco State University.

24. Jess/Kevin Killian interview, November 4, 1990.

25. Paul Alexander to Lewis Ellingham, August 28, 1982; and see Duncan's notes to the staged reading of the play (March 1957) in the Poetry Center files, Bancroft Library, University of California, Berkeley.

26. Spicer to Robin Blaser, [n.d., 1957?] in *line* 9 (Simon Fraser University, Spring 1987), pp. 48–49.

27. Richard Duerden, conversation with Lewis Ellingham, May 11, 1983. The Olsons "had the pleasure of having Ruth Witt-Diamant tell them how great Dylan Thomas was," remembered Richard Duerden. "They were sleeping in the room Dylan had slept in. Olson was being told, of course, that in comparison to Dylan Thomas, he was a second-rate poet."

28. Robert Duncan, p. 25 of an unpublished manuscript fragment for an introduction to a Spicer bibliography sponsored by the Gotham Book Mart in New York, but never realized (c. 1970). The chronology of Olson's visit to San Francisco has been clarified by Ralph Maud, editor of *The Minutes of the Charles Olson Society* (Vancouver), in a letter to Kevin Killian (December 29, 1995) and in an interview on January 7, 1996.

29. The Coexistence Bagel Shop: founded by Jay Hoppe in the mid-1950s and surviving about five years, with Leo Krikorian—owner, too, of The Place—a part owner with Hoppe. The storefront, exactly at the southeast corner of Grant Avenue (1398 Grant) and Green Street—served beer, wine, and food, and was an early Beatnik center.

30. Lewis Ellingham/Richard Duerden interview, pp. 1–6, 10–13.

31. Michael Rumaker, "Robert Duncan in San Francisco," *Credences* 5/6 (SUNY, Buffalo, March 1978), p. 34. In 1996 Grey Fox Press published the revised memoir *Robert Duncan in San Francisco* in book form.

32. Gerrit Lansing described the "back story" of Olson's horror of Tarot in a telephone conversation with Kevin Killian in February 1997.

33. Robert Duncan, interviewed by Lewis Ellingham, 1983.

34. John Allen Ryan, interviewed by Kevin Killian, June 19, 1993.

35. "A Postscript for Charles Olson," *Admonitions*, CB, p. 65.

36. Robert Duncan, interviewed by Lewis Ellingham, 1983.

37. Spicer to Olson, n.d. [1958, but dated 1957 by George Butterick], Charles Olson papers, Literary and Cultural Archives, University of Connecticut, Storrs, Library.

38. Ralph Maud, *Charles Olson's Reading: A Biography* (Carbondale, Ill.: Southern Illinois University Press, 1966), p. 318. Robin Blaser sent Olson the later *The Heads of the Town Up to the Aether*, but it was not found in Olson's library at the time of his death. We would like to thank Ralph Maud for sharing his knowledge of Olson's San Francisco visit with us on several occasions.

39. Robert Duncan, interviewed by Lewis Ellingham, 1983.

40. Spicer, "Letters to Robin Blaser," in *line* 9, p. 40.

41. Spicer to Blaser, February 21, 1957, in *line* 9, p. 44.

42. Spicer to Blaser, in *line* 9, p. 44.

43. Duncan/Blaser correspondence, Bancroft Library, University of California (italics are in the original); Charles Olson's "Against Wisdom as Such" is a meditation upon some ideas of Robert Duncan—see *Human Universe and Other Essays*, ed.Donald M. Allen (San Francisco: Auerhahn, 1965; New York: Grove Press, 1967), pp. 67–71. "Black Mountain" probably refers to the *Black Mountain Review*, edited by Robert Creeley, in this context.

44. Michael Rumaker, *Robert Duncan in San Francisco* (San Francisco: Grey Fox Press), 1996; Spicer's correspondence with Donald Allen is at the Bancroft Library, University of California, Berkeley.

45. Lewis Ellingham/Bob Connor interview, pp. 26–27.

46. Kristen Prevallet found the typescript of "Initiation to the Magic Workshop" among the Helen Adam papers at the Poetry/Rare Books Collection at the Lockwood Library, State University of New York, Buffalo, and incorporated some of the material into a slide presentation she gave at "In Recovery of the Public World," the Robin Blaser Conference in Vancouver, B.C., in June 1995. She later made this text available to us. Thanks also to Robert J. Bertholf, head of the Poetry/Rare Books Collection, and to the family of Helen Adam, for permission to quote from it here.

47. James Broughton to Kevin Killian, April 18, 1997.

48. Harry Redl, interviewed by Kevin Killian, March 1997.

49. George Stanley, interviewed by Lewis Ellingham, 1983.

50. Robert Duncan, interviewed by Lewis Ellingham; and Robin Blaser, *CB*, "The Practice of Outside," p. 273.

51. Spicer to Blaser, n.d., in *line* 9, p. 45.

52. Ibid.

53. Ibid., p. 47.

54. Robert Duncan to Robin Blaser, June 4, 1957, Bancroft Library, University of California, Berkeley.

55. Jack Goodwin, "Spicer and All the Poets," *Hanging Loose* 58, pp. 35–36.

56. Walter E. Kidd correspondence (10/26/56–4/7/57) in the Poetry Center files, Bancroft Library, University of California, Berkeley.

57. Robert Duncan, "Notes on Jack Spicer/Memoirs of our Time and Place," [March 17, 1957], files of the Poetry Center at San Francisco State University.

58. This section of Spicer's reading can be heard on the CD accompanying *Exact Change Yearbook* 1 (Boston: Exact Change/Manchester: Carcanet, 1995), ed. Peter Gizzi, together with a transcription of the "Elegies" and an account of their revision by Kevin Killian ("Under the Influence," pp. 133–40).

59. Conversations with Robert Berg, Myrsam Wixman, and Richard Bratset, all of whom knew Spicer and who, in the cases of Berg and Bratset, worked at San Francisco State.

60. Merle Ellis, interviewed by Kevin Killian, November 14, 1990.

61. Wesley Day, interviewed by Kevin Killian, October 25, 1991.

62. Pauline Oliveros, interviewed by Kevin Killian, December 27 and 30, 1996.

63. Jack Spicer, "Letters to Robin Blaser," *line* 9, p. 41.

64. Landis Everson, interviewed by Lewis Ellingham.

65. John Allen Ryan, interviewed by Lewis Ellingham.

66. Michael McClure, interviewed by Kevin Killian, July 19, 1992.

67. J. F. Goodwin, "Spicer and All the Poets," pp. 1–5.

68. John Gibbons ("Jack") Langan, interviewed by Kevin Killian, July 17, 1992.

69. Rumaker, "Robert Duncan in San Francisco," pp. 31–32.

70. Ebbe Borregaard and Joanne Kyger, interviewed by Lewis Ellingham, 1982.

71. Nemi Frost, interviewed by Lewis Ellingham, 1987.

72. Nemi Frost and Tom Field, interviewed by Lewis Ellingham, 1987.

73. Joanne Kyger, *The Dharma Committee* (Bolinas: Smithereens Press, 1986), p. 16.

74. George Stanley, interviewed by Lewis Ellingham, 1982.

75. Harold Dull, interviewed by Lewis Ellingham, 1982.

76. George Stanley, interviewed by Lewis Ellingham, 1983.

77. It's tempting to see this seaside floating seminar as Spicer's attempt to recreate the postwar Santa Monica beach scene of Christopher Isherwood and Billy Caskey, summer of 1946, in which Isherwood had played the wise, vatic "guru" with a taste for young flesh, and in which Spicer had briefly participated.

78. George Stanley, interviewed by Lewis Ellingham, 1983.

79. Fran Herndon, interviewed by Lewis Ellingham, 1982.

80. Jim Herndon, interviewed by Lewis Ellingham, 1982.

81. Clayton Eshleman, in his *Boundary 2* essay, "The Lorca Working," in the Spicer special issue (Fall 1977, pp. 39–40), observes that "Forest" is "accurately translated." Eshleman adds this remark: "There is an increase of poems in which living as well as dead boys appear after the 'Whitman Ode,'" meaning poems following Spicer's translation of the book's centerpiece effort, the Lorca "Ode for Walt Whitman," to the end of *After Lorca*. Eshleman points out, too, that the letter to Lorca quoted here was Spicer's choice to describe his own poetics in Donald M. Allen's *The New American Poetry, 1945–1960*.

82. This is no coincidence, of course, since both O'Hara and Spicer were strongly influenced by the poet Paul Goodman's thinking on the subject. As Brad Gooch has noted, in his life of O'Hara, Goodman's 1951 article on "Advance-Guard Writing" profoundly thrilled the New York poet with its celebration of "occasional poetry" as the "genre of the highest integrated art." Spicer and Goodman had argued over these issues in Berkeley during Goodman's 1949–50 tenure there, Spicer resisting, but now he came back to the fold. Brad Gooch, *City Poet: The Life and Times of Frank O'Hara* (New York: Alfred A. Knopf, 1993), p. 187.

83. Bob Connor, interviewed by Lewis Ellingham.

84. *CB*, p. 34.

85. John L. Spicer, "The Poems of Emily Dickinson," *Boston Public Library Quarterly* (July 1956), p. 140.

86. "Letters to Robin Blaser," in *line* 9, pp. 26–55.

87. Ibid.

88. Donald Allen, interviewed by Kevin Killian, October 4, 1990.

89. Both the context of the letter and the text suggest that Duncan had access to the original version of this "letter," which did not see print until 1993 when it was published as "'Letter to Robin Blaser,' from *Admonitions* (earlier draft)" in *Lyric& 2* (San Francisco, July 1993), pp. 85–89; this version differs significantly from the later one printed in *CB*, p. 46.

90. Duncan/Blaser correspondence, Bancroft Library, University of California, Berkeley.

91. James Broughton to Kevin Killian, October 9, 1990.

92. Joanne Kyger, interviewed by Lewis Ellingham, 1982.

93. Tom Field, interviewed by Lewis Ellingham, 1982.

94. Rumaker, "Robert Duncan in San Francisco," p. 29.

95. "The Question," from a letter to Blaser from Duncan, undated [1958], Bancroft Library, University of California, Berkeley.

96. Harold Dull, interviewed by Lewis Ellingham, 1982.

97. Dora FitzGerald to Lewis Ellingham, September 23, 1990.

98. Dora FitzGerald, "A Jack Memoir," pp. 4–5.

99. Ida Hodes, "San Francisco Poetry," in Program, Eleventh Annual Arts Festival, September 26–29, 1957, Washington Square Park; from the files of the Poetry Center at San Francisco State University.

100. Spicer's comments on the Arts Festival are from his letter to Don Allen, September 30, 1957, Bancroft Library, University of California, Berkeley.

101. *Manroot* 10 (San Francisco, 1974), p. 25.

102. Joanne Kyger, *The Tapestry and the Web* (San Francisco: Four Seasons, 1965).

103. Joanne Kyger, interviewed by Lewis Ellingham, 1982.

104. David Meltzer, interviewed by Lewis Ellingham, 1983. Letter, George Stanley to Lewis Ellingham, December 19, 1982: "having come in late, Broughton didn't realize it was part 1 of Part I."

105. Ron Loewinsohn, interviewed by Lewis Ellingham, 1982.

106. Joe Dunn, interviewed by Lewis Ellingham, 1986.

107. Alastair Johnston, "Introduction," *Bibliography of White Rabbit Press* (Berkeley, Calif.: Poltroon Press, 1985).

108. George Stanley, interviewed by Lewis Ellingham, 1982.

109. Joe Dunn, interviewed by Lewis Ellingham, 1986. Jack Goodwin, in his memoir "Spicer and All the Poets" (p. 34), offers another version of the name's origin. "Little Joe Dunn was a Black Mountain poet, and he and his wife sat on the floor one night listening to records of my opera 'The White Rabbit Caper,' and the next day he started the White Rabbit Press."

110. Robert Duncan, in telephone conversation with Lewis Ellingham, October 22, 1983.

111. The poem's title, "Partington Ridge" (*CB*, p. 136), derives from a location by this name in Big Sur coastal country where Spicer spent some time in the 1940s; it was also the home of novelist Henry Miller, whose book *Remember to Remember* was the subject for one of Spicer's very few reviews (in *Occident*, 1948).

112. Joe Dunn, interviewed by Lewis Ellingham, 1986.

113. Joe Dunn, undated letter to Robin Blaser, Bancroft Library, University of California, Berkeley.

114. "Letters to Robin Blaser," in *line* 9, p. 35.

115. Spicer to Blaser, n.d., in *line* 9, p. 45.

116. Joe Dunn, interviewed by Lewis Ellingham, 1986.

117. Joanne Kyger, interviewed by Lewis Ellingham, 1982.

118. Gary Snyder to Ruth Witt-Diamant, December 17, 1958, Bancroft Library, University of California, Berkeley.

119. Robert Duncan to Robin Blaser, August 6, 1958, Bancroft Library, University of California, Berkeley.

120. George Stanley, interviewed by Lewis Ellingham, 1982.

121. Dora [Geissler] FitzGerald, interviewed by Kevin Killian, 1991.

122. Harold Dull, interviewed by Lewis Ellingham, 1982.

123. Robert Duncan to Robin Blaser, March 24, 1958, Bancroft Library, University of California, Berkeley.

5. Honey in the Groin (pp. 118–139)

1. Letter, dated by note of receipt, September 30, 1957, Jack Spicer/Donald Allen correspondence, Bancroft Library, University of California, Berkeley.

2. The *Howl* trial concluded September 9, 1957, dismissing charges of obscenity against City Lights Books, the publisher of the Ginsberg poem, brought by the U.S. Government. See *Literary San Francisco*, Lawrence Ferlinghetti and Nancy Peters (San Francisco: City Lights Books and Harper & Row, 1980), pp. 180–81, for a discussion of the case.

3. Kaufman's self-inventing persona recalls Spicer's drive to obscure his previous

life. Maria Damon's pioneering detective work tracing the real origins of Kaufman appear in her book *The Dark End of the Street: Margins in American Vanguard Poetry* (Minneapolis, University of Minnesota Press), 1993. What's important to this narrative is what Spicer, FitzGerald, and (later) Duncan thought to be Kaufman's ancestry.

4. Russell Fitzgerald, Diary, November 9, 1958.

5. Anxious Asp: a beer-and-wine bar at 528 Green Street, the north side, in San Francisco, at first bohemian and by the 1960s partly a gay bar, owned by Arlene Arbuckle, also owner of other gay bars in North Beach (The Capri, the Paper Doll/524) in the 1960s.

6. Russell FitzGerald, Diary, November 7, 1958.

7. George Stanley, interviewed by Lewis Ellingham.

8. Jack Spicer to Robin Blaser, [n.d. 1958?], in *line* 9 (Simon Fraser University, Spring 1987), p. 52.

9. Myrsam Wixman, interviewed by Lewis Ellingham. Among Spicer's activities at Berkeley beyond the Linguistic Atlas project, he helped grade examinations, with Professor Josephine Miles, after Professor Thomas Parkinson was shot in his office, January 18, 1961. The assailant proposed to open World War III by an assault on "liberals" in this still highly charged aftermath of the McCarthy era. He wounded Parkinson and killed a graduate student who happened to be conferring at the professor's desk. Thomas Parkinson, letter to Lewis Ellingham, October 13, 1983.

10. Ron Primack, interviewed by Lewis Ellingham, 1982.

11. Jack Spicer, "For Kids," Joanne Kyger Papers (MSS 8), Archive for New Poetry, Mandeville Department of Special Collections, University of California, San Diego; Richard H. F. Lindemann, Special Collections Librarian; Joanne Kyger, telephone conversation with Kevin Killian, September 9, 1991.

12. Duncan to Blaser, January 6, 1958 [misdated 1957 by RD], Bancroft Library, University of California, Berkeley.

13. Robert Berg's diary contains many acerbic remarks about "Toughy" Judson. Also, Myrsam Wixman, interviewed by Lewis Ellingham, April 17, 1997.

14. *CB, Admonitions*, "For Judson," p. 62.

15. Subscription list for Denise Levertov's reading appended to letter from Duncan to Ruth Witt-Diamant, January 8, 1958, Poetry Center files, Bancroft Library, University of California, Berkeley.

16. James Broughton, letter to Kevin Killian, April 18, 1997.

17. *CB, Admonitions*, "For Joe," p. 62.

18. Robert Duncan, interviewed by Lewis Ellingham, 1983.

19. Michael Davidson, *The San Francisco Renaissance: Poetics and Community at Mid-century* (Cambridge: Cambridge University Press, 1989), pp. 172–73.

20. *CB, Admonitions*, "Dear Joe," p. 55.

21. Denise Levertov, *O Taste and See*, "Hypocrite Women" (New York: New Directions, 1962), p. 70.

22. *CB, Language*, "Love Poems" no. 6, p. 227.

23. Denise Levertov to Lewis Ellingham, March 26, 1984.

24. *Caterpillar* 12 (New York: July 1970), p. 204, "Vancouver Lecture #1," with "writing to a conscious metaphor" as opposed to "dictation" under discussion: "Well, the only good poet who I think does it [deliberate, planned writing which nevertheless succeeds] to some extent is Denise Levertov, and the poems I like of hers are all poems that scared her and that she didn't really want to have written."

25. James Broughton to Kevin Killian, April 18, 1997.

26. "George Stanley," by Jack Spicer [Introductory Notes for Borregaard/Stanley

reading, March 16, 1958], Poetry Center files, Bancroft Library, University of California, Berkeley.

27. Robert Duncan to Robin Blaser, April 3, 1958, Bancroft Library, University of California, Berkeley.

28. Robert Duncan to Jack Spicer, April 4, 1958, Bancroft Library, University of California, Berkeley.

29. The novel was never finished, but six chapters remain, and part of a seventh. Chapter 1 was published in the magazine *Caterpillar* in 1970 and was later to form the centerpiece for Michael Davidson's chapter on Spicer and his circle in his marvelous book *The San Francisco Renaissance*. In 1994 Zasterle Books (Tenerife, Canary Islands) published Chapter 3 as "The Train of Thought," and later the same year Talisman House (Hoboken, N.J.) produced the complete extant text under the title *The Tower of Babel: Jack Spicer's Detective Novel*.

30. See "The Battle between the Poets and the Painters," in *Carnal Matters*, as by "Alexander Goodman" (Washington, D.C.: Guild Press, 1969).

31. Robin Blaser, interviewed by Lewis Ellingham, 1983.

32. Jack Spicer to Graham Mackintosh, letter of October 22 [1954], in *Caterpillar* 12 (New York, July 1970), p. 91, ed. Clayton Eshleman.

33. Jack Spicer to Jonathan Williams, n.d. [Spring 1955?], Jonathan Williams papers, Poetry/Rare Books Collection of the University Libraries, State University of New York at Buffalo.

34. Spicer's letters to Olson are to be found among the Charles Olson papers, Literary and Cultural Archives, at the University of Connecticut, Storrs, Library.

35. Robert Duncan to Robin Blaser, April 30, 1957, Bancroft Library, University of California, Berkeley.

36. Letter to Lewis Ellingham, October 4, 1987; and see Jack Spicer/Donald M. Allen correspondence, Bancroft Library, University of California, Berkeley, especially the exchange for 1958. Interviewed about the novel, Allen described it as a failure in terms of its genre—"one hundred pages and no murder!" Kevin Killian/Donald Allen interview, October 4, 1990.

37. Spicer, *The Tower of Babel*, pp. 15–16.

38. Robin Blaser, interviewed by Lewis Ellingham, 1983.

39. Russell FitzGerald, Diary, January 1958.

40. *CB*, p. 57.

41. Spicer to Russell Fitzgerald, *ACTS* 6, "A Book of Correspondences for Jack Spicer" (San Francisco, 1987), p. 60, ed. David Levi Strauss and Benjamin Hollander.

42. Russell Fitzgerald, Diary, April 22, 1959.

43. Ibid., February 1958.

44. Ibid., undated entry [January 1958].

45. Dora FitzGerald to Lewis Ellingham, September 4, 1986; *CB*, p. 83; see *Boundary* 2 (New York: SUNY Binghamton, 1977), pp. 25–28, and *ACTS* 6, "Book of Correspondences for Jack Spicer" (San Francisco, 1987), pp. 50–51, for, respectively, an outline by Spicer of a "plan for a book on Tarot," and "four Tarot cards by Russell FitzGerald."

46. Russell FitzGerald, Diary, June 1, 1958.

47. *CB*, pp. 55 and 82.

48. Gail Chugg, interviewed by Lewis Ellingham, and conversation between Lewis Ellingham and Robert Berg, summer 1984: both Berg and Chugg remembered occasions of Spicer's enthusiasm for Paul Newman's portrayal of the Billy-the-Kid subject in *The Left-Handed Gun*. In conversation with Robert Duncan and Lewis Ellingham in

San Francisco, after a reading by George Stanley at Small Press Traffic bookstore, Stanley agreed that Jack Spicer had "seen Billy" as Russell FitzGerald while writing the poem.

49. James Broughton to Kevin Killian, October 1, 1990.

50. In contrast to FitzGerald's fantasy of June 27, Spicer was cremated and his ashes disposed of without ceremony. Russell FitzGerald, too, was cremated and his ashes scattered over water near Vancouver, B.C.

51. Jess, interviewed by Kevin Killian, November 4, 1990.

52. Robert Duncan to Robin Blaser, June 27, 1958, Bancroft Library, University of California, Berkeley. "Conspiracy," from *A Book of Music, CB,* p. 75.

53. Louis Zukofsky, "Some Time," *Jargon* 15 (1956), pp. 48–51. Dora FitzGerald's unpublished essay "Picture *Billy the Kid*" is an invaluable guide to the Spicer-Zukofsky connection.

54. Robert Duncan to Robin Blaser, June 27, 1958, Bancroft Library, University of California, Berkeley.

55. Russell FitzGerald, Diary, June 7, 1958.

56. Joanne Kyger to Michael Rumaker, July 17, 1958, Joanne Kyger archive, Archive for New Poetry, Mandeville Department of Special Collections, University of California, San Diego.

57. Jim Herndon, interviewed by Lewis Ellingham, 1982.

58. Russell FitzGerald, Diary, August 4, 1958.

59. Russell FitzGerald, Diary, August 5, 1958.

60. Conversation, Robert Duncan and Lewis Ellingham, March 26, 1983.

61. Russell FitzGerald, Diary, May 6, 1959.

62. N. A. Diaman, "Memories of Jack and The Poets Table," manuscript article for *The Advocate* (Spring 1983), par. 14.

63. Dora FitzGerald to Lewis Ellingham, September 4, 1986.

6. "The Hell of Personal Relations" (pp. 140–179)

1. Ida Hodes to Robert Duncan, September 15, 1958, files of Poetry Center at San Francisco State University.

2. Ida Hodes to Robert Duncan and Jess Collins, September 16, 1958, Poetry Center files, San Francisco State University.

3. Joe Dunn to Ida Hodes, September 4, 1958, Poetry Center files, San Francisco State University.

4. Jack Anderson, "The Poetry of Jack Spicer," *Mouth of the Dragon 9* (New York, July 1976), pp. 62–63.

5. Diane Wakoski, letter to Kevin Killian, January 10, 1997.

6. Mackintosh's ideas were rather different than Jess's. Jess's handwritten indications, for example, for what should be typeset, were reproduced in his hand and spoiled, he feels, the look of the book.

7. "Of course," Jess added, "you should ask Fran [Herndon] for her opinion." Spicer's drawings can be seen in the illustrated deluxe copies of *The Heads of the Town Up to the Aether.*

8. Nikos A. Diaman, "Memories of Jack and The Poets' Table," manuscript article for *The Advocate* (Spring 1983), pars. 3–8, for the texts in this chapter; also, see Diaman's *roman à clef, Second Crossing* (San Francisco: Persona Press, 1982), chapters 3–7, pp. 21ff, for an only slightly fictionalized account of the life of Spicer-circle personalities from this novelist's viewpoint.

9. Nikos A. Diaman, "Memories of Jack and The Poets' Table," manuscript, article for *The Advocate* (Spring 1983), par. 8.

10. Joanne Kyger, *The Dharma Committee* (Bolinas, Calif.: Smithereens Press, 1986), p. 7.

11. Ebbe Borregaard and Joanne Kyger, interviewed by Lewis Ellingham.

12. Dora FitzGerald, interviewed by Kevin Killian, May 1992.

13. Dora FitzGerald, "A Jack Memoir," pp. 2–3.

14. N. A. Diaman, "Memories of Jack Spicer at the Poets' Table," pp. 9–11, an early version of an article in *The Advocate* 385 (January 10, 1984), pp. 38–41 (Writers Section).

15. N. A. Diaman, "Memories of Jack Spicer at the Poets' Table," pp. 9–11.

16. George Stanley to Kevin Killian, December 5, 1990.

17. Marianne Moore, "If I Were Sixteen Today," *World Week* 33 (7 November 1958), pp. 16–17; reprinted in *The Complete Prose of Marianne Moore*, ed. Patricia C. Willis (New York: Penguin Books, 1987), pp. 502–504.

18. George Stanley, interviewed by Lewis Ellingham, 1982.

19. Marianne Moore to Ruth Witt-Diamant, January 28, 1958, Poetry Center files, Bancroft Library, University of California, Berkeley.

20. Marianne Moore, "The Ways Our Poets Have Taken In Fifteen Years Since the War," (Review of *The New American Poetry: 1945–1960*, ed. Donald M. Allen [Grove Press]), New York *Herald Tribune Book Review*, 26 June 1960; reprinted in *The Complete Prose of Marianne Moore*, ed. Patricia C. Willis (New York: Penguin Books, 1987), pp. 502–504.

21. Myrsam Wixman, interviewed by Lewis Ellingham, April 17, 1997; Robert Berg's diary gives a running account of the Wendy Murphy case.

22. "Notes from the Poets," autobiographical statement by Boyd, March 30, 1958, in Poetry Center files, Bancroft Library, University of California at Berkeley.

23. Stan Persky, interviewed by Lewis Ellingham, 1983.

24. Ronald Primack, interviewed by Lewis Ellingham, 1982.

25. Russell FitzGerald, Diary, November 24, 1958.

26. Russell FitzGerald, Diary, December 10, 1958.

27. Joanne Kyger, *The Dharma Committee* (Bolinas: Smithereens Press, 1958), p. 5.

28. Russell FitzGerald, Diary, December 15, 1958.

29. Russell FitzGerald, Diary, January 4, 1959.

30. Introduction to Kyger, *The Dharma Committee*, p. 1.

31. John Wieners, *The Hotel Wentley Poems* (San Francisco: Auerhahn Press, 1958).

32. George Stanley, interviewed by Lewis Ellingham, 1982.

33. Jack Spicer, "Harold Dull," notes for Dull/Turner Wright/Wieners reading June 21, 1959, Poetry Center files, Bancroft Library, University of California, Berkeley.

34. Duncan's letter to Ruth Witt-Diamant, quoted in Witt-Diamant to Glenn Lewis, July 8, 1959, Poetry Center files, Bancroft Library, University of California, Berkeley.

35. John Wieners, notes for Dull/Turner Wright/Wieners reading June 21, 1959, Poetry Center files, Bancroft Library, University of California at Berkeley.

36. John Wieners, interviewed by Kevin Killian, 1991.

37. George Stanley, interviewed by Lewis Ellingham, 1982.

38. Jack Spicer, "What Is The Main Theme Of The Poem," *An Exercise*, ed. Robin Blaser and John Granger, *Boundary 2* vol. 6, no. 1 (SUNY, Binghamton, 1977), p. 6.

39. Ida Hodes, interviewed by Kevin Killian, February 1991.

40. Robin Blaser to Donald Allen, November 12, 1959, Donald Allen archive, Archive for New Poetry, Mandeville Department of Special Collections, University of California, San Diego. Blaser: "I took this to be junkey doldrums, but Jack got very

fussed in the old way and told them to shut up, not to up-stage him. It turned out they want to get Jack because he's spreading the word they're all on heroine (Jack claims Duncan's the blabber mouth). I fear for him a little; there's a whole underworld behind her, but he knows that as well as I." Thanks to Curtis Leitz, University of Minnesota, for bringing this letter to our attention.

41. Joe Dunn, phone interview with Kevin Killian, October 9, 1996.

42. Paul Alexander to Lewis Ellingham, August 28, 1982.

43. Dora FitzGerald, interviewed by Kevin Killia, 1991.

44. James Alexander, *The Jack Rabbit Poem* (San Francisco: White Rabbit Press, 1966).

45. James Alexander to Lewis Ellingham, August 29 and December 11, 1982.

46. JS, *"The Tower of Babel": Jack Spicer's Detective Novel* (Hoboken, N.J.: Talisman House, 1994), p. 72.

47. Gail Chugg, interviewed by Lewis Ellingham, 1982.

48. See Terry Ludwar's introduction to Spicer's "Letters to Robin Blaser: 1955–1958," *line* 9 (Simon Fraser University, Spring 1987), p. 27: "[Lori Chamberlain] proposes the blur of distinctions: 'Letters as poems, poems as letters. We can read them as a dialogue between a public I and a private I.'" See Jack Spicer, "Letters to James Alexander" and "Letters to Graham Mackintosh," in *Caterpillar* 12 (Los Angeles, 1970). The letters to Allen Joyce appeared in *Sulfur 10* (Los Angeles, 1984), pp. 140–53, ed. Clayton Eshleman.

49. *Caterpillar* 12 (New York, July 1970), p. 165. Spicer's reference to a post office suggests the *"Fake Novel about the Life of Arthur Rimbaud"* section of *The Heads of the Town Up to the Aether*, which would occupy much of his time over the next few years. The Drew House had been Stinson Beach's original post office at the turn of the twentieth century. A small frame of glass between living room and porch remained from the day when it had been the postal desk or window.

50. Dora FitzGerald, "A Jack Memoir," p. 4; "Homage to Creeley" was completed in the spring of 1960, without the "Explanatory Notes" at the bottom of the poems.

51. George Stanley to Lewis Ellingham, Christmas/December 27, 1983, p. 3.

52. Russell FitzGerald, Diary, February 23, 1959.

53. A year later, however, the Spicer anathema relented to a forbearance; at least Dora believed Jack may have visited the household in its second year, then situated at the Kashia reservation. Dora FitzGerald to Lewis Ellingham, January 11, 1985.

54. Robert Duncan to Robin Blaser, February 28, 1959, Bancroft Library, University of California, Berkeley. The "anonymous admirer in New Orleans" mentioned by Duncan was in fact a woman, the poet Kay Johnson, whom Spicer later that year published in his magazine, *J.*

55. Russell FitzGerald, Diary, March 3, 1959.

56. Ruth Witt-Diamant to JS, March 12, 1959, Poetry Center files, Bancroft Library, University of California.

57. DeLattre's recollections are drawn from Lyman Gilmore's interviews with him while preparing a paper, "Pierre DeLattre: The Beat Priest," for the 1994 NYU "Beat Generation" conference. Thanks to Mr. Gilmore and Mr. DeLattre for sharing them with us. In the spring of 1959 Stephen Spender was Beckmann Professor at the UC Berkeley campus: see his *Journals 1939–1983*, ed. John Goldsmith (New York: Random House, 1986), pp. 131, 186, for details of his visit.

58. Letters, James Alexander to Lewis Ellingham, August 29 and December 11, 1982.

59. Russell FitzGerald, Diary, June 26, 1959.

60. JS to Don Allen, September 24, 1959, Bancroft Library, University of California, Berkeley.

61. Donald M. Allen, interviewed by Kevin Killian, October 14, 1990.

62. Jack Spicer and Fran Herndon, "[Announcement of "J"], from the collection of Fran Herndon.

63. Stan Persky to Joanne Kyger, March 16, 1959. Joanne Kyger archive, Archive for New Poetry, Mandeville Special Collections, University of California, San Diego.

64. Fran Herndon, interviewed by Lewis Ellingham; James Herndon, *Everything as Expected* (San Francisco: privately printed, 1973).

65. Larry Eigner, interviewed by Kevin Killian, November 12, 1990.

66. Jack Spicer to Don Allen, undated letter, Bancroft Library, University of, Berkeley.

67. Robert Duncan, "Dream Data" (J 1) and "Dear Carpenter" (J 2), *Roots and Branches* (New York: New Directions, 1964), pp. 10, 16–21.

68. Robert Duncan, *Roots and Branches* (New York: New Directions, 1964), pp. 11–16.

69. Jack Spicer, "Jacob," *ONS*, p. 85.

70. Fran Herndon, interviewed by Kevin Killian, February 1, 1997.

71. Joanne Kyger, *The Dharma Committee*, p. 12.

72. Ebbe Borregaard and Joanne Kyger, interviewed by Lewis Ellingham, 1982.

73. Russell FitzGerald, Diary, February 23, 1959.

74. George Stanley, interviewed by Lewis Ellingham, 1982.

75. Dora [Geissler] Dull to Joanne Kyger, July 18, 1960, Joanne Kyger Papers, Archive for New Poetry, Mandeville Department of Special Collections, University of California at San Diego.

76. George Anthony Stanley, "It Happened to Me: Between Us There is a Gulf," *Search* (August 1959), pp. 45–46. Thanks to Darin De Stefano and Edmund Berrigan for bringing this article to our attention.

77. The Jack Spicer/Donald M. Allen correspondence, Bancroft Library, University of California, Berkeley, offers a picture of the exceptions to the admonition to others not to distribute Spicer-influenced publications outside the Bay Area.

78. Stan Persky, interviewed by Lewis Ellingham, 1982.

79. Stan Persky letter to Lewis Ellingham, undated—May or June 1982. See Stan Persky, *Lives of the French Symbolist Poets* (San Francisco: White Rabbit Press, 1967).

80. Stan Persky, interviewed by Lewis Ellingham, 1982.

81. Ibid.

82. Dora Geissler's recollections drawn from her interview with Kevin Killian, May 24, 1992.

83. George Stanley, interviewed by Lewis Ellingham.

84. Russell FitzGerald, Diary, November 17, 1959.

85. "They Came To The Briers And The Briers Couldn't Find 'Em," *CB*, p. 123. Gail Chugg told Lewis Ellingham—without factual support, only memory—Jack Spicer associated "goops" with Alfred Hitchcock's film *The 39 Steps*. The humorist Gelett Burgess (d. 1951) had written *Goops And How To Be Them* in 1900, and perhaps Spicer was familiar with this book as well.

86. George Stanley, interviewed by Lewis Ellingham, 1982; and letter to Lewis Ellingham, Christmas/December 27, 1983, p. 3.

87. Richard Duerden, interviewed by Lewis Ellingham; "Right Now 1" and "Right Now 2," *J* 5 (San Francisco, 1959); Richard Duerden, *The Air's Almost Perfect Elasticity* (Bolinas, Calif.: Tombouctou Press, 1979), pp. 18–19.

88. Jack Spicer to Don Allen, Bancroft Library, University of California, Berkeley.

89. Fran Herndon to Lewis Ellingham, telephone conversation, September 29, 1983.

90. In fact, there were eight issues of *J*. "J 1–5 were put out by Jack [1959], 6 [1960] was put out by me in San Francisco, 7 [1960] was an 'apparition'—run off, by the way, on a mimeograph belonging to L. Ron Hubbard at the Dianetics office in New

York [also edited by Stanley]—and 8 was produced by Harold Dull [1961] in Rome (it must be quite a rarity!)" George Stanley to Lewis Ellingham, December 25, 1983, p. 5. Inspired by the Italian edition, Joanne Kyger began editing *J-Kyoto* 8 in Japan.

91. Dora FitzGerald, interviewed by Kevin Killian, May 24, 1992.

92. Gail Chugg, interviewed by Lewis Ellingham, 1982.

93. *CB*, p. 118.

94. Jack Spicer, "Epilog for Jim," *J* 2.

95. Lewis Ellingham/Jess Sawyer Statement, pp. 10–11.

96. *J* 2 (San Francisco, 1959).

97. George Stanley, interviewed by Lewis Ellingham, 1982.

98. Lewis Ellingham/Jess Sawyer Statement, pp. 4–6.

99. Myrsam Wixman, interviewed by Lewis Ellingham, 1982.

100. Russell FitzGerald, Diary, April 19, 1960.

101. Letters, James Alexander to Lewis Ellingham, August 29 and December 11, 1982.

7. Heads of the Town (pp. 180–219)

1. Robin Blaser, interviewed by Kevin Killian, May 22, 1992.

2. Their 1956–59 correspondence has recently been published in *The Minutes of the Charles Olson Society* 9 (May/June 1995), annotated by Robin Blaser.

3. Robin Blaser to Ruth Witt-Diamant, November 8, 1959, Poetry Center files, Bancroft Library, University of California, Berkeley.

4. Jim Herndon, interviewed by Lewis Ellingham, 1982.

5. Jess, interviewed by Kevin Killian, November 4, 1990.

6. Robin Blaser, interviewed by Lewis Ellingham, 1983.

7. Collection of Robert Duncan, no date.

8. Gail Chugg, interviewed by Lewis Ellingham, 1982.

9. Fran Herndon, interviewed by Lewis Ellingham, 1982.

10. Robin Blaser, "Cups," *The Holy Forest* (Toronto: Coach House Press, 1993), pp. 1–17.

11. Robin Blaser, "The Park," Ibid., p. 27.

12. Jack Spicer, "Sonnet for the Beginning of Winter," *ONS*, p. 58.

13. Fran Herndon's lithographic illustrations for Spicer's "Homage to Creeley" appear in the first edition of *The Heads of the Town Up to the Aether* (San Francisco: Auerhahn Press, 1962).

14. Fran Herndon, interviewed by Lewis Ellingham, 1982.

15. Gail Chugg, interviewed by Lewis Ellingham, 1983.

16. Jean Doresse, *The Secret Books of the Egyptian Gnostics* (New York: Viking, 1960), p. 50. Thanks to Bruce Boone for pinpointing this reference.

17. Russell FitzGerald, Diary, March 20, 1960.

18. *CB*, p. 119.

19. *CB*, p. 132.

20. See Blaser's discussion of this poem in his essay, *CB*, pp. 280–81.

21. Gail Chugg, interviewed by Lewis Ellingham.

22. Alfred Bester, *The Demolished Man* (New York: Signet, 1954), p. 34.

23. On Halloween 1960 the first public presentation of Helen and Pat Adam's musical play *San Francisco's Burning!* took place there.

24. George Stanley to Joanne Kyger, April 19, 1960, Joanne Kyger Papers, Archive

for New Poetry, Mandeville Department of Special Collections, University of California, San Diego.

25. George Stanley to Joanne Kyger, April 12, 1960, Joanne Kyger papers, Archive for new Poetry, Mandeville Department of Special Collections, University of California, San Diego. "Enoch Soames" was Max Beerbohm's fictional character who sold his soul to Satan for the chance to transport himself in time 100 years forward (to June 3, 1997) in order to see what references to himself he could find at the British Museum. When he got there he found only one reference to himself, that he had been the subject of a story by Max Beerbohm.

26. *The Californians: Writings of their Past & Present*, ed. Robert Pearsall and Ursula Spier Erickson (San Francisco: Hesperian House, 1961). Three poems by Spicer ("The Dancing Ape," "Berkeley in Time of Plague," "Psychoanalysis: An Elegy"—all previously seen in the "San Francisco Scene" issue of *The Evergreen Review*) are printed in volume 2, pp. 547–50. Spicer wrote this description of himself for *The Californians*: "Jack Spicer: Southern Californian by origin (b. 1925), Jack Spicer roamed widely before settling in San Francisco's North Beach, where he now writes and lives." "Roamed widely" stretched the truth a bit, but Spicer might have felt the exaggeration necessary to focus emphasis on his then-resolute commitment to North Beach.

27. Spicer's views on Duncan, Blaser, Ferlinghetti, Don Allen, and John Crowe Ransom are given in a letter from Dora [Geissler] Dull to Joanne Kyger, June 24, 1960, Joanne Kyger papers, Archive for New Poetry, Mandeville Department of Special Collections, University of California, San Diego.

28. Jack Spicer to Lawrence Ferlinghetti, July 13, 1960, City Lights papers, Bancroft Library, University of California, Berkeley.

29. *CB*, p. 133.

30. George Stanley, interviewed by Lewis Ellingham, 1982.

31. Jack Spicer to Robert Duncan, letter, printed in *ACTS* 6, "A Book of Correspondences for Jack Spicer" (San Francisco, 1987), p. 27. [Note: in *ACTS* 6 Duncan misdates this letter to 1959.] In his memoir of The Place, Jack Goodwin wrote: "There was more than a whiff of the anti-intellectual to it, though. Knowing nothing of any foreign language, they started a chic style of mispronouncing all foreign words, and their idea of classic literature seemed to be Gertrude Stein." J. F. Goodwin, "Spicer and All the Poets (or *After Spicer*)," *Hanging Loose* 58, pp. 1–5.

32. Robin Blaser to Robert Duncan, and Robin Blaser to Jess Collins, May 7, 1960, Bancroft Library, University of California, Berkeley.

33. Jack Spicer to Robert Duncan, undated letter, printed in *ACTS* 6, p. 27.

34. Robin Blaser to Robert Duncan, August 10, 1960, Bancroft Library, University of California, Berkeley.

35. See Lewis Ellingham, telephone conversation with Robin Blaser, December 1, 1983.

36. Prospectus for "The History of Poetry," in Auerhahn archive, Bancroft Library, University of California, Berkeley.

37. Robert Duncan, "An Open Letter Regarding Borregaard's Museum. April 21, 1961"; Ebbe Borregaard, "A Reply to Mr. Duncan's Open Letter [April 27, 1961]," Robert Duncan papers, Bancroft Library, University of California at Berkeley.

38. Jack Spicer, letter to Ebbe Borregaard, *ACTS 6*, p. 30.

39. Paul Alexander, interviewed by Lewis Ellingham, April 8, 1997.

40. Cid Corman to Kevin Killian, January 8, 1991.

41. See letters, Jack Spicer to Robin Blaser (unpublished [1951?]), from Minneapolis (in Robin Blaser's possession).

Notes

42. The late Robert Berg's diary is unpublished and remains in private hands.

43. Perhaps the names of some of the other witnesses referred to by Robert Berg need clarification. Max Deskin was a Spicer friend from Berkeley; the "Parkinsons" refers to Professor Thomas and Mrs. Ariel Parkinson; John Button was "wasted" because he was under treatment for cancer. Myrsam Wixman and Landis Everson were friends of Spicer's from his Berkeley life. Though two "Alans" are referred to with identical spelling of the names, "Allen" is the correct spelling for "Allen Joyce," who died in 1980.

44. Robin Blaser, telephone conversation with Lewis Ellingham, October 2, 1983.

45. "The Poet and Poetry—A Symposium," *ONS*, pp. 90–92; Lewis Ellingham/Gail Chugg interview, p. 126.

46. Robin Blaser, telephone conversation with Lewis Ellingham, October 2, 1983.

47. Robert Duncan to Jack Spicer, Bancroft Library, University of California, Berkeley.

48. Helen Adam told this story to Lewis Ellingham not long after the Patchen event.

49. "San Francisco Tribute to Kenneth Patchen," [program and press releases], Patchen folder, Poetry Center files, Bancroft Library, University of California, Berkeley.

50. Jack Goodwin, "Spicer and All the Poets," p. 33. The painter Charlie Walker was one of Spicer's students at the San Francisco Art Institute and appears in at least one photograph of the members of his 1957 Magic Workshop.

51. George Stanley, in conversation with Lewis Ellingham, 1984.

52. Robert Duncan, "A Play with Masks"—a "Halloween entertainment written for Paul Alexander, October 1961"—in *Audit*, vol. 4, no. 3 (Buffalo, 1967), pp. 2–24.

53. Helen and Pat Adam, *San Francisco's Burning!* (Berkeley, Calif.: Oannes Press, 1963); while this edition has errors, it is the first complete publication of the play—a very rare book—and is the only edition not disclaimed or disapproved by the authors. Of one published in the mid-1980s, for example, Helen Adam wrote: "The edition of *San Francisco's Burning!* that you mention is so full of so many hopeless mistakes & atrocious muddles that I hate to think of any of my friends seeing it. It is just another of my miseries." (Letter to Lewis Ellingham, March 7, 1987).

54. Robert Duncan, "What Happend: Prelude," *Roots and Branches* (New York: New Directions, 1964), pp. 97–106.

55. See Robert Duncan's review of James Broughton's *True and False Unicorn*, in *Poetry* (Chicago) 91, no. 5 (February 1958), pp. 328–32.

56. Robert Duncan, "Some Notes for *Open Space*, January 1964," *Open Space*, ed. Stan Persky (San Francisco, February 1964), and a Duncan note to Spicer, Spring 1962, accompanying Duncan's three Dante sonnets on deposit in the University of California Bancroft Library, which mentions that John Wieners rejected "What Happend: Prelude" for *Measure* at the same time the poem was rejected for *M.*

57. Kristin Prevallet, "The Reluctant Pixie Poole: A Recovery of Helen Adam's San Francisco Years," published by the Electronic Poetry Center at the State University of New York at Buffalo in 1995 at http://wings.buffalo.edu/epc/authors/prevallet/adam.html.

58. Gail Chugg, interviewed by Lewis Ellingham, 1982.

59. Stan Persky, interviewed by Lewis Ellingham, 1983.

60. Jack Spicer, "Dear Lew," *Manroot-10*, p. 144; the reference in Spicer's letter to "George's plum-colored volume" is to George Stanley's *Love Root*, an early White Rabbit Press book; the reference to the "major poet now dead" is, of course, to Robert Duncan.

61. Gail Chugg, interviewed by Lewis Ellingham, 1982.

62. *M 1* (San Francisco, 1962), ed. Lewis Ellingham and Stan Persky.

63. George Stanley, "The Death of Orpheus," *You* [Poems 1957–1967] (Vancouver,

B.C.: New Star Books, 1974); "The Death of Orpheus" also appeared in a review of the time, *Locus Solus* (second issue), published internationally.

64. *M 1*.

65. Larry Fagin, interviewed by Lewis Ellingham, 1983; Stan Persky, interviewed by Lewis Ellingham, 1983; Ron Loewinsohn, interviewed by Lewis Ellingham, 1982.

66. Larry Fagin, interviewed by Kevin Killian, September 19, 1993.

67. Ron Loewinsohn, interviewed by Lewis Ellingham, 1982.

68. In the chronology of Spicer's works printed in *The Collected Books of Jack Spicer*, Blaser states that work on this poem interrupted that on *The Heads of the Town Up to the Aether*, but there are a number of discrepancies in this account. Gail Chugg, who typed the manuscripts of both books, was adamant that *Heads* was completely finished before *Lament* was begun.

69. See *CB*, "A Textbook of Poetry," no. 29, p. 183; Gail Chugg, interviewed by Lewis Ellingham, 1982.

70. Matthew Arnold's famous liberal poem was one of Spicer's models—the one great "beach poem about politics," as Gail Chugg recalled. Another model was Pope. "Jack said, 'I would like to ask Alexander Pope how he was able to write poetry in an age when you couldn't write poetry.' Spicer had been calling this poem 'The Duncaniad' as a take-off on Pope's *Dunciad*." Gail Chugg, interviewed by Lewis Ellingham, 1982.

71. *CB*, p. 380—Blaser remarks here that the first printed version of *Lament for the Makers* differs from the text presented in *CB*: the main difference is that "Robert Browning" is used instead of "Robert Duncan" in "Dover Beach," the contemporary poet appearing in *CB*; the model for these lines is Ezra Pound, *Cantos*, II, opening two lines.

72. *ONS*, "Psychoanalysis: An Elegy," p. 38.

73. *CB*, p. 112.

74. Gail Chugg, interviewed by Lewis Ellingham, 1982.

75. Spicer's comments on Dunbar and *Lament for the Makers* are drawn from his third lecture in Vancouver in June 1965.

76. Graham Mackintosh, interviewed by Lewis Ellingham, 1983.

77. Ibid.

78. Ibid.

79. Herb Caen, interviewed by Kevin Killian, 1992.

80. Jack Spicer to Don Allen, undated letter, Bancroft Library, University of California, Berkeley.

81. Donald Allen, interviewed by Kevin Killian, October 4, 1990.

82. Russell FitzGerald, Diary, March 1, 1960.

83. Ron Loewinsohn, interviewed by Lewis Ellingham, 1982.

84. Amiri Baraka to Kevin Killian, October 25, 1990. Their friendly meeting came after a barbed exchange of letters with Spicer, Spicer's dated May 24, 1961, criticizing Jones's mimeographed magazine "Floating Bear" for its failure to treat poetry and politics seriously; and Jones/Baraka's dated May 27, 1961, cutting Spicer deliciously. These letters are preserved in the LeRoi Jones/"Floating Bear" archive at the Lilly Library, Indiana University, Bloomington.

85. Larry Kearney, interviewed by Lewis Ellingham, 1982.

86. Jim Herndon, interviewed by Lewis Ellingham, 1982.

87. Larry Fagin, interviewed by Lewis Ellingham, 1983.

88. Bill Brodecky, interviewed by Lewis Ellingham, 1982.

89. Ibid.

90. Tom Field, interviewed by Lewis Ellingham, 1982; supported by Paul Alexander to Lewis Ellingham, December 1, 1982.

91. Bill Brodecky, interviewed by Lewis Ellingham, 1982.

92. Cf. the following item in *Open Space* (1964): "Mr. Berg was gracious enough to entertain, the other evening, for cocktails, a Goldwater man from Los Angeles, myself, and others. Conversation turned through Diderot to contemporary events.

"Mr. Ellingham: 'Oh well, he's so gorgeous I could suck his cock around the clock.'

"Mr. Blaser: 'I love the rhyme.'"

93. Larry Fagin, interviewed by Lewis Ellingham, 1983.

94. George Stanley, interviewed by Lewis Ellingham, 1982.

95. *CB*, p. 187.

96. *CB*, p. 224.

97. Charles Olson, "Against Wisdom as Such," *Human Universe and Other Essays* (New York: Grove Press, 1967), pp. 67–71.

98. *CB*, p. 226.

99. See George Stanley, *Beyond Love* (San Francisco: Open Space/Dariel Press, 1967); Harold Dull, *The Star Year* (San Francisco: White Rabbit, 1967); Robert Duncan, *Bending the Bow* (New York: New Directions, 1968); George Stanley, interviewed by Lewis Ellingham.

100. Bill Brodecky, interviewed by Lewis Ellingham, 1982.

101. Robert Duncan, interviewed by Lewis Ellingham, 1983.

102. Robert Duncan, interviewed by Lewis Ellingham, 1983; *ONS*, Robert Duncan, "Preface," pp. ix–xxvii.

8. The Holy Grail (pp. 220–245)

1. George Stanley, interviewed by Lewis Ellingham, 1982.

2. For advice on which Tony (Sherrod or Aste) serves as partial model or source for *The Holy Grail* poem, Lewis Ellingham relied in the first place on Gail Chugg's comment (telephone conversation, July 2, 1984) and second on his own impression. Tony Sherrod was literally beautiful, explicitly heterosexual, talkative, agreeable. He was insecure, touchy, used light drugs and drank as we all did; for jobs he drove a taxi, tended bar; while I knew him he married and fathered a child. For some people he seemed to register no great impression, but was reasonably popular. For others he was regarded as too lightweight to be taken seriously; but that presupposed being taken seriously was something to be valued. Helen Adam and Lewis Ellingham were godparents to his child of these years by his wife, Marie, who lived and worked in North Beach for a time. There had been a birth celebration in Berkeley, Helen and Lew attending, among many others; a large event. Driving back to San Francisco, Tony sideswiped the railing of the Bay Bridge, scaring Helen badly; their relation soured thereafter. Tony published writing of Ellingham in a one-issue magazine he started, *Mythrander*, and a mediocre poem of his own, a bad pastiche of Joe Dunn's kookiest style, in George Stanley's magazine *The Capitalist Bloodsucker: N.* Tony was a bird of passage, a lovely birdquick, avoiding controversy. "To be casual and have the wish to heal . . . Gawain no ghostman, guest who could not gather / Anything" ("Book of Gawain," no. 1).

3. Tony Aste's monologue provided by Gail Chugg when interviewed by Lewis Ellingham, 1982.

4. Letter, Samuel R. Delany to Lewis Ellingham, May 6, 1987.

5. Letter, George Bowering to Kevin Killian, November 24, 1996.

6. Dora FitzGerald, interviewed by Kevin Killian, May 24, 1992.

7. Telephone interview, Kevin Killian and Robin Blaser, August 3, 1995.

8. Ron Loewinsohn, interviewed by Lewis Ellingham, 1982; this interview preceded Richard Brautigan's suicide in the autumn of 1984 in Bolinas, California.

9. Gail Chugg, interviewed by Lewis Ellingham, 1982.

10. Robert Duncan to Richard Brautigan, December 6, 1956, Poetry Center files, Bancroft Library, University of California, Berkeley.

11. Spicer, "For Dick" (from *Admonitions*), *CB*, p. 59.

12. James Herndon, *Everything as Expected* (San Francisco, 1973); Fran Herndon, interviewed by Lewis Ellingham.

13. Jack Spicer, undated letter to Ariel Parkinson, courtesy of Ms. Parkinson. *The Holy Grail* was begun in December 1961 or January 1962; "27 poems in 4 books" would indicate a date for this letter at Eastertime, 1962. The book was completed by August 25, 1962.

14. Herndon's "Grail Series" was exhibited at the Peacock Gallery in San Francisco the following year (October-November 1963).

15. *CB*, p. 196.

16. Robin Blaser, interviewed by Lewis Ellingham, 1983.

17. See *CB*, "Book of Merlin" 2; in Spicer's own voice the rendering was sunny, pleasant.

18. See *CB*, "Book of Merlin" no. 7, p. 205.

19. Peter Riley, "The Narratives of the Holy Grail," *Boundary* 2, vol. 6, no. 1 (SUNY, Binghamton, 1977), pp. 163–90.

20. Duncan's "Dante Sonnets" are to be found in *Roots and Branches* (New York: New Directions, 1964).

21. Stan Persky, interviewed by Lewis Ellingham, 1983.

22. In this letter, Duncan alludes to three of his poems that later appeared in *Roots and Branches*: "Set of Romantic Hymns," "Thank You for Love," "Forced Images." "Thank You for Love" is Duncan's response to the then-new Creeley collection, *For Love* (New York: Charles Scribner's & Sons, 1962). "The H.D. Book" is Duncan's own title of a long-ongoing work just then beginning. Duncan also quotes from a line of "The Book of Gawain" 5, *CB, The Holy Grail*, p. 189. Harry Jacobus was a painter and friend of Duncan and Jess from the Berkeley days, who knew, but was not close to, Spicer. Lewis Brown, with Deneen Peckinpah Brown, had just arrived at this time on the San Francisco scene in North Beach, both as writers (and actors on occasion). The letter from Duncan to Spicer is on deposit in the Bancroft Library, University of California, Berkeley.

23. Ron Loewinsohn, interviewed by Lewis Ellingham, 1982.

24. *Foot* 2 (1962), p. 21.

25. Philip Whalen, interviewed by Kevin Killian, November 5, 1991.

26. Philip Whalen, letter to Joanne Kyger, May 25, 1963, Joanne Kyger Papers, Archive for New Poetry, Mandeville Department of Special Collections, University of California, San Diego.

27. Philip Whalen, "For Jack Spicer (23:IV:62)," Joanne Kyger Papers, Archive for New Poetry, Mandeville Department of Special Collections, University of California, San Diego.

28. The letter from Duncan to Spicer is on deposit in the Bancroft Library, University of California, Berkeley. James Schevill had succeeded Ruth Witt-Diamant as director of the Poetry Center at San Francisco State Poetry Center. Harry Jacobus, the painter and intimate of Duncan, told Ellingham that Duncan had wondered if somehow he were connected by name with the Anglo-Irish nineteenth-century poet William Allingham: the confusion, or snub, carried into Duncan's letter.

29. Larry Fagin, interviewed by Lewis Ellingham, 1983.

30. Arthur Kloth, interviewed by Kevin Killian, November 4, 1990.

31. Stan Persky, interviewed by Lewis Ellingham, 1983.

32. Bill Brodecky, interviewed by Lewis Ellingham, 1982. "Of course there was always something very exciting whenever *Jack* greeted you in his social presence, too—when he would come over for dinner or when we would go out to a movie or something together."

33. Stan Persky, interviewed by Lewis Ellingham, 1983.

34. Guests who remember no reading are John Button ("Some Memories," *No Apologies* 2 [San Francisco, May 1984]) and Bill Brodecky (conversation, Brodecky, Robert Berg, Lewis Ellingham, June 3, 1984); and those remembering a partial or possibly complete reading (of *The Holy Grail*) are Robert Duncan (interviewed by Lewis Ellingham, 1983) and Robin Blaser (conversations with Lewis Ellingham, November 17, 1983, and June 29, 1984; letter, November 1, 1983).

35. John Button, "Some Memories," p. 31. Button died at 53, December 12, 1982, in New York City.

36. Robin Blaser, conversations with Lewis Ellingham, November 17, 1983, and June 29, 1984.

37. Gerald Fabian to Lewis Ellingham, November 1, 1983.

38. Persky, interviewed by Lewis Ellingham, 1983.

39. John Button, "Some Memories."

40. Gerald Fabian to Lewis Ellingham, November 1, 1983.

41. Jess, interviewed by Kevin Killian, November 4, 1990.

42. Bill Brodecky, conversation, Brodecky, Robert Berg, Lewis Ellingham, June 3, 1984.

43. Ron Primack, interviewed by Lewis Ellingham, 1982.

44. Robert Duncan, interviewed by Lewis Ellingham, 1983.

45. Robert Duncan to Robin Blaser, August 29, 1962, Bancroft Library, University of California, Berkeley.

46. Telephone conversation between Robin Blaser and Lewis Ellingham, December 1, 1983; Alastair Johnston's *A Bibliography of the White Rabbit Press* incorrectly gives David Schaff as the sponsor of Spicer's *The Heads of the Town Up to the Aether* in the Auerhahn edition, pp. 55–56.

47. Dora FitzGerald, "A Jack Memoir," p. 7.

48. Ron Primack, interviewed by Lewis Ellingham, 1983.

49. In Spicer's lifetime, U.S. copyright laws did not automatically include all written material as they do today. One then had to declare intention of copyright, properly file application with the appropriate governmental agency, and pay a fee.

50. Letter, Gail Chugg to Lewis Ellingham, March 16, 1984.

51. Fran Herndon, interviewed by Lewis Ellingham, 1982.

52. Robin Blaser to Dave Haselwood and Andrew Hoyem, September 25, 1962, Auerhahn archive, Bancroft Library, University of California, Berkeley.

53. Dave Haselwood to Robert Creeley, March 13, 1963, Auerhahn archive, Bancroft Library, University of California, Berkeley.

54. George Bowering, for example, wrote on November 6, 1962, for a copy of the book, and his review appeared a mere six weeks later (December 14) in *Tish*.

55. James Laughlin to Dave Haselwood, July 31, 1962; Gerrit Lansing to Andrew Hoyem, November 29, 1962; Dave Haselwood to Cid Corman, June 28, 1962; Auerhahn archive, Bancroft Library, University of California, Berkeley.

56. Donald Hall to Dave Haselwood and Andrew Hoyem, December 24, 1962, Auerhahn archive, Bancroft Library, University of California, Berkeley.

57. Tram Combs to Andrew Hoyem, August 25, 1962, Auerhahn archive, Bancroft Library, University of California, Berkeley.

58. Rizzoli/Auerhahn correspondence of October 2, 1962; October 5, 1962, January 18, 1963, Auerhahn archive, Bancroft Library, University of California, Berkeley. A unique copy of *Heads of the Town* can be seen at the University of California's Bancroft Library. Printed on pink-paper divider sheets, this silly, foppish volume was Hoyem's "secret revenge against the author's bitchery." Hoyem's cover letter for his Bancroft donation is dated May 24, 1971: typescripts and texts of Jack Spicer's *The Heads of the Town Up to the Aether* are all located in the Bancroft Library, University of California, Berkeley.

59. Telephone conversation between Dave Haselwood and Lewis Ellingham, December 31, 1983; Haselwood letter to Lewis Ellingham, January 31, 1984; Stan Persky, letter to Lewis Ellingham, January 13, 1984; Andrew Hoyem, letter to Lewis Ellingham, March 19, 1984.

60. Robert Creeley to Dave Haselwood, March 1963, Auerhahn archive, Bancroft Library, University of California, Berkeley.

61. Gail Chugg, interviewed by Lewis Ellingham, 1982.

62. Robert Duncan, interviewed by Lewis Ellingham, 1983.

63. After saying that he had met Jack Spicer at Joe Dunn's earlier, that Spicer told him his anxiety over Dunn's "sadly fading scene then," which Creeley felt "characteristic" of Jack's "generosity," Creeley went on to say that "I got on with Jack very simply." Saying that Spicer once admonished him in Berkeley after a reading for not having read anything new, that Spicer had gone away shaking his head—"Jack was a hard man to excuse oneself to, like they say"—Creeley finished this letter by saying that Jack Spicer had sent him his books and his magazine, *J.*

64. Robert Creeley to Lewis Ellingham, May 6 and May 26, 1983; in a letter from George Butterick, curator of the Olson archives at the University of Connecticut, August 14, 1984: "I have been through Creeley's letters to Olson from 1956 through 1962, and the only thing I come up with is, 12 August 1959, written from Guatemala after a visit to San Francisco: 'I had a chance to play it [tape of Olson reading] for Jack Spicer, whom I like, very much, *i.e.* a weight I go with.'"

65. *CB*, p. 121.

66. George Bowering, "Holes in the San Francisco Fog," *Tish* 16 (December 14, 1962), pp. 2–3; see Bowering to Auerhahn.

67. Robert Duncan, "Adam's Way," *Roots and Branches* (New York: New Directions, 1964), pp. 127–63. *Also see* Robert Duncan, *Bending the Bow*, "Narrative Bridges for *Adam's Way*" (New York: New Directions, 1968), pp. 101–11.

68. Robin Blaser, interviewed by Lewis Ellingham, 1983.

69. Stan Persky to Joanne Kyger, September 27, 1962, Joanne Kyger papers, Archive for New Poetry, Mandeville Library of Special Collections, University of California, San Diego.

70. Robin Blaser, interviewed by Lewis Ellingham, 1983.

71. Robin Blaser, "Image-Nation 5," *Image-Nations 1–12* (London: The Ferry Press, 1974), pp. 17–18; for the same material, condensed but covering the entire interview, Blaser and Ellingham, see *No Apologies* 1 (San Francisco, November 1983), specifically pp. 9–10, and overall, pp. 6–20.

72. Robin Blaser to Jess Collins, October 10, 1962, Bancroft Library, University of California, Berkeley.

73. Robert Duncan to Robin Blaser, October 11, 1962, Bancroft Library, University of California, Berkeley.

74. Graham Mackintosh, interviewed by Lewis Ellingham. "There are five different variant copies of this book around," Mackintosh enumerated. "Jamie MacInnis got one; Jack got another, which he said he trashed; I never got one, the variant."

75. George Stanley, interviewed by Lewis Ellingham, 1982. The San Francisco Giants defeated the Los Angeles Dodgers for the National League pennant in 1962.

76. *ONS*, "October 1, 1962," p. 87.

77. The *Book of Resemblances* fiasco is detailed in letters from Duncan, Jess, Hoyem, and Haselwood, October 3—November 26, 1962, in the Auerhahn archive, Bancroft Library, University of California, Berkeley; see also Robert J. Bertholf's *Robert Duncan: A Descriptive Bibliography* (Santa Rosa: Black Sparrow Press, 1986), pp. 79–82.

78. This account of Blaser's withdrawal from Auerhahn is drawn from two letters from Robin Blaser to Jess Collins, October 17, 1962, Bancroft Library, University of California, Berkeley.

79. Robert Duncan to Robin Blaser, February 12, 1963, Bancroft Library, University of California, Berkeley.

9. The Long Silence (pp. 246–277)

1. John Allen Ryan, interviewed by Lewis Ellingham, 1982.

2. Knute Stiles, interviewed by Lewis Ellingham, 1982.

3. Ron Primack, interviewed by Lewis Ellingham, 1982.

4. Ibid.

5. George Stanley, letter to Lewis Ellingham, April 25, 1983, p. 1; see FitzGerald diary, entry for June 6, 1959, for the dating of the "Epithalamium" poem.

6. Ron Primack, interviewed by Lewis Ellingham, 1982.

7. Letter from Stan Persky to Lewis Ellingham, July 13, 1983.

8. Robin Blaser, interviewed by Kevin Killian, May 22, 1992.

9. Ron Primack, interviewed by Lewis Ellingham, 1982. When Jack and Ron split up, he gave Ron a final gift—the appliquéd hanging, "Uncle Louie." Shortly afterward, after another fight, he asked Ron to return it. Two years later, Jack was dead and his executor—Robin Blaser—was going through his estate. He asked Ron if there was some token of Jack's he'd like to remember him by. Ron remembered the pharaoh appliqué, and told Robin the circumstances under which he once had owned it. And so "Uncle Louie" returned once more to Ron's possession, his legacy from the Spicer estate. Ron hung it, framed, behind glass, to preserve its fabulous decay and his memories of the poet who gave it to him, then demanded it back.

10. Ron Primack, interviewed by Lewis Ellingham, 1982.

11. James Broughton to Kevin Killian, October 1, 1990.

12. Ron Primack, interviewed by Lewis Ellingham, 1982.

13. Two years later, the mural was chipped from the wall, when the premises became the Caffè Sport, and Katie moved her business to another storefront around the corner on Grant Avenue. "Bourbon Street," Katie's "old" bar, was located at 574 Green Street; her "new" bar was at 1441 Grant Avenue.

14. Ron Primack, interviewed by Lewis Ellingham, 1982.

15. Graham Mackintosh, interviewed by Lewis Ellingham, 1983.

16. Ron Primack, interviewed by Lewis Ellingham, 1982.

17. *CB*, "A Fake Novel about the Life of Arthur Rimbaud," no. 6, p. 158.

18. Stan Persky to Joanne Kyger, July 9, 1963, Joanne Kyger papers, Archive for New Poetry, Mandeville Library, University of California, San Diego.

19. Graham Mackintosh, interviewed by Lewis Ellingham, 1983.

20. See Ron Primack, *The Late Major Horace Bell of the Los Angeles Rangers* (San Francisco: White Rabbit Press, 1963), for poems occurring throughout the text without acknowledgment.

21. Ron Primack, interviewed by Lewis Ellingham, 1982.

22. Graham Mackintosh, interviewed by Lewis Ellingham, 1983.

23. Gerald Fabian, interviewed by Kevin Killian, September 19, 1993.

24. Dick Bratset, interviewed by Kevin Killian, October 3, 1993.

25. "Homage to Creeley," *CB*, pp. 117–48.

26. Jim Herndon, interviewed by Lewis Ellingham, 1982.

27. Fran Herndon, interviewed by Kevin Killian, February 1, 1997.

28. Ron Primack, interviewed by Lewis Ellingham, 1982.

29. Fran Herndon, interviewed by Lewis Ellingham, 1982.

30. Harold Dull, *The Wood Climb Down Out Of* (San Francisco: White Rabbit Press, 1963).

31. Dora [Geissler] Dull to Joanne Kyger, September 29, 1962, Joanne Kyger papers, Archive for New Poetry, Mandeville Department of Special Collections, University of California, San Diego.

32. Dora FitzGerald, "A Jack Memoir," pp. 8–9.

33. Dora FitzGerald, interviewed by Kevin Killian, May 24, 1992.

34. Ron Primack, interviewed by Lewis Ellingham, 1982.

35. Ibid.

36. John Allen Ryan, interviewed by Lewis Ellingham, 1982.

37. Tom Field, interviewed by Lewis Ellingham, 1982.

38. Robin Blaser to James Schevill, April 25, 1963 (Blaser refers to Primack's *Long Poem for Major Bell*), and Schevill to Blaser, May 6, 1963, Poetry Center files, San Francisco State University, 1982.

39. Dora FitzGerald, "A Jack Memoir," pp. 8–9.

40. *CB*, p. 239.

41. Harris Schiff, interviewed by Kevin Killian, May 6, 1991.

42. Ibid.

43. Robert Duncan to LeRoi Jones, January 14, 1963, Washington University Libraries, St. Louis, Missouri.

44. Robert Duncan, interviewed by Lewis Ellingham, 1983.

45. Robert Duncan, "A Part-Sequence for *Change*," in *Change* (San Francisco, Spring 1963), ed. Richard Brautigan and Ron Loewinsohn.

46. David Bromige, interviewed by Kevin Killian, July 5, 1991.

47. Stan Persky, interviewed by Lewis Ellingham, 1983.

48. Letter, Duncan to Blaser, June 8, 1963, Bancroft Library, University of California, Berkeley.

49. Jim Felts lived with Robin Blaser from undergraduate years at UC Berkeley through the early 1960s. In a telephone conversation in San Francisco in the late summer of 1984, he told Lew Ellingham that "when Robin and I were still together in Berkeley [early/middle 1950s] he told me he wasn't going to get his Ph.D. there, that the faculty wasn't good enough. I asked him how he would earn his living? He finally settled on library school. When he got that degree we went to Boston, he to Harvard library."

50. Harris Schiff, interviewed by Kevin Killian, May 6, 1991.

51. Lewis Warsh, interviewed by Kevin Killian, September 30, 1994.

52. Warren Tallman, interviewed by Terry Ludwar, January 1991.

53. Harris Schiff, interviewed by Kevin Killian, May 6, 1991.

54. Fred J. Wah to Kevin Killian, August 10, 1996.

55. Armando Navarro, interviewed by Lewis Ellingham, 1983.

56. Dora FitzGerald, "A Jack Memoir," p. 6.

57. Robert Duncan, "The Structure of Rime, XIII," *The Opening of the Field* (New York: New Directions, 1960), p. 83; telephone conversation, Duncan with Ellingham, August 14, 1984, confirmed the writing of the end of *The Opening of the Field* (and the beginning of *Roots and Branches*) at Stinson Beach.

58. Exhibition Catalogue for Peacock Gallery Exhibition sponsored by Fire Bird Fund (October 12–November 23, 1963), Bancroft Library, University of California, Berkeley.

59. William McNeill, interviewed by Lewis Ellingham, 1982. McNeill died in 1984, an early victim of AIDS.

60. Paul Alexander to Lewis Ellingham, May 3, 1985.

61. Nemi Frost, interviewed by Lewis Ellingham, 1987.

62. Harris Schiff, interviewed by Kevin Killian, May 6, 1991.

63. Allen Ginsberg, interviewed by Kevin Killian, October 16, 1990.

64. See "Letters: Jack Spicer to Robin Blaser," letter return-addressed and dated "Los Angeles, December 31, 1956," *line* 9 (Simon Fraser University, Spring 1987), p. 38.

65. Warren Tallman, interviewed by Terry Ludwar, January 1991.

66. Allen Ginsberg, interviewed by Kevin Killian, October 16, 1990.

67. George Stanley to Kevin Killian, December 5, 1990.

68. Cf. Russell FitzGerald, Diary, May 21, 1959: "Last eve. Ginsberg reads at the Mission. Many thoughts in reaction. A prophet: 'Is[a]iah.' The poetry/the muse seems willing to allow the needs of public-forming to interrupt and even prevent a certain amount of poetry. That maybe the amount of art that can be wasted varies, is more, for those who built art a public. That Allen himself is very charming & does flirt with his public." For June 1: "Annapolis—after legendary party at the Transylvanian Countess's in Berkeley (*complete* with Ginsberg on his knees before Spicer) Jack admitted that I was right about some things and asked/offered to reopen our 'correspondence.' 'The Sixth Elegy' [the sixth of Spicer's *Imaginary Elegies*] is another technical marvel, compressed & classical."

69. Larry Fagin, interviewed by Lewis Ellingham, 1983.

70. *CB*, p. 300.

71. Allen Ginsberg, interviewed by Kevin Killian, October 16, 1990, and November, 1996.

10. Crisis (pp. 278–316)

1. See *An Art of Wondering: The King Ubu Gallery 1952–1953*, curated by Christopher Wagstaff (Davis: Natsoulas Novelozo Gallery, 1989).

2. William McNeill, interviewed by Lewis Ellingham, 1982.

3. Telephone conversation, Lewis Ellingham, Ken Botto, Joanne Kyger, September 28, 1984.

4. Jess, interviewed by Kevin Killian, November 4, 1990.

5. *CB*, p. 217.

6. Stan Persky, interviewed by Lewis Ellingham, 1983.

7. George Stanley, interviewed by Lewis Ellingham, 1982.

8. Robin Blaser to Robert Duncan, January 5, 1964, Bancroft Library, University of California, Berkeley.

9. Robert Duncan to Robin Blaser, February 22, 1964, Bancroft Library, University of California, Berkeley.

10. Helen Adam, "I Love My Love," *The New American Poetry*, pp. 116–17.

11. *CB*, pp. 219–20.

12. See *CB, Language*, "Morphemics" 1, p. 234.

13. Stan Persky, interviewed by Lewis Ellingham, 1983.

14. Letter, Samuel R. Delany to Lewis Ellingham, May 6, 1987.

15. *A Controversy of Poets: An Anthology of Contemporary American Poetry*, ed. Paris Leary and Robert Kelly (New York: Anchor Books/Doubleday), 1965, pp. 551–52; Robert Kelly, letter to Kevin Killian, December 21, 1996.

16. Robert Kelly, interviewed by Kevin Killian, February 25, 1991.

17. Lawrence Lipton to Dave Haselwood, June 8, 1964, Auerhahn archive, Bancroft Library, University of California, Berkeley.

18. *Open Space* 2; *CB*, p. 218.

19. Robin Blaser, interviewed by Lewis Ellingham, 1983.

20. Robert Lowell to Ruth Witt-Diamant, March 30, 1959, Poetry Center files, Bancroft Library, University of California, Berkeley.

21. The story of Helen Adam's Merrill Award is told in her correspondence with the Poetry Center at San Francisco State University, which has kept it in their archives. Ida Hodes, interviewed by Kevin Killian in January 1991, contributed some detail.

22. "Intermission II," *CB*, p. 231.

23. Harris Schiff, interviewed by Kevin Killian, May 6, 1991.

24. Jim Herndon, interviewed by Lewis Ellingham, 1982.

25. David Reed, interviewed by Lewis Ellingham. Tom Parkinson recalled that Reed, who was not familiar with San Francisco poetics, "had no idea" about Spicer's nonacademic life, and that a "brief glimpse" into Allen Ginsberg's *Howl* so shocked him he "didn't know what to do": Thomas Parkinson, interviewed by Lewis Ellingham and Kevin Killian, June 22, 1991.

26. Robin Blaser, interviewed by Lewis Ellingham, 1983.

27. Fran Herndon, interviewed by Lewis Ellingham, 1982.

28. Nemi Frost, interviewed by Lewis Ellingham, 1987.

29. Jim Herndon, interviewed by Lewis Ellingham, 1982.

30. Kate Mulholland, interviewed by Lewis Ellingham, 1984, mentioned Spicer's therapy while a student at UC Berkeley, at Cowell Hospital Annex.

31. Fran Herndon, interviewed by Lewis Ellingham, 1982.

32. Ibid.

33. Knute Stiles, interviewed by Lewis Ellingham, 1982.

34. This quote exists only in the manuscript/proof version, as well as the anecdote from George Stanley about Lawrence Ferlinghetti and *Howl* that follows. See *A Bibliography of the White Rabbit Press* (Berkeley: Poltroon Press in association with Anacapa Books, 1985), p. 41, for the surviving text minus the bits quoted here.

35. George Stanley, interviewed by Lewis Ellingham, 1983.

36. David Meltzer, interviewed by Lewis Ellingham, 1983.

37. Graham Mackintosh, interviewed by Lewis Ellingham, 1983.

38. Spicer told Robin Blaser (interviewed by Kevin Killian, May 22, 1992) that John Lovely Spicer had known Rosa Luxemburg (1870–1919) in his Wobbly days. It's *possible*.

39. Ariel Parkinson to Lewis Ellingham and Kevin Killian, June 25, 1991.

40. Lawrence Ferlinghetti, interviewed by Kevin Killian, November 5, 1990.

41. Fran Herndon, interviewed by Lewis Ellingham, 1982.

42. This information, gathered from contemporary press releases on the IMSSS, is preserved in the Stanford University News Service, Biographical Vertical Files: "Suppes,

Patrick (General and Bio) Folder." Patrick Suppes, philosopher, enterpreneur, learning researcher, was the director of the IMSSS at the time of Spicer's appointment in 1964. Our thanks to Gerald Koskovich for locating these details of Spicer's employment at Stanford.

43. Harry Z. Coren, interviewed by Lewis Ellingham, 1987.

44. Paul Alexander, interviewed by Lewis Ellingham, April 8, 1997.

45. Paul Alexander to Lewis Ellingham, August 28, 1982, pp. 6–7.

46. Harry Z. Coren, interviewed by Lewis Ellingham, 1987.

47. Ibid.

48. Tové Neville, "Impressions of an 'Estranged' Poet," San Francisco *Chronicle*, August 29, 1965.

49. Spicer told Dr. Coren that he'd last been "truly interested" in a girl he'd met while working; this description might fit either Mary Rice, his student in Minnesota (1951), or the librarian Ellen Oldham (1955).

50. Harry Z. Coren, interviewed by Lewis Ellingham, 1987. The "green hair," of course, is also a reference to Joseph Losey's 1949 film *The Boy with Green Hair*, a complex parable about tolerance, anti-Communist hysteria, and sexual difference.

51. Fran Herndon, interviewed by Lewis Ellingham, 1982.

52. Harry Z. Coren, interviewed by Lewis Ellingham, 1987.

53. Ibid.

54. Arthur Kloth, interviewed by Kevin Killian, November 4, 1990.

55. George Haimsohn, as reported by Gerald M. Ackerman, interviewed by Kevin Killian, November 3, 1991.

56. Harry Z. Coren, interviewed by Lewis Ellingham, 1987.

57. Ibid.

58. Ibid.

59. Larry Kearney, interviewed by Lewis Ellingham, 1982.

60. James Merrill, interviewed before his death, denied Spicer's version of these events. Telephone interview, James Merrill to Kevin Killian, October 1992.

61. Nemi Frost, interviewed by Lewis Ellingham, 1987.

62. Larry Kearney, interviewed by Lewis Ellingham, 1982.

63. Spicer discussed his idea of the "Pacific Nation" in an interview that appeared after his death in the San Francisco *Chronicle*: Tové Neville, "Impressions of an 'Estranged' Poet."

64. Harold Dull, in "Pacific Nation," *A Selection of Poems for Jack Spicer on the Tenth Anniversary of His Death* (San Francisco, August 1975).

65. *A Controversy of Poets*, ed. Leary and Kelly, pp. 551–52.

66. Larry Kearney, interviewed by Lewis Ellingham, 1982.

67. Larry Kearney interviewed by Kevin Killian, November 24, 1995.

68. Alexander Star, "The God in the Trash: The Fantastic Life and Oracular Work of Philip K. Dick," *New Republic* (December 6, 1993).

69. Spicer/Persky letters, *Open Space* 7.

70. Larry Kearney, interviewed by Lewis Ellingham, 1982.

71. George Stanley, interviewed by Lewis Ellingham, 1982.

72. The manuscript of "Love Poems," at Simon Fraser University, reveals an original title, lightly crossed out: "Three Poems for Larry."

73. The poem in "Love Poems" [8] most closely resembling Kearney's memory here ends with the line, "I have seen your locked lips and come home sweating." *CB*, p. 228.

74. Larry Kearney, interviewed by Lewis Ellingham, 1982.

75. *CB*, p. 221.

76. Robin Blaser, interviewed by Kevin Killian, May 22, 1992.

77. *Open Space*, 9.

78. A year later, McClure was later to complain good-naturedly to his bibliographer that "*Open Space* pirated an early poem of mine." See Marshall Clements to Dave Hasel-wood, August 5, 1965, Auerhahn archive, Bancroft Library, University of California, Berkeley.

79. George Stanley, interviewed by Lewis Ellingham, 1982.

80. Joanne Kyger, "Joanne Kyger," entry in *Contemporary Authors Autobiography Series* (Chicago: Gale Research, 1991), vol. 14.

81. Larry Fagin, interviewed by Kevin Killian, September 19, 1993.

82. George Stanley, interviewed by Lewis Ellingham, 1982.

83. Ron Loewinsohn, interviewed by Lewis Ellingham, 1982; see *Manroot* 10, p. 78, for Loewinsohn's "Lots of Lakes." In 1965, at the time of his Vancouver Lectures, Spicer thought "a poem written by an idea belonged on the editorial pages. He blamed Ron Loewinsohn for writing such a poem. Jack said, 'Why didn't you write a letter to the editor instead?'" Warren Tallman, interviewed by Terry Ludwar, January 1991.

84. Stan Persky, interviewed by Lewis Ellingham, 1983.

85. Gail Chugg, interviewed by Lewis Ellingham, 1982.

86. Larry Fagin, interviewed by Lewis Ellingham, 1983.

87. Kate Mulholland, interviewed by Lewis Ellingham, 1984.

88. Spicer to Blaser, letter [1956?], in *line 9* (Simon Fraser University, Spring 1987), p. 36.

89. George Stanley, interviewed by Lewis Ellingham, 1982.

90. Larry Kearney, interviewed by Lewis Ellingham, 1982.

91. Paul Alexander, interviewed by Lewis Ellingham, April 8, 1997.

92. Larry Kearney, interviewed by Lewis Ellingham, 1982.

93. Dora FitzGerald, interviewed by Kevin Killian, May 24, 1992.

94. Larry Kearney, interviewed by Lewis Ellingham, 1982; interviewed by Kevin Killian, November 25, 1995.

95. David Bromige, interviewed by Kevin Killian, July 5, 1991.

96. Ron Loewinsohn, interviewed by Lewis Ellingham, 1982.

97. Richard Duerden, interviewed by Lewis Ellingham, 1982.

98. Larry Kearney, interviewed by Lewis Ellingham, 1982.

99. Ibid.

100. Larry Fagin, interviewed by Lewis Ellingham, 1983.

101. Jamie MacInnis, "Ducks for Grownups," in *Open Space* 12, and her *Practicing* (Bolinas, Calif.: Tombouctou Press, 1980), p. 15.

102. Lawrence Fagin, poems from *Procris and Cephalus*, in *Open Space* 12.

103. Lawrence Kearney, "For Jamie," *Open Space* 12, and (for his first book of poems) *Fifteen Poems* (San Francisco: White Rabbit Press, 1964).

104. Jack Spicer, "Graphemics" no. 5, in *Open Space* 11 and *CB*, p. 241. Kearney, interviewed by Kevin Killian, November 25, 1995, suggested that if any poem corresponded to Spicer's feelings toward MacInnis, it would be "Transformation III," also from *Language*. "This is the maiden all forlorn, a crumpled cow with a crumpled horn / Who lived in the house that Jack built."

11. "The Chill in My Bones" (pp. 317–343)

1. Larry Kearney, interviewed by Lewis Ellingham, 1982.

2. After being invited to Vancouver to read, Spicer's confidence soared, and before

leaving he boasted to his psychiatrist, Dr. Coren, that Herb Caen, San Francisco's popular gossip columnist, had named him one of the best poets in the City in one of his columns. Asked for verification in 1990, Caen submitted the following item from January 5, 1965: "Two of our very best poets, Gary Snyder and Jack Spicer, were deep in North Beach conversation the other day. Jack, disgruntled: 'The trouble with poets today is that too many of 'em are whores, not poets.' Gary: 'And what's your definition of a poet who had turned prostitute?' Jack: 'Any one whose name appears in Herb Caen's column.' Welcome to the club." San Francisco *Chronicle*, January 5, 1965; Harry Z. Coren, interviewed by Lewis Ellingham, 1987. One would think that this item, with its allusions to prostitution, would depress Spicer, but apparently all he "saw" was the reference to "best poets."

3. Warren Tallman, interviewed by Terry Ludwar, January 1991.

4. Gladys Hindmarch, interviewed by Terry Ludwar, July 1991.

5. Maxine Gadd, interviewed by Kevin Killian, May 25, 1992.

6. Warren Tallman, interviewed by Terry Ludwar, January 1991. Perhaps one of these books was *The Chill* (1964), Macdonald's current novel? Cf. "I am headed north looking for the source of the chill in my bones" ("Poems for the Vancouver Festival," *Book of Magazine Verse*).

7. Ellen Tallman, interviewed by Kevin Killian, July 3, 1991.

8. Harry Z. Coren, interviewed by Lewis Ellingham, 1987.

9. Larry Kearney, interviewed by Lewis Ellingham, 1982.

10. Ibid.

11. Stan Persky to Dave Haselwood, April 29, 1965, Auerhahn archive, Bancroft Library, University of California, Berkeley.

12. Sam Hardin, interviewed by Kevin Killian, January 31, 1993.

13. Harold Dull, interviewed by Lewis Ellingham, 1982.

14. See a brochure/preface ("A Note to . . . ") by Robert Duncan for Richard Grossinger, *Solar Journal*, first edition (Los Angeles: Black Sparrow Press, 1970).

15. Robin Blaser, interviewed by Lewis Ellingham. The exact quote, from Granger's M.A. thesis, is: "Thus the poet composes a world from the fragments of division. According to Jack Spicer, you see division and then you see God." See John Granger, *The Idea of the Alien in Jack Spicer's Dictated Books* (unpublished Master of Arts thesis, Simon Fraser University, Burnaby, B.C., 1982), p. 148; *No Apologies* 1 (San Francisco, November 1983), p. 11, ed. Bryan Monte; and *Ironwood* 28 (Tucson, 1986), p. 185, ed. Michael Cuddihy.

16. Robert Duncan, "The Chimeras of Gerard de Nerval," *Audit*, vol. 4, no. 3 (Buffalo, N.Y., 1967), pp. 38–64, mentions Jack Spicer in various connections, usually unsympathetically.

17. See Charles Olson, "Causal Mythology," *Muthologus*, vol. 1 (Bolinas, Calif.: Four Seasons Foundation, 1978), pp. 91–93 specifically. The essay is a lecture given at the University of California, Berkeley Poetry Conference, July 20, 1965.

18. Robin Blaser, interviewed by Lewis Ellingham, 1983.

19. *The New American Poetry 1945–1965*, pp. 400–408, 432–36.

20. *CB*, p. 227.

21. Rainer Maria Rilke, *The Duino Elegies* (any edition—the Spender/Leishman was favored in Spicer's day), first line of "The First Elegy."

22. Robin Blaser, interviewed by Lewis Ellingham, 1983.

23. Robin Blaser, interviewed by Kevin Killian, May 22, 1992.

24. Karen Tallman De Beck, interviewed by Kevin Killian, May 24, 1992.

25. Gladys Hindmarch, interviewed by Terry Ludwar, July 1991.

26. Stan Persky, interviewed by Lewis Ellingham, 1983.

27. Gladys Hindmarch, interviewed by Terry Ludwar, July 1991.

28. Neap and Leni Hoover, interviewed by Terry Ludwar, July 1991.

29. Warren Tallman, interviewed by Terry Ludwar, April 5, 1991.

30. Gladys Hindmarch, interviewed by Terry Ludwar, July 1991.

31. Warren Tallman, interviewed by Terry Ludwar, April 5, 1991.

32. Warren Tallman, interviewed by Terry Ludwar, April 5, 1991.

33. Today the tape of this reading can be heard at Simon Fraser University, where it rests among their special collections.

34. Warren Tallman, interviewed by Terry Ludwar, April 5, 1991.

35. Robin Blaser, interviewed by Lewis Ellingham, 1983.

36. Warren Tallman, interviewed by Terry Ludwar, April 5, 1991.

37. Robin Blaser, interviewed by Lewis Ellingham. Perhaps as few as ten or fifteen copies of *Language* were bound with blank pages where several of the "Love Poems" should be (pages 13, 15, 17). These are today extremely rare collectors' items.

38. Graham Mackintosh, interviewed by Lewis Ellingham, 1983.

39. Stan Persky, interviewed by Lewis Ellingham, 1983.

40. *CB*, pp. 247, 249; in the first of "Three Poems for *Tish*," Spicer renders Diaghilef's command, *"Etonnez-moi!"* as one directed to Nijinsky (*CB*, p. 25) and not, as it was, to Cocteau. Whether this error was noticed, it would not have been corrected by Spicer, according to the practice of dictation, at this late stage of his life.

41. Graham Mackintosh, interviewed by Lewis Ellingham, 1983.

42. See the final lines of "Four Poems for the St. Louis Sporting News" no. 4, and, in general, *CB*, pp. 253–55, 258.

43. A generation after his death, only one of the lectures has been published, the first lecture (on "dictation"), in *Caterpillar* 10 (1970), pp. 175–212, but Peter Gizzi is preparing an edition of the Vancouver Lectures, as well as Spicer's lecture at the Berkeley Poetry Conference.

44. *CB*, pp. 11–52, 60–61.

45. *ONS*, pp. 90–92.

46. George Bowering to Lewis Ellingham, September 17, 1983.

47. Gladys Hindmarch, interviewed by Terry Ludwar, July 1991.

48. Dorothy Livesay to Kevin Killian, August 5, 1991.

49. Dorothy Livesay, "Making the Poem for Jack Spicer before his death," *The Unquiet Bed* (Toronto: The Ryerson Press, 1967), pp. 22–23.

50. Robin Blaser, interviewed by Lewis Ellingham, 1983.

51. Ibid.

52. George Stanley, interviewed by Lewis Ellingham, 1983.

53. Karen Tallman De Beck, interviewed by Kevin Killian, May 24, 1992.

54. The quotes from Spicer are taken from Peter Gizzi's transcriptions of the Vancouver Lectures, as they will appear in Gizzi's forthcoming edition of *The House that Jack Built: The Collected Lectures of Jack Spicer.* Thanks for making these available to us.

55. Warren Tallman, interviewed by Terry Ludwar, April 5, 1991.

56. Robin Blaser, interviewed by Lewis Ellingham, 1983.

57. Warren Tallman, interviewed by Terry Ludwar, January 1991.

58. Stan Persky, interviewed by Lewis Ellingham, 1983.

59. Jack Spicer to the editors of *Poetry*, n.d [1957?], Joseph Regenstein Library, University of Chicago.

60. George Bowering, letter to Lewis Ellingham, September 17, 1983.

61. Ibid.

62. Ibid.

63. *CB*, p. 259.

1. Henry Rago to Jack Spicer, June 3, 1965, courtesy of the Manuscripts Department, Lilly Library, Indiana University, Bloomington, Indiana.
2. Larry Kearney, interviewed by Lewis Ellingham, 1982.
3. George Tysh, interviewed by Kevin Killian, October 30, 1990, *Work* 2, dedicated to Spicer, contained Tysh's review of *Language*.
4. Ellen (King) Tallman, interviewed by Kevin Killian, July 3, 1991.
5. Karen Tallman, interviewed by Kevin Killian, May 24, 1992.
6. Neap Hoover, interviewed by Terry Ludwar, July 1, 1991.
7. Knute Stiles, interviewed by Lewis Ellingham, 1982.
8. Karen Tallman, interviewed by Kevin Killian, May 24, 1992.
9. Warren Tallman, interviewed by Terry Ludwar, January 1991.
10. Robin Blaser, interviewed by Lewis Ellingham, 1983.
11. Larry Fagin, interviewed by Lewis Ellingham, 1983.
12. Tom Parkinson, interviewed by Lewis Ellingham, 1982.
13. Josephine [Fredman] Stewart, interviewed by Kevin Killian, March 8, 1992.
14. Larry Kearney, interviewed by Lewis Ellingham, 1982.
15. Gerald Fabian, interviewed by Kevin Killian, September 19, 1993.
16. Robin Blaser, interviewed by Lewis Ellingham, 1983.
17. Larry Fagin, interviewed by Lewis Ellingham, 1983.
18. Robin Blaser, interviewed by Lewis Ellingham, 1983.
19. Josephine Miles, interviewed by Lewis Ellingham, 1982.
20. Kate Mulholland, interviewed by Lewis Ellingham, 1984.
21. "Statement" to the editors of the San Francisco *Chronicle* and *Examiner*, July 15, 1965. Lew Welch Papers, Mandeville Department of Special Collections, University of California at San Diego. The "Statement" was also signed by George Stanley, Blaser, Persky, Dull, Lew Welch, Gary Snyder, Tom Parkinson, Richard Duerden, Ron Loewinsohn, Victor Coleman, Robert Creeley, Ken Irby, Robert Duncan, Joanne Kyger ("I cannot feel the word immoral expresses the action. They *know.*"), John Wieners, Ellen Tallman, Ron Primack, Allen Ginsberg, Philip Whalen, Peter Orlovsky, and many others.
22. Harold Dull, interviewed by Lewis Ellingham, 1982.
23. Karen Tallman, interviewed by Kevin Killian, May 24, 1992.
24. Jack Spicer to Sister Mary Norbert Korte, July 1965, *Cow: The San Francisco Magazine of Livestock/Cow Soup Issue* (San Francisco, November 1965). A poet who in time left Catholic orders (in the photograph she is wearing a Dominican habit), she became a prominent figure in the Haight-Ashbury in the 1960s.
25. *CB*, p. 265. Hunce Voelcker later moved to northern California. Until his death from AIDS in 1990, Voelcker continued to write, much of his work focusing on Hart Crane.
26. Hunce Voelcker, *Sillycomb* (San Francisco: Panjumdrum Press, 1973), pp. 70–71.
27. Link's looks and attitude were described by Gerald Fabian, interviewed by Kevin Killian, September 19, 1993.
28. Samuel R. Delany to Lewis Ellingham, May 6, 1987.
29. Paul Mariah, telephone conversation with Kevin Killian, March 6, 1991. "Link" continued to publish *Cow*, moved to New York in 1967, and in the seventies embarked on a spiritual quest to Nepal, where he is said to have died in Kathmandu.
30. Two such memoirs are by David Schaff, "I met Jack Spicer after he walked . . . ," *Ephemeris II* (New York and San Francisco, 1970); and Richard Tagett, "Mono/Graphic

Letter: Jack Spicer & Proximities," *Manroot* 10, "Jack Spicer Issue" (San Francisco, 1974–75), pp. 160–62.

31. Larry Fagin, interviewed by Kevin Killian, September 19, 1993.

32. Lewis Warsh, interviewed by Kevin Killian, September 30, 1994.

33. Stan Persky, interviewed by Lewis Ellingham, 1983.

34. Mary Rice Moore in two telephone conversations with Lewis Ellingham, September 17, 1984.

35. Fran Herndon, interviewed by Lewis Ellingham, 1982.

36. Jim Herndon, interviewed by Lewis Ellingham, 1982.

37. "Ten Poems for Downbeat," no. 5 ("For Huntz"), *Book of Magazine Verse, CB,* p. 265.

38. *CB,* p. 267.

39. Harold Dull, interviewed by Lewis Ellingham, 1982.

40. Robin Blaser, interviewed by Lewis Ellingham, 1983.

41. Ibid.

42. Jim Herndon, interviewed by Lewis Ellingham, 1982.

43. Harry Z. Coren, interviewed by Lewis Ellingham, 1987. Dr. Coren had obtained the notes of Dr. Frank Lewis of San Francisco General Hospital, and read them to, and interpreted them for, Lewis Ellingham.

44. Robin Blaser, interviewed by Lewis Ellingham, 1983.

45. Karen Tallman, interviewed by Kevin Killian, May 24, 1992.

46. Ellen Tallman, interviewed by Kevin Killian, July 3, 1991.

47. Graham Mackintosh, interviewed by Lewis Ellingham, 1983.

48. Kate Mulholland, interviewed by Lewis Ellingham, 1989.

49. Mary Rice Moore, interviewed by Kevin Killian, June 23, 1991.

50. Jess, interviewed by Kevin Killian, November 4, 1990.

51. Robert Duncan to Henry Wenning, August 3–6, 1965, Washington University Libraries, St. Louis, Missouri.

52. Fran Herndon, interviewed by Lewis Ellingham, 1982.

53. Larry Kearney, interviewed by Lewis Ellingham, 1982.

54. Herb Caen, San Francisco *Chronicle,* August 9, 1965.

55. Warren Tallman, interviewed by Terry Ludwar, April 5, 1991.

56. Karen Tallman, interviewed by Kevin Killian, May 24, 1992.

57. Lew Brown and Deneen Peckinpah Brown, a young married couple, came to North Beach by way of Lew, who had been a friend of Larry Fagin and Bill Brodecky in Germany before the latters' arrivals in 1962. Both made friendships in every quarter of the community, developed skills in acting, collected painting.

58. Duncan's visit to Spicer when dying: Robert Duncan, telephone conversation with Lewis Ellingham, December 11, 1984.

59. Notes from Deneen Peckinpah Brown to Robert Duncan, Robert Duncan papers, Poetry/Rare Books Collection, State University of New York, Buffalo.

60. Bill Brodecky, interviewed by Lewis Ellingham, 1982.

61. In 1983 Duncan told a joke, saying that Jess, knowing of Robin's interest in the final utterances of poets, had promised Robert that, should occasion arise that Blaser be present at Duncan's deathbed, he would hang the room with microphones attached to a recorder to assure accuracy for posterity's record. Robert Duncan interview, March 21, 1983 (but unrecorded).

62. Paul Alexander, letter to Lewis Ellingham, August 28, 1982.

63. Stan Persky, interviewed by Lewis Ellingham, 1983.

64. Robin Blaser, interviewed by Lewis Ellingham, 1983.

65. Lewis Ellingham/Holt Spicer Statement, 1983.

66. Robin Blaser, telephone conversation with Lewis Ellingham, October 2, 1983.

67. Stan Persky, interviewed by Lewis Ellingham, 1983.

68. Fran Herndon, interviewed by Lewis Ellingham, 1982.

69. Lewis Ellingham/Holt Spicer Statement, 1983.

70. Fran Herndon, interviewed by Lewis Ellingham, 1982.

71. Lewis Ellingham/Holt Spicer Statement, 1983.

72. Ibid.

73. Robin Blaser, interviewed by Kevin Killian, May 22, 1992.

74. Ibid.

75. Lewis Ellingham/Holt Spicer Statement, 1983.

76. Larry Kearney, interviewed by Lewis Ellingham, 1982.

77. Ebbe Borregaard, letter to Lewis Ellingham, June 30, 1983.

78. Dora FitzGerald, letter to Lewis Ellingham, December 2, 1990.

79. Helen Adam to James Broughton, August 20, 1965, Broughton archives, Kent State University Library.

80. Steve Jonas's statement, "I have been moved by the death of Jack Spicer," was made available to us by Raffael De Gruttola and Gerrit Lansing, Jonas's literary executors.

81. Donald Allen, interviewed by Kevin Killian, October 4, 1990.

82. James Devlin, interviewed by Kevin Killian, November 26, 1990.

83. George Bowering, *Baseball: a poem in the magic number 9* (Toronto: Coach House Press, 1967). *Baseball* is reprinted in Bowering's book of selected poems, *Particular Accidents*, ed. Robin Blaser (Vancouver: Talonbooks, 1980), pp. 50–59.

84. Harry Z. Coren, interviewed by Lewis Ellingham, 1987.

85. Lewis Ellingham/Holt Spicer Statement, 1983.

Epilogue (pp. 367–374)

1. Gerrit Lansing, "Test of Translation: IX," *Caterpillar* 7, 1966, pp. 77–91. Lansing's article analyzes several translations of de Nerval's *Les Chimères*, one of them by Duncan (as "The Chimeras of Gerard de Nerval," they form a part of his *Bending the Bow*).

2. *Audit*, vol. 4, no. 3 (Buffalo, N.Y., 1967), a special Robert Duncan issue; Robert Duncan, "The Chimeras of Gerard de Nerval," *Bending the Bow* (New York: New Directions, 1968), pp. 84–91—the first edition omits 24 lines at the end of these poems, the typesetter's error, discussed by Gerrit Lansing in his *Caterpillar* 7 article.

3. Robin Blaser, interviewed by Lewis Ellingham, 1983.

4. Robert Duncan, interviewed by Lewis Ellingham, 1983.

5. Stan Persky, interviewed by Lewis Ellingham, 1983.

6. Bill Brodecky, interviewed by Lewis Ellingham, 1982.

7. Jim Herndon, interviewed by Lewis Ellingham, 1982.

8. Robert Duncan, interviewed by Lewis Ellingham, 1983.

9. Robin Blaser, interviewed by Lewis Ellingham, 1983.

Acknowledgments (*continued from page iv*)

Unpublished letter of Robert Creeley to Lew Ellingham quoted with the permission of Robert Creeley.

Excerpt from Michael Davidson's *The San Francisco Renaissance* courtesy of the author and Cambridge University Press.

Lyman Gilmore's interviews with Pierre DeLattre are drawn from here with the kind permission both of Mr. Gilmore and Mr. DeLattre.

Permission to quote from N. A. Diaman's article "Memories of Jack and the Poets' Table" granted by Mr. Diaman.

Published and unpublished material (unpublished poems, letters, and Duncan's "Program Notes" for Jack Spicer's 1957 poetry reading at San Francisco State University) by the late Robert Duncan quoted by his permission and with the permission of Robert J. Bertholf, Curator, The Literary Executor of the Estate of Robert Duncan. Copyright by The Literary Estate of Robert Duncan.

"Sonnet 3: From Dante's Sixth Sonnet" and "A Part-Sequence for Change," by Robert Duncan, from *Roots and Branches*. Copyright © 1964 by Robert Duncan. Reprinted by permission of New Directions Publishing Corp.

Excerpt from "Procris and Cephalus" quoted by permission of Larry Fagin.

"A Jack Memoir," by Dora FitzGerald, quoted by permission of Dora FitzGerald.

Russell FitzGerald's diaries printed by arrangement with Dora FitzGerald.

Excerpt from "For Jamie," by Larry Kearney, quoted by permission of Larry Kearney.

Excerpt from *The Dharma Committee,* by Joanne Kyger, printed with her permission.

Unpublished material from Joe LeSueur's work-in-progress, *Personal Notes on Poems by Frank O'Hara,* quoted with the permission of Mr. LeSueur.

"Hypocrite Woman," by Denise Levertov, from *Poems 1960–1967.* Copyright ©1966 by Denise Levertov. Reprinted by permission of New Directions Publishing Corp.

Permission to use materials by Dorothy Livesay is granted by Jay S. Stewart, Literary Executrix for Dorothy Livesay.

Permission to quote from Marianne Moore's letter of January 28, 1958, to Ruth Witt-Diamant granted by Marianne Craig Moore, Literary Executor for the Estate of Marianne Moore. All rights reserved.

Permission to quote from Marianne Moore's essay "The Ways Our Poets Have Taken in Fifteen Years Since the War" (1960), from *The Complete Prose of Marianne Moore,* edited by Patricia C. Willis, courtesy of Penguin USA.

"At the Old Place," by Frank O'Hara, from *Collected Poems* by Frank O'Hara. Copyright © 1955 by Maureen Granville-Smith, Administratix of the Estate of Frank O'Hara. Reprinted by permission of Alfred A. Knopf, Inc.

Description of Jack Spicer by Ariel Parkinson printed with her permission.

Unpublished letters by Stan Persky to Joanne Kyger quoted by permission of Stan Persky.

Excerpt from "The Reluctant Pixie Poole: A Recovery of Helen Adam's San Francisco Years," by Kristin Prevallet, printed with the permission of Kristin Prevallet.

Photographs by Harry Redl, copyright © 1997 by Harry Redl, printed with his permission.

Excerpts from Michael Rumaker's *Robert Duncan in San Francisco* (San Francisco: Grey Fox Press, 1996) quoted with the permission of Michael Rumaker.

Excerpts from *The Collected Books of Jack Spicer,* copyright © 1975 by the Estate of Jack Spicer and reprinted with the permission of Black Sparrow Press.

Excerpts from the following poems by Jack Spicer published in *One Night Stand and Other Poems* (Grey Fox Press, 1980), printed by permission of Donald Allen: "A Heron for Mrs. Altrocchi," "The Dancing Ape," "Train Song for Gary," "Sonnet for the Beginning of Winter," "Five Words for Joe Dunn on his 22nd Birthday," "Song for Bird and Myself," "October 1, 1962," "Three Marxist Essays," "The Poet and Poetry—A Symposium." Copyright © 1980 by the Estate of Jack Spicer.

Excerpts from *The Tower of Babel: Jack Spicer's Detective Novel* quoted by permission of the Jack Spicer Estate and by Talisman House, publishers.

Excerpts from Jack Spicer's letters to Richard-Gabriel Rummonds (from *Some Things from Jack* [Verona: Plain Wrapper Press, 1972]) printed with permission of Mr. Rummonds.

Jack Spicer's letters to Jonathan Williams, Ariel Parkinson, Robert Duncan, and Ebbe Borregaard appear courtesy of Robert J. Bertholf, Curator, The Poetry/Rare Books Collection, SUNY at Buffalo. Copyright by The Literary Estate of Jack Spicer.

Unpublished letter of Jack Spicer to Charles Olson is from the Charles Olson papers, Archives and Special Collections, University of Connecticut Libraries. Used by permission.

Unpublished collaboration between Jack Spicer and Fran Herndon granted by permission of Robin Blaser, Literary Executor for the Estate of Jack Spicer, and by Mrs. Herndon.

All published and unpublished material by Jack Spicer printed with the permission of Robin Blaser, Literary Executor of the Estate of Jack Spicer.

"It Happened to Me: Between Us There is a Gulf," by George Stanley, printed with the permission of George Stanley.

Unpublished letter from George Stanley to Joanne Kyger printed with his permission.

Unpublished letter from Philip Whalen to Joanne Kyger quoted with the permission of Philip Whalen.

Unpublished correspondence by Ruth Witt-Diamant printed with the permission of her son and executor, Stephen Diamant.

Photo credits:

Page 4, Jack and Holt Spicer at summer camp, by permission of Robin Blaser, Literary Executor of the Estate of Jack Spicer.

Photos on pages 16–17 appear courtesy of Ariel Parkinson.

Page 19, photographs by Mary Morehart are printed with her permission.

Page 36, Spicer in Minneapolis, courtesy of Gary Bottone.

Page 82, "Magic Workshop" photo by Harry Redl, courtesy of the Poetry Center at San Francisco State University.

Page 93, "Brains Trust" photo of Ida Hodes, Jack Spicer, Ruth Witt-Diamant and Robert Duncan in 1957, copyright © 1997 by Harry Redl, and printed here for the first time with his permission.

Photos on pages 107, 126, 144, 157, 201 by Helen Adam appear by permission of Robert J. Bertholf, Curator, The Poetry/Rare Books Collection, State University of New York at Buffalo. Copyright by the Literary Estate of Helen Adam.

Page 119, photo of Russell FitzGerald courtesy of Dora FitzGerald.

Page 145, photo of Joanne Kyger by Tom Field, courtesy of Joanne Kyger; reprinted with her permission.

Photos on pages 186–187 courtesy of Fran Herndon.

Page 194, photo by Joanne Kyger, reprinted with her permission.

Page 270, photo of Harold and Dora Dull, courtesy of Dora FitzGerald.

Page 308, etching of Jack Spicer by Ariel, printed with her permission.

Page 331, photo by Karen Tallman, printed courtesy of Terry Ludwar, the late Warren Tallman, and Karen Tallman DeBeck.

All other photos from the collection of the authors.

Index

UNIVERSITY PRESS OF NEW ENGLAND publishes books under its own imprint and is the publisher for Brandeis University Press, Dartmouth College, Middlebury College Press, University of New Hampshire, Tufts University, and Wesleyan University Press.

LEWIS ELLINGHAM is a freelance editor and writer living in San Francisco. He is the author of a volume of poetry, *The Jefferson Airplane* (1972).

KEVIN KILLIAN is a novelist living in San Francisco. He is the author of two novels, *Shy* (1989) and *Arctic Summer* (1997); a book of stories, *Little Men* (1997); a memoir, *Bedrooms Have Windows* (1989); and a play, with Leslie Scalapino, *Stone Marmalade* (1996). He has also written a number of critical essays on Spicer, Blaser, and Duncan.

LIBRARY OF CONGRESS CATALOGING-IN-PUBLICATION DATA
Ellingham, Lewis.
    Poet be like God : Jack Spicer and the San Francisco renaissance / Lewis Ellingham and Kevin Killian.
        p.   cm.
    Includes bibliographical references and index.
    ISBN 0–8195–5308–5 (alk. paper)
    1. Spicer, Jack.   2. Homosexuality and literature—California—Berkeley—History—20th century.   3. American poetry—California—Berkeley—History and criticism.   Duncan, Robert Edward, 1919–—Friends and associates.   5. Berkeley (Calif.)—Intellectual life—20th century.   6. Poets, American—20th century—Biography.   7. Blaser, Robin—Friends and associates.   8. Gay men—United States—Biography.   I. Killian, Kevin.   II. Title.
PS3569.P47Z65   1998
811'.54—dc21   97-32883